T0185818

Mastering Oracle GoldenGate

Ravinder Gupta

⟨IOUG⟩
Independent oracle users group

Apress®

Mastering Oracle GoldenGate

Ravinder Gupta
Chicago, Illinois, USA

ISBN-13 (pbk): 978-1-4842-2300-0   ISBN-13 (electronic): 978-1-4842-2301-7
DOI 10.1007/978-1-4842-2301-7

Library of Congress Control Number: 2016957837

Copyright © 2016 by Ravinder Gupta

This work is subject to copyright. All rights are reserved by the Publisher, whether the whole or part of the material is concerned, specifically the rights of translation, reprinting, reuse of illustrations, recitation, broadcasting, reproduction on microfilms or in any other physical way, and transmission or information storage and retrieval, electronic adaptation, computer software, or by similar or dissimilar methodology now known or hereafter developed.

Trademarked names, logos, and images may appear in this book. Rather than use a trademark symbol with every occurrence of a trademarked name, logo, or image we use the names, logos, and images only in an editorial fashion and to the benefit of the trademark owner, with no intention of infringement of the trademark.

The use in this publication of trade names, trademarks, service marks, and similar terms, even if they are not identified as such, is not to be taken as an expression of opinion as to whether or not they are subject to proprietary rights.

While the advice and information in this book are believed to be true and accurate at the date of publication, neither the authors nor the editors nor the publisher can accept any legal responsibility for any errors or omissions that may be made. The publisher makes no warranty, express or implied, with respect to the material contained herein.

Managing Director: Welmoed Spahr
Lead Editor: Jonathan Gennick
Development Editor: Laura Berendson
Technical Reviewer: Arup Nanda
Editorial Board: Steve Anglin, Pramila Balan, Laura Berendson, Aaron Black, Louise Corrigan, Jonathan Gennick, Todd Green, Robert Hutchinson, Celestin Suresh John, Nikhil Karkal, James Markham, Susan McDermott, Matthew Moodie, Natalie Pao, Gwenan Spearing
Coordinating Editor: Jill Balzano
Copy Editor: Kim Wimpsett
Compositor: SPi Global
Indexer: SPi Global
Artist: SPi Global

Distributed to the book trade worldwide by Springer Science+Business Media New York, 233 Spring Street, 6th Floor, New York, NY 10013. Phone 1-800-SPRINGER, fax (201) 348-4505, e-mail orders-ny@springer-sbm.com, or visit www.springer.com. Apress Media, LLC is a California LLC and the sole member (owner) is Springer Science + Business Media Finance Inc (SSBM Finance Inc). SSBM Finance Inc is a **Delaware** corporation.

For information on translations, please e-mail rights@apress.com, or visit www.apress.com.

Apress and friends of ED books may be purchased in bulk for academic, corporate, or promotional use. eBook versions and licenses are also available for most titles. For more information, reference our Special Bulk Sales–eBook Licensing web page at www.apress.com/bulk-sales.

Any source code or other supplementary materials referenced by the author in this text are available to readers at www.apress.com. For detailed information about how to locate your book's source code, go to www.apress.com/source-code/. Readers can also access source code at SpringerLink in the Supplementary Material section for each chapter.

Printed on acid-free paper

For my dear friend, Vandana Mishra.
I admire you more than the Seven Wonders of the World.

About IOUG Press

*IOUG Press is a joint effort by the **Independent Oracle Users Group (the IOUG)** and **Apress** to deliver some of the highest-quality content possible on Oracle Database and related topics. The IOUG is the world's leading, independent organization for professional users of Oracle products. Apress is a leading, independent technical publisher known for developing high-quality, no-fluff content for serious technology professionals. The IOUG and Apress have joined forces in IOUG Press to provide the best content and publishing opportunities to working professionals who use Oracle products.*

Our shared goals include:

- Developing content with excellence
- Helping working professionals to succeed
- Providing authoring and reviewing opportunities
- Networking and raising the profiles of authors and readers

To learn more about Apress, visit our website at **www.apress.com**. Follow the link for IOUG Press to see the great content that is now available on a wide range of topics that matter to those in Oracle's technology sphere.

Visit **www.ioug.org** to learn more about the Independent Oracle Users Group and its mission. Consider joining if you haven't already. Review the many benefits at www.ioug.org/join. Become a member. Get involved with peers. Boost your career.

www.ioug.org/join

Apress®

Contents at a Glance

Contents

About the Author

Ravinder Gupta is a DBA by profession and Oracle Certified GoldenGate Specialist. He has worked in Hyderabad, Mumbai, and Chicago for reputed IT firms. He worked as a technology lead consultant for a major telecom giant and Fortune 50 company.

He developed his passion for Oracle GoldenGate in 2010 and since then has worked on setting up GoldenGate systems on various platforms. Through this book he has attempted to share his admiration for this powerful replication technology.

When not working, he is an active social service volunteer and loves participating in activities that aim to make a difference to society. He loves to write poetry and travel.

Feel free to contact him via ravinder.rg.gupta@gmail.com.

About the Technical Reviewer

Arup Nanda has been an Oracle DBA for more than 20 years with experience spanning all aspects, from modeling to performance tuning and Exadata. He has delivered more than 300 sessions, authored about 500 articles, and co-authored six books. He blogs at `http://arup.blogspot.com` and mentors new and seasoned DBAs. He won Oracle's DBA of the Year in 2003 and Enterprise Architect of the Year in 2012, and he is an ACE director and a member of Oak Table Network.

Acknowledgments

First, thank you to Jonathan Gennick, my lead editor, for believing in me and giving me this opportunity to put my experience and admiration of Oracle GoldenGate into this book. You have helped me a lot at every stage of the publication.

Thank you, Jill Balzano and Laura Berendson, for helping me while the book was taking shape. You have been extremely helpful and great to work with.

Thank you, Arup Nanda, my technical reviewer. You did a great job reviewing each chapter and sharing ideas throughout the book. You helped me understand the expectations from the readers' perspective, both beginners and professionals.

Thank you to my mom and dad who have always believed in my abilities to succeed on whatever path I take in my life.

Thank you to my dear friend, Ramesh Waje, who listened to me patiently while I kept blabbering about ideas and topics I was working on to include in the book. You were always there "almost" when I needed to hear myself.

Thank you, Prateek Upadhyay, for always believing in my abilities and giving me confidence. This book in some ways is a product of the confidence you have shown in me.

Thank you to my friends, Shweta, Umesh, Ajay, Sree, Seetha, Mohit, and all the other wonderful people who have been around me while I was busy writing this book.

Finally, thank you to my sweetheart for it was you and it is you who inspires me as well as tempts me to do things I wouldn't do if it wasn't for you.

Introduction

Oracle GoldenGate is Oracle's strategic replication solution not limited to Oracle databases. It supports a wide variety of popular platforms; I discuss the most popular ones in this book. As per Oracle's marketing statistics, Oracle GoldenGate has more than 400 customers with 4,000+ implementations across Fortune 500 companies.

It is used in a wide range of industries including financial services, communications, healthcare, the public sector, retail, and utilities.

- It is used in the top three of the five largest commercial banks.

- It is used in the top three of the three busiest ATM networks.

- It is used in the top seven of the ten financial data services companies.

- It is used in the top four of the five telecommunications providers.

- It is used in the top three of the five largest food and drug stores.

Mastering Oracle GoldenGate is a detailed illustration of Oracle GoldenGate concepts, tools, and add-ons using illustrative examples. The book discusses Oracle GoldenGate for Oracle databases as well as how to set up other popular databases such as IBM DB2, Sybase ASE, MySQL, and Microsoft SQL Server.

This book discusses the new features included in Oracle GoldenGate 12*c*. It discusses both classic and integrated capture and delivery. You will also learn about Oracle GoldenGate security and performance tuning to keep your system secure and high performing.

You will learn to monitor your GoldenGate system using both tools that come with the Oracle GoldenGate Management Pack and shell/batch scripts. Troubleshooting is illustrated with examples.

Few sections of the book are as handy as the Oracle GoldenGate command and property reference guide that comes with examples.

This book also discusses Oracle GoldenGate high availability, Big Data, and cloud systems.

With this book I've made an attempt to provide a master reference for learning and implementing Oracle GoldenGate. Thank you for taking the time to read this book. I wish you all the best for mastering the Oracle GoldenGate technology.

PART I

Getting Started

CHAPTER 1

■ ■ ■

Introduction to Oracle GoldenGate (OGG)

GoldenGate Software Inc. was founded by Eric Fish and Todd Davidson in 1995. The San Francisco–based company was named after the famous Golden Gate Bridge. The company quickly became popular in the financial industry. Banks started using the data synchronization and integration tool to send transactional data information from their ATM machines to central mainframe systems.

The GoldenGate software captures and routes transactions over a variety of computer systems and platforms. Some of the clients of GoldenGate Software Inc. were DirecTV, Adventis, Chase, and Pulse. It was later acquired by Oracle in 2009.

Today, GoldenGate is Oracle's strategic replication solution but is not limited to Oracle databases. It supports a wide variety of popular platforms discussed later in this book. As per Oracle marketing statistics, Oracle GoldenGate has more than 400 customers with 4,000+ implementations across Fortune 500 companies.

It covers a wide domain of industries including financial services, communications, healthcare, public sector, retail, and utilities.

This will give you an idea of the popularity of Oracle GoldenGate, which is growing every day:

- It is used in the top three of the five largest commercial banks.

- It is used in the top three of the three busiest ATM networks.

- It is used in the top seven of the ten financial data services companies.

- It is used in the top four of the five telecommunications providers.

- It is used in the top three of the five largest food and drug stores.

What's So Magical About Oracle GoldenGate?

Oracle GoldenGate is the best-in-class replication solution that enables near real-time data integration and continuous availability by capturing and routing information as the changes occur. The data flow is across the TCP/IP network, and change is visible on the receiver system within subseconds. Oracle GoldenGate is a near real-time data integration solution that works across heterogeneous platforms and has been time- and stress-tested by transaction-intensive applications across industries since its release in 1995.

Being a true heterogeneous player, Oracle GoldenGate supports most of the popular databases and platforms. Table 1-1 lists the supported databases, operating systems, and hardware platform combinations.

© Ravinder Gupta 2016
R. Gupta, *Mastering Oracle GoldenGate*, DOI 10.1007/978-1-4842-2301-7_1

Table 1-1. *Supported Technologies Matrix*

Database	Operating System	Hardware Platform
Enscribe	HP Nonstop	NSK
IBM DB2 UDB	AIX	IBM PowerPC
IBM DB2 UDB	Red Hat AS	AMD/Intel x64
IBM DB2 UDB	Red Hat AS	Intel x86
IBM DB2 UDB	Solaris	Sun SPARC
IBM DB2 UDB	z/OS	Mainframe
IBM DB2 UDB	SUSE	Intel x86
IBM DB2 UDB	Windows	AMD/Intel x64
Microsoft SQL Server	Windows	Intel x86
Microsoft SQL Server	Windows	AMD/Intel x64
Microsoft SQL Server	Windows	Intel IA64
MySQL	Red Hat AS	Intel x86
MySQL	Red Hat AS	Intel IA64
MySQL	Red Hat AS	AMD/Intel x64
MySQL	Windows	Intel x86
MySQL	Windows	AMD/Intel x64
Oracle	AIX	IBM PowerPC
Oracle	HP-UX	HP Intel IA64
Oracle	HP-UX	HP PA-RISC
Oracle	Oracle Linux	AMD/Intel x64
Oracle	Oracle Linux	Intel x86
Oracle	Oracle Linux	Intel IA64
Oracle	Solaris	Sun SPARC
Oracle	SUSE	Opteron
Oracle	SUSE	Intel x86
Oracle	Tru64	HP OSF
Oracle	Windows	AMD/Intel x64
Oracle	Windows	Intel x86
Oracle	Red Hat AS	AMD/Intel x64
Oracle	Red Hat AS	Intel x86
TimesTen	Oracle Linux	AMD/Intel x64
Sybase ASE	AIX	IBM PowerPC
Sybase ASE	HP-UX	HP Intel IA64
Sybase ASE	HP-UX	HP PA-RISC

(*continued*)

Table 1-1. (continued)

Database	Operating System	Hardware Platform
Sybase ASE	Red Hat AS	AMD/Intel x64
Sybase ASE	Red Hat AS	Intel x86
Sybase ASE	Solaris	Sun SPARC
Sybase ASE	Windows	Intel x86
Teradata	Red Hat AS	Intel x86
Teradata	Windows	Intel x86
Teradata	Red Hat AS	AMD/Intel x64
Teradata	Windows	AMD/Intel x64
SQL/MX	Windows	Intel x86
SQL/MX	HP Nonstop	NA
Enscribe	HP Nonstop	Itanium
SQL/MX	HP Nonstop	NSK
SQL/MX	HP Nonstop	Itanium
SQL/MP	HP Nonstop	NSK
SQL/MP	HP Nonstop	Itanium
TimesTen	Red Hat AS	AMD/Intel x64

Visit www.oracle.com/technetwork/middleware/goldengate/certify-100402.html for a list of databases and platforms currently supported by Oracle GoldenGate.

Types of Replication

There are two types of replication based on whether it is performed in a synchronous or asynchronous way.

- *Synchronous replication*: Data is replicated as soon as the change occurs on the source. This guarantees that at any point in time the target database is an almost identical copy of the source database. However, there will be some latency between the time the change happens on the source and the time it gets applied on the target. This latency depends on the replication technology in use. For Oracle GoldenGate, the latency is usually in subseconds.

- *Asynchronous replication*: Transactions are written only to the primary database system and sent to the remote database at a later time. Because of this lag, the target database may not be an identical copy of the source.

Available Replication Options

Replicating your database to another database may serve various purposes such as fault tolerance, backup, high performance, load balancing, zero downtime migrations, and so on.

There are various replication technologies available to you for your replication requirement. For example, for a once-a-day replication of a couple of tables from a source database to a target database, you may find easy to set up Oracle materialized views to refresh to the latest data at specified times during a day, while in some situations Oracle advanced replication or Oracle Streams replication may serve the purpose for your replication requirement. The primary factors while choosing your replication solution are the rate of data change at the primary site, the link speed, and the distance between the sites. Let's quickly discuss various replication options available for Oracle and when to use them. Later in this chapter, we will discuss some of the other popular replication solutions by non-Oracle vendors.

- *Materialized views (snapshots)*: A materialized view creates a copy of the source at a single point in time on the target database. The advantage of creating materialized views is that it enables local access to data and thus improves response time and availability. It offloads the source database by enabling the users to query materialized views on the target instead of the source table.

  The disadvantage of materialized views is that they are not real time. There is no continuous availability. They can replicate only data and in one direction only. However, they are quick to set up and are suitable in some of the replication requirements.

- *Oracle advanced replication*: Oracle supports multimaster replication in which replication happens via creating push jobs on each replication site. Setting up advanced replication is complex to configure and needs maintenance because it often involves conflicts to be resolved.

- *Oracle Streams replication*: Oracle Streams allows movement of data, transactions, or events in data streams either within a database or from one database to another. The user can control what information to put into the stream, how the stream will flow from one node to another, how the stream events behave when they move through a node, and the termination of the streams. Depending on how the three stages of Oracle Streams (Capture, Stage, and Apply) are configured, they are effective for addressing a variety of replication requirements like hub-and-spoke replication and message queuing. Oracle Streams provides near real-time replication. Implementing Advanced Queuing with Oracle Streams has resolved problems associated with other replication technologies.

  The downsides of Oracle Streams replication are that it is not instantaneous and is prone to update collisions.

- *Oracle Data Guard*: Oracle Data Guard provides a software infrastructure to manage, monitor, and automate the creation of one or more standby databases. Data Guard is a unique replication solution among other Oracle replication solutions as it supports both synchronous and asynchronous configurations. The switchover to a standby database can be done manually or automatically in situations of disaster for mission-critical applications. The standby database can be both physical and logical. Physical standby databases use Redo Apply to maintain an exact replica of the primary database. However, logical standby uses SQL Apply to create logical replica of primary database. The physical structure of the database can be different in the case of logical standby. Oracle Data Guard provides typically a disaster recovery option rather than a high availability option.

- *Oracle GoldenGate*: Oracle GoldenGate is a real-time replication solution offering by Oracle for heterogeneous environments. This is by far the best and most reliable replication solution that can be implemented across different types of databases. For a list of supported databases, please refer to Table 1-1.

  Database transaction logs are read for any transactional changes on the source and are replicated across a TCP/IP network to target the database (or databases) in real time.

Advantages of Oracle GoldenGate

Oracle GoldenGate replication has quickly become one of the most popular replication technologies today. It offers a real-time and secure replication solution with high throughput. It can be implemented and customized for multiple business requirements, which we will discuss as we progress further in this book. The following are some of the major benefits of Oracle GoldenGate:

- *Real time*: Replication happens in real time. Changes flow from the source to the target within subseconds.

- *High performance*: It supports thousands of records flowing in batches with almost no performance impact on the source and target systems.

- *Reliability*: All committed records are delivered even in the event of a network disruption.

- *Heterogeneity*: It supports different database systems and platforms.

- *Flexible topology support*: It supports different database topologies like unidirectional, bi-directional, one to one, one to many, and multimaster.

- *Conflict detection and resolution*: In a multimaster configuration where multiple systems can modify separate instances of same table, conflicts may occur. Oracle GoldenGate comes with the capability to handle such conflicts.

- *Data encryption*: Data can be encrypted at the source and sent over a TCP/IP network to a the target system where it is decrypted and then applied to the target database.

- *Routing and compression*: Since Oracle GoldenGate uses TCP/IP network for routing information, it can compress and route information in different database topologies irrespective of geographical distances.

- *Deferred apply*: The user has the option for both immediate and deferred application of transactional changes on the target system.

When to Use Oracle GoldenGate?

You have read about the popularity of Oracle GoldenGate and the major advantages it offers. The following are some of the most popular business requirements where you can implement and take advantage of Oracle GoldenGate:

- The business needs load balancing in a production environment. An active-active configuration of the source and the target can help balance the load among multiple database systems.

- The business wants to implement query offloading. Long-running read-only transactions can be offloaded to an active standby database and thus improve the overall performance of production systems.

- The business wants to create and manage a live, active standby database with up-to-the-minute data. This minimizes recovery time for mission-critical systems.

- The business needs to integrate an Oracle database with a non-Oracle database or a non-Oracle database with another non-Oracle database.

- The business requires zero downtime migrations and upgrades.

Oracle GoldenGate vs. Streams

Keeping in mind that Oracle Streams is free to use while Oracle GoldenGate requires licensing, Table 1-2 helps you differentiate between the two replication technologies.

Table 1-2. *Oracle GoldenGate vs. Oracle Streams*

Oracle GoldenGate	Oracle Streams
Strategic solution for all replication needs	Oracle Streams is deprecated in Oracle Database 12*c*. It will be continued to be supported, but no new features will be added to existing Oracle Streams.
Easy to install and configure	Installation and configuration are comparatively complicated as they require API-based, stored database packages and execution of a list of packages to set up Oracle Streams.
Works in both homogeneous and heterogeneous environments	Oracle Streams allows replication between Oracle databases only.
Sends only COMMITED transactions to the target system where they are applied by the Apply process	Oracle Streams immediately captures changes and sends them to the target's apply queue. If a transaction is rolled back on the source, it is removed from the target apply queue.
Offers high performance in high transaction environments	Oracle Streams works well in high-throughput environments. But Oracle GoldenGate is the leader as it delivers high-volume data changes with subsecond latency.

Oracle GoldenGate vs. Data Guard

Oracle Data Guard is a popular replication solution implemented across industries. Oracle GoldenGate is not a replacement for Oracle Data Guard and is sometimes used along with Oracle Data Guard to support specific business needs such as downstream real-time replication, which we will discuss in Chapter X. There are two types of standby databases that can be created with Data Guard: physical standby and logical standby. For physical standby , Oracle Data Guard uses the Redo Apply technique. The target database is read-only. On the other hand, a logical standby database can be read-write, and changes are applied using the SQL Apply method. Table 1-3 identifies some of the key differences between Oracle GoldenGate and Oracle Data Guard.

Table 1-3. *Oracle GoldenGate vs. Oracle Data Guard*

Oracle GoldenGate	Oracle Data Guard
Oracle GoldenGate supports multiple replication topologies.	Oracle Data Guard supports simple one-way replication only.
The target database can be read-write.	The physical standby database is read-only when using an Active Data Guard configuration. In the rest of the other cases, to make your standby database open and read-only, you will have to pause the sync process. The logical standby database, however, is read-write.
There is I/O overhead and capture processing overhead on primary databases.	There is no I/O overhead or capture processing overhead on the primary.
Few data types are not supported.	There is no restriction of data types.
Oracle GoldenGate comes as middleware installed separately from the Oracle database.	It is integrated with Oracle database software.
Oracle GoldenGate is a heterogeneous player supporting a wide range of database environments.	It supports replication only between Oracle databases.
The source and target databases can be of different versions.	The standby database used for replication should be the same version as the primary Oracle database.
The Oracle GoldenGate source and target databases can be on different OS platforms.	Oracle Data Guard requires both the primary and standby databases to be on the same OS platform.

Oracle GoldenGate vs. SharePlex

SharePlex is a proprietary technology from Dell Software. It is comparatively older and is the closest competitor to Oracle GoldenGate in terms of features it provides for database replication needs. It was originally made for Oracle database replication needs and now supports a range of heterogeneous environments too. Table 1-4 lists a few differences between the two technologies.

Table 1-4. *Oracle GoldenGate vs. Dell SharePlex*

Oracle GoldenGate	Dell SharePlex
Add-ons such as Oracle GoldenGate Management Pack and Veridata need to be purchased separately.	It is a low-cost solution for database replication needs. The GUI comes packaged with the original license for SharePlex.
It is a true heterogeneous player that supports most of the popular database environments.	It is a heterogeneous database replication solution limited to a few popular databases only.

Oracle GoldenGate 12*c* New Features

Oracle GoldenGate 12*c* is a new, improved, and enhanced version of Oracle GoldenGate. Listed here are some important new and significant features of Oracle GoldenGate 12*c*. We will be discussing them throughout the book.

- Support for Oracle Database 12*c* multitenant architecture.

- Oracle Universal Installer support.

- Integrated replicat feature for Oracle databases.

- Coordinated replicat feature for non-Oracle databases.

- Inclusion of metadata in trail files via a table definition record (TDR). Thus, you are no longer required to create definition files containing table metadata on the target system.

- Ease of monitoring channel lags using an automatic heartbeat table.

- Improved trail file recovery. In the case of a bad trail file or missing trail files, you can delete the bad trail files and bounce the extract process. It will automatically rebuild the required trail files.

- Support for quick-and-easy logical design of GoldenGate solutions using GoldenGate Studio.

- Nine-digit trail file sequence to support 1 billion files per trail.

- Expanded heterogeneous support.

- Enhanced security with the introduction of a wallet and master key.

- Support for Big Data.

- Support for private and public cloud systems.

- Repair capabilities in Oracle GoldenGate Veridata.

Summary

In this chapter, we discussed a brief history of Oracle GoldenGate and its popularity as compared to other replication options. We talked about synchronous and asynchronous replications and few popular replication options available to you. We also looked at the various advantages that Oracle GoldenGate has to offer as compared to other replication solutions and some common business requirements for when you should implement Oracle GoldenGate. We briefly listed the Oracle GoldenGate 12c new features, which we will be discussing in detail as we proceed through the book.

Now that you have an understanding of what we are talking about in this book, let's proceed to the next chapter, which discusses the architecture and components of Oracle GoldenGate. Pay special attention to the different replication topologies in which you can configure Oracle GoldenGate and the business scenarios when a particular replication topology should be implemented.

CHAPTER 2

███

Architecture

In the previous chapter, you learned about data replication and some popular replication solutions available for your business. You also got an idea of what Oracle GoldenGate has to offer for your replication needs. We'll discuss the Oracle GoldenGate architecture in this chapter. Oracle GoldenGate has a modular architecture with each component integrated to work with each other.

Figure 2-1 shows the basic Oracle GoldenGate architecture. The extract process captures database changes from the database transaction logs and writes them to the source trails. These source trails are *pumped* (or passed) by data pumps to the target system where a dynamic collector process writes them to disk as remote trails. A replicat reads these remote trails and writes the database changes on the target system.

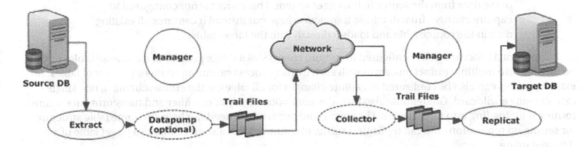

Figure 2-1. *Oracle GoldenGate basic architecture*

Both the source and the target have a manager control process. The manager process manages each of the other components of GoldenGate.

Oracle GoldenGate consists of following components:

- Extract
- Data pump
- Replicat
- Trails
- Collector
- Manager
- Checkpoints

© Ravinder Gupta 2016

R. Gupta, *Mastering Oracle GoldenGate*, DOI 10.1007/978-1-4842-2301-7_2

Overview of the Components

Let's discuss in detail each of the main components of Oracle GoldenGate listed in the previous section. Understanding how these components work will help you in customizing Oracle GoldenGate for your specific replication needs and will also help you effectively troubleshoot any errors encountered during setup.

Extract

An *extract* is a capture process that captures an insert, update, or delete performed on a source schema. An extract process can also be configured to capture DDL changes performed on the source DB and send them across the target DB in the form of trails (or trail files) routed across a TCP/IP network. The extract process captures these changes from database transaction logs, and only committed changes are captured and written to trail files.

There are primarily three types of extracts.

- *Local extracts*: This is the extract process that captures changes from database transaction logs and writes the changes in local trail files.

- *Data pumps*: This is the extract process that reads the local trails generated from the local extracts and sends them to the target server. Having a data pump in your GoldenGate configuration is highly recommended. The advantages of having a data pump are discussed in the following section.

- *Initial load extracts*: This type of extract process is configured for the initial load of the data from the source to the target system. This extract is not configured to capture changes from database transaction logs, but instead it captures all existing data in the source table and loads it directly into the target table.

The extract process can be configured to capture changes as a single process to capture all tables or can be divided into multiple extract processes with each extract process capturing changes for a set of tables. An extract process can also be configured to capture changes for all tables in the entire schema in one single extract using a wildcard. GoldenGate also provides numerous ways you can filter and transform data before routing it for loading into target tables. The source and target tables need not have the same table structure for setting up replication. You can replicate a subset of columns from a source table to a target table of a different name.

Data Pump

Data pumps are similar to GoldenGate extract processes. These are the secondary extract processes that read from the source trails written by the local extract and pump them to the target over a TCP/IP network. Having data pumps is not absolutely necessary but is highly recommended. If you do not have data pumps configured, extracts must be configured to send the trails to the target system. The following are some of the advantages of having a data pump:

- *Protection against losing connectivity to target system*: Assume that your target system has gone down or there is a network connectivity issue. In such a scenario, not having a data pump will mean the extract process directly tries to send trails to an unreachable target host. The extract process in this situation will *abend* since it is no longer able to communicate and send trails to the target host. No more capturing will happen until the network connectivity or failed target system is restored. To reduce the dependency of the source on connectivity to the target system, Oracle recommends using data pumps in your GoldenGate setup.

Now assume that you have data pumps reading from source trails and pumping the trails to target over a TCP/IP network. In case of any connectivity issue to target system, the data pump will abend (stop working) as it will not be able to communicate to the target system. But you still have extracts running on the source and capturing and writing the changes in form of source trails on the source system. Thus, data pump also facilitates the storage facility by letting the extract capture change and store them on disk until the data pump processes them.

- *Filter and transformation*: When you are filtering and transforming data, it is good to do this with the data pump as it may greatly reduce the unnecessary data being sent over the network and then later filtered at the target system.

- *One-to-many replication*: If you have multiple targets, you can configure individual data pumps for each target. When one target goes down, only the corresponding data pump is affected, and the other target systems continue to receive data.

- *Many-to-one replication*: In a configuration of data being consolidated from many sources to one target, data pumps allow you to store extracted trails at the source database itself and send one trail at a time to the target. This way of diving storage load between multiple sources and the targets avoids huge space requirements on the target system for storing these trails.

Replicat

The extract process captures changes on the source system and writes them to local trail files. These trail files are then sent to the target system over a TCP/IP network. A replicat is the delivery process that is configured on the target system to read the trails and apply the changes to the target system. The changes are applied in the database in same order as they were committed on the source system. There are two types of extracts based on how and what changes are captured.

- *Initial load replicat*: An initial load replicat is a special replicat that is configured for the initial load of the target tables from the source tables. These replicats are used only one time during the initial load and can be deleted once their job is done.

- *Replicat for change synchronization*: These replicats are configured for reading changes from the remote trails and applying these changes to the target database by reconstructing the captured DML or DDL. These are the typical delivery processes of your GoldenGate configuration that will be reading captured database changes in the trail files and continuously applying them on the target database.

Like the extract, the replicat can also be configured as a single process for delivery changes for the entire schema or can be split into multiple processes for delivering the changes for each set of source tables. Data filter and transformation can also be applied in the replicat process before writing the changes to the target systems.

Trails

The extract process captures and writes the committed transactions sequentially into files called *trails*. These trails are then sent across the network where they are written on the remote machine before being read by the replicat.

There are two types of trails.

- *Source trails*: Trails written by the extract process on the local staging area are called *source trails* or *local trails*.

- *Remote trails*: Source trails are received on the target system by a background process called a *collector* and written to a similar trails called *remote trails*. These remote trails are the one that will be read by the replicat, and changes will be written to the target database.

Collector

The collector is a process that runs in the background on the target system, receives trails from extracts, and writes them locally into remote trails for processing by the replicat. If you are using a dynamic port configuration, when identifying a connection request from the extract to the manager, the collector scans an available port and sends this port information to the manager for establishing a connection with the extract process. The collector process is a background process, and you will not need to configure it in your GoldenGate setup.

Manager

The manager is the main process that runs and controls all other Oracle GoldenGate processes and components. It contains control information for processes configured on the specific Oracle GoldenGate instance. For your extract or replicat to be running, the manager should also be running. GoldenGate Manager has the following main functions:

- Maintains the port number for communication over the network

- Starts and stops the extracts and replicat

- Generates reports for the processes

- Contains control parameters like "Purge old trails," and so on

- Manages trail files

Checkpoints

Checkpoints are the way GoldenGate keeps track of which transaction it has replicated. GoldenGate extracts create checkpoints for their position in the source database and trail. Since extract captures only committed transactions, it tracks all the open transactions. Once a transaction is committed, extracts look behind the oldest open transaction position. This information is written by the extract on the disk in the form of checkpoint files.

The replicat, on the other hand, creates checkpoints for its position in the trail. This information is more effectively stored in checkpoint tables created in the target database. GoldenGate also stores this information on the disk in the form of checkpoint files.

The checkpoint facilitates database recovery and ensures data consistency. It guarantees that a transaction is applied only once even if the replicat is restarted after a failure.

Support for Non-Oracle Databases

Oracle GoldenGate supports capture and delivery on most of the popular databases, as listed in Table 2-1. However, you cannot install Oracle GoldenGate as the source on the DB2 for i and TimesTen databases. You still have the option to send feeds from other supported databases and apply the transactions on the DB2 for i or TimesTen databases.

Table 2-1. *Support for Capture and Delivery on Popular Databases*

Database	Supports Extract	Supports Replicat
DB2 for i	No	Yes
DB2 for Linux, Unix, Windows, zOS	Yes	Yes
Oracle	Yes	Yes
MySQL	Yes	Yes
Microsoft SQL Server	Yes	Yes
Sybase	Yes	Yes
Teradata	Yes	Yes
TimesTen	No	Yes

Supported Topologies

The flexible and decoupled architecture of GoldenGate allows it to support a varied range of replication topologies. The following are some of the most common supported replication topologies:

- Unidirectional replication
- Bidirectional replication
- One-to-many replication
- Many-to-one replication
- Peer-to-peer replication

We will discuss each of these topologies and examples of scenarios when the replication topology is suitable.

Unidirectional Replication

A unidirectional replication between a source and a target is the simplest replication topology. Any database change on the source is replicated to the target. In this architecture, the target is read-only, and the changes are made only at the source database.

This type of replication topology is best suited for query offloading and reporting purpose. Figure 2-2 shows a simple view of a unidirectional replication between a source database and a target database.

Source DB   **Target DB**

Figure 2-2. *Unidirectional replication*

When to Use Unidirectional Replication?

The following are some of the business scenarios when you would need to implement a simple unidirectional replication between two database systems.

- To maintain a hot standby database for failover purpose

- For query offloading on a standby database

- For zero-downtime database upgrades or migration

Figure 2-3 shows components of Oracle GoldenGate in a unidirectional replication configuration. You would need to install two separate Oracle GoldenGate instances, one for each database. The source instance will capture changes and send it to the target system over the network. The second instance on the target database will read from the trail files and apply the transactions on the target database in real time.

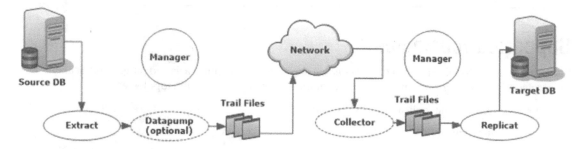

Figure 2-3. *Oracle GoldenGate unidirectional replication configuration*

Bidirectional Replication

In a bidirectional replication configuration, database changes may occur on either of the two systems. Either of the two systems can be the source or the destination. This is also known as two-way replication or an active-active replication since both the systems are active and receive transaction changes. A bidirectional active-active configuration should have identical objects and data. Transactions can be performed on either database and are replicated to the other database by Oracle GoldenGate for consistency. Figure 2-4 shows a simple view of two systems in a bidirectional replication configuration.

Figure 2-4. *Bidirectional replication*

Limitations of Bidirectional Configuration

For data consistency, often one of the two sites is considered to be the master. We will discuss this in detail in Chapter X when we set up a bidirectional replication using Oracle GoldenGate. Truncates are not supported in bidirectional replication. This means you cannot allow truncate operations to replicated from any of the two sites. However, you can configure your replication to allow truncates in one direction, and truncates should always happen on one particular database that acts as a master in your bidirectional replication configuration.

Figure 2-4 shows a simple view of bidirectional replication between two databases.

When to Use Bidirectional Replication?

The following are some of the business scenarios when you would need to set up a bidirectional replication:

- *Active-active high availability system*: In a high availability configuration, if one database server crashes because of software or hardware failure, the application can be restarted to point another database without having to wait for the crashed database to be fixed. The application user can use either of the databases for business processing. Such a configuration can be effectively achieved using Oracle GoldenGate in a bidirectional replication configuration.

- *Load sharing*: This configuration is used for load sharing among the two databases. This boosts the overall database system performance to a higher grade. To allow load sharing without any changes to the application and database configuration, the two databases participating in load sharing should be identical. This can be effectively achieved by using Oracle GoldenGate bidirectional replication.

- *Disaster tolerance*: A bidirectional replication configuration can be used for disaster tolerance as well. When one database goes down, the other database continues to support application. Once the failed database is back, it is synchronized and made consistent with the other database.

- *Zero-downtime upgrades*: A bidirectional replication configuration can be used for database upgrades with zero downtime involved. You can set up bidirectional replication between the existing and new databases. If the upgraded database doesn't work as expected, you can switch back to the older database that was kept in sync by Oracle GoldenGate.

Figure 2-5 shows interaction between components of Oracle GoldenGate in a bidirectional replication configuration.

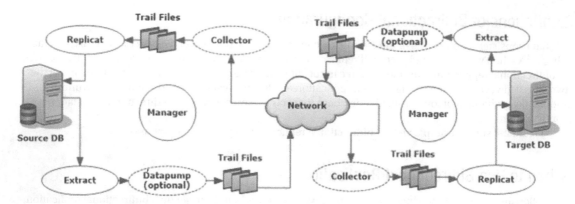

Figure 2-5. *Oracle GoldenGate bidirectional replication configuration*

One-to-Many Replication

In this configuration, a source database is synchronized across multiple target databases. This can include both homogeneous and heterogeneous systems. Data from the source is captured and manipulated if required and is sent across multiple target databases. It is significantly important to use data pumps in this configuration for fault tolerance. If one target goes down, the corresponding data pump will get affected, but other data pumps can continue sending data to the remaining target systems. Figure 2-6 shows a simple view of a one-to-many replication configuration.

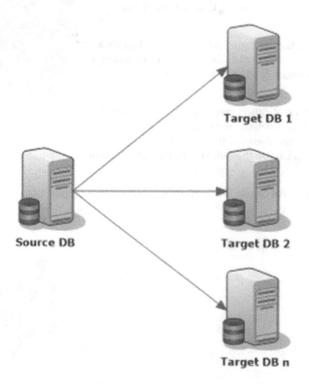

Figure 2-6. *One-to-many replication*

When to Use One-to-Many Replication?

Here are some of the common business scenarios when you would need to implement one-to-many replication configuration. These business requirements can be effectively achieved using Oracle GoldenGate real-time replication.

- For reporting purpose, when source data is to be distributed across multiple target databases

- For multiple standby database to serve as backups in case of the failure of production database

Figure 2-7 shows the interaction between various components of Oracle GoldenGate in a one-to-many replication configuration.

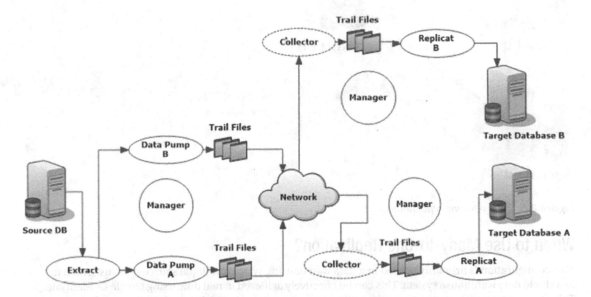

Figure 2-7. *Oracle GoldenGate one-to-many replication configuration*

Many-to-One Replication

Data is sent from multiple source databases to one repository target database. This kind of many-to-one replication can be between both homogeneous and heterogeneous databases. Figure 2-8 shows a simple view of many-to-one replication between databases.

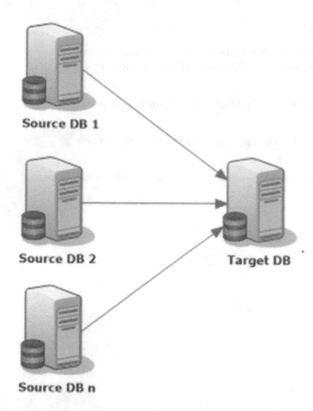

Figure 2-8. *Many-to-one replication*

When to Use Many-to-One Replication?

This configuration is primarily needed in a data warehousing system. Multiple source systems send data to a single data warehouse system. This can be effectively achieved in real time using Oracle GoldenGate. This allows data warehouse users to effectively generate reports using real-time data. Figure 2-9 shows components of Oracle GoldenGate in a many-to-one replication configuration.

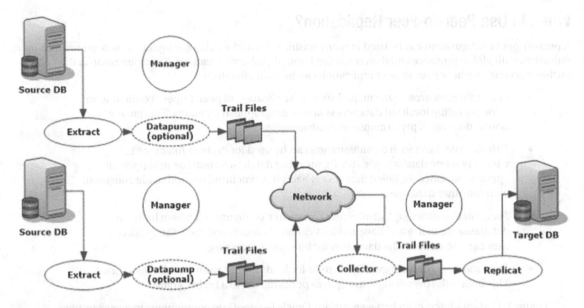

Figure 2-9. *Oracle GoldenGate many-to-one replication configuration*

Peer-to-Peer Replication

Peer-to-peer or multimaster replication contains multiple master sites. It is also called an *update anywhere* model, where changes made on one site are propagated to all other sites in the architecture. This ensures global transaction concurrency and data integrity. Each database is an exact replica of all other databases in the peer-to-peer configuration. Figure 2-10 shows a simple view of peer-to-peer replication configuration.

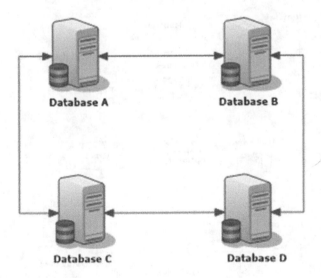

Figure 2-10. *Peer-to-peer replication*

When to Use Peer-to-Peer Replication?

A peer-to-peer configuration can be used in many business scenarios. This configuration is common among industries with global presence and data is received from distributed locations. These are some of the business scenarios where peer-to-peer replication can be used effectively:

- *Localized data access*: One major business application of peer-to-peer configuration is for providing localized data access across geographical locations. This greatly boosts the overall performance of database system.

- *Disaster tolerance*: Such a configuration can be used for disaster tolerance as well. When one database goes down, the other databases continue to support the application. Once the failed database is back, it is synchronized and made consistent with the other databases.

- *For an active-active high availability system*: In a configuration where both the databases are active and have an identical set of objects and data, the application user can use either of the databases for business processing.

- *Load sharing*: This configuration is used for load sharing among each master site. This boosts the overall database system performance to a higher grade.

Figure 2-11 shows interaction between various Oracle GoldenGate components in a peer-to-peer replication.

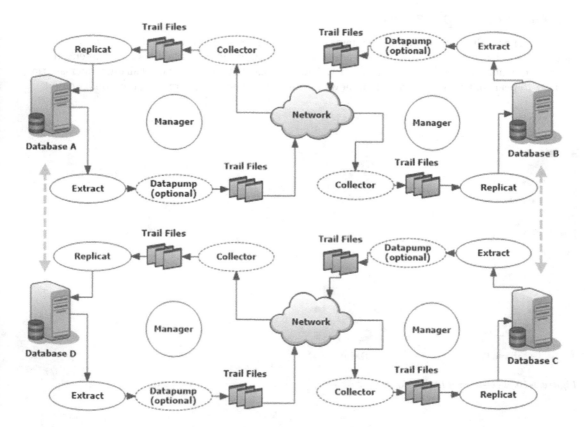

Figure 2-11. *Oracle GoldenGate peer-to-peer replication configuration*

Summary

To be able to effectively implement and use a technology, it is necessary that you understand the overall architecture and have a clear picture of how the various components interact with each other. In this chapter, we discussed various components of Oracle GoldenGate and how they interact with each other for providing you with a near real-time replication system with subseconds of latency. We discussed the various types of capture and the apply process. We also discussed various replication topologies in which you can configure Oracle GoldenGate and the business scenarios when the particular replication topology should be implemented.

Having reached this point, you are now ready to begin installing the Oracle GoldenGate software to configure your first replication environment. In the next chapter, we will discuss pre-installation tasks, including designing your Oracle GoldenGate replication environment and configuring the source and target databases.

CHAPTER 3

■ ■ ■

Oracle GoldenGate Pre-installation Tasks

The Oracle GoldenGate pre-installation preparation involves three major categories.

- Design considerations and requirements
- Oracle GoldenGate replication setup
- Database privileges for GoldenGate users

The first step when planning to set up Oracle GoldenGate replication between your source and target databases is to make sure your databases and OS platforms are supported. For a list of supported platforms for Oracle GoldenGate, refer to Table 1-1 in Chapter 1.

Memory Requirements

The amount of memory needed by you is directly related to the bulk of transactions that happen on your source database and the retention period of the trail files. More memory will be required for tables with bulk transactions as compared to tables with fewer transactions. The capture processes will be reading these transactions and writing them into trail files. Oracle GoldenGate supports up to 5,000 extract and replicat processes per GoldenGate instance. Each extract needs a minimum of 25 MB to 55 MB of memory for processing. The amount of RAM available to Oracle GoldenGate can significantly affect the overall performance by reducing or increasing the number of swapping to disk.

Disk Space Requirements

You will need only around 400 MB of disk space for the Oracle GoldenGate binaries. A large amount of disk storage is, however, needed for the trail files. A good rule of thumb is to have at least 2 GB of free disk space reserved for GoldenGate trails.

Network Requirements

The effectiveness of high-speed, minimal-latency, real-time replication using Oracle GoldenGate is also dependent on the network used for transferring trail files from the source system to the target system. The following are some key requirements for a high-performing network to be used for Oracle GoldenGate.

© Ravinder Gupta 2016
R. Gupta, *Mastering Oracle GoldenGate*, DOI 10.1007/978-1-4842-2301-7_3

- Use the fastest network available to you for the optimal performance of Oracle GoldenGate. Good performance of the network is essential for real-time and reliable replication.

- The network should be configured to use TCP/IP services. Oracle GoldenGate supports both IPv4 and IPv6 protocols.

- Configure the network with the host and IP addresses of the systems with which Oracle GoldenGate will be connecting, in other words, the source and target database servers.

- Make sure that ports are available for Oracle GoldenGate. The default port used by GoldenGate is 7,840, but depending on the number of concurrent processes, it's good to use a range of ports. We will discuss later in this book how to use a range of ports for GoldenGate replication.

- The network firewall should allow connections through Oracle GoldenGate ports.

Ensure that you have appropriate permissions on the directory where you are installing Oracle GoldenGate. You need to have read-write privileges to troubleshoot and maintain Oracle GoldenGate replication environment.

Configuring Your Database and Server for Oracle GoldenGate

Once you ensure that your OS/network meets the desired criteria for the GoldenGate installation, you need to configure your database for replication. The first step is to configure environment variables specific to your database and operating system. For example, if you are installing Oracle GoldenGate for an Oracle database, you would need to set up ORACLE_HOME and ORACLE_SID if they are not already set up. These parameters should be correctly set up as they will be referred to by Oracle GoldenGate processes while connecting to the Oracle database.

If you have more than one database instance on the same server, then you would need to set ORACLE_HOME and ORACLE_SID for each GoldenGate process using SETENV statements in parameter files of each Oracle GoldenGate process.

```
SETENV (ORACLE_HOME = "oracle home directory path here")
SETENV (ORACLE_SID = "SID")
```

Oracle GoldenGate processes use the database shared libraries. You will need to set the shared library variable for this purpose.

Set LD_LIBRARY_PATH if you are using HP-UX, Linux, or Sun Solaris OS and LIBPATH if you are using the IBM AIX operating system.

```
export PATH=$PATH:/app/ggs/tiger/:.
export LD_LIBRARY_PATH=$LD_LIBRARY_PATH:/app/oracle/product/orcl/lib/
```

Oracle GoldenGate uses redo logs to capture transactions for replication. For this purpose, you would need supplemental logging enabled for your source database so it can add additional undo information to redo logs, which can be used to locate rows when ROWID information is unavailable. This is especially required while applying update transactions on the target database. Enabling supplemental logging in Oracle databases creates a supplemental log group for each table; this log group contains the list of columns for which supplemental logging will be captured. Let's discuss briefly how to enable supplemental logging for some of the popular supported databases.

Enable Logging for Oracle Databases

Log in as the DBA user in the Oracle database and verify whether supplemental logging is already enabled.

```
SELECT supplemental_log_data_min, force_logging FROM v$database;
```

If both of the previous are already YES, your database is already configured for the logging needed by Oracle GoldenGate. Setting up force logging is optional; you can only set supplemental minimal logging and add table/schema-level supplemental logging from the GoldenGate Software Command Interface (GGSCI). This is especially recommended when only a few tables/schema are to be replicated. This will in turn reduce logging overhead for the entire database.

Enable minimal supplemental logging at the database level, as follows:

```
SQL> ALTER DATABASE ADD SUPPLEMENTAL LOG DATA;
```

Optionally, you can enable force logging for the entire database.

```
SQL> ALTER DATABASE FORCE LOGGING;
```

After changing logging option, either FORCE LOGGING or MINIMAL SUPPLEMENTAL LOGGING, you must switch log files, as follows:

```
SQL> ALTER SYSTEM SWITCH LOGFILE;
```

You must enable GoldenGate replication before you can add supplemental logging information for Oracle GoldenGate. Run the following using the sysdba user:

```
SQL> ALTER SYSTEM SET ENABLE_GOLDENGATE_REPLICATION=TRUE;
System altered.
```

Log in to GGSCI and enable supplemental logging for the GoldenGate table/schema, as follows:

```
GGSCI> DBLOGIN USERID user_name, PASSWORD password
GGSCI> ADD SCHEMATRANDATA schema_name ALLCOLS
```

or as follows:

```
GGSCI> ADD SCHEMATRANDATA schema_name NOSCHEDULINGCOLS
```

To enable logging for particular tables, use ADD TRANDATA. You can specify the container name, column list, and so on, with this command. Refer to Chapter 8 for more details on using options for Oracle GoldenGate commands.

```
GGSCI> ADD TRANDATA schema_name.table_name
```

Enable Logging for Sybase Databases

Log in to GGSCI and enable transaction logging for all the tables.

```
GGSCI> DBLOGIN SOURCEDB database_name USERID user_name
```

Issue one of the following commands to enable trandata for a Sybase table based on how you want to handle LOB data. You can choose not to replicate LOB using LOBSNEVER or always replicate LOB using LOBSALWAYS. LOBSIFCHANGED means supplemental information for LOB is captured only if there is a change in LOB data. Here are several examples:

```
GGSCI> ADD TRANDATA table_name
```

or

```
GGSCI> ADD TRANDATA table_name, LOBSNEVER
```

or

```
GGSCI> ADD TRANDATA table_name, LOBSALWAYS
```

or

```
GGSCI> ADD TRANDATA table_name, LOBSIFCHANGED
```

The extract process refers to the secondary truncate point in a Sybase source database to determine the transactions to be processed. Set this secondary log truncation point as shown here:

```
isql> use tigerdb
isql> go
isql> dbcc settrunc( 'ltm', valid )
isql> go
```

Enable Logging for Microsoft SQL Server Databases

If your source database is Microsoft SQL Server, make sure it is set to full recovery model. Log in to GGSCI and enable supplemental logging.

```
GGSCI> DBLOGIN SOURCEDB <dsn>, USERID user_name, PASSWORD password
GGSCI> ADD TRANDATA owner_name.table_name
```

The previous command creates a secondary truncation log point in the SQL Server database. You can either manage it via the Oracle GoldenGate extract process or through the SQL Server database.

Use the MANAGESECONDARYTRUNCATIONPOINT command for managing the secondary truncation log point in the extract process.

```
TRANLOGOPTIONS MANAGESECONDARYTRUNCATIONPOINT
```

Define the interval for moving the secondary log point in SQL Server as shown here:

```
EXEC sp_repldone @xactid = NULL, @xact_segno = NULL, @numtrans = 0, @time = 0, @reset = 1
```

Enable logging for an IBM DB2 Database on the Linux/Unix/Windows platform.

The first step is to do one of the following; either enable USEREXIT or use LOGRETAIN RECOVERY:

```
db2 update db cfg for database_name using USEREXIT ON
```

or

```
db2 update db cfg for database_name using LOGRETAIN RECOVERY
```

Next, set your source database to retain the transaction log for roll-forward recovery.

```
db2 update db cfg for database_name using LOGARCHMETH1 LOGRETAIN
db2 update db cfg for database_name using LOGARCHMETH2 OFF
```

or

```
db2 update db cfg for database_name using LOGARCHMETH1 DISK
db2 update db cfg for database_name using LOGARCHMETH2 TSM
```

Verify the log retention parameters.

```
db2 connect to database_name USER user_name using password
db2 get db cfg for database_name
```

Before you restart extract process, ensure that you have taken a full backup of the database.

```
db2 backup db database_name to device_name
```

You will also need to set the `OVERFLOWLOGPATH` parameter to the archive log directory.
Log in to GGSCI and enable supplemental logging for the tables to be replicated.

```
GGSCI> DBLOGIN SOURCEDB dsn, USERID user_name , PASSWORD password
```

Issue one of the following to add trandata to the table based on how you want to handle long data.

```
GGSCI> ADD TRANDATA table_name
```

or

```
GGSCI> ADD TRANDATA table_name, EXCLUDELONG
```

Supported Data Types

Before you start designing your Oracle GoldenGate replication environment, let's take a look at the supported data types for a few popular databases.

Supported Data Types for Oracle Databases

Oracle GoldenGate supports many of the Oracle database data types, as listed here:

- Abstract data type
- BASICFILE Lob
- BINARY DOUBLE
- BINARY FLOAT

- `BLOB`
- `CHAR`
- `CLOB`
- Clustered table
- `DATE`
- `DATETIME`
- Index organized tables
- `LONG`
- `LONG RAW`
- Materialized view
- `NCHAR`
- `NCLOB`
- Nested tables
- `NUMBER`
- `NVARCHAR2`
- Object table
- `PDML`
- `RAW`
- `SECUREFILE` Lob
- Sequence
- `TIMESTAMP`
- Transparent data encryption
- `VARCHAR2`
- `VARRAY`
- `XA`
- XML stored as `CLOB/Binary`

Oracle GoldenGate supports DDL operations approximately up to 2 MB for the following Oracle objects:

- Cluster
- Function
- Index
- Materialized view
- Package
- Procedure

- Role
- Sequence
- Synonym
- Table
- Tablespace
- Trigger
- Type
- User
- View

Supported Data Types for SYBASE Databases

The following are the Sybase ASE data types that can be replicated using Oracle GoldenGate:

- BIGDATETIME
- BIGTIME
- BINARY
- BIT
- CHAR
- DATE
- DATETIME
- DECIMAL
- DOUBLE
- FLOAT
- IDENTITY
- IMAGE
- INT
- MONEY
- NCHAR
- NUMERIC
- NVARCHAR
- REAL
- SMALLDATETIME
- SMALLINT
- SMALLMONEY

- TEXT
- TIME
- TINYINT
- UNICHAR
- UNIVARCHAR
- VARBINARY
- VARCHAR

Supported Data Types for MySQL Databases

Oracle GoldenGate effectively supports many commonly used MySQL data types for replication:

- BIG INT
- BINARY
- BIT(M)
- BLOB
- CHAR
- DATE
- DATETIME
- DECIMAL
- DOUBLE
- ENUM
- FLOAT
- INT
- LONGBLOB
- LONGTEXT
- MEDIUM INT
- MEDIUMBLOB
- MEDIUMTEXT
- SMALL INT
- TEXT
- TIME
- TIMESTAMP
- TINYBLOB
- TINYINT

- `TINYTEXT`
- `UINT64`
- `VARBINARY`
- `VARCHAR`
- `YEAR`

Supported Data Types for SQL Server Databases

Oracle GoldenGate supports all SQL Server data types except `SQL_VARIANT`.

Supported Data Types for DB2 Databases on LUW

On the Linux, Unix, or Windows platform, Oracle GoldenGate supports all IBM DB2 data types except the XML data type, user-defined data types, and negative dates.

Supported Data Types for DB2 Databases on z/OS

On a z/OS platform, Oracle GoldenGate supports all DB2 data types except XML, user-defined data types, negative dates, and `DECFLOAT`.

Supported Operations

Oracle GoldenGate supports many but has limitations with some of the database operations. Here we discuss the database operations captured by Oracle GoldenGate for the popular databases.

Database Operations Captured for Oracle Databases

The following are supported: insert, update, and delete operations on regular tables, index organized tables, clustered tables, and materialized views. There are, however, few limitations, as listed here:

- Virtual columns are not captured.
- Tables created as `EXTERNAL` are not captured.
- Tables created with table compression are not supported.
- Materialized views created with `ROWID` are not supported.

`SEQUENCES` are supported in an active-passive replication structure. The source and target sequence must have identical cache size and incremental interval values.

DDL operations approximately up to 2 MB are supported on the following Oracle objects:

- Cluster
- Function
- Index
- Materialized view

- Package

- Procedure

- Role

- Sequence

- Synonym

- Table

- Tablespace

- Trigger

- Type

- User

- View

The TRUNCATE statement is supported, however, in active-active bidirectional replication. TRUNCATES must always originate on the same server.

No DDL operations are supported on Oracle reserved schemas.

Database Operations Captured on Sybase Databases

Insert, update, and delete operations on tables with row lengths of up to 512 KB are supported.

Deferred inserts, deferred indirect inserts, deferred updates, and deferred deletes are supported.

TRUNCATE TABLE is supported. However, the table name should be unique across all databases/schemas of the Sybase DB server.

Encrypted data in the database with system-encrypted passwords are supported for replication. If the encrypted data uses a user-defined password, they cannot be replicated.

DDL operations are not replicated.

BATCHSQL used in the Oracle GoldenGate replicat is not available when the target database is Sybase.

Database Operations Captured on MySQL Databases

INSERT, UPDATE, DELETE, START TRANSACTION, COMMIT TRANSACTION, ROLLBACK TRANSACTION, and TRUNCATE are, supported for transactional tables with no limit on row size or maximum number of columns in table.

Oracle GoldenGate also supports the AUTO_INCREMENT attribute on a column.

DDL replication is not supported for the MySQL database.

BATCHSQL used in the Oracle GoldenGate replicat is not available when the target database is MySQL.

Database Operations Captured on SQL Server Databases

Oracle GoldenGate supports INSERT, UPDATE, and DELETE operations on tables with a row length of up to 512 KB. However, TEXT, NTEXT, IMAGE, VARBINARY, VARCHAR (MAX), and NVARCHAR (MAX) columns are supported to their full size limit in SQL Server.

Data compression and tables with partitions are also supported. The partitioned table should have the same physical layout across all partitions.

DDL replication is not supported.

BATCHSQL used in the Oracle GoldenGate replicat is supported.

Database Operations Captured on DB2 Databases for LUW

INSERT, UPDATE, DELETE, and TRUNCATE operations on tables are supported for replication by Oracle GoldenGate.

Multidimensional clustered tables (MDC tables) are supported.

Base tables of the materialized query tables (MQT) are supported for replication.

DDL replication is not supported.

Database Operations Captured on Sybase Databases for z/OS

INSERT, UPDATE, and DELETE operations are supported for tables with a row length of up to 512 KB.

TRUNCATE TABLE is always captured on the source and is ignored if IGNORETRUNCATES is specified in the replicat parameter files.

DDL replication is not supported.

Designing Your GoldenGate Replication Setup

An important pre-step of setting up Oracle GoldenGate replication is to understand the standard naming conventions and best practices while designing your setup. Using a well-designed and intuitive naming convention while designing the overall architecture of your GoldenGate real-time replication configuration will serve multiple benefits.

Why Choose Standard Naming Conventions?

You are free to use your own naming conventions while designing your Oracle GoldenGate replication. However, choosing standard naming conventions brings several benefits that you must consider. These benefits of using standard naming conventions include the following:

- Standard names are intuitive and easy to remember.
- They are significant in saving time during maintenance.

Naming Capture and Delivery Process

In this section, we will list the standard practice followed while naming your capture and delivery processes. This, however, is not mandatory but a recommended convention that will be used in the examples in this book. For naming your extract, replicat, and data pump, you can use the following recommendations:

- An extract should start with *E* followed by seven alphanumeric characters.
- A data pump can start with either *P* or *D* followed by seven alphanumeric characters.
- A replicat should start with *R* followed by seven alphanumeric characters.

Each character in the name of your capture or delivery process can have a meaningful abbreviation. Before you decide on the name of these processes, you may need to know the source and the target applications, the tables to be replicated, and so on. In the following section, I explain the naming conventions that I will be using in the examples in this book.

Know Your Application

Before you begin designing your Oracle GoldenGate replication architecture for your business, it is good to know your application and environment. This will help you choose proper naming conventions for your capture and delivery processes. Table 3-1 lists the example system that we will be using for the examples in this book.

Table 3-1. *Example Source and Target Application*

Source Application	TIGER	T
Target Application	FOX	F
Source Location	TENNESSEE	TN
Target Location	DALLAS	DL

Next, you group the tables to be replicated. These groups indicate individual extract/replicat processes in which different table groups will be added. This grouping choice often depends on the number of transactions per group. The best practice would be to keep the load distributed on different extract/replicat channels. Table 3-2 shows the three groups in which I have clubbed tables of the `tiger` schema to be replicated through three different extract and replicat channels.

Table 3-2. *Table Groups Based on Transactional Load*

Group 1	Group 2	Group 3
COUNTRY	ORDER_DTL	BILLING
CUSTOMER_INFO	ORDER_TYPE	BILLING_SUMMARY
ACCOUNT_DTL	PRODUCTS	
ACCOUNT_TYPE	ORDER_HIST	

Based on whether you are setting up replication on a development, test, user acceptance testing (UAT), or production environment, you can choose a single character in your extract, data pump, and replicat group names to identify the application environment. Table 3-3 shows the abbreviation that we will use in the examples of this book.

Table 3-3. *Application Environment for Replication*

Development	D
Test	T
UAT	U
Production	P

Based on the information from Tables 3-1 to 3-3 or other additional information for your specific application environment, choose the names for your capture and delivery process. For the later examples in the book, I will be using the GoldenGate channel names shown in Table 3-4. Yes! You guessed it right. Extract, data pump, and replicats are also commonly called GoldenGate *channels* for replication.

Table 3-4. *Example GoldenGate Channels*

Extract	Data Pump	Replicat
ETTND001	PFTND001	RFDLD001
ETTND002	PFTND002	RFDLD002
ETTND003	PFTND003	RFDLD003

Just by looking at the channel names, you can interpret some specific information, as listed in Table 3-5. This kind of naming convention may take a while to get used to, but I have found it useful in large database environments where I had hundreds of servers with a complex network of replication among them.

Table 3-5. *Interpreting Your Channel Name*

1st Letter (Process Type)	Extract	E
	Data Pump	P
	Replicat	R
2nd Letter (Database User/Schema)	TIGER	T
	FOX	F
3rd and 4th Letters (Location of Database)	TENNESSEE	TN
	DALLAS	DL
5th Letter (Application Environment)	Development	D
	Test	T
	UAT	U
	Production	P
6th, 7th, and 8th Letters (Channel Number)	001, 002, and so on	

Next, you will need to identify the names for your local and remote trails. A trail file name starts with two unique alphanumeric characters, and the remaining eight characters are numeric characters managed by GoldenGate itself.

In the examples in this book, I will use the trail name initials listed in Table 3-6.

Table 3-6. *Trail Sequence for Extract, Data Pump, and Replicat*

Extract	Local Trail	Data Pump	Remote Trail	Replicat
ETTND001	t1	PFTND001	f1	RFDLD001
ETTND002	t2	PFTND002	f2	RFDLD002
ETTND003	t3	PFTND003	f3	RFDLD003

It is good practice to document the entire design before you are ready to implement your setup. Once you have your architectural design ready for the GoldenGate real-time replication, you can start with creating scripts and commands, as discussed in the next chapter.

Based on your replication environment to be unidirectional, bidirectional, one-to-many, or many-to-one, you will need to consider the following points for designing your GoldenGate setup:

- Know the type of replication you need.

- Are you planning to replicate only data changes or are structural changes also involved?

- Know the various capture process groups into which you will divide the tables to be replicated. This grouping can be based on various application-specific factors such as transactional load, criticality of the tables, and so on. Keep in mind, if one channel goes down because of any reason, all the tables in the channel are affected. Also, loading all the tables or a large number of tables in same channel may delay replication in the case of heavy transactional load on the tables.

Database Privileges for GoldenGate Users

Oracle GoldenGate processes, specifically the extract and replicat processes, require database credentials to perform replication. Table 3-7 lists the significant privileges that are required for the GoldenGate users used in the extract and replicat processes.

Table 3-7. Database Privileges for Oracle GoldenGate User

	Extract		Replicat	
Privilege	Classic Mode	Integrated Mode	Nonintegrated Mode	Integrated Mode
CREATE SESSION	Y	Y	Y	Y
RESOURCE	Y	Y	Y	Y
ALTER SYSTEM	Y	Y		
dbms_goldengate_auth.grant_ admin_privilege	Y	Y	Y	Y
INSERT, UPDATE, DELETE on target schema tables			Y	Y
CREATE TABLE			Y	Y
DDL privileges on target schema (if DDL replication is required)			Y	Y
DBA	Y	Y	Y	Y

I recommend creating separate users for managing GoldenGate replication and granting the required table privileges from the owner schema to this user. However, in this book, for convenience I will use the TIGER and FOX owner schemas for GoldenGate replication as well.

OGG User Permissions in Oracle Databases

The base privileges required by the Oracle GoldenGate user in Oracle databases are given through the dbms_ goldengate_auth.grant_admin_privileges package.

Use following to grant base privileges to the GoldenGate user ggsuser. Execute the following command to grant privilege to both the capture and apply processes.

```
SQL> exec dbms_goldengate_auth.grant_admin_privilege('ggsuser')
```

Optionally, you can specify whether you are providing the privilege to the capture or apply process as shown here:

```
SQL> exec dbms_goldengate_auth.grant_admin_privilege('ggsuser','capture');
SQL> exec dbms_goldengate_auth.grant_admin_privilege('ggsuser','apply');
```

OGG User Permissions in Sybase Databases

In the Sybase ASE database, you can either grant system administration role sa_role to the GoldenGate user or more specifically grant replication_role as shown here:

```
isql> sp_role 'grant', replication_role, 'ggsuser'
```

or shown here:

```
isql> use database_name
isql> go
isql> grant role replication_role to ggsuser
isql> go
```

OGG User Permissions in IBM DB2 Databases

Privileges required by the Oracle GoldenGate user are managed by the SYSADM or DBADM roles in the IBM DB2 database. The role can be granted as follows in the IBM DB2 database:

```
SQL> grant DBADM to ggsuser;
```

The use on the replicat side, however, only needs connect and select on the system catalog and DML permissions on the replicated tables. These required privileges for the Oracle GoldenGate user on the target using the IBM DB2 database can be granted as shown here:

```
SQL> grant connect to ggsuser;
SQL> grant select, insert, update, delete on table_name to ggsuser;
```

OGG User Permissions in MySQL Databases

The Oracle GoldenGate user for MySQL databases requires read permission on the INFORMATION_SCHEMA database. Apart from this, an extract requires the following privileges:

- SELECT ANY TABLE
- Read and Execute on the MySQL configuration file and its directory
- Read and Execute on binary logs
- Read and Execute on the tmp directory

The replicat user (in other words, the Oracle GoldenGate user) on the target database needs the following permissions for applying changes on the target database:

- INSERT, DELETE, and UPDATE on the target database tables

- EXECUTE on stored procedures

- CREATE TABLE (required only when using the checkpoint table)

OGG User Permissions in Teradata Databases

Oracle GoldenGate is frequently used for Teradata databases for real-time replication. Create a user dedicated for GoldenGate replication in a Teradata database and provide grants as listed here:

```
GRANT SELECT ON DBC.REPGROUP TO ggsuser;
GRANT REPLCONTROL TO ggsuser;
GRANT SELECT ON DBC.TVM TO ggsuser;
GRANT SELECT ON DBC.INDEXES TO ggsuser;
GRANT SELECT ON DBC.INDOUBTRESLOG TO ggsuser;
GRANT SELECT ON DBC.DBASE TO ggsuser;
GRANT SELECT ON DBC.ERRORMSGS TO ggsuser;
GRANT SELECT ON DBC.TVFIELDS TO ggsuser;
GRANT ALL ON database_name TO ggsuser;
GRANT ALL ON SYSUDTLIB TO ggsuser WITH GRANT OPTION;
```

Summary

The chapter discussed pre-installation tasks to do before downloading and installing your Oracle GoldenGate software. Pre-installation preparations can be broadly divided into three categories: design considerations and requirements, designing OGG replication for your specific application environment, and database privileges for Oracle GoldenGate users.

The chapter discussed these pre-installation tasks for some of the popular databases like Oracle, SQL Server, IBM DB2, Sybase ASE, and Teradata. The Oracle GoldenGate configuration for different database types is more or less similar. Sound knowledge and experience with two or three of popular databases is enough to give you the confidence to set up Oracle GoldenGate replication for any of the supported databases in a homogeneous or heterogeneous environment.

At this stage, you are ready to set up basic one-directional replication. In the next chapter, you will perform your first Oracle GoldenGate installation for replication between two Oracle databases. The chapter will present a step-by-step guide for installing and configuring replication between the TIGER and FOX schemas discussed in this chapter.

CHAPTER 4

■ ■ ■

Installing Oracle GoldenGate

It's time to begin your first Oracle GoldenGate installation. The example in this chapter is a simple one-directional replication between two Oracle databases. We will, however, discuss heterogeneous and more complex replication structures in later sections of this book.

This chapter explains how to install Oracle GoldenGate 12.1.2 on Oracle Database 12c.

Download the Installer

Based on your database and operating system platform, download the appropriate installer from the Oracle web site (https://edelivery.oracle.com). You need to create an Oracle Technology Network (OTN) account to be able to download the software from the Oracle web site. Oracle GoldenGate is available as part of Oracle Fusion Middleware Pack. Here's an outline of the steps to follow:

1. Navigate to https://edelivery.oracle.com.

2. Sign in if you already have an OTN account; if not, register. Figure 4-1 shows the welcome screen for the Oracle Software Delivery Cloud site.

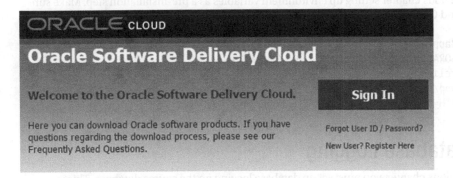

Figure 4-1. Welcome page of the Oracle Software Delivery Cloud site

3. Once logged in, search for *Oracle Fusion Middleware* and select the appropriate platform. Figure 4-2 shows the search window where you can select the product and platform.

© Ravinder Gupta 2016
R. Gupta, *Mastering Oracle GoldenGate*, DOI 10.1007/978-1-4842-2301-7_4

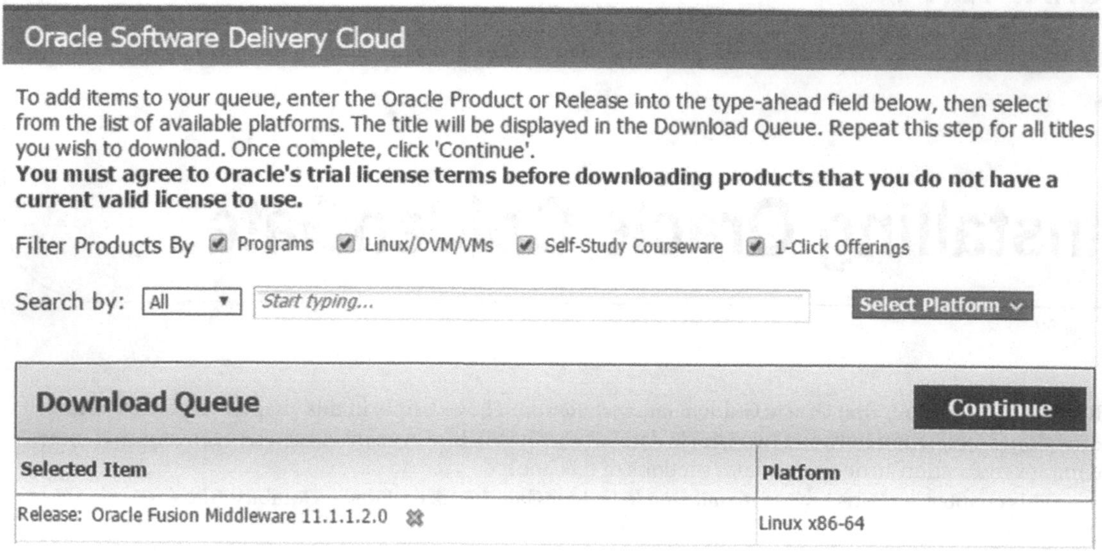

Oracle Software Delivery Cloud

To add items to your queue, enter the Oracle Product or Release into the type-ahead field below, then select from the list of available platforms. The title will be displayed in the Download Queue. Repeat this step for all titles you wish to download. Once complete, click 'Continue'.
You must agree to Oracle's trial license terms before downloading products that you do not have a current valid license to use.

Filter Products By ☑ Programs ☑ Linux/OVM/VMs ☑ Self-Study Courseware ☑ 1-Click Offerings

Search by: | All ▼ | | Start typing... | | Select Platform ∨ |

Download Queue		Continue
Selected Item		Platform
Release: Oracle Fusion Middleware 11.1.1.2.0 ✖		Linux x86-64

Figure 4-2. Selecting the software and platform

4. Click Continue to proceed.

5. You must read and accept Oracle's terms and conditions to download software.

6. Click Download and save your media pack file.

Setting Up Environmental Variables

We discussed in the previous chapter setting up environment variables as a pre-installation step. Make sure your Oracle database and Oracle GoldenGate environment variables are set as follows:

```
export ORACLE_BASE=/app/oracle
export ORACLE_HOME=$ORACLE_BASE/product/12.1.0.2/dbhome_1
export ORACLE_SID=orcl1
export PATH=$PATH:/app/ggs/tiger/:.
export LD_LIBRARY_PATH=$LD_LIBRARY_PATH:$ORACLE_HOME/lib/
```

Setting Up Database Logging

As discussed in the previous chapter, you must set up database logging on the source database. This is, however, not required on the target database in a one-directional replication setup. Supplemental logs are required only by extract processes to capture transactions for replication.

Enable minimal supplemental logging at the database level.

```
SQL> ALTER DATABASE ADD SUPPLEMENTAL LOG DATA;
Database altered.
```

Switch the log file.

```
SQL> ALTER SYSTEM SWITCH LOGFILE;
System altered.
```

Log in to GGSCI and enable supplemental logging for the GoldenGate table/schema.

```
GGSCI> DBLOGIN USERID tiger, PASSWORD tiger123_
Successfully logged into database
GGSCI> ADD SCHEMATRANDATA tiger ALLCOLS
```

Setting Up User Privileges

Set up an Oracle GoldenGate user in the database and grant the appropriate permissions as discussed in the previous chapter. You need to set up database privileges for both the source and target GoldenGate users. In this example, the source user is TIGER on the orcl1 database, and the target user is FOX on the orcl2 database.

We have already installed and set up the two Oracle databases orcl1 and orcl2, the source and target schemas, and some sample tables, as listed in Chapter 3's Table 3-1 and Table 3-2. You can use an existing database schema/user for your Oracle GoldenGate replication, or you can create a dedicated user just for OGG replication. It is preferable to create a dedicated OGG user and give SELECT, INSERT, UPDATE, and DELETE grants on the tables from the owner schema to the OGG user. Let's configure the two schemas for OGG replication.

On the source database, set up the following privileges for the TIGER user:

```
SQL> dbms_goldengate_auth.grant_admin_privilege('tiger','capture');
SQL> GRANT CREATE SESSION TO username WITH ADMIN OPTION;
SQL> GRANT RESOURCE TO TIGER;
SQL> GRANT ALTER SYSTEM TO TIGER;
```

On the target database, set up the following privileges for the FOX user:

```
SQL> dbms_goldengate_auth.grant_admin_privilege('fox','apply');
SQL> GRANT CREATE SESSION TO username WITH ADMIN OPTION;
SQL> GRANT RESOURCE TO FOX;
SQL> GRANT ALTER SYSTEM TO FOX;
```

Installing Oracle GoldenGate on Unix/Linux

Here we will discuss installing and configuring Oracle GoldenGate on Oracle Database 12c on the Linux platform. The steps for installation on the Linux and Unix platforms are the same. To install Oracle GoldenGate and set up your first replication configuration, follow the steps outlined in the next sections.

Step 1: Log In as the Linux Superuser

You should be logged into the server as the Linux user under which you are installing GoldenGate. The Linux user should have read and write privileges for the directory in which you want to install GoldenGate software. You can switch to the desired Linux user by issuing the following command in the terminal:

```
su - oracle
```

I installed Oracle GoldenGate under the oracle user.

Step 2: Navigate to the GoldenGate Directory

Once you are logged in as your Linux user on the server, navigate to the directory where the GoldenGate installation will be done. For example, I have used the following location for setting up Oracle GoldenGate on my source machine:

```
cd /app/ggs/tiger
```

Step 3: Copy or FTP the GoldenGate Software File from the Local System or Remote Server

Place the .zip file in the /app/ggs/tiger directory where Oracle GoldenGate is to be installed. If you have a compressed .zip file, unzip the file. You can issue following command to unzip the compressed GoldenGate software you downloaded from the Oracle web site:

```
[oracle@ravin-ravinpc tiger]$ unzip 121200_fbo_ggs_Linux_x64_shiphome.zip
```

Step 4: Locate the Installer

Up until GoldenGate 11.2, installing GoldenGate binaries was pretty much a single step task. Just untar the compressed binaries into the desired location and it's done.

For Oracle GoldenGate 12, Oracle has included a GUI installer that takes care of configuring your manager process and creating Oracle GoldenGate subdirectories.

Navigate to Disk1 from the unzipped contents, as shown here:

```
[oracle@ravin-ravinpc tiger]$ cd /app/ggs/tiger/fbo_ggs_Linux_x64_shiphome/Disk1


[oracle@ravin-ravinpc Disk1]$ ls -lrt
total 12
drwxr-xr-x.  4 oracle oinstall 4096 Apr 29 17:15 install
drwxr-xr-x.  2 oracle oinstall   24 Apr 29 17:15 response
-rwxr-xr-x.  1 oracle oinstall  918 Apr 29 17:15 runInstaller
drwxr-xr-x. 11 oracle oinstall 4096 Apr 29 17:16 stage
```

Step 5: Begin Installation

If you are installing on a remote host from a Windows machine, you need to use an X Server for Windows. I usually use Xming X Server for Windows. Once your X Server is started, set your display variable on the remote host as follows:

```
export DISPLAY=<your windows machine IP where X server is running>:0.0
```

Kick off the runInstaller file, which will do a quick space and display check and take you to a GUI installer. You can follow along with the screenshots in Figure 4-3 to 4-9.

```
[oracle@ravin-ravinpc tiger]$ ./runInstaller
```

If you are going to use Oracle Database 12c features, select the first option, as shown in Figure 4-3.

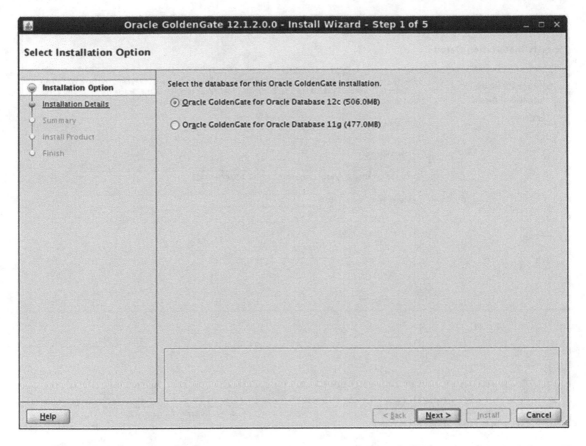

Figure 4-3. *Choosing the installation option*

Next, as shown in Figure 4-4, specify the Oracle GoldenGate base directory where your GoldenGate software will be installed, and all the OGG process directories will be created inside this directory.

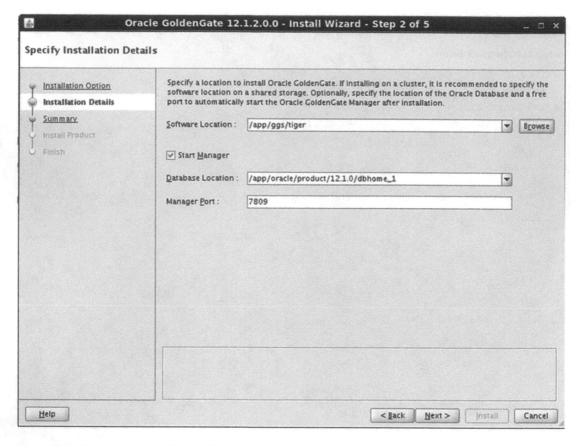

Figure 4-4. *Entering the installation details*

If you have your database already installed, it will automatically pick the database location.

The default manager port is 7809. You can specify DYNAMICPORTLIST in the parameter file later if you do not want to use a dedicated port.

As shown in Figure 4-5, it asked me if I want to continue installing to my nonempty directory /app/ggs/tiger. My installer files are also present in same directory. This is absolutely fine, and I can delete the .zip file and any installer file after installation to reclaim space.

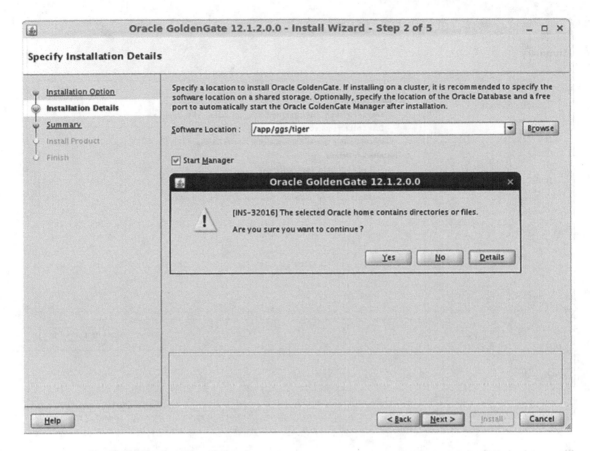

Figure 4-5. *Verifying your installation details*

Figure 4-6 shows the installation summary. Review your installation summary and click Install to begin the installation.

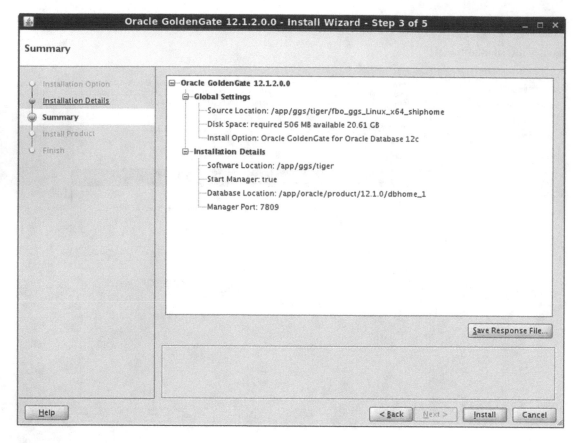

Figure 4-6. *Installation summary*

It asks you twice to make sure you are not going to overwrite anything that you need and then later blame the Oracle Installer (OUI) for messing with your useful files. So, be very careful about any warning messages the OUI gives you before clicking Yes, as shown in Figure 4-7.

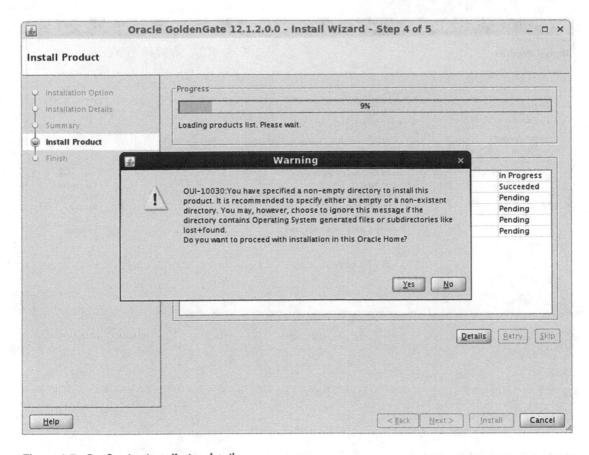

Figure 4-7. *Confirming installation details*

The installation is quick and took less than ten minutes to complete on my machine. Figure 4-8 shows the Succeeded and In Progress installation tasks.

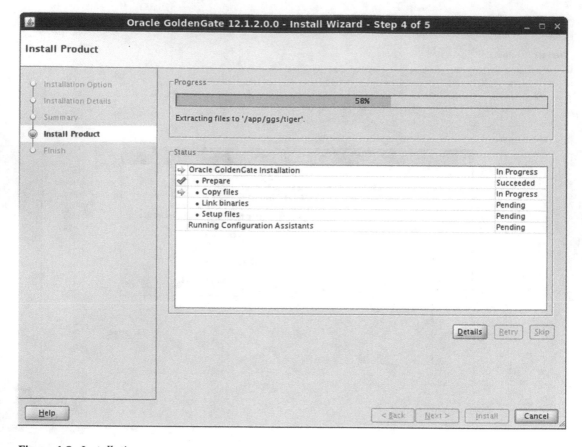

Figure 4-8. *Installation progress*

Figure 4-9 shows that the Oracle GoldenGate software installation was successfully completed on the source machine.

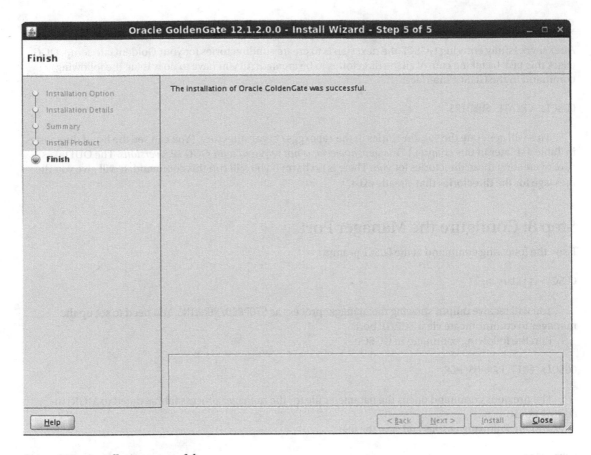

Figure 4-9. Installation successful

Step 6: Execute GGSCI

Now that your binaries have been installed, you can try running GGSCI. (As mentioned in Chapter 3, GGSCI is an acronym for the GoldenGate Software Command Interface). For GGSCI to run, you need to set up the ORACLE_HOME and LD_LIBRARY_PATH environment variables. They should be set up in your user profile. When I executed GGSCI on my machine, I was successfully able to start GGSCI, as shown in Figure 4-10.

```
[oracle@ravin tiger]$ export ORACLE_HOME=/app/oracle/product/12.1.0/dbhome_1
[oracle@ravin tiger]$ export LD_LIBRARY_PATH=$ORACLE_HOME/lib
[oracle@ravin tiger]$ ./ggsci

Oracle GoldenGate Command Interpreter for Oracle
Version 12.1.2.0.0 17185003 OGGCORE_12.1.2.0.0_PLATFORMS_130924.1316_FBO
Linux, x64, 64bit (optimized), Oracle 12c on Sep 25 2013 02:33:54
Operating system character set identified as UTF-8.

Copyright (C) 1995, 2013, Oracle and/or its affiliates. All rights reserved.


GGSCI (ravin.ravinpc) 1> ▮
```

Figure 4-10. Logging into GGSCI

Step 7: Create Subdirectories

After successfully entering GGSCI, the next step is to create subdirectories for your GoldenGate setup. OGG eases this task by taking care of all the directories to be created. All you have to do is issue the following command in the GGSCI interface:

```
GGSCI> CREATE SUBDIRS
```

This will generate the subdirectories in the /app/ggs/tiger directory. (You can see the list of directories in Table 4-1 later in this chapter.) *This step, however, is not required with OGG 12.x versions.* The OUI takes care of creating these directories for you. There is no harm if you still run this command. It will give you the message for the directories that already exist.

Step 8: Configure the Manager Port

Issue the following command at the GGSCI prompt:

```
GGSCI> status all
```

You will receive output showing the manager process as STOPPED/RUNNING. You need to set up the manager to communicate via a TCP/IP port.

Run the following command in GGSCI:

```
GGSCI> EDIT PARAMS MGR
```

The previous command opens the parameter file for the manager process (abbreviated to MGR) in editing mode.

Add the following entries and save the file:

```
PORT 7809
AUTOSTART E*
LAGINFOMINUTES 5
LAGCRITICALMINUTES 5
```

Only the PORT 7809 part is mandatory for getting your manager process running.

PORT 7809 tells GoldenGate to communicate via TCP/IP port 7809. You can also set up a dynamic port list by adding the following command:

```
DYNAMICPORTLIST 7809-7879
```

LAGINFOMINUTES specifies how often lag information is reported to the error log file ggserror.log.

AUTOSTART automatically starts the specified extract/replicat process when the manager starts. Here we have specified to start all processes (channels) starting with *E* when the manager starts. This is specifically useful during system reboots.

Step 9: Start/Stop the Manager

Once you have set up the manager process, you can start the manager process by issuing the following command:

```
GGSCI> START MGR
```

Check the status of the manager by issuing following command at the GGSCI prompt:

```
GGSCI> status all
```

The manager should be in running status. If your manager process is stopped or abended, you can view the report file for errors as follows:

```
GGSCI> view report mgr
```

The most common reason for your manager to be stopped is that the TCP/IP port is already in use. Try using another port number in the parameter file for the manager process.

You can stop the manager process after you are able to successfully start it.

```
GGSCI> STOP MGR
```

You can again check the status by issuing the following command at the GGSCI prompt:

```
GGSCI> status mgr
or
GGSCI> status all
```

The manager should now be in stopped status.

Step 10: Check Supplemental Logging for the Database

Log in to the DBA user in the Oracle database and verify whether supplemental logging is already enabled. Since you have configured your OGG user with dba access, you can log in using the tiger schema as well.

```
SELECT supplemental_log_data_min, force_logging FROM v$database;
```

If both of the previous are already YES, your database is already configured for the logging needed by Oracle GoldenGate. Setting up force logging is optional; you can only set supplemental minimal logging and add table/schema-level supplemental logging from GGSCI. This is especially recommended when only few tables/schemas are to be replicated. It will in turn reduce the logging overhead for the entire database. If you have already enabled supplemental logging before OGG installation, you can skip this step.

Enable minimal supplemental logging at the database level.

```
SQL> ALTER DATABASE ADD SUPPLEMENTAL LOG DATA;
```

Optionally, you can enable force logging for the entire database.

```
SQL> ALTER DATABASE FORCE LOGGING;
```

After changing the logging option, either FORCE logging or MINIMAL SUPPLEMENTAL LOGGING, you must switch log file.

```
SQL> ALTER SYSTEM SWITCH LOGFILE;
```

Step 11: Add Extracts

Execute the following command on GGSCI to create your extract process:

```
GGSCI> ADD EXTRACT ETTND001, TRANLOG, BEGIN NOW
```

Or execute this

```
GGSCI> ADD EXTRACT ETTND001, TRANLOG, BEGIN 2015-11-10 04:03
```

You use the BEGIN timestamp if you want to start a transaction capture sometime after you actually create the extract.

Assign a local trail file sequence to the extract.

```
GGSCI> ADD RMTTRAIL /app/ggs/tiger/dirdat/t1, EXTRACT ETTND001, MEGABYTES 60
```

Next, you need to create the parameter file with instructions for replication for this extract. Run the following command from GGSCI:

```
GGSCI> EDIT PARAMS ETTND001
```

Add the following entries in the parameter file:

```
EXTRACT ETTND001
USERID TIGER, PASSWORD tiger123_
RMTHOST node2.ravin-pc.com, MGRPORT 7809
RMTTRAIL /app/ggs/fox/dirdat/f1
TABLE TIGER.ORDER_DTL;
```

■ **Note**   The login schema should have access to v$database and v$log and complete access on tables to be captured for changes.

Save the parameter file. It is optional to create the data pump process at this stage. We will discuss it in a more detailed setup example later in this book. For now, the simple installation of GoldenGate will have only one extract communicating to one replicat process.

Before we start the extract process, you need to install Oracle GoldenGate on your target machine and add the replicat process.

Step 12: Install Oracle GoldenGate on the Target Machine

Follow steps 1 to 9 and install Oracle GoldenGate on your target machine where data will be replicated. You can choose same manager port on your target machine or a different manager port. The source and target machine manager ports do not need to be same. You just need to specify the correct port number being used on the target in the extract parameter file on the source.

I installed OGG on my target machine node2.ravin-pc.com at location /app/ggs/fox.

Step 13: Add the Replicat

Execute the following command at the GGSCI prompt to create the replicat process:

```
GGSCI> ADD REPLICAT RFDLD001, EXTTRAIL /app/ggs/fox/dirdat/f1, NODBCHECKPOINT
```

Create the parameter file for this replicat. Run the following command from GGSCI:

```
GGSCI> EDIT PARAMS RFDLD001
```

Add the following entries in the parameter file for the replicat:

```
REPLICAT RFDLD001
PURGEOLDEXTRACTS
ASSUMETARGETDEFS
DISCARDFILE /app/ggs/fox/dirrpt/rfdld001.dsc, PURGE, MEGABYTES 599
USERID fox, PASSWORD fox123_
MAP TIGER.ORDER_DTL, TARGET FOX.ORDER_DTL;
```

Step 14: Create the Definition File

If your source and target table structure and name are different, you need to create a definition file on your source and transfer it to your target. This definition file is then referred to by the Oracle GoldenGate replicat process for mapping the source and target tables and applying the replicated transactions.

Create a temporary parameter file temp.prm in the /app/ggs/tiger/dirprm directory on the source machine and add the following entries:

```
DEFSFILE /app/ggs/tiger/dirdef/rfdld001.def
USERID TIGER, PASSWORD tiger123_
TABLE TIGER.ORDER_DTL;
```

Run the following command from the OGG home directory /app/ggs/tiger. This will generate the definition file.

```
defgen paramfile dirprm/temp.prm
```

A definition file gets generated at /app/ggs/tiger/dirdef/rfdld001.def and is ready to be copied to the target server.

Copy /app/ggs/tiger/dirdef/rfdl001.def from the source machine to /app/ggs/fox/dirdef/rfdl001.def on the target machine.

Remove ASSUMETARGETDEFS and add the following to your replicat parameter file:

```
SOURCEDEFS /app/ggs/fox/dirdef/rfdld001.def
```

Step 15: Enable Supplemental Logging for Oracle GoldenGate

Log in to GGSCI on the source and enable supplemental logging for GoldenGate table/schema. This needs to be done only on the capture side. Replicat processes do not need supplemental logging.

```
GGSCI> DBLOGIN USERID tiger, PASSWORD tiger123_
GGSCI> ADD SCHEMATRANDATA tiger ALLCOLS
or
GGSCI> ADD SCHEMATRANDATA tiger NOSCHEDULINGCOLS
```

To enable logging only for specific tables, use ADD TRANDATA. You can specify the database container name, column list, and so on with this command. Refer to Chapter 8 for more details on using options for Oracle GoldenGate commands.

```
GGSCI> ADD TRANDATA tiger.order_dtl
```

Step 16: Initial Data Synchronization

All the existing source data of tables to be replicated needs to be copied to the target database in order for any replication to succeed. There is more than one way that data copying can be done. The copy method used is dependent on the volume of data in the source database that needs to be copied over.

In most cases, the export and import of data can be performed by copying the source data to the target environment. Oracle provides utilities like expdp and impdp for this purpose.

Another method is to set up the initial extract and replicat processes for one-time synchronization.

Setting Up the Initial Extract Process on Source

Add the initial load extract process by executing the following command. Here, SOURCEISTABLE informs Oracle GoldenGate that the extract process is the initial load extract and the entire table content needs to be captured for replication.

```
GGSCI> ADD EXTRACT INITEXT1, SOURCEISTABLE
```

Edit the extract parameter file.

```
GGSCI> EDIT PARAMS INITEXT1
EXTRACT INITEXT1
RMTHOST node2.ravin-pc.com, MGRPORT 7809
RMTTASK REPLICAT, GROUP INITREP1
USERID tiger, PASSWORD tiger123_
TABLE TIGER.ORDER_DTL;
```

Setting Up the Initial Replicat Process on the Target

Add the initial load replicat on the target machine's GoldenGate instance, SPECIALRUN informs GoldenGate that the replicat process is the initial load replicat and will process trails received from an initial load extract.

```
GGSCI> ADD REPLICAT INITREP1, SPECIALRUN
```

Edit the replicat parameter file.

```
GGSCI> EDIT PARAMS INITREP1

REPLICAT INITREP1
ASSUMETARGETDEFS
DISCARDFILE /app/ggs/fox/dirrpt/initrep1.dsc, MEGABYTES 599, append
USERID FOX, PASSWORD fox123_

MAP TIGER.ORDER_DTL, TARGET FOX.ORDER_DTL;
```

Start the initial load extract and replicat process. Let all the data get copied once before proceeding to the next step, where you start your regular extract and replicat processes to begin the real-time replication.

Initial data synchronization methods are discussed in detail in Chapter 7.

Step 17: Start the Manager, Extract, and Replicat, and Test the Result

You should be able to start your GoldenGate processes now. First start the GoldenGate manager and replicat processes on the target followed by the GoldenGate manager and extract processes on the source system.

A replicat is a listener process and should be started before extract or extract will stop again with a TCP/IP communication error.

Log in to the target machine and start the manager.

```
GGSCI> START MGR
```

Verify whether the manager is running and troubleshoot any error during the starting manager process. Start the replicat process.

```
GGSCI> start RFDLD001
```

Check whether the replicat is running.

```
GGSCI> status RFDLD001
```

or use this:

```
GGSCI (node2.ravin-pc.com) 1> info all
```

Program	Status	Group	Lag at Chkpt	Time Since Chkpt
MANAGER	RUNNING			
REPLICAT	RUNNING	RFDLD001	00:00:00	00:00:10

If the replicat is abended/stopped, view the report file for errors. Refer to Chapter 15 for troubleshooting Oracle GoldenGate errors.

Next, log in to the source machine and start the manager on the source.

```
GGSCI> START MGR
```

Verify whether the manager is running and troubleshoot any errors during the starting manager process.

You can start the extract now to begin capturing transactions from the source database.

```
GGSCI> start ETTND001
```

Check whether the extract is running.

```
GGSCI> status ETTND001
```

or use this:

```
GGSCI (node1.ravin-pc.com) 1> info all

Program      Status       Group        Lag at Chkpt    Time Since Chkpt

MANAGER      RUNNING
EXTRACT      RUNNING      ETTND001     00:00:00        00:00:10
```

If the extract is abended/stopped, view the report file for errors. Refer to Chapter 15 for troubleshooting Oracle GoldenGate errors.

Now that you have your extract running, verify that the extract has started generating trail files at the local trail location /app/ggs/tiger/dirdat/t1. Your first trail file name will be t1000000.

Check stats on the extract and replicat to see the transaction counts being captured and applied.

```
GGSCI> stats ETTND001
GGSCI> stats RFDLD001
```

Silent Installation

Before version 12.*x* of Oracle GoldenGate, there was the option to simply uncompress into the directory where you want to install GoldenGate. OUI replaced this with a GUI installer that does a couple of background pre- and post-setups to simply the overall installation.

There still might be a situation where you do not want to use the OUI and instead perform a silent install without intervention.

This installation method will require you to configure a response file first. Once you unzip the compressed installer binaries, go to the response directory to find the response file.

```
[oracle@ravin fox]$ unzip ./121200_fbo_ggs_Linux_x64_shiphome.zip –d ggate
[oracle@ravin fox]$ cd /app/ggs/fox/fbo_ggs_Linux_x64_shiphome/Disk1/response
```

The response file name provided with the installer is oggcore.rsp.

Parameters in the Response File

```
INSTALL_OPTION=
ORA12c or ORA11g
```

```
SOFTWARE_LOCATION=
Where to install the software
```

```
START_MANAGER=
TRUE or FALSE
```

```
MANAGER_PORT=
Any port number, default 7809
```

```
DATABASE_LOCATION=
Set to $ORACLE_HOME
```

```
INVENTORY_LOCATION=
Specify location for oraInventory
```

```
UNIX_GROUP_NAME=
Group that should own the installation of Golden Gate
```

Once you have configured your response file, you can run it with the runInstaller script.

```
[oracle@ravin response]$ ../runInstaller -silent -responseFile /app/ggs/fox/fbo_ggs_Linux_
x64_shiphome/Disk1
/response/oggcore.rsp
Starting Oracle Universal Installer...
Checking Temp space: must be greater than 120 MB.    Actual 38378 MB    Passed
Checking swap space: must be greater than 150 MB.    Actual 7804 MB    Passed
Preparing to launch Oracle Universal Installer from /tmp/OraInstall2015-11-09_12-32-23AM.
Please wait ...
[oracle@ravin response]$ You can find the log of this install session at:
/oracle/oraInventory/logs/installActions2015-11-09_12-32-23AM.log
The installation of Oracle GoldenGate Core was successful.
Please check '/oracle/oraInventory/logs/silentInstall2015-11-09_12-32-23AM.log' for more
details.
```

OGG Subdirectories

Both the OUI and silent installation for Oracle 12c create the subdirectories as part of installation. For earlier versions, you must issue the CREATE SUBDIRS command in GGSCI to create the subdirectories. Table 4-1 lists the GGSCI directories and their usage.

Table 4-1. *Oracle GoldenGate Directories*

Directory	Files It Stores
dirprm	Parameter files
dirrpt	Report files
dirchk	Checkpoint files
dirpcs	Process status files
dirsql	SQL script files
dirdef	Database definitions files
dirdat	Extract data files
dirtmp	Temporary files
dirver	Veridata files
dirver/lock	Veridata lock files
dirver/oos	Veridata out-of-sync files
dirver/oosxml	Veridata out-of-sync XML files
dirver/params	Veridata parameter files
dirver/report	Veridata report files
dirver/status	Veridata status files
dirver/trace	Veridata trace files
dirout	Stdout files

Handling Character Set

Oracle GoldenGate provides globalization support, which means data can be processed in its own native language.

Before discussing in detail how Oracle GoldenGate preserves character sets when out-of-sync source and target database character sets are different, take a look at Table 4-2, which lists some of the Oracle character sets. There are about 200 Oracle character sets currently supported by Oracle GoldenGate. For a complete list, refer to the Oracle documentation.

Table 4-2. *Supported Oracle Character Sets*

Character Set	Description
ar8ados710t	Arabic MS-DOS 710 8-bit Latin/Arabic
ar8arabicmact	Mac 8-bit Latin/Arabic
ar8hparabic8t	HP 8-bit Latin/Arabic
ar8iso8859p6	ISO 8859-6 Latin/Arabic
ar8mswin1256	MS Windows Code Page 1256 8-Bit Latin/Arabic
az8iso8859p9e	ISO 8859-9 Azerbaijani

(continued)

Table 4-2. (*continued*)

Character Set	Description
bg8pc437s	IBM-PC Code Page 437 8-bit (Bulgarian Modification)
blt8iso8859p13	ISO 8859-13 Baltic
blt8pc775	IBM-PC Code Page 775 8-bit Baltic
hu8abmod	Hungarian 8-bit Special AB Mod
in8iscii	Multiple-Script Indian Standard 8-bit Latin/Indian
ja16dbcs	IBM EBCDIC 16-bit Japanese
ko16mswin949	MS Windows Code Page 949 Korean
s8ebcdic1143	EBCDIC Code Page 1143 8-bit Swedish
th8tisebcdics	Thai Industrial Standard 620-2533 - EBCDIC Server 8-bit
we8dec	DEC 8-bit West European
we8iso8859p1	ISO 8859-1 West European

Table 4-3 lists some of the non-Oracle character sets supported by OGG. There are more than 150 non-Oracle character sets supported by OGG. For a complete list, you can check the Oracle documentation on supported character sets.

Table 4-3. *Supported Non-Oracle Character Sets*

Character Set	Description
UTF-8	ISO-10646 UTF-8, surrogate pairs are 4 bytes per character
UTF-16	ISO-10646 UTF-16
UTF-32	ISO-10646 UTF-32
US-ASCII	US-ASCII, ANSI X34-1986
windows-1250	Windows Central Europe
ibm-867	DOS Hebrew/IBM
IBM277	IBM 277-1/697-1 EBCDIC, Denmark, Norway
IBM500	IBM 500-1/697-1 EBCDIC, International
ibm-942	IBM Windows Japanese

For preserving the character set while processing data, Oracle GoldenGate takes into account the character set of database metadata, the character data types, the session character set for database connection, the character sets of input and output commands on the command line, and the character set of human-readable text files such as report files, definition files, discard files, parameter files, and so on.

Using CHARSET

By default, the parameter files of Oracle GoldenGate are created using the character set of the operating system. If you need to use a different character set to support characters not supported by the operating system character set, you can specify the CHARSET parameter in your EXTRACT, REPLICAT, MANAGER, DEFGEN, and GLOBALS parameter files.

It should be the first line in the parameter file. The syntax to use CHARSET is as follows:

```
CHARSET character_set_name
```

You can alternatively use escape sequence to specify a characters not supported by your operating system character set.

Using Escape Sequences

To use a character in your parameter file that is not supported by your operating system character set, you can use an escape sequence in this format: \<escape sequence type>.

Types of Escape Sequences in OGG

The following are types of escape sequences in OGG:

- *Unicode escape sequence*: \uFFFF

- *Octal escape sequence*: \377

- *Hexadecimal escape sequence*: \xFF

Escape sequences can be used anywhere in a parameter file. These are frequently used in TABLE or MAP statements of the extract and replicat parameter files. Here's an example:

```
TABLE TIGER."\u3000XYZ";
```

Using SOURCECHARSET

Until Oracle GoldenGate 11.2.1, the OGG extract process did not write source character set information in the trail file. If your source and target character sets are different, you need to use the SOURCECHARSET parameter in your replicat parameter file to let Oracle GoldenGate on the target know the source character set.

```
SOURCECAHRSET we8dec
```

However, this conversion is taken care by default in version 11.2.1 and later.

This, however, does not mean the SOURCECHARSET parameter has become obsolete. In situations when you do not want the automatic character set conversion to happen to protect data integrity, you can use SOURCECHARSET PASSTHRU. This is required when a character set conversion causes data to be mispresented on the target system.

In some less frequent scenarios, you may also need to override the source character set and use another character set instead for conversion.

```
SOURCECHARSET OVERRIDE
```

This can be used while doing database migrations.

Using NLS_LANG

You can also use the NLS_LANG parameter in your extract or replicat parameter file to take care of the character set conversion.

```
setenv (NLS_LANG="AMERICAN_AMERICA.AL32UTF8")
```

For OGG 11.2 and earlier, when dealing with the destination character set, which is a superset of source character set, you must specify the NLS_LANG parameter. The character set of your extract process should match with the database character set to correctly read the redo logs. Similarly, the replicat character set should match the character set of the trail files it is reading from.

■ **Tip**   For a quick fix where a character in the trail file cannot be stored in the target database, you can use the REPLACEBADCHAR parameter in the replicat parameter file.

Summary

In this chapter, we discussed the steps to install, configure, and test a basic, one-directional Oracle GoldenGate real-time replication between two Oracle databases. We also discussed configuring the response file that can be used for silent installations of Oracle GoldenGate. We also discussed the Oracle GoldenGate directory structure and types of files stored in each subdirectory created with the CREATE SUBDIR command. Some of the subdirectories may be different depending on your version of Oracle GoldenGate.

We also discussed handling character sets when replicating between two databases with different character sets.

In the next chapter, we will discuss how to implement the classic and integrated capture and apply processes. We will also discuss the coordinated replicat process, which was recently introduced with Oracle GoldenGate 12*c*.

CHAPTER 5

■ ■ ■

Classic vs. Integrated Capture and Apply

In the previous chapter, we discussed the role of the capture and delivery processes in Oracle GoldenGate replication. The capture process in Oracle GoldenGate is called *extract*, and the apply process is called *replicat*.

Until Oracle GoldenGate 11, you had only the classic capture and delivery modes. However, Oracle GoldenGate 11.2 introduced an optional and efficient processing mode, namely, integrated capture. Later Oracle GoldenGate 12 introduced integrated apply as well. *Integrated* refers to the processing capability being integrated with database features. This is native to Oracle database, so if you are using any non-Oracle database, then you will not be able to use integrated capture and apply. Let's discuss what these capture modes are. Then you will look at which capture mode to choose for what kind of replication requirement. Figure 5-1 shows the capture modes available with Oracle GoldenGate 12.*x*. We will discuss each of them in detail.

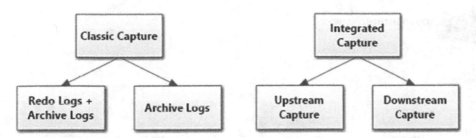

Figure 5-1. *OGG capture modes*

OGG Capture Process

By now you have already been introduced to two OGG capture modes. Let's discuss how they work and how to set up each of them. We will also discuss how to upgrade an existing classic capture to integrated capture mode.

Classic Capture

In the classic capture mode, data changes are captured from the Oracle redo logs/archive logs. This is the initial capture mode developed and used by GoldenGate Software Inc. The classic capture process is supported for all databases that are supported by Oracle GoldenGate. Figure 5-2 shows an Oracle GoldenGate replication configuration when using classic capture.

© Ravinder Gupta 2016
R. Gupta, *Mastering Oracle GoldenGate*, DOI 10.1007/978-1-4842-2301-7_5

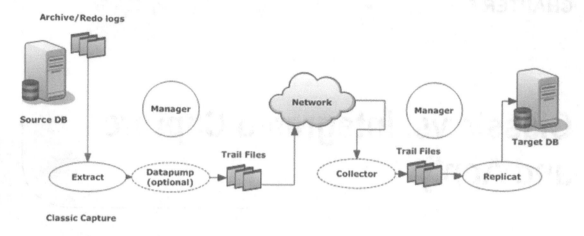

Figure 5-2. *OGG replication using classic capture*

Integrated Capture

This capture mode is specific to Oracle Database 11.2 onward. In the integrated capture mode, the extract process communicates with the database log mining server and receives information in the form of a logical change record (LCR). The database log mining server mines redo log and captures changes in the form of an LCR. Figure 5-3 shows an Oracle GoldenGate replication configuration when using integrated capture.

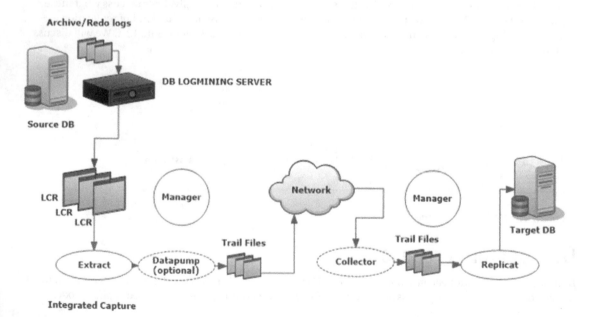

Figure 5-3. *OGG replication using Integrated Capture*

Integrated capture was recently introduced and is a more efficient mode of data capture. Let's discuss a few benefits of integrated capture mode compared to classic capture mode, as listed here:

- It supports more Oracle data types compared to classic capture mode.

- Interaction with the database log mining server allows you to switch automatically between copies of archived logs and mirror images of redo logs. This is useful in the case of disk block corruption of the archived/redo logs.

- It supports a multitenant container database containing multiple pluggable databases. This is not possible with classic capture.

- It has easy configuration for Oracle RAC and ASM.

- It requires Oracle Database 11.2.0.3 or higher.

- It requires more memory, and hence you need to increase the size of MEMORY_TARGET and STREAMS_POOL.

Integrated Capture Modes

Integrated capture supports two types of configuration:

- *On-source capture*: The capture process runs on the actual source database server. Changes will be captured locally and routed to the target in real time. This might add additional workload on the source database server but provides the best real-time option.

- *Downstream capture*: The capture process runs on a remote database server. The Log Writer (LGWR) or Archiver (ARCH) process is configured on the primary database, and redo data is transferred to the standby database server. When using the Archiver process, the redo data is archived whenever a log switch happens on the primary server, whereas LGWR writes redo data to standby redo logs on the downstream server. The changes are then mined from the standby redo logs on the downstream server. This kind of architecture has inherent latency since redo data has to be transferred first on the remote server and then mined to be sent to the target server. This, however, reduces the workload and resource usage from the source database server. Figure 5-4 shows components of the Oracle GoldenGate downstream capture configuration.

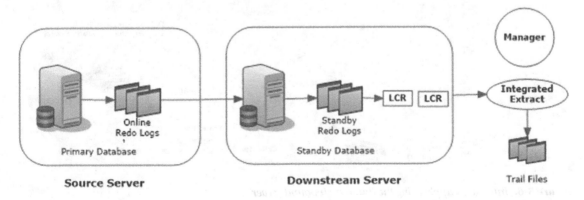

Figure 5-4. *Integrated capture in downstream configuration*

OGG Apply Process

The replicat process can work either in nonintegrated mode or in integrated mode. We will discuss each of these in detail.

Nonintegrated Apply

The replicat process makes use of standard SQL to apply DML or DDL changes to the target system. A change is read from the trail, data conversion or filtering is applied, and a SQL statement is constructed that is then applied on the target database. Figure 5-5 shows the components of Oracle GoldenGate configuration using nonintegrated apply.

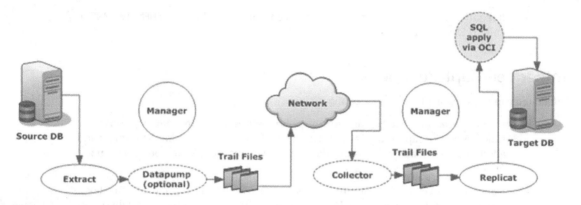

Figure 5-5. Nonintegrated apply using the Oracle Calling Interface (OCI)

Integrated Apply

In this configuration, the Oracle internal apply process is used by the replicat. A change is read from the trail, and the data conversion and filtering takes place. The apply process then constructs an LCR for the DML change. The LCR is then applied to the target database by the inbound server. This mode makes use of parallel apply while keeping intact the atomicity of the transaction. It thereby has higher/faster throughput. Figure 5-6 shows the components of the Oracle GoldenGate configuration using integrated apply.

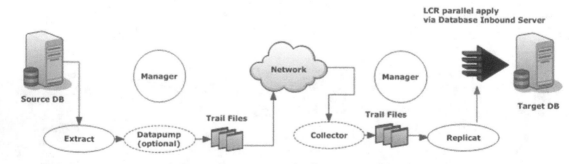

Figure 5-6. Integrated apply using the database inbound server

As is the case with integrated capture, integrated apply is native to Oracle databases only. For other database types, you can use the original capture and apply methods, which are classic capture and classic apply. Oracle GoldenGate 12c has also introduced the coordinated replicat for supporting non-Oracle databases. We will discuss it in detail later in this chapter. Before we look into the implementation of the capture and apply methods, let's look at the advantages of using integrated apply over classic apply.

- The apply processes can be configured with the parameters PARALLELISM and MAX_PARALLELISM to define the degree of parallelism. This allows the apply processes to work in parallel for applying multiple transactions concurrently during heavy workloads.

- Integrated apply is easier to configure when compared to classic apply.

- It supports pluggable databases.

Support for Multitenant Databases

Oracle GoldenGate 12c supports the new Oracle multitenant container databases (CDBs). These container databases provide a common pool of resources. A CDB with a user database is called a *pluggable database* (PDC). These PDBs can be unplugged and plugged into different CDBs.

Oracle GoldenGate 12c now allows you to mine multiple PDBs with a single integrated capture process and write them to a single trail file. Thus, resources are required at the CDB level only to capture from multiple PDBs. This reduces overhead and increases throughput. The delivery process then can apply the captured changes to single or multiple PDBs. Figure 5-7 shows the Oracle GoldenGate capture and apply configuration for multitenant source and target databases.

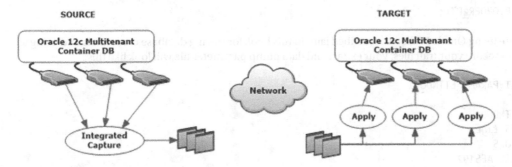

Figure 5-7. *Support for multitenant databases*

Implementing Classic and Integrated Captures

We already discussed classic capture during your first Oracle GoldenGate setup in Chapter 4. We will revisit classic capture here along with implementing a classic data pump. You will next see how to set up an integrated capture.

Creating a Classic Capture

To create a classic capture process named ETTND001, issue the following command at the GGSCI prompt:

```
GGSCI> ADD EXTRACT ETTND001, TRANLOG, BEGIN NOW
```

Next, assign a local trail to this extract.

```
GGSCI> ADD EXTTRAIL /app/ggs/tiger/dirdat/t1, EXTRACT ETTND001
```

You can create an intermediate data pump called PFTND001 to read these local trails.

```
GGSCI> ADD EXTRACT PFTXD001, EXTTRAILSOURCE /app/ggs/tiger/dirdat/t1
```

Edit the extract parameter file and add the following parameters:

```
GGSCI> EDIT PARAMS ETTND001

EXTRACT ETTND001
USERID tiger, PASSWORD tiger123_
EXTTRAIL /app/ggs/tiger/dirdat/t1
TABLE TIGER.ORDER_DTL;
```

Edit the data pump parameter file and add the following parameters:

```
GGSCI> EDIT PARAMS PFTND001

EXTRACT PFTND001
USERID tiger, PASSWORD tiger123_
RMTHOST node2.ravin-pc.com, MGRPORT 7809
RMTTRAIL /app/ggs/fox/dirdat/f1
PASSTHRU
TABLE TIGER.ORDER_DTL;
```

If you are using Oracle Wallet as described later in this book for storing database credentials and using encryption to secure your trail files, your extract and data pump parameter file will look like this:

```
GGSCI> EDIT PARAMS ETTND001

EXTRACT ETTND001
USERIDALIAS tiger
LOGALLSUPCOLS
ENCRYPTTRAIL AES192
EXTTRAIL /app/ggs/tiger/dirdat/t1
TABLE TIGER.ORDER_DTL;

GGSCI> EDIT PARAMS PFTND001

EXTRACT PFTND001
USERIDALIAS tiger
RMTHOST node2.ravin-pc.com, MGRPORT 7809 ENCRYPT AES192, KEYNAME mykey1
RMTTRAIL /app/ggs/fox/dirdat/f1
PASSTHRU
TABLE TIGER.ORDER_DTL;
```

Save and close the parameter files. Start the extract and data pump processes.

```
GGSCI> start *
```

Creating an On-Source Integrated Capture

To create an integrated capture process, you need to specify INTEGRATED TRANLOG along with the ADD EXTRACT command.

```
GGSCI> ADD EXTRACT ETTND001 INTEGRATED TRANLOG, BEGIN NOW
```

Then in the extract parameter file, you need to use the TRANLOGOPTIONS INTEGRATEDPARAMS parameter.

```
TRANLOGOPTIONS INTEGRATEDPARAMS (max_sga_size 200, parallelism 2)
```

The max_sga_size value here should be 75 percent of streams_pool_size. Parallelism specifies the number of processes supporting the database log mining server. The default value for parallelism is 2 if not specified explicitly.

Here's the parameter file for an integrated extract ETTND001 when the source database is the mining database.

```
GGSCI> EDIT PARAMS ETTND001

EXTRACT ETTND001
USERID tiger, PASSWORD tiger123_
LOGALLSUPCOLS
UPDATERECORDFORMAT COMPACT
ENCRYPTTRAIL AES192
TRANLOGOPTIONS INTEGRATEDPARAMS (max_sga_size 200, parallelism 2)
EXTTRAIL /app/ggs/tiger/dirdat/t1
TABLE TIGER.*;
```

And here's the corresponding data pump parameter file pftnd001.prm:

```
GGSCI> EDIT PARAMS PFTND001

EXTRACT PFTND001
USERID tiger, PASSWORD tiger123_
RMTHOST node2.ravin-pc.com, MGRPORT 7809 ENCRYPT AES192, KEYNAME mykey1
RMTTRAIL /app/ggs/fox/dirdat/f1
PASSTHRU
TABLE TIGER.*;
```

If you are setting up the extract and data pump on a source database that is a multitenant Oracle database, your extract and data pump parameter files will have the following configuration. In this example, I have used USERIDALIAS for specifying the login credentials. This requires you to set up Oracle GoldenGate Wallet and define the alias in it. We will discuss setting up Oracle Wallet in Chapter 10.

```
EXTRACT ETTND001
USERIDALIAS tiger
LOGALLSUPCOLS
UPDATERECORDFORMAT COMPACT
ENCRYPTTRAIL AES192
EXTTRAIL /app/ggs/tiger/dirdat/t1
SOURCECATALOG pdb1
```

```
TABLE TIGER1.*;
SOURCECATALOG pdb2
TABLE TIGER2.*;
```

Here's the data pump parameter file for a multitenant database:

```
EXTRACT PFTND001
USERIDALIAS tiger
RMTHOST node2.ravin-pc.com, MGRPORT 7809 ENCRYPT AES192, KEYNAME mykey1
RMTTRAIL /app/ggs/fox/dirdat/f1
SOURCECATALOG pdb1
TABLE TIGER1.*;
SOURCECATALOG pdb2
TABLE TIGER2.*;
```

In a classic capture setup, there is no need to register the extract with the database, whereas in an integrated capture, the extract is first registered with the database to be able to read the redo logs. This registration integrates the database log mining server to receive changes in the form of LCRs.

```
GGSCI> DBLOGIN USER tiger PASSWORD tiger123_
GGSCI> REGISTER EXTRACT ETTND001 DATABASE
```

Creating an Integrated Capture Using a Downstream Mining Database

For integrated capture using downstream mining, the downstream database must be running in ARCHIVELOG mode. Also, you need to set up standby redo log files, which receive redo logs from online redo log files on the source database. You also need to configure your downstream database to archive the standby redo log files locally.

Add the extract integrated extract process on the mining database server.

```
GGSCI> ADD EXTRACT ETTND001 INTEGRATED TRANLOG BEGIN NOW
EXTRACT added.
```

```
GGSCI> ADD EXTTRAIL /app/ggs/tiger/dirdat/t1, EXTRACT ETTND001
EXTTRAIL added.
```

Log into the mining database to register the extract as follows:

```
GGSCI> DBLOGIN USERID tiger@orcl1 PASSWORD tiger123_
Successfully logged into database.
```

```
GGSCI> MININGDBLOGIN USERID tiger, PASSWORD tiger123_
Successfully logged into mining database.
```

```
GGSCI> REGISTER EXTRACT ETTND001 DATABASE
2015-06-23 12:03:54  INFO    OGG-02003  Extract ETTND001 successfully registered with
database at SCN 65420125.
```

Add the following parameters to your extract and data pump processes' parameter files.

```
GGSCI> EDIT PARAMS ETTND001

EXTRACT ETTND001
USERID tiger, PASSWORD tiger123_
TRANLOGOPTIONS MININGUSER tiger@orcl2 MININGPASSWORD tiger123_
TRANLOGOPTIONS INTEGRATEDPARAMS (downstream_real_time_mine Y)
EXTTRAIL /app/ggs/tiger/dirdat/t1
TABLE TIGER.*;
```

The data pump parameter file configuration remains essentially the same as classic mode.

```
GGSCI> EDIT PARAMS PFTND001

EXTRACT PFTND001
USERID tiger, PASSWORD tiger123_
RMTHOST node2.ravin-pc.com, MGRPORT 7809 ENCRYPT AES192, KEYNAME mykey1
RMTTRAIL /app/ggs/fox/dirdat/f1
PASSTHRU
TABLE TIGER.*;
```

If you are using an Oracle 12*c* multitenant database, your extract and data pump parameter file will have the following configuration:

```
EXTRACT ETTND001
USERIDALIAS tiger1
TRANLOGOPTIONS MININGUSERALIAS tiger2
TRANLOGOPTIONS INTEGRATEDPARAMS (MAX_SGA_SIZE 164, &
DOWNSTREAM_REAL_TIME_MINE y)
LOGALLSUPCOLS
UPDATERECORDFORMAT COMPACT
ENCRYPTTRAIL AES192
EXTTRAIL /app/ggs/tiger/dirdat/t1
SOURCECATALOG pdb1
TABLE TIGER1.*;
SOURCECATALOG pdb2
TABLE TIGER2.*;
```

Here is the data pump parameter configuration for a multitenant database:

```
EXTRACT PFTND001
USERIDALIAS tiger
RMTHOST node2.ravin-pc.com, MGRPORT 7809 ENCRYPT AES192, KEYNAME mykey1
RMTTRAIL /app/ggs/fox/dirdat/f1
SOURCECATALOG pdb1
TABLE TIGER1.*;
SOURCECATALOG pdb2
TABLE TIGER2.*;
```

Monitoring an Integrated Capture

Since this type of capture process is integrated with the database features, you can efficiently use integrated capture monitoring views to check and monitor the progress of extracts.

The first things to look for are the capture processes, which are configured in the source database or the mining database.

```
col CAPTURE_NAME for a20;
col QUEUE_NAME for a15;
col START_SCN for 9999999999;
col STATUS for a10;
col CAPTURED_SCN for 9999999999;
col APPLIED_SCN for 9999999999;
col SOURCE_DATABASE for a10;
col LOGMINER_ID for 9999999;
col REQUIRED_CHECKPOINTSCN for a30;
col STATUS_CHANGE_TIME for a15;
col ERROR_NUMBER for a15;
col ERROR_MESSAGE for a10;
col CAPTURE_TYPE for a10;
col START_TIME for a30

SELECT CAPTURE_NAME, QUEUE_NAME, START_SCN, STATUS,
CAPTURED_SCN, APPLIED_SCN, SOURCE_DATABASE,
LOGMINER_ID, REQUIRED_CHECKPOINT_SCN,
STATUS_CHANGE_TIME, ERROR_NUMBER, ERROR_MESSAGE,
CAPTURE_TYPE, START_TIME
FROM DBA_CAPTURE;
```

You can also query the dynamic statistics from the GoldenGate views in the database.

```
col state for a30;


SELECT sid, serial#, capture#, CAPTURE_NAME, STARTUP_TIME, CAPTURE_TIME,
state, SGA_USED, BYTES_OF_REDO_MINED,
to_char(STATE_CHANGED_TIME, 'mm-dd-yy hh24:mi') STATE_CHANGED_TIME
FROM V$GOLDENGATE_CAPTURE;
```

The following query gives additional details about the capture message's create time and its number:

```
col capture_message_create_time for a30;
col enqueue_message_create_time for a27;
col available_message_create_time for a30;

SELECT capture_name,
to_char(capture_time, 'mm-dd-yy hh24:mi') capture_time,
capture_message_number,
to_char(capture_message_create_time ,'mm-dd-yy hh24:mi') capture_message_create_time,
to_char(enqueue_time,'mm-dd-yy hh24:mi') enqueue_time,
enqueue_message_number,
```

```
to_char(enqueue_message_create_time, 'mm-dd-yy hh24:mi') enqueue_message_create_time,
available_message_number,
to_char(available_message_create_time,'mm-dd-yy hh24:mi') available_message_create_time
FROM GV$GOLDENGATE_CAPTURE;
```

You can monitor the number of open transactions and LCRs for each capture processes using the following query:

```
SELECT component_name capture_name, count(*) open_transactions,
sum(cumulative_message_count) LCRs
FROM GV$GOLDENGATE_TRANSACTION
WHERE component_type='CAPTURE'
group by component_name;
```

You can query LogMiner views for LogMiner sessions and statistics as shown here:

```
col db_name for a15;
select INST_ID, SESSION_ID,SESSION_NAME,SESSION_STATE, DB_NAME,
NUM_PROCESS,START_SCN,END_SCN,SPILL_SCN, PROCESSED_SCN, PREPARED_SCN,
READ_SCN MAX_MEMORY_SIZE,USED_MEMORY_SIZE PINNED_TXN, PINNED_COMMITTED_TXN
from GV$LOGMNR_SESSION;
SELECT SESSION_ID, NAME, VALUE
FROM V$LOGMNR_STATS;
```

Upgrading Classic Capture Mode to Integrated Capture Mode

There may come a time when you want to upgrade a classic capture to an integrated capture. GoldenGate makes such upgrades possible. The following subsections show first how to create a classic capture and then how to upgrade that classic capture to an integrated capture.

Creating a Classic Capture

Here's an example of a classic extract TESTEXT1 that you will upgrade to an integrated extract:

```
GGSCI> ADD EXTRACT TESTEXT1, TRANLOG BEGIN NOW
EXTRACT added.
GGSCI> ADD RMTTRAIL /app/ggs/tiger/dirdat/t1 EXTRACT TESTEXT1
RMTTRAIL added.
```

Configure the extract parameter file.

```
GGSCI> EDIT PARAMS TESTEXT1

EXTRACT TESTEXT1
USERID tiger, PASSWORD tiger123_
RMTHOST node2.ravin-pc.com, MGRPORT 7809
RMTTRAIL /app/ggs/fox/dirdat/f1
TABLE TIGER.*;
```

Start the extract.

```
GGSCI> START EXTRACT TESTEXT1
Sending START request to MANAGER ...
EXTRACT TESTEXT1 starting
```

To verify that TESTEXT1 is a classic capture, you can view information about the extract; notice that it should be reading the Oracle redo logs of the database.

```
GGSCI> INFO EXTRACT TESTEXT1
EXTRACT      TESTEXT1    Last Started 2015-11-08 12:42    Status RUNNING
Checkpoint Lag        00:00:00 (updated 00:01:15 ago)
Log Read Checkpoint   Oracle Redo Logs
                      2015-11-08 12:42:42  Seqno 455, RBA 458721
                      SCN 0.0 (0)
```

Upgrading to an Integrated Capture

Upgrading a classic capture to integrated capture for an Oracle database source is an easy task. You will need to stop your extract process, and your replication will stop while the upgrade is taking place. Also, it is not mandatory to upgrade the corresponding replicat group. An integrated extract can work with a classic replicat. These are the steps to upgrade the extract process:

- Stop the extract and register it with the database.

- Test whether the extract can be upgraded.

- Use UPGRADE INTEGRATED TRANLOG to upgrade the extract.

- Start and verify whether the extract has been upgraded.

Stop the extract TESTEXT1.

```
GGSCI> STOP EXTRACT TESTEXT1
Sending STOP request to EXTRACT TESTEXT1 ...
Request processed.
```

Register the extract with the database.

```
GGSCI> REGISTER EXTRACT TESTEXT1 DATABASE
2015-11-08 12:56:18  INFO    OGG-02003  Extract TESTEXT1 successfully registered with
database at SCN 458780.
```

Test whether the extract is ready for an upgrade.

```
GGSCI> INFO TESTEXT1 UPGRADE
ERROR: Extract TESTEXT1 is not ready to be upgraded because recovery SCN 458742 has not
reached SCN 458780.
```

To overcome the previous error, you can start the extract from the current timestamp using the following command:

```
GGSCI> ALTER EXTRACT TESTEXT1 TRANLOG BEGIN NOW
```

```
EXTRACT altered.
GGSCI> START EXTRACT TESTEXT1
Sending START request to MANAGER ...
EXTRACT TESTEXT1 starting
```

View the information to check whether the extract is running now.

```
GGSCI> INFO EXTRACT TESTEXT1
EXTRACT      TESTEXT1     Last Started 2015-11-08 12:58    Status RUNNING
Checkpoint Lag        00:00:00 (updated 00:02:06 ago)
Log Read Checkpoint   Oracle Redo Logs
                      2015-11-08 12:58:07   Seqno 455, RBA 458721
                      SCN 0.0 (0)
```

Stop the extract.

```
GGSCI> STOP EXTRACT TESTEXT1
Sending STOP request to EXTRACT TESTEXT1 ...
Request processed.
```

Verify again whether the extract is ready to be upgraded.

```
GGSCI> INFO TESTEXT1 UPGRADE
Extract TESTEXT1 is ready to be upgraded to integrated capture.
```

Use the UPGRADE INTEGRATED TRANLOG command to upgrade the extract.

```
GGSCI> ALTER EXTRACT TESTEXT1, UPGRADE INTEGRATED TRANLOG
Extract TESTEXT1 successfully upgraded to integrated capture.
```

Start the extract.

```
GGSCI> START EXTRACT TESTEXT1
Sending START request to MANAGER ...
EXTRACT TESTEXT1 starting
```

Your extract is upgraded. You can check the information of the upgraded extract.

```
GGSCI> INFO EXTRACT TESTEXT1
EXTRACT      TESTEXT1     Initialized   2015-11-08 13:12    Status RUNNING
Checkpoint Lag        00:00:00 (updated 00:01:26 ago)
Log Read Checkpoint   Oracle Integrated Redo Logs
                      2015-11-08 13:12:59
                      SCN 0.458790 (458790)
```

Note the difference between the classic capture and integrated capture.
Here's the classic capture:

```
Log Read Checkpoint   Oracle Redo Logs
                      2015-11-08 12:58:07   Seqno 455, RBA 458721
                      SCN 0.0 (0)
```

Here's the integrated capture:

```
Log Read Checkpoint  Oracle Integrated Redo Logs
                     2015-11-08 13:12:59
                     SCN 0.458790 (458790)
```

A queue called OGG$Q_TESTEXT1 and a queue table called OGG$Q_TAB_TESTEXT1 get created in the database. You can query them in the database using the following queries:

```
SQL> select CAPTURE_NAME, QUEUE_NAME, STATUS from DBA_CAPTURE;
SQL> select OWNER, QUEUE_TABLE, QUEUE_TYPE from dba_queues where NAME='OGG$Q_TESTEXT1';
```

Implementing Classic and Integrated Apply

When using an Oracle database as the target database, you can utilize the benefit of parallel apply by implementing integrated apply. We will first discuss a classic apply and then discuss the additional configuration required to configure an integrated apply.

Creating a Classic Apply

To add a classic apply/replicat, use the following commands:

```
GGSCI> ADD REPLICAT RFDLD001, EXTTRAIL /app/ggs/fox/dirdat/f1, NODBCHECKPOINT
```

Configure the replicat parameter file to have the following parameters:

```
GGSCI> EDIT PARAMS RFDLD001
```

```
REPLICAT RFDLD001
PURGEOLDEXTRACTS
ASSUMETARGETDEFS
DISCARDFILE /app/ggs/fox/dirrpt/rfdld001.dsc, PURGE, MEGABYTES 599
USERID fox, PASSWORD fox123_
MAP TIGER.ORDER_DTL, TARGET FOX.ORDER_DTL;
```

We will discuss in detail how to add both the extract and replicat processes later in this book when you set up your first GoldenGate replication environment.

Creating an Integrated Apply

The integrated apply process or integrated replicat works only for an Oracle database version 11.2.0.4 or higher. It cannot be implemented for a non-Oracle database. For an integrated replicat, some new parameters are required in the extract process that were introduced only in Oracle GoldenGate 12c. So if you are using an Oracle GoldenGate version lower than 12c, integrated apply will not work for your environment.

The extract parameter needs to have LOGALLSUPCOLS and UPDATERECORDFORMAT COMPACT.

LOGALLSUPCOLS tells the extract to capture a before image for all supplemental log columns for the update and delete operations. By default before and after images are captured in a separate record, which incurs processing overhead and disk I/O for both capture and apply processes, and also the overall trail files size is larger. UPDATERECORDFORMAT COMPACT allows extract to write both before and after images to a single record that will have all the information required for the update.

Let's take a look at how to add integrated replicat RFDLD001.

```
GGSCI> DBLOGIN USERID fox@orcl2, PASSWORD fox123_
Successfully logged into database.
```

Add replicat RFDLD001 with the INTEGRATED option.

```
GGSCI> ADD REPLICAT RFDLD001 INTEGRATED EXTTRAIL /app/ggs/fox/dirdat/f1
REPLICAT (Integrated) added.
```

Configure the replicat parameter file to contain the following parameter:

```
GGSCI> edit params RFDLD001

REPLICAT RFDLD001
SETENV (ORACLE_SID='orcl3')
DBOPTIONS INTEGRATEDPARAMS(parallelism 6)
USERID fox@orcl3, PASSWORD fox123_
ASSUMETARGETDEFS
MAP TIGER. *, TARGET FOX. *;
```

Start the newly added replicat and run INFO on it.

```
GGSCI> info replicat RFDLD001
REPLICAT    RFDLD001    Last Started 2015-11-08 13:25    Status RUNNING
INTEGRATED
Checkpoint Lag      00:00:00 (updated 00:01:09 ago)
Process ID         38172
Log Read Checkpoint File /app/ggs/fox/dirdat/f1000000
First Record  RBA 0
```

An inbound server named OGG$RFDLD001 and a queue named OGGQ$RFDLD001 get created in the database. You can query the newly created replicat information from the database using the following queries:

```
SQL> select REPLICAT_NAME,SERVER_NAME from DBA_GOLDENGATE_INBOUND;
SQL> select APPLY_NAME,QUEUE_NAME,status from dba_apply;
SQL> select apply_ame,state from V$GG_APPLY_COORDINATOR ;
```

In this example, we have set parallelism to 6 for the replicat, which means there will be six apply processes that you can query from the database, as shown here:

```
SQL> select server_id,TOTAL_MESSAGES_APPLIED from V$GG_APPLY_SERVER where apply_
name='OGG$RFDLD001';
 SERVER_ID TOTAL_MESSAGES_APPLIED
---------- ----------------------
         4                      0
         2                      0
         6                      0
         5                      0
         3                      0
         1                      0
```

Capture and Apply Modes, Mix and Match

When using a classic capture on the source database, it is not mandatory for you to use only nonintegrated replicat on the target database. Similarly, an integrated capture on the source database can work with both integrated and nonintegrated replicats.

Table 5-1 shows the database and capture/apply mode combinations that you can have in your OGG replication setup.

Table 5-1. *Supported Combination of Classic and Integrated Capture and Apply*

Source Database	Capture Mode	Target Database	Replicat Mode
Any OGG-supported DB	Classic	Any OGG-supported DB	Nonintegrated
Any OGG-supported DB	Classic	Oracle DB	Integrated
Oracle DB	Integrated	Any OGG-supported DB	Nonintegrated
Oracle DB	Integrated	Oracle DB	Integrated

Coordinated Replicat

The integrated capture and delivery processes are limited only to Oracle databases. With an Oracle GoldenGate 12*c* release, a new delivery process called *coordinated replicat* was introduced. This type of replicat is multithreaded. They can read multiple trails independently and apply transactions in parallel. Unlike integrated replicat where GoldenGate automatically adds additional apply processes depending on the workload, in coordinated replicat the user defines thread partitioning using the THREADS and MAXTHREADS parameters.

Later in this book, we will discuss in detail how, in earlier versions, the RANGE partition was implemented by splitting a replicat group. This turns out to be a great performance booster for a high-workload replicat group.

Here is replicat 1:

```
MAP TIGER.TABLEA, TARGET FOX.TABLEA, FILTER (@RANGE (1, 2, WORKID));
```

Here is replicat 2:

```
MAP TIGER.TABLEA, TARGET FOX.TABLEA, FILTER (@RANGE (2, 2, WORKID));
```

In Oracle GoldenGate 12*c*, a single replicat parameter file is created, and additional replicat groups are added automatically with a coordinator process assigning workloads to individual replicat groups. This partitioning is done using the THREADRANGE parameter, as in the following example:

```
MAP TIGER.TABLEA, TARGET FOX.TABLEA, THREADRANGE (1-3, WORKID));
```

You can use either classic or integrated extract groups on the source that delivers trails to the target with the coordinated replicat. The replicat you configure is called *coordinator*, and its name is limited to five characters. The additional replicat created by this coordinator will have this name appended with three numeric digits in sequence based on the number of threads specified by the MAXTHREADS parameter. Let's see an example of creating a coordinated replicat.

```
GGSCI> DBLOGIN USERIDALIAS fox
Successfully logged into database FOX.
```

Add a coordinated replicat as shown next. Please note here the replicat group name is only five characters; remaining characters are automatically assigned by the coordinated replicat process.

```
GGSCI> add replicat RFDLD, coordinated, EXTTRAIL /app/ggs/fox/dirdat/f1, maxthreads 5
REPLICAT (Coordinated) added.
```

Configure the coordinated replicat with the THREADRANGE parameter as shown here:

```
GGSCI> view params RFDLD
REPLICAT RFDLD
USERIDALIAS fox
ASSUMETARGETDEFS
MAP TIGER.TABLEA, TARGET FOX.TABLEA, THREADRANGE (1-5, WORKID));
```

Start the coordinated replicat.

```
GGSCI> start replicat RFDLD
Sending START request to MANAGER ...
REPLICAT RFDLD001 starting
```

use INFO on the replicat to see the details.

```
GGSCI> info replicat RFDLD

REPLICAT  RFDLD      Last Started 2016-04-13 18:49   Status RUNNING
COORDINATED          Coordinator                     MAXTHREADS 5
Checkpoint Lag       00:00:00 (updated 00:00:07 ago)
Process ID           35421
Log Read Checkpoint  File /app/ggs/fox/dirdat/f1000000
                     First Record  RBA 0
```

Perform some transactions on the source and check the status of the replicat group on the target. You will see that the replicat has created five additional threads, and the replicat groups RFDLD001 to RFDLD005 are created. Each replicat thread is sharing approximately one-fifth of the total load.

```
GGSCI> info replicat RFDLD detail

REPLICAT  RFDLD      Last Started 2016-04-13 18:49   Status RUNNING
COORDINATED          Coordinator                     MAXTHREADS 5
Checkpoint Lag       00:00:00 (updated 00:00:07 ago)
Process ID           35421
Log Read Checkpoint  File /app/ggs/fox/dirdat/f1000000
                     2016-04-13 19:06:14.245621  RBA 41253121

Lowest Log BSN value:

Active Threads:
ID  Group Name PID    Status   Lag at Chkpt  Time Since Chkpt
1   RFDLD001   35424  RUNNING  00:00:00      00:00:20
2   RFDLD002   35425  RUNNING  00:00:00      00:00:20
3   RFDLD003   35426  RUNNING  00:00:00      00:00:20
4   RFDLD004   35427  RUNNING  00:00:00      00:00:20
5   RFDLD005   35428  RUNNING  00:00:00      00:00:20
```

You can view the information on any or all replicat group names created by the coordinated replicat group RFDLD.

```
GGSCI> info replicat RFDLD001

REPLICAT    RFDLD001   Last Started 2016-04-13 18:49    Status RUNNING
COORDINATED            Replicat Thread                  Thread 1
Checkpoint Lag         00:00:00 (updated 00:00:04 ago)
Process ID             35424
Log Read Checkpoint    File /app/ggs/fox/dirdat/f1000000
                       2016-04-13 19:08:55.214642   RBA 54562143
```

■ **Note** Both coordinated delivery and integrated delivery were introduced in Oracle GoldenGate 12*c*. The major advantage of coordinated delivery is that it is not limited to Oracle databases; it supports all the popular databases supported by OGG.

Summary

In this chapter, we discussed in detail how to implement different types of extract and replicat processes and their advantages. We also discussed coordinated replicat, which makes use of the multithreading concept to achieve high performance. The coordinated replicat is not limited to Oracle databases and supports all OGG-supported databases.

Now that you have installed and configured Oracle GoldenGate replication of data in real time, you will look at replicating DDL for Oracle databases. DDL support is available only for Oracle databases and is discussed in detail in the next chapter.

CHAPTER 6

■ ■ ■

Capturing DDL Changes

Oracle GoldenGate supports replication of DDL statements from one database to another database. Currently, DDL replication is supported only for Oracle databases. In this chapter, we will discuss how to configure Oracle GoldenGate to capture and replicate DDL changes. By default DDL replication is disabled on the extract side (source database) and enabled only on the replicat side (target database).

What Is DDL Replication?

A change in the structure of an object or creating new object in an Oracle database is called Data Definition Language (DDL). Oracle GoldenGate supports DDL on the following objects of Oracle databases:

- Clusters
- Functions
- Indexes
- Materialized views
- Packages
- Procedures
- Roles
- Sequences
- Synonyms
- Tables
- Tablespaces
- Triggers
- Types
- Users
- Views

In addition to using DDL on the previous objects, Oracle GoldenGate supports TRUNCATE TABLE, ALTER TABLE, and TRUNCATE PARTITION.

© Ravinder Gupta 2016
R. Gupta, *Mastering Oracle GoldenGate*, DOI 10.1007/978-1-4842-2301-7_6

■ **Note**   If you are using Oracle Database 10*g*, the recycle bin must be turned off to support DDL replication with Oracle GoldenGate. This was because of a known bug in Oracle Database 10*g*. For Oracle 11*g* and above, the recycle bin need not be turned off.

DDL replication is not supported by Oracle GoldenGate for database systems other than Oracle. However, the TRUNCATE statement is supported.

Types of DDL Replication

There are two types of DDL Replication supported by Oracle GoldenGate as listed the following:

- *Trigger-based or classic DDL replication*: This is the classic DDL capture method supported for Oracle database versions earlier than 11.2.0.4. It requires you to install triggers and supporting objects for capturing and applying DDL changes.

- *Triggerless or native DDL replication*: The triggerless, also called native, DDL replication was introduced with Oracle Database 11.2.0.4. This type of replication uses the database log mining server for capturing and applying DDL changes. For a multitenant database, native replication is the only supported DDL replication method.

Limitations with DDL Replication

DDL replication is slightly trickier when compared to replicating data. Before setting up DDL replication between two systems, you must be aware of the limitations with DDL replication. The most important ones are as follows:

- The maximum length of a DDL statement to be replicated is between 2 MB to 4 MB. If the DDL length exceeds this size, the extract process will issue a warning message and ignore the DDL statement. These ignored DDL statements will be stored in the marker table. The GoldenGate ddl_ddl2file.sql file allows you to dump all the DDL statements at a location specified by the USER_DUMP_DEST directory. You can find this file in your OGG home directory.

- The source and target database objects on which the DDL replication will happen should be identical.

- DDL replication is not supported on standby databases.

- DDL replication can be mapped to different object names only by the primary extract process. Data pumps support DDL replication in as it is PASSTHRU mode.

- A DML/DDL operation within a DDL trigger is not captured.

- It is mandatory to use ASSUMETARGETDEFS instead of SOURCEDEFS in the replicat configured for DDL replication.

DDL Scope

The DDL scope defines how a DDL operation is handled by Oracle GoldenGate. There are three DDL scopes in which you can classify DDL operations to be replicated. These DDL scopes are as follows:

- *Mapped*: Objects are specified in the TABLE and MAP statements in the extract/replicat process. Both DDL and DML changes are applicable using the instructions in the TABLE and MAP statements.

Here's an example:
If your extract on the source has this:

```
TABLE TIGER.ORDER_DTL;
```

and the replicat on the target has the following MAP statement:

```
MAP TIGER.ORDER_DTL, TARGET FOX.BILLING;
```

then the DDL code on the source will look like this:

```
ALTER TABLE TIGER.ORDER_DTL ADD COMMENTS VARCHAR2 (200);
```

It is applied on the target as the following statement:

```
ALTER TABLE FOX.BILLING ADD COMMENTS VARCHAR2 (200);
```

Unmapped: The object name is not included in TABLE and MAP statements in the extract/replicat process. Only DDL changes are replicated. DDL statements are applied to the same schema name as on the source. The replicat automatically switches from the current schema to the source schema and then after applying the DDL, it switches back to the current schema.
Here's an example:

```
CREATE TABLE NEW_TABLE1
(
ID NUMBER,
DESCRIPTION VARCHAR2(30)
);
```

- *Other*: The object is not mapped to the MAPPED or UNMAPPED scope that comes under this scope, such as CREATE USER, ALTER TABLESPACE, and so on. DDLs are applied at the target with the same schema and object names as on the source.

Here's an example:

```
CREATE USER ravin IDENTIFIED by ravin123_;
```

How Does DDL Replication Work?

DDL replication is same as DML replication. The only difference is how a DDL statement is captured, written to the trail file, and applied on the target. Figure 6-1 shows a complete DDL path for an ALTER statement on a table.

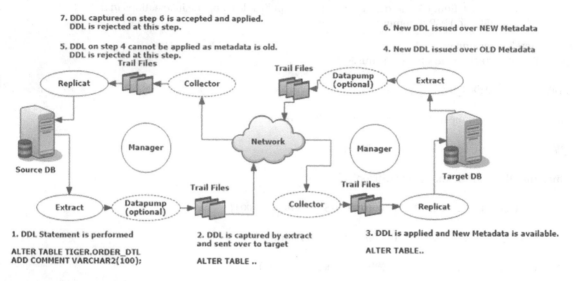

Figure 6-1. *DDL replication cycle in bidirectional configuration*

On the Source Machine

A DDL statement is captured by the extract process on the source machine. Comments are separated with the actual DDL statement. The extract process will look for DDL parameters. If IGNOREREPLICATES is found and the DDL was produced by a replicat process on the machine, the DDL statement will be ignored. A RENAME statement will be processed as ALTER TABLE RENAME. If a DDLOPTIONS REMOVECOMMENTS BEFORE is found, the comments are removed from the DDL statement. The next step is to assign the scope for the DDL statement. The DDL statement will be checked for any EXCLUDE or INCLUDE parameter filtering. If the DDLSUBST parameter is defined, the DDL statement substitution happens accordingly. If the DDL statement is a CREATE TABLE and DDLOPTIONS ADDTRANDATA is specified, the extract process will trigger an ALTER TABLE table_name ADD SUPPLEMENTAL LOG GROUP statement.

The final DDL statement is written to the trail file and sent over to the target machine.

On the Target Machine

The replicat will read the DDL statement from the trail. If there is a comment present, it will be separated from the main statement. If DDLOPTIONS REMOVECOMMENTS BEFORE is specified, the comments are removed from the DDL statement. The next step is to identify the DDL scope for the DDL statement. For the DDL statement with a MAPPED scope, the replicat will look for the MAP statements in its parameter file. Based on the object name specified in the corresponding TARGET clause, the DDL statement is modified to replace the object name in it. If a DDL statement includes a derived object, it will look for DDLOPTIONS MAPDERIVED. If present, the source derived name is replaced by the target derived name. If INCLUDE or EXCLUDE clauses are present, the DDL statement is evaluated against them. It next looks for the DDLSUBST parameter and performs the necessary string substitution. If the REMOVECOMMENTS AFTER parameter is found, the replicat will now remove the comments from the DDL statement. Finally, the DDL statement is executed on the target machine. If an error is encountered, replicat looks for the DDLERROR parameter to handle the error. If no error handling is specified, either the DDL statement will be ignored or the channel will be abended based on the specified rule.

DDL Capture in Classic Capture Mode

DDL capture in classic capture mode is a trigger-based DDL capture mode. The first step to set up a DDL capture is to install the DDL trigger and supporting database objects. Table 6-1 lists the database objects to be created for this purpose.

Table 6-1. *Database Objects for Trigger-Based DDL*

DDL Synchronization Object	Usage
GGS_MARKER	This is the DDL marker table that stores the DDL information. The table will have only insert statements on it.
GGS_DDL_SEQ	This is used as a sequence in the marker table.
GGS_DDL_HIST	This is the DDL history table that stores the object metadata history. This table will receive inserts, updates, and deletes.
GGS_DDL_HIST_ALT	The table contains object IDs of configured objects.
GGS_DDL_TRIGGER_BEFORE	The DDL trigger fires on DDL operations. The information about the operation is written to the marker and history tables.
DDL Schema	This contains the DDL synchronization objects. It must be specified during installation and in the GLOBALS file.
GGS_GGSUSER_ROLE	This role is needed to execute DDL operations.
ddl_pin	This pins DDL tracing, the DDL package, and the DDL trigger for performance improvements.
ddl_cleartrace.sql	This is the SQL to remove the DDL trace file.
ddl_status.sql	This verifies whether GoldenGate DDL objects are installed.
marker_status.sql	This verifies whether the GGS_MARKER table is installed.
ddl_tracelevel.sql	This sets the level of DDL tracing.

To set up your DDL replication, you must install DDL objects as follows:

1. Choose a schema (for example GGSUSER) that will contain the GoldenGate DDL objects.

2. Grant execute privileges on the utl_file package to the GoldenGate user. This gives the GoldenGate user access to the operating system files in the UTL_FILE directory.

```
GRANT EXECUTE ON utl_file TO GGSUSER;
```

3. Set up a default tablespace for the previous schema you created (GGSUSER). Make sure that this tablespace is solely used by the previous DDL schema and no other objects are created in it. It is a good idea to keep AUTOEXTEND ON for this tablespace as the DDL history and marker table may grow with time.

4. Create or edit the GLOBALS parameter file. You will need to specify the schema_ name in the GLOBALS file.

```
EDIT PARAMS ./GLOBALS
GGSCHEMA ggsuser
```

5. To recognize Oracle invisible indexes for DDL replication, set allow_invisible_ index_keys to TRUE in the params.sql file.

6. define allow_invisible_index_keys = 'TRUE'

7. Save and close the globals and params files and exit all Oracle sessions to proceed to the next step.

8. You now need to run some SQL files to set up your DDL replication environment. You should be logged in as the SYSDBA user for running these SQL files. These SQL files are present in the GoldenGate installation directory where all the OGG software binaries are extracted during installation.

Execute the marker_setup.sql file. This will prompt for the Oracle GoldenGate schema. Provide GGSUSER when prompted.

```
SQL>@marker_setup.sql
```

Next, execute the ddl_setup.sql file. This will prompt for the DDL schema. This will fail if the tablespace you specified for this schema is shared by any other user.

```
SQL>@ddl_setup.sql
```

Set up the role by executing the role_setup.sql file. This will prompt for the DDL schema. This takes care of the role setup required for DDL synchronization.

```
SQL>@role_setup.sql
```

Use GRANT role (the default is GGS_GGSUSER_ROLE) for the Oracle extract users.

```
SQL>GRANT role TO ggsuser;
```

Enable the DDL trigger.

```
SQL>@ddl_enable.sql
```

Optionally, to improve the performance of the DDL trigger, the script pins the PL/SQL package being used by the trigger into the memory.

```
SQL>@ddl_pin DDL_user
```

9. To replicate DDL operations on any new table, you can use wildcards in the parameter files as follows:

- In the TABLE statement of the extract parameter file:

```
TABLE source_schema.*;
```

- In the MAP and TARGET statements of the replicat parameter file:

```
MAP source_schema.TAB*. TARGET target_schema.HIST_*;
```

An Example of Classic Capture DDL

Let's take a look at an example of setting up DDL replication between the TIGER and FOX schemas. For this example, I am going to set up DDL replication using the TIGER and FOX schemas as GoldenGate users. All the tables to be replicated are owned by these users.

Once the GoldenGate users have received the required privileges for setting up DDL replication, you are required to run several setup scripts. The privileges were discussed in detail in Chapter X. The scripts need to be run as SYSDBA.

You will be prompted to enter the GoldenGate schema name.

You should stop any DDL replication before starting with the execution of the following scripts. Let's first install the marker table GGS_MARKER by executing marker_setup.sql.

```
sqlplus / as sysdba
SQL> @marker_setup.sql

Marker setup script

You will be prompted for the name of a schema for the Oracle GoldenGate database objects.
NOTE: The schema must be created prior to running this script.
NOTE: Stop all DDL replication before starting this installation.

Enter Oracle GoldenGate schema name:TIGER

Marker setup table script complete, running verification script…
Please enter the name of a schema for the GoldenGate database objects:
Setting schema name to TIGER

MARKER TABLE
-------------------------------
OK

MARKER SEQUENCE
-------------------------------
OK

Script complete.
```

This step is optional. You can turn off the recycle bin for the source database. Turning off the recycle bin is not required for 11g or higher.

There is a known issue in Oracle 10g: if the recycle bin is enabled, the GoldenGate DDL trigger session receives implicit recycle bin DDL operations that cause the trigger to fail. For an 11g or higher source, it can be on/enabled.

```
SQL> alter session set recyclebin=OFF;

Session altered.
```

Before moving on to installing DDL objects, make sure that DDL schema has its own exclusive tablespace not shared by any other user. Otherwise, you will see the following error during your pre-check of ddl_setup.sql:

```
declare
*
ERROR at line 1:
ORA-20783:
ORA-20783:
Oracle GoldenGate DDL Replication setup:
*** Please move TIGER to its own tablespace
ORA-06512: at line 34
```

Execute ddl_setup.sql to install the DDL objects required for GoldenGate DDL replication.

```
SQL> @ddl_setup.sql

Oracle GoldenGate DDL Replication setup script

Verifying that current user has privileges to install DDL Replication…

You will be prompted for the name of a schema for the Oracle GoldenGate database objects.
NOTE: For an Oracle 10g source, the system recycle bin must be disabled. For Oracle 11g and
later, it can be enabled.
NOTE: The schema must be created prior to running this script.
NOTE: Stop all DDL replication before starting this installation.

Enter Oracle GoldenGate schema name:TIGER

Working, please wait …
Spooling to file ddl_setup_spool.txt

Checking for sessions that are holding locks on Oracle Golden Gate metadata tables …

Check complete.

Using TIGER as a Oracle GoldenGate schema name.

Working, please wait …

DDL replication setup script complete, running verification script…
Please enter the name of a schema for the GoldenGate database objects:
Setting schema name to TIGER
```

CLEAR_TRACE STATUS:

```
Line/pos   Error
---------- ----------------------------------------------------------------
No errors  No errors
```

CREATE_TRACE STATUS:

```
Line/pos   Error
---------- ----------------------------------------------------------------
No errors  No errors
```

TRACE_PUT_LINE STATUS:

```
Line/pos   Error
---------- ----------------------------------------------------------------
No errors  No errors
```

INITIAL_SETUP STATUS:

```
Line/pos   Error
---------- ----------------------------------------------------------------
No errors  No errors
```

DDLVERSIONSPECIFIC PACKAGE STATUS:

```
Line/pos   Error
---------- ----------------------------------------------------------------
No errors  No errors
```

DDLREPLICATION PACKAGE STATUS:

```
Line/pos   Error
---------- ----------------------------------------------------------------
No errors  No errors
```

DDLREPLICATION PACKAGE BODY STATUS:

```
Line/pos   Error
---------- ----------------------------------------------------------------
No errors  No errors
```

DDL IGNORE TABLE
```
-----------------------------------
OK
```

DDL IGNORE LOG TABLE
```
-----------------------------------
OK
```

```
DDLAUX PACKAGE STATUS:

Line/pos   Error
---------- -----------------------------------------------------------------
No errors  No errors

DDLAUX PACKAGE BODY STATUS:

Line/pos   Error
---------- -----------------------------------------------------------------
No errors  No errors

SYS.DDLCTXINFO  PACKAGE STATUS:

Line/pos   Error
---------- -----------------------------------------------------------------
No errors  No errors

SYS.DDLCTXINFO  PACKAGE BODY STATUS:

Line/pos   Error
---------- -----------------------------------------------------------------
No errors  No errors

DDL HISTORY TABLE
------------------------------------
OK

DDL HISTORY TABLE(1)
------------------------------------
OK

DDL DUMP TABLES
------------------------------------
OK

DDL DUMP COLUMNS
------------------------------------
OK

DDL DUMP LOG GROUPS
------------------------------------
OK

DDL DUMP PARTITIONS
------------------------------------
OK

DDL DUMP PRIMARY KEYS
------------------------------------
OK
```

```
DDL SEQUENCE
------------------------------------
OK

GGS_TEMP_COLS
------------------------------------
OK

GGS_TEMP_UK
------------------------------------
OK
DDL TRIGGER CODE STATUS:

Line/pos   Error
----------  -----------------------------------------------------------------
No errors  No errors

DDL TRIGGER INSTALL STATUS
------------------------------------
OK

DDL TRIGGER RUNNING STATUS
------------------------------------
ENABLED

STAYMETADATA IN TRIGGER
------------------------------------
OFF

DDL TRIGGER SQL TRACING
------------------------------------
0

DDL TRIGGER TRACE LEVEL
------------------------------------
0

LOCATION OF DDL TRACE FILE
---------------------------------------------------------------------------------------
/app/oracle/product/12.1.0/dbhome_1/rdbms/log/ggs_ddl_trace.log

Analyzing installation status…

VERSION OF DDL REPLICATION
---------------------------------------------------------------------------------------
OGGCORE_12.1.2.1.0_PLATFORMS_140727.2135.1

STATUS OF DDL REPLICATION
---------------------------------------------------------------------------------------
```

SUCCESSFUL installation of DDL Replication software components

Script complete.

Execute role_setup.sql to set up GGS_GGSUSER_ROLE.

SQL> @role_setup.sql

GGS Role setup script

This script will drop and recreate the role GGS_GGSUSER_ROLE
To use a different role name, quit this script and then edit the params.sql script to change
the gg_role parameter to the preferred name. (Do not run the script.)

You will be prompted for the name of a schema for the GoldenGate database objects.
NOTE: The schema must be created prior to running this script.
NOTE: Stop all DDL replication before starting this installation.

Enter GoldenGate schema name:TIGER
Wrote file role_setup_set.txt

PL/SQL procedure successfully completed.

Role setup script complete

Grant this role to each user assigned to the Extract, GGSCI, and Manager processes, by using
the following SQL command:

GRANT GGS_GGSUSER_ROLE TO loggedUser>

where loggedUser> is the user assigned to the GoldenGate processes.

Let's grant the newly set up role to GGSUSER. In this example, we are using the TIGER schema for DDL
setup on the source database.

SQL> grant ggs_ggsuser_role to TIGER;

Grant succeeded.

Next, enable the DDL support. By default DDL replication support is as follows:

- Disabled for the extract process
- Enabled for the replicat process

SQL> @ddl_enable.sql
Trigger altered.

Execute `ddl_pin.sql`, which pins DDL tracing, the DDL package, and the DDL trigger for performance improvements.

```
SQL> @ddl_pin.sql TIGER

PL/SQL procedure successfully completed.

PL/SQL procedure successfully completed.

PL/SQL procedure successfully completed.
```

Next, you need to enable supplemental logging at the table level. This is again mandatory for DDL replication. Use the `ADD TRANDATA` command for this purpose.

Optionally, if all the tables in the schema are to be replicated, you can use `ADD SCHEMATRANDATA` to enable supplemental logging for all the tables in the schema.

```
GGSCI> DBLOGIN USERID TIGER, PASSWORD tiger123_
Successfully logged into database.

GGSCI> ADD TRANDATA tiger.CNTRY
Logging of supplemental redo data enabled for table tiger.cntry.
```

Now, you can configure the parameter files for the extract process for DDL synchronization. Add the following entry to your extract process:

```
DDL INCLUDE MAPPED
```

This means all mapped objects are included in DDL replication. Make use of parameters like `EXCLUDE ALL` and `INCLUDE ALL` to specify tables for DDL replication. `EXCLUDE` has priority over `INCLUDE`. If an `EXCLUDE` clause is specified, a corresponding `INCLUDE` clause must exist. It's not mandatory the other way round. You can just have an `INCLUDE` clause with no corresponding `EXCLUDE` clause.

Here are the parameters for the extract process (ETTND001):

```
EXTRACT ETTND001
USERID tiger, PASSWORD tiger123_
EXTTRAIL /app/ggs/tiger/dirdat/t1
DDL INCLUDE ALL
TABLE tiger.t*;
```

Here are the parameters for the data pump process (PFTND001):

```
EXTRACT PFTND001
USERID tiger, PASSWORD tiger123_
RMTHOST node2.ravin-pc.com, MGRPORT 7809
RMTTRAIL /app/ggs/fox/dirdat/f1
DDL INCLUDE ALL
TABLE tiger.t*;
```

Here are the parameters for the replicat process (RFDLD001):

```
REPLICAT RFDLD001
```

```
USERID fox, PASSWORD fox123_
ASSUMETARGETDEFS
DISCARDFILE /app/ggs/fox/dirrpt/rfdld001.dsc, PURGE
DDL INCLUDE ALL
DDLERROR DEFAULT IGNORE
MAP tiger.*, TARGET fox.*;
```

The DDLERROR DEFAULT IGNORE parameter will prevent the replicat process from abending if there is a mismatch between the source and target environments.

DDL Capture in Integrated Capture Mode

The integrated capture and apply processes are exclusive to Oracle Database since they use the Oracle log mining server for replication. If you have an integrated capture on an Oracle Database 11.2.0.4 or later, you can configure DDL replication through the log mining server.

You do not need to install a trigger or DDL replication support objects. You will need to include the DDL INCLUDE MAPPED or DDL INCLUDE ALL parameter in your capture parameter files to tell OGG that DDL changes need to be captured for replication. This is also called OGG native DDL replication.

Selective DDL Replication with an Oracle Source DB

If your source database is Oracle and you have classic captures with trigger-based DDL replication, you can make use of PL/SQL code to filter DDLs sent to the extract process. This kind of filtering will also aid in improving the overall performance of your replication setup.

OGG software comes with a set of SQL files. Copy ddl_filter.sql from the OGG software directory to another system for editing and testing your code.

You will have a filterDDL function in the ddl_filter.sql file, which you can modify for filtering what to replicate and what not. Table 6-2 lists the parameters you will work with in this function.

Table 6-2. *filterDDL Parameters*

Parameter	Description
ora_login_user	User who executed the DDL statement
ora_owner	DDL schema/username
ora_name	Object name
ora_objtype	Object type
ora_optype	Operation type
retVal	INCLUDE or EXCLUDE

Here's an example of excluding some specific DDL statements from replication.
Exclude any DDL statement from the SYS user, as follows:

```
if ora_owner='SYS' then
retVal:='EXCLUDE';
end if;
```

Exclude DROP USER statements, as follows:

```
if ora_objtype='USER' and ora_optype ='DROP' then
retVal:='EXCLUDE';
end if;
```

Exclude DDL on TEMP% tables, as follows:

```
if ora_owner='TIGER' and ora_name like 'TEMP%' then
retVal:='EXCLUDE';
end if;
```

Save your ddl_filter.sql file and execute it. Make sure there is no DDL activity on the source when you do this. TIGER is the source DDL schema name in this example:

```
@ddl_filter.sql TIGER
```

It is recommended that you perform the previous on a test machine before implementing it on a production environment.

Selective DDL Replication Using DDLAUX.addRule()

Once you run the ddl_setup.sql file in your Oracle GoldenGate schema, it installs DDL objects including the DDLAUX.addRule() function. You can use this function to filter DDL at the source.

Here's the function definition of DDLAUX.addRule(). Table 6-3 lists the parameters and their descriptions used in this function.

```
FUNCTION addRule( obj_name IN VARCHAR2 DEFAULT NULL,
base_obj_name IN VARCHAR2 DEFAULT NULL,
owner_name IN VARCHAR2 DEFAULT NULL,
base_owner_name IN VARCHAR2 DEFAULT NULL,
base_obj_property IN NUMBER DEFAULT NULL,
obj_type IN NUMBER DEFAULT NULL,
command IN VARCHAR2 DEFAULT NULL,
inclusion IN boolean DEFAULT NULL ,
sno IN NUMBER DEFAULT NULL)
RETURN NUMBER;
```

Table 6-3. *addRule() Parameters*

Parameter	Description
obj_name	Object name.
base_obj_name	Name of the base object for the DDL object.
owner_name	DDL schema/username of the object.
base_owner_name	Schema of the base object.
base_obj_property	Base object property; see the following list.
obj_type	Object type; see the following list.
Command	See the following list.
Inclusion	When TRUE, indicates the specified object type needs to be captured.
Sno	Serial number of the rule.

The following is a list of different commands, object types, and base object properties that you will be using while implementing filter rules using DDLAUX.addRule().

The following are the commands that you can pass as parameters to the addRule() function:

- CMD_CREATE
- CMD_ALTER
- CMD_DROP
- CMD_TRUNCATE

The following are the object types you can pass to the addRule() function to set rules based on particular object types:

- TYPE_TABLE
- TYPE_VIEW
- TYPE_INDEX
- TYPE_SYNONYM
- TYPE_TRIGGER
- TYPE_PROCEDURE
- TYPE_FUNCTION
- TYPE_PACKAGE
- TYPE_SEQUENCE

The base object properties that can be used with the addRule() function are as follows:

- TB_IOT
- TB_NESTED
- TB_CLUSTER
- TB_TEMP
- TB_EXTERNAL

Here are a few examples to illustrate the method.

Include all tables that contain 'TIGER_%' in the name, as follows:

```
DECLARE sno NUMBER;
BEGIN sno := DDLAUX.ADDRULE(obj_name => 'TIGER_%' , obj_type => TYPE_TABLE); END
```

Exclude temporary tables, as follows:

```
DDLAUX.ADDRULE(base_obj_property => TB_TEMP, obj_type => TYPE_TABLE);
```

Exclude DDL from a particular owner, as follows:

```
DDLAUX.ADDRULE(owner_name => 'RAVIN');
```

Exclude truncate on tables, as follows:

```
DDLAUX.ADDRULE(obj_type => TYPE_TABLE, command => CMD_TRUNCATE)
```

Selective DDL Replication Using the DDL Parameter

You can use a DDL parameter with the INCLUDE and EXCLUDE option in the capture parameter. Only one DDL parameter can be used in a parameter file. Please note that the DDL option can be used only in the primary extract and not in a data pump extract.

The basic syntax is DDL <INCLUDE or EXCLUDE> <Filter option>.

If you are creating an EXCLUDE, you must use an INCLUDE to pair it. This, however, is not mandatory if you are simply using DDL INCLUDE. Also, DDL EXCLUDE ALL does not require INCLUDE with it.

Here are some examples of DDL filters:

```
DDL INCLUDE ALL, EXCLUDE OBJNAME TIGER.*
DDL INCLUDE OBJNAME TIGER.* EXCLUDE OBJNAME TIGER.CNTRY
DDL INCLUDE OBJNAME TIGER.* ALLOWEMPTYOBJECT
DDL INCLUDE OBJNAME orcl.TIGER.* ALLOWEMPTYOWNER
DDL INCLUDE OBJNAME tiger.*
DDL INCLUDE OBJNAME tiger."cntry"
DDL INCLUDE OBJTYPE 'INDEX'
DDL INCLUDE OBJTYPE 'SNAPSHOT'
DDL INCLUDE OPTYPE ALTER
DDL INCLUDE ALL EXCLUDE INSTR 'CREATE INDEX'
DDL INCLUDE ALL EXCLUDE INSTRCOMMENTS 'NOT REPLICATED'
```

The following is how you can combine multiple INCLUDE and EXCLUDE statements for generating your filter requirement:

```
DDL  &
INCLUDE UNMAPPED &
    OPTYPE alter &
    OBJTYPE 'table' &
    OBJNAME users.tab* &
INCLUDE MAPPED OBJNAME * &
EXCLUDE MAPPED OBJNAME temporary.tab
```

You can also opt to block DDL replication using an EXCLUDE ALL filter.

```
DDL EXCLUDE ALL
```

Using DUMPDDL

As discussed previously in this book, OGG maintains a DDL history table. You can use the DUMPDDL command in GGSCI to view the contents of the DDL history table. DUMPDDL will dump all the contents of the DDL history table. Since the DDL history table usually has large volume of data, only the first 4,000 bytes are dumped for performance reasons.

The following is the syntax to use when invoking DUMPDDL:

```
GGSCI> DUMPDDL
```

or the following:

```
GGSCI> DUMPDDL SHOW
```

It's important to note the DDL history table gets data from DDL before the trigger; hence, it contains the before state of all DDLs. Therefore, there will not be any CREATE operations in the DUMPDDL output. DUMPDDL dumps DDL contents from the history table to certain SQL tables listed in the next table.

Table 6-4 shows a list of tables in Oracle databases that store the output of your DUMPDDL command.

Table 6-4. *Tables That Store Output of DUMPDDL*

Table	Description
GGS_DDL_OBJECTS	Contains information about objects involved in DDL replication. The primary key is SEQNO and is referred to by all other tables that have SEQNO as a foreign key to GGS_DDL_OBJECTS.
GGS_DDL_COLUMNS	Contains information about columns of objects involved in DDL.
GGS_DDL_LOG_GROUPS	Contains information on supplemental log groups.
GGS_DDL_PARTITIONS	Contains information about the DDL object partitions .
GGS_DDL_PRIMARY_ KEYS	Contains information about primary keys of the DDL objects.

DDL Replication in Active-Active Mode (Bidirectional Replication)

In a bidirectional replication environment, the extract must know how to differentiate between DDL operations by an application user and OGG. Table 6-5 lists the options you can use with DDLOPTIONS in you extract parameter to control which transactions are captured and which are ignored.

Table 6-5. *DDLOPTIONS for Filtering Users for DDL Replication*

Parameter	Usage
GETREPLICATES	Captures DDL from GoldenGate user.
IGNOREREPLICATES	Ignores DDL from GoldenGate user. This is the default when not specified.
GETAPPLOPS	Captures DDL from the Application user.
IGNOREAPPLOPS	Ignores DDL from the Application user. This is the default when not specified.
UPDATEMETADATA	Used in the replicat parameter file when GETREPLICATS is enabled in the extract.

In bidirectional configuration, the extract and replicat on the primary and secondary database servers should have the following parameters.

- Extract on both servers:

```
DDLOPTIONS GETREPLICATES, GETAPPLOPS
```

- Replicat on both servers:

```
DDLOPTIONS UPDATEMETADATA
```

DDL Replication in a Cascading Replication Setup

In a cascading replication environment, your extracts need to be configured to capture DDL by the OGG user as follows:

```
DDLOPTIONS GETREPLICATES, IGNOREAPPLOPS
```

DDL Replication in a Heterogeneous Environment

Each database has its own DDL statement structures and varies in the syntax. Hence, Oracle GoldenGate DDL replication can be configured only between two Oracle databases. Non-Oracle databases are not supported.

Summary

This chapter discussed how to configure Oracle GoldenGate to capture and replicate DDL statements between two Oracle databases. It discussed in detail the two types of DDL replication available for Oracle GoldenGate: trigger based and native DDL replication. We also discussed how to perform selective DDL replication to filter DDLs sent to the extract process. Finally, you also learned about a special DDL replication parameter for configuring the replication of DDL statements in bidirectional and cascading replication configurations.

So, you have learned how to install and configure DML and DDL replication. In the next chapter, we will demonstrate different initial load options for performing a first-time data load from the source to target environment.

CHAPTER 7

Performing the Initial Load

Once you have installed Oracle GoldenGate and have set up your extract/replicat processes, the next step before you can begin replication is the initial load of existing data from the source database to the target database. There are two ways this can be done, as listed here:

- Using database copy options such as CTAS (Create Table As Select) over DBLINK, EXPDP and IMPDP, SQLLOADER, and so on.

- Using the initial load extract and replicat processes. This is known as GoldenGate *direct load*.

Preparing for the Initial Load

Before you can begin the initial load to the target database system, there are a few pre-steps, shown here:

1. Disable the DDL replication before starting the initial load.

2. Empty the target tables or they might throw up unique constraint errors in case of a conflict.

3. Disable the foreign key and check constraints on the target tables. A check constraint slows the load process.

4. Preferably, drop indexes from the target tables because they might slow the load process. They can be added later after the initial load is complete.

5. In the case of Oracle databases, normally redo logs are not generated for sequences until the current cache is exhausted. To start capturing sequences immediately after the extract process is started, issue the following command on the source:

GGSCI> FLUSH SEQUENCE owner_name.sequence_name

Or the following:

GGSCI> FLUSH SEQUENCE *owner_name.* *

6. The chapter discusses using the initial load extract and replicat processes. Ensure that you have your regular extract and replicat processes ready as configured during the GoldenGate setup on your system. Always start the regular extract process first and then the initial load extract. On the other hand, wait for the initial load replicat to complete and then start your regular replicat.

© Ravinder Gupta 2016
R. Gupta, *Mastering Oracle GoldenGate*, DOI 10.1007/978-1-4842-2301-7_7

Here's the script to disable all the foreign keys in the Oracle target database before the initial load process:

```
declare
    v_sql_stmt varchar2(1024);
  BEGIN
    FOR fk IN (SELECT table_name, constraint_name
                 FROM user_constraints
                 WHERE constraint_type='R')
    LOOP
      v_sql_stmt := 'alter table ' || fk.table_name ||
                    ' enable constraint "' || fk.constraint_name || '"';
      DBMS_OUTPUT.PUT_LINE(v_sql_stmt || ';');
      EXECUTE IMMEDIATE v_sql_stmt;
    END LOOP;
  END ;
/
```

Here's a script to enable all the foreign keys in the Oracle target database after the initial load process. Alternatively, you can also spool the output of the previous script that disables foreign keys and then convert the enable statements to disable statements and run them. This ensures that all keys that were disabled are enabled and none of them are missed.

```
set serveroutput on size 1000000
  declare
    v_sql_stmt varchar2(1024);
  BEGIN
    FOR fk IN (SELECT table_name, constraint_name
                 FROM user_constraints
                 WHERE constraint_type='R'
                   AND status != 'ENABLED')
    LOOP
      v_sql_stmt := 'alter table ' || fk.table_name ||
                    ' enable constraint "' || fk.constraint_name || '"';
      DBMS_OUTPUT.PUT_LINE(v_sql_stmt || ';');
      BEGIN
      EXECUTE IMMEDIATE v_sql_stmt;
      EXCEPTION
      WHEN OTHERS
      THEN
        DBMS_OUTPUT.PUT_LINE(SQLERRM);
        DBMS_OUTPUT.PUT_LINE(v_sql_stmt);
      END;
    END LOOP;
  END ;
/
```

Before the initial load on the target database, you must ensure the target tables are empty. You can use the following PL/SQL code in the Oracle database to truncate all tables in a particular schema.

■ **Caution**   Be cautious while executing the following code. You don't want to be logged in as the wrong user and then run the following. All application data will be lost.

```
set serveroutput on size 1000000
spool truncate_wseprod_uat_20110914.log
BEGIN
FOR rec IN (select 'truncate '|| object_type || ' ' || object_name AS drop_sql
FROM user_objects WHERE object_type IN ('TABLE')
LOOP
DBMS_OUTPUT.PUT_LINE(rec.drop_sql);
EXECUTE IMMEDIATE(rec.drop_sql);
END LOOP;
END;
/
```

Table 7-1 lists the parameters that are used in the direct initial load extract/replicat process. We will use these parameters in our examples in this chapter.

Table 7-1. *Direct Load Parameters*

Parameter	Used In	Description
SOURCEISTABLE	Extract	The extract is an initial load extract that extracts directly from the source table.
SPECIALRUN	Replicat	The replicat is a one-time run replicat that runs without using checkpoints.
BULKLOAD	Replicat	The replicat will directly interface with the Oracle SQLLOADER utility on the target to load data into the target tables.
GENLOAD	Replicat	This generates run and control files for the specified database utility.
RMTFILE	Extract	This specifies the extract file name.
FORMATASCII	Extract	This instructs the extract to write output in ASCII text in flat files. These can be used by the database utility on the target machine to load data directly without setting up the replicat process.
SQLLOADER	Extract	This is used along with the FORMATASCII parameter to extract data into ASCII-format flat files.

Initial Load Using the Database Utility

This is the simplest mode of the initial load. Here a static copy of the source is taken and applied to the target. Keep the extract processes running so that it captures any changes done during the static copy and so that the same is available on the target when the replicat is started after the initial load completes.

The replicat process should have the HANDLECOLLSION parameter to handle errors after the initial load. Turn off HANDLECOLLISION once pending transactions from the extract have flown to the replicat. To turn off HANDLECOLLISSION, you can simply remove the parameter from the replicat parameter file and bounce the replicat or issue the following command in GGSCI.SEND REPLICAT RFDLD001, NOHANDLECOLLISIONS

Initial Load Using SQLLOADER

One way to perform the initial load using SQLLOADER is to capture data from the source database using the initial load extract process into external ASCII-format flat files. These flat files are then used by tools like Oracle's SQLLOADER, IBM's LOADUTIL, and so on, which are flat-file processing tools to load into the target database. Figure 7-1 shows the OGG components for the initial load using SQLLoader.

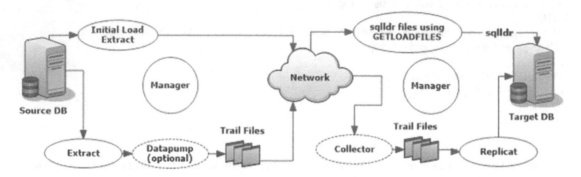

Figure 7-1. *Initial load using SQLLoader template*

Create an initial load extract on the source machine.

GGSCI> ADD EXTRACT INITEXT1, SOURCEISTABLE

Configure the extract parameter file to have the following parameters:

GGSCI> EDIT PARAMS INITEXT1

```
SOURCEISTABLE
SETENV (NLS_LANG = "AMERICAN_AMERICA.AL32UTF8")
userid tiger, password tiger123_
FORMATASCII, SQLLOADER
RMTHOST node2-ravinpc, MGRPORT 7809
RMTFILE /app/ggs/tiger/dirdat/load_cntry.dat PURGE
TABLE tiger.cntry;
```

Create the initial load replicat on the target machine. This replicat only generates control and run files to be used by the database utility for loading data.

GGSCI> ADD REPLICAT INITREP1, SPECIALRUN

Configure the replicat parameter file.

GGSCI> EDIT PARAMS INITREP1

```
SPECIALRUN
END RUNTIME
GENLOADFILES sqlldr.tpl
```

```
userid fox, password fox123_
extfile /app/ggs/fox/dirdat/load_cntry.dat
assumetargetdefs
MAP TIGER.CNTRY, TARGET FOX.CNTRY;
```

GETLOADFILES specifies the name of the template that generates the control and run file. This in turn will be used by SQLLOADER. The template file sqlldr.tpl can be found in the GoldenGate installation directory.

First start your regular extract process and then start your initial load extract process.

```
$ GGSCI> START EXTRACT ETLDT0001
```

```
$ /app/ggs/tiger/extract paramfile dirprm/initext1.prm reportfile initext1.rpt
```

You can verify the report file to see whether the extraction has completed. The report file should have similar to the following information indicating your flat file for the load has been extracted.

```
2015-11-13 05:57:27 INFO    OGG-01478 Output file ./dirdat/load_data.dat is using format
ASCII.
```

```
2015-11-13 05:57:33 INFO    OGG-01226 Socket buffer size set to 27985 (flush size 27985).
```

```
Processing table TIGER.CNTRY
```

```
Report at 2015-11-13 05:57:35 (activity since 2015-11-13 05:57:24)
```

```
Output to /app/ggs/tiger/dirdat/load_cntry.dat:
```

```
From Table TIGER.CNTRY:
```

```
       #              inserts:    50014
       #              updates:        0
       #              deletes:        0
       #              discards:       0
```

Start the replicat process and verify the load after it completes.

```
$ /app/ggs/fox/replicat paramfile dirprm/initrep1.prm reportfile initrep1.rpt
```

You can send the INFO command on the replicat INITREP1 to see the progress. The report file for the replicat should look like the following information indicating completion:

```
File created for loader initiation: LOAD_CNTRY.run
```

```
File created for loader control:    LOAD_CNTRY.ctl
```

```
Load files generated successfully.
```

The .run file generated will have the sqlldr command load the database in the target environment, which will make use of the .c+tl file generated with it.

You can copy the .dat, .run, and .ctl file to your target database server and run them as follows:

```
./LOAD_CNTRY.run
```

Verify the target table count after the load is finished.

You should start the initial load extract along with the regular extract that will keep capturing any changes during and after the initial load process.

Similarly, configure your regular replicat process for applying the changes captured during and after the initial load.

Once the initial load is complete, start your regular replicat processes that will load changes captured during and after the initial load.

```
GGSCI> START REPLICAT RFDLD001
```

```
GGSCI> SEND REPLICAT RFDLD001, NOHANDLECOLLISIONS
```

Initial Load Using the Direct Load Method

For this mode of the initial load, special extract and replicat processes are created. The initial load extract captures all of the source records and is sent to the initial load replicat task. The initial load replicat task is dynamically started by the manager process. Figure 7-2 shows the components of Oracle GoldenGate when using the direct load method for initial load.

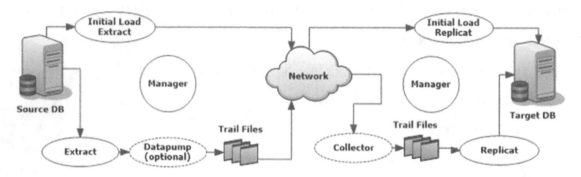

Figure 7-2. *Initial load using direct load*

Let's start with creating an initial load extract named INITEXT1.

```
GGSCI> ADD EXTRACT INITEXT1, SOURCEISTABLE
```

```
GGSCI> EDIT PARAMS INITEXT1
```

```
EXTRACT INITEXT1
SOURCEISTABLE
RMTHOST ravin-ravinpc, MGRPORT 7809
RMTTASK REPLICAT, GROUP INITREP1

USERID tiger, PASSWORD tiger123_
TABLE TIGER.*;
```

Save and close the parameter file. Now, create an initial load replicat called INITREP1 on the target.

```
GGSCI> ADD REPLICAT INITREP1, SPECIALRUN
```

```
GGSCI> EDIT PARAMS INITREP1
```

```
REPLICAT INITREP1
--ASSUMETARGETDEFS
SOURCEDEFS /app/ggs/fox/dirdef/INITREP1.def
DISCARDFILE /app/ggs/fox/dirrpt/INITREP1.dsc, MEGABYTES 599, append
USERID fox, PASSWORD fox123_
MAP TIGER.*, TARGET FOX.*;
```

Save and close the parameter file.
First start your regular extract process and then start your initial load extract process.

```
$ GGSCI> START EXTRACT ETLDT0001
```

```
$ /app/ggs/tiger/extract paramfile dirprm/initext1.prm reportfile initext1.rpt
```

On the target machine, view the initial load replicat report file to monitor whether the initial load is complete. Once the initial load is complete, start your regular replicat processes that will load changes captured during and after the initial load.

```
GGSCI> START REPLICAT RFDLD001
```

```
GGSCI> SEND REPLICAT RFDLD001, NOHANDLECOLLISIONS
```

Initial Load Using BULKLOAD to sqlloader

In this method, the initial load extract sends data to the initial load replicat. The replicat task then interfaces with the sqlloader API to bulk-load data in the target Oracle database. Figure 7-3 shows the components of Oracle GoldenGate when using the direct bulk load to sqlloader method for initial load.

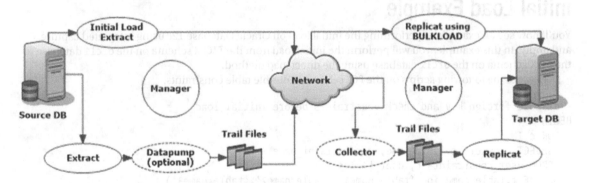

Figure 7-3. *Initial load using direct bulk load to SQLLoader*

Create the initial load extract as follows:

```
GGSCI> ADD EXTRACT INITEXT1, SOURCEISTABLE
```

```
GGSCI> EDIT PARAMS INITEXT1
```

```
EXTRACT INITEXT1
RMTHOST node2-ravinpc, MGRPORT 7809
```

```
RMTTASK REPLICAT, GROUP INITREP1
USERID tiger, PASSWORD tiger123_
TABLE TIGER.*;
```

Create an initial load replicat called INITREP1 on the target as shown here:

```
GGSCI> ADD REPLICAT INITREP1, SPECIALRUN

GGSCI> EDIT PARAMS INITREP1

REPLICAT INITREP1
BULKLOAD
--ASSUMETARGETDEFS
SOURCEDEFS /app/ggs/fox/dirdef/INITREP1.def
DISCARDFILE /app/ggs/fox/dirrpt/INITREP1.dsc, MEGABYTES 599, append
USERID fox, PASSWORD fox123_
MAP TIGER.*, TARGET FOX.*;
```

Follow the similar process explained for the direct load method. Start the initial load extract named INITEXT1 and let it complete.

```
$ /app/ggs/tiger/extract paramfile dirprm/initext1.prm reportfile initext1.rpt
```

Verify the report file to see whether the extraction has completed. Start the replicat process and verify the load after it completes. You can send the INFO command on the replicat INITREP1 to see the progress.

```
GGSCI> START REPLICAT RFDLD001
GGSCI> SEND REPLICAT RFDLD001, NOHANDLECOLLISIONS
```

Initial Load Example

You'll now see an example of performing the initial load on Oracle Database 12c using integrated capture and apply. In this example, you will perform the initial load from the TIGER schema on the orcl1 database to the FOX schema on the orcl2 database using the direct load method.

Execute the following scripts on the FOX schema to disable table constraints.

```
--disable foreign key and check constraints before initial load
BEGIN
  FOR c IN
  (SELECT c.owner, c.table_name, c.constraint_name
   FROM user_constraints c, user_tables t
   WHERE t.table_name in ('table_name1','table_name2','table_name3')
   AND c.table_name = t.table_name
   AND c.constraint_type!='P'
   AND c.status = 'ENABLED'
   ORDER BY c.constraint_type DESC)
  LOOP
    dbms_utility.exec_ddl_statement('alter table "' || c.owner || '"."' || c.table_name ||
'" disable constraint ' || c.constraint_name);
  END LOOP;
END;
/
```

Next, truncate tables from the FOX schema on the orcl2 database. If you are replicating only specific tables, you should truncate only those tables.

```
set serveroutput on size 1000000
spool truncate_wseprod_uat_20110914.log
BEGIN
FOR rec IN (select 'truncate '|| object_type || ' ' || object_name AS drop_sql
FROM user_objects WHERE object_type IN ('TABLE')
LOOP
DBMS_OUTPUT.PUT_LINE(rec.drop_sql);
EXECUTE IMMEDIATE(rec.drop_sql);
END LOOP;
END;
/
```

Add supplemental logging for tables to be replicated on the source. For this example, I have only the ORDER_DTL table in the TIGER schema.

```
GGSCI> DBLOGIN USERID tiger@orcl1 PASSWORD tiger123_
Successfully logged into database.

GGSCI> ADD TRANDATA TIGER.ORDER_DTL
Logging of supplemental redo data enabled for table TIGER.ORDER_DTL.
TRANDATA for scheduling columns has been added on table 'TIGER.ORDER_DTL'.
```

Add the extract on the source:

```
GGSCI> ADD EXTRACT ETTND001, integrated tranlog, begin now

GGSCI> add exttrail /app/ggs/tiger/dirdat/t1, extract ETTND001, megabytes 5
```

Add the following entries in the parameter file.

```
EXTRACT ETTND001
USERID TIGER, PASSWORD tiger123_
EXTTRAIL /app/ggs/tiger/dirdat/t1
LOGALLSUPCOLS
UPDATERECORDFORMAT compact
TABLE TIGER.ORDER_DTL;
```

Log in to the GoldenGate user from GGSCI and register the extract with the database.

```
GGSCI> DBLOGIN USERID tiger@orcl1 PASSWORD tiger123_

GGSCI> REGISTER EXTRACT ETTND001 DATABASE
2016-04-23 19:13:22  INFO    OGG-02003  Extract ETTND001 successfully registered with
database at SCN 254214.
```

Add the data pump to the pump trail files from the target to the fox GoldenGate instances.

```
GGSCI> add extract DTTND001, exttrailsource /app/ggs/tiger/dirdat/t1
GGSCI> add rmttrail /app/ggs/fox/dirdat/f1, extract DTTND001, megabytes 5
```

```
GGSCI> edit params DTTND001

EXTRACT DTTND001
PASSTHRU
RMTHOST node2-ravinpc, MGRPORT 7840
RMTTRAIL /app/ggs/fox/dirdat/f1
TABLE TIGER.ORDER_DTL;
```

Start the extract and data pump.

```
GGSCI> start extract *
```

Create a replicat group on the target machine's FOX OGG instance.

```
GGSCI> edit params RFDLD001

REPLICAT RFDLD001
ASSUMETARGETDEFS
DISCARDFILE /app/ggs/fox/dirrpt/rfdld001.dsc, purge
USERIDALIAS DB2 domain admin
MAP hr.*, TARGET hr.*;

GGSCI> add replicat RFDLD001, integrated, exttrail /app/ggs/fox/dirdat/f1
```

Get the current SCN of the source database.

```
SQL> select current_scn from v$database;

CURRENT_SCN
-----------
    1642141
```

Once you have set up your regular extract, data pump, and replicat processes for capturing and applying change, set up the initial load extract called INITEXT1 and the initial load replicat called INITREP1.

```
GGSCI> edit params INITEXT1

EXTRACT INITEXT1
SOURCEISTABLE
USERID tiger@orcl1 PASSWORD tiger123_
RMTHOST node2-ravinpc, MGRPORT 7809
RMTFILE /app/ggs/fox/dirdat/initld, MEGABYTES 2, PURGE
TABLE TIGER.*, SQLPREDICATE 'AS OF SCN 1642141';
TABLEEXCLUDE TIGER.RAVIN_ORDERS;
```

Here, TABLEEXCLUDE will inform OGG not to capture the table RAVIN_ORDERS.
Next, create and start the INITEXT1 extract channel.

```
GGSCI> add extract INITEXT1, sourceistable

GGSCI> start extract INITEXT1
Sending START request to MANAGER …
EXTRACT INITLOAD starting
```

View the report file for the `initext1` initial load extract to monitor the progress.

```
GGSCI> view report INITEXT1
```

Add the initial load replicat.

```
GGSCI> add replicat INITREP1, specialrun

REPLICAT INITREP1
USERID fox@orcl1 PASSWORD fox123_
SPECIALRUN
END RUNTIME
ASSUMETARGETDEFS
EXTFILE /app/ggs/fox/dirdat/initld
MAP TIGER.*, TARGET FOX.*;
```

Start the initial load replicat.

```
GGSCI> start replicat INITREP1
```

You can view the report file for INITREP1 to monitor the progress. Once the INITREP1 has finished loading data in the FOX schema, you can start your regular replicat RFDLD001.

```
GGSCI> start replicat RFDLD001, aftercsn 1642141
Sending START request to MANAGER ...
REPLICAT RFDLD001 starting
```

You can perform updates on the source in the TIGER schema for ORDER_DTL now, and it should show up in the target database.

■ **Tip** For a large source database, doing the initial load using a database utility is faster than using Oracle GoldenGate direct load.

Summary

In this chapter, we discussed different initial load options for performing a first-time data load from the source to the target environment. We discussed various pre- and post-initial load steps. We discussed initial load both using Oracle GoldenGate special extract/replicat processes and using database native copy and load options.

In the next chapter, we will discuss an overview of most commonly used OGG commands. These commands will be useful during the advanced data processing discussed in the subsequent chapter.

PART II

■ ■ ■

Advanced Configurations

CHAPTER 8

■■■

Oracle GoldenGate Commands

This chapter discusses Oracle GoldenGate commands, command-line utilities and functions. You will use these commands and functions frequently while performing advanced configuration and monitoring of your Oracle GoldenGate replication environment.

Data Transformation Using Column Conversion Functions

Let's first take a look at the GoldenGate functions for column conversion, filtering, and transforming data during the extract or replicat process. Column conversion functions provide you with the capabilities of extract, transform, and load using GoldenGate. Table 8-1 lists the conditional analysis functions that you can use in your Oracle GoldenGate extract or replicat parameter files.

Table 8-1. Conditional Analysis Functions

Function	Usage	Example
IF	This is for the conditional return of a value.	BALANCE = @IF (BAL > 0, BAL, 0) JOB_STATUS = @IF (@VALONEOF (STATUS, 'P', 'A', 'D'), 'VALID', 'INVALID')
CASE	This is the regular CASE statement to choose conditional output based on a series of possible values. The syntax is @ CASE(Variable,compare_value1, result_ value1, compare_value2, result_ value2, ..., default_result).	@CASE(DISCOUNT,5, 95, 10, 90, 100)
EVAL	This returns a value based on multiple independent tests. This works like multiple IFs where the first true condition returns the result and exits.	value=@EVAL(condition1,result1,condition2 ,result2,...,default) discount=@EVAL(cart_value<1000,'5%',cart_ value<2000,'10%','15%')

© Ravinder Gupta 2016

R. Gupta, *Mastering Oracle GoldenGate*, DOI 10.1007/978-1-4842-2301-7_8

Table 8-2 shows commonly used date functions available for date conversion and manipulation in Oracle GoldenGate.

Table 8-2. *Date Functions*

Function	Usage	Example
DATE	Returns the date and time in specified format	update_time = @DATE ('YYYY-MM-DD HH:MI:SS', 'YYYYMMDDHHMISS', record_date) update_time = @DATE ('YYYY-MM-DD HH:MI:00', 'YYMMDD', record_date, 'HHMI', record_time)
DATENOW	Returns the current date and time in YYYY-MM-DD HH:MI:SS format	update_time=@DATENOW()
DATEDIFF	Calculates the difference between two dates in days or seconds	num_of_days = @DATEDIFF ('DD', '2012-07-01', @DATENOW ()) num_of_days = @DATEDIFF ('SS', '2014-07-01', @DATENOW ())

Table 8-3 shows the COMPUTE function that can be used to do arithmetic calculations.

Table 8-3. *Math Function*

Function	Usage	Example
COMPUTE	Evaluates an arithmetic operation and returns the result	DISCOUNT=@(0.5*AMOUNT)

You can perform a variety of string operations for the conversion and transformation of your string data, as listed in Table 8-4.

Table 8-4. *String Functions*

Function	Usage	Example
NUMSTR	Converts a string value into a number.	@NUMSTR(value)
STRCAT	Concatenates one or more strings.	@STRCAT(FIRST_NAME, ' ',LAST_NAME)
STRCMP	Compares two string literals and returns -1,0,1 depending on first string that is less, equal to, or greater than the second string.	@STRCMP('GOLDEN','GATE')
STREXT	Extracts a part (substring) of the string.	@STREXT (string, begin_position, end_position)
STREQ	Checks whether two strings are equal. Returns 1 if true; else 0.	@IF (@STREQ (STATUS, 'P'), 'Processed', 'Other')
STRFIND	Determines the position of a pattern within a string.	@STRFIN(string,search_pattern,start_position)
STRLEN	Returns the length of the string.	@STRLEN('GoldenGate')
STRLTRIM	Trims the leading spaces.	@STRLTRIM(FULL_NAME)
STRRTRIM	Trims the training spaces.	@STRRTRIM(FULL_NAME)
STRSUB	Substitutes a pattern within a string.	@STRSUB(String,pattern,replacement_string)
STRTRIM	Trims both the leading and trailing spaces.	@STRTTRIM(FULL_NAME)
STRUP	Converts a string to uppercase.	@STRUP('employee')
VALONEOF	Compares a string with a list. If matched, 1 is returned; else 0.	@VALONEOF (STATUS, 'P', 'A', 'D')

Table 8-5 lists some common miscellaneous functions that you may find useful for your column conversion requirements.

Table 8-5. *Miscellaneous Functions*

Function	Usage	Example
AFTER	Returns an after image of the specified columns.	@AFTER(column_name)
BEFORE	Returns a before image of the specified columns. This is to be used with the EXTRACT parameters GETUPDATEBEFORES and GETBEFORECOLS.	@BEFORE(column_name)
BEFOREAFTER	Returns a before image if available; if not, it returns an after image. This is to be used with the EXTRACT parameters GETUPDATEBEFORES and GETBEFORECOLS.	@BEFOREAFTER(column_name)
GETENV	Returns information about the GoldenGate environment.	@GETENV ('STATS','TABLE','schema_name. table_name','CDR_CONFLICTS') @GETENV ('STATS','TABLE','schema_name. table_name', 'CDR_RESOLUTIONS_FAILED') @GETENV ('STATS','CDR_RESOLUTIONS_ SUCCEEDED') @GETENV ('STATS', 'TRUNCATE') @GETENV ('STATS', 'DML') @GETENV ('OSVARIABLE', 'variable')
GETVAL	Extracts a value from a stored procedure or a query and passes it to the FILTER and COLMAP attributes.	MAP source_schema.table_name, TARGET target_schema.table_name, SQLEXEC (SPNAME dummy, PARAMS (var = dummy_col)), COLMAP (target_col = @GETVAL (dummy. var));

GGSCI Commands

GGSCI commands are executed directly from the GGSCI prompt. These commands can be frequently used to interact with various GoldenGate processes and databases. Table 8-6 lists the GGSCI commands for giving instructions to the manager process.

Table 8-6. *GGSCI Commands for the Manager Process*

Command	Usage	Example
INFO MANAGER	Gives information about the host IP and port on which the manager is running.	INFO MANAGER
SEND MANAGER	Retrieves the status of the active process and dynamic port information.	SEND MANAGER GETPORTINFO SEND MANAGER CHILDSTATUS SEND MANAGER CHILDSTATUS DEBUG
START MANAGER	Starts the manager process.	START MANAGER
STATUS MANAGER	Checks the status of the manager process (running/stopped).	STATUS MANAGER
STOP MANAGER	Stops the manager. This optional and is used to bypass the confirmation for stopping the manager.	STOP MANAGER!

You will be working frequently with your extract and replicat processes. Table 8-7 lists the commands to send instructions to your extract and replicat processes.

Table 8-7. *GGSCI Commands for Extract and Replicat*

Command	Usage	Example
ADD EXTRACT	Creates an EXTRACT group. SOURCEISTABLE is used only when it is an initial load extract.	ADD EXTRACT extract_name, TRANLOG, BEGIN NOW ADD EXTRACT extract_name, EXTFILESOURCE trail_name, BEGIN NOW ADD EXTRACT INITEXT, SOURCEISTABLE
ADD REPLICAT	Creates a REPLICAT group. SPECIALRUN is used only when it is an initial load replicat.	ADD REPLICAT replicat_name, EXTTRAIL dirdat/aa ADD REPLICAT replicat_name, EXTTRAIL /app/ggs/tiger/dirdat/aa, NODBCHECKPOINT ADD REPLICAT INITREP, SPECIALRUN
ALTER EXTRACT/ REPLICAT	Changes or assigns an attribute to an extract or replicat group.	ALTER EXTRACT extract_name, BEGIN 2014-01-01 ALTER EXTRACT extract_name, ETROLLOVER ALTER EXTRACT extract_name, EXTSEQNO 06, EXTRBA 250311
DELETE EXTRACT/ REPLICAT	Deletes an EXTRACT/REPLICAT group.	DELETE EXTRACT extract_name DELETE EXTRACT extract_name!
CLEANUP EXTRACT/ REPLICAT	Deletes the run history on the specified EXTRACT/REPLICAT group.	CLEANUP EXTRACT extract_name CLEANUP EXTRACT extract_name,5 CLEANUP EXTRACT *
INFO EXTRACT/ REPLICAT	Views various information related to the EXTRACT/REPLICAT.	INFO EXTRACT extract_name INFO EXTRACT extract_name, DETAIL INFO EXTRACT extract_name, SHOWCH

(continued)

Table 8-7. (*continued*)

Command	Usage	Example
KILL EXTRACT/ REPLICAT	Kills an EXTRACT/REPLICAT when it can't be stopped gracefully.	KILL EXTRACT extract_name
LAG EXTRACT/ REPLICAT	Determines the exact lag time between the extract and the data source.	LAG EXTRACT extract_name
SEND EXTRACT/ REPLICAT	Sends commands to a running extract or replicat.	SEND EXTRACT extract_name, ROLLOVER SEND EXTRACT extract_name, STOP SEND EXTRACT extract_ name, TRANLOGOPTIONS TRANSCLEANUPFREQUENCY 10 SEND EXTRACT extract_name, SHOWTRANS COUNT 5
START EXTRACT/ REPLICAT	Starts an extract. Optionally, ATCSN specifies an alternate start point.	START EXTRACT extact_name START EXTRACT extract_name ATCSN 10005464 START EXTRACT extract_name AFTERCSN 10005464
STATS EXTRACT/ REPLICAT	Displays statistics of one or more extract groups. Optionally, you can use statistics options such as TOTAL, HOURLY,DAILY,TABLE, and so on.	STATS EXTRACT extract_name STATS EXTRACT extract_name, TOTAL, HOURLY, TABLE schema_name. table_name, REPORTRATE MIN, RESET, REPORTFETCH
STOP EXTRACT/ REPLICAT	Stops an extract gracefully.	STOP EXTRACT extract_name

ER refers to extract and replicat. You can send common instructions to the extract or replicat processes using wildcards for their group names. This allows you to work on multiple extract and replicat groups together. Table 8-8 lists the GGSCI commands to send instructions to the extract or replicat groups using wildcards and patterns.

Table 8-8. *GGSCI Commands Using the ER Parameter*

Command	Usage	Example
INFO	Gives information about multiple extract and replicat groups	INFO ER *T*
KILL	Kills multiple extract and replicat groups	KILL ER T*
LAG	Checks the LAG on multiple extract and replicat groups	LAG ER *
SEND	Communicates with multiple extract and replicat groups	SEND ER T*, START
START	Starts multiple extract and replicat groups	START ER T*
STATS	Displays statistics on multiple extract and replicat groups	STATS ER T*
STATUS	Displays the status of multiple extract and replicat groups	STATUS ER *
STOP	Stops multiple extract and replicat groups	STOP ER *

We will discuss creating and working with Oracle GoldenGate Wallet in Chapter 10. Table 8-9 lists the commands that you can use while working with OGG Wallet.

Table 8-9. *Oracle GoldenGate Wallet Commands (Available Only in GoldenGate 12 and Higher Versions)*

Command	Usage	Example
CREATE WALLET	Creates a master-key wallet. It is used by GoldenGate processes to encrypt the encryption keys. The wallet is created at the location specified by the GLOBALS parameter WALLETLOCATION if specified; otherwise, the default location is dirwlt.	CREATE WALLET
OPEN WALLET	Opens the wallet to decrypt the content and load it into GGSCI memory. A wallet must be open before you can add or delete a master key.	OPEN WALLET
PURGE WALLET	Permanently removes the master-key versions that were marked for deletion by the DELETE MASTERKEY command.	PURGE WALLET
ADD MASTERKEY	A master-key is used by GGSCI processes (extracts and replicats) to secure the encryption keys being sent across the network.	ADD MASTERKEY
INFO MASTERKEY	Displays the contents of the currently open master-key wallet. It will display the version history of the master key.	INFO MASTERKEY INFO MASTERKEY VERSION 5
RENEW MASTERKEY	Renews the master key to new version.	RENEW MASTERKEY
DELETE MASTERKEY	Marks the master key as deleted so it can't be used any longer. This is later purged with the PURGE MASTERKEY command.	DELETE MASTERKEY VERSION 2 DELETE MASTERKEY RANGE FROM 2 to 5
UNDELETE MASTERKEY	Removes the deletion mark from a master-key version.	UNDELETE MASTERKEY VERSION 3

Table 8-10 lists the commands to add, alter, delete, and get info on local as well as remote trail files.

Table 8-10. *GGSCI Commands for Trail Files*

Command	Usage	Example
ADD EXTRAIL	Creates a trail on the local machine and assigns it to an extract group.	ADD EXTTRAIL ggs/tiger/dirdat/ aa, EXTRACT extract_name, MEGABYTES 200 ADD EXTTRAIL ggs/tiger/dirdat/aa
ADD RMTTRAIL	Creates a trail on the remote machine and assigns it to an extract group.	ADD RMTTRAIL ggs/tiger/dirdat/ bb, EXTRACT extract_name, MEGABYTES 200 ADD RMTTRAIL ggs/tiger/dirdat/bb
ALTER EXTRAIL	Alters attributes of a trail created on the local machine.	ADD EXTTRAIL ggs/tiger/dirdat/ aa, EXTRACT extract_name, MEGABYTES 200
ALTER RMTTRAIL	Alters attributes of a trail created on a remote machine.	ADD RMTTRAIL ggs/tiger/dirdat/ bb, EXTRACT extract_name, MEGABYTES 200
DELETE EXTRAIL	Deletes the checkpoints for the trail created on the local machine. These checkpoints are stored in the dirchk directory with the same name as the extract group. Please note that it does not delete the trail files. Trail files can be deleted using standard OS commands to remove files.	DELETE EXTTRAIL ggs/tiger/ dirdat/aa
DELETE RMTTRAIL	Deletes the checkpoints for the trail created on the remote machine.	DELETE RMTTRAIL ggs/tiger/ dirdat/bb
INFO EXTRAIL	Displays information related to the local trail such as the name of the trail, the extract that writes to the trail, and so on.	INFO EXTRAIL trail_name
INFO RMTTRAIL	Displays information related to the remote trail such as the name of the trail, the extract that writes to the trail, and so on.	INFO RMTTRAIL trail_name INFO RMTTRAIL *

Parameter files in Oracle GoldenGate are key configuration files that you will look for replication, transformation, and troubleshooting errors. Table 8-11 lists the commands to view and edit parameter files.

Table 8-11. *GGSCI Commands for Parameter Files*

Command	Usage	Example
EDIT PARAMS	Creates or changes a parameter file for a manager, extract, or replicat process.	EDIT PARAMS MGR EDIT PARAMS extract_name
SET EDITOR	Changes the default text editor for the current GGSCI session	SET EDITOR VIM
VIEW PARAMS	Views the parameter file for a manager, extract, or replicat process	VIEW PARAMS MGR VIEW PARAMS extract_name VIEW PARAMS replicat_name

There will be times when you need to interact with your database through the GGSCI interface. Table 8-12 lists the frequently used GGSCI commands to send or receive information from the database.

Table 8-12. *GGSCI Commands for Database*

Command	Usage	Example
DBLOGIN	Logs in to the database from the GGSCI prompt to be able to issue GoldenGate commands that affect database. The user who issues DBLOGIN must have grants on the dbms_goldengate_auth. grant_admin_privilege procedure.	DBLOGIN USERID tiger@ogg_demo, PASSWORD AACAAAAAAAAAAAAJAUEUGODSCVGJEEIUGKJDJTF NDKEJFFFTCAES128, ENCRYPTKEY securekey1 DBLOGIN SOURCEDB ogg_demo USERIDALIAS tgr DOMAIN demo
DUMPDDL	Views all the records in the DDL history table. You will need to log in to the database using DBLOGIN to query the history table.	DUMPDDL DUMPDDL SHOW
ENCRYPT PASSWORD	Encrypts a password to be used in the extract or replicat parameter files. Available encryption keys are AES128, AES192, AES256, and BLOWFISH.	ENCRYPT PASSWORD tiger_123 BLOWFISH ENCRYPTKEY DEFAULT ENCRYPT PASSWORD tiger_123 AES192 ENCRYPTKEY tgrsuperkey
FLUSH SEQUENCE	This is executed during initial synchronization when the extract is started for the first time. It updates the Oracle sequence so that the initial redo logs are available when the extract starts capturing data. This is needed since redo is not generated until the current cache for the sequence is exhausted.	FLUSH SEQUENCE schema_name.sequence_name
LIST TABLES	Lists all tables in the database that matches the specified pattern.	LIST TABLES ACCOUNT*

Trandata consists of the instructions you can give from GGSCI to the database to capture supplemental logging information. Table 8-13 lists the commands for adding, deleting, and querying supplemental logging status for the schema or tables.

Table 8-13. *GGSCI TRANDATA Commands*

Command	Usage	Example
ADD SCHEMATRANDATA	Enables schema-level supplemental logging. The user will require the dbms_ streams_auth.grant_admin_privilege privilege to be able to enable schema-level supplemental logging.	ADD SCHEMATRANDATA tiger ADD SCHEMATRANDATA tiger ALLCOLS
ADD TRANDATA	Enables supplemental logging at the table level.	ADD TRANDATA schema_name. table_name ADD TRANDATA table_name ALLCOLS ADD TRANDATA schema_name. table_name, COLS (column_ name1, column_name2)
DELETE SCHEMATRANDATA	Deletes schema-level supplemental logging.	DELETE SCHEMATRANDATA tiger DELETE SCHEMATRANDATA tiger ALLCOLS
DELETE TRANDATA	Deletes table-level supplemental logging.	DELETE TRANDATA schema_name. table_name DELETE TRANDATA schema_name. tabl*
INFO SCHEMATRANDATA	Displays whether schema-level supplemental logging is enabled.	INFO SCHEMATRANDATA schema_ name
INFO TRANDATA	Displays table-level supplemental logging details.	INFO TRANDATA schema_name. table_name

Oracle GoldenGate by default maintains checkpoint information for recovery in the dirchk directory in the form of checkpoint files. It is, however, recommended to use the checkpoint table stored in the database. This will be especially helpful in the case of disaster recovery to a failover server when the checkpoint files on the primary server are not reachable. Table 8-14 lists the commands for working with the checkpoint table.

Table 8-14. *GGSCI CHECKPOINTABLE Commands*

Command	Usage	Example
ADD CHECKPOINTTABLE	Creates the checkpoint table in the target database. This will be used by the replicat process to keep track of read points. This is used during the recovery process. This value is specified in the GLOBALS parameter file.	ADD CHECKPOINT TABLE ADD CHECKPOINTTABLE schema_name.ggs_check
CLEANUP CHECKPOINTTABLE	Removes unused checkpoint records.	CLEANUP CHECKPOINTTABLE schema_name.ggs_check
DELETE CHECKPOINTTABLE	Deletes a checkpoint table. The replicat process will need to be stopped and re-created for this.	DELETE CHECKPOINTTABLE schema_name.ggs_check
INFO CHECKPOINTTABLE	Displays the checkpoint table and its creation date time.	INFO CHECKPOINTTABLE schema_name.ggs_check
UPGRADE CHECKPOINTTABLE	Upgrades a checkpoint table when you upgrade GoldenGate 11.2 or earlier.	UPGRADE CHECKPOINTTABLE schema_name.ggs_check

Trace tables are used in bidirectional replication to prevent data loopbacks. Table 8-15 shows the commands for working with TRACETABLE.

Table 8-15. *GGSCI TRACETABLE Commands*

Command	Usage	Example
ADD TRACETABLE	A trace table is required in bidirectional replication to prevent replicat transactions from being extracted again.	ADD TRACETABLE ggs_trace
DELETE TRACETABLE	Deletes the tracetable.	DELETE TRACETABLE ggs_ trace
INFO TRACETABLE	Displays the trace table and its creation date time.	INFO TRACETABLE ggs_ trace

Table 8-16 lists miscellaneous GGSCI commands that are helpful while working with GGSCI.

Table 8-16. *Miscellaneous GGSCI Commands*

Command	Usage	Example
!	Executes the previous (most recent) command.	!
CREATE SUBDIRS	Used during the GoldenGate installation to create default directories in the GoldenGate home directory.	CREATE SUBDIRS
FC	Displays and edits the previously executed command and reexecutes it.	FC 3 FC FC STA
HELP	Displays information about a GoldenGate command.	HELP STATS
HISTORY	Displays a list of recently executed commands.	HISTORY HISTORY 5
INFO ALL	Displays status and lag information for all processes (manager, extract, replicat).	INFO ALL
OBEY	Runs batches of GoldenGate commands in a file.	OBEY filename
SHELL	Executes shell commands from the GGSCI prompt.	SHELL ls -lrt
SHOW	Displays GoldenGate commands.	SHOW
VERSIONS	Displays the OS and DB version information. You need to connect via DBLOGIN to view the DB version information.	VERSIONS
VIEW GGSEVT	Displays the GoldenGate error log (ggserr.log).	VIEW GGSEVT
VIEW REPORT	Displays the process report for the manager, extract, and replicat processes.	VIEW REPORT channel_name

Native Non-GGSCI Commands and Utilities

In this section we will discuss some important Oracle GoldenGate commands that can be run directly through the operating system command line or through a script. These commands are available in the GoldenGate installation directory.

DEFGEN

DEFGEN is a GoldenGate utility found in the Oracle GoldenGate installation's home directory. The utility generates definition files to be used by the replicat process.

If the source and target table structures are identical, you can simply include the parameter ASSUMETARGETDEFS in the replicat.

```
ASSUMETARGETDEFS
MAP TIGER.CNTRY, TARGET FOX.CNTRY;
```

But if your source and target table structures in the particular replicat group differ, you will need to generate a definition file at the source using the DEFGEN utility and use this file on the target.

Create a temporary parameter file in the dirprm directory, say temp01.prm, with the following content:

```
DEFSFILE /app/ggs/tiger/dirdef/ETTND001.def
USERID "tiger", PASSWORD "tiger123_"
```

```
TABLE TIGER.TABLEA;
TABLE TIGER.TABLEB;
```

To generate a definition file, switch to the GoldenGate installation directory where the DEFGEN utility can be found and run the following command:

```
defgen paramfile dirprm/temp01.prm
```

This will generate the definition file with the name as specified using the parameter DEFSFILE. You will need to transfer this definition file to the target machine and place it in the dirprm directory. Use the file in the replicat process corresponding to the extract process you generated the definition file for.

Add the following parameter to the replicat process:

```
SOURCEDEFS /app/ggs/fox/dirdef/ETTXD001.def
```

KEYGEN

KEYGEN generates encryption keys to be used in the ENCKEYS file. These are used for adding security to GoldenGate replication.

The syntax for using the KEYGEN utility is as follows:

```
KEYGEN length_of_key number_of_key_to_generate
```

```
KEYGEN 128 1
```

length_of_key can be any value up to 256 bits (32 bytes).
We will discuss KEYGEN in more detail and show examples in Chapter 10.

LOGDUMP

The LOGDUMP utility allows you to view transactions and records within the trail files and gather statistical information. You can also save the data within the trail files.

Every trail file has a file header attached to it that contains information about the physical system that produced the trail. The trail file has many transaction records, and with all these transactions a record header is attached that contains information such as the source table name, a before/after image, the database operation type and timestamp, the source database row ID and change number (LOGCSN), and so on. Figure 8-1 shows a simplified version of the information contained in an Oracle GoldenGate trail file.

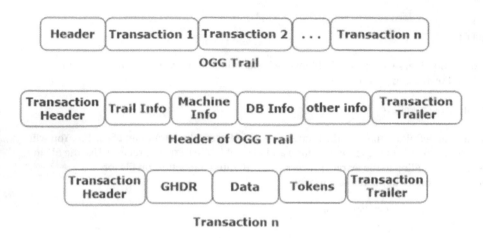

Figure 8-1. *Oracle GoldenGate trail file structure*

The trail information contains the following: creation time, character set, file name, trail sequence number, file size, first CSN, last CSN, first I/O time, last I/O time, and so on.

The machine information consists of the following: OS name, node if it's a multinode system, version, and hardware information.

The database information includes the following: vendor, character set, version, database object meta information, and database time zone.

The transaction record contains the following: GoldenGate header (GHDR), data, GGS tokens, and user tokens.

Starting LOGDUMP

Enter LOGDUMP from the GoldenGate installation directory. It will start by displaying a banner showing version information like the following:

```
[ravin-ravinpc]$ ./logdump
Oracle GoldenGate Log File Dump Utility for Oracle
Version 12.1.2.0.0 17185003 OGGCORE_12.1.2.0.0_PLATFORMS_130924.1316
Copyright (C) 1995, 2013, Oracle and/or its affiliates. All rights reserved.

Logdump>
```

Opening a Trail

To open a trail, issue open <trail_file> at the LOGDUMP prompt.

```
Logdump 15>open ./dirdat/t1000004
Current LogTrail is /app/ggs/tiger/dirdat/t1000004
```

The numeric value next to the LOGDUMP prompt is the count of history commands in the buffer. These commands can be accessed/reused by using FC or !.

Record Count

The COUNT command returns various counts like the total and average data bytes, count of database operations, and number of before and after images.

```
Logdump 24 >open /app/ggs/tiger/dirdat/t1000087
Current LogTrail is /app/ggs/tiger/dirdat/t1000087
Logdump 25 >count
LogTrail /app/ggs/tiger/dirdat/t1000087 has 208767 records
Total Data Bytes            78742616
  Avg Bytes/Record               377
Delete                        12635
Insert                       161612
FieldComp                     12872
LargeObject                   21647
Others                            1
Before Images                 12635
After Images                 196131

Average of 220 Transactions
     Bytes/Trans .....       403470
     Records/Trans ...          948
     Files/Trans .....           26
```

Here, you notice two new database operations types: FieldComp and LargeObject.

FieldComp indicates a compressed update operation in the transaction log of the source database. LargeObject indicates the count of LOB operations.

To view a list of all the available Oracle GoldenGate operation types, type show rectype at the Logdump prompt.

```
Logdump 45 >show rectype
LogTrail record types
    1 - Abort                   2 - Commit
    3 - Delete                  4 - EndRollBack
    5 - Insert                  6 - Prepared
    7 - TMF-Shutdown            8 - TransBegin
    9 - TransRelease           10 - Update
   11 - UpdateComp             12 - FileAlter
   13 - FileCreate             14 - FilePurge
   15 - FieldComp              16 - FileRename
   17 - AuxPointer             18 - NetworkCommit
   19 - NetworkAbort           20 - CurrentPos
   90 - GGSSQLCol             100 - GGSPurgedata
  108 - GGSPurgedataPartonly  101 - GGSPurgeFile
  102 - GGSCreateFile         103 - GGSAlterFile
  104 - GGSRenameFile         105 - GGSSetmode
  107 - GGSControl            106 - GGSChangeLabel
  115 - GGSPKUpdate           117 - GGSPKUpdate32
  116 - LargeObject           132 - Sequence OP
  150 - RestartAbend          151 - RestartOK
  152 - RecoveryEnd           160 - DDLOP
```

```
161 - RecordFragment          200 - GGSBulkio
201 - GGSFileClose            202 - GGSLoggerTS
203 - GGSExtractTS            204 - GGSCollectTS
205 - GGSComment              250 - LibOpenTrace
251 - LibCloseTrace           252 - LoggerOpenTrace
253 - LoggerCloseTrace        254 - LoggerAddedInfo
249 - LoggerAddedStats        255 - FileHeader
```

Table-Level Details

To get table-level details of information similar to what you got with the COUNT command, issue DETAIL ON as follows:

```
Logdump 26 >detail on
Logdump 27 >count
LogTrail /app/ggs/tiger/dirdat/t1000087 has 208767 records
Total Data Bytes            78742616
  Avg Bytes/Record               377
Delete                         12635
Insert                        161612
FieldComp                      12872
LargeObject                    21647
Others                             1
Before Images                  12635
After Images                  196131

Average of 220 Transactions
     Bytes/Trans .....     403470
     Records/Trans ...        948
     Files/Trans .....         26

*                    FileHeader*        Partition 0
Total Data Bytes           1393
  Avg Bytes/Record         1393
Others                        1

TIGER.ACCOUNT_DTL                       Partition 4
Total Data Bytes           1611
  Avg Bytes/Record          268
Insert                        6
After Images                  6

TIGER.BILLING                           Partition 4
Total Data Bytes          68327
  Avg Bytes/Record          669
Insert                      102
After Images                102

TIGER.ORDER_DTL                         Partition 4
Total Data Bytes            106
  Avg Bytes/Record          106
```

```
Insert                               1
After Images                         1


TIGER.ORDER_HIST                              Partition 4
Total Data Bytes              7728
  Avg Bytes/Record             168
Insert                          46
After Images                    46


TIGER.ORDER_TYPE                              Partition 4
Total Data Bytes             88024
  Avg Bytes/Record             647
Insert                         136
After Images                   136


TIGER.PRODUCTS                                Partition 4
Total Data Bytes              3214
  Avg Bytes/Record             169
Insert                          19
After Images                    19
```

File Header Detail

You can view each file header token by issuing the fileheader detail command. You should start with the beginning of the trail file, position 0, and enter n or next to scroll through the trail file.

```
Logdump 28 >fileheader detail
Logdump 29 >n

2016/05/24 10:30:38.025.328 FileHeader          Len  1393 RBA 0
Name: *FileHeader*
 3000 01c7 3000 0008 4747 0d0a 544c 0a0d 3100 0002 | 0...0...GG..TL..1...
 0003 3200 0004 2000 0000 3300 0008 02f2 59cb b1ea | ..2... ...3.....Y...
 d670 3400 002f 002d 7572 693a 7a6c 7476 3635 3433 | .p4../.-uri:rvpc6543
 3a3a 6f70 743a 6170 703a 7431 6331 6436 3031 3a67 | ::opt:app:rvpctst2:g
 6773 3a31 312e 322e 312e 302e 3336 0000 2f00 2d2f | gs:11.2.1.0.36../.-/
 6f70 742f 6170 702f 7431 6331 6437 3637 2f67 6773 | opt/app/rvpctst1/ggs
 2f63 7572 7265 6e74 2f64 6972 6461 742f 7268 3030 | /current/dirdat/rh00


GroupID x30 'O' TrailInfo         Info x00 Length  455
 3000 01c7 3000 0008 4747 0d0a 544c 0a0d 3100 0002 | 0...0...GG..TL..1...
 0003 3200 0004 2000 0000 3300 0008 02f2 59cb b1ea | ..2... ...3.....Y...
 d670 3400 002f 002d 7572 693a 7a6c 7476 3635 3433 | .p4../.-uri:rvpc6543
 3a3a 6f70 743a 6170 703a 7431 6331 6436 3031 3a67 | ::opt:app:rvpctst2:g
 6773 3a31 312e 322e 312e 302e 3336 0000 2f00 2d2f | gs:11.2.1.0.36../.-/
 6f70 742f 6170 702f 7431 6331 6437 3637 2f67 6773 | opt/app/rvpctst1/ggs
 2f63 7572 7265 6e74 2f64 6972 6461 742f 7268 3030 | /current/dirdat/rh00
 3030 3837 3700 0001 0138 0000 0400 0000 5739 0000 | 00877....8......W9..
 0800 0000 0005 f5e0 cf3a 0000 810e 3134 3532 3130 | .........:....145210
 3931 3931 3439 3831 0000 0000 0000 0000 0000 0000 | 91914981............
 0000 0000 0000 0000 0000 0000 0000 0000 0000 0000 | ..................
```

```
0000 0000 0000 0000 0000 0000 0000 0000 0000 0000 | ....................
0000 0000 0000 0000 0000 0000 0000 0000 0000 0000 | ....................
0000 0000 0000 0000 0000 0000 0000 0000 0000 0000 | ....................
0000 0000 0000 0000 0000 0000 0000 0000 0000 0000 | ....................
0000 3b00 0081 0e31 3435 3231 3039 3231 3831 3933 | ..;....1452109218193
3000 0000 0000 0000 0000 0000 0000 0000 0000 0000 | 0...................
0000 0000 0000 0000 0000 0000 0000 0000 0000 0000 | ....................
0000 0000 0000 0000 0000 0000 0000 0000 0000 0000 | ....................
0000 0000 0000 0000 0000 0000 0000 0000 0000 0000 | ....................
0000 0000 0000 0000 0000 0000 0000 0000 0000 0000 | ....................
0000 0000 0000 0000 0000 0000 0000 003c 0000 0802 | ...............<....
f259 cbb1 db31 403d 0000 0802 f259 e9             | .Y...1@=.....Y.
TokenID x30 '0' Signature          Info x00   Length   8
4747 0d0a 544c 0a0d                               | GG..TL..
TokenID x31 '1' Compatibility      Info x00   Length   2
0003                                              | ..
TokenID x32 '2' Charset            Info x00   Length   4
2000 0000                                         | ...
TokenID x33 '3' CreationTime       Info x00   Length   8
02f2 59cb b1ea d670                               | ..Y....p
TokenID x34 '4' URI                Info x00   Length   47
002d 7572 693a 7a6c 7476 3635 3433 3a3a 6f70 743a | .-uri:rvpc6543::opt:
6170 703a 7431 6331 6436 3031 3a67 6773 3a31 312e | app:rvpctst2:ggs:11.
322e 312e 302e 33                                 | 2.1.0.3
TokenID x36 '6' Filename           Info x00   Length   47
002d 2f6f 7074 2f61 7070 2f74 3163 3164 3736 372f | .-/opt/app/rvpctst1/
6767 732f 6375 7272 656e 742f 6469 7264 6174 2f72 | ggs/current/dirdat/r
6830 3030 3038 37                                 | h000087
TokenID x37 '7' MultiPart          Info x00   Length   1
01                                                | .
TokenID x38 '8' Seqno              Info x00   Length   4
0000 0057                                         | ...W
TokenID x39 '9' FileSize           Info x00   Length   8
0000 0000 05f5 e0cf                               | ........
TokenID x3a ':' FirstCSN           Info x00   Length  129
0e31 3435 3231 3039 3139 3134 3938 3100 0000 0000 | .14521091914981.....
0000 0000 0000 0000 0000 0000 0000 0000 0000 0000 | ....................
0000 0000 0000 0000 0000 0000 0000 0000 0000 0000 | ....................
0000 0000 0000 0000 0000 0000 0000 0000 0000 0000 | ....................
0000 0000 0000 0000 0000 0000 0000 0000 0000 0000 | ....................
0000 0000 0000 0000 0000 0000 0000 0000 0000 0000 | ....................
0000 0000 0000 0000 00                            | .........
TokenID x3b ';' LastCSN            Info x00   Length  129
0e31 3435 3231 3039 3231 3831 3933 3000 0000 0000 | .14521092181930.....
0000 0000 0000 0000 0000 0000 0000 0000 0000 0000 | ....................
0000 0000 0000 0000 0000 0000 0000 0000 0000 0000 | ....................
0000 0000 0000 0000 0000 0000 0000 0000 0000 0000 | ....................
0000 0000 0000 0000 0000 0000 0000 0000 0000 0000 | ....................
0000 0000 0000 0000 0000 0000 0000 0000 0000 0000 | ....................
0000 0000 0000 0000 00                            | .........
TokenID x3c '<' FirstIOTime        Info x00   Length   8
```

```
  02f2 59cb b1db 3140                          | ..Y...1@
TokenID x3d '=' LastIOTime        Info x00  Length   8
  02f2 59e9 e64e a380                          | ..Y..N..


GroupID x31 '1' MachineInfo       Info x00  Length   109
  3100 006d 3000 0007 0005 4c69 6e75 7831 0000 0a00 | 1..m0.....Linux1....
  087a 6c74 7636 3534 3332 0000 1b00 1932 2e36 2e33 | .rvpc65432.....2.6.3
  322d 3530 342e 382e 312e 656c 362e 7838 365f 3634 | 2-504.8.1.el6.x86_64
  3300 0025 0023 2331 2053 4d50 2046 7269 2044 6563 | 3..%.##1 SMP Fri Dec
  2031 3920 3132 3a30 393a 3235 2045 5354 2032 3031 |  19 12:09:25 EST 201
  3434 0000 0800 0678 38                       | 44.....x8
TokenID x30 '0' Sysname           Info x00  Length   7
  0005 4c69 6e75 78                             | ..Linux
TokenID x31 '1' Nodename          Info x00  Length   10
  0008 7a6c 7476 3635 3433                      | ..rvpc6543
TokenID x32 '2' Release           Info x00  Length   27
  0019 322e 362e 3332 2d35 3034 2e38 2e31 2e65 6c36 | ..2.6.32-504.8.1.el6
  2e78 3836 5f36 34                             | .x86_64
TokenID x33 '3' Version           Info x00  Length   37
  0023 2331 2053 4d50 2046 7269 2044 6563 2031 3920 | .##1 SMP Fri Dec 19
  3132 3a30 393a 3235 2045 5354 2032 3031 34    | 12:09:25 EST 2014
TokenID x34 '4' Hardware          Info x00  Length   8
  0006 7838 365f 3634                           | ..x86_64


GroupID x32 '2' DatabaseInfo      Info x00  Length   359
  3200 0167 3000 0002 0007 3100 000a 0008 5431 4331 | 2..g0.....1.....T1C1
  4436 3031 3200 000a 0008 7431 6331 6436 3031 3300 | D6012.....rvpctst23.
  0004 0000 0408 3400 0002 000b 3500 0002 0002 3600 | ......4.....5.....6.
  00e7 00e5 4f72 6163 6c65 2044 6174 6162 6173 6520 | ....Oracle Database
  3131 6720 456e 7465 7270 7269 7365 2045 6469 7469 | 11g Enterprise Editi
  6f6e 2052 656c 6561 7365 2031 312e 322e 302e 342e | on Release 11.2.0.4.
  3020 2d20 3634 6269 7420 5072 6f64 7563 7469 6f6e | 0 - 64bit Production
  0a50 4c2f 5351 4c20 5265 6c65 6173 6520 3131 2e32 | .PL/SQL Release 11.2
  2e30 2e34 2e30 202d 2050 726f 6475 6374 696f 6e0a | .0.4.0 - Production.
  434f 5245 0931 312e 322e 302e 342e 3009 5072 6f64 | CORE.11.2.0.4.0.Prod
  7563 7469 6f6e 0a54 4e53 2066 6f72 204c 696e 7578 | uction.TNS for Linux
  3a20 5665 7273 696f 6e20 3131 2e32 2e30 2e34 2e30 | : Version 11.2.0.4.0
  202d 2050 726f 6475 6374 696f 6e0a 4e4c 5352 544c |  - Production.NLSRTL
  2056 6572 7369 6f6e 2031 312e 322e 302e 342e 3020 | Version 11.2.0.4.0
  2d20 5072 6f64 7563 7469 6f6e 0a37 0000 0440 0000 | - Production.7...@..
  0038 0000 0c00 0a31 312e 322e 302e 342e 3039 0000 | .8.....11.2.0.4.09..
  0400 0000 013a 0000 0200 003b 0000 0400 0000 013c | .....:.....;.......<
  0000 1400 0000 1014 1414 1414 1414 1414 1414 14    | ................
TokenID x30 '0' Vendor            Info x00  Length   2
  0007                                          | ..
TokenID x31 '1' Name              Info x00  Length   10
  0008 5431 4331 4436 3031                      | ..RVPCTST2
TokenID x32 '2' Instance          Info x00  Length   10
  0008 7431 6331 6436 3031                      | ..rvpctst2
TokenID x33 '3' Charset           Info x00  Length   4
  0000 0408                                     | ....
```

```
TokenID x34 '4' MajorVersion      Info x00   Length    2
000b                                                |  ..
TokenID x35 '5' MinorVersion      Info x00   Length    2
0002                                                |  ..
TokenID x36 '6' VerString         Info x00   Length  231
00e5 4f72 6163 6c65 2044 6174 6162 6173 6520 3131 |  ..Oracle Database 11
6720 456e 7465 7270 7269 7365 2045 6469 7469 6f6e |  g Enterprise Edition
2052 656c 6561 7365 2031 312e 322e 302e 342e 3020 |   Release 11.2.0.4.0
2d20 3634 6269 7420 5072 6f64 7563 7469 6f6e 0a50 |  - 64bit Production.P
4c2f 5351 4c20 5265 6c65 6173 6520 3131 2e32 2e30 |  L/SQL Release 11.2.0
2e34 2e30 202d 2050 726f 6475 6374 696f 6e0a 434f |  .4.0 - Production.CO
5245 0931 312e 322e 302e 342e 3009 5072 6f64 7563 |  RE.11.2.0.4.0.Produc
7469 6f6e 0a54 4e53 2066 6f72 204c 696e 7578 3a20 |  tion.TNS for Linux:
5665 7273 696f 6e20 3131 2e32 2e30 2e34 2e30 202d |  Version 11.2.0.4.0 -
2050 726f 6475 6374 696f 6e0a 4e4c 5352 544c 2056 |   Production.NLSRTL V
6572 7369 6f6e 2031 312e 322e 302e 342e 3020 2d20 |  ersion 11.2.0.4.0 -
5072 6f64 7563 7469 6f6e 0a                        |  Production.
TokenID x37 '7' ClientCharset     Info x00   Length    4
4000 0000                                           |  @...
TokenID x38 '8' ClientVerString   Info x00   Length   12
000a 3131 2e32 2e30 2e34 2e30                       |  ..11.2.0.4.0
TokenID x39 '9' ClientNCharset    Info x00   Length    4
0000 0001                                           |  ....
TokenID x3a ':' DbLocale          Info x00   Length    2
0000                                                |  ..
TokenID x3b ';' DbNCharset        Info x00   Length    4
0000 0001                                           |  ....
TokenID x3c '<' DbObjNameMetadata Info x00   Length   20
0000 0010 1414 1414 1414 1414 1414 1414 1114 1414 |  ....................

GroupID x33 '3' ProducerInfo      Info x00   Length  128
3300 0080 3000 000a 0008 4532 4538 5545 5854 3100 |  3...0.....ETTNP0011.
0002 0003 3200 0002 000b 3300 0002 0002 3400 0002 |  ....2.....3.....4...
0001 3500 0002 0000 3600 0002 0001 3700 004a 0048 |  ..5.....6.....7..J.H
5665 7273 696f 6e20 3131 2e32 2e31 2e30 2e33 2031 |  Version 11.2.1.0.3 1
3434 3030 3833 3320 4f47 4743 4f52 455f 3131 2e32 |  4400833 OGGCORE_11.2
2e31 2e30 2e33 5f50 4c41 5446 4f52 4d53 5f31 3230 |  .1.0.3_PLATFORMS_120
3832 332e 3132 3538                                 |  823.1258
TokenID x30 '0' Name              Info x00   Length   10
0008 4532 4538 5545 5854                            |  ..ETTNP001
TokenID x31 '1' DataSource        Info x00   Length    2
0003                                                |  ..
TokenID x32 '2' MajorVersion      Info x00   Length    2
000b                                                |  ..
TokenID x33 '3' MinorVersion      Info x00   Length    2
0002                                                |  ..
TokenID x34 '4' MaintLevel        Info x00   Length    2
0001                                                |  ..
TokenID x35 '5' BugFixLevel       Info x00   Length    2
0000                                                |  ..
TokenID x36 '6' BuildNumber       Info x00   Length    2
```

```
 0001                                              |..
TokenID x37 '7' VerString        Info x00  Length  74
 0048 5665 7273 696f 6e20 3131 2e32 2e31 2e30 2e33 | .HVersion 11.2.1.0.3
 2031 3434 3030 3833 3320 4f47 4743 4f52 455f 3131 |  14400833 OGGCORE_11
 2e32 2e31 2e30 2e33 5f50 4c41 5446 4f52 4d53 5f31 | .2.1.0.3_PLATFORMS_1
 3230 3832 332e 3132 3538 5f46 424f               | 20823.1258_FBO

GroupID x34 '4' ContinunityInfo  Info x00  Length  322
 3400 0142 3000 0004 0000 0001 3100 0081 0e31 3435 | 4..B0.......1....145
 3231 3039 3139 3134 3634 3600 0000 0000 0000 0000 | 21091914646.........
 0000 0000 0000 0000 0000 0000 0000 0000 0000 0000 | ....................
 0000 0000 0000 0000 0000 0000 0000 0000 0000 0000 | ....................
 0000 0000 0000 0000 0000 0000 0000 0000 0000 0000 | ....................
 0000 0000 0000 0000 0000 0000 0000 0000 0000 0000 | ....................
 0000 0000 0000 0000 0000 0000 0000 0000 0000 0000 | ....................
 0000 0000 0032 0000 0f32 0000 0b00 0931 2e39 2e39 | .....2...2.....1.9.9
 3630 3034 3300 0081 0e31 3435 3231 3039 3139 3134 | 60043....14521091914
 3938 3100 0000 0000 0000 0000 0000 0000 0000 0000 | 981.................
 0000 0000 0000 0000 0000 0000 0000 0000 0000 0000 | ....................
 0000 0000 0000 0000 0000 0000 0000 0000 0000 0000 | ....................
 0000 0000 0000 0000 0000 0000 0000 0000 0000 0000 | ....................
 0000 0000 0000 0000 0000 0000 0000 0000 0000 0000 | ....................
 0000 0000 0000 0000 0000 0000 0000 0000 0034 0000 | .................4..
 0d00 0b37 2e31 382e 3133 3631 3835 3500 0008 02f2 | ...7.18.1361855.....
 59cb                                              | Y.
TokenID x30 '0' RecoveryMode     Info x00  Length  4
 0000 0001                                         | ....
TokenID x31 '1' LastCompletedCSN Info x00  Length  129
 0e31 3435 3231 3039 3139 3134 3634 3600 0000 0000 | .14521091914646.....
 0000 0000 0000 0000 0000 0000 0000 0000 0000 0000 | ....................
 0000 0000 0000 0000 0000 0000 0000 0000 0000 0000 | ....................
 0000 0000 0000 0000 0000 0000 0000 0000 0000 0000 | ....................
 0000 0000 0000 0000 0000 0000 0000 0000 0000 0000 | ....................
 0000 0000 0000 0000 0000 0000 0000 0000 0000 0000 | ....................
 0000 0000 0000 0000 00                            | .........
TokenID x32 '2' LastCompletedXID Info x00  Length  15
 3200 000b 0009 312e 392e 3936 3030 34            | 2.....1.9.96004
TokenID x33 '3' LastCSN          Info x00  Length  129
 0e31 3435 3231 3039 3139 3134 3938 3100 0000 0000 | .14521091914981.....
 0000 0000 0000 0000 0000 0000 0000 0000 0000 0000 | ....................
 0000 0000 0000 0000 0000 0000 0000 0000 0000 0000 | ....................
 0000 0000 0000 0000 0000 0000 0000 0000 0000 0000 | ....................
 0000 0000 0000 0000 0000 0000 0000 0000 0000 0000 | ....................
 0000 0000 0000 0000 0000 0000 0000 0000 0000 0000 | ....................
 0000 0000 0000 0000 00                            | .........
TokenID x34 '4' LastXID          Info x00  Length  13
 000b 372e 3138 2e31 3336 3138 35               | ..7.18.136185
TokenID x35 '5' LastCSNTS        Info x00  Length  8
 02f2 59cb b1db 3140                              | ..Y...1@
Logdump 30 >
```

You will see a lot of information about the database and transactions. Make particular note of the tokens FirstCSN and LastCSN. This field information can be useful during a database recovery or starting a channel to read from a specific CSN point in the trail.

Other useful commands to scan through a trail file using the logdump utility are ghdr on, sfh, detail data, and ggstoken detail.

GHDR is an acronym for "GoldenGate header," and sfh is acronym for ScanForHeader.

Scanning the Trail File for Data

Let's take a look at how you can scan a trail file to locate records for specific tables and how to save them to a new trail file.

Let's first set a data filter for a table, say, TIGER.ORDER_DTL. To do so, issue the following command:

```
Logdump 34 >filter inc filename TIGER.ORDER_DTL
Logdump 35 >pos eof
Reading forward from RBA 99999951
Logdump 36 >pos rev
Reading in reverse from RBA 99999951
Logdump 37 >n

2016/05/25 22:32:46.000.921 Insert              Len    47 RBA 99924705
Name: TIGER.ORDER_DTL
After  Image:                                   Partition 4   G  m
 0000 000a 0000 0000 0000 02b7 0ae8 0001 0016 0000 | ...................
 0012 5458 5f48 5354 4e5f 5045 4152 4c41 4e44 5f4e | ..TX_HSTN_PEARLAND_N
 0002 0003 0000 54                                 | ......T
Column     0 (x0000), Len    10 (x000a)
Column     1 (x0001), Len    22 (x0016)
Column     2 (x0002), Len     3 (x0003)


Filtering suppressed    243 records
Logdump 38 >n

2016/05/25 22:32:46.000.921 Insert              Len    38 RBA 99924563
Name: TIGER.ORDER_DTL
After  Image:                                   Partition 4   G  m
 0000 000a 0000 0000 0000 02b7 0ae8 0001 000d 0000 | ...................
 0009 5458 5f54 5845 535f 4e00 0200 0300 0049      | ..TX_TXES_N......I
Column     0 (x0000), Len    10 (x000a)
Column     1 (x0001), Len    13 (x000d)
Column     2 (x0002), Len     3 (x0003)
```

Here I want to locate the last record for this table in the trail. To do so, I will position to the end of file.

```
Logdump > pos eof
```

Now to scan the last records, you instruct logdump to scan the trail backward.

```
Logdump > pos rev
```

Now, issue n to scan backward and display the first record for the table TIGER.CNTRY.

```
Logdump > n
```

The GGS token LOGCSN shows the Oracle SCN number for the transaction. You can also find out all the records for a particular LOGCSN number.

```
Logdump > filter clear all
```

This will reset all the existing filters on logdump.

```
Logdump > filter logcsn 1234567
```

This sets a new filter to scan for all records associated with LOGCSN 1234567. Now you can use the count and pos commands to count the number of records for this LOGCSN and scan through them one by one.

You can save records to new trail file as shown here:

```
Logdump 43 >open /app/ggs/tiger/dirdat/t1000087
Current LogTrail is /app/ggs/tiger/dirdat/t1000087
Logdump 44 >save /app/ggs/tiger/dirdat/rg000015 2 records
Saved 2 records to /app/ggs/tiger/dirdat/rg000015
```

■ **Note** The Logdump utility is a useful tool during troubleshooting replication issues in Oracle GoldenGate. It helps you view transactions and identify any missing or bad transactions. We will visit troubleshooting in Chapter 16.

Summary

In this chapter, we discussed some of the most useful and commonly used OGG commands and utilities. We classified these commands as data transformation and column conversion functions, GGSCI commands to be executed at the GGSCI prompt, and native non-GGSCI commands and utilities.

In the next chapter, we will discuss advanced Oracle GoldenGate processing on the extract as well replicat sides. We will discuss using data transformation and manipulation functions, OGG user tokens, user exits, SQLEXEC, and macros in Oracle GoldenGate replication.

■ ■ ■

## CHAPTER 9

Advanced Processing

In this chapter, we will discuss in detail the advanced data transformation techniques available in Oracle GoldenGate. This chapter then takes you through advanced processing by using tokens, macros, SQLEXEC, and user exits.

Data Transformation in Oracle GoldenGate

During Oracle GoldenGate replication, while the changes are captured in local trails and before they get applied on the target system, you can perform data transformation and manipulation on the extract or replicat or both. The mapping and transformation can be performed on the source, on the target, or on an intermediary system.

Data Filter Methods

Data can be filtered between the source and target systems. You can skip sets of columns or records based on a specified filter condition. To filter data, you can use one or more of the following options:

- Using FILTER or WHERE clauses in TABLE/MAP statements
- Using SQLEXEC to execute SQL queries or stored procedures
- Using user exits

Data Transformation Methods

Data manipulation or transformation can be achieved using one or more of the following options:

- Using the Oracle GoldenGate conversion functions discussed in Tables 8-1 to 8-5
- Using user exits from the extract or replicat process to apply a database routine and return the result to Oracle GoldenGate
- Using the replicat to deliver data directly to another ETL engine

If your source and target databases differ in structure, you will require either a source or target definition file for Oracle GoldenGate to compare and map metadata between the two systems.

If the mapping and conversion are performed by the replicat process, specify the SOURCEDEFS parameter in the replicat. This is the most common scenario. However, in some scenarios, when mapping and conversion have to be done on the extract, you must specify the TARGETDEFS parameter in the extract parameter file. For example, when replicating from a Linux, Unix, or Windows (LUW) system to a NonStop system, conversion must be done with an extract process.

© Ravinder Gupta 2016
R. Gupta, *Mastering Oracle GoldenGate*, DOI 10.1007/978-1-4842-2301-7_9

Using COLMAP for Column Mapping

The COLMAP parameter can be used with the MAP and TABLE parameters to map column names between the source and target database tables if the column names are different. It can also be used to specify default mapping between columns using the USEDEFAULTS argument. A general syntax of COLMAP usage is as follows:

```
MAP <table_name >, TARGET <table_name>, COLMAP ([USEDEFAULTS, ] <target column> = <source expression>);
```

Data Transformation Examples

Let's see some examples of how FILTER, WHERE, and COLMAP work for data transformation.

Replicate only those records that have GROUPTYPE ='J' in the source table JOB_GROUPS and map it to the target table FX_JG.

```
MAP TIGER.JOB_GROUPS, FILTER (@STRFIND (GROUPTYPE,"J") > 0), TARGET FOX.FX_JG;
```

Replicate only records with RELATIONTYPE='A' and AREATYPE='T' in the source table. Also, map the AREA_NM and TURF_NM columns on the target to AREANAME and TURFNAME in the source table.

```
MAP TIGER.AREA, FILTER (@STRFIND (RELATIONTYPE,"A") > 0 AND @STRFIND (AREATYPE,"T") > 0),
TARGET FOX.FX_AREA_DETAIL,COLMAP (USEDEFAULTS,AREA_NM=AREANAME,TURF_NM=TURFNAME);
```

Replicate only the records with GROUPNAME as NULL and map GRP_NM on the target to GROUPNAME on the source. Also, update the LAST_UPDATE_TS column on the target with the current date and time. Finally, set the REPL_SITE value as null on the target table for the replicated record.

```
MAP TIGER.JOB_TYPE, WHERE (GROUPNAME <> @NULL), TARGET FOX.FX_JTYPE,COLMAP (USEDEFAULTS,GRP_
NM=GROUPNAME,LAST_UPDATE_TS = @DATENOW(),REPL_SITE=@COLSTAT(NULL));
```

Use the COLSTAT function while setting the NULL value expression. The COLSTAT function returns an indicator to the extract or replicat process stating that a column is NULL, MISSING, or INVALID.

You can also use the operation type in your filter statement. The syntax to use a filter on the source and target are as follows:

- In extract parameter file:

```
TABLE source_table, FILTER (ON INSERT | ON UPDATE| ON DELETE]
[, IGNORE INSERT | IGNORE UPDATE | IGNORE DELETE]
, filter_clause);
```

- In replicat parameter file:

```
MAP source_table, TARGET target_table, FILTER (ON INSERT | ON UPDATE| ON DELETE]
[, IGNORE INSERT | IGNORE UPDATE | IGNORE DELETE]
[, RAISEERROR error_number]
, filter_clause);
```

For example, the following statement instructs the extract process to select only those records with an amount less than 10 for update and delete operations.

```
TABLE TIGER.ORDER_DTL, FILTER (ON UPDATE, ON DELETE, AMOUNT > 10);
```

Refer to Tables 8-1 to 8-5 for a list of frequently used column conversion functions.

Using COLMATCH

While COLMAP is used to map columns for specific tables, you can use another parameter, COLMATCH, to map the columns for all tables in a particular extract or replicat group.

The syntax to use COLMATCH is as follows:

```
COLMATCH {NAMES target_column = source_column | PREFIX prefix | SUFFIX suffix | RESET}
```

Let's see an example to understand how COLMATCH works.

I have a table called ORDER_DETAIL on the source database with the following table structure:

Table Name: ORDER_DETAIL

Column 1: ORD_NMBR

Column 2: ORD_DATE

Column 3: USR_NAME

I have a similar table called ORD_DTL on the target database with the following table structure:

Table Name: ORD_DTL

Column 1: NMBR

Column 2: DATE

Column 3: USER_NAME

Now, here's the replicat parameter file using the COLMATCH parameter.

```
COLMATCH NAMES USER_NAME = USR_NAME
COLMATCH PREFIX ORD_
MAP TIGER.ORDER_DETAIL, TARGET FOX.ORD_DTL, COLMAP (USEDEFAULTS);
COLMATCH RESET
MAP TIGER.ACCOUNT_DTL, TARGET FOX.ACCOUNT_DTL;
```

To control duplicate MAP and TARGET statements for the same pair of source and target tables, use ALLOWDUPTARGETMAP or NOALLOWDUPTARGETMAP.

OGG User Tokens

A user token is information that can be stored in and captured from the user token area in an Oracle GoldenGate trail header. User tokens are typically used to store environment information but can also be used to store any type of information and then used in OGG replication in multiple ways.

Here's the syntax to use the TOKEN option on the source:

```
TABLE <table_name>, TOKENS (<token name> = <token data> [, ...]) ;
```

For example, the following sets token values to be written to a trail file header:

```
TABLE TIGER.AUDIT_LOG,
TOKENS (TKN-OSUSER = @GETENV("GGENVIRONMENT","OSUSERNAME"),
TKN-TRANSACTION-CSN =@GETENV("TRANSACTION","CSN"),
TKN-DBNAME = @GETENV ("DBENVIRONMENT","DBNAME"),
TKN-HOSTNAME = @GETENV ("GGENVIRONMENT","HOSTNAME"),
```

```
TKN-COMMITTIME = @GETENV("GGHEADER","COMMITTIMESTAMP"),
TKN-REC-FILESEQNO=@GETENV ("RECORD", "FILESEQNO"),
TKN-REC-FILERBA=@GETENV ("RECORD", "FILERBA"));
```

Here's the syntax to use the TOKEN option on the target:

```
COLMAP (target_column_name = @TOKEN ('token_name'))
```

For example, the following map statement uses the token values for trail file header and maps them to the columns of the target table:

```
MAP TIGER.AUDIT_LOG, TARGET FOX.AUDIT_LOG,
COLMAP (USEDEFAULTS,
OSUSER = @TOKEN("TKN-OSUSER"),
TRANSACTION_CSN = @TOKEN("TKN-TRANSACTION-CSN"),
DBNAME = @TOKEN("TKN-DBNAME"),
HOSTNAME = @TOKEN("TKN-HOSTNAME"),
COMMITTIME = @TOKEN("TKN-COMMITTIME"),
RECFILESEQNO = @TOKEN ("TKN-REC-FILESEQNO"),
REC-FILERBA = @TOKEN ("TKN-REC-FILERBA"));
```

User Exits

User exits are user-defined callbacks to C/C++ functions from within Oracle GoldenGate. These can be called from either the extract or replicat process by using the CUSEREXIT parameter.

User exits can work as an alternative to and along with column conversion functions. The major advantage is that data is processed only once when it is extracted at the source. This is unlike the column conversion functions where data is first extracted and then read again to perform the transformation.

User exits can be used to

- Perform column conversion and manipulation for data transformation

- Repair bad data

- Compute delta information from before and after update values of any record

- Perform complex filters on the extraction and replication of data

- Accumulate statistic data

- Respond to database events

The following is the syntax of the CUSEREXIT command:

```
CUSEREXIT {DLL | shared_object} routine
[, PASSTHRU]
[, INCLUDEUPDATEBEFORES]
[, PARAMS 'string']
```

To use user exits, create a shared object or DLL in C and create a routine to be called from the extract or replicat. The routine must accept the parameters listed in Table 9-1. These parameters provide the communication between GoldenGate and the C program. It accepts event calls from an extract or replicat process, processes desired information, and returns results to the extract or replicat process. Table 9-1 lists the user exit routine parameters.

Table 9-1. *User Exits Routine Parameters*

Parameter	Description
EXIT_CALL_TYPE	Specifies the user exit call type when it is called
EXIT_CALL_RESULT	Specifies the response returned to the user exit by the routine
EXIT_PARAMS	Specifies additional information to the user exit for processing
ERCALLBACK	Executes user callback routine that retrieves context value from the OGG process that called it and sets context values

The following are user exit calls that you will be using in your user exits:

- EXIT_CALL_START
- EXIT_CALL_STOP
- EXIT_CALL_BEGIN_TRANS
- EXIT_CALL_ABORT_TRANS
- EXIT_CALL_END_TRANS
- EXIT_CALL_CHECKPOINT
- EXIT_CALL_DISCARD_ASCII_RECORD
- EXIT_CALL_DISCARD_RECORD
- EXIT_CALL_FATAL_ERROR
- EXIT_CALL_PROCESS_MARKER
- EXIT_CALL_PROCESS_RECORD
- EXIT_CALL_RESULT

You will use EXIT_CALL_RESULT to send responses to the routine. The following are the user responses that can be returned to the user exit:

- EXIT_ABEND_VAL
- EXIT_IGNORE_VAL
- EXIT_STOP_VAL
- EXIT_OK_VAL
- EXIT_PROCESSED_REC_VAL

Next, include the usrdecs.h header file in the C code. The header file is located in the OGG Home directory. You must recompile your user exit routines every time if you have upgraded OGG to a higher version with a higher version of usrdec.h in it.

Use ERCALLBACK in the shared code to implement callback routines. This is not mandatory for all user exits. You can implement it only when a callback routine is required.

```
ERCALLBACK (function_code, buffer, result_code);
```

Some of the function codes used with ERCALLBACK are as follows:

- COMPRESS_RECORD

- DECOMPRESS_RECORD

- GET_BEFORE_AFTER_IND

- GET_ERROR_INFO

- GET_OBJECT_NAME

- GET_RECORD_LENGTH

- GET_TABLE_NAME

- SET_SESSION_CHARSET

- STRNCMP

Some of the result code used with ERCALLBACK is as follows:

- EXIT_FN_RET_BAD_COLUMN_DATA

- EXIT_FN_RET_BAD_DATE_TIME

- EXIT_FN_RET_COLUMN_NOT_FOUND

- EXIT_FN_RET_OK

- EXIT_FN_RET_TABLE_NOT_FOUND

Refer to the Oracle GoldenGate reference documentation for a complete list of supported functions and return codes.

Use CUSEREXIT in the extract or replicat parameter file.

Here's an example in Unix:

```
CUSEREXIT eruserexit.so user_exit1
```

Here's an example in Windows:

```
CUSEREXIT eruserexit.dll user_exit1
```

Here are some additional examples of using CUSEREXIT in your OGG processes:

```
CUSEREXIT userexit.dll tiger_userexit, PARAMS 'init.properties'
CUSEREXIT userexit.dll tiger_userexit, INCLUDEUPDATEBEFORES, PASSTHRU, & PARAMS 'init.
properties'
```

Navigate to the UserExitExamples directory in the OGG Home to view sample user exit files included with the OGG installation files.

```
$ cd UserExitExamples
ravin@ravin-pc /app/ggs/tiger/UserExitExamples
$ ls -lrt
total 20
drwxrws--- 2 oracle oinstall 4096 Aug 23  2012 ExitDemo_pk_befores
drwxrws--- 2 oracle oinstall 4096 Aug 23  2012 ExitDemo_passthru
drwxrws--- 2 oracle oinstall 4096 Aug 23  2012 ExitDemo_more_recs
drwxrws--- 2 oracle oinstall 4096 Aug 23  2012 ExitDemo_lobs
drwxrws--- 2 oracle oinstall 4096 Aug 23  2012 ExitDemo
```

```
$ cd ExitDemo_pk_befores
ravin@ravin-pc /app/ggs/tiger/UserExitExamples/ExitDemo_pk_befores
$ ls -lrt
total 80
-rwxrwx--- 1 oracle oinstall 13554 Oct 15  2010 exitdemo_pk_befores.vcproj
-rwxrwx--- 1 oracle oinstall  8722 Oct 15  2010 readme.txt
-rwxrwx--- 1 oracle oinstall  1905 Oct 15  2010 Makefile_pk_befores.SOLARIS
-rwxrwx--- 1 oracle oinstall  1956 Oct 15  2010 Makefile_pk_befores.LINUX
-rwxrwx--- 1 oracle oinstall  1944 Oct 15  2010 Makefile_pk_befores.HPUX
-rwxrwx--- 1 oracle oinstall  1950 Oct 15  2010 Makefile_pk_befores.AIX
-rwxrwx--- 1 oracle oinstall 36396 Jun 17  2011 exitdemo_pk_befores.c
```

Open the user exits C files and check the program description in the comments for a detailed explanation of each sample user exit. The readme.txt files have detailed explanation of each sample user exit and their usage. You can use these user exits to write your own custom user exit routines.

SQLEXEC

With SQLEXEC you allow the Oracle GoldenGate extract and replicat processes to communicate with the database to execute queries, commands, and stored procedures. This greatly enhances Oracle GoldenGate's capability to perform complex processing. The SQLEXEC command can be used in multiple ways. Let's discuss each of them one by one.

Using SQLEXEC as a Parameter to a TABLE or MAP Statement

You can use SQLEXEC as a parameter to the TABLE or MAP statement in your extract and replicat parameter file, respectively. The syntax for SQLEXEC is as follows:

```
SQLEXEC (SPNAME sp_name, PARAMS (param_specification))
```

or as follows:

```
SQLEXEC (SPNAME sp_name, NOPARAMS)
```

or as follows:

```
SQLEXEC (ID logical_name, QUERY ' query ', PARAMS (param_specification))
```

or as follows:

```
SQLEXEC (ID logical_name, QUERY ' query ', NOPARAMS)
```

Here's an example:

```
TABLE TIGER.ORDER_DTL,
SQLEXEC (id lookup, query "select product_name from products where productid= :p1_
productid",
PARAMS (p1_productid =productid)),
TOKENS (TKN-product_name = @GETVAL(lookup.product_name));
```

If the table product in the previous example is in another database, say orcl3 and the schema ravin, then you can use the following statement in your extract process:

```
TABLE TIGER.ORDER_DTL,
SQLEXEC (id lookup, query "select product_name from orcl3:ravin:products  where productid=
:p1_productid",
PARAMS (p1_productid =productid)),
TOKENS (TKN-product_name = @GETVAL(lookup.product_name));
```

Using SQLEXEC to Run Stored Procedures

In previous example, we discussed how to run a query using SQLEXEC. Let's see an example of how you can execute a database stored procedure and use its OUT parameter or return value to process data for replication.

I have a database procedure called check_product as follows:

```
CREATE OR REPLACE PROCEDURE check_product OUT parameter (CODE_IN_PARAM IN NUMBER, CODE_OUT_
PARAM OUT VARCHAR2)
BEGIN
SELECT product_name
INTO CODE_OUT_PARAM
FROM products
WHERE productid = CODE_IN_PARAM;
END;
```

The value returned by CODE_OUT_PARAM can be retrieved using the @GETVAL function.

```
MAP TIGER.ORDER_DTL, TARGET FOX.ORDER_DTL,
SQLEXEC (SPNAME check_product,
PARAMS (CODE_IN_PARAM = productid)),
COLMAP (USEDEFAULTS, PRODUCT_NAME = @GETVAL(check_product.CODE_OUT_PARAM));
```

Alternatively, you can embed the query within the MAP statement, as shown here:

```
MAP TIGER.ORDER_DTL, TARGET TIGER.ORDER_DTL,
SQLEXEC (ID lookup1,
QUERY "SELECT PRODUCT_NAME FROM PRODUCTS WHERE PRODUCTID = :CODE_IN_PARAM",
PARAMS (CODE_IN_PARAM = productid)),
COLMAP (USEDEFAULTS,
PRODUCT_NAME = @GETVAL(lookup1.PRODUCT_NAME));
```

The following example runs a query to get a sequence value and then uses the value in COLMAP to apply on the target database:

```
Map TIGER.ORDER_DETAIL, TARGET FOX.ORDR_DTL,
KEYCOLS(ORDER_ID), WHERE (DELETED_FLAG = "N"), &
SQLEXEC (ID LOOKUP_SEQ, &
QUERY "SELECT FOX.GROUP_ID_SEQ.NEXTVAL FROM DUAL ", NOPARAMS), &
COLMAP (USEDEFAULTS, &
GROUP_ID = @GETVAL (LOOKUP_SEQ.FOX.GROUP_ID_SEQ.nextval), &
FLAG = 1, &
MODIFIED_USER = "RG", &
DEFAULT_LOCALE = "US");
```

Using SQLEXEC to Run as a Stand-Alone Parameter

You can run SQLEXEC in your extract or replicat parameter file to execute a stored procedure, query, or database command as follows:

```
SQLEXEC 'call db_procedure_name()'
```

or as follows:

```
SQLEXEC 'some sql query'
```

or as follows:

```
SQLEXEC 'dbcommand'
```

Macros in Oracle GoldenGate

Macros in Oracle GoldenGate help you to reuse commands and parameters. A macro is a built-in automation tool that can execute a stored set of processing steps. Macros can be nested among each other and can also be stored in libraries and used via library calls.

You can use macros for the extract, replicat, and defgen parameter files. The following is the syntax for defining a macro:

```
MACRO #macro_name
PARAMS (#p1, #p2 ...)
BEGIN
macro_body
END;
```

Here's how you can call the macro in the same parameter file where it is defined:

```
target=macro_name (value1,value2, ...)
```

or as follows:

```
macro_name (value1,value2, ...)
```

For example, the following example macro simplifies the task of mapping the schema, table, and key columns.

```
MACRO #macro1
PARAMS (#s, #t, #k)
BEGIN
MAP #s.#t, TARGET #s.#t, KEYCOLS (#k), COLMAP (USEDEFAULTS);
END;
```

Here's another example, where a macro executes a set of commands:

```
MACRO #includeinall
BEGIN
```

```
INSERTDELETES
REPERROR 0001, DISCARD
END;
```

Now, call `macro1` as shown here:

```
#macro1 (TIGER, ORDER_DETAIL, ORDER_ID)
```

Similarly, call `#includeinall` as shown here:

```
#includeinall()
MAP TIGER.ORDER_DTL, TARGET FOX.ORDER_DTL;
```

Let's see another example of a macro that is used directly in a `MAP` statement.

```
MACRO #format_dt
PARAMS (#year, #month, #day)
BEGIN
@DATE ('YYYY-MM-DD', 'CC', @IF (#year < 50, 20, 19), 'YY', #year, 'MM', #month, 'DD', #day)
END;
```

Next, call the macro in the `COLMAP` parameter as shown here:

```
MAP tiger.order_detail, TARGET fox.order_detail,
COLMAP
(
USEDEFAULTS,
Update_dt = #format_dt(yr, mo, day),
);
```

You can also save the macro in the `.mac` file in the `dirprm` directory and then use it in extract or replicat parameter files. You can have multiple macros in the same `.mac` file or create separate `.mac` files for individual macros.

Use `INCLUDE` in the extract or replicat parameter file to include the macro library as follows:

```
INCLUDE /ggs/fox/dirprm/macro_lib1.mac
```

Oracle GoldenGate Auditing

You can capture the history of changes on each record in Oracle GoldenGate along with the operation type that caused the change. This historical data of changes done along with meta information about the change can be used to generate reports or audit what changed and how.

To store an update on a column, the entire record is converted into an insert and entered into the audit table. For converting an update into an insert, it is essential that all columns are logged in transaction logs mined by the OGG extract processes.

You can use the following command to log all the columns of a table:

```
GGSCI> ADD TRANDATA schema_name.table_name ALLCOLS
GGSCI> ADD TRANDATA schema_name.table_name,, COLS(col1, col2,  col3...)
```

Table 9-2 lists the parameters that you can include in your Oracle GoldenGate replicat parameter file to capture change information and store them in your audit table where you will maintain historical information of these changes.

Table 9-2. *Parameters Used in Capturing and Storing Historical Information of Record Changes*

Parameter	Description
INSERTUPDATES	Converts updates into insert statements and stores them in the specified table
INSERTDELETES	Converts delete operations into insert statements
UPDATEDELETES	Converts delete operations into update statements
INSERTALLRECORDS	Converts any record change on the source into an insert statement on the target

Use tokens to pass meta information from the source to the target and use the tokens to insert additional information along with the record change information in audit tables.

Let's see an example.

Include the following in the source extract parameter file:

```
TABLE TIGER.ORDER_DETAIL,
TOKENS (TKN-COMMITTIME = @GETENV("GGHEADER","COMMITTIMESTAMP"),

TKN-REC-FILESEQNO=@GETENV ("RECORD", "FILESEQNO"),
TKN-REC-FILERBA=@GETENV ("RECORD", "FILERBA"));
```

Include the following in the target replicat parameter file:

```
INSERTALLRECORDS
MAP TIGER.ORDER_DETAIL, TARGET FOX.ORDER_DETAIL_AUDIT,
COLMAP (USEDEFAULTS,
TRAN_TIME= @GETENV("GGHEADER","COMMITTIMESTAMP"),
OP_TYPE= @GETENV("GGHEADER", "OPTYPE"),
BEFORE_AFTER_IND = @GETENV("GGHEADER", "BEFOREAFTERINDICATOR"),
REC-FILESEQNO = @TOKEN ("TKN-REC-FILESEQNO")
REC-FILERBA = @TOKEN ("TKN-REC-FILERBA"));
```

You can also use SQLEXEC for executing database stored procedures for handling the storage of historical changes in the audit tables.

```
MAP TIGER.ORDER_DETAIL, TARGET FOX.ORDER_DETAIL_AUDIT,
SQLEXEC (SPNAME AUDIT_PROCEDURE,
PARAMS (@GETENV ("GGENVIRONMENT","HOSTNAME"),
@GETENV("GGENVIRONMENT","OSUSERNAME"),
@GETENV ("GGHEADER", "OPTYPE"),
@GETENV("GGHEADER","COMMITTIMESTAMP"),
@GETENV ("GGHEADER", "TABLENAME"),
@GETENV ("GGHEADER","USERID"),
@GETENV ("GGHEADER","TIMESTAMP"),
ALLPARAMS REQUIRED, ERROR REPORT, DBOP)
```

Summary

In this chapter, we discussed in detail the advanced data transformation techniques available in Oracle GoldenGate. We discussed advanced data filtering and processing techniques by using tokens, SQLEXEC, and user exits. We also discussed using macros in Oracle GoldenGate, a built-in automation tool for reusing commands and parameters.

In the next chapter, we will discuss using the advanced features in Oracle GoldenGate in three main categories, such as collision handling, OGG performance tuning, and OGG security.

CHAPTER 10

■ ■ ■

Advanced Features

In this chapter, we will discuss some of Oracle GoldenGate's advanced features that you can implement to make your replication environment more robust and efficient. We will discuss how to implement advanced Oracle GoldenGate configurations in these three major categories:

- Collision handling

- Oracle GoldenGate performance tuning

- Encryption and security

Collision Handling

Collision handling, better known as *conflict detection and resolution* (CDR), is a technique used primarily in active-active configurations.

In an active-active bidirectional replication, the OLTP transaction load is shared by both the servers, and thus any or both sides get transactions. This is different from an active-passive, unidirectional replication, where transactions happen on one server and failover receives the data from the primary server in passive mode. In the event of a failover, the OLTP transaction load is shifted to the failover database. At any time, only the capacity of one server is utilized.

In an active-active bidirectional replication, where transactions happen on both sides, it's important to handle any conflicts and resolve them to maintain data integrity.

HANDLECOLLISION

The simplest form of conflict resolution is HANDLECOLLISION. During the initial load, when the target schema tables are being loaded manually, the extract process keeps capturing any changes made to the tables on the source. After the initial load, when the replicat process is started, duplicate rows or missing row errors (conflicts) may happen. To handle these conflicts, Oracle GoldenGate provides the HANDLECOLLISION parameter for the replicat. This can smartly handle duplicate/missing record conflicts.

HANDLECOLLISION can be defined globally for each MAP statement in the parameter file as follows:

```
HANDLECOLLISION
MAP fox.table_name1, TARGET tiger.table_name1;
MAP fox.table_name2, TARGET tiger.table_name2;
MAP fox.table_name3, TARGET tiger.table_name3;
```

© Ravinder Gupta 2016
R. Gupta, *Mastering Oracle GoldenGate*, DOI 10.1007/978-1-4842-2301-7_10

You can also specify HANDLECOLLISION for specific MAP statements as follows:

```
MAP fox.table_name1, TARGET tiger.table_name1;
MAP fox.table_name2, TARGET tiger.table_name2, HANDLECOLLISIONS;
MAP fox.table_name3, TARGET tiger.table_name3;
```

If you want to specify HANDLECOLLISION for all MAP statements and exclude a few specific ones, you can specify your parameter file as follows:

```
HANDLECOLLISIONS
MAP fox.table_name1, TARGET tiger.table_name1;
MAP fox.table_name2, TARGET tiger.table_name2, NOHANDLECOLLISIONS;
MAP fox.table_name3, TARGET tiger.table_name3;
```

The NOHANDLECOLLISION parameter specifies that this table or group of tables is excluded from collision handling.

The HANDLECOLLISION and NOHANDLECOLLISION parameters are ideal for the initial load time only and should be commented out after the initial load is finished. For handling conflicts in real time, you should implement CDR, which gives you more control in dealing with different kinds of conflicts.

CDR for Active-Active Replication

CDR is a major improvement over the previous conflict handling technique for an active-active two-way replication. Previously, the replicat parameter files had to contain SQLEXEC commands that were used to query the target table before applying any DML change. This added an additional call to the database and slowed the overall performance.

In the new, enhanced technique, extra information (in other words, a before image of the records being processed) is sent to the target. In the case of any conflicts while replicating data, the conflict is handled by matching against the before image and using the CDR option as specified. For this to work, tables should have the key column defined either at the table level or in GoldenGate using the KEYCOL parameter.

Supported Data Types for CDR

A data type for which a before image and an after image can be compared against each other for resolving conflicts is a supported data type for CDR. Here's a list of data types that are supported:

- NUMERIC
- DATE
- TIMESTAMP
- CHAR/NCHAR
- VARCHAR/NVARCHAR

Types of Conflicts

Data conflicts can happen during insert, update, and delete operations. Figure 10-1 shows various types of conflicts during insert, update, and delete operations and ways to resolve the conflicts.

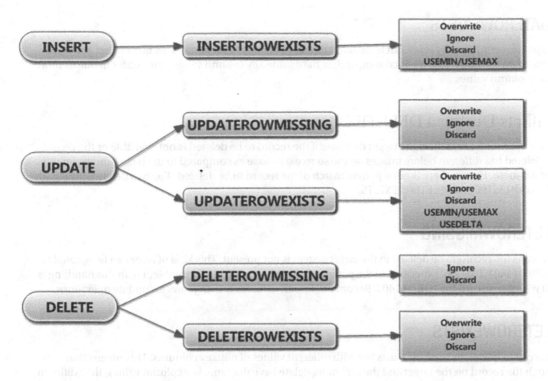

Figure 10-1. *Types of data conflict*

Conflicts During an INSERT Operation

A conflict in simpler terms means the operation applying a data change on the target has failed. There is only one type of conflict that is possible when applying an insert on the target database.

INSERTROWEXISTS

This conflict means that during an insert operation on the target, a unique constraint error is encountered. The key column (or columns) of the table already has a matching record compared to the incoming insert.

Conflicts During an UPDATE Operation

An update operation can fail on the target when the record to be updated is not available in the target database or the record to be updated has a different before and after image as compared to the before and after image of the updated record on the source database. The two types of update conflicts are UPDATEROWMISSING and UPDATEROWEXISTS.

UPDATEROWMISSING

The row being updated is missing on the target. In the absence of CDR, the update will fail, and no records will show up on the target system to the end user.

155

UPDATEROWEXISTS

The update record already exists but with different values of nonkey columns. This means that although the record on the target and the incoming update have same key column values, they differ in one or more nonkey column values.

Conflicts During a DELETE Operation

A delete operation may fail on the target database if the record to be deleted is not available or the record to be deleted has different before images on the source database as compared to the before image on the target database. Hence, there is not a perfect match of the record to be deleted. The two delete conflicts are DELETEROWMISSING and DELETEROWEXISTS.

DELETEROWMISSING

This means the record to be deleted in the target system is not present. This kind of error can be ignored using REPERROR (1403,DISCARD) specified in the parameter file of the replicat. The problem with this handling is that it will also discard the "ORA-01403: Record not found" error for missing rows for update operations.

DELETEROWEXISTS

The record to be deleted already exists but with different values of nonkey columns. This means that although the record on the target and the incoming delete have the same key column values, they differ in one or more nonkey column values.

CDR Parameters

Table 10-1 lists the CDR parameters used in the extract and replicat parameter files to identify and resolve conflicts.

Table 10-1. *CDR Parameters*

CDR Parameter	Description	Applicable to Extract/Replicat
GETUPDATEBEFORES	Specifies to capture before and after images of transactions, which will be used by the replicat process for conflict resolution	Extract
GETBEFORECOLS	Captures a before image for the operation types UPDATE and DELETE	Extract
COMPARECOLS	Specifies the list of columns to be compared for conflicts	Replicat
RESOLVECONFLICT	Specifies the conflict, resolution type, and resolution method to resolve conflicts	Replicat

The conflict resolution parameters can be configured to consider one data source as the master and always overwrite the other data source value. Another way to resolve conflict is to utilize the timestamp column and determine the most recent data to resolve the conflict. In certain situations, you will also use delta value to make adjustments at both sites to resolve conflicts.

Table 10-2 lists the conflict resolution methods used to resolve conflicts via the CDR technique. We will discuss these resolution methods in detail with examples.

Table 10-2. *Conflict Resolution Methods*

RESOLVECONFLICT Parameters	Description	Example
OVERWRITE	Applicable to all conflicts except DELETEROWMISSING. If UPDATEROWMISSING, it converts updates into inserts. If UPDATEROWEXISTS, it applies the updates from the trail record. If INSERTROWEXISTS, it converts inserts into updates to resolve conflicts. If DELETEROWEXISTS, applies delete based on columns in the WHERE clause.	RESOLVECONFLICT (UPDATEROWMISSING, (DEFAULT, OVERWRITE))
IGNORE	Applicable to all conflicts. The trail record is ignored.	RESOLVECONFLICT (DELETEROWMISSING, (DEFAULT, IGNORE))
DISCARD	Applicable to all conflicts. The trail record is discarded, and information is written into the discard file of the replicat process.	RESOLVECONFLICT (DELETEROWMISSING, (DEFAULT, DISCARD))
USEMIN	If the value of the column in the trail record is less than the value of the column in the database, the trail record gets preference, and the insert/update happens as per the trail record. Applicable to conflicts INSERTROWEXISTS and UPDATEROWEXISTS.	RESOLVECONFLICT (UPDATEROWEXISTS, (DEFAULT, USEMIN (last_updated)) RESOLVECONFLICT (INSERTROWEXISTS, (DEFAULT, USEMIN (last_updated))
USERMAX	If the value of the column in the trail record is greater than the value of the column in the database, the trail record gets preference, and the insert/update happens as per the trail record. Applicable to conflicts INSERTROWEXISTS and UPDATEROWEXISTS.	RESOLVECONFLICT (UPDATEROWEXISTS, (DEFAULT, USEMAX (last_updated)) RESOLVECONFLICT (INSERTROWEXISTS, (DEFAULT, USEMAX (last_updated))
USEDELTA	Adds the difference between the AFTER and BEFORE values of the column in the trail record to the current value in the database. This is used with columns having a numeric value in a multinode environment, where only the difference is propagated. Eventually, it syncs up all the nodes. Applicable to UPDATEROWEXISTS conflicts only.	RESOLVECONFLICT (UPDATEROWEXISTS,(delta_ res_method, USEDELTA, COLS (discount)),(DEFAULT, USEMAX (last_updated)))

In addition to using the CDR technique in a bidirectional system, I also implemented it in a one-directional system to deal with the occasional loss of transactions into a discard file because of data sync issues in nonproduction environments that were not maintained.

My target machine was not in sync with the source, and even after resyncing, there were times when the source and the target were out of sync. These transaction losses were due to long abended channels, server reboots, and network glitches. Implementing CDR in a unidirectional nonproduction environment where data sync is not critical can help you save effort when identifying tables that are out of sync and fixing them. With CDR in place, new transactions won't fail to replicate, and appropriate action is taken in case of conflicts because of an out-of-sync target. Oracle provides a tool called Veridata to deal with these sync issues. If you want to avoid the additional cost of a Veridata license, there is no harm in implementing CDR for a one-directional setup as well.

CDR Example

The following are two common conflict scenarios that show which CDR resolution method will be used to resolve conflicts and keep the data on the source and target databases in sync.

- *Conflict Situation 1*: Suppose an account with an initial balance of 2,000 was simultaneously credited with 400 on site B and debited 200 on site A. The result should be 2,200 on both site A and site B.

    Resolution: You can use USEDELTA to resolve this conflict situation. The balance on site B will be applied as an existing balance + (400 - 200).

- *Conflict Situation 2*: A seat 7E is booked first by Ray on site A and at about the same time by George on site B. The seat should be allotted to the first user who booked the seat irrespective of the site.

    Resolution: You can use the USEMIN timestamp method to resolve conflicts in a seat booking situation.

In the following section, I show you an example setup for CDR between the TIGER and FOX schemas.

Enable Supplemental Logging at the Column Level

As discussed earlier in this book, to add supplemental logging for a table, you issue the following command:

```
ADD TRANDATA schem_name.table_name
```

By default, this only adds key columns to supplemental logging. If you want to capture a before image of all nonkey columns or a set of them and use them for conflict detection at the target, issue the following commands:

```
ADD TRANDATA TIGER.CNTRY, COLS (CNTRY_NAME)
```

You can view the columns that are currently present in supplemental logging by issuing the following command:

```
INFO TRANDATA TIGER.CNTRY
```

While adding supplemental logging for columns for a particular table, those columns should not be present already in the supplemental log or you will get duplicate column in the list error, as shown here:

```
WARNING OGG-00706 Failed to add supplemental log group on table schema_name.table_name due
to ORA-00957: duplicate column name
```

If there is no key column in the table, supplemental logging can be added by issuing the following command:

```
ADD TRANDATA TIGER.ENTRY_LOG, NOKEY
```

Capture a Before Image on the Source

The GETBEFORECOLS parameter instructs the extract process to write a before image of the changed record in the trail files along with the after image once the change is applied. You can instruct the extract process to capture a before image for update operations, delete operations, or both.

The following shows how I did this on the source schema TIGER:

```
TABLE TIGER.CNTRY, GETBEFORECOLS (ON UPDATE KEYINCLUDING (LAST_UPDATED), ON DELETE
KEYINCLUDING (LAST_UPDATED));
TABLE TIGER.SCHOOL_LOC, GETBEFORECOLS (ON UPDATE ALL, ON DELETE ALL);
TABLE TIGER.EDUCATION_MODE, GETBEFORECOLS (ON UPDATE ALL);
```

Configure CDR on the Target

COMPARECOLS specifies the list of columns to be compared for detecting conflicts. I have used the DEFAULT resolution type and specified the appropriate resolution methods for resolving any detected conflict. The following are the changes done to the REPLICAT parameter on the target:

```
MAP TIGER.CNTRY, TARGET FOX.CNTRY,
COMPARECOLS(ON UPDATE KEYINCLUDING (LAST_UPDATED), ON DELETE KEYINCLUDING (LAST_UPDATED)),
RESOLVECONFLICT (UPDATEROWEXISTS, (DEFAULT, USEMIN (LAST_UPDATED))),
RESOLVECONFLICT (INSERTROWEXISTS, (DEFAULT, OVERWRITE)),
RESOLVECONFLICT (DELETEROWEXISTS, (DEFAULT, OVERWRITE)),
RESOLVECONFLICT (UPDATEROWMISSING, (DEFAULT, OVERWRITE)),
RESOLVECONFLICT (DELETEROWMISSING, (DEFAULT, DISCARD));

MAP TIGER.SCHOOL_LOC, TARGET FOX.SCHOOL_LOC,
COMPARECOLS(ON UPDATE ALL), ON DELETE ALL),
RESOLVECONFLICT (UPDATEROWEXISTS, (DEFAULT, USEMAX (LAST_UPDATED)));

MAP TIGER.EDUCATION_MODE, TARGET FOX.EDUCATION_MODE,
COMPARECOLS(ON UPDATE ALL, ON DELETE ALL),
RESOLVECONFLICT (UPDATEROWEXISTS, (DEFAULT, USEMAX (LAST_UPDATED))),
RESOLVECONFLICT (UPDATEROWMISSING, (DEFAULT, OVERWRITE));
```

Now you are ready to start your extract and replicat processes. To check the collision handling statistics on a replicat group, issue the following command in GGSCI:

```
GGSCI> STATS REPLICAT  replicat_name , REPORTCDR
```

The CDR statistics are also written by the replicat in a report file, as shown here:

```
Total CDR conflicts          7
CDR resolutions succeeded    6
CDR resolutions failed       1
```

```
CDR INSERTROWEXISTS conflicts        1
CDR UPDATEROWEXISTS conflicts        4
CDR DELROWEXISTS conflicts           1
CDR DELROWMISSING conflicts          1
```

Oracle GoldenGate Performance Tuning

In a high-volume transaction environment, you might see a lag of sometimes more than 30 minutes, and in rare cases of a poorly configured replicat process, the lag may shoot up to hours during peak transaction hours. This definitely is not acceptable to real-time businesses. There are some performance improvements that can be implemented to deal with such situations.

Best Practices for Configuring Your Oracle GoldenGate Replication Environment

Following best practices while setting up Oracle GoldenGate replication can avoid latency and boost overall performance to a great extent. The following are some of the important best practices you should keep in mind while setting up your replication environment:

- Enable supplemental logging to ensure data is replicated to the target database with the correct information.

- If using an Oracle database, configure the Oracle GoldenGate extract in integrated capture mode to take advantage of the database's LogMiner server.

- Configure the Oracle GoldenGate integrated replicat processes to take advantage of the apply processing functionality that is available within the Oracle database. For non-Oracle databases, leverage coordinated replicate as discussed in Chapter 5.

- Configure multiple parallel replicat processes using batched SQL for improved apply performance.

The first step for Oracle GoldenGate tuning is to determine the current performance.

Determining the Current Performance Statistics

Usually performance tuning begins after you first encounter an unacceptable lag. Lag is the time since the change occurred in the source database and the current time.

If you are using integrated extract or integrated replicat, you can query the current lag from the database using the following queries:

- Lag for integrated extract:

```
SQL> SELECT capture_name,
        86400 * (available_message_create_time - capture_message_create_time)
          lag_in_seconds
   FROM GV$GOLDENGATE_CAPTURE;
```

- Lag for integrated replicat:

```
SQL> SELECT r.apply_name,
        86400 * (r.dequeue_time - c.lwm_message_create_time)
```

160

```
      latency_in_seconds
  FROM GV$GG_APPLY_READER r, GV$GG_APPLY_COORDINATOR c
HERE r.apply# = c.apply# AND r.apply_name = c.apply_name;
```

Add the following parameters in the manager parameter file (`mgr.prm`) to capture lag alerts in the `ggserror.log` file. You can then write a shell script to mine the log for lag alerts and send a notification. You can specify different values for the following parameters depending on your particular replication need:

```
LAGREPORTMINUTES 5
LAGINFOMINUTES 5
LAGCRITICALMINUTES 15
```

You can also monitor the extract/replicat report file for Oracle GoldenGate performance statistics. Add REPORTCOUNT to the extract, data pump, and replicat parameter files.

```
REPORTCOUNT EVERY 10000 records, rate
REPORT at 1:00
REPORTROLLOVER at 1:15
```

The output of the previous commands gets written in the report file that can be viewed to note the current performance metric. Here's an example:

```
14214154 records processed as of 2016-05-05 09:35:15 (rate 124124,delta 134152)
141743251 records processed as of 2016-05-05 09:39:13 (rate 124314,delta 124315)
```

It is often additionally helpful to gather CPU and I/O statistics using OS tools such as `top`, `iostat`, `oswatcher`, and so on.

You can monitor latency using the heartbeat table. How to set this up is discussed in Appendix A.

Configure Your Database

Enable `ARCHIVELOG` mode for your database. The extract process mines data from Oracle redo logs if configured in integrated capture mode, and the LogMiner server efficiently mines redo from the log buffer, online, and archive log files.

You should also enable `FORCE LOGGING` of the database to generate redo information for all the tables in the database. If you are replicating only part of the tables instead of entire tables, you can have `FORCE LOGGING` enabled at the tablespace level. It's recommended you check the Oracle documentation on `FORCE LOGGING` before enabling it for your environment.

Enable Supplemental Logging

You can enable supplemental logging for each table using the `ADD TRANDATA` command in GGSCI. Alternatively, if all the tables of the schema are to be replicated, you can use the `ADD SCHEMATRANDATA` command.

PASSTHRU or NOPASSTHRU

A data pump essentially serves the function of reading extract trail files and copying them to the target machine. In some cases, data pumps are also configured to filter some information before the actual copying or mapping of the source to the target tables when the table names or structures differ.

Make use of PASSTHRU for tables with no filtering required and when the table structures on the source and the target match exactly. You can define PASSTHRU and NOPASSTHRU in same data pump as follows:

```
PASSTHRU TABLE TIGER.TABLE1;
NOPASSTHRU TABLE TIGER.TABLE2, WHERE (REGION< 10);
```

Tuning TCPBUFSIZE and TCPFLUSHBYTES

You should tune the RMTHOST parameters (in other words, TCPBUFSIZE and TCPFLUSHBYTES) to send a larger TCP/IP packet size. The default packet size for Oracle GoldenGate is 30,000 bytes. You can set it to roughly 1 MB each.

```
RMTHOST targetserver, MGRPORT 7809, TCPBUFSIZE 1000000, TCPFLUSHBYTES 1000000
or
RMTHOST targetserver, MGRPORT 7809, TCPBUFSIZE 10000000, COMPRESS
```

Here's how you can calculate values to be set for TCPBUFSIZE and TCPFLUSHBYTES:

1. Ping to the remote server to obtain the average round-trip time (RTT).

2. Calculate BDP (Bandwidth-Delay Product) values as

    BDP=(Network Speed in MB)*Network Round Trip Time (calculated using the ping command) in seconds.

3. Set TCPBUFSIZE and TCPFLUSHBYTES equal to three times the BDP values calculated in the previous step.

Additionally, use the COMPRESS parameter to compress the trails before sending. This is useful when there is limited network bandwidth available between the source and the target. COMPRESS will help to reduce the overall bandwidth requirement.

Batch Transactions

By default, SQL statements are applied one at a time on the target database by the OGG replicat. This often causes a performance bottleneck because the replicat process is not able to apply the changes as fast as the extract delivers new trails. Using BATCHSQL organizes similar SQLs in batches that are applied together. The maximum size of a statement batch processed by the replicat is controlled by the following parameters:

```
BATCHSQL, BATCHTRANSOPS, GROUPTRANSOPS
```

Setting these parameters too high or too low can also result in performance degradation. The values should be altered in a manner that new and old performance metrics can be compared. The default value for BATCHTRANOPS is 50. You can set a different value to tune your batch size. If an error is encountered in any batched SQL, the entire batch is rolled back.

Use Compression

If you have limited network bandwidth and enough CPU, you can compress the trail files and then transfer them over the network. The compression is handled by the data pump extract by including one of the following:

```
RMTHOST node2-ravinpc, MGRPORT 7809, COMPRESS, COMPRESSTHRESHOLD 512
```

Or, you can specify additional remote host options using the RMTHOSTOPTIONS parameter as shown here:

```
RMTHOSTOPTIONS COMPRESS, COMPRESSTHRESHOLD 750, TCPBUFSIZE 1000000, TCPFLUSHBYTES 2000000,
STREAMING
```

COMPRESSTHRESHOLD specifies the minimum block size for which compression should happen. The compressed trail files are received by the collector on the target server, and then it decompresses it at the target before writing it to the target trail files. The compression can save network bandwidth by approximately 3:1 to 4:1 compared to utilization when compression is not used. This, however, comes at the cost of increased CPU utilization.

Streams Pool for Integrated Extract and Replicat

When using an Oracle database as the source or target and using the extract and replicat in integrated mode, you can improve the performance of the extract and replicat processes by configuring the streams pool in the system global area (SGA). Since the integrated extract and replicat use LogMiner, you can first monitor the AWR reports to find instances of high waits on the LogMiner preparer, reader, builder, and capture background processes. In such an event, increasing the value of MAX_SGA_SIZE by 20 percent to 25 percent can improve the performance of the extract and replicat processes.

For example, include the following in the extract parameter file:

```
TRANLOGOPTIONS INTEGRATEDPARAMS (MAX_SGA_SIZE 2560, PARALLELISM 2)
```

Here, PARALLELISM specifies the number of LogMiner preparer processes to be used by the LogMiner server. The default value is 2.

Now, with MAX_SGA_SIZE 2560 and PARALLELISM as 2, set STREAMS_POOL_SIZE in your database initialization parameter file as shown here:

```
STREAMS_POOL_SIZE = (MAX_SGA_SIZE * PARALLELISM) + (20 to 25)% overhead
```

For the target database with the integrated replicat processes, this value can be calculated as shown here:

```
STREAMS_POOL_SIZE = (MAX_SGA_SIZE * number of integrated replicat processes) + (20 to 25)%
overhead
```

Refer to the Oracle Streams Performance Advisor (SPADV) to collect statistics on the performance of the integrated extract and replicat processes. These statistics can help you diagnose performance bottlenecks.

RANGE Splitting

A large table with a high volume of transactions can be range split, and you can assign the processing of certain row ranges to multiple extract or replicat groups.

You can use the RANGE function for this purpose. Here's the syntax:

```
@RANGE ({range}, {total ranges} [, {column}] [, {column}] [, …])
```

Let's see an example where a table is split into two ranges based on the column used.

The column name is an optional field. If no column name is specified, Oracle GoldenGate uses the primary key to assign the row ranges.

- Replicat 1, RFDLD001:

```
MAP TIGER.ORDER_DTL, TARGET FOX.ORDER_DTL, FILTER (@RANGE (1, 2, WORKID));
```

- Replicat 2, RFDLD002:

```
MAP TIGER.ORDER_DTL, TARGET FOX.ORDER_DTL, FILTER (@RANGE (2, 2, WORKID));
```

Similarly, the RANGE function can be used for the extract processes.

- Extract 1, ETTND001:

```
TABLE TIGER.ORDER_DTL, FILTER (@RANGE(1, 3));
TABLE TIGER.BILLING_SUMMARY,  FILTER (@RANGE(1, 3));
```

- Extract 2, ETTND002:

```
TABLE TIGER.ORDER_DTL, FILTER (@RANGE(2, 3));
TABLE TIGER.BILLING_SUMMARY,  FILTER (@RANGE(2, 3));
```

- Extract 3, ETTND003:

```
TABLE TIGER.ORDER_DTL, FILTER (@RANGE(3, 3));
TABLE TIGER.BILLING_SUMMARY,  FILTER (@RANGE(3, 3));
```

Using the extract to calculate the ranges is more efficient than using the replicat. Calculating ranges on the target side requires the replicat to read through the entire trail to find the data that meets each range specification.

Encryption and Security

Today it's important to secure data being processed and transported over a network. This is especially required in financial institutions or where customer-related information is being replicated.

There are three types of encryption that Oracle GoldenGate can provide for securing information.

- Encrypting passwords used in the extract and replicat parameter files

- Encrypting trail files on both the extract and the replicat

- Data being sent over the TCP/IP network for replication

Encrypting Database Passwords

The simplest way to encrypt a password is from the GGSCI command line. Run the encrypt command using the default algorithm. The Oracle GoldenGate default algorithm is called Blowfish. Other standard encryption algorithms used in Oracle GoldenGate are AES182, AES192, and AES256.

```
GGSCI> ENCRYPT PASSWORD ggsuser4u, ENCRYPTKEY default
```

The output of the previous command will be something like this:

```
Using Blowfish encryption with DEFAULT key.
Encrypted password:  AACAAAAAAAAAAAGAIFAAUDVHCFUGFIYF
Algorithm used:  BLOWFISH
```

You can use this encrypted password directly in the extract or replicat parameter file. If you want to test the password, you can also issue DBLOGIN to test it as shown here:

```
GGSCI> DBLOGIN USERID tiger, PASSWORD AACAAAAAAAAAAAGAIFAAUDVHCFUGFIYF, ENCRYPTKEY DEFAULT
```

Besides using a standard encryption key, you can generate your own custom encryption key.

Generating a Custom Encryption Key

Run the KEYGEN command from the GoldenGate software installation home.

```
KEYGEN (key length) (n)
```

The key length is the encryption key length and can be up to 128 bits, and n is the number of encryption keys to generate.

Here's an example:

```
./keygen 128 4
0x0A0E5C624211E87040B50129726C0371
0x0D44A10F0A6A05101FCE1E2003F0B405
0x0F7AE63CD1C2222FFEE63B179373661A
0xBB5A266A0AFF58158771E5599E5AB84C
```

Now create a file called enckeys and specify logical names for your keys generated earlier.

```
vi ENCKEYS
securekey1 0x0A0E5C624211E87040B50129726C0371
securekey2 0x0D44A10F0A6A05101FCE1E2003F0B405
securekey3 0x0F7AE63CD1C2222FFEE63B179373661A
securekey4 0xBB5A266A0AFF58158771E5599E5AB84C
```

Copy this file if not already generated in the GoldenGate software home directory. Now you are ready to generate the encrypted password using one of your secure keys.

```
GGSCI> encrypt password tiger encryptkey securekey1
Encrypted password: AACAAAAAAAAAAAJAUEUGODSCVGJEEIUGKJDJTFNDKEJFFFTC
```

You can test the key by using it in the DBLOGIN command in GGSCI.

Wallet and a Master Key

One option to secure your trail files and data sent over the network is to use Oracle Wallet and a master key for encryption.

With every trail file, Oracle GoldenGate generates a new encryption key to encrypt trails. A master key is then used to encrypt the encryption keys. The master key is also used to generate a session key for secure transferring trail files over the network.

Please note that encryption using Oracle Wallet and a master key is not supported on the z/OS, iSeries, and NonStop OS platforms.

You can create the wallet on a shared file system or create the wallet on the source system and then copy it over to each system in your Oracle GoldenGate replication environment. If there is any change in the master key, you will have to update the wallet to reflect the change on each machine.

Steps for Creating a Wallet and Master Key

The following are the steps you should follow for creating an Oracle GoldenGate wallet.

1. The wallet is by default stored in your Oracle GoldenGate `dirwlt` directory. If you want to secure your wallet in a different location, specify the location in your GLOBALS parameter file.

    ```
    WALLETLOCATION /app/ggs/wallet/
    ```

2. Create the wallet.

    ```
    GGSCI> CREATE WALLET
    ```

3. Add the master key to the wallet.

    ```
    GGSCI> ADD MASTERKEY
    ```

4. Check the master key version.

    ```
    GGSCI> INFO MASTERKEY
    ```

5. Use the version number from step 4 and get the AES hash value of your master key as shown here:

    ```
    GGSCI> INFO MASTERKEY VERSION version_number
    ```

Copy the master key to all other machines in your Oracle GoldenGate replication environment and issue the commands in step 4 and step 5. The version and AES hash value for your master key should match on all systems.

Renew the Master Key

Organizational security policies require renewing your master key periodically. If your wallet is configured on multiple systems, you will need to stop OGG on all instances and update the wallet to have the master key with the same version across. The steps to renew your master key are as follows:

1. Stop the extract on the source.

2. Check for the status of each replicat group until it returns EOF, marking the completion of all pending trails.

    ```
    GGSCI> SEND REPLICAT replicat_name STATUS
    ```

3. Once the replicat has finished processing, stop the replicat. You can leave the data pump running or stop the data pump at this stage.

```
GGSCI> STOP replicat_name
GGSCI> STOP datapump_name
```

4. Open the wallet and check the master key version.

```
GGSCI> OPEN WALLET
GGSCI> INFO MASTERKEY
```

5. Renew the master key.

```
GGSCI> RENEW MASTERKEY
```

6. Check the version and hash value of the renewed key.

```
GGSCI> INFO MASTERKEY
GGSCI> INFO MASTERKEY VERSION new_version
```

7. Copy the new wallet to all other systems in your OGG replication environment and check for the version and hash value on each system. They should match on all the systems.

8. Start the extract, data pump, and replicat processes.

Encrypt and Decrypt Trail Files

To secure your trail files, encrypt them before sending them across the network. You use the ENCRYPTTRAIL parameter along with EXTTRAIL, RMTTRAIL, EXTFILE, and RMTFILE to instruct Oracle GoldenGate to encrypt data in the trail files. Another complementary parameter called DECRYPTTRAIL is used to decrypt the trail files before applying transactions to the database.

```
EXTRACT ETTND001
USERID tiger, PASSWORD AACAAAAAAAAAAAJAUEUGODSCVGJEEIUGKJDJTFNDKEJFFFTC, ENCRYPTKEY
securekey1
RMTHOST targetserver, MGRPORT 7809, ENCRYPT BLOWFISH, KEYNAME securekey1
ENCRYPTTRAIL RMTTRAIL /app/ggs/tiger/dirdat/ab
TABLE tiger.ORDER_DTL;
```

The corresponding replicat parameter file will have DECRYPTTRAIL, as shown here:

```
REPLICAT RFDLD001
HANDLECOLLISIONS
DECRYPTTRAIL
ASSUMETARGETDEFS
USERID tiger, PASSWORD AACAAAAAAAAAAAJAUEUGODSCVGJEEIUGKJDJTFNDKEJFFFTC, ENCRYPTKEY securekey1
Map TIGER.ORDER_DTL, Target FOX.ORDER_DTL;
```

For a setup with EXTRACT, DATAPUMP, and REPLICAT, you should instruct OGG to encrypt the data in trail files once transactions are written by the extract process. It should then decrypt the trail files for the data pump to read and process. Once the data pump has processed the trail file data for any filter and transformed it, it then encrypts it again before sending it to the target.

The encryption and decryption of the trail follow this order:

```
EXTRACT ETTND001
USERID tiger, PASSWORD AACAAAAAAAAAAAJAUEUGODSCVGJEEIUGKJDJTFNDKEJFFFTC, ENCRYPTKEY
securekey1
ENCRYPTTRAIL EXTRAIL /app/ggs/tiger/dirdat/t1
TABLE tiger.ORDER_DTL;

EXTRACT PFTND001
DECRYPTTRAIL
ENCRYPTTRAIL
USERID tiger, PASSWORD AACAAAAAAAAAAAJAUEUGODSCVGJEEIUGKJDJTFNDKEJFFFTC, ENCRYPTKEY
securekey1
RMTHOST node2-ravinpc, MGRPORT 7809
RMTTRAIL /app/ggs/fox/dirdat/f1
PASSTHRU
TABLE TIGER.ORDER_DTL;

REPLICAT RFDLD001
HANDLECOLLISIONS
DECRYPTTRAIL
ASSUMETARGETDEFS
USERID tiger, PASSWORD AACAAAAAAAAAAAJAUEUGODSCVGJEEIUGKJDJTFNDKEJFFFTC, ENCRYPTKEY
securekey1
Map TIGER.ORDER_DTL, Target FOX.ORDER_DTL;
```

Encrypt Data Sent Over a Network

As important it is to secure data on the system, it is equally important to secure the data set over the network to the target machine. The target system OGG then decrypts the data before writing into the trail files.

For example, add the following to your extract parameter file to instruct your extract to encrypt trail files using the encryption key securekey1:

```
RMTHOST targetserver, MGRPORT 7809, ENCRYPT BLOWFISH
```

Or the following:

```
RMTHOSTOPTIONS ENCRYPT BLOWFISH
```

Using an Oracle GoldenGate Credential Store

Credential stores have been introduced with Oracle GoldenGate 12c. They allow you to manage the user ID and password used in Oracle GoldenGate. You will be storing your username and passwords used in the OGG processes in the credential store and will be using an alias instead in your extract and replicat processes. The credential store also can be used to store usernames and passwords that you use for DBLOGIN through GGSCI.

This shields the original credentials from being displayed and provides an extra layer of security.

Create a Credential Store

Use the ADD CREDENTIALSTORE command to create a credential store. By default the credential store is created in the OGG directory dircrd.

```
GGSCI> ADD CREDENTIALSTORE
Credential store created in ./dircrd/.
```

The credential store gets created in the dircrd directory in your OGG home. Alternatively, you can specify CREDENTIALSTORELOCATION in the GLOBALS parameter file to create a wallet at another location.

```
$ cd dircrd
$ ls
cwallet.sso
```

Add, Replace, and Delete Users in the Credential Store

You would need to alter your credential store every time you want to add, modify, or delete your user details. Here's the syntax of an ALTER CREDENTIALSTORE command:

```
ALTER CREDENTIALSTORE {
ADD USER userid |
REPLACE USER userid |
DELETE USER userid }
[PASSWORD password]
[ALIAS alias]
[DOMAIN domain]
```

Let's start with adding a user to the credential store without specifying an alias to it. By default it takes an alias name that's the same as the username.

```
GGSCI> ALTER CREDENTIALSTORE ADD USER tiger
Password:
Credential store in ./dircrd/ altered.
```

Here, it prompts you for a password since you have not specified the password in the command itself. View the credential store. It should reflect the new user and its alias.

```
GGSCI> INFO CREDENTIALSTORE
Reading from ./dircrd/:
Domain: OracleGoldenGate
Alias: tiger
Userid: tiger
```

Alternatively, you can specify a password, alias, and domain name.

```
GGSCI> ALTER CREDENTIALSTORE ADD USER tiger PASSWORD tiger123_ ALIAS ggs_tiger domain ggs

GGSCI> ALTER CREDENTIALSTORE ADD USER tiger PASSWORD tiger123_ ALIAS ggs_tiger domain ggs

GGSCI> ALTER CREDENTIALSTORE ADD USER tiger PASSWORD tiger123_ ALIAS ggs_tiger DOMAIN ggs
Credential store in ./dircrd/ altered.
```

Now you can get information about the credential store for a specific domain name. Providing a domain name is mandatory if you have added or altered a user with a specific domain.

```
GGSCI> INFO CREDENTIALSTORE DOMAIN ggs
Reading from ./dircrd/:
Domain: ggs
Alias: ggs_tiger
Userid: tiger
```

If you do not provide a domain name with the INFO CREDENTIALSTORE command, you will not be able to see users created in the domain.

```
GGSCI> INFO CREDENTIALSTORE
Reading from ./dircrd/:
No information found in credential store.
```

Once your credential store is set up and you have added users to it, you can use the alias to connect to the database. Here's the syntax for the DBLOGIN command using an alias:

```
GGSCI> DBLOGIN USERIDALIAS alias_name
GGSCI> DBLOGIN USERIDALIAS alias_name DOMAIN domain_name
```

Here again, if your user was added to the credential store with a domain name, you must specify the domain name along with the alias name.

DBLOGIN Without Using the Credential Store

If you have not set up or are not using a credential store, you can log in to your underlying database as shown here:

```
GGSCI> DBLOGIN USERID tiger, PASSWORD tiger123_
Successfully logged into database.
```

DBLOGIN with Using the Credential Store

When using a credential store, your DBLOGIN command can be rewritten as shown here:

```
GGSCI> DBLOGIN USERIDALIAS ggs_tiger
Successfully logged into database.
```

Delete a User from the Credential Store

You can delete users from your credential store using the ALTER CREDENTIALSTORE command.

```
GGSCI> ALTER CREDENTIALSTORE DELETE USER tiger
Credential store in ./dircrd/ altered.
```

```
GGSCI> ALTER CREDENTIALSTORE DELETE USER tiger ALIAS ggs_tiger DOMAIN ggs
Credential store in ./dircrd/ altered.
```

Finally, let's take a look at how to update user information in the credential store.

If your user password has changed and you have not reflected this in your credential store, you will see the following error:

```
SQL> alter user tiger identified by tiger321_;
User altered.

GGSCI> DBLOGIN USERIDALIAS ggs_tiger DOMAIN ggs
ERROR: Unable to connect to database using user tiger. Please check privileges.
ORA-01017: invalid username/password; logon denied.
```

You can replace the user information in the credential store as follows:

```
GGSCI> ALTER CREDENTIALSTORE REPLACE USER tiger ALIAS ggs_tiger DOMAIN ggs
Password:
Credential store in ./dircrd/ altered.
```

Please note this does not allow you to replace the alias or domain name. You will have to delete the user and re-create it with the new alias or domain.

Using an Alias in Your Extract Parameter File

You can now use the alias created in the credential store for your OGG processes. Here, you can see USERIDALIAS used in extract ETTND001 to connect to the database.

```
GGSCI> edit params ETTND001


EXTRACT ETTND001
USERIDALIAS ggs_tiger domain ggs
LOGALLSUPCOLS
EXTTRAIL /app/ggs/tiger/dirdat/t1
TABLE TIGER.ORDER_DTL;
```

Summary

In this chapter, we discussed advanced configurations for Oracle GoldenGate in three categories: collision handling, OGG performance tuning, and security in OGG.

The collision handling technique makes Oracle GoldenGate even smarter and enables it to identify conflicts and resolve them without manual intervention. We then discussed OGG performance tuning to identify performance bottlenecks and take preventive as well as corrective actions to boost performance. Finally, we discussed encrypting the passwords and securing the data being replicated. At the end of this chapter, you saw how to create an OGG credential store to manage IDs and passwords.

In the next chapter, we will discuss how to upgrade a previous Oracle GoldenGate version to a higher version. By upgrading to the latest version, you can use the new features introduced with new versions.

CHAPTER 11

■ ■ ■

Upgrading Oracle GoldenGate

If you have an existing Oracle GoldenGate setup and you want to move to the newer version of OGG, chances are rare that you want to re-create everything. You can simply upgrade the binaries of the Oracle GoldenGate software and keep your custom channels, trails, and so on, as they are. These are the main steps for upgrading your GoldenGate setup:

1. Let the current transactions under processing be completely processed by the Oracle GoldenGate extract process.

2. Let the replicat processes read all the trails on the target system and write them to the database. Ensure there are no pending trails on the target.

3. Back up the existing GoldenGate instance directory. This is just in case something goes wrong and you want to back out of the upgrade process.

4. Create a new directory to install the latest version of Oracle GoldenGate.

5. Copy the contents of the new directory to the existing Oracle GoldenGate install directory. This overwrites the GoldenGate binaries with the new version binaries. No changes are made to existing the dirdat, dirprm, dirdef, dirpcs, dirtmp, and so on, directories. Thus, the existing setup of the extract and replicat are unaffected.

6. Restart Oracle GoldenGate with the extract and replicat communicating with the new set of trails.

Log in to the server that has the Oracle GoldenGate instance to be upgraded. Take a backup of the existing Oracle GoldenGate installation directory where all your binaries and other GoldenGate files are. In my example, I am upgrading GoldenGate from 11.2 to 12.0.

Download the Patch

Since you already have Oracle GoldenGate installed on your machine, you can download a new version from http://support.oracle.com. Log in to Oracle Support using your Oracle ID and go to Patches and Upgrades. Click Products or Family. Type **Oracle GoldenGate** in the Product field. Select appropriate release and platform and click Search. Select and download the patch from the available patches list.

Install the Patch

Temporarily set ORACLE_HOME as the Oracle GoldenGate Home and add the ORACLE_HOME/OPatch directory in the PATH variable. Run the following command to confirm the OPatch directories are available:

```
$ opatch lsinventory
```

Extract the compressed .zip file of the OGG patch you downloaded from the Oracle Support web site into a new directory, say, /app/ggs/patch_dir.

Stop the OGG Manager and the extract and replicat processes.

```
GGSCI> STOP MGR
GGSCI> STOP ER *
```

Navigate to the location of the patch in the patch directory and apply the patch as follows:

```
$ opatch apply
```

Once the patch is installed, reset ORACLE_HOME to the Oracle Database home directory. You should configure the Oracle GoldenGate parameter files to include any new parameters that came with the new version of Oracle GoldenGate. Finally, restart the Oracle GoldenGate manager and channels.

```
GGSCI> START MGR
GGSCI> START ER *
```

Pre-upgrade Tasks

If your extract process was processing an open transaction at the time you stopped it and the archived log for this transaction is no longer on the system, you first need to restore the archived log to allow the extract to begin from the old transaction. Note the output of the following command:

```
GGSCI> INFO ETTND001, SHOWCH
```

Alternatively, you can skip the transaction and let your extract process begin with the next available transaction. This, however, will lead to data loss, and your source and target tables will be out of sync. If the tables are fairly small, you can sync them manually or use OGG Veridata.

```
GGSCI> SEND EXTRACT ETTND001, SHOWTRANS
```

Note the transaction ID and use the following command to skip the transaction:

```
GGSCI> SEND EXTRACT ETTND001, SKIPTRANS transaction_id
```

Once you skip old running transactions for which no logs are available on the system, you can force a bounded recovery checkpoint as shown here:

```
GGSCI> SEND EXTRACT ETTND001, BR BRCHECKPOINT IMMEDIATE
```

Wait until the extract has finished reading the pending transactions. Compare the SCN value from the database and extract the report file. Once your extract has picked up old open transactions and is currently processing recent transactions, you can also issue LOGEND to the extract until it returns YES.

```
GGSCI> SEND EXTRACT ETTND001 LOGEND
```

Stop the extract process.

```
GGSCI> STOP ETTND001
```

If Oracle GoldenGate is upgraded only on the source and not on the target, there will be compatibility issues with the trail file format version on the two systems. To handle this, include the following parameter in your extract parameter files to instruct Oracle GoldenGate on the source to write trails in a specific format version compatible with your target system.

Include the following command in the extract parameter file:

```
EXTTRAIL /app/ggs/tiger/dirdat/t1, FORMAT RELEASE 11.2
```

In the data pump parameter file, include the following command:

```
RMTTRAIL /app/ggs/fox/dirdat/f1, FORMAT RELEASE 11.2
```

Next, you must rebuild DDL objects. Execute the following scripts to remove DDL objects. You can then set up trigger-based DDL objects again using the steps discussed in Chapter 6. If you upgrade to Oracle GoldenGate 12c on an Oracle database, you can use integrated DDL capture as well. This is the recommended method of DDL capture for an Oracle database and requires minimal configuration. Execute the following scripts with a sysdba account or a user with sysdba privileges:

```
SQL> @ddl_disable.sql
SQL> @ddl_remove.sql
SQL> @marker_remove.sql
```

Log in to your target machine in GGSCI and execute the following on the replicat processes:

```
GGSCI> SEND REPLICAT RFDLD001 STATUS
```

Continue executing the previous command until you see At EOF in the output. You can also use ! to execute the previously executed command without retyping it.

Once your replicat process has reached EOF, stop the replicat.

```
GGSCI> STOP RFDLD001
```

Repeat this process for each replicat process in your OGG instance.

Now, you can stop the manager process.

```
GGSCI> STOP MANAGER
```

Upgrading Oracle GoldenGate on the Source

Up until now you have handled your extract and replication processes and rebuilt DDL objects. Once you have done this much, back up your current OGG directories on both the source and target machines and perform the upgrade as discussed next.

Take a Backup

This source OGG instance is set up at /app/ggs/tiger. Let's take a backup of this using the following command:

```
cp -fR tiger tiger_bkp
```

Install the New Version of GoldenGate

Install the new version of Oracle GoldenGate using the OUI in the existing directory /app/ggs/tiger. Make sure to select the Start Manager option during installation to prevent overwriting your existing manager parameter file.

Convert Supplemental Log Group Version

On the source system, the DBA should run the ulg.sql script as SYSDBA. This script converts the existing supplemental log groups to the new format that is required for the new version of OGG you have upgraded to. The script should return "Upgrade completed successfully." If it does not return this message, contact Oracle Support.

```
SQL> @ulg.sql
```

Verify the Upgrade

I have upgraded from Oracle GoldenGate 11.2 to 12.1. This can be confirmed when I log in to GGSCI in the tiger instance as shown here:

```
$ ./ggsci
Oracle GoldenGate Command Interpreter for Oracle
Version 12.1.2.0.0 OGGCORE_12.1.2.0.0_PLATFORMS_10924.1316_FBO
LINUX, x64, 64bit (optimized), Oracle 12c on Nov 6 2015 05:03:51
Copyright (C) 1995, 2015, Oracle and/or its affiliates. All rights reserved.
```

Upgrading Oracle GoldenGate on the Target

Once you have upgraded the source Oracle GoldenGate instance, you can upgrade your target Oracle GoldenGate instance as discussed here. It is, however, not mandatory to upgrade both the source and target Oracle GoldenGate instances. You can have different versions of Oracle GoldenGate on the source and target systems.

Take a Backup

The target OGG instance is set up at /app/ggs/fox. Let's take a backup of this using the following command:

```
cp -fR fox fox_bkp
```

Install the New Version of GoldenGate

Install a new version of Oracle GoldenGate using the OUI in the existing directory /app/ggs/fox. Make sure to select the Start Manager option during installation to prevent overwriting your existing manager parameter file.

Upgrade the Checkpoint Table

If you have implemented a checkpoint table in your target GoldenGate instance, the checkpoint table will need to be upgraded. This is because the table structure of CHECKPOINT TABLE may differ in different versions of Oracle GoldenGate.

```
GGSCI>dblogin userid fox, password fox123_
GGSCI>upgrade checkpointtable fox.chkptab
```

Verify the Upgrade

I have upgraded from GoldenGate 11.2 to 12.0. This can be confirmed when I log in to the GGSCI interface in the fox instance as shown here:

```
$ ./ggsci
Oracle GoldenGate Command Interpreter for Oracle
Version 12.1.2.0.0 OGGCORE_12.1.2.0.0_PLATFORMS_10924.1316_FBO
LINUX, x64, 64bit (optimized), Oracle 12c on Nov 6 2015 06:08:12
Copyright (C) 1995, 2015, Oracle and/or its affiliates. All rights reserved.
```

Post-upgrade Tasks

Once your upgrade is finished, it is important to start your extract and replicat processes and monitor replication. Let's discuss these post-upgrade tasks in this section.

Start GoldenGate and Monitor Replication

Start the manager process on the source and target. You now want the extract process to write to the newer version of the trail files, so use ETROLLOVER to force the new file sequence and start the extract process.

```
GGSCI> ALTER EXTRACT ETTND001, etrollover
```

Instruct the data pump and replicat processes to start reading from the new trail files. Navigate to the dirdat directory and note the new trail sequences.

```
GGSCI> ALTER EXTRACT PTTND001, EXTSEQNO 023, EXTRBA 0
GGSCI> START PTTND001
```

```
GGSCI> ALTER REPLICAT RFDLD001, EXTSEQNO 032, EXTRBA 0
GGSCI> START RFDLD001
```

Monitor both the extract and replicat. Check the respective report files for any error.

If your Oracle GoldenGate instance is on a non-Oracle database, you can follow the previous upgrade steps except DDL replication, which is not supported for non-Oracle databases.

Summary

In this chapter, we discussed how to apply a new patch for Oracle GoldenGate and upgrade from OGG 11.2 to OGG 12*c*. The upgrade process is simple and requires you to install a new version of OGG on top of an existing OGG version to be upgraded. Your parameter files, checkpoints, and trail files all remain intact. You may have to perform a rollover on the extract process to instruct it to start writing to the new trail files because of the difference in trail file formats for different versions of Oracle GoldenGate.

In the next chapter, we will discuss Oracle GoldenGate bidirectional replication configuration.

CHAPTER 12

■ ■ ■

Bidirectional Replication

Bidirectional replication, or active-active replication, has two systems with an identical set of data. Each set can be changed by the application users on either system. The job of a bidirectional replication setup is to replicate the transactional changes from one system to the other and thus keep the two data sets identical.

This kind of active-active replication is essential in a high availability environment for load sharing and disaster recovery. Figure 12-1 shows a simple view of two database systems in a bidirectional replication configuration.

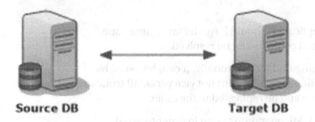

Source DB   **Target DB**

Figure 12-1. *Bidirectional replication between two databases*

Oracle GoldenGate supports active-active bidirectional replication on both Oracle and the supported non-Oracle databases listed here:

- Oracle

- MySQL

- SQL Server

- Sybase

- Teradata

- DB2 on z/OS, LUW, and IBM i

- SQL/MX

An active-active configuration typically has a complete OGG setup on each system. Figure 12-2 shows a local extract and a local replicat setup on the source and target machines.

© Ravinder Gupta 2016
R. Gupta, *Mastering Oracle GoldenGate*, DOI 10.1007/978-1-4842-2301-7_12

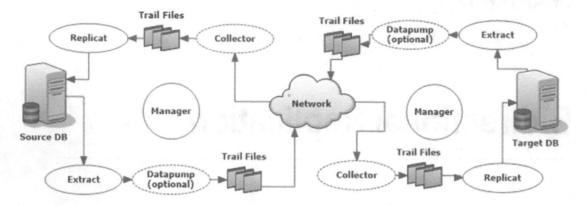

Figure 12-2. *Oracle GoldenGate bidirectional replication configuration*

Key Points Before Setting Up OGG Bidirectional Replication

The following are some key points to consider before setting up bidirectional replication. Thinking about and solving these points beforehand can save you headaches when encountering subtle issues after your replication is set up and running.

- Both the systems in an active-active replication should have the same time zone. This is required so that timestamp-based conflicts can be resolved.

- The TRUNCATE statement cannot be configured bidirectionally. It can, however, be configured to originate from one machine to another, but not vice versa. All truncates should originate from only one machine and be replicated to the other.

- If triggers on tables exist and generate DML operations, then in order to avoid conflicts between the local DML and the replicated triggered DML, modify your triggers to handle the local DML and replicated DML. The OGG replicat in integrated mode allows the handling of triggers.

- Do not replicate DB-generated values such as sequences to avoid conflicts. Also, you can use even sequences on one database and odd sequences on another to avoid conflicts.

- Tables should have a primary or unique key to identify rows. This will be needed for resolving conflicts.

Handling Data Loopbacks

Imagine a situation where the data capture on Machine A is replicated to Machine B and the same transaction on Machine B gets captured by the extract on Machine B and gets replicated back to Machine A. This will lead to an endless loop. You will need to configure your bidirectional replication to distinguish between user transactions and local replicat transactions to avoid such data loopbacks.

Different databases will have different ways to identify local replicat transactions, as discussed next.

Handling Data Loopbacks in Oracle Databases

Since Oracle databases have two capture modes, you handle data loopbacks differently for each type of capture mode, as discussed next.

Classic Capture Mode

When running classic capture, use EXCLUDEUSER in the extract parameter file to exclude transactions from the replicat user. This will require you to use different usernames or user IDs on Machine A and Machine B.

```
TRANLOGOPTIONS EXCLUDEUSER user_name
OR
TRANLOGOPTIONS EXCLUDEUSERID user_id
```

Classic/Integrated Mode

Alternatively, you can prevent data loopbacks in an Oracle GoldenGate bidirectional configuration on Oracle databases by using the following tags:

- Set a numeric tag on the replicat on System A. For example, I have set the tag as 542 on System A. You can set the tag as any numeric value except 0.

```
DBOPTIONS SETTAG 542
```

- Exclude transactions to be captured on Machine B by adding the following to the extract process:

```
TRANLOGOPTIONS EXCLUDETAG 542
```

Handling Data Loopbacks in All Supported Databases

If Oracle GoldenGate is running in classic capture mode on any of the supported databases including Oracle databases, you can include the following parameters to identify application and replicat transactions to prevent data loopback:

- To control whether the DML performed by application users is captured by the extract or not, use the following parameter in your extract parameter file. (APPL here means "application.")

```
GETAPPLOPS | IGNOREAPPLOPS
```

- To control whether a replicat transaction is captured by the extract process or ignored, use the following parameters in your extract parameter file:

```
GETREPLICATES | IGNOREREPLICATES
```

Handling Data Loopbacks in Teradata Databases

You can instruct Teradata to override replication from the OGG replicat by including the following statement in your replicat parameter file. This will instruct Oracle GoldenGate to set up a separate replicat session when a replicat is started.

```
SQLEXEC 'SET SESSION OVERRIDE REPLICATION ON;'
SQLEXEC 'COMMIT;'
```

Handling Data Loopbacks by Identifying Replicat Transactions

You can handle data loopback in a bidirectional replication configuration by identifying replicat transactions. You can identify replicat transactions in Oracle databases by setting the tag in the replicat parameter file and then excluding these tagged transactions from the extract process on the opposite side.

- Set the tag in the replicat on System A as shown here:

```
DBOPTIONS SETTAG 542
```

- Exclude transactions to be captured on Machine B by adding the following to the extract process:

```
TRANLOGOPTIONS EXCLUDETAG 542
```

Identifying Replicat Transactions on Sybase

You can instruct Oracle GoldenGate on Sybase databases to exclude users or transactions as shown here:

```
TRANLOGOPTIONS EXCLUDETRANS transaction_name
TRANLOGOPTIONS EXCLUDEUSER user_name
```

The default transaction name of replicat transactions is ggs_repl. When using the default transaction name, you do not need to use EXECLUDETRANS. This is handled automatically by Oracle GoldenGate.

Identifying Replicat Transactions on SQL Server

For SQL Server databases, you can exclude replicat transactions as shown here. You do not need to include this statement in your extract parameter file if using the default transaction name ggs_repl.

```
TRANLOGOPTIONS EXCLUDETRANS transaction_name
```

CDR in Bidirectional Replication

Conflict detection and resolution (CDR) plays an important role in a bidirectional replication. It ensures any insert, update, or delete conflicts between two machines are handled in real time.

We already discussed CDR in detail in Chapter 11. We will implement CDR in this chapter for a bidirectional replication setup.

Setting Up OGG Bidirectional Replication

In this example, we will have two machines, Machine A and Machine B, between which we are going to set up bidirectional replication. Table 12-1 shows the application user (or schema), location of the database, and the abbreviations that I used to represent the information in my channel names.

Table 12-1. Bidirectional Replication Machines A and B

Machine A Application User	TIGER	T
Machine B Application User	FOX	F
Machine A Location	TENNESSEE	TN
Machine B Location	DALLAS	DL

Table 12-2 shows the name of extract, data pump, and replicat on the two machines between which we will set up bidirectional replication.

Table 12-2. Extract and Replicat Processes on Machine A and Machine B

	Extract	Local Trail	Data Pump	Remote Trail	Replicat
Machine A	ETTND001	t1	PFTND001	f1	RFDLD002
Machine B	ETTND002	t2	PFTND002	f2	RFDLD001

For this example, I have table CNTRY on both the TIGER and FOX schemas. I have created a trigger as shown here on both the databases (on Machine A and Machine B):

```
--On Machine A, TIGER Schema

CREATE OR REPLACE TRIGGER TIGER_CDR_TRG
BEFORE UPDATE
ON TIGER.CNTRY
REFERENCING NEW AS New OLD AS Old
FOR EACH ROW
BEGIN
IF SYS_CONTEXT ('USERENV', 'SESSION_USER') != 'FOX'
THEN
:NEW.LAST_UPDATED := SYSTIMESTAMP;
END IF;
END;
/

--On Machine B, FOX Schema

CREATE OR REPLACE TRIGGER FOX_CDR_TRG
BEFORE UPDATE
ON FOX.CNTRY
REFERENCING NEW AS New OLD AS Old
FOR EACH ROW
BEGIN
IF SYS_CONTEXT ('USERENV', 'SESSION_USER')!= 'TIGER'
THEN
:NEW.LAST_UPDATED := SYSTIMESTAMP;
END IF;
END;
/
```

Next, create the extract and data pump on Machine A as shown here:

```
GGSCI> ADD EXTRACT ETTND001 TRANLOG BEGIN NOW
GGSCI> ADD EXTTRAIL /app/ggs/tiger/dirdat/t1 EXTRACT ETTND001
GGSCI> ADD EXTRACT PFTND001 EXTTRAILSOURCE /app/ggs/tiger/dirdat/t1
GGSCI> ADD RMTTRAIL /app/ggs/fox/dirdat/f1 EXTRACT PFTND001
```

Configure the parameter file for the extract ETTND001.

```
GGSCI> EDIT PARAMS ETTND001

EXTRACT ETTND001
USERID tiger, PASSWORD tiger123_
EXTTRAIL /app/ggs/tiger/dirdat/t1
TRANLOGOPTIONS EXCLUDEUSER fox
TABLE TIGER.CNTRY,
GETBEFORECOLS (
ON UPDATE KEYINCLUDING (CNTRY_NAME,LAST_UPDATED),
ON DELETE KEYINCLUDING (CNTRY_NAME,LAST_UPDATED));
```

Configure the parameter file for the data pump extract PFTND001.

```
GGSCI> EDIT PARAMS PFTND001

EXTRACT PFTND001
USERID tiger, PASSWORD tiger123_
RMTHOST ravinpc2, MGRPORT 7809, TCPBUFSIZE 100000
RMTTRAIL /app/ggs/fox/dirdat/f1
PASSTHRU
TABLE TIGER.CNTRY;
```

Add the corresponding replicat on Machine B with the parameters shown here:

```
GGSCI> ADD REPLICAT RFDLD001 EXTTRAIL /app/ggs/fox/dirdat/f1
GGSCI> EDIT PARAMS RFDLD001

REPLICAT RFDLD001
ASSUMETARGETDEFS
USERID GGATE, PASSWORD GGATE
DISCARDFILE /app/ggs/fox/dirrpt/rfdlD001.dsc, APPEND,
MAP TIGER.CNTRY, TARGET FOX.CNTRY;
```

To actively capture transactions on Machine B, you need to set up local extract processes on this machine as well. Create the capture process on Machine B as shown here:

```
GGSCI> ADD EXTRACT ETTND002 TRANLOG BEGIN NOW
GGSCI> ADD EXTTRAIL /app/ggs/fox/dirdat/t2 EXTRACT ETTND002
GGSCI> ADD EXTRACT PFTND002 EXTTRAILSOURCE /app/ggs/fox/dirdat/t2
GGSCI> ADD RMTTRAIL /app/ggs/tiger/dirdat/f2 EXTRACT PFTND002
```

Configure the extract parameter file on Machine B.

```
GGSCI> EDIT PARAMS ETTND002

EXTRACT ETTND002
USERID tiger, PASSWORD tiger123_
EXTTRAIL /app/ggs/fox/dirdat/t2
TRANLOGOPTIONS EXCLUDEUSER fox
TABLE TIGER.CNTRY,
GETBEFORECOLS (
ON UPDATE KEYINCLUDING (CNTRY_NAME,LAST_UPDATED),
ON DELETE KEYINCLUDING (CNTRY_NAME,LAST_UPDATED));
```

Configure the data pump extract on Machine B.

```
GGSCI> EDIT PARAMS PFTND002

EXTRACT PFTND002
USERID fox, PASSWORD fox123_
RMTHOST ravinpc1, MGRPORT 7809, TCPBUFSIZE 100000
RMTTRAIL /app/ggs/tiger/dirdat/f2
PASSTHRU
TABLE TIGER.CNTRY;
```

Now, create the corresponding replicat on Machine A.

```
GGSCI> ADD REPLICAT RFDLD002 EXTTRAIL /app/ggs/tiger/dirdat/f2
```

Configure the replicat parameter file on Machine A.

```
GGSCI> EDIT PARAMS RFDLD002

REPLICAT RFDLD002
ASSUMETARGETDEFS
USERID tiger, PASSWORD tiger123_
DISCARDFILE /app/ggs/tiger/dirrpt/rfdlD002.dsc, APPEND,
MAP TIGER.CNTRY, TARGET FOX.CNTRY;
```

Since your Oracle GoldenGate setups will be actively capturing transactions on both Machine A and Machine B, add trandata on both Machine A and Machine B.

Here's how to add supplemental logging on Machine A:

```
GGSCI> dblogin userid tiger password tiger123_
Successfully logged into database.

GGSCI> add trandata tiger.cntry cols (cntry,name,last_updated)
Logging of supplemental redo data enabled for table tiger.cntry.

GGSCI> info trandata tiger.cntry
Logging of supplemental redo log data is enabled for table tiger.cntry.
Columns supplementally logged for table tiger.cntry: CNTRY_ID,CNTRY_NAME,LAST_UPDATED.
```

Here's how to add supplemental logging on Machine B:

```
GGSCI> dblogin userid fox password fox123_
Successfully logged into database.

GGSCI> add trandata fox.cntry cols (cntry,name,last_updated)
Logging of supplemental redo data enabled for table fox.cntry.

GGSCI> info trandata fox.cntry
Logging of supplemental redo log data is enabled for table fox.cntry.
Columns supplementally logged for table fox.cntry: CNTRY_ID, CNTRY_NAME,LAST_UPDATED.
```

Adding Conflict Detection and Resolution

We discussed CDR earlier in this book. Here, I will show how to implement it for our bidirectional replication setup. Here's a list of key parameters you can use for identifying conflicts and resolving them in an active-active replication setup.

- TRANLOGOPTIONS EXCLUDEUSER: To have the extract process avoid capturing DML transactions applied by the replicat process to the database, you have to tell the extract to skip any transactions from a particular user. In our case, the extract on TIGER will exclude the FOX user, and vice versa.

- GETBEFORECOLS: With this parameter, you instruct your extract process to capture a before image and write it to the trail files. This before image is used on the target database for comparison and resolving conflicts.

- KEYINCLUDING: This parameter is followed by an explicit list of column names for the table. It instructs the extract process to capture a before image for the primary key on the table including the columns specified.

- COMPARECOLS and RESOLVECONFLICT: These CDR parameters will be used in the replicat process to compare and resolve conflicts.

CDR When Machine A is a Trusted Source and Always Wins

Let's consider that Machine A is a trusted source, and with any conflict between Machine A and Machine B the transaction on Machine A wins. Please note that we have RESOLVECONFLICT (UPDATEROWEXISTS, (DEFAULT, IGNORE)) in the replicat on Machine A. This means if there is a conflict on Machine A with the incoming data from Machine B, the data of Machine B is ignored. On the other hand, the replicat on Machine B has RESOLVECONFLICT (UPDATEROWEXISTS, (DEFAULT, OVERWRITE)). This means if there is any conflict in the data on Machine B with the incoming data from Machine A, the Machine A data overwrites the data on Machine B.

Here's the extract parameter configuration on Machine A:

```
EXTRACT ETTND001
USERID tiger, PASSWORD tiger123_
EXTTRAIL /app/ggs/tiger/dirdat/t1
TRANLOGOPTIONS EXCLUDEUSER fox
TABLE TIGER.CNTRY,
GETBEFORECOLS (
ON UPDATE KEYINCLUDING (CNTRY_NAME, LAST_UPDATED),
ON DELETE KEYINCLUDING (CNTRY_NAME, LAST_UPDATED));
```

Here's the replicat parameter configuration on Machine A:

```
REPLICAT RFDLD001
ASSUMETARGETDEFS
USERID tiger, PASSWORD tiger123_
DISCARDFILE /app/ggs/fox/dirrpt/rfdlD001.dsc, APPEND,
MAP FOX.CNTRY, TARGET TIGER.CNTRY,
COMPARECOLS (ON UPDATE ALL, ON DELETE ALL),
RESOLVECONFLICT (UPDATEROWEXISTS,
(DEFAULT, IGNORE));
```

Here's the extract parameter configuration on Machine B:

```
EXTRACT ETTND002
USERID fox, PASSWORD fox123_
EXTTRAIL /app/ggs/fox/dirdat/t2
TRANLOGOPTIONS EXCLUDEUSER tiger
TABLE FOX.CNTRY,
GETBEFORECOLS (
ON UPDATE KEYINCLUDING (CNTRY_NAME,LAST_UPDATED),
ON DELETE KEYINCLUDING (CNTRY_NAME,LAST_UPDATED));
```

Here's the replicat parameter configuration on Machine B:

```
REPLICAT RFDLD002
ASSUMETARGETDEFS
USERID fox, PASSWORD fox123_
DISCARDFILE /app/ggs/tiger/dirrpt/rfdlD002.dsc, APPEND,
MAP TIGER.CNTRY, TARGET FOX.CNTRY,
COMPARECOLS (ON UPDATE ALL, ON DELETE ALL),
RESOLVECONFLICT (UPDATEROWEXISTS,
(DEFAULT, OVERWRITE));
```

You can query conflict resolution statistics in GGSCI as shown here:

```
GGSCI> stats replicat RFDLD001 latest reportcdr
```

CDR When Both Sites Are Equally Trusted

In a bidirectional replication configuration where both Machine A and Machine B are equally trusted, you can identify and resolve conflicts at the table level on each side as shown in the following example.

Here's the extract parameter configuration on Machine A:

```
EXTRACT ETTND001
USERID tiger, PASSWORD tiger123_
EXTTRAIL /app/ggs/tiger/dirdat/t1
TRANLOGOPTIONS EXCLUDEUSER fox
TABLE TIGER.CNTRY,
GETBEFORECOLS (
ON UPDATE KEYINCLUDING (CNTRY_NAME, LAST_UPDATED),
ON DELETE KEYINCLUDING (CNTRY_NAME, LAST_UPDATED));
```

Here's the replicat parameter configuration on Machine A:

```
REPLICAT RFDLD001
ASSUMETARGETDEFS
USERID tiger, PASSWORD tiger123_
DISCARDFILE /app/ggs/fox/dirrpt/rfdlD001.dsc, APPEND,
MAP FOX.CNTRY, TARGET TIGER.CNTRY,
COMPARECOLS (ON UPDATE ALL, ON DELETE ALL),
RESOLVECONFLICT (UPDATEROWEXISTS, (DEFAULT, USEMIN (LAST_UPDATED))),
RESOLVECONFLICT (INSERTROWEXISTS, (DEFAULT, USEMAX (LAST_UPDATED))),
RESOLVECONFLICT (DELETEROWEXISTS, (DEFAULT, OVERWRITE)),
RESOLVECONFLICT (DELETEROWMISSING, (DEFAULT, DISCARD));
```

Here's the extract parameter configuration on Machine B:

```
EXTRACT ETTND002
USERID fox, PASSWORD fox123_
EXTTRAIL /app/ggs/fox/dirdat/t2
TRANLOGOPTIONS EXCLUDEUSER tiger
TABLE FOX.CNTRY,
GETBEFORECOLS (
ON UPDATE KEYINCLUDING (CNTRY_NAME,LAST_UPDATED),
ON DELETE KEYINCLUDING (CNTRY_NAME,LAST_UPDATED));
```

Here's the replicat parameter configuration on Machine B:

```
REPLICAT RFDLD002
ASSUMETARGETDEFS
USERID fox, PASSWORD fox123_
DISCARDFILE /app/ggs/tiger/dirrpt/rfdlD002.dsc, APPEND,
MAP TIGER.CNTRY, TARGET FOX.CNTRY,
COMPARECOLS (ON UPDATE ALL, ON DELETE ALL),
RESOLVECONFLICT (UPDATEROWEXISTS, (DEFAULT, USEMIN (LAST_UPDATED))),
RESOLVECONFLICT (INSERTROWEXISTS, (DEFAULT, USEMAX (LAST_UPDATED))),
RESOLVECONFLICT (DELETEROWEXISTS, (DEFAULT, OVERWRITE)),
RESOLVECONFLICT (DELETEROWMISSING, (DEFAULT, DISCARD));
```

DBFS Configuration for OGG Bidirectional Replication

DBFS is Oracle's native database file system introduced with Oracle 11g. Files such as medical images, pictures, documents, and so on, are stored in the database in the form of SecureFiles LOBs. File access operations such as open, read, write, create, and so on, are handled through PL/SQL procedures and packages.

To configure Oracle GoldenGate bidirectional replication when the source or target (or both) databases are Oracle databases using SecureFiles LOBs, you follow the steps covered in the next sections.

Step 1: Install the Patch for bug-9651229

Verify whether the Oracle DBFS patch for bug-9651229 is applied on the database. If not, please apply the patch before moving to the next step.

Step 2: Configure DBFS Sequences

DBFS uses internal sequences to construct unique names and IDs. To avoid conflicts with DBFS operations related to creating and altering the file systems, you must range partition the sequences.

```
select max(last_number) + 1 as CURRENT_MAXIMUM_VALUE from dba_sequences where sequence_owner
= 'SYS' and sequence_name = 'DBFS_SFS_$FSSEQ'
```

Considering that you have two systems named Machine A and Machine B, run the following procedure to partition the indexes on the two systems:

- Machine A:

```
dbms_dbfs_sfs_admin.partition_sequence(nodes => 2, myid => 0, newstart =>
CURRENT_MAXIMUM_VALUE);
commit;
```

- Machine B:

```
dbms_dbfs_sfs_admin.partition_sequence( nodes => 2, myid => 1, newstart =>
CURRENT_MAXIMUM_VALUE);
commit;
```

Step 3: Create the New DBFS File Systems for OGG Replication

You must now create the new DBFS file systems and use these new file systems for the Oracle GoldenGate replication. Both the file systems should be created on each machine participating in the replication.

```
dbms_dbfs_sfs.createfile system('MY_DBFS1');
dbms_dbfs_sfs.createfile system('MY_DBFS2');

dbms_dbfs_content.registerStore('MY_DBFS1','posix', 'DBMS_DBFS_SFS');
dbms_dbfs_content.registerStore('MY_DBFS2','posix', 'DBMS_DBFS_SFS');
```

Configure read-write access for the file systems. Make the local file system read-write and the remote file system read-only.

- Machine A:

```
dbms_dbfs_content.mountStore('MY_DBFS1', 'local');
dbms_dbfs_content.mountStore('MY_DBFS2', 'remote', read_only => true);
```

- Machine B:

```
dbms_dbfs_content.mountStore('MY_DBFS1', 'remote',read_only => true);
dbms_dbfs_content.mountStore('MY_DBFS2', 'local');
```

For each DBFS file system or mount store, a table and a ptable are created. Query these table names on both machines.

```
select fs.store_name, tb.table_name, tb.ptable_name
from table(dbms_dbfs_sfs.listTables) tb,
table(dbms_dbfs_sfs.listfile systems) fs
where    fs.schema_name = tb.schema_name
and fs.table_name = tb.table_name
and fs.store_name in ('MY_DBFS1', 'MY_DBFS2');
```

The results are shown here:

- Machine A:

```
STORE NAME      TABLE_NAME      PTABLE_NAME
-------------   -------------   -------------
MY_DBFS1        SFS$_FST_10     SFS$_FSTP_10
MY_DBFS2        SFS$_FST_14     SFS$_FSTP_14
```

- Machine B:

```
STORE NAME      TABLE_NAME      PTABLE_NAME
-------------   -------------   -------------
MY_DBFS1        SFS$_FST_11     SFS$_FSTP_11
MY_DBFS2        SFS$_FST_15     SFS$_FSTP_15
```

Step 4: Configure the Extract/Replicat Processes

Your DBFS configuration for Oracle GoldenGate bidirectional replication is complete. You can now set up your extract and replicat processes on Machine A and Machine B as follows:

- Here's the extract parameter configuration on Machine A:

```
EXTRACT ETTND001
USERID tiger, PASSWORD tiger123_
EXTTRAIL /app/ggs/tiger/dirdat/t1
TRANLOGOPTIONS EXCLUDEUSER fox
TABLE TIGER.SFS$_FST_10;
TABLE TIGER.SFS$_FSTP_10;
```

- Here's the replicat parameter configuration on Machine A:

```
REPLICAT RFDLD001
ASSUMETARGETDEFS
USERID tiger, PASSWORD tiger123_
DISCARDFILE /app/ggs/fox/dirrpt/rfdlD001.dsc, APPEND,
MAP FOX.SFS$_FST_15, TARGET TIGER.SFS$_FST_14;
MAP FOX.SFS$_FSTP_15, TARGET TIGER.SFS$_FSTP_14;
```

- Here's the extract parameter configuration on Machine B:

```
EXTRACT ETTND002
USERID fox, PASSWORD fox123_
```

```
EXTTRAIL /app/ggs/fox/dirdat/t2
TRANLOGOPTIONS EXCLUDEUSER tiger
TABLE FOX.SFS$_FST_15;
TABLE FOX.SFS$_FSTP_15;
```

- Here's the replicat parameter configuration on Machine B:

```
REPLICAT RFDLD002
ASSUMETARGETDEFS
USERID fox, PASSWORD fox123_
DISCARDFILE /app/ggs/tiger/dirrpt/rfdlD002.dsc, APPEND,
MAP TIGER.SFS$_FST_10, TARGET FOX.SFS$_FST_11;
MAP TIGER.SFS$_FSTP_10, TARGET FOX.SFS$_FSTP_11;
```

Summary

This chapter discussed how to implement Oracle GoldenGate for bidirectional replication configuration. We discussed key considerations before you begin setting up OGG for bidirectional replication. We also discussed in detail how to handle data loopback and implement conflict detection and resolution. You also saw how to set up DBFS for OGG bidirectional replication.

In the next two chapters, we will discuss the Oracle GoldenGate Management Pack for managing and monitoring OGG instances.

Managing Oracle GoldenGate

CHAPTER 13

∎∎∎

Oracle GoldenGate Management Pack Part I

In earlier chapters of this book, you learned how to set up and configure different replication solutions using Oracle GoldenGate. The job doesn't end there. Ensuring that the replication happens smoothly, while troubleshooting any issues, is an even more important task for a GoldenGate admin.

Oracle provides the GoldenGate Monitor as part of the Management Pack for Oracle GoldenGate. Besides the Oracle GoldenGate Monitor, the Management Pack includes the Oracle GoldenGate Director and the Oracle GoldenGate Enterprise Manager plug-in.

The OGG Management Pack will be discussed in two chapters of this book. This chapter discusses in detail the OGG Monitor and the Monitor Agent. You will learn how to configure the OGG Monitor and learn about its prerequisite software in this chapter. Chapter 14 discusses how to install the OGG plug-in for Oracle Enterprise Manager and how to configure the OGG Monitor Agent for the Oracle Enterprise Manager plug-in. It then discusses the Oracle GoldenGate Director, which allows you to remotely configure and manage OGG instances.

Specifically, in this chapter, we will discuss how to install, configure, and use the components of the Oracle GoldenGate Monitor.

Oracle GoldenGate Monitor

The Oracle GoldenGate Monitor provides you with a web interface for viewing OGG instances and the associated databases. It allows you to monitor OGG processes for any performance issues. It comes with built-in capabilities to send alerts for lags, abended channels, errors, and so on.

The OGG processes (namely, extract, replicat, and manager) are configured to send information to a Java agent called the Monitor Agent. The OGG Manager process communicates with the Monitor Agent and sends information to it. The Monitor Agent for each GoldenGate instance in turn communicates to the Monitor Server. The Monitor Server uses a set of GUIs to monitor the GoldenGate instances remotely. The Monitor Server has its own dedicated Monitor Server repository. You will learn how to configure it as well during installation.

Figure 13-1 shows the components of an Oracle GoldenGate Monitor configuration.

© Ravinder Gupta 2016
R. Gupta, *Mastering Oracle GoldenGate*, DOI 10.1007/978-1-4842-2301-7_13

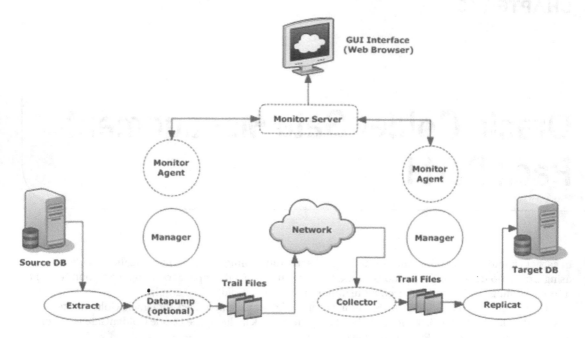

Figure 13-1. *Oracle GoldenGate Monitor configuration*

Installation Overview

We will discuss how to install OGG Monitor 12*c* (12.2.1) in this chapter. The OGG Monitor installation involves the following steps. We will discuss each of these one by one in the following sections.

1. Install Oracle WebLogic Server 12*c* with Java Required Files (JRF) or Java Database Connection (JDBC).

2. Install the Oracle GoldenGate Monitor server.

3. Create the OGG Monitor repository using the Repository Creation Utility (RCU).

4. Create the WebLogic Server domain using the Configuration Wizard.

5. Configure the OGG Monitor server.

6. Start the OGG Monitor server.

7. Install the Oracle GoldenGate Monitor Agent.

8. Create and configure the OGG Monitor Agent instances.

Install Oracle WebLogic Server

Before you can begin installing the Oracle GoldenGate Monitor server, it is important that you have Oracle WebLogic Server with JRF installed on your machine. This is required because the Oracle GoldenGate Monitor runs as a plug-in to Oracle WebLogic Server.

You can download Oracle WebLogic Server from `https://edelivery.oracle.com`. Search for *Oracle WebLogic Server 12.2.1*, select your operating system platform, and hit Download.

You need to unzip the compressed archive you downloaded and locate the JAR file. Execute the following command to launch the installer:

```
$ java -jar -Xmx1024m fmw_12.2.1.0.0_wls.jar
```

Let's take a quick look at installing Oracle WebLogic Server 12*c*. Figures 13-2 to 13-10 show the installation steps for Oracle WebLogic Server. Specifically, Figure 13-2 shows the Welcome screen.

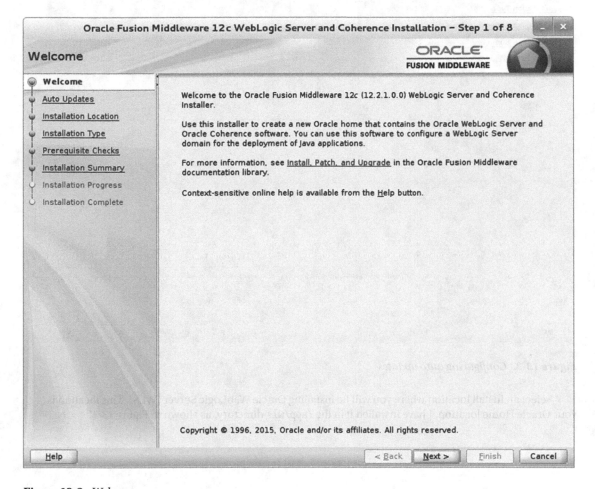

Figure 13-2. Welcome screen

Next, the installer asks you if you want to apply patch or updates, as shown in Figure 13-3. You can provide your Oracle Support ID or skip this step.

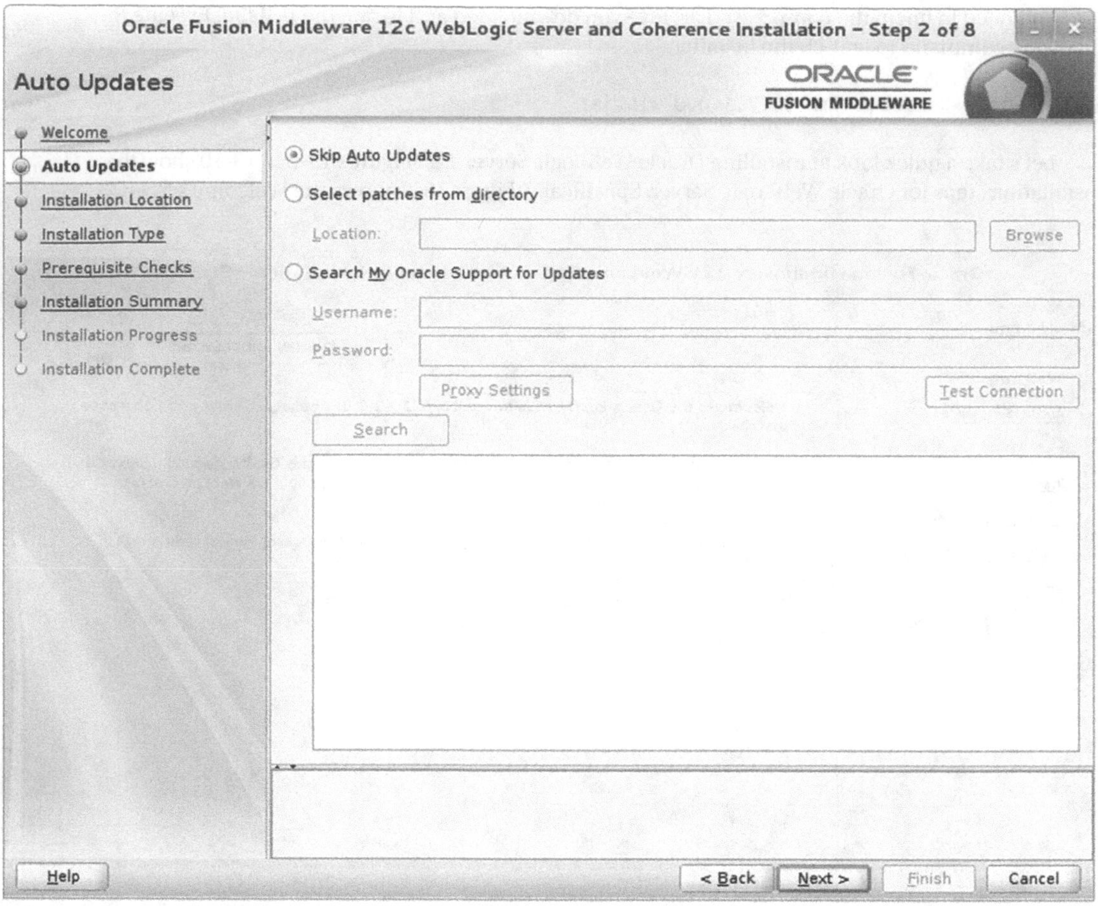

Figure 13-3. *Configuring auto updates*

Select an install location where you will be installing Oracle WebLogic Server (WLS). This location is your Oracle Home location. I have installed it in the /app/wls directory, as shown in Figure 13-4.

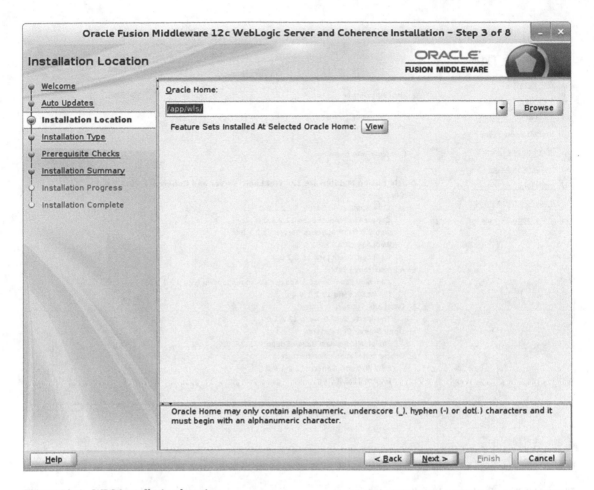

Figure 13-4. *WLS installation location*

Figure 13-5 shows the various installation types you can choose. Coherence is an in-memory data grid that comes with WLS. It distributes application objects and logic across multiple physical servers and thus avoids any single bottleneck or failure. For our setup, we will install only WebLogic Server.

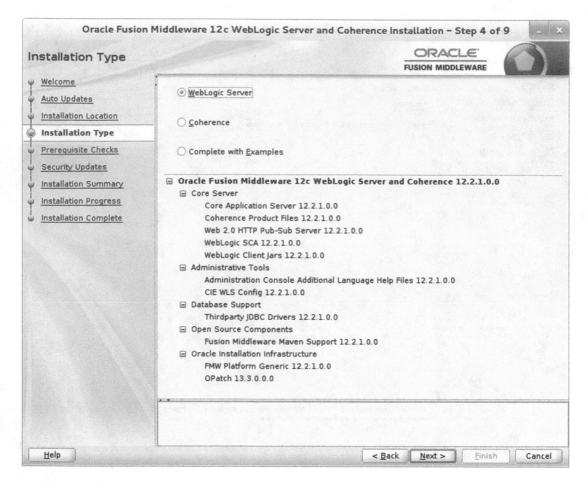

Figure 13-5. *Selecting an installation type*

Once you have selected your installation type and location, the installer performs some basic prerequisite checks such as for the OS certification and Java version. Figure 13-6 shows a successful prerequisites check. Click Next to continue.

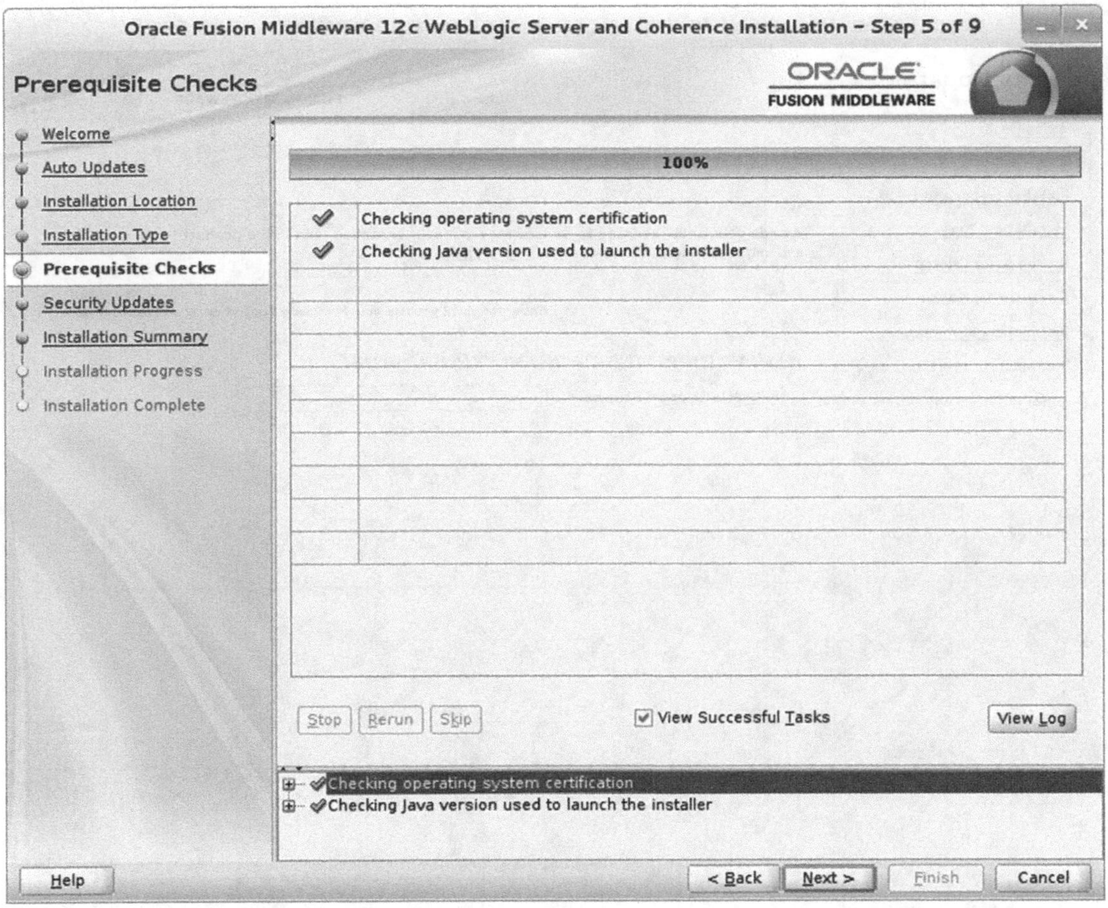

Figure 13-6. Checking for prerequisites

If you have an Oracle Support ID and want to receive security updates, you can provide your Oracle Support details in step 6, as shown in Figure 13-7. Since I am setting this up on a nonproduction environment for demonstration purposes only, I have chosen to skip this step by opting not to receive security updates.

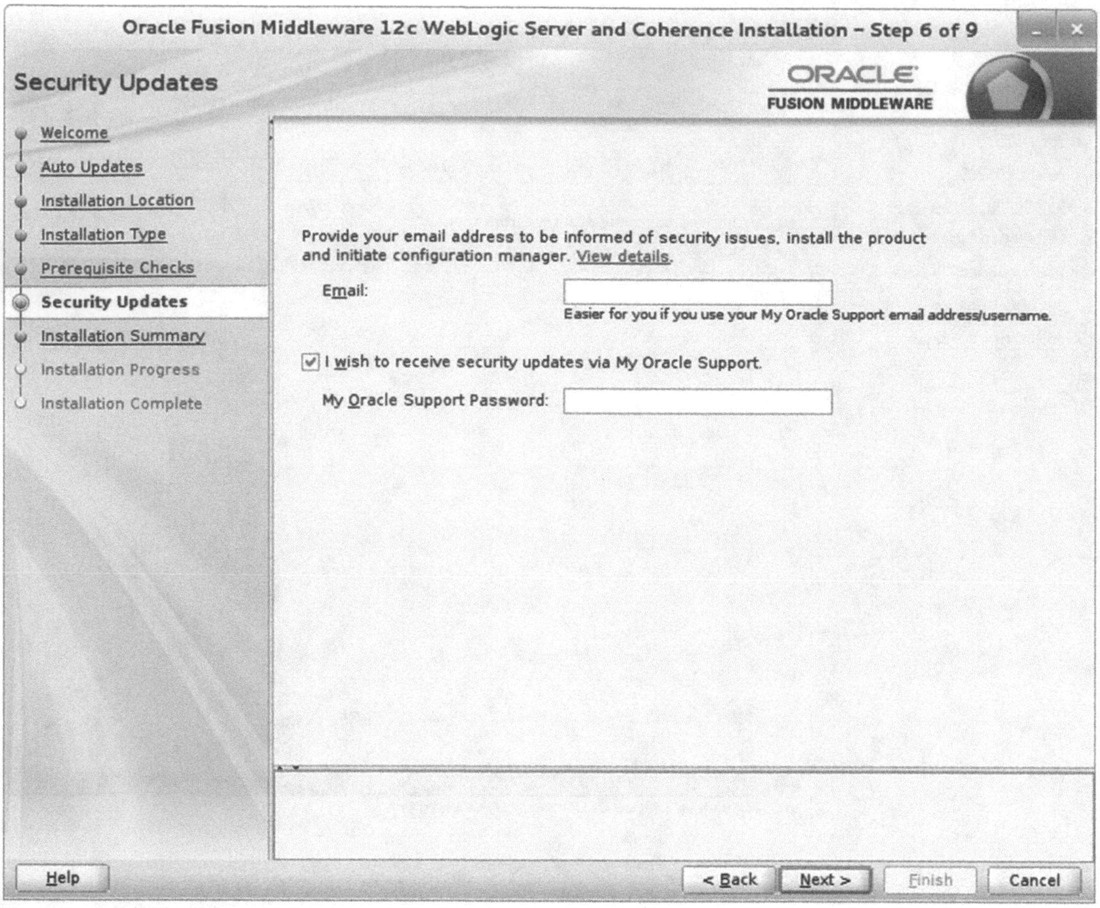

Figure 13-7. *Providing Oracle Support details if security updates are required*

Figure 13-8 shows an installation summary. Please review it before continuing to the next step. You can also choose to save your response file in case you want to reuse it for silent installations.

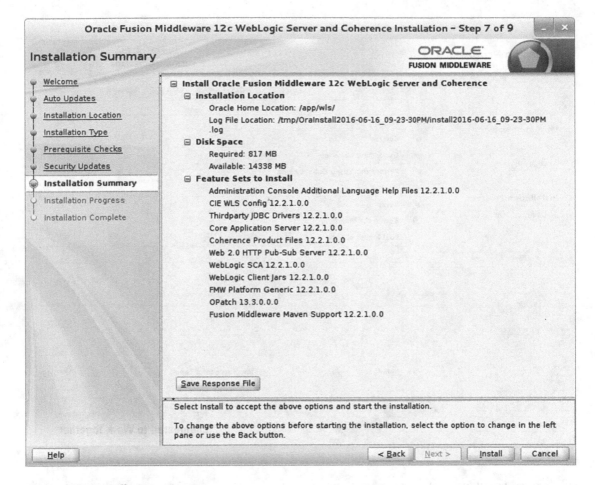

Figure 13-8. *Installation summary*

Figure 13-9 shows the installation tasks and their status. Wait until it finishes. This may take up to 15 minutes.

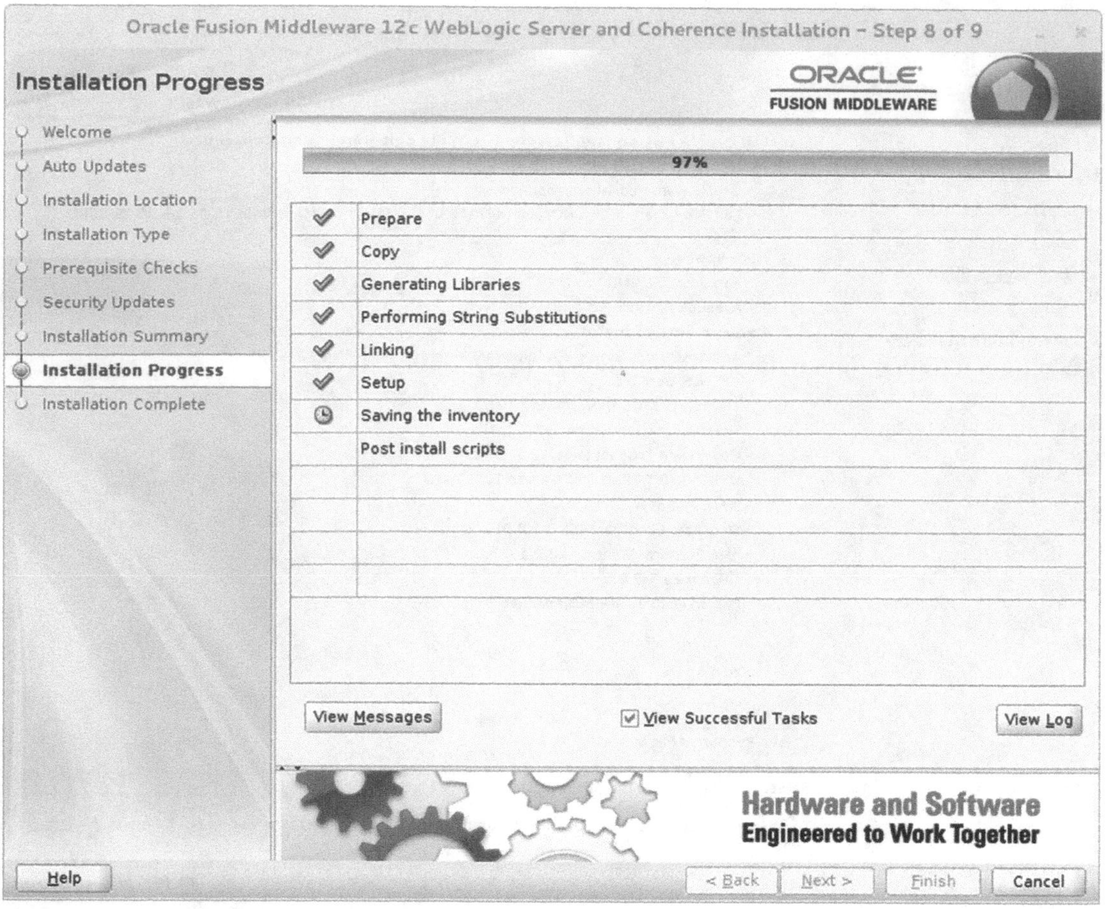

Figure 13-9. *Installation tasks and progress*

You have finished installing your Oracle WebLogic Server. You can choose to start the Configuration Wizard by selecting the relevant check box. The Configuration Wizard will help you set up the node manager and managed servers. You can perform this step once you have installed the Oracle GoldenGate Monitor and database repository. Figure 13-10 shows a successful installation of Oracle WebLogic Server 12*c*.

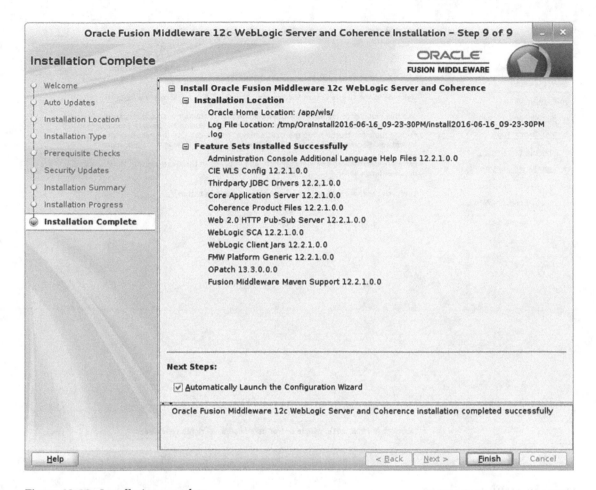

Figure 13-10. *Installation complete*

In addition to Oracle WebLogic Server 12*c*, I also installed Oracle Fusion Middleware (FMW) Infrastructure 12*c* in the same Oracle Home. This installs additional features such as WLS for FMW, which is required when you install Fusion Middleware products.

You can download Oracle FMW Infrastructure from https://edelivery.oracle.com. Search for *Oracle Fusion Middleware Infrastructure 12.2.1*, select your operating system platform, and hit Download.

You need to unzip the compressed archive you have downloaded and locate the JAR file. Execute the following command to launch the installer:

```
$ java -jar -Xmx1024m fmw_12.2.1.0.0_infrastructure.jar
```

Figures 13-11 to 13-18 show the steps to install Oracle Fusion Middleware Infrastructure 12*c*. Specifically, Figure 13-11 shows the Welcome screen for Oracle FMW Infrastructure. Click Next to continue.

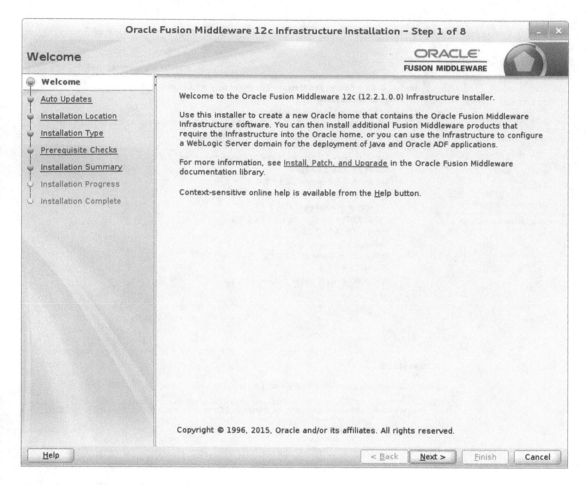

Figure 13-11. *Welcome screen*

Next, the installer asks you if you want to apply patches or updates, as shown in Figure 13-12. You can provide your Oracle Support ID or skip this step.

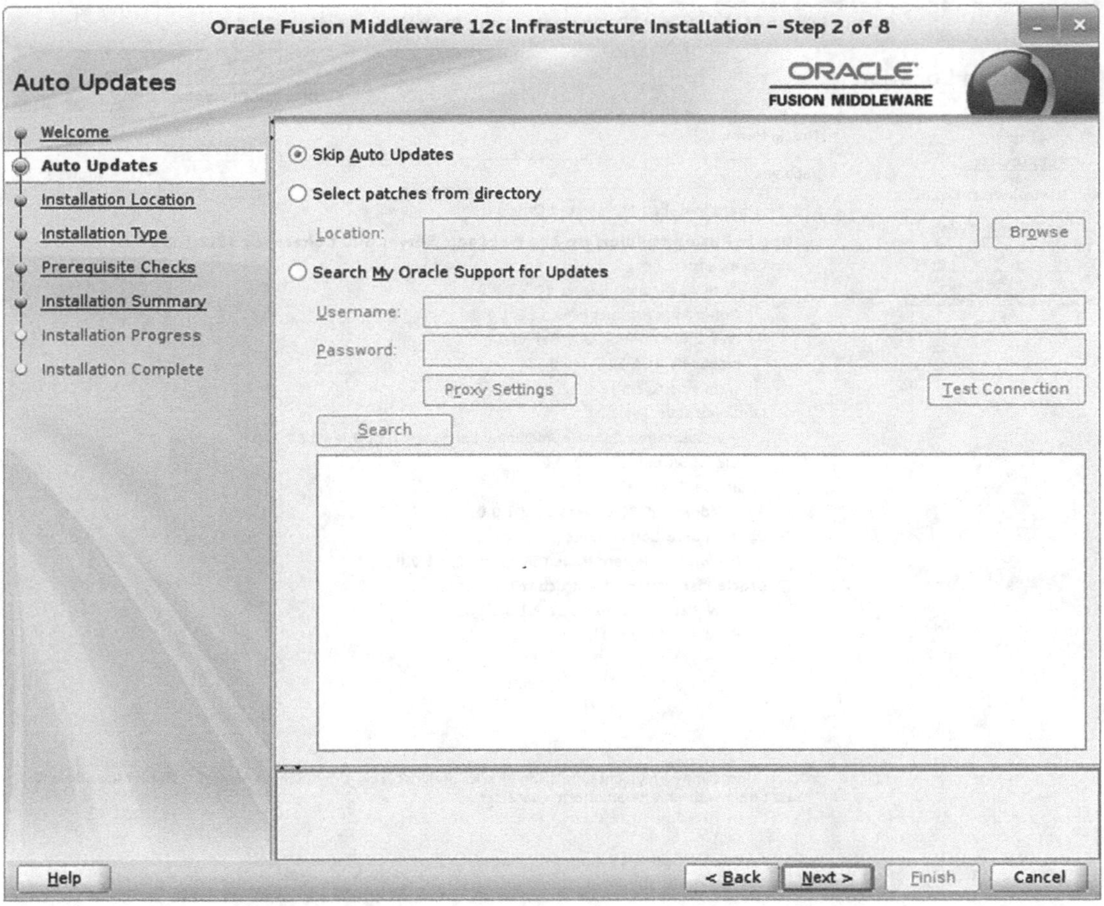

Figure 13-12. *Configuring auto updates*

Select the Oracle Home location where you have installed Oracle WebLogic Server 12*c*. Click the View button to see the feature sets installed in the Oracle Home, as shown in Figure 13-13. The Oracle FMW Infrastructure installation will install only the features not already available to your installed WLS version.

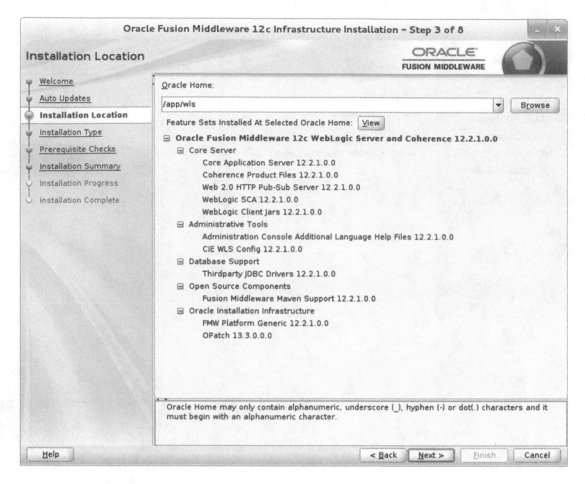

Figure 13-13. *Selecting the Oracle Home location*

Figure 13-14 shows the two installation types you have to choose from, installing FMW Infrastructure or installing FMW Infrastructure with Examples. Since you only need FMW Infrastructure to be able to install other Fusion Middleware products, we will skip installing the examples.

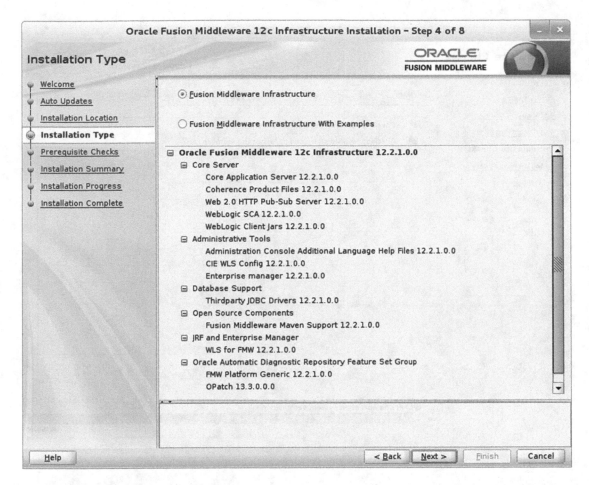

Figure 13-14. Selecting the installation type

Once you have selected your installation type and location, the installer performs some basic prerequisite checks such as the OS certification and Java version. Figure 13-15 shows a successful prerequisites check. Click Next to continue.

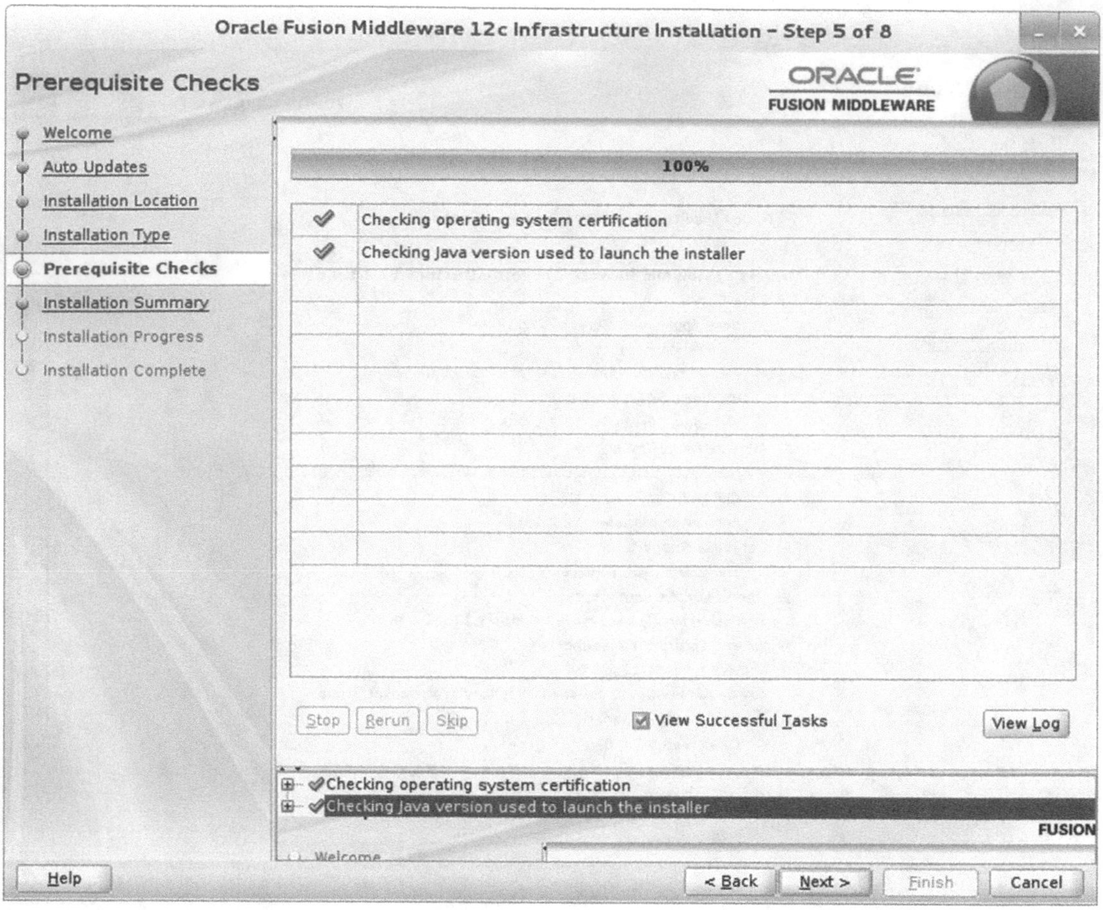

Figure 13-15. *Prerequisites check*

Figure 13-16 shows the installation summary for the features that will be installed. Please notice that only those features that are not installed in your Oracle Home will be installed. Review the summary and click Next.

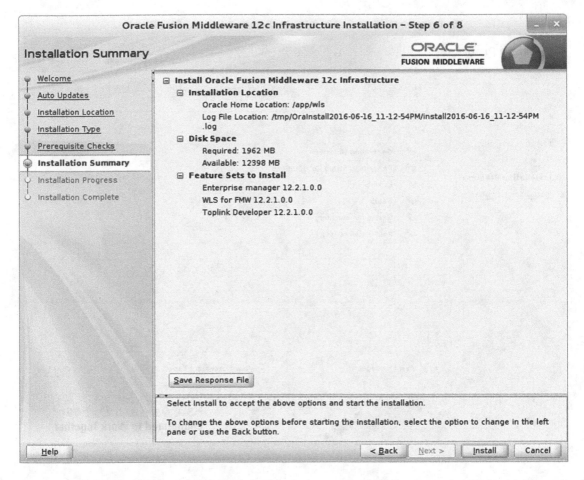

Figure 13-16. FMW Infrastructure installation summary

Figure 13-17 shows the installation tasks and their progress. Wait for all the tasks to complete. This may take up to 15 minutes. Click Next to continue.

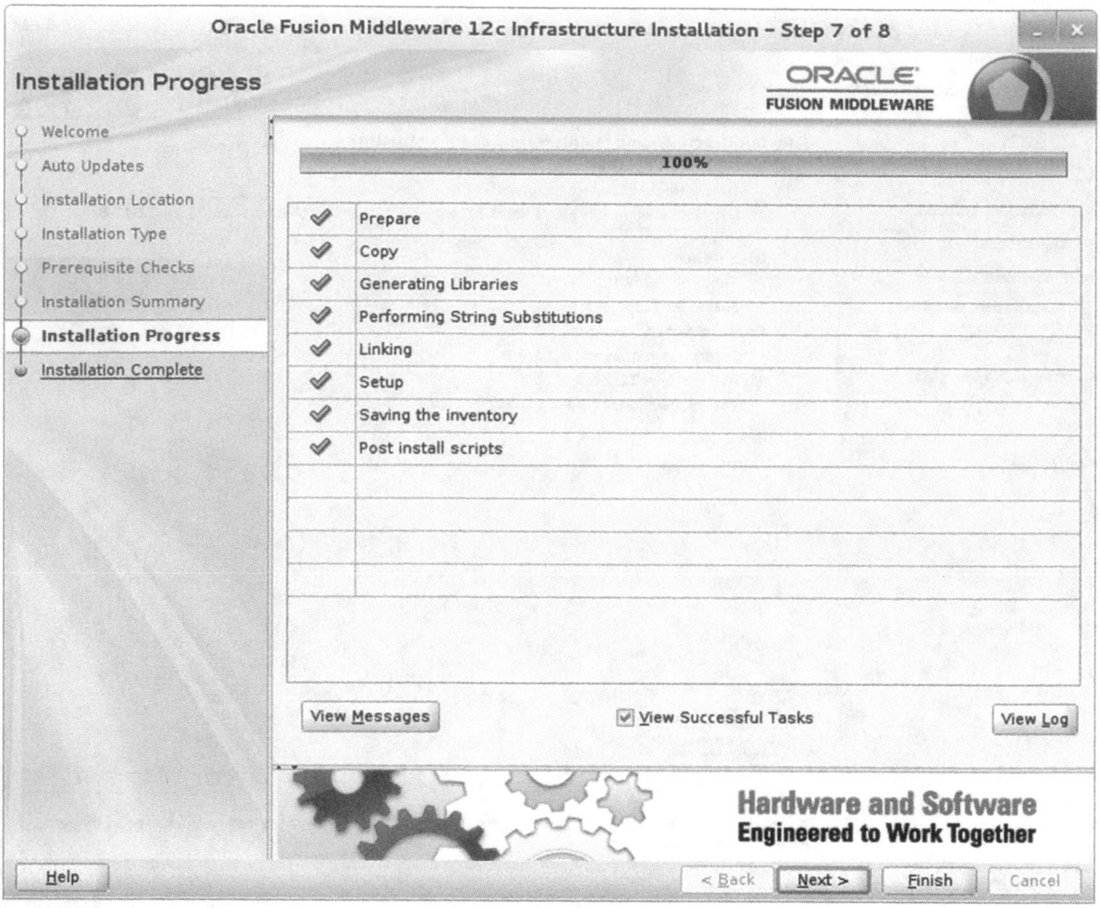

Figure 13-17. *FMW Infrastructure installation progress*

Figure 13-18 shows that the installation completed successfully. Review the installation details and click Finish.

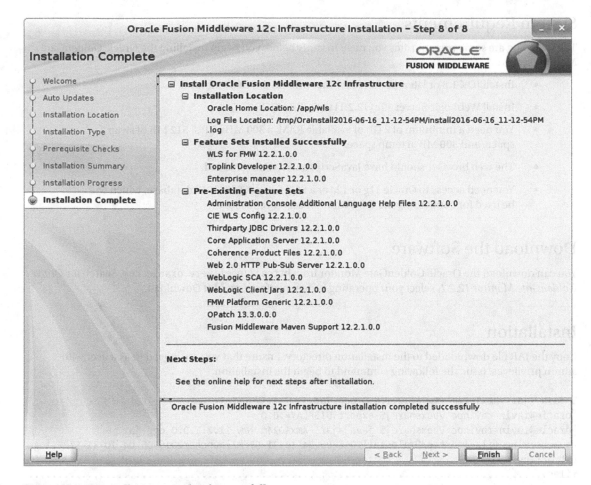

Figure 13-18. *Installation completed successfully*

Install the Oracle GoldenGate Monitor Server

We will now begin installing the Oracle GoldenGate Monitor server that runs as a plug-in to Oracle WebLogic Server. Please review that your system meets all the prerequisites as listed in the next section.

System Requirements

The following are some prerequisites you need to verify before you begin installing the Oracle GoldenGate Monitor server:

- Install JDK 1.8 or later on the server that will run the OGG Monitor.

- Install WebLogic Server 12*c* (12.2.1) with JRF or JDBC.

- You need a minimum of 2 GB of available RAM, a 300 MHz CPU, 512 MB of swap space, and 300 MB of temp space.

- The web browser should have JavaScript and cookies enabled.

- You need access to Oracle 11*g* or 12*c* or a SQL Server 2008/2012 database, which will be used for configuring the OGG Monitor server repository.

Download the Software

You can download the Oracle GoldenGate Monitor from https://edelivery.oracle.com. Search for *Oracle GoldenGate Monitor 12.2.1*, select your operating system platform, and hit Download.

Installation

Copy the JAR file downloaded to the installation directory. Ensure that you are logged in as a user with admin privileges. Issue the following command to begin the installation:

```
$ java -jar -Xmx1024m fmw_12.2.1.0.0_ogg.jar
[oracle@ravin-ravinpc vboxshare]$ export DISPLAY=:0.0
[oracle@ravin-ravinpc vboxshare]$ java -jar -Xmx1024m fmw_12.2.1.0.0_ogg.jar
Launcher log file is /tmp/OraInstall2016-06-04_10-31-57PM/launcher2016-06-04_10-31-57PM.log.
Extracting
files..........................................................................................
.................................................................................................
.................................................................................................
.................................................................................................
....................................
Starting Oracle Universal Installer

Checking if CPU speed is above 300 MHz.   Actual 2527.012 MHz     Passed
Checking monitor: must be configured to display at least 256 colors.   Actual
16777216     Passed
Checking swap space: must be greater than 512 MB.   Actual 2047 MB     Passed
Checking if this platform requires a 64-bit JVM.   Actual 64     Passed (64-bit not required)
Checking temp space: must be greater than 300 MB.   Actual 19343 MB     Passed

Preparing to launch the Oracle Universal Installer from /tmp/OraInstall2016-06-04_10-31-57PM
Log: /tmp/OraInstall2016-06-04_10-31-57PM/install2016-06-04_10-31-57PM.log
```

Figure 13-19 shows the Fusion Middleware 12*c* banner preparing to load the installer. Navigate through the installation screens and follow the steps.

Figure 13-19. *Fusion Middleware 12c installer prelaunch banner*

Fusion Middleware 12*c* is a single bundle of middleware products that helps you install the following products:

- Oracle GoldenGate Veridata Server
- Oracle GoldenGate Veridata Agent
- Oracle GoldenGate Veridata Server and Agent
- Oracle GoldenGate Monitor Server
- Oracle GoldenGate Monitor Agent
- Oracle GoldenGate Monitor Server and Agent
- Complete Install, which includes all of the previously listed products

Figure 13-20 shows the Welcome screen for Oracle Fusion Middleware 12*c*. Click Next to navigate to the next step.

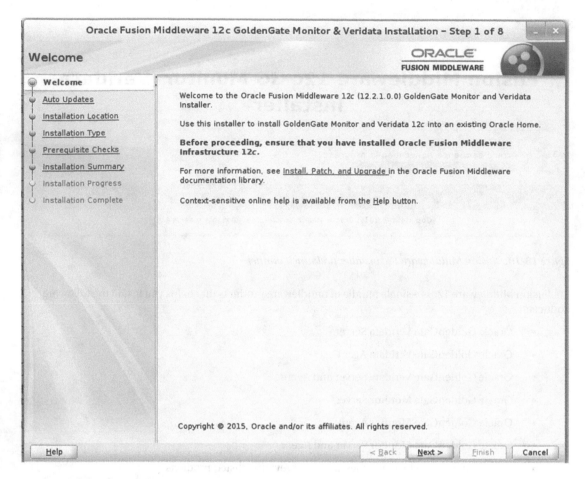

Figure 13-20. Oracle GoldenGate Monitor Welcome screen

The installer will prompt you to search and apply any patches or updates, as shown in Figure 13-21. You can also choose to skip this step.

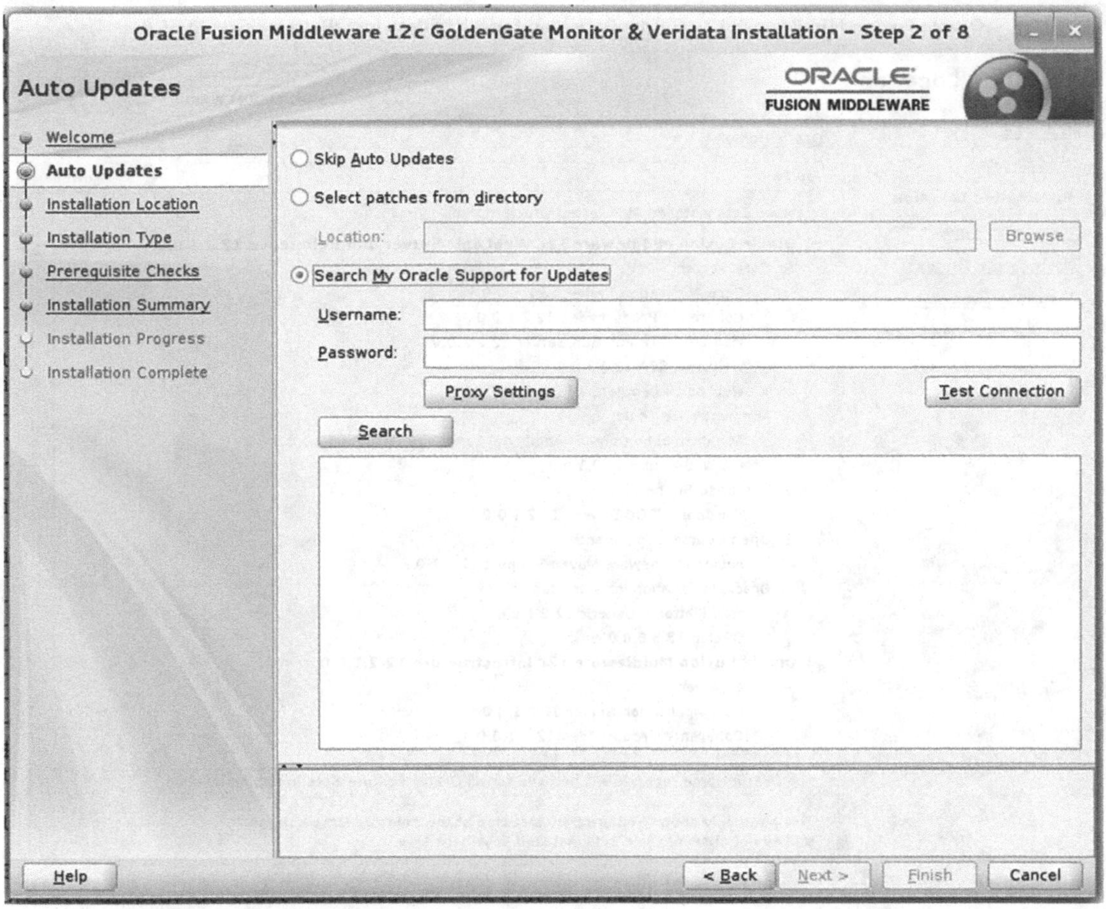

Figure 13-21. *Oracle GoldenGate Monitor applying updates*

Specify the Oracle Home directory location where you have dependent features for the Oracle GoldenGate Monitor installed, as shown in Figure 13-22. Select the directory where you have Oracle WebLogic 12*c* and JRF installed. If you have not installed Oracle WebLogic and JRF prior to this step, the installer will not proceed. The Oracle GoldenGate Monitor runs as a plug-in to Oracle WebLogic Server and hence needs it to be pre-installed to continue. Notice the error in Figure 13-23 when I selected an empty Oracle Home directory.

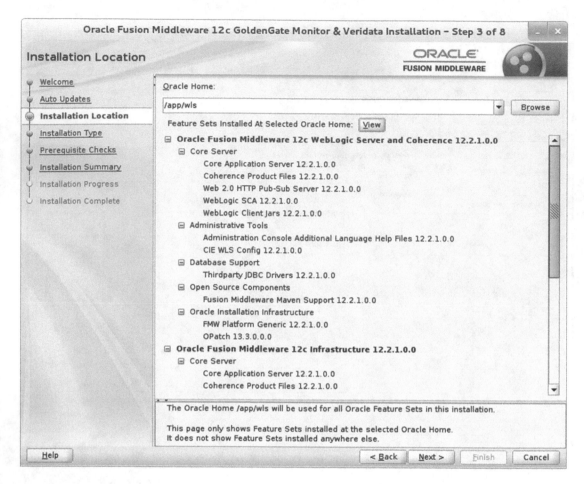

Figure 13-22. *Selecting the installation location*

Once you have WebLogic and JRF in place and have selected the correct Oracle Home directory, select Oracle GoldenGate Monitor Server as the type of installation in step 4, as shown in Figure 13-23. You will use the same installation program later to install the Oracle GoldenGate Monitor Agent.

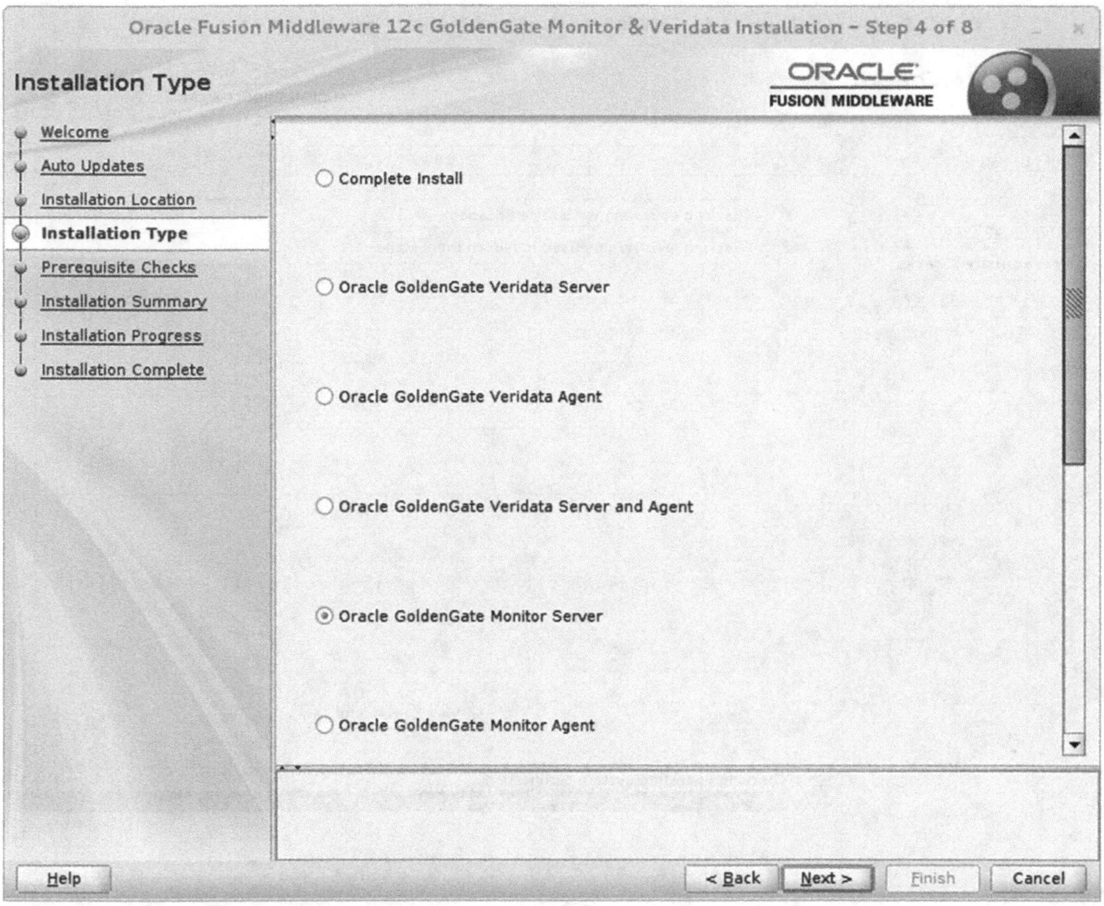

Figure 13-23. *Selecting the installation component name*

Once you have selected the desired product to install, click Next. The wizard will begin checking for certain prerequisites including the Java version and OS platform. Click Next to continue once the prerequisite checks are complete and have passed, as shown in Figure 13-24.

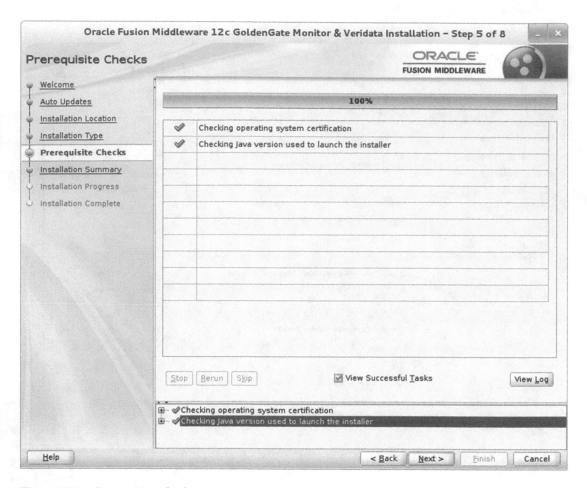

Figure 13-24. *Prerequisites check*

Figure 13-25 shows the installation summary screen. It lists the features you have selected for installation along with disk space consumption. You can also select to save the response file to save the installation configuration. You can then reuse this response file for silent installations on other servers if required.

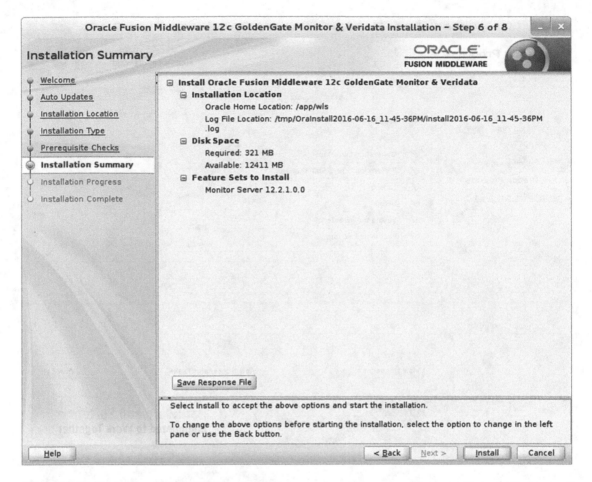

Figure 13-25. *Reviewing the installation summary*

Review the installation summary and click Install to begin the installation.

Figure 13-26 shows the installation stages in progress. You can view the installation messages for the current step by clicking View Messages. You can also view the installer log by clicking the View Log button.

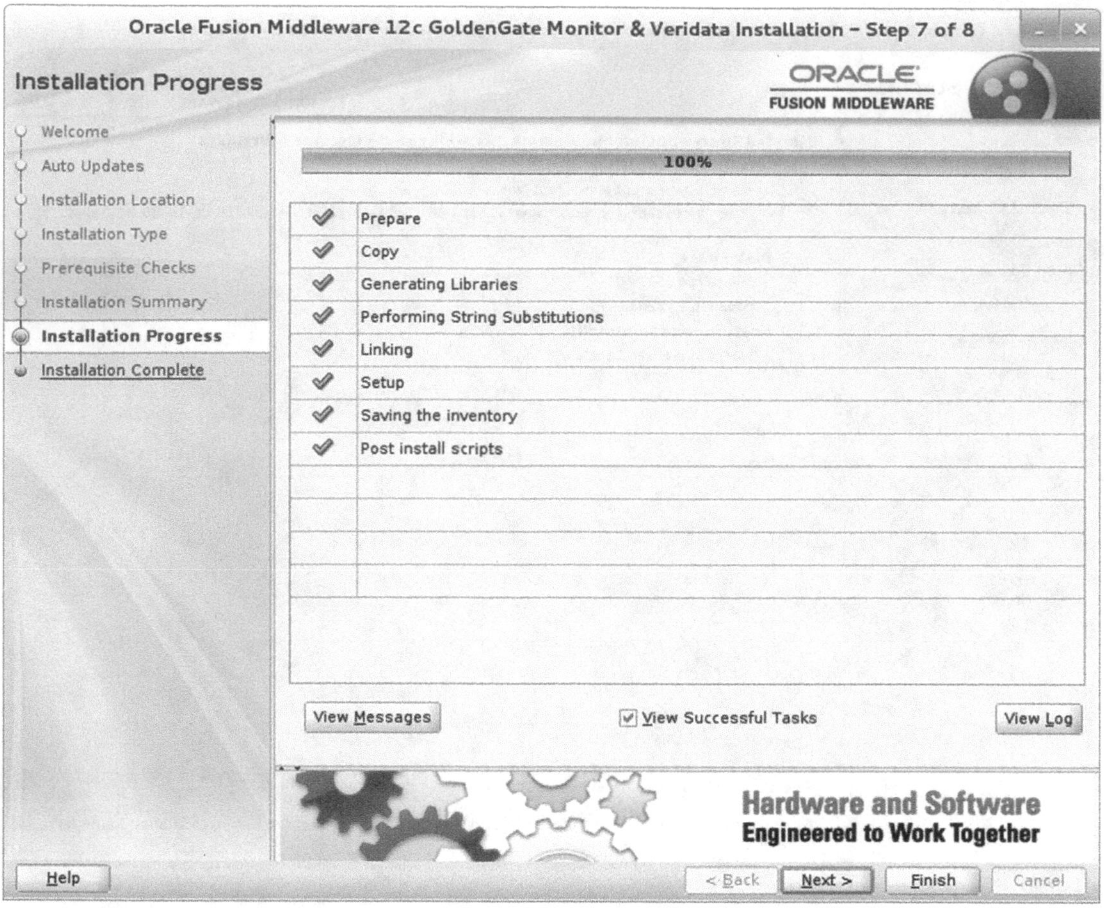

Figure 13-26. *Installing components*

Figure 13-27 shows that installation has successfully completed. Congrats for the achievement!

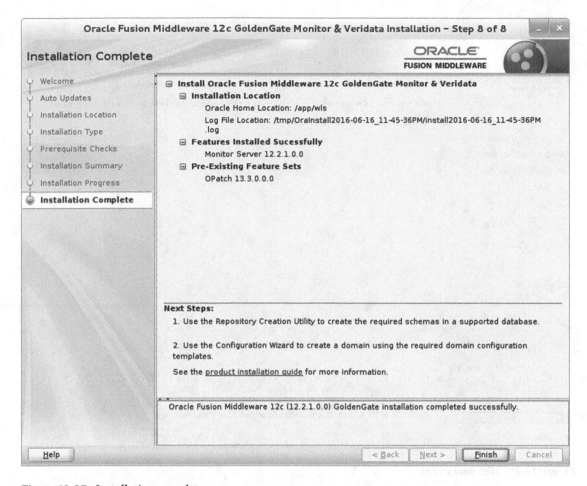

Figure 13-27. Installation complete

Create the OGG Monitor Repository Using RCU

Now that you have achieved your first checkpoint of installing the Oracle GoldenGate Monitor server, you are ready to install the OGG Monitor repository. Navigate to the Oracle Home to locate the RCU. It is located in your ORACLE_HOME/oracle_common/bin/ directory. Launch RCU as shown here:

```
$./rcu
```

If you are using a Windows machine, run rcu.bat from the command prompt.

```
rcu.bat
```

Navigate through the installation screens and create the repository. Figure 13-28 shows the Welcome screen of Repository Creation Utility 12.2.1 for Oracle Fusion Middleware. Click Next to continue.

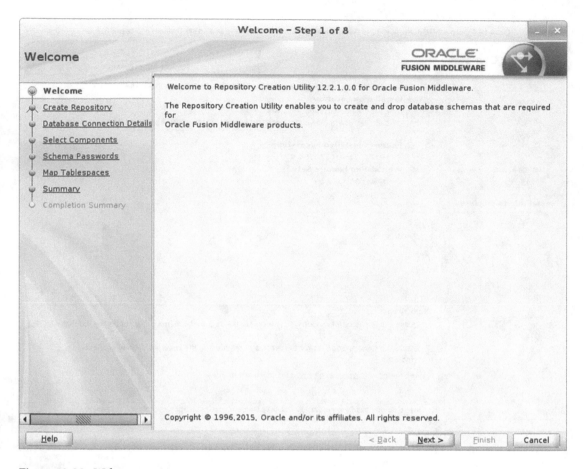

Figure 13-28. *Welcome screen*

Since you are creating a new repository for the Oracle GoldenGate Monitor server, select Create Repository and under it select System Load and Product Load, as shown in Figure 13-29. Make sure you have DBA privileges to create the repository.

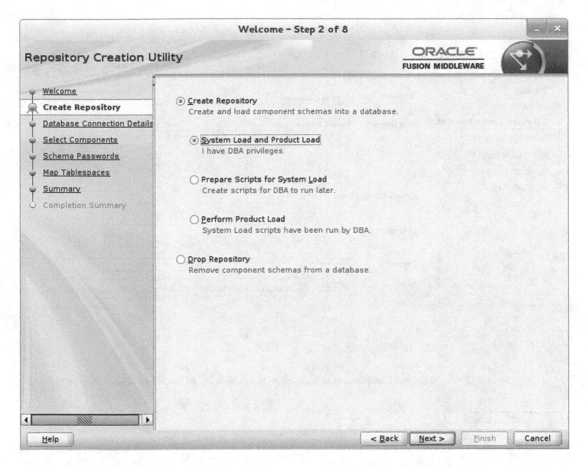

Figure 13-29. Creating a repository

Provide the connection details of the database you are connecting to in order to create the repository. Make sure the user has the SYSDBA role. Figure 13-30 shows the connection details I used for connecting to the orcl database on node1.ravin-pc.com.

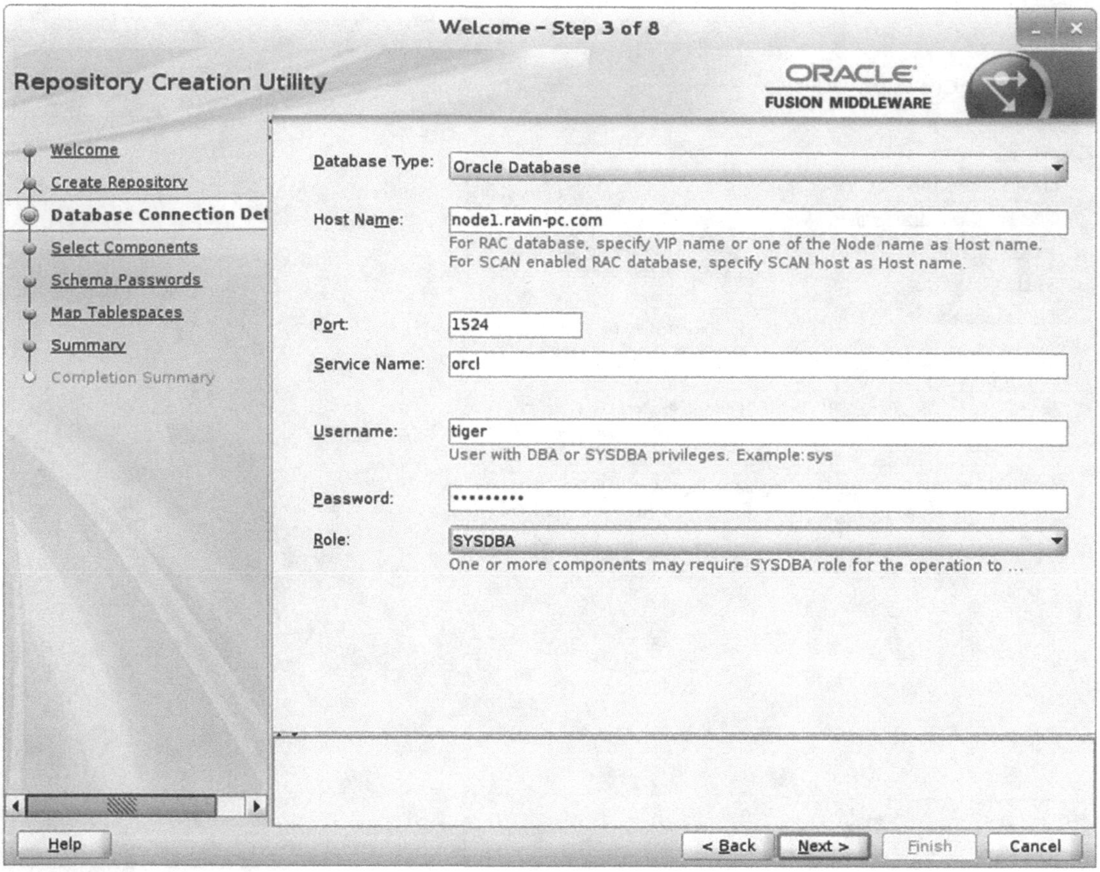

Figure 13-30. *Database connection details*

Figure 13-31 shows the prerequisites check for the database you specified for repository creation.

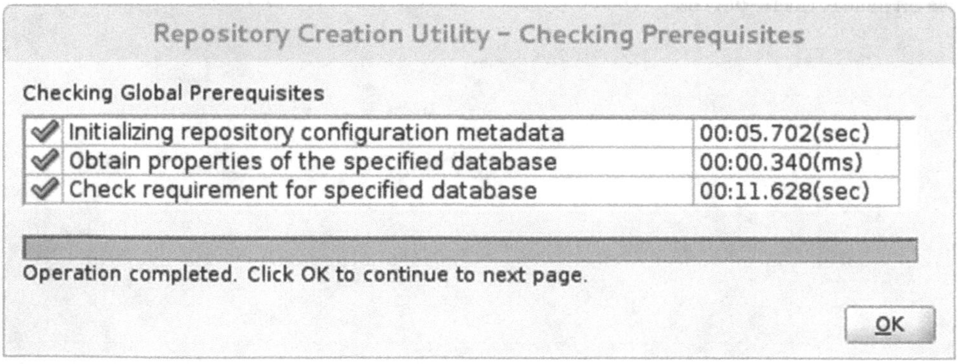

Figure 13-31. *Repository database prerequisites check*

Next, you are asked to select the components to be installed. You must also select a prefix to generate unique names for various schemas that get created with the repository. Figure 13-32 shows the repository components I selected and the prefix TST1 for schema names.

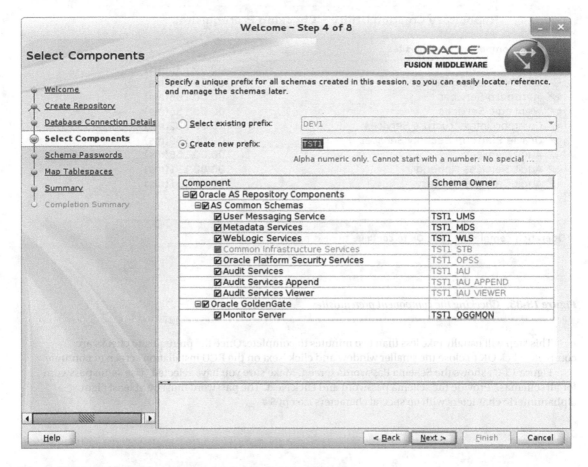

Figure 13-32. *Selecting the repository components to install*

Note that the prefix (TST1) will automatically be appended with _STB and will be used when configuring the WLS domain. In addition to TST1_STB, the installer will create a few more schemas based on the components you have selected.

- TST1_OGGMON

- TST1_UMS

- TST1_MDS

- TST1_STB

- TST1_OPSS

- TST1_IAU

- TST1_IAU_APPEND

- TST1_IAU_VIEWER

Once you select the repository components and click Next, the installer will pop up a window indicating the prerequisite checks for the selected repository components, as shown in Figure 13-33.

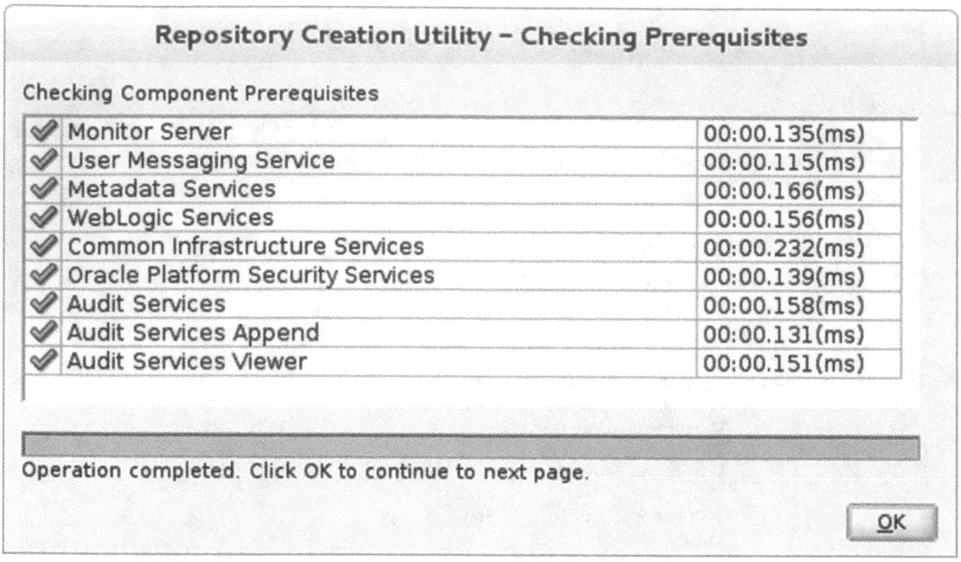

Repository Creation Utility – Checking Prerequisites

Checking Component Prerequisites

✅ Monitor Server	00:00.135(ms)
✅ User Messaging Service	00:00.115(ms)
✅ Metadata Services	00:00.166(ms)
✅ WebLogic Services	00:00.156(ms)
✅ Common Infrastructure Services	00:00.232(ms)
✅ Oracle Platform Security Services	00:00.139(ms)
✅ Audit Services	00:00.158(ms)
✅ Audit Services Append	00:00.131(ms)
✅ Audit Services Viewer	00:00.151(ms)

Operation completed. Click OK to continue to next page.

OK

Figure 13-33. *Checking the component prerequisites*

This step will usually take less than two minutes to complete. Once the prerequisite checks are complete, click OK to close the smaller window and click Next on the RCU installation screen to continue.

Figure 13-34 shows the Schema Passwords screen. Make sure you have selected "Use same password for all schemas." Provide the schema password and click Next. The password must be at least eight alphanumeric characters with no special characters except $ # . _.

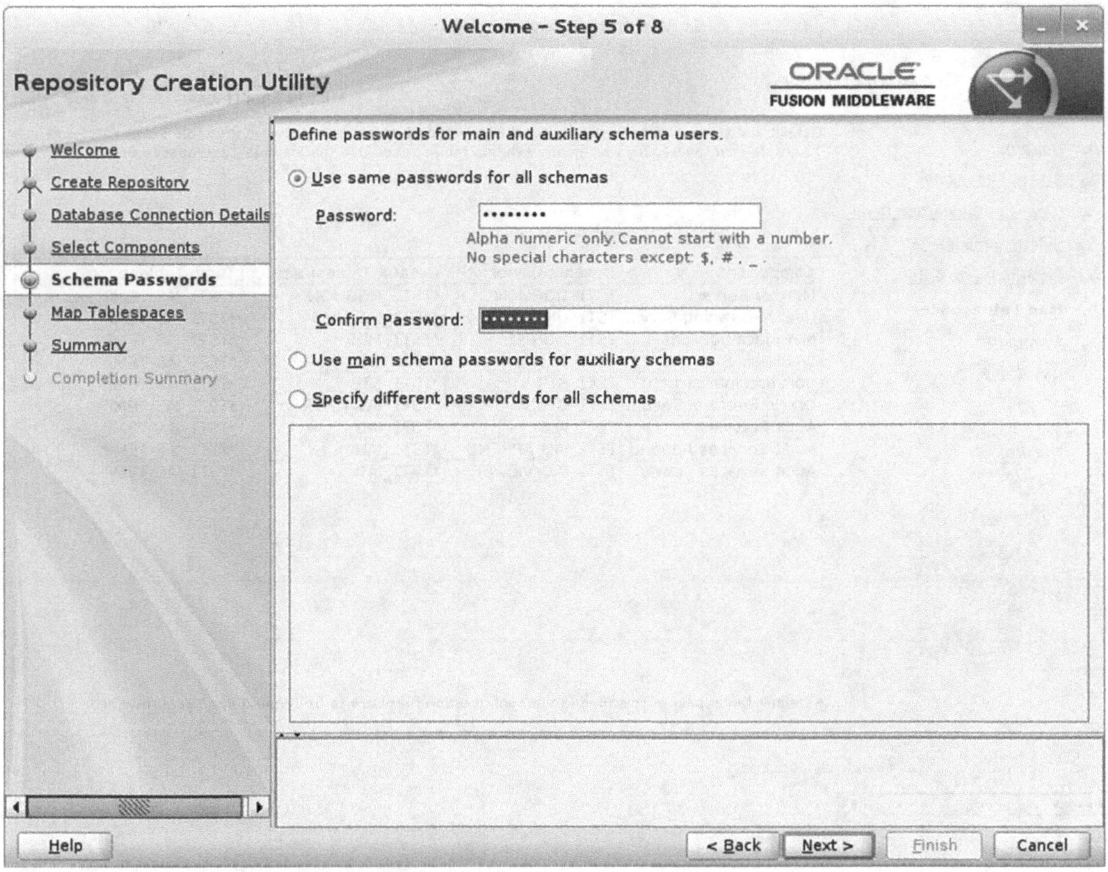

Figure 13-34. *Providing the schema passwords*

The next step shows the Map Tablespaces page. The default and temporary tablespaces for all the components you selected in step 4 are displayed in a table, as shown in Figure 13-35. You can create new tablespaces or modify existing tablespaces by clicking the Manage Tablespaces button.

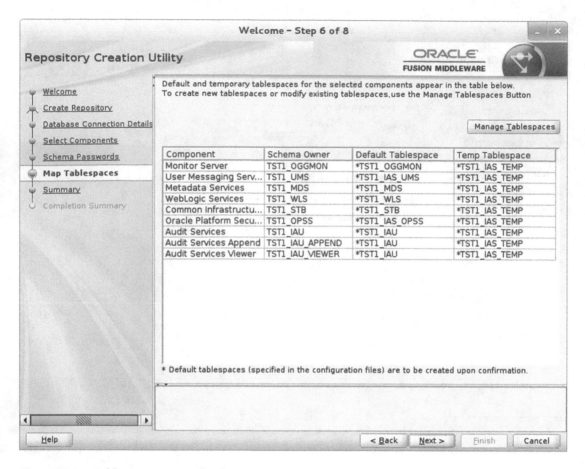

Figure 13-35. *Tablespace mapping for the repository database*

Figure 13-36 shows the Manage Tablespaces window that opens when I click the Manage Tablespaces button in step 6. I will not perform any changes and will use only the default tablespaces for our example.

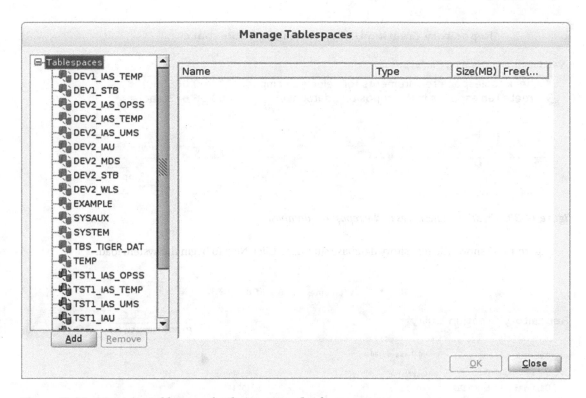

Figure 13-36. *Managing tablespaces for the repository database*

A small dialog box appears, as shown in Figure 13-37, to confirm the creation of the tablespace before moving to the next step.

Figure 13-37. *Confirming the tablespace creation*

Figure 13-38 shows the creation of the tablespace in progress in the repository database. This usually takes a couple of minutes to complete.

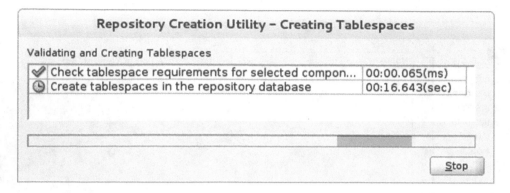

Figure 13-38. *Creating tablespaces in the repository database*

Figure 13-39 shows the repository database summary. Click Next to begin the system load.

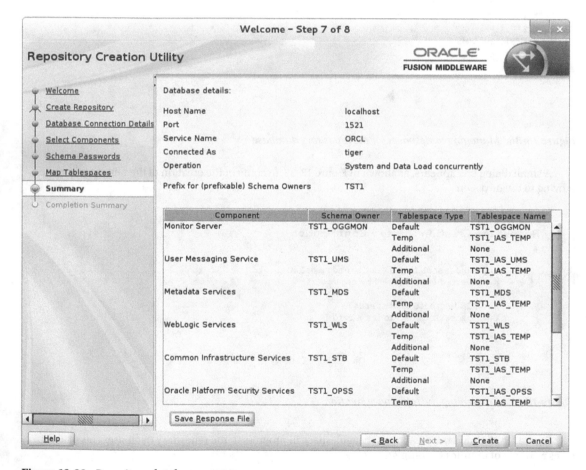

Figure 13-39. *Repository database summary*

Figure 13-40 shows the progress of the repository system load. This step may take up to 15 minutes unless you are using a supercomputer.

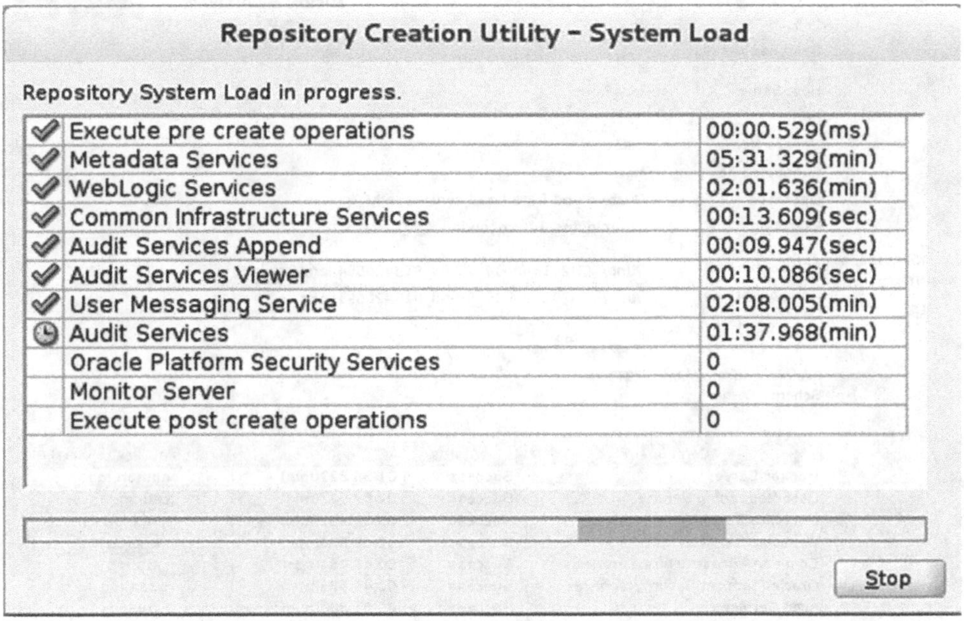

Repository Creation Utility – System Load	
Repository System Load in progress.	
✔ Execute pre create operations	00:00.529(ms)
✔ Metadata Services	05:31.329(min)
✔ WebLogic Services	02:01.636(min)
✔ Common Infrastructure Services	00:13.609(sec)
✔ Audit Services Append	00:09.947(sec)
✔ Audit Services Viewer	00:10.086(sec)
✔ User Messaging Service	02:08.005(min)
🕓 Audit Services	01:37.968(min)
Oracle Platform Security Services	0
Monitor Server	0
Execute post create operations	0
	Stop

Figure 13-40. *System load progress for the repository*

The system load and product load are the final steps of your repository creation. I chose to perform both the system load and the product load. The installer runs them concurrently, and the installation logs are available to you for review, as shown in Figure 13-41.

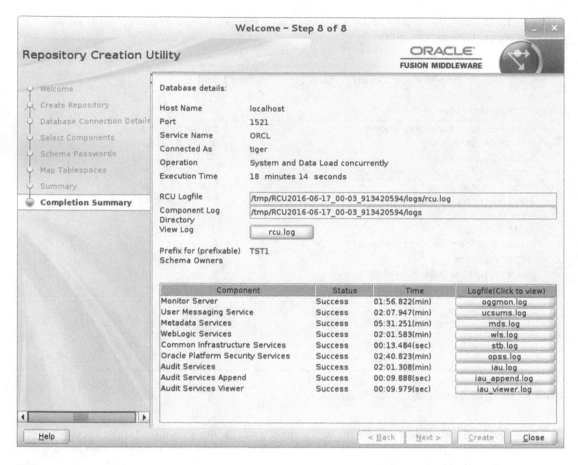

Figure 13-41. *Completion summary*

Create the WebLogic Server Domain Using the Configuration Wizard

Install Oracle WebLogic Server if it's not already installed. Navigate to ORACLE_HOME/oracle_common/common/bin/ and locate config.sh or config.cmd (when installing on Windows).

Launch the Configuration Wizard, as follows:

```
$ ./config.sh
```

Or as follows:

```
config.cmd
```

Figure 13-42 shows the Oracle WebLogic Server Configuration Wizard banner, the first screen that launches when you execute config.sh.

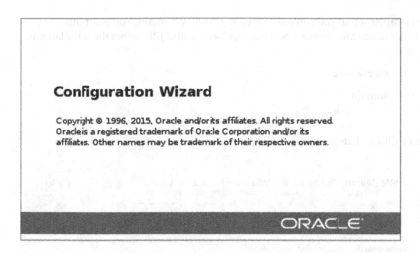

Figure 13-42. WLS Configuration Wizard

We will be creating a new domain. Select "Create a new domain," as shown in Figure 13-43.

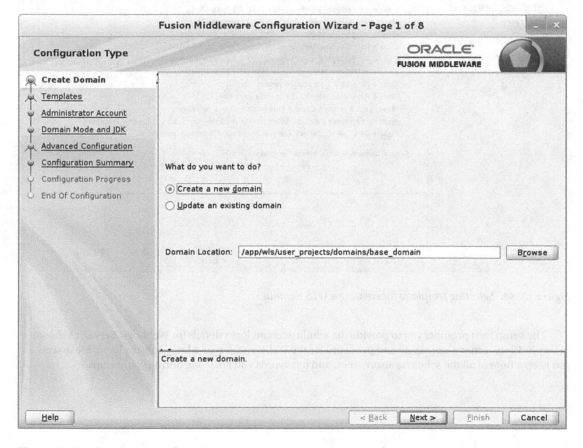

Figure 13-43. Creating a new domain

Figure 13-44 shows a list of templates that you can use to create your new domain. You want this domain to support the Oracle GoldenGate Monitor server, WebLogic Server, and JRF. Select the templates as listed here:

- Oracle GoldenGate Monitor Server

- Basic WebLogic Server Domain

- Oracle JRF

- WebLogic Coherence Cluster Extension

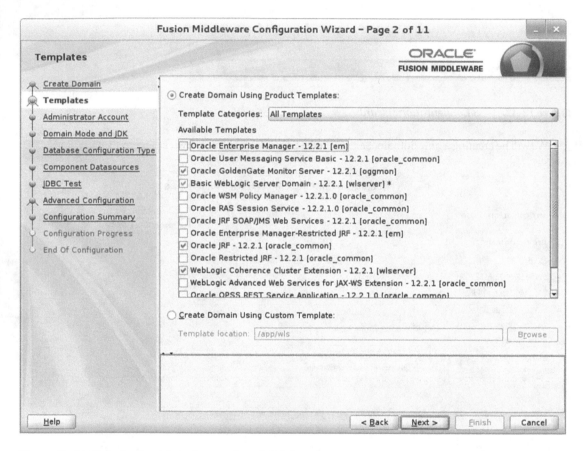

Figure 13-44. *Selecting templates for creating a WLS domain*

The setup next prompts you to provide the admin account login details for WebLogic Server, as shown in Figure 13-45. Enter a username and password for the WebLogic Server admin console login. Make sure you keep a note of all the schemas, usernames, and passwords you are using during your setups.

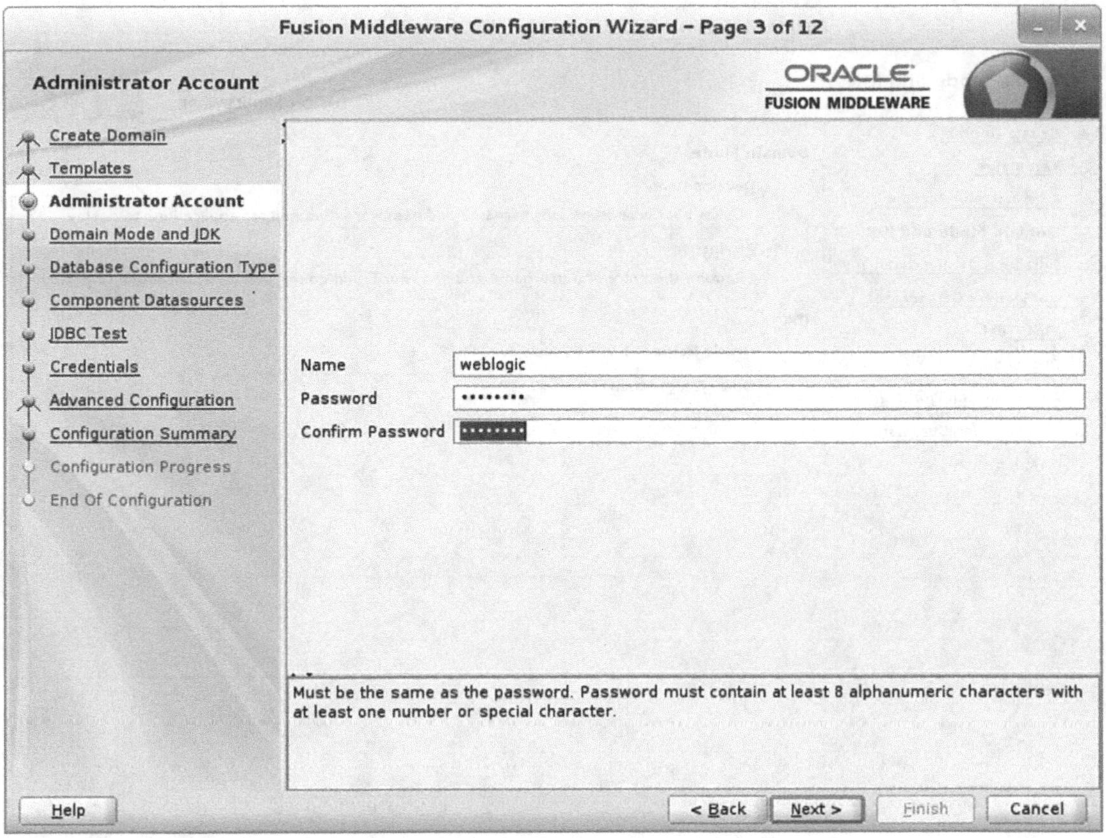

Figure 13-45. *Providing a username and password for the WLS admin account*

Select Domain Mode and JDK, as shown in Figure 13-46.

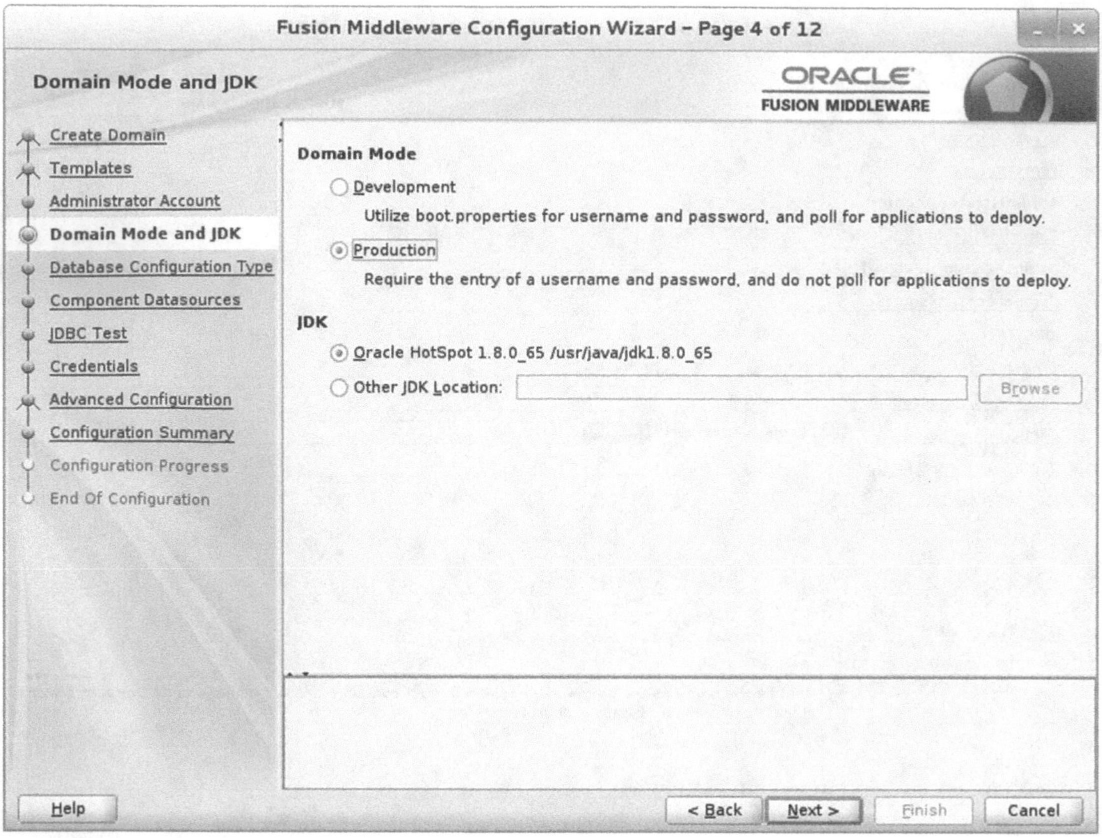

Figure 13-46. Selecting a domain mode and JDK

Development mode is usually needed when your applications are still developing. The security is relatively relaxed in this mode. Development mode also allows you to auto-deploy any changes in your application.

Production mode, on the other hand, is best suited when you have a running application. We will choose production mode in this demonstration.

The Configuration Wizard offers you two ways to select and configure information for schemas used in your WebLogic domain.

If you select RCU Data, it will allow you to connect to the database to automatically retrieve schema information for all the templates you selected in Figure 13-44. Fill in the details for your repository database that you set up in the previous section in this chapter. Click the Get RCU Configuration button to retrieve the schema information.

Figure 13-47 shows the connection result log for the RCU data.

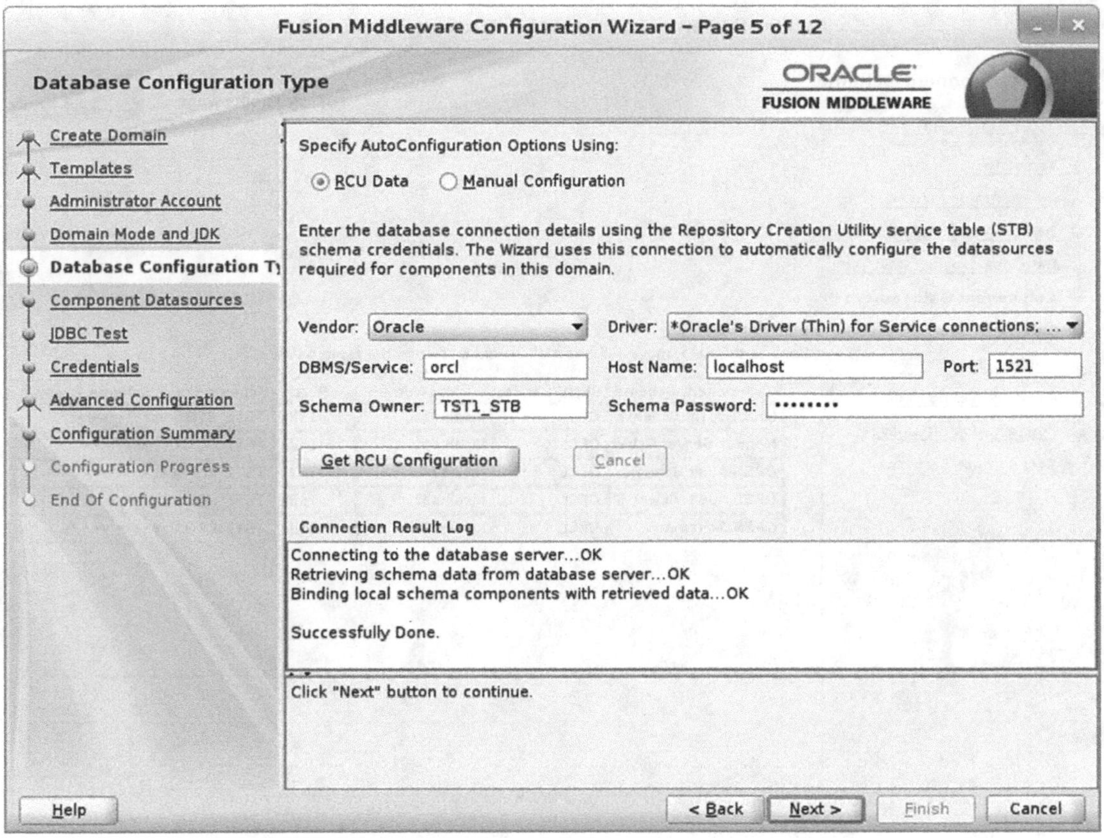

Figure 13-47. Providing the database type and details

Figure 13-48 shows the JDBC component schema details. These schemas were created when installing components using RCU. Click Next to continue.

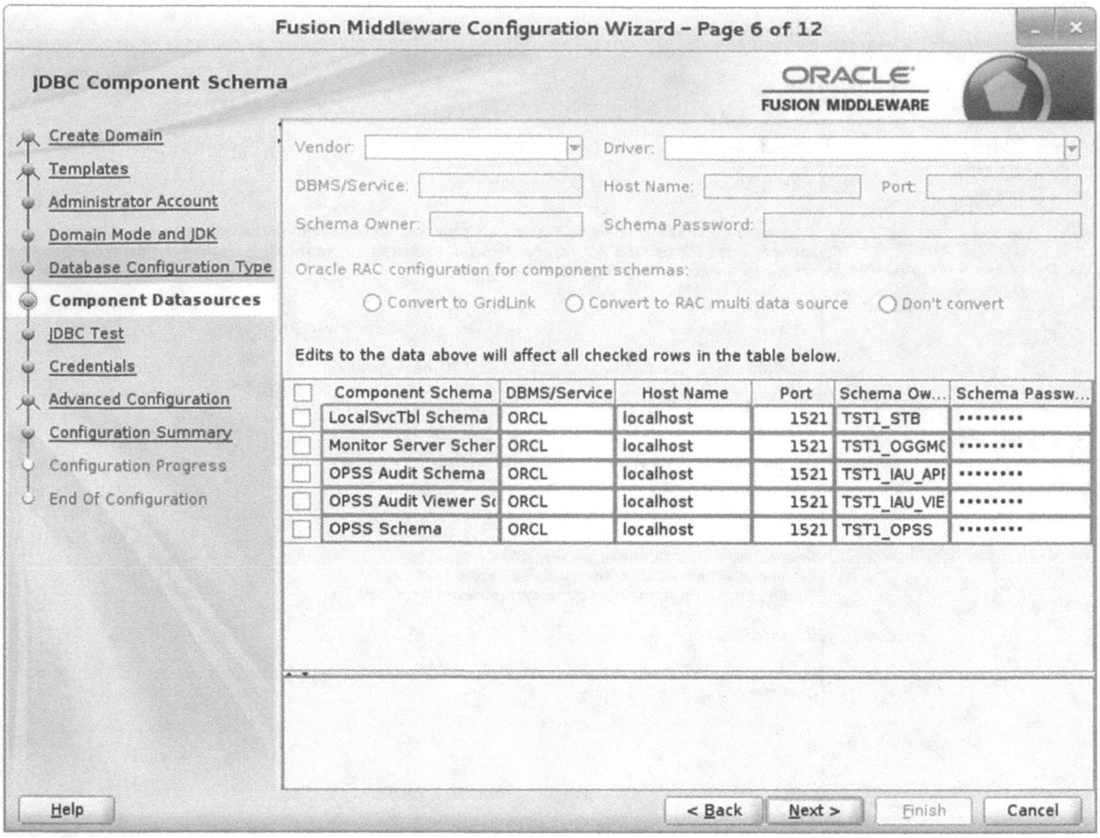

Figure 13-48. *Entering a password for component data sources*

In this step, you can test the data source configurations for the data sources in the previous screen. Select the check boxes for which you want to test the configuration and click Test Selected Connections. The Configuration Wizard tests connections for each component schema, and the result is displayed in the Status column. Details of the connection results are displayed as shown in Figure 13-49.

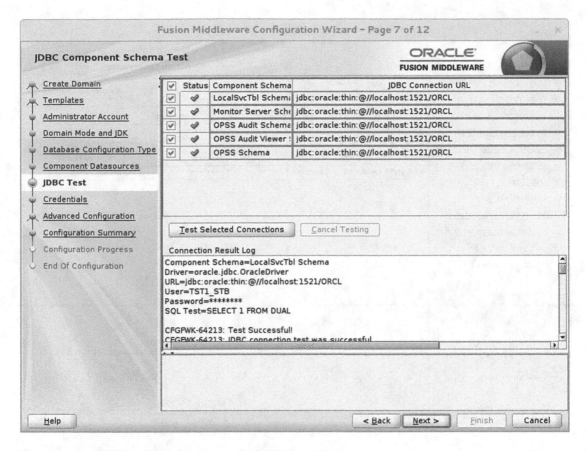

Figure 13-49. *JDBC test for each component schema*

Figure 13-50 shows the key names in the domain and the store name. Provide the username and password for each key in the store and click Next.

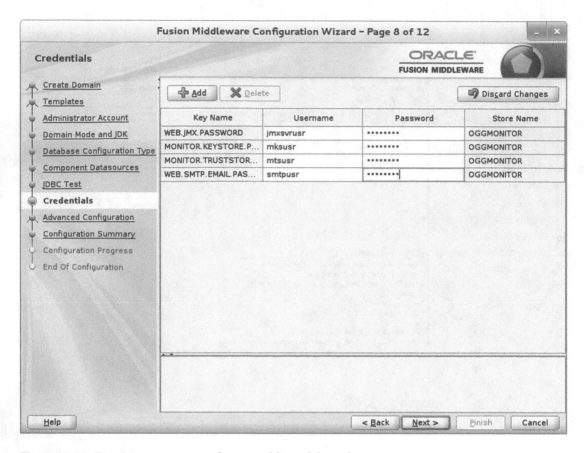

Figure 13-50. *Entering a username and password for each key value*

Figure 13-51 shows the advanced configuration options for the WLS domain. I have selected to configure settings for the administration server, node manager, and managed server.

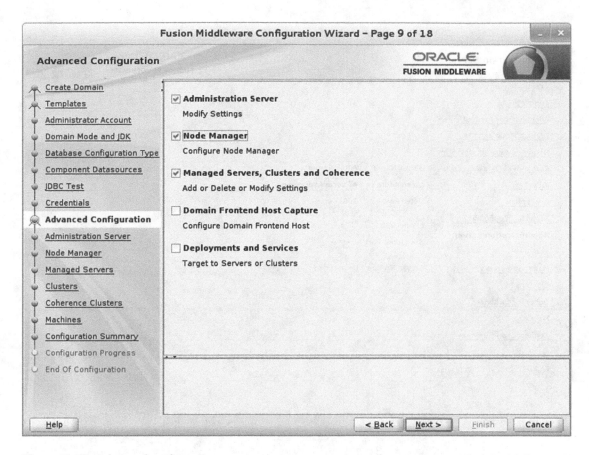

Figure 13-51. *Advanced configuration*

The administration server is where you can manage your WLS domain. The URL format for the administration server is protocol://listen-address:listen-port. AdminServer and 7001 are the default server name and listen port, respectively. You can opt to enable SSL, although the default is disabled. Figure 13-52 shows the configuration of the administration server for this example.

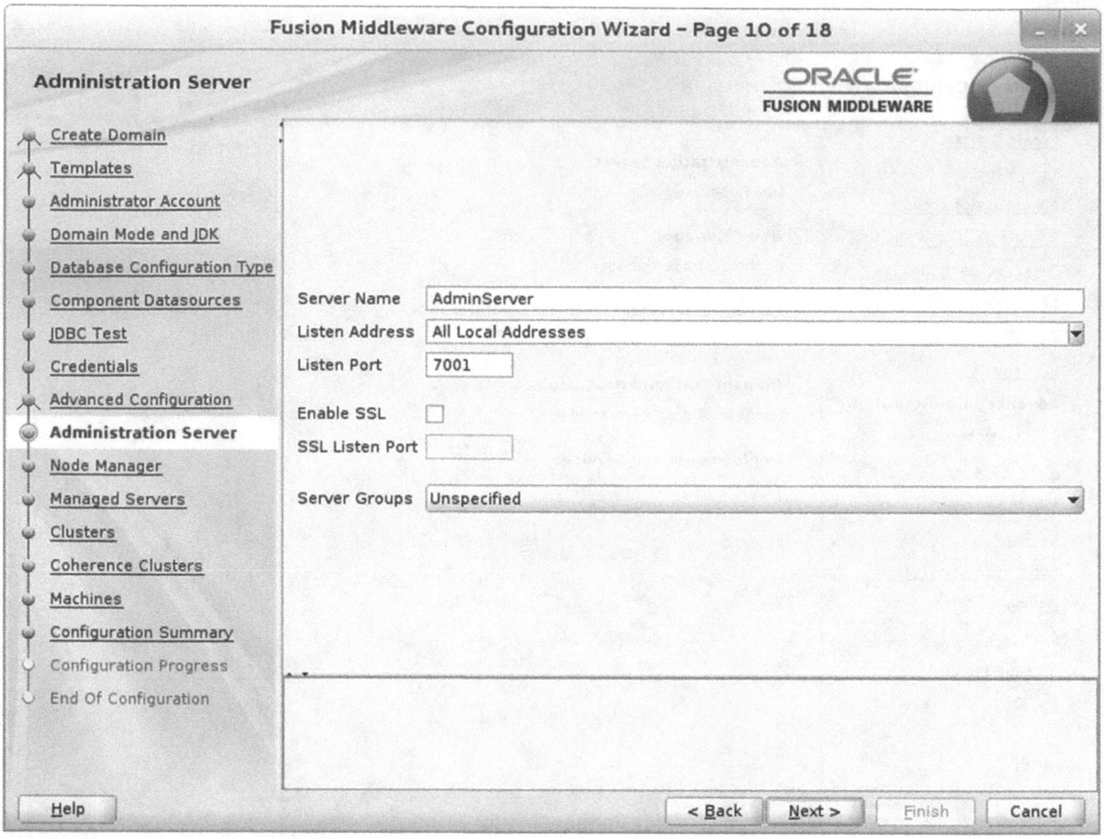

Figure 13-52. *Administration server details*

Select Node Manager Type and provide the node manager credentials, as shown in Figure 13-53.

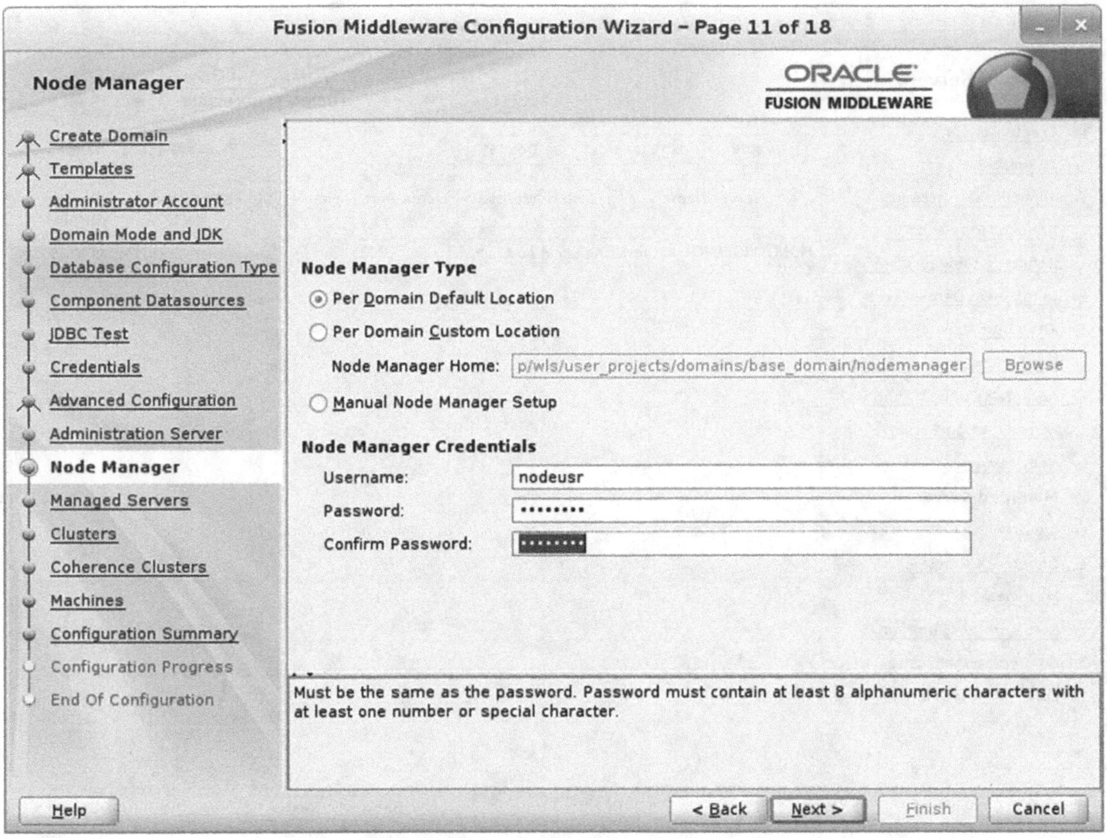

Figure 13-53. *Configuring the node manager*

Configure the managed server, as shown in Figure 13-54. You can add multiple managed servers in this step.

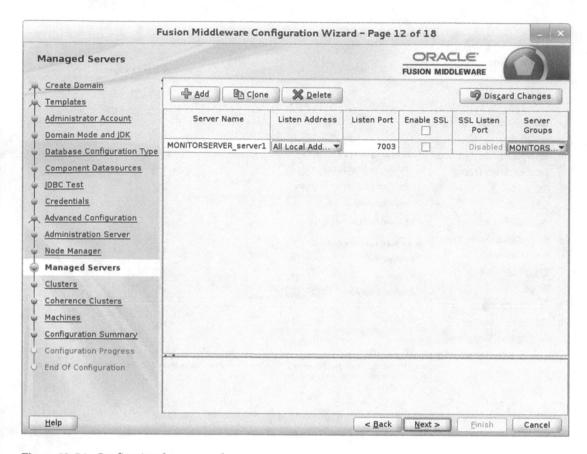

Figure 13-54. Configuring the managed server

Figure 13-55 shows the cluster configuration screen. You can add a cluster in this step to group WLS instances to work together to provide scalability and high availability. You do not need to configure clusters for this example. Simply click Next to continue.

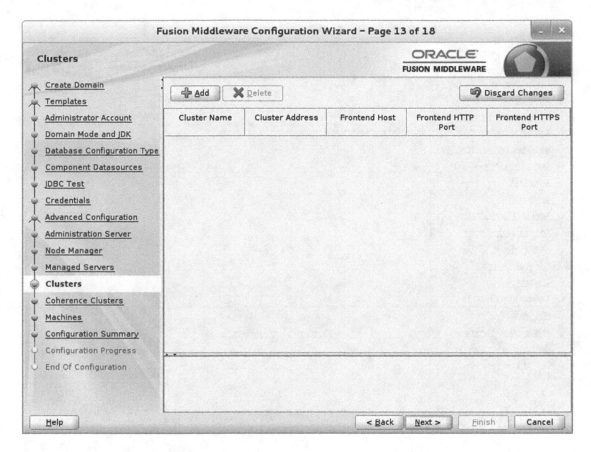

Figure 13-55. *Cluster configuration*

Figure 13-56 shows the coherence cluster details. This screen is shown only if you selected to install coherence during WLS installation. You can either accept the default cluster name or type a custom cluster name. Enter a port to be used for the cluster listen port and click Next to continue.

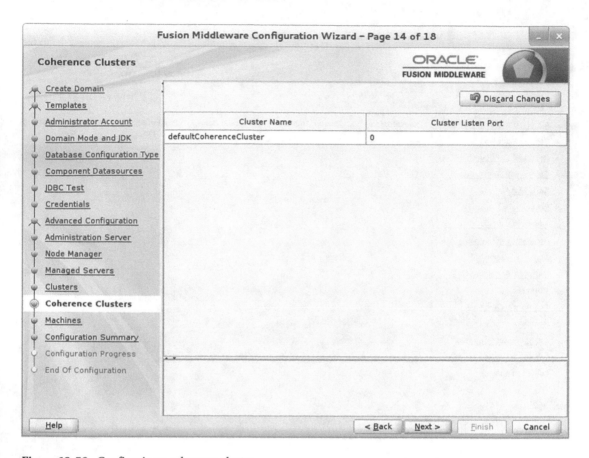

Figure 13-56. *Configuring a coherence cluster*

Figure 15-57 shows the machine configuration screen. Machines are the physical unit of hardware and are associated with the WLS instances that are hosted on them. You will not need to configure machines for this setup. Click Next to continue.

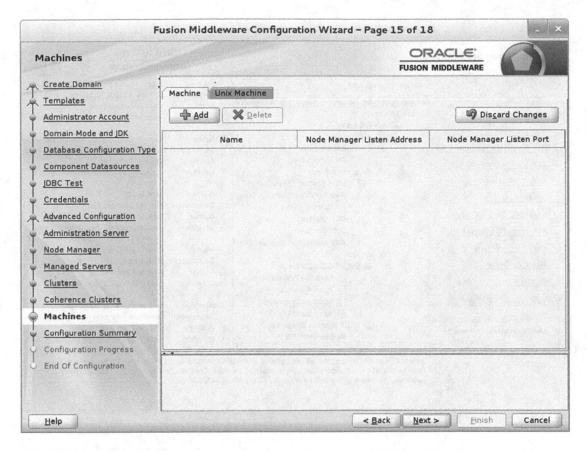

Figure 13-57. Adding machines

Figure 13-58 shows the detailed configuration summary. It provides a summary of all the configurations you have chosen until now. Review the detailed summary before continuing to create the WLS domain. If you want to change some information, click Back to navigate to the appropriate screen and modify the configuration as required.

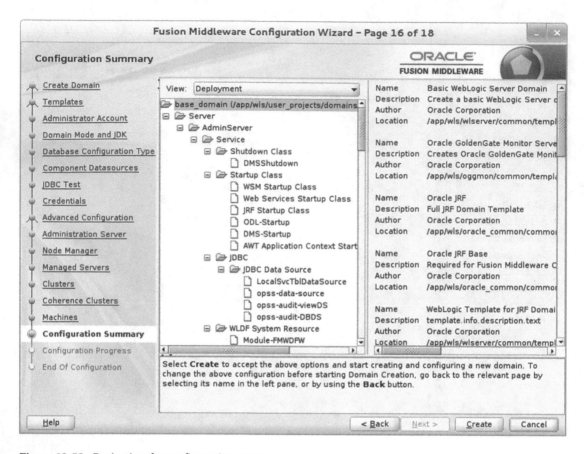

Figure 13-58. *Reviewing the configuration summary*

Figure 13-59 shows the configuration progress. Once the domain is created successfully, you are pretty much done. Click Next to continue.

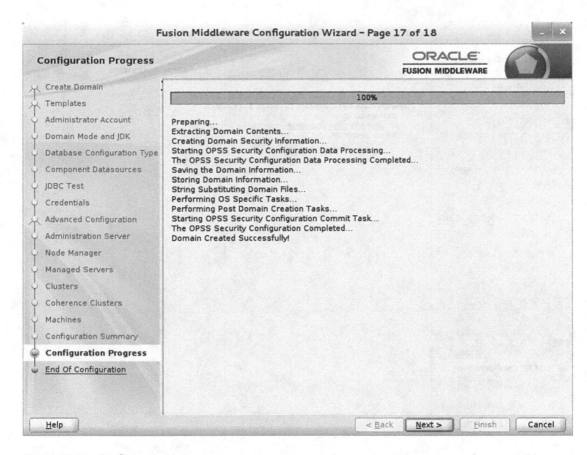

Figure 13-59. *Configuration in progress*

Figure 13-60 shows that the Oracle WebLogic Server configuration succeeded. The new domain name is base_domain. Click Finish to exit the setup.

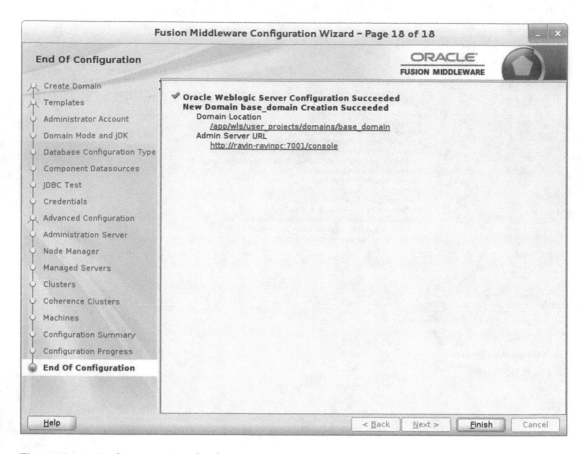

Figure 13-60. *Configuration completed successfully*

Configure the OGG Monitor Server

You can configure your Oracle GoldenGate Monitor server by editing monitor.properties located in the OGG Monitor domain you created using the Configuration Wizard.

In this example, the file is at the following location:

/app/wls/user_projects/domains/base_domain/config/monitorserver/cfg/monitor.properties

The following is the content of the monitor.properties file:

```
# Copyright (c) 2009, 2014, Oracle and/or its affiliates. All rights reserved.
#Oracle GoldenGate Monitor
#Thu May 02 16:27:01 PDT 2013
#JMX server is enabled by default (otherwise Agents cannot register), so property is
optional
monitor.jmx.server.enabled=true

#JMX server's host name
# underscore in JMX server's hostname is not valid e.g. XXX_YZW is invalid JMX server's host
name
```

```
monitor.jmx.server.host=ravin-ravinpc

#Port that is bound by the JMX server
monitor.jmx.server.port=5502

#JMX server's user
monitor.jmx.server.user=oggmsjmxusr

#Whether internal components are exposed as MBeans - useful for troubleshooting
#monitor.jmx.internal.mbeans.enabled=false

#Number of attempts to connect before giving up (0 or negative numbers means unlimited
attempts)
#monitor.default_agent_connection.max_attempts=0

#Interval (in seconds) between each attempt
monitor.default_agent_connection.interval=30

#interval (in seconds) before each attempt to reconnect (after an existing connection was
broken)
#monitor.default_agent_connection.reconnect_interval=5

#The version of meta-data currently supported by CM when the agents attempt to register
monitor.supported.agent.metadata.version=1.0

#Number of threads for the event dispatcher
monitor.events.dispatcher.threads_size=30

#Flavor of the EclipseLink dialect
#This property underlines the database that eclipselink will be talking to.
#Accordingly it provides pointer to eclipselink to use the appropriate dialect according to
the target database.

#Please use this property value when the Monitor repository database is Oracle.
eclipselink.target-database=org.eclipse.persistence.platform.database.OraclePlatform

#Please use this property value when the Monitor repository database is SQL Server.
#eclipselink.target-database=org.eclipse.persistence.platform.database.SQLServerPlatform

#Please use this property value when the Monitor repository database is MySql.
#eclipselink.target-database=org.eclipse.persistence.platform.database.MySQLPlatform

#EclipseLink weaving mode
eclipselink.weaving=static

#Enable this property to create database objects on server re-start if the administrator
wants to re-point the server install to a new database
#eclipselink.ddl-generation=create-tables

#Interval for Interval Renderer in seconds. To disable interval renderer set to 0
#monitor.web.rendering_interval=15
```

```
#Time out in milli seconds for Solution Discovery to pick up events
monitor.cm.event.timeout=2000

#Monitor SSL Enabled property
monitor.ssl=false

#Keystore file - value for SSL property javax.net.ssl.keyStore
monitor.keystore.file=monitorKeyStore

#truststore file - value for SSL property javax.net.ssl.trustStore
monitor.truststore.file=jagentKeyStore

#Maximum events before Solution Discovery to pick up
monitor.cm.event.max.size=1000

# SSO WEB PARAMETERS

# This property specifies the SSO (Single Sign On) Log Out URL.
# if monitor is accessed in SSO environment, then monitor.ssoLogOutUrl is considered as log
out URL for Monitor application.
#
# If the logout URL format for subsequent OAM (Oracle Access Manager) version changes, then
this property shall have to be
# modified accordingly. However, server restart shall not required in such an event.
monitor.ssoLogOutUrl=/oamsso/logout.html?end_url=/monitor
```

Configure the JMX Server Properties

To configure the JMX server settings, set the following parameters in your monitor.properties file:

```
#JMX server's host name
monitor.jmx.server.host=ravin-ravinpc

#Port that is bound by the JMX server
monitor.jmx.server.port=5502
```

Depending on your target database, uncomment one of the following lines from your monitor.properties file:

```
eclipselink.target-database=org.eclipse.persistence.platform.database.OraclePlatform

#eclipselink.target-database=org.eclipse.persistence.platform.database.SQLServerPlatform

#eclipselink.target-database=org.eclipse.persistence.platform.database.MySQLPlatform
```

SMTP, SNMP, and CLI Alert Properties

Alerts can be set up from the OGG user interface to notify events such as stopped processes (extract, replicat, or manager) or if there is a lag threshold reached by any extract or replicat process. The alerts can be configured to be sent to e-mail accounts. Let's discuss some of these configurations here. You can find more information in the online help section in the OGG Monitor user interface.

If you selected SMTP during the OGG Monitor installation, you can navigate to the User Management tab in the OGG Monitor user interface. Provide the e-mail address where alerts need to be sent. Then go to the User Profile tab and select Email as the notification type. You can also configure command-line interface (CLI) alerts to run a script on the OGG Monitor server when an alert is triggered. Another alert type, Simple Network Management Protocol (SNMP), can be set to send alerts in the form of datagrams, which will be received by the SNMP trap recipient.

Add the following parameters to set the SMTP, SNMP, and CLI alert settings:

```
monitor.smtp.alerts.enabled=true
monitor.smtp.secure=false
monitor.smtp.host=smtp.ravin-ravinpc
monitor.smtp.port=25
monitor.smtp.from=oggm@ravin-ravinpc
monitor.smtp.user=ravig@ravin-ravinpc
monitor.snmp.alerts.enabled=true
monitor.cli.alerts.enabled=true
```

Some other important files present in the directory are SNMPJMXMapping.xml, CommandLineHandlers.xml, and CommandLineHandlers.xsd.

SNMPJMXMapping.xml contains the SNMP alert configurations. The only changes that you should make are setting the SNMP version and target tags as shown here:

```
<notification version="1" enabled="false">
<targets>
<target>localhost/162
</target>
</targets>
</notification>
```

The CommandLineHandlers.xml file located in the cfg directory contains the configuration for CLI. The definitions for this file are present in CommandLineHandlers.xsd, which you can use to regenerate your CommandLineHandler.xml file using an XML generation tool. You need to bounce (stop and start) the Oracle GoldenGate Monitor if you make any configuration changes.

Start the OGG Monitor Server

The first step to start the OGG Monitor server is to start the WLS server. This is located in the OGG Monitor domain you created.

```
$ cd /app/wls/user_projects/domains/base_domain
$./startWebLogic.sh
```

If you are using Windows, locate and run startWebLogic.cmd.

```
Enter username to boot WebLogic server:weblogic
Enter password to boot WebLogic server:
```

Enter the username and password for the WLS admin user when prompted.
Notice the startup messages on the screen; starting WebLogic Server may take a few minutes.

```
<19-Jun-2016 11:35:22 o'clock EDT> <Notice> <WebLogicServer> <BEA-000365> <Server state
changed to STARTING.>
<19-Jun-2016 11:35:23 o'clock EDT> <Info> <WorkManager> <BEA-002900> <Initializing
self-tuning thread pool.>

Oracle Coherence Version 12.2.1.0.0 Build 60603
 Grid Edition: Production mode
Copyright (c) 2000, 2015, Oracle and/or its affiliates. All rights reserved.

<19-Jun-2016 11:41:44 o'clock EDT> <Notice> <WebLogicServer> <BEA-000365> <Server state
changed to STANDBY.>
<19-Jun-2016 11:41:44 o'clock EDT> <Notice> <WebLogicServer> <BEA-000365> <Server state
changed to STARTING.>

<19-Jun-2016 11:48:51 o'clock EDT> <Notice> <WebLogicServer> <BEA-000365> <Server state
changed to ADMIN.>
<19-Jun-2016 11:48:53 o'clock EDT> <Notice> <WebLogicServer> <BEA-000365> <Server state
changed to RESUMING.>

<19-Jun-2016 11:48:56 o'clock EDT> <Notice> <WebLogicServer> <BEA-000329> <Started the
WebLogic Server Administration Server "AdminServer" for domain "base_domain" running in
production mode.>

<19-Jun-2016 11:48:56 o'clock EDT> <Notice> <WebLogicServer> <BEA-000360> <The server
started in RUNNING mode.>
<19-Jun-2016 11:48:57 o'clock EDT> <Notice> <WebLogicServer> <BEA-000365> <Server state
changed to RUNNING.>
```

Once you have started WebLogic Server, you can navigate to the admin console or use the command line to start the WLS managed server you created for the Oracle GoldenGate Monitor.

For starting the WLS managed server through the command line, use this:

```
$./startManagedWebLogic.sh MONITORSERVER_server1 http://ravin-ravinpc:7001
```

Enter the username and password for the WLS admin user when prompted.

Log in to the WLS Server admin console using the admin login you created during installation. The URL for the admin console is in this format:

```
http://ravin-ravinpc:7001/console
```

Figure 13-61 shows the admin console login page.

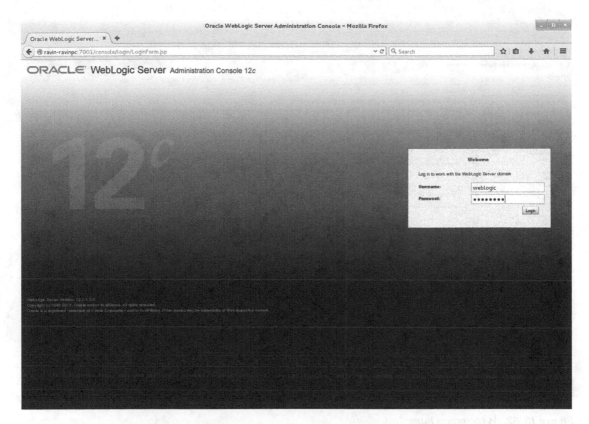

Figure 13-61. *WLS admin console login page*

Expand your OGG Monitor domain under the domain structure and click Servers, as shown in
Figure 13-62.

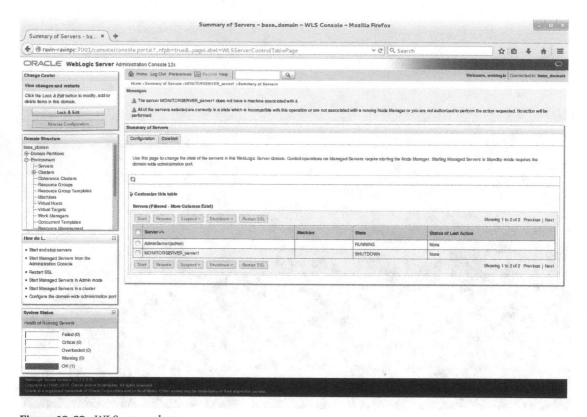

Figure 13-62. *WLS servers home*

Please note the error in Figure 13-62 that says the server MONITORSERER_server1 cannot be restarted as it is not associated with a machine. A *machine* is a component of hardware resources that hosts your WLS server. Click Machines under Domain Structure and create a new machine. I have selected the default machine name MACHINE-0, as shown in Figure 13-63.

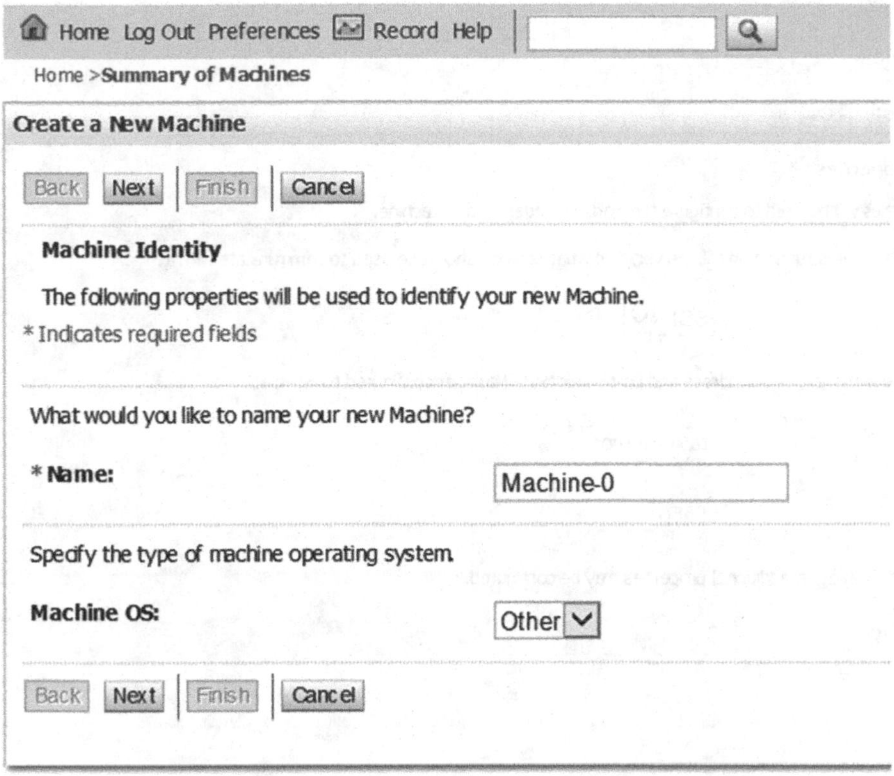

Figure 13-63. *Creating a new machine to host the WLS server*

Select Machine OS from the drop-down. If your host operating system is not listed, select Other from the drop-down.

Click Next to continue to the node manager configuration for the machine. The node manager is a utility that lets you start and stop your server remotely. Select the appropriate configuration as shown in Figure 13-64. The default value for Listen Port is 5556. Click Finish to complete your machine configuration.

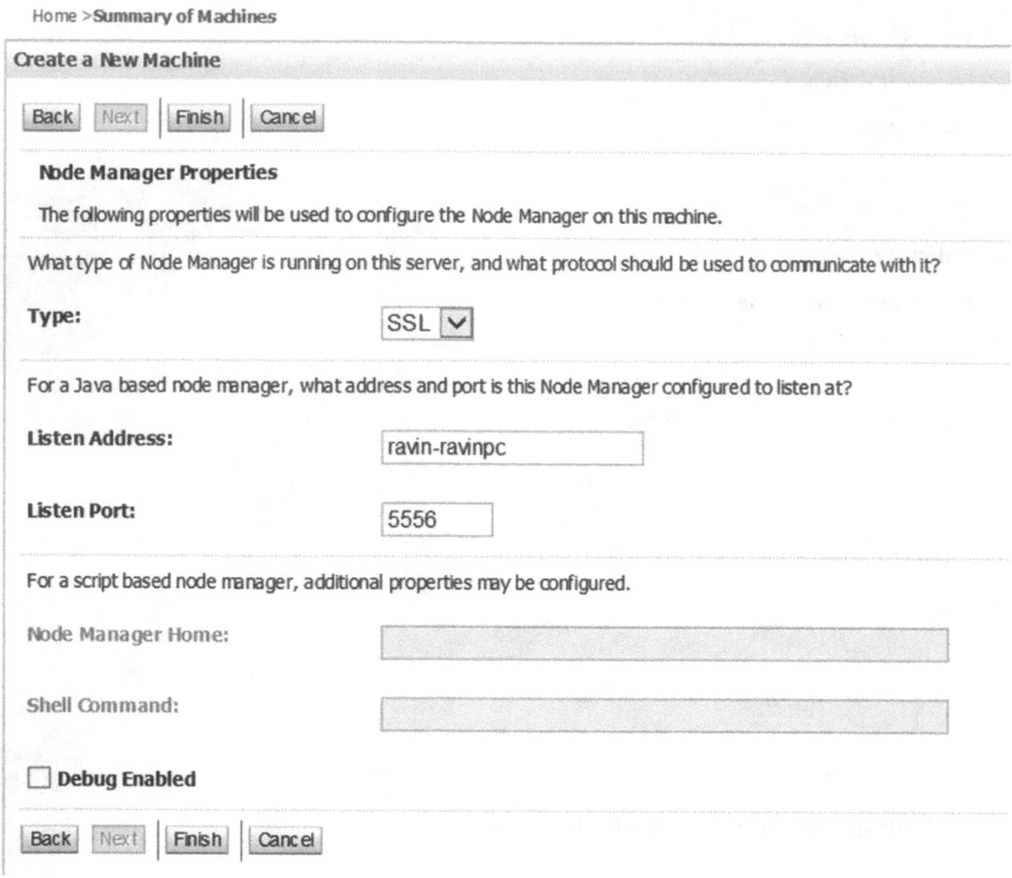

Home >**Summary of Machines**

Create a New Machine

| Back | Next | Finish | Cancel |

Node Manager Properties

The following properties will be used to configure the Node Manager on this machine.

What type of Node Manager is running on this server, and what protocol should be used to communicate with it?

Type: SSL ▼

For a Java based node manager, what address and port is this Node Manager configured to listen at?

Listen Address: ravin-ravinpc

Listen Port: 5556

For a script based node manager, additional properties may be configured.

Node Manager Home:

Shell Command:

☐ **Debug Enabled**

| Back | Next | Finish | Cancel |

Figure 13-64. *Finishing the machine configuration*

It is important that your node manager is in Reachable status. Since you have created a new machine configuration, you need to restart WebLogic Server again. Figure 13-65 shows that the node manager was not reachable before I restarted WebLogic Server.

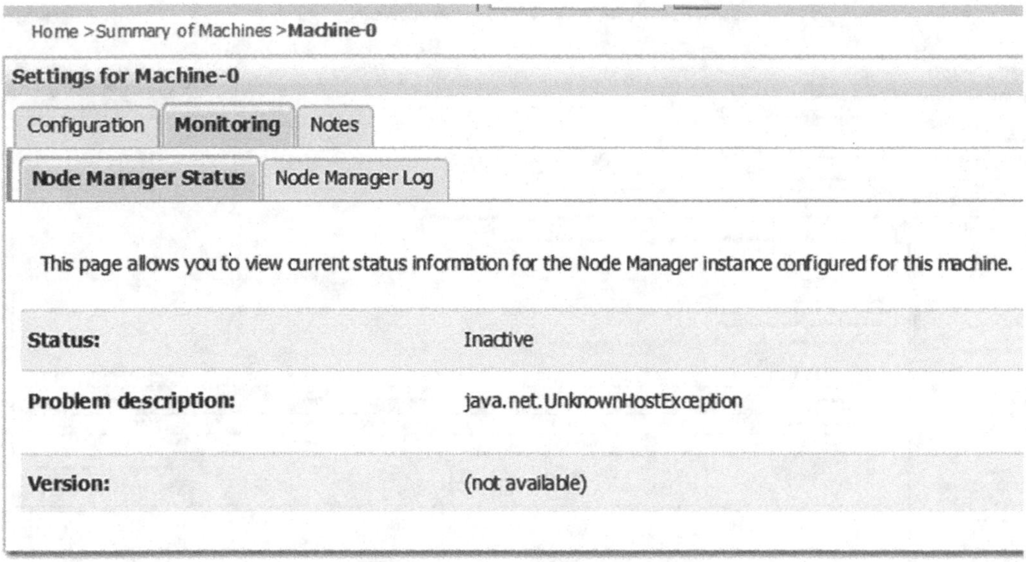

Home >Summary of Machines >**Machine-0**

Settings for Machine-0

| Configuration | **Monitoring** | Notes |

| **Node Manager Status** | Node Manager Log |

This page allows you to view current status information for the Node Manager instance configured for this machine.

Status:	Inactive
Problem description:	java.net.UnknownHostException
Version:	(not available)

Figure 13-65. *Check the node manager status for a new machine*

Check the node manager's status again after you have successfully restarted WebLogic Server. Figure 13-66 shows that the node manager is now reachable.

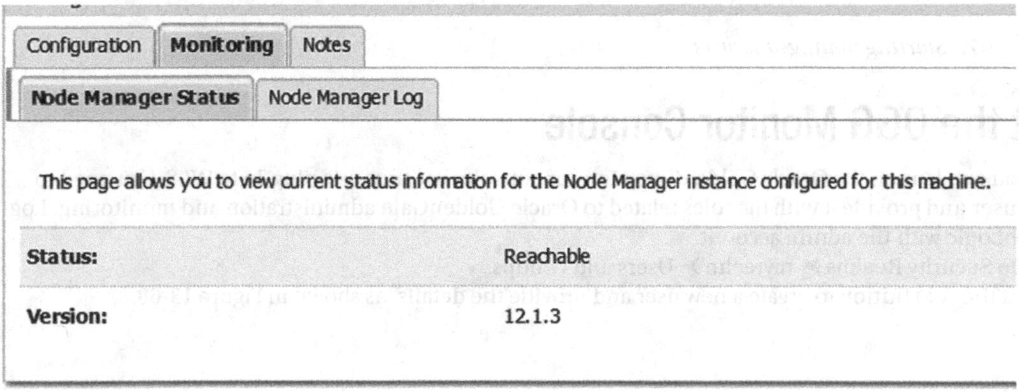

| Configuration | **Monitoring** | Notes |

| **Node Manager Status** | Node Manager Log |

This page allows you to view current status information for the Node Manager instance configured for this machine.

| **Status:** | Reachable |
| **Version:** | 12.1.3 |

Figure 13-66. *Node manager status after WebLogic restart*

Navigate to the server's home and click the Control tab. Select the check box for the managed server you want to restart and click Start. This may take a few minutes. View the log file at ../<domain name>/servers/<server_name>/logs/ for any errors and warnings. Figure 13-67 shows that both the admin server and Oracle GoldenGate managed server MONITORSERVER_server1 are running.

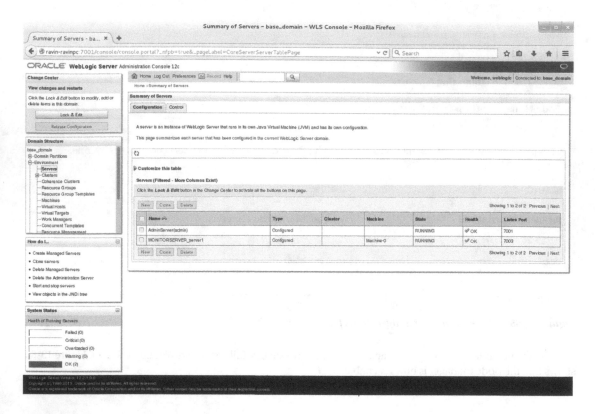

Figure 13-67. *Starting managed servers*

Start the OGG Monitor Console

Before you can launch the Oracle GoldenGate Monitor console that runs as a plug-in to WLS, you need to create a user and provide it with the roles related to Oracle GoldenGate administration and monitoring. Log in to WebLogic with the admin account.

Go to Security Realms ➤ myrealm ➤ Users and Groups.

Click the Add button to create a new user and provide the details, as shown in Figure 13-68.

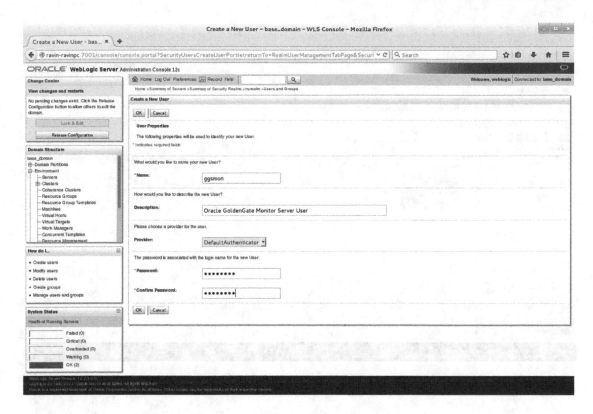

Figure 13-68. *Creating a new user*

Click the Groups tab and look through the available groups. You can assign the new OGG user to one or more groups.

Assign the new user to one or more groups. I added my user to all five groups, as shown in Figure 13-69.

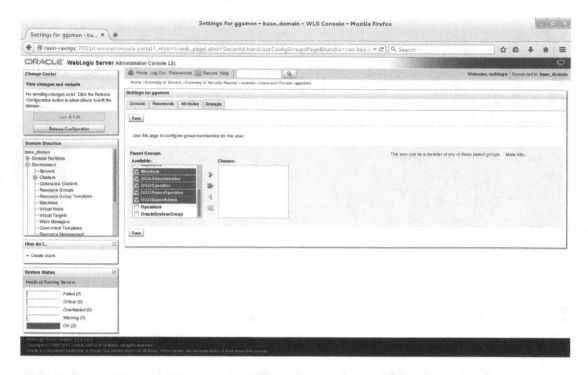

Figure 13-69. *Assigning a role to the new user*

Click the Save button. You need to click the Activate Changes button in the left-top section of the window to activate the new changes.

You are ready to launch the OGG Monitor console from a web browser. The URL for the OGG Monitor console is in the following format:

```
http://hostname:portNumber/monitor/faces/loginPage.jspx
```

In our example, the Oracle GoldenGate Monitor console can be accessed by launching `http://ravin-ravinpc:7003/monitor/faces/loginPage.jspx` in any JavaScript-enabled web browser.

Use the user (`ggsmon`) and password that you created in the previous step to log in to the OGG Monitor server console.

Figure 13-70 shows the Oracle GoldenGate Monitor home page.

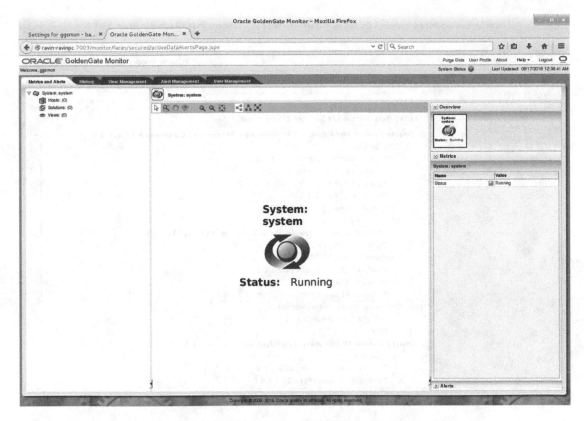

Figure 13-70. *OGG Monitor server console*

Install the Oracle GoldenGate Monitor Agent

The Oracle GoldenGate Monitor Agent communicates with the OGG instance, collects information, and sends it to OGG Monitor server. It can also send the information to Oracle Enterprise Manager if you are using the Oracle GoldenGate plug-in with it. We will discuss it in Chapter 14.

Make sure you have JDK 1.7 or later installed before installing the OGG Monitor Agent. The agent is installed on servers running OGG instances.

You already have download the Oracle Fusion Middleware 12*c* Media Pack (Oracle Fusion Middleware 12c [12.2] GoldenGate Monitor and Veridata) from the Oracle Software Delivery Cloud site for installing the Oracle GoldenGate Monitor. Use the same JAR file to install the Oracle GoldenGate Monitor Agent as discussed in this section.

Copy the downloaded files to the OGG Monitor Agent installation directory and launch the installer.

```
$ java -jar -Xmx1024m fmw_12.2.1.0.0_ogg.jar
```

Follow these steps to complete the installation.

Click Next on the Welcome and Auto Updates screens. Select the Oracle Home where you will be installing the Monitor Agent. For this example, you will install the agent at /app/wls. You already have WebLogic Server and JRF installed at this location. Figure 13-71 shows the installation location and feature sets installed at this location. Click Next to continue.

265

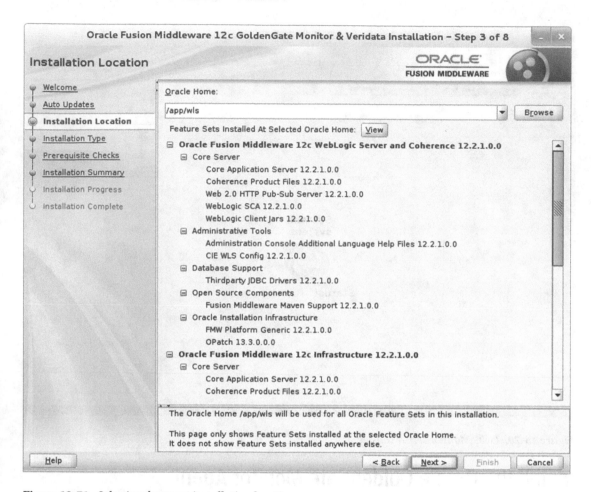

Figure 13-71. *Selecting the agent installation location*

In the next step, you are presented with various installation types for Oracle Fusion Middleware 12*c*. Select Oracle Golden Gate Monitor Agent as the installation type, as shown in Figure 13-72.

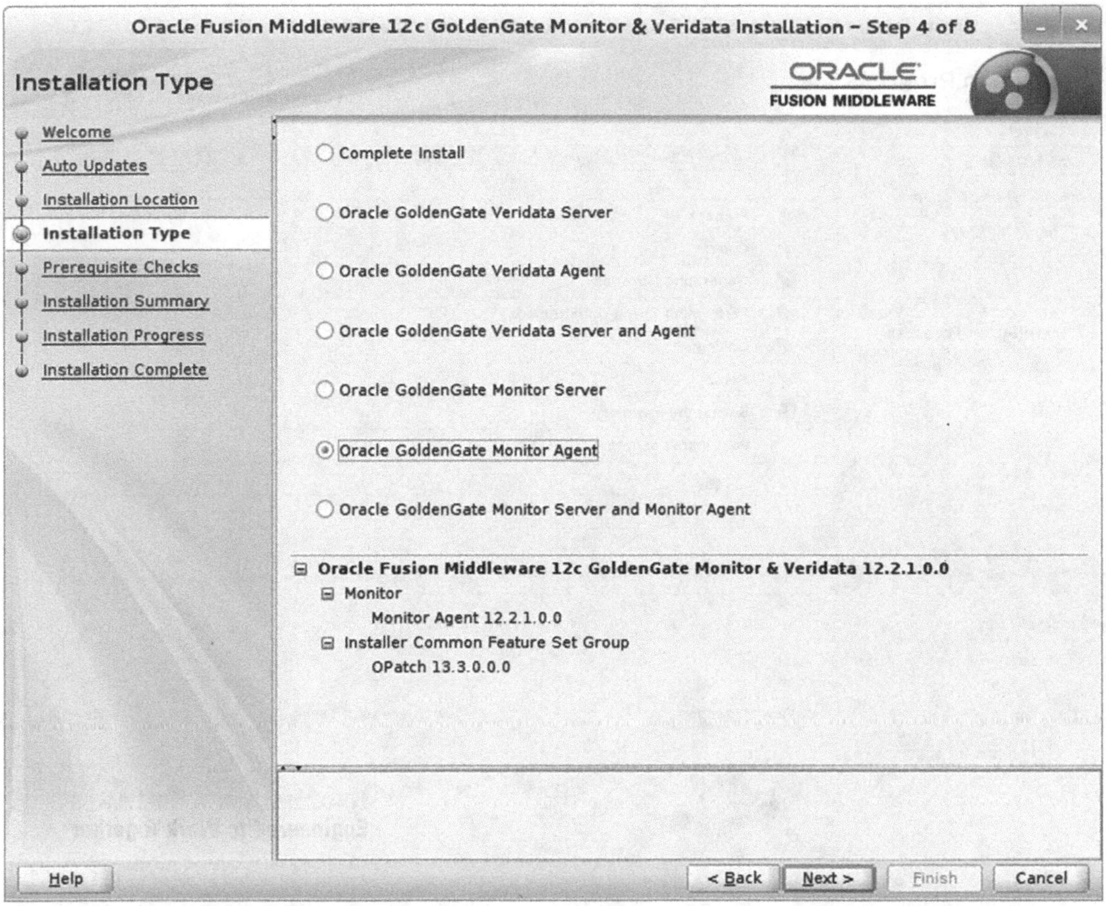

Figure 13-72. *Selecting an installation type*

The installer performs prerequisite checks similar to checks while installing the OGG Monitor server. Click Next to review the installation summary.

Figure 13-73 shows the installation tasks and their status in progress. Wait until it finishes. This may take up to 15 minutes. You can view the installation messages for the current step by clicking View Messages. You can also view the installer log by clicking the View Log button.

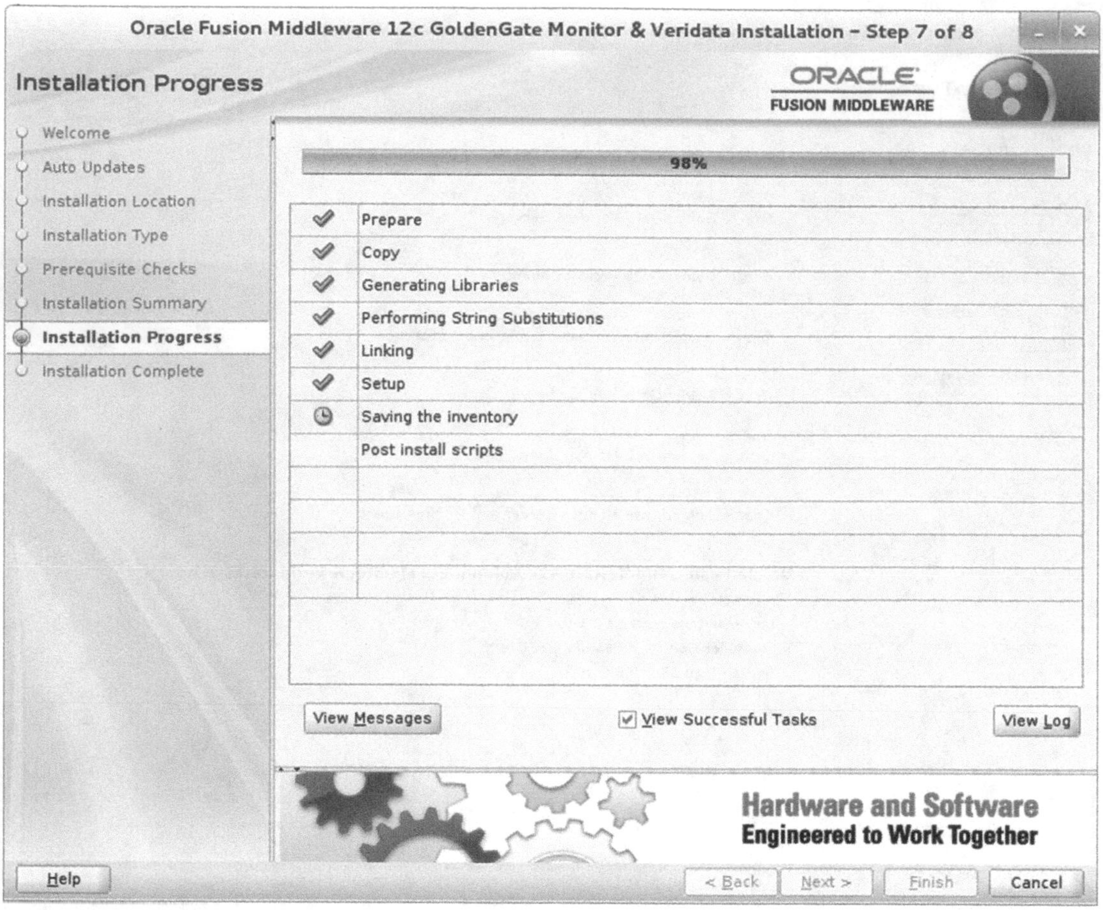

Figure 13-73. *Installation in progress*

Figure 13-74 shows that the Oracle GoldenGate Monitor Agent installation has successfully completed.

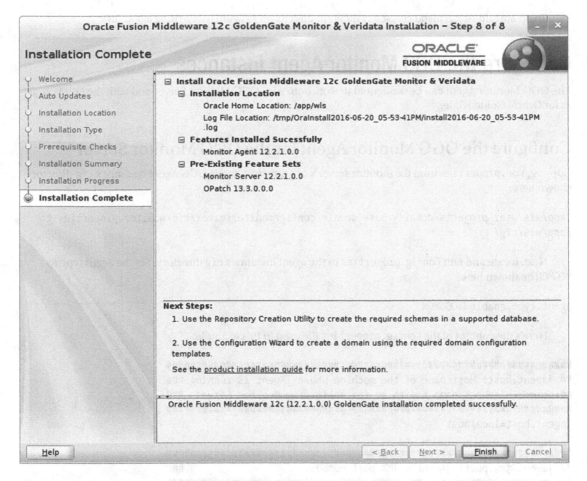

Figure 13-74. Installation successfully completed

Create the OGG Monitor Agent Instances

Navigate to the OGG Monitor Agent home directory where you have installed the agent. Locate and execute the agent instance creation script as follows:

```
$ cd /app/wls/oggmon/ogg_agent
$ ./createMonitorAgentInstance.sh
```

The system prompts you to enter the absolute path for the OGG home directory and OGG Agent instance and other parameters. Follow the steps shown here:

```
Please enter absolute path of Oracle GoldenGate home directory : /app/ggs/tiger
Please enter absolute path of OGG Agent instance : /app/wls
OGG Agent instance directory already exists, do you want to overwrite the contents
(yes | no) : yes
Please enter unique name to replace timestamp in startMonitorAgent script
(startMonitorAgentInstance_20160620161309.sh) : agent4tiger
Sucessfully created OGG Agent instance.
```

To create additional instances, select different directories to avoid overwriting agent files.

Configure the OGG Monitor Agent Instances

The OGG Monitor Agent can be configured to work both with OGG Monitor Server and with the OEM plug-in for Oracle GoldenGate.

Configure the OGG Monitor Agent for the OGG Monitor Server

Copy oggmon.properties from the monitor server's cfg directory to the OGG Agent instance's cfg directory, shown here:

/app/wls/user_projects/domains/base_domain/config/monitorserver/cfg/monitor.properties to /app/wls/cfg/

Next, locate and edit Config.properties in the agent instance's cfg directory. Set the agent type to OGGMON as shown here:

agent.type.enabled=OGGMON

Here's the content of the Config.properties file used in this example:

```
####################################################################
## jagent.host: Host name of the machine where jAgent is running ###
## Note: This host name has to be reachable from Monitor Server  ###
####################################################################
jagent.host=localhost

####################################################################
## jagent.jmx.port: jAgent's JMX port number                    ###
####################################################################
jagent.jmx.port=5555


####################################################################
## interval.regular, interval.quick:                            ###
## jAgent's regular and quick polling interval for new          ###
## Monitoring Point values.                                     ###
## Default values are 60 and 30 seconds                         ###
####################################################################
interval.regular=60
interval.quick=30


####################################################################
## monitor.host: Monitor Server host name.                      ###
## Note: This property has to be the same with the property:    ###
## monitor.jmx.server.host in monitor.properties file           ###
## on Monitor Server side                                       ###
####################################################################
monitor.host=localhost
```

```
########################################################################
## monitor.jmx.port: Monitor Server JMX port number            ###
########################################################################
monitor.jmx.port=5502


########################################################################
## monitor.jmx.username: Monitor Server JMX username           ###
## This is the JMX username defined during Monitor Installation  ###
########################################################################
monitor.jmx.username=oggmsjmxusr


########################################################################
## jagent.username: jAgent username                            ###
## It can be any name. This jAgent username will be passed to   ###
## Monitor Server during jAgent registration.                  ###
########################################################################
jagent.username=oggmajmxusr


########################################################################
## reg.retry.interval: jAgent incremental registration          ###
## retry interval in seconds; when connection exception         ###
## occurs while jAgent is connecting to Monitor Server for the   ###
## first time                                                   ###
## Default value is 60 seconds                                  ###
########################################################################
reg.retry.interval=10


########################################################################
## instance.query.initial.interval:                            ###
## If only manager process is running, jAgent will wait for     ###
## 15 seconds by default before starting to register           ###
## to Monitor Server. After this waiting period of time,         ###
## if there are still no other running processes such as        ###
## extract and replicat beside the manager process, JAgent will  ###
## go ahead and register to Monitor Server.                     ###
########################################################################
instance.query.initial.interval=5


########################################################################
## incremental.registration.quiet.interval:                    ###
## jAgent will incrementally register to Monitor Server after    ###
## a new process is configured. However, jAgent will wait for    ###
## a period of 5 seconds by default before each                 ###
## incremental registration started.                           ###
########################################################################
incremental.registration.quiet.interval=5


########################################################################
## maximum.message.retrieval:                                  ###
## Maximum number of message to retrieve from cagent/core when   ###
## jagent starts                                               ###
```

271

```
######################################################################
maximum.message.retrieval=500

######################################################################
## mgr.host: Host name of the machine where Manager is running    ###
## Note: This host name has to be reachable from JAgent           ###
## There is no need to define this property if JAgent is          ###
## running on the same machine with OGG Deployment                ###
######################################################################
#mgr.host=localhost

######################################################################
## mgr.port: Manager port number                                  ###
## There is no need to define this property if JAgent is          ###
## running on the same machine with OGG Deployment                ###
######################################################################
#mgr.port=7089

######################################################################
## jagent.rmi.port                                                ###
## RMI Port which EM Agent will use to connect to JAgent          ###
## RMI Port will only be used if agent.type.enabled=OEM           ###
######################################################################
jagent.rmi.port=5559

######################################################################
## agent.type.enabled : Choose either OEM or OGGMON               ###
## Choosing OGGMON will allow JAgent to register to               ###
## Monitor Server and JMX RMI connector will not be enabled.      ###
## Choosing OEM will enable JMX RMI connector which will be used  ###
## by EM Agent to connect to JAgent and JAgent will not register  ###
## to Monitor Server.                                             ###
######################################################################
agent.type.enabled=OGGMON

######################################################################
## status.polling.interval: polling interval for status changes  ###
## in second. Newly added process will be detected based on this  ###
## polling interval.Default is 5 seconds.                         ###
######################################################################
status.polling.interval=5

######################################################################
## message.polling.interval: polling interval for message         ###
## changes in second. Default is 5 seconds.                       ###
######################################################################
message.polling.interval=5

## This property is not being used at the moment
reg.retry.times=-1

######################################################################
```

```
## jagent backward compatibility                              ###
####################################################################
jagent.backward.compatibility=false

################## Start SSL Properties #########################

####################################################################
## jagent SSL Enabled property                                ###
####################################################################
jagent.ssl=false

####################################################################
## keystore file - value for SSL property javax.net.ssl.keyStore ###
####################################################################
jagent.keystore.file=jagentKeyStore

####################################################################
## truststore file-value for SSL property javax.net.ssl.trustStore #
####################################################################
jagent.truststore.file=jagentKeyStore

################## End SSL Properties ###########################

####################################################################
## jagent restful web service timeout (in millisecond)        ###
####################################################################
jagent.restful.ws.timeout=15000

####################################################################
##              jagent GGSCI timeout (in second)              ###
####################################################################
jagent.ggsci.timeout=30
```

Configure the OGG Monitor Agent When Using the OEM Plug-in for Oracle GoldenGate

Edit Config.properties in the agent instance's cfg directory. Set the agent type to OEM as shown here:

```
agent.type.enabled=OEM
```

Next, you will be creating a wallet for storing credentials as discussed in the next section.

Create a Wallet When Using the OGG Monitor

Locate and delete the existing dirwlt directory from your agent's home directory.
Execute the following from the bin directory in your agent instance's home/bin and follow these steps:

```
$ cd /app/wls/bin
$ ./pw_agent_util.sh -create
Please create a password for Java Agent:
```

```
Please confirm password for Java Agent:
Please enter Monitor Server JMX password:
Please confirm Monitor Server JMX password:
Jun 20, 2016 5:11:33 PM oracle.security.jps.JpsStartup start
INFO: Jps initializing.
Jun 20, 2016 5:11:35 PM oracle.security.jps.JpsStartup start
INFO: Jps started.
Wallet is created successfully.
```

This will create two files, cwallet.sso.lck and cwallet.sso, in the dirwlt wallet directory, as shown here:

```
$ cd /app/wls/dirwlt
$ ls -lrt
total 4
-rw-r--r--. 1 oracle oinstall   0 Jun 20 20:45 cwallet.sso.lck
-rw-r--r--. 1 oracle oinstall 613 Jun 20 20:45 cwallet.sso
```

Create a Wallet When Using the OGG OEM Plug-In

Execute the following from the bin directory in your agent instance's home/bin:

```
$ ./pw_agent_util.sh -jagentonly
```

Enable Monitoring

To enable monitoring, add the parameter ENABLEMONITORING to the GLOBALS file. Create the GLOBALS file if it does not exist in the agent instance's home directory.

```
GGSCI> edit ./GLOBALS
ENABLEMONITORING
```

Start the OGG Monitor Agent

Navigate to the OGG Home and execute the following from GGSCI:

```
GGSCI> start jagent

Sending START request to MANAGER ...
GGCMD JAGENT starting

GGSCI> status all

Program     Status      Group      Lag at Chkpt  Time Since Chkpt

MANAGER     RUNNING
JAGENT      RUNNING
```

Check ogg_agent.log in the OGG agent instance's home /logs directory if needed. The OGG Monitor Agent can be configured to send information to the OGG Monitor server or OGG plug-in for Oracle Enterprise Manager. This chapter discussed using the OGG Monitor Agent with the OGG Monitor server. We will cover using the OGG plug-in for OEM and configuring the OGG Monitor Agent to send information to the OEM in Chapter 14.

Summary

In this chapter, our discussion focused on Oracle GoldenGate Monitor 12*c*. We discussed the OGG Monitor architecture and prerequisites, as well as the steps to install and configure the OGG Monitor server and agent. You will use the OGG Monitor to view the related OGG instances through a web interface. It allows you to monitor the OGG processes for any performance issues. It comes with built-in capabilities to send alerts for lags, abended channels, errors, and so on.

In the next chapter, we will configure the Oracle Enterprise Manager plug-in for OGG, and then we will discuss the Oracle GoldenGate Director, which allows you to remotely configure and manage OGG instances.

CHAPTER 14

■ ■ ■

Oracle GoldenGate Management Pack Part II

In the previous chapter, we discussed how to set up the Oracle GoldenGate Monitor for monitoring your Oracle GoldenGate replication environment. We also showed how to configure the Oracle GoldenGate Monitor Agent for the Monitor server as well as the Oracle Enterprise Manager plug-in for Oracle GoldenGate.

In this chapter, we will show you how to configure the Oracle Enterprise Manager plug-in for OGG, and then we will discuss the Oracle GoldenGate Director, which allows you to remotely configure and manage OGG instances.

Oracle GoldenGate Enterprise Manager Plug-In

The Oracle GoldenGate plug-in for Oracle Enterprise Manager (OEM) extends the capability of OEM 12*c* to support, monitor, and manage Oracle GoldenGate instances and processes.

With the Oracle GoldenGate plug-in for OEM, you can perform a range of management and monitoring tasks remotely, such as the following:

- Stop/start processes

- Modify parameter files

- View error logs, report files, and discard files

- View and monitor OGG metrics and historical trends

- Configure automatic alerts

Installing the OGG Plug-in for EM

In this chapter, we will discuss the Oracle GoldenGate plug-in for OEM 12*c* Release 3 (12.1.0.3).

System Requirements

You should have Enterprise Manager Cloud Control 12*c* Release 3 (12.1.0.3) and later. Also, your Oracle GoldenGate version should be 11.2.1 or later to configure it with OEM 12*c*. You must also verify if your OS platform is supported for running the OEM plug-in for the specific version. You can view this information on the Oracle Support web site on the Certification tab.

© Ravinder Gupta 2016
R. Gupta, *Mastering Oracle GoldenGate*, DOI 10.1007/978-1-4842-2301-7_14

Make sure you have JDK 1.7 or above installed on your machine and validate whether the JAVA_HOME environment variable is set. If not, please set it to point to the JDK installation directory.

Downloading the Plug-In

In Oracle EM, navigate to Setup ➤ Extensibility ➤ Self Update. In the Type column, select Plug-In. On the updates page, you should see an update for Oracle GoldenGate. Select Oracle GoldenGate under the Plug-in Name column and click the Download button. Once the download is complete, the status will change from Available to Downloaded.

Alternatively, you can navigate to www.oracle.com/technetwork/middleware/goldengate/downloads/index.html and download the OGG plug-in for OEM, called "Oracle GoldenGate Plug-in for Oracle Enterprise Manager V13.1.1.0.0."

Download and install the Enterprise Manager command-line interface (EM CLI) if it's not already set up on your machine.

Next, execute the following commands to import the OGG plug-in for OEM that you downloaded from the Oracle web site:

```
emcli login -username=ravin -password=ravin123_
emcli sync
emcli import_update -file=/app/downloads/13.1.1.0.0_oracle.fmw.gg_2000_0.opar
```

Deploying the Plug-In

Navigate to Setup ➤ Extensibility ➤ Plug-ins.

You will see how to deploy the plug-in first on the management server and then on the servers where the management agents are running. In the Deploy On drop-down, select Management Servers. This will open a dialog box where you will specify the OGG version and repository SYS password. Click Continue to begin the prerequisite check. Once the prerequisite check is complete, click Next to begin the deployment.

While a plug-in is deployed, the Oracle Management Server (OMS) remains down. You can query this using following command in the bin subdirectory of your EM installation directory:

```
./emctl status oms

Oracle Enterprise Manager Cloud Control 12c Release 12.1.0.3.0
Copyright (c) 1996, 2011 Oracle Corporation.  All rights reserved.
WebTier is Down
Oracle Management Server is Down

This may be due to the following plug-ins being deployed on the management server or
undeployed from it:
Plugin name:     : Oracle GoldenGate
Version:         : 12.1.0.1.0
ID:              : oracle.fmw.gg
```

You can monitor the status of the deployment job via the command emctl status oms –details. Alternatively, you can use the EM CLI to check the deployment status as follows:

```
emcli login -username=ravin -password=ravin123_
emcli sync
emcli get_plugin_deployment_status -plugin_id=oracle.fmw.gg -omslocal
```

After the deployment job is complete, the OMS starts up again automatically.

When you connect to OEM 12c again and go to the Plug-ins page, you now see that the GoldenGate plug-in has been deployed on the OMS. The next step is to deploy the plug-in on all the nodes of the RAC cluster where the GoldenGate instances are running. In the Deploy On drop-down, select Management Agent. This will open another dialog box. Click Add to search and add the management agents on which the plug-in needs to be deployed.

You can navigate to Plug-ins ➤ Deployment Activities. You should see that the plug-in has been deployed on both the OMS as well as the management agents where the plug-in has been deployed.

After the deployment is complete, go to the Targets drop-down. A new entry of GoldenGate should appear in the list.

Navigate to Setup ➤ Configure Auto Discovery ➤ All Discovery Modules. Select the agent host name and click Run Discovery Now. You need to add the JAgent username and password here. Then the entries with a target type of GoldenGate will appear under Non-Host Targets. Select the target name and click Promote.

Your OGG plug-in is ready.

Click the Targets menu to get to the GoldenGate home page. Here you can monitor your GoldenGate processes and perform other actions for monitoring your Oracle GoldenGate instances.

■ **Note**   Make sure you have applied OEM patch#20460402 before deploying the Oracle GoldenGate plug-in.

Creating an Oracle Wallet

You are required to create an Oracle wallet to add the password that the Oracle Management Agent will use to connect to the Oracle GoldenGate Agent to receive metric values.

Locate the pw_agent_util script in your Oracle GoldenGate installation directory and run it as follows:

- On a Windows command shell:

```
pw_agent_util.bat -jagentonly
```

- On a Unix/Linux command shell:

```
./pw_agent_util.sh -jagentonly
```

The utility will ask you to create a password for the Java agent. If a wallet already exists, you can create the password for JAgent as follows:

- On a Windows command shell:

```
pw_agent_util.bat -updateAgentJMX
```

- On a Unix/Linux command shell:

```
./pw_agent_util.sh -updateAgentJMX
```

Configuring the OGG Instance to Run with OEM

Navigate to the OGG installation directory and locate cfg/Config.properties. You will need to edit this file to set the properties as follows:

- Set the monitoring type as Oracle Enterprise Manager:

```
agent.type.enabled=OEM
```

Refer to Chapter 13 for the values of the other parameters in the Config.properties file.

Starting the OGG Instance

You need to bounce your manager if it's already running. The manager also starts the agent.

If you are starting the OGG manager for the first time after enabling monitoring in the GLOBALS file, you need to create a database for persisting the monitoring data as follows:

```
GGSCI> CREATE DATASTORE
```

Next, stop and start the manager.

```
GGSCI> STOP MGR
GGSCI> START MGR
```

Start the OGG agent.

```
GGSCI> START JAGENT
```

Oracle GoldenGate Director

Part of the Oracle GoldenGate Management Pack, the OGG Director allows you to configure and manage OGG instances from a remote client. Figure 14-1 shows the architecture of the OGG director.

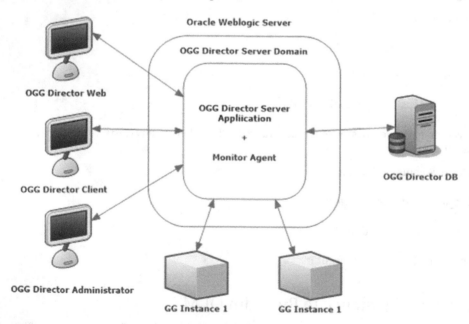

Figure 14-1. *Oracle GoldenGate Director architecture*

Let's discuss these components, and then we will discuss how to configure and use the OGG Director.

OGG Director Server

The OGG Director server is installed in the Oracle WebLogic server domain and is used to manage OGG instances. Each OGG instance is identified in the OGG Director as a combination of the host name, the port on which the manager process is listening, and a data source name.

The OGG Director server has two components: the OGG Director server application and the Monitor Agent. We will discuss them as we get further into understanding and configuring the OGG Director.

OGG Director Database

The central repository database is used by the OGG Director to store information. The user can log in to OGG Director client on his own machine and view this information.

OGG Director Web

This is the web-based interface hosted on the OGG Director server. It can be used to configure and manage OGG instances without the need to install any software on client machines.

OGG Director Client

The OGG Director client is a GUI interface to manage OGG instances. It can be installed on any platform that supports Java and desktop GUI application features.

OGG Director Administrator

This is a client of the OGG Director server used to configure and perform administrative tasks on the OGG Director server. You can add users and OGG instances and configure the OGG Director server using this interface.

Why Use the OGG Director?

The Oracle GoldenGate Director can greatly add to your capability of managing Oracle GoldenGate implementations in your organization. The OGG Director enables you to perform the following tasks:

- Manage and administer Oracle GoldenGate instances remotely
- Issue GGSCI commands remotely from the OGG Director
- Start/stop processes and instances
- Add new extract or replicat processes
- View error and report files for troubleshooting
- Present a graphical view of Oracle GoldenGate implementations in your company network

Installing the OGG Director Server

The first step of using the Oracle GoldenGate Director is installing the OGG Director server on a shared server, which will communicate with various Oracle GoldenGate instances.

System Requirements

Before you can begin your installation process, verify that the system on which you are installing the Oracle GoldenGate Director meets the following requirements:

- Make sure a dedicated port is available for the OGG Director.

- Make sure you have a minimum of 1 GB available RAM.

- The OGG Director software needs a minimum of 400 MB free disk space. Further, based on number of instances that will be monitored, additional disk space for storage will be required.

- The web browser should have JavaScript and cookies enabled.

- You need access to Oracle 9*i* or later, MySQL 5.*x*, or SQL Server 2005/2008, which will be used for configuring the OGG Director server repository.

- You need a currently supported OS; options are Windows, Red Hat, Solaris, HPUX, and AIX.

Downloading the Software

The Oracle GoldenGate Director can be downloaded from www.oracle.com/technetwork/middleware/goldengate/downloads/index.html. Look for the Oracle GoldenGate Director server in the Management Pack for Oracle GoldenGate. Click the appropriate version for your operating system environment. For demonstration in this chapter, I downloaded "Oracle GoldenGate Director V12.1.2.0.1 Server on UNIX Based Platforms."

Installing the Server

There are two ways to install the OGG Director server. You can use either the GUI installer or the command line. Let's discuss each of them.

Using the GUI Installer

Unzip the compressed file you downloaded in either previous step and run the .exe or .sh file. If you are using Windows OS, run the .exe file, gg-director-serversetup_<release>.exe.

If you are using Unix OS and you have X Windows configured, run the shell script gg-director-serversetup_<release>.sh.

EXPORT DISPLAY=:0.0
./gg-director-serversetup_unix_v12_1_2_0_1.sh

Follow the onscreen instructions and provide the appropriate values.

Figure 14-2 shows the welcome screen for installing Oracle GoldenGate Server using the GUI wizard. Click Next to continue installing the Oracle GoldenGate Director server.

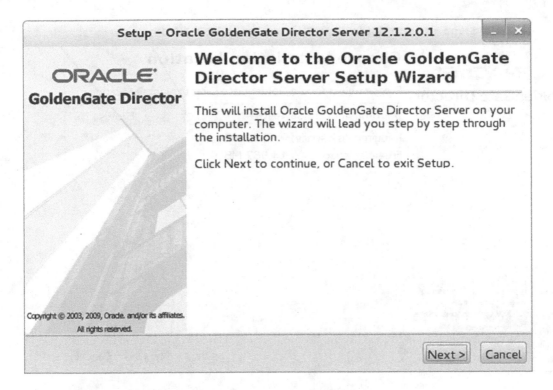

Figure 14-2. Oracle GoldenGate Director server setup welcome screen

Figure 14-3 shows the installation location screen for the OGG Director server setup. Choose the installation location where you want to install the Oracle GoldenGate Director server and click Next.

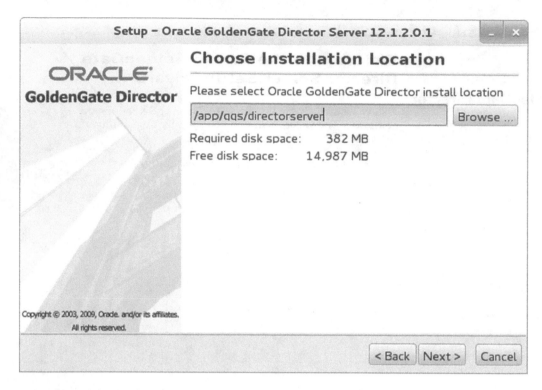

Figure 14-3. *Selecting the installation location*

The OGG Director server runs on the Oracle WebLogic Server domain. Select the WebLogic installation directory. Here I chose a directory just one step above the directory where WebLogic Server (WLS) is installed. If WebLogic Server is not already installed, you must install it before installing the OGG Director server.

Figure 14-4 shows the WebLogic Server location I am using for this example. Unless you choose a valid location with a pre-installed Oracle WebLogic Server, the installer will not let you proceed.

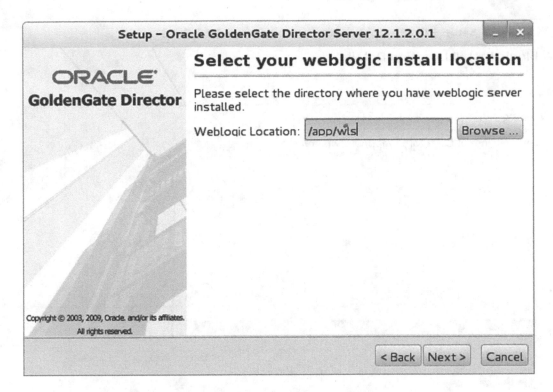

Figure 14-4. *Selecting a valid WebLogic installation directory*

The setup detects if the Oracle WebLogic directory you selected has a valid Oracle WLS installation. Please review the WLS version and click Next, as shown in Figure 14-5.

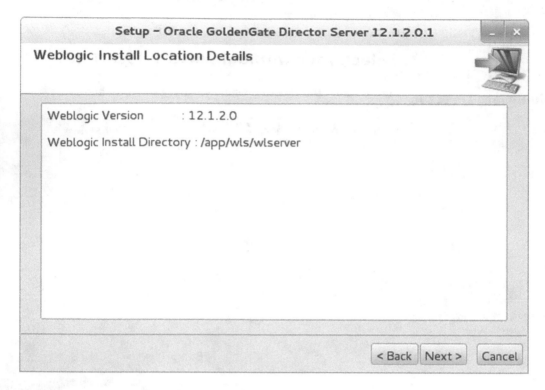

Figure 14-5. *Reviewing the WebLogic installation details*

The Oracle GoldenGate Director server processes HTTP requests from the web interface. The default HTTP port is 7001. You can use another HTTP port if 7001 is dedicated to another program installed on your machine.

Figure 14-6 shows the HTTP port I have selected for this example.

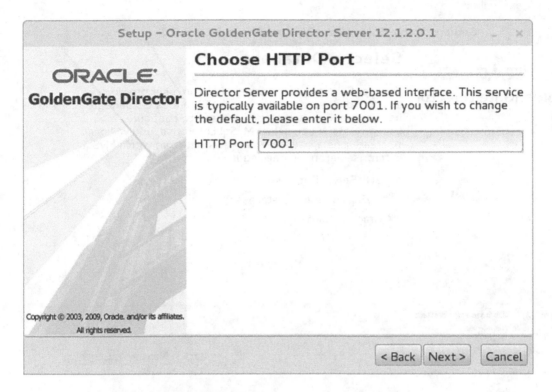

Figure 14-6. HTTP port for Oracle GoldenGate Director web interface requests

The Oracle GoldenGate Director server uses a database repository to store information and work with various Oracle GoldenGate instances. Select one of the available database types, as shown in Figure 14-7. Make sure you have the selected database installed and configured on your system with a username and password that you will use for the repository. Click Next to continue.

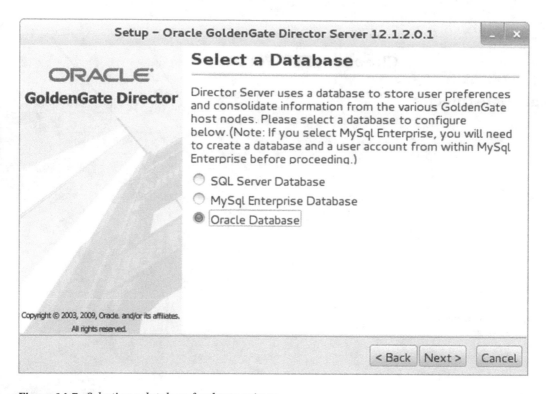

Figure 14-7. Selecting a database for the repository

Provide your database connection details that will be used to create a database driver for connecting to the repository database. Values on this screen depend on the type of database you selected in the previous step. Figure 14-8 shows the connection details for the orcl database, which is listening on port 1521.

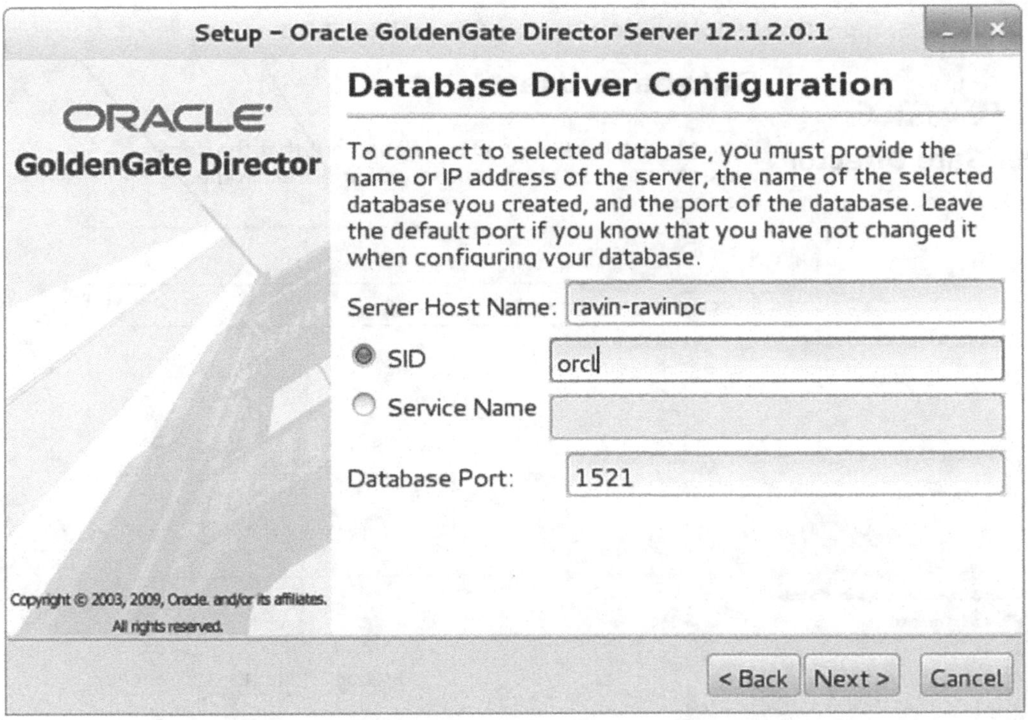

Figure 14-8. *Connection details for the database driver*

Provide a username and password for the database user that will be used by the OGG Director, as shown in Figure 14-9.

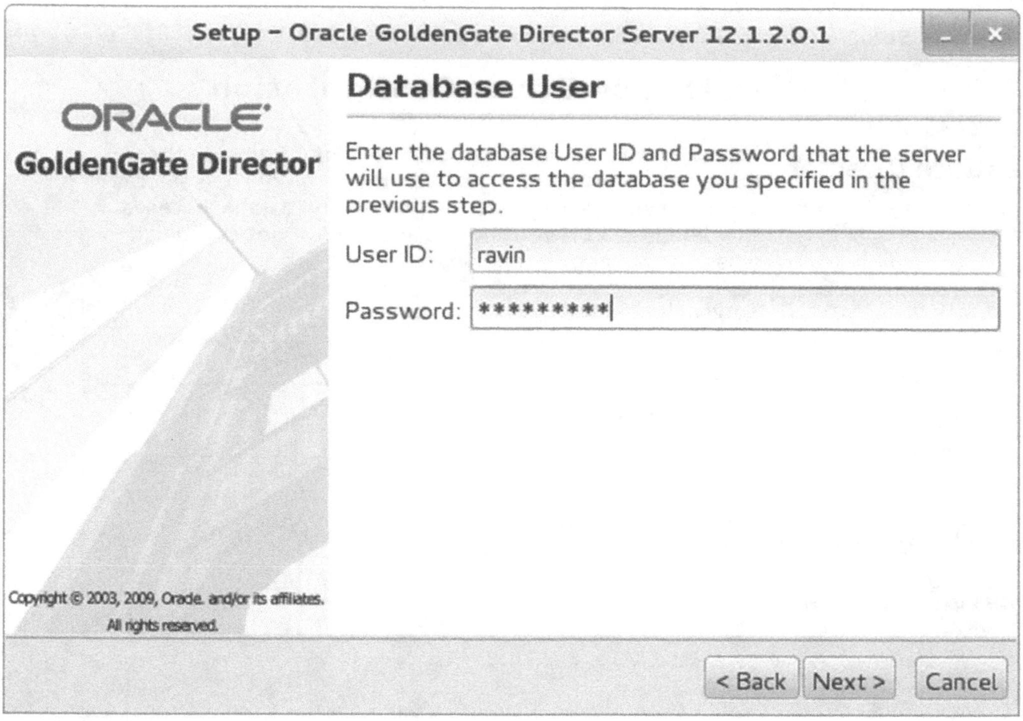

Figure 14-9. *Providing a database user and password*

Figure 14-10 shows the installation summary. Review the installation summary and click Next to begin installing the OGG Director server.

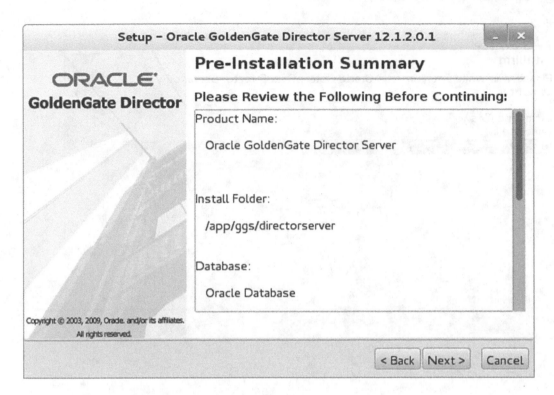

Figure 14-10. *Reviewing the pre-installation summary*

Figure 14-11 shows the installation is in progress. This is fairly quick and completes in a couple of minutes.

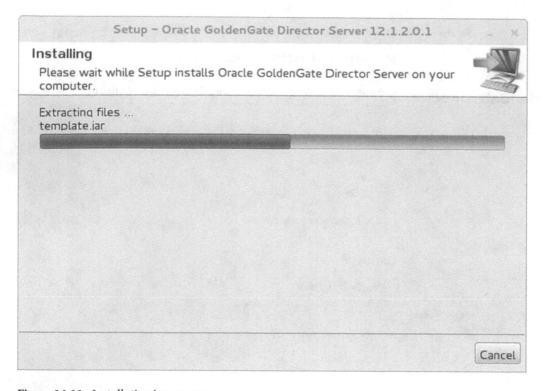

Figure 14-11. *Installation in progress*

Figure 14-12 shows an error. This could happen because of a number of reasons. Before you click OK at this step, navigate to the Oracle GoldenGate Director installation directory and locate the cds-tool. log file. Check for the cause of the error and resolve it; then try running the installer again with the same configurations. In addition to cds-tool.log, you can see certain other files in the directory. Once you fix the issue, you can run the run-cds-tool.sh script to quickly recheck if the issue is fixed. The moment you click OK on the screen shown in Figure 14-12, the installer abends and drops all files except the log file.

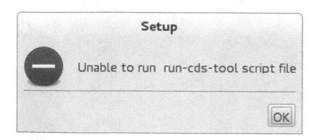

Figure 14-12. *cds-tool error during installation*

Here are some common reasons for this error:

- The installer cannot connect to the database specified in the configuration.
- JAVA_HOME and PATH are not properly set.
- The database version is not supported.

The following is one of the sample errors I produced when I tried to use SQL Server as the repository database type without having a SQL Server database installed on the machine.

```
Canonicaly: /app
Testing connection with: jdbc:sqlserver://localhost:1433;databaseName=ggsdb
Execption while processing db setup.  Cannot continue.  Exception follows…
com.microsoft.sqlserver.jdbc.SQLServerException: The TCP/IP connection to the host  has
failed. java.net.ConnectException: Connection refused
        at com.microsoft.sqlserver.jdbc.SQLServerException.makeFromDriverError(Unknown
        Source)
        at com.microsoft.sqlserver.jdbc.SQLServerConnection.connectHelper(Unknown Source)
        at com.microsoft.sqlserver.jdbc.SQLServerConnection.loginWithoutFailover(Unknown
        Source)
        at com.microsoft.sqlserver.jdbc.SQLServerConnection.connect(Unknown Source)
        at com.microsoft.sqlserver.jdbc.SQLServerDriver.connect(Unknown Source)
        at com.goldengate.gdsc.util.ConfigDirectorServer.startDBSetup(ConfigDirectorServer.
        java:704)
        at com.goldengate.gdsc.util.ConfigDirectorServer.main(ConfigDirectorServer.java:955)
```

Using Command-Line Installation

Command-line installation is similar to GUI installation, only that the installer prompts you to specify inputs and waits for your response. To begin the command-line installation, execute the .exe or .sh file on your operating system shell with the –c option, as shown here:

- On Windows:

  ```
  gg-director-serversetup_<release>.exe –c
  ```

- On Unix/Linux:

  ```
  ./gg-director-serversetup_<release>.sh -c
  ```

Start and Stop the OGG Director Server

The script to start and stop the OGG Director server is in the domain and domain/bin subdirectory of your OGG Director installation directory.

On the Unix/Linux command shell, execute one of the following. The option -b means executing in the background.

```
directorControl.sh start
directorControl.sh -b start
directorControl.sh stop
directorControl.sh -b stop
startWebLogic.sh
stopWebLogic.sh
```

On the Windows command shell, execute one of the following:

```
startWebLogic.cmd
stopWebLogic.cmd
```

Installing the OGG Director Client

Now you have installed and successfully started your Oracle GoldenGate Director server. You are all set to install the OGG Director client. The client will provide you with a graphical interface to manage Oracle GoldenGate instances.

System Requirements

Before you can begin your installation process, verify that your system meets the following requirements:

- The OGG Director client version should be the same as the OGG Director server.

- Your machine should have JRE installed.

- Verify that the host and port for the OGG Director server is accessible from the machine you are installing the OGG Director client on. You may opt to install the server and client on the same machine.

Downloading Software

The Oracle GoldenGate Director can be downloaded from www.oracle.com/technetwork/middleware/goldengate/downloads/index.html. Look for the Oracle GoldenGate Director Client under Management Pack for Oracle GoldenGate. Click the appropriate version for your operating system environment. For demonstration in this chapter, I downloaded "Oracle GoldenGate Director V12.1.2.0.1 Client on UNIX Based Platforms."

Installing the Client

Unzip the compressed installer and execute the following at the command shell to launch the installer:

```
$ ./gg-director-clientsetup_unix_v12_1_2_0_1.sh
```

Follow the onscreen instructions and provide the appropriate values. Figure 14-13 shows the welcome screen for the Oracle GoldenGate Director client setup.

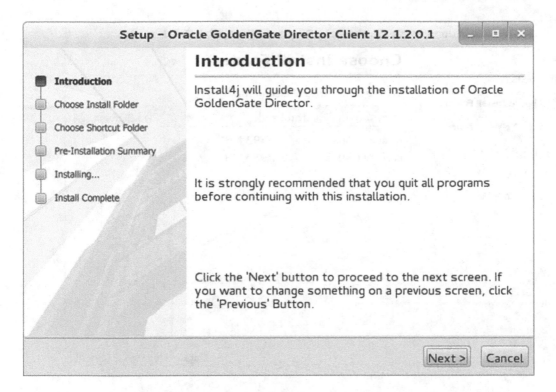

Figure 14-13. *OGG Director client setup welcome screen*

Choose the installation folder where you want to install the OGG Director client. The client software is fairly a light tool and requires less than 100 MB disk space. The installation steps are pretty easy, and the complete installation takes less than five minutes (unless you fall asleep during the work!).

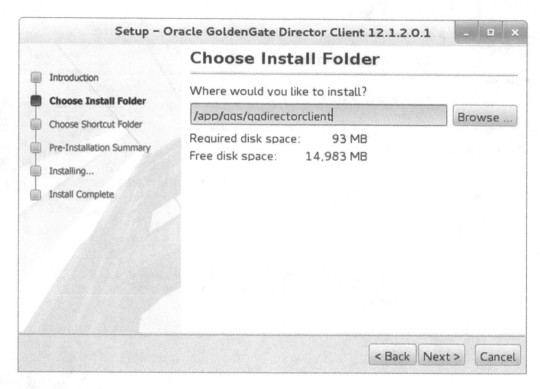

Figure 14-14. *Choosing an installation location*

The Director client creates symlinks to the executables for quick access. You can create them in your home directory or any other frequently used convenient location. I have chosen to create symlinks in the /app/ggs location as shown in Figure 14-15.

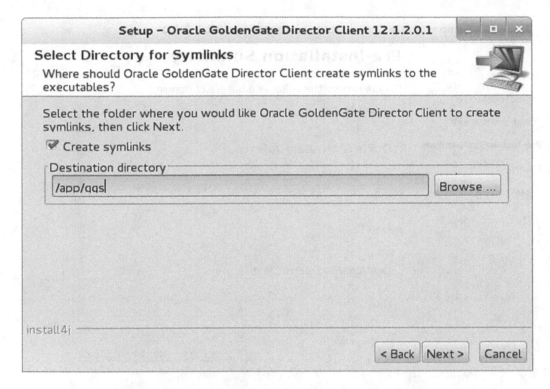

Figure 14-15. *Creating symlinks to executables*

Review the installation summary as shown in Figure 14-16 and click Next to begin the installation.

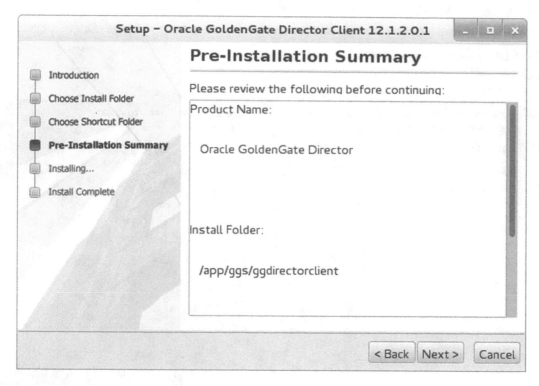

Figure 14-16. Reviewing the installation summary

Figure 14-17 shows that the installation is in progress. Hold on, it won't take long.

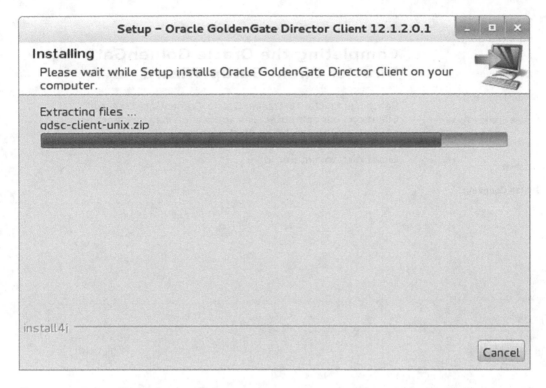

Figure 14-17. *Installation in progress*

The installation process has completed successfully, as shown in Figure 14-18. Click Finish.

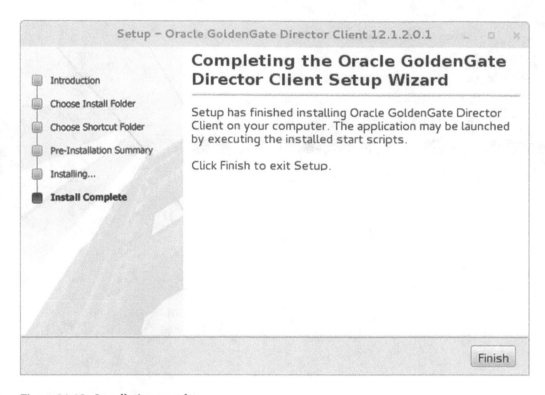

Figure 14-18. *Installation complete*

Starting the OGG Director Client

Locate and execute the `run-director.sh` script from the `bin` directory inside the installation directory. When prompted, provide the username and password for the admin user for the OGG Director and the host name and port for the OGG Director server.

```
$ ./run-director.sh
```

Wait for the OGG Director client interface to launch. Go to the File menu and click Login. Figure 14-19 shows the OGG Director client login screen.

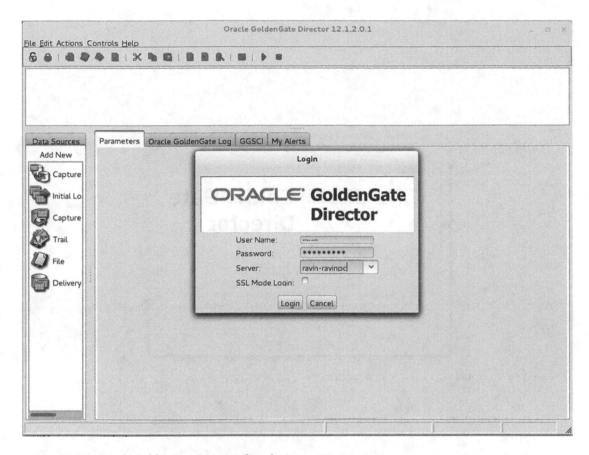

Figure 14-19. *Oracle GoldenGate Director client login screen*

Starting the OGG Director Administrator

Locate and execute the run-admin.sh script from the bin directory inside the installation directory.

Figure 14-20 shows the login screen for the OGG Director client.

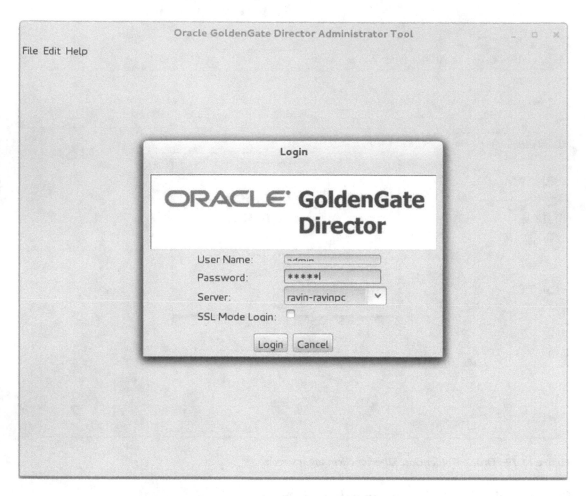

Figure 14-20. *Oracle GoldenGate Director admin login*

Provide the admin username and password and specify the server and port. For a first-time login, the username/password is admin/admin. You should change the admin password for future logins instead of using the default password.

You are ready to use your Oracle GoldenGate Director admin to set up users and data sources and to configure and start the Monitor Agent on each particular tab, as shown in Figure 14-21.

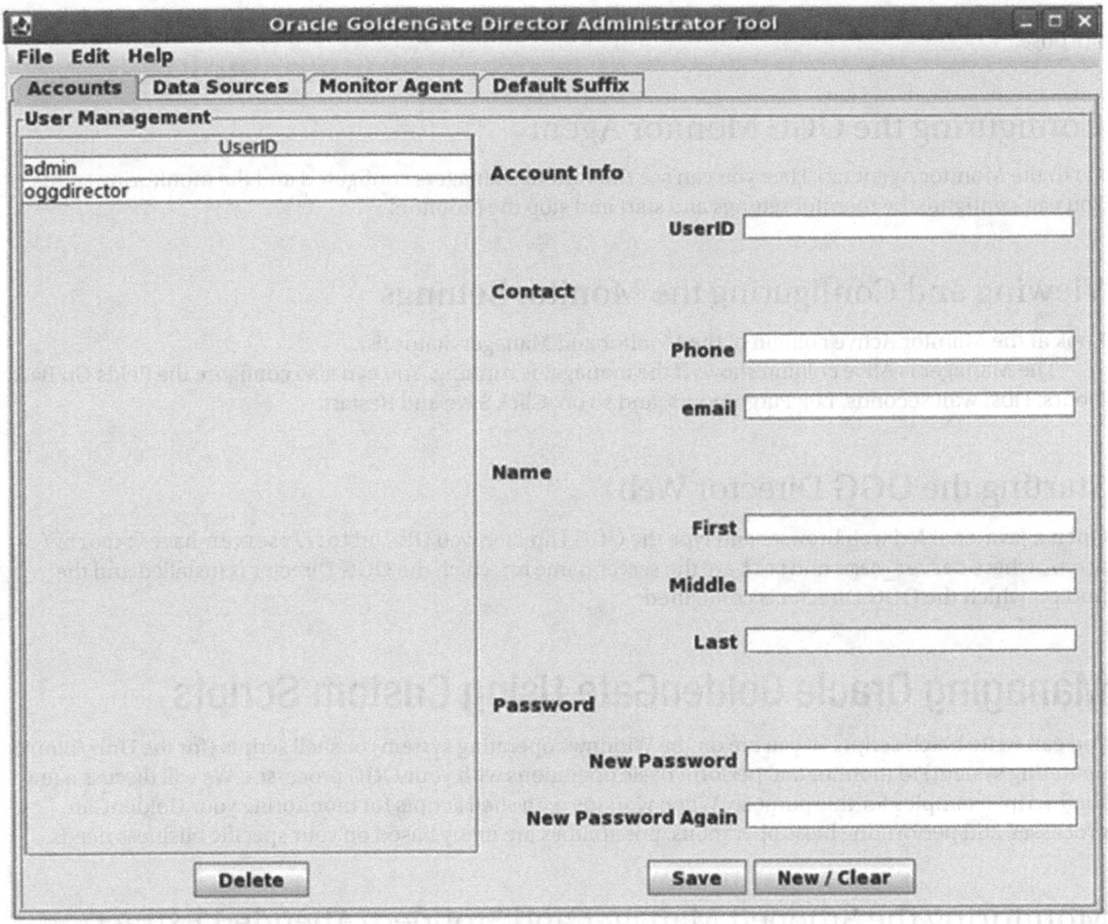

Figure 14-21. OGG Director admin home

Adding, Changing, and Deleting User Accounts

To add a user, go to the Accounts tab, click New/Clear, and provide the information on the screen.

Similarly, if you want to change information for an existing user, click the user ID on the Accounts tab and edit the information as required.

To delete the user, simply select the user under the user ID of the Accounts tab and click the Delete button.

Adding the OGG Data Source

Start the manager process for the OGG instance for which you are going to add the data source.

Go to the Data Sources tab and click New/Clear.

Enter the information on the screen. You need to provide the host identity, manager port, and data source name. It is a user-defined name, for example, ggs_dev1.

Go to the GoldenGate info and enter the requested information on the screen. You need to enter the host operating system, database type, and GoldenGate version in this section.

Enter the default DB credentials and access control information and click Save.

Similarly, you can go to the Data Sources tab and select the appropriate data source to edit and delete purpose.

Configuring the OGG Monitor Agent

Go to the Monitor Agent tab. Here you can see the various managers configured and the monitoring status. You can configure the monitor settings and start and stop the monitors.

Viewing and Configuring the Monitor Settings

Look at the Monitor Active column of the Monitor and Manager Status list.

The Manager is Alive column shows if the manager is running. You can also configure the fields Go Back Hours, Host wait seconds, Log Purge Hours, and so on. Click Save and Restart.

Starting the OGG Director Web

Open a Java-enabled web browser and type the OGG Director web URL, `http://<server_name>:<port>/acon/`, where `server_name` and `port` are the server name on which the OGG Director is installed and the port on which the OGG Director is configured.

Managing Oracle GoldenGate Using Custom Scripts

You can write batch scripts (if you are on the Windows operating system) or shell scripts (for the Unix/Linux operating system) to monitor and perform basic operations with your OGG processes. We will discuss a few shell script examples for this purpose. When working with shell scripts for monitoring your GoldenGate processes and performing basic operations, possibilities are many based on your specific business needs.

Monitoring the Stopped Manager and Stopped/Abended Extract/Replicat Processes

The script uses the `status all` command to print the status of the OGG processes of your OGG instance. It then scans this output and sends the appropriate notification if any process is stopped or abended or has a lag greater than the threshold.

```
#!/bin/sh -a
############################################################################
#  Script:  ggmon.sh                                                      #
#  Usage:                                                                  #
#  ggmon.sh <ORA_SID> <OGG instance directory path>                       #
############################################################################

### Verify if all required parameters are passed ###
 if [[ $# -ne 2 ]]; then
    echo " Syntax : "
    echo " $0 <ORA_SID> <GoldenGate Directory>"
    exit
fi
```

```
LOG_DIR=/app/ggs/scripts/gglogs
SCRIPT_DIR=/app/ggs/scripts
DB_NAME=$1
GG_INSTANCE=$2


### 	LOAD PROFILE PARAMETERS 	#####
. /orasoft/local/bin/oraprof $DB_NAME


### 	CONFIGURE VARIABLES 	###
vTimestamp=`date +"%Y%m%d%H%M"`
HOST=`nslookup $(hostname) | grep 'Name:' | awk '{print $2}'`

GG_STATUS_LOG=${LOG_DIR}/ggsci_status_all.log
OUT_FILE=${LOG_DIR}/err_chn_lst.out
MAIL_IDs=${SCRIPT_DIR}/mail.lst


### 	CHECK GoldenGate Manager down, Channels down/lag 	###
checkerror()
{
    echo " " |awk ' BEGIN { mgr_up=0; } {
        while ("grep -e '"RUNNING"' -e '"STOPPED"' -e '"ABENDED"' '"$GG_STATUS_LOG"'"|
getline info) {
            if ( info == "" ) {
                continue;
            }
            split(info, data_list, " ");
                if ((data_list[1] == "MANAGER" && data_list[2] == "RUNNING") || mgr_up == 1
) {
                    if ( mgr_up == 1 ) {
                        if ( data_list[2] == "RUNNING" && data_list[4] != "" ) {
                            split(data_list[4],lag,":");
                            act_lag=lag[1] lag[2];
                            if (act_lag > "0015" ) {
                                #Lag list
                                print "CHANNEL_LAG: "info;
                            }
                        } else {
                            #Channel down
                            print "CHANNEL_DOWN: "info;
                        }
                    }
                    mgr_up=1;
                } else {
                    #Manager down
                    print "MANAGER_DOWN: "info;
                    break;
                }
        }
        }' >> $OUT_FILE
}
```

305

```
###    SEND ALERTS    ###
send_mail()
{
    checkerror
    v_mailIds=`cat $MAIL_IDs | grep -v "^#"`
    if [[ $(grep -c MANAGER_DOWN $OUT_FILE) -ge 1 ]] ; then
        cat $OUT_FILE | cut -d" " -f2- | mailx -s "GoldenGate Manager DOWN for $GG_INSTANCE
instance on (`hostname`)" $v_mailIds
    elif [ $(grep -c CHANNEL_DOWN $OUT_FILE) -ge 1 ] && [ $(grep -c CHANNEL_LAG $OUT_FILE)
-eq 0 ] ; then
        cat $OUT_FILE | cut -d" " -f2- | mailx -s "GoldenGate Channel(s) DOWN for $GG_
INSTANCE instance on (`hostname`)" $v_mailIds
    elif [ $(grep -c CHANNEL_LAG $OUT_FILE) -ge 1 ] && [ $(grep -c CHANNEL_DOWN $OUT_FILE)
-eq 0 ] ; then
        cat $OUT_FILE | cut -d" " -f2- | mailx -s "GoldenGate Channel(s) LAG for $GG_
INSTANCE instance on (`hostname`)" $v_mailIds
    elif [ $(grep -c CHANNEL_LAG $OUT_FILE) -ge 1 ] && [ $(grep -c CHANNEL_DOWN $OUT_FILE)
-ge 1 ] ; then
        cat $OUT_FILE | cut -d" " -f2- | mailx -s "GoldenGate Channel(s) DOWN and LAG for
$GG_INSTANCE instance on (`hostname`)" $v_mailIds
    else
        echo "All GoldenGate Instances Running fine !!!"
    fi
}


###    GET GoldenGate Status    ###
get_status_all()
{
cd $GG_INSTANCE
ggsci <<EOF | grep -e MANAGER -e REPLICAT -e EXTRACT > $GG_STATUS_LOG
status all
quit
EOF
}


#####################################################
#              Main Script Here                     #
#####################################################

> $GG_STATUS_LOG
> $OUT_FILE
echo -e " Following channel(s) is/are down or has lag in GoldenGate : \n" > $OUT_FILE
echo -e " Program     Status      Group       Lag            Time Since Chkpt\n" >> $OUT_FILE
get_status_all
send_mail

### END OF SCRIPT ####
```

Here's some sample output for the previous script:

```
Following channel(s) is/are down or lag in GoldenGate:

Program     Status      Group       Lag             Time Since Chkpt

EXTRACT     ABENDED     ETTND001    00:00:00        00:08:04


Following channel(s) is/are down or lag in GoldenGate:

Program     Status      Group       Lag             Time Since Chkpt

MANAGER     STOPPED
```

You can create your shell script to extract information from report files such as ggserror.log, perform stats and other GGSCI commands, extract information from the output, and send e-mail/pager notifications. The possibilities are practically endless.

Summary

Oracle Enterprise Manager is a great GUI-based monitoring utility for Oracle Enterprise servers and databases. Oracle GoldenGate can be installed as a plug-in and extends the capability of OEM to monitor and manage Oracle GoldenGate instances. This chapter discussed how to configure OEM to install and use the OGG plug-in. We also discussed the Oracle GoldenGate Director, which allows you to remotely configure and manage OGG instances.

In addition to using proprietary software in the Oracle GoldenGate Management Pack, you can create custom scripts to monitor OGG processes. An example of such a monitoring script was discussed at the end of this chapter.

In the next chapter, we will discuss how to use Oracle GoldenGate Veridata for data integrity. It comes as separately licensed software and is not part of the OGG Management Pack. The tool compares two data sets and lets you know what data is out of sync. This tool is especially significant in high-volume live environments where downtime to verify data integrity and repair inconsistencies is not an option. The best part of this tool is that your replication keeps on happening and still produces accurate reports.

CHAPTER 15

■ ■ ■

Ensuring Data Integrity with Veridata

Oracle GoldenGate comes with a nice data comparison and repair tool called Veridata. The tool compares two data sets and lets you know what data is out of sync. This tool is especially significant in high-volume live environments where downtime to verify data integrity and repair inconsistencies is not an option. The best part of this tool is that your replication keeps on happening and still produces accurate reports.

Why Use OGG Veridata?

In today's ever-complex IT environment, data distributed across multiple systems is prone to inconsistencies because of several reasons, as listed here:

- Hardware and network issues such as system failures, disk corruptions/failures, and network failures/glitches can lead to data inconsistencies. These inconsistencies might get introduced after a system is brought back from a failure.

- Errors can happen during the initial load of data before replication can actually be started. This may happen based on the initial data migration tool used and the way it handles specific data. Also, sometimes a difference in the character sets of the two systems may introduce bad characters in the target system during the initial load. These may go unnoticed until you have a transaction that fails because of inconsistency on the two systems.

- It is extremely important to ensure that the source and target database systems match in terms of the table constraints that limit the data entered into them. For example, if you missed the primary/unique constraint or did not enable a foreign key after the initial load, it may result in duplicates in your target tables when replication is turned on.

- Sometimes even though replication is working absolutely fine, transactions on the source are done in a compromised manner that prevents them from being captured by the capture process. For example, a bulk data load using the NOLOGGING feature in Oracle databases will boost the performance of the load.

- Sometimes replication is unidirectional and the applications, users, or DBAs on the target machine are not supposed to modify data on the target machine. However, they may do it anyway, which may lead to inconsistencies in data.

© Ravinder Gupta 2016
R. Gupta, *Mastering Oracle GoldenGate*, DOI 10.1007/978-1-4842-2301-7_15

These situations can be prevented completely, but there are some that cannot be guaranteed all the time. OGG Veridata can work with Oracle GoldenGate replication and can also work with another similar product. Hence, you don't need to have Oracle GoldenGate replication to use OGG Veridata.

OGG Veridata 12c can compare data and repair data inconsistencies for heterogeneous database systems including Oracle, SQL Server, Sybase ASE, DB2, and Teradata databases. Also, it can identify inconsistencies and generate reports for HP Enscribe and NonStop SQL/MP without the repair capability.

OGG Veridata uses fast hashing, ordering, and comparison techniques that enable it to compare high-volume data easily without any performance impact on the replicating systems. OGG Veridata uses its own repository for this purpose.

Moreover, OGG Veridata comes with a graphically rich user interface that can be used by both technical and business users for common activities and monitoring.

How Does It Work?

Working with OGG Veridata consists of the following three broad steps:

1. *Initial comparison*: OGG Veridata queries and retrieves rows to be compared from the source and target databases. The columns are converted to standard data types for comparison in this step if using a heterogeneous database environment. Primary key columns are compared value by value, and a hash key is generated for nonkey values. The hash key techniques reduce the overall data volume to be transferred over the network for comparison. The unique hash key values are compared against each other for each row. This, however, is not a guaranteed confirmation that the data in the nonkey columns matches exactly. OGG Veridata can also be configured to match nonkey columns, value by value, at the cost of increased network utilization and reduced performance.

2. *Maybe out of sync*: The rows that do not match are put in the MOOS queue. There are chances that these rows do not match on the source and target because of transactions in trails that are yet not applied on target.

3. *Confirm out of sync (COOS)*: A specified replication latency threshold is used to decide whether the rows in the MOOS queue are really out of sync and put them into another queue called COOS. The rows in the queue waits for the specified replication latency threshold to expire before they are evaluated again and marked with one of the three status listed here:

    *   *In-flight*: Veridata could not confirm if the rows are not in sync because of an update on the same row after the initial comparison step.

    *   *In-sync*: The two rows are in sync.

    *   *Persistently out-of-sync*: The two rows are out of sync.

The results of comparisons can be viewed in the form of reports using the OGG Veridata web UI. Figure 15-1 shows the components of OGG Veridata.

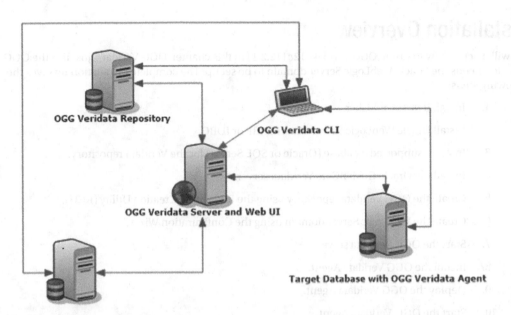

Figure 15-1. *Oracle GoldenGate Veridata components*

Listed here are the components of Oracle GoldenGate Veridata:

- *Veridata server*: This is the controller of all the Veridata activity. It compares the data set, detects and validates data mismatches, and generates a report for it.

- *Veridata web user interface*: This is a browser-based GUI that lets the end user interact with and issue instructions to Veridata. The user can configure any data comparison rule and view the reports of the comparisons.

- *Veridata repository*: Persistent information related to Veridata is stored in the Veridata repository.

- *Veridata Agent*: This interacts with the source and target databases, fetches the data set to be compared, and returns it to the Veridata server or command-line interface (CLI).

- *Veridata CLI*: Oracle GoldenGate Veridata comes with a command-line interface called Vericom. You can run data set comparison and stop and stop the Veridata server using Vericom.

Installation Overview

We will discuss how to install OGG Veridata 12c (12.2.1) in this chapter. OGG Veridata, just like the OGG Monitor, needs the Oracle WebLogic Server domain to be set up. The complete installation involves the following steps:

1. Install JDK 1.8 or higher.

2. Install Oracle WebLogic Server 12c with JRF or JDBC.

3. Install a supported database (Oracle or SQL Server) for the Veridata repository.

4. Install the Oracle GoldenGate Veridata server.

5. Create the OGG Veridata repository using the Repository Creation Utility (RCU).

6. Create the WebLogic Server domain using the Configuration Wizard.

7. Start the OGG Veridata server.

8. Install the OGG Veridata Agent.

9. Deploy the OGG Veridata Agent.

10. Start the OGG Veridata Agent.

System Requirements

Up to Oracle GoldenGate Veridata 12c, you can use Veridata for data comparison on the following databases. Please check the Oracle documentation for the latest list of supported databases for your version of OGG Veridata.

- DB2 LUW and z/OS

- Enscribe

- Oracle

- NonStop SQL/MP

- SQL Server

- Sybase Adaptive Server Enterprise (ASE)

- Teradata

Make sure your system meets the necessary requirements for the Veridata Agent, Veridata server, and web user interface, as listed here:

- The Veridata Agent is installed for each database instance (on the source as well as the target). This is because one Veridata Agent can fetch data from multiple schemas on the same database instance but not from multiple database instances.

- A Java agent is required on all database platforms except for NonStop, which uses a C-Agent. Download and install either the Java Software Development Kit (SDK) or the Java Runtime Environment (JRE).

- A minimum of 1 GB RAM and 200 MB disk space are required for each Veridata Agent on each database server.

- The Oracle GoldenGate Veridata server and the web UI are installed as part of a single installer. The Veridata server needs around 200 MB of RAM for performing basic tasks. Most of the other RAM requirements are for the sort operations on the dataset for comparison. For an in-memory sort, which typically is the fastest of all sorting methods, the Veridata server requires around 2.5 times the memory of the data set size. For larger sets of data, usually other sort operations that take much less memory are implemented.

- The Veridata repository needs storage space to store objects for persistent information related to Veridata. These objects usually do not need much space. You can create the repository on Oracle or SQL Server.

- The Veridata user typically needs CREATE SESSION, TABLE, VIEW, CREATE, and DROP INDEXES privileges on the repository. You need to grant INSERT, UPDATE, DELETE, and SELECT privileges on each table to the user.

- For the Veridata web UI, all you need is a Java-enabled web browser.

Installing the OGG Veridata Server

Assuming you have already installed the appropriate JDK and Oracle WebLogic Server as discussed during the OGG Monitor installation in Chapter 13, you can begin installing the OGG Veridata server.

Download the Software

Oracle GoldenGate Veridata can be downloaded from https://edelivery.oracle.com. Search for *Oracle GoldenGate Veridata 12.2.1*, select your operating system platform, and hit Download. This step requires the creation of an OTN account. We already discussed the steps for downloading software from the Oracle Software Delivery Cloud site in Chapter 4.

Figure 15-2 shows the OGG Veridata version and platform I downloaded for our demonstration in this chapter.

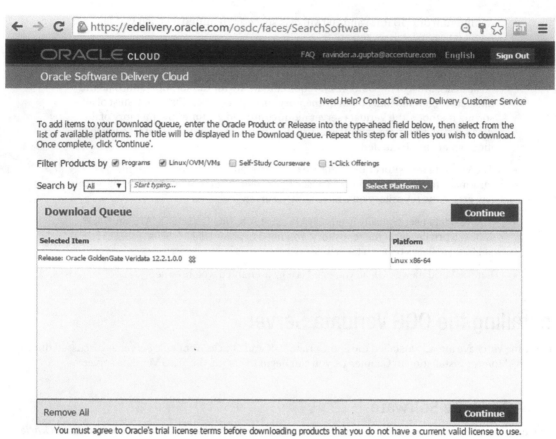

Figure 15-2. *Downloading the OGG Veridata software*

Installation

Let's start with installing the GoldenGate Veridata server. Here I will discuss the installation steps on a Linux server. Copy the JAR file downloaded to the installation directory. Ensure that you are logged in as a user with admin privileges. Issue the following command to begin the installation:

```
$ java -jar -Xmx1024m fmw_12.2.1.0.0_ogg.jar
[oracle@ravin-ravinpc vboxshare]$ export DISPLAY=:0.0
[oracle@ravin-ravinpc vboxshare]$ java -jar -Xmx1024m fmw_12.2.1.0.0_ogg.jar
Launcher log file is /tmp/OraInstall2016-07-04_10-16-14PM/launcher2016-07-04_10-16-14PM.log.
Extracting
files.............................................................................................
.................................................................................................
.................................................................................................
.................................................................................................
.............................................
Starting Oracle Universal Installer
```

```
Checking if CPU speed is above 300 MHz.    Actual 2527.012 MHz    Passed
Checking monitor: must be configured to display at least 256 colors.    Actual
16777216    Passed
Checking swap space: must be greater than 512 MB.    Actual 2047 MB    Passed
Checking if this platform requires a 64-bit JVM.    Actual 64    Passed (64-bit not required)
Checking temp space: must be greater than 300 MB.    Actual 19343 MB    Passed

Preparing to launch the Oracle Universal Installer from /tmp/OraInstall2016-07-04_10-16-14PM
Log: /tmp/OraInstall2016-07-04_10-16-14PM/install2016-07-04_10-16-14PM.log
```

Figure 15-3 shows the Welcome screen for Oracle Fusion Middleware 12*c*. Click Next to navigate to the next step.

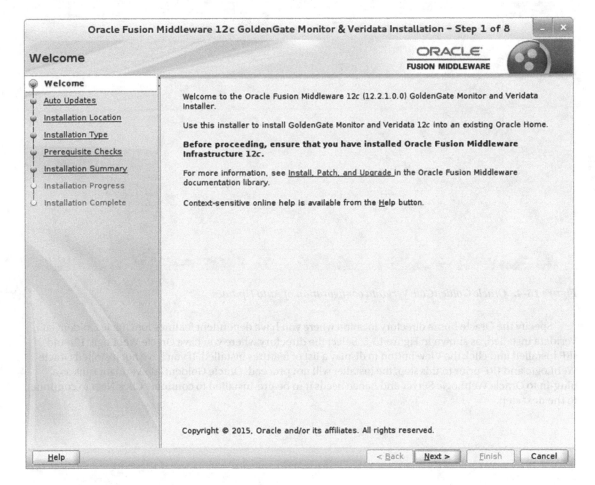

Figure 15-3. *Oracle GoldenGate Veridata server installation Welcome screen*

The installer will prompt you to search and apply any patches or updates, as shown in Figure 15-4. You can also choose to skip this step.

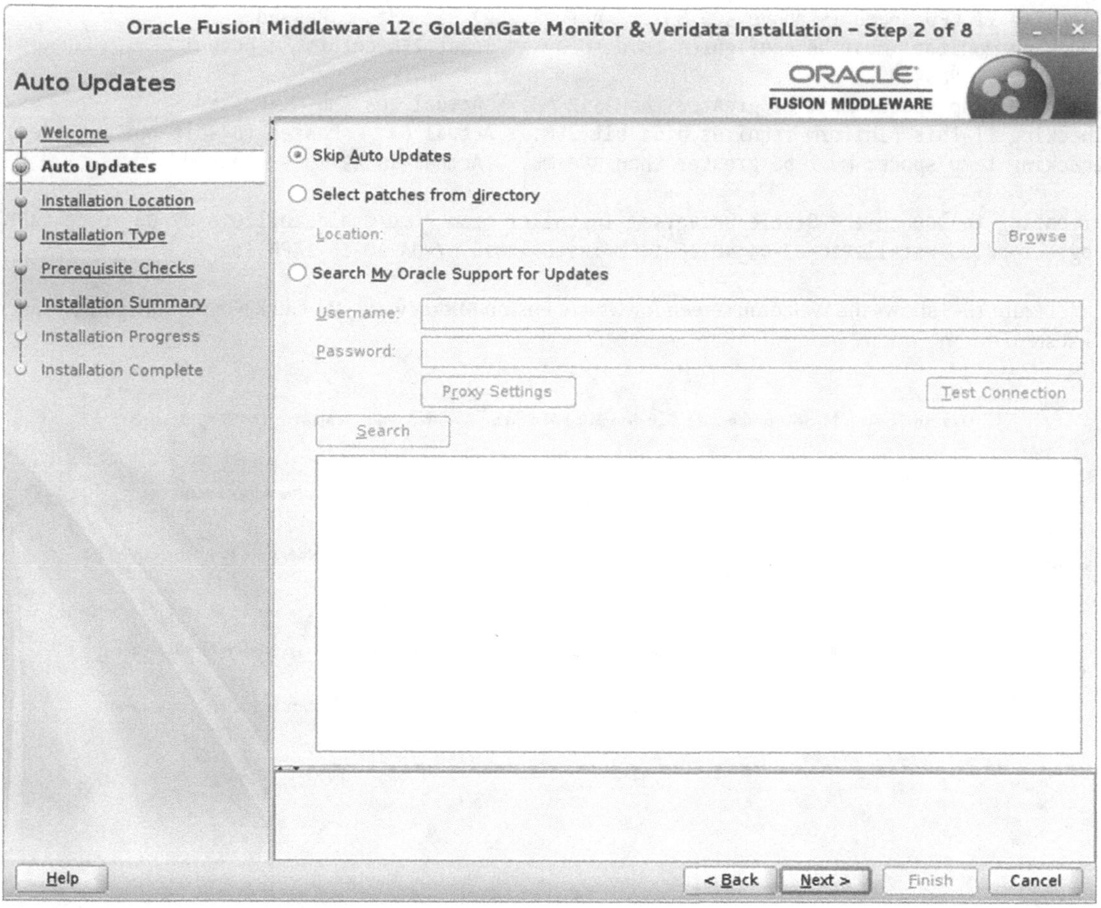

Figure 15-4. *Oracle GoldenGate Veridata configuration of Auto Updates*

Specify the Oracle home directory location where you have dependent features for Oracle GoldenGate Veridata installed, as shown in Figure 15-5. Select the directory where you have Oracle WebLogic 12*c* and JRF installed and click the View button to display a list of features installed. If you have not installed Oracle WebLogic and JRF prior to this step, the installer will not proceed. Oracle GoldenGate Veridata runs as a plug-in to Oracle WebLogic Server and hence needs it to be pre-installed to continue. Click Next to continue to the next step.

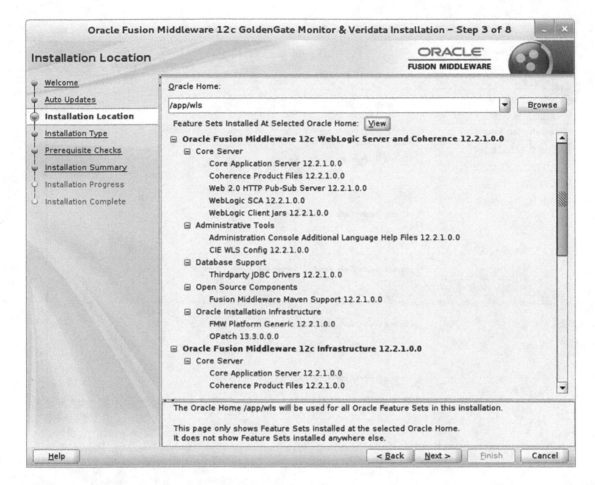

Figure 15-5. *Selecting the installation location*

Once you have WebLogic and JRF in place and have selected the correct Oracle Home directory, select Oracle GoldenGate Veridata Server as the type of installation in step 4, as shown in Figure 15-6. You will use the same installation program later to install the Oracle GoldenGate Veridata Agent.

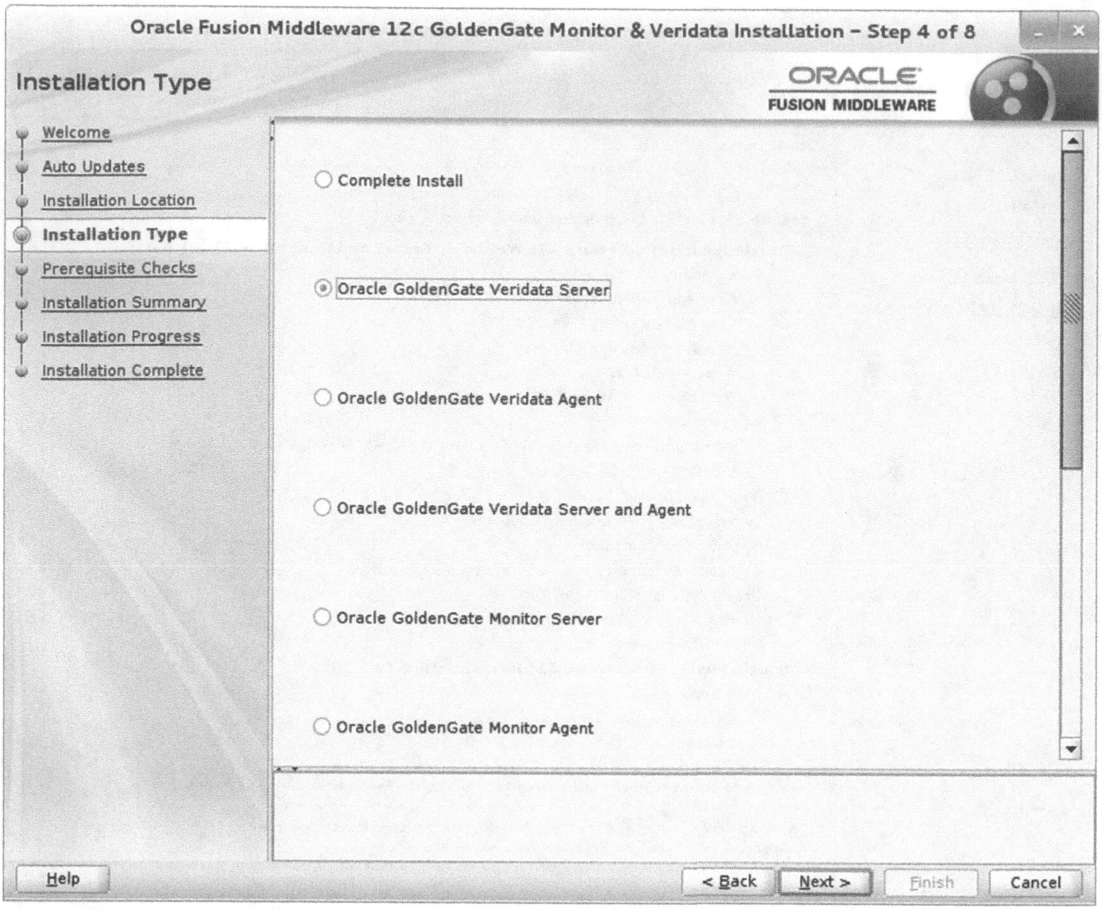

Figure 15-6. Selecting the installation component name

Once you have selected the desired product to install, click Next. The wizard will begin checking for certain prerequisites including the Java version and OS platform. Click Next to continue once the prerequisite checks are complete and have passed, as shown in Figure 15-7.

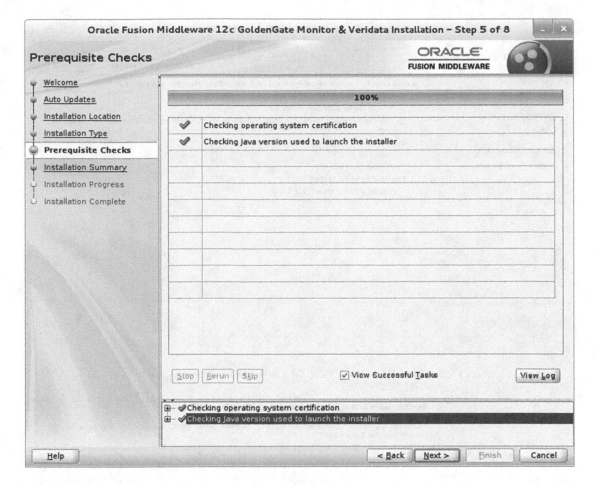

Figure 15-7. Prerequisites check

Figure 15-8 shows the installation summary screen. It lists the features you have selected for installation along with disk space consumption. You can also select Save Response File to save the installation configuration. You can then reuse this response file for silent installations on other servers if required.

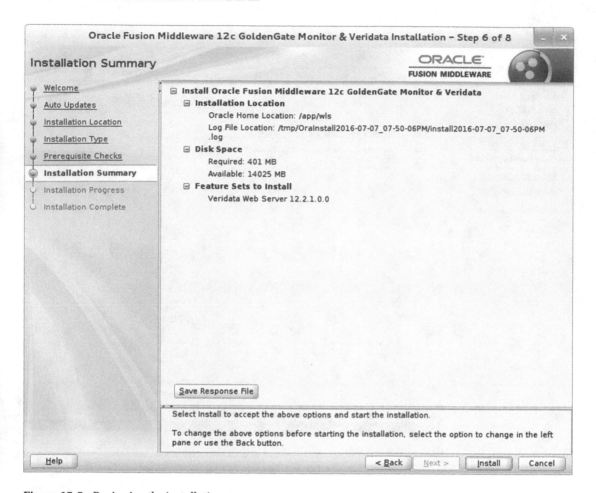

Figure 15-8. *Reviewing the installation summary*

Review the installation summary and click Install to begin the installation.

Figure 15-9 shows the installation stages in progress. You can view installation messages for the current step by clicking View Messages. You can also view the installer log by clicking the View Log button.

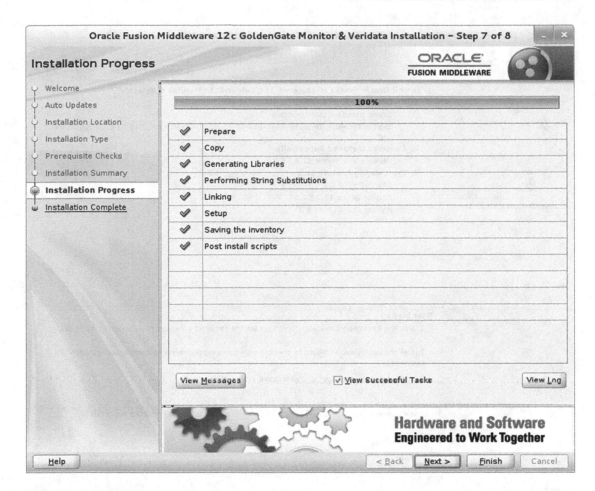

Figure 15-9. *Installing components*

Figure 15-10 shows that the installation has successfully completed.

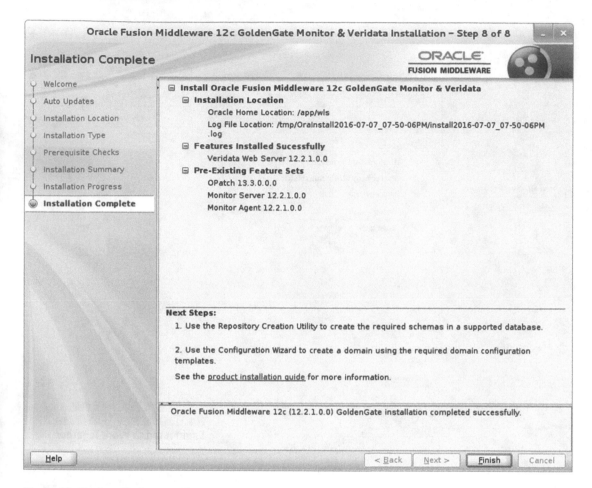

Figure 15-10. *Installation complete*

Create the OGG Veridata Repository Using RCU

Now that you have achieved your first checkpoint of installing the Oracle GoldenGate Veridata server, you are ready to install the OGG Veridata repository. Navigate to the Oracle Home to locate the RCU. It is located in your ORACLE_HOME/oracle_common/bin/ directory. Launch RCU as shown here:

```
$./rcu
```

Or if you are using a Windows machine, run rcu.bat from the command prompt.

```
rcu.bat
```

If you are creating the repository on MySQL, first run the following commands at the SQL prompt before starting RCU:

```
mysql> SET GLOBAL INNODB_FILE_PER_TABLE="ON";
mysql> SET GLOBAL INNODB_FILE_FORMAT="Barracuda";
```

```
mysql> SET GLOBAL INNODB_LARGE_PREFIX="ON";
mysql> SET GLOBAL LOG_BIN_TRUST_FUNCTION_CREATORS="ON";
```

Navigate through the installation screens and create the repository. Figure 15-11 shows the Welcome screen of Repository Creation Utility 12.2.1 for Oracle Fusion Middleware. Click Next to continue.

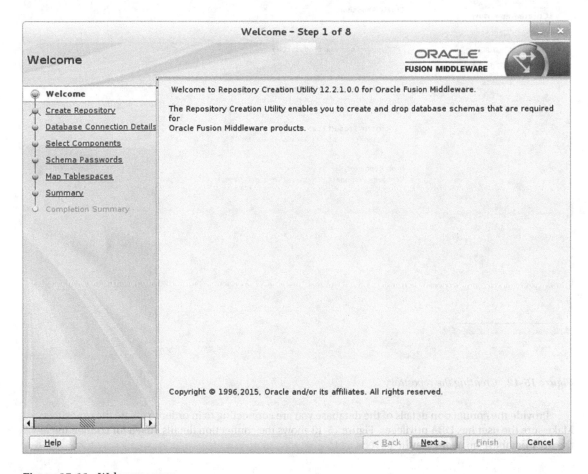

Figure 15-11. *Welcome screen*

Since you are creating a new repository for the Oracle GoldenGate Veridata server, select Create Repository and under it select System Load and Product Load, as shown in Figure 15-12. Make sure you have DBA privileges to create the repository.

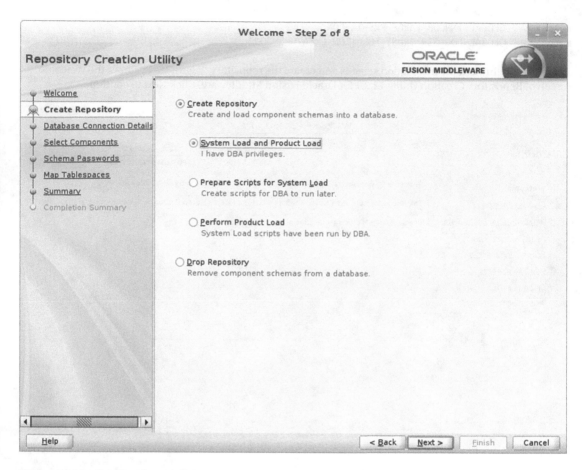

Figure 15-12. Creating the repository

Provide the connection details of the database you are connecting to in order to create the repository. Make sure the user has DBA privileges. Figure 15-13 shows the connection details I used for connecting to the orcl database on node1.ravin-pc.com.

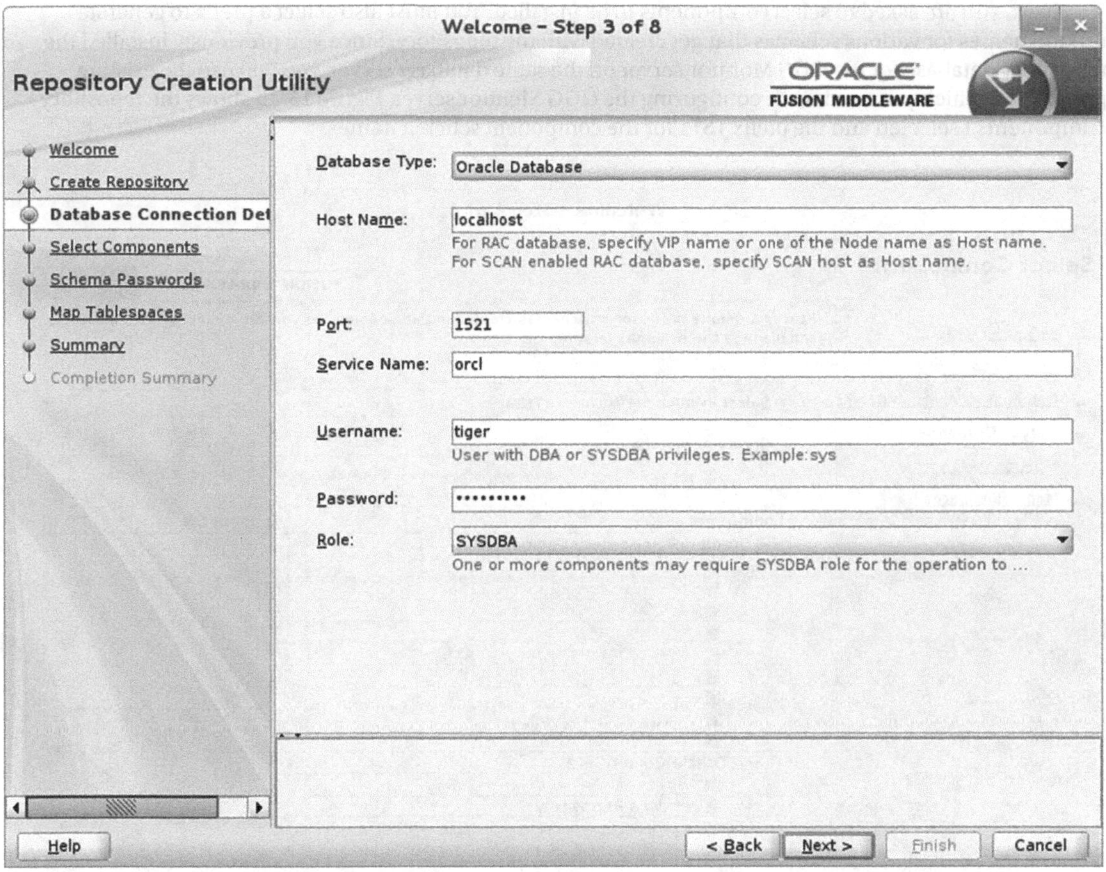

Figure 15-13. *Database connection details*

Figure 15-14 shows the prerequisite checks for the database you specified for the repository creation.

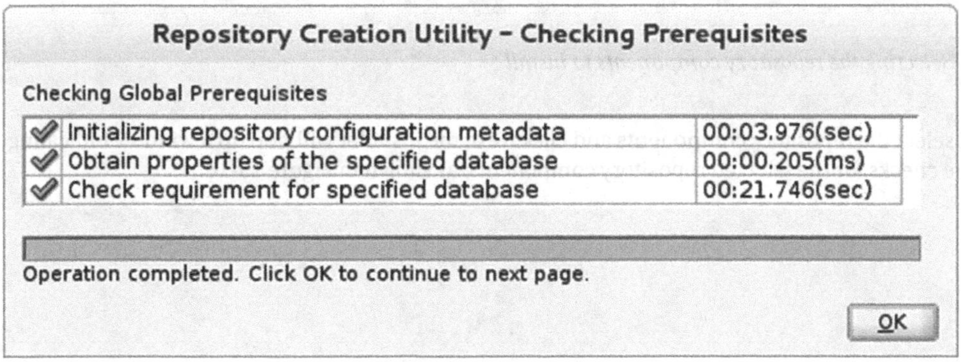

Figure 15-14. *Repository database prerequisites check*

Next, you are asked to select components to be installed. You must also select a prefix to generate unique names for various schemas that get created with the repository. Since you previously installed the repository database for the OGG Monitor server on the same database server, you will use the existing prefix TST1, which you used while configuring the OGG Monitor server. Figure 15-15 shows the repository components I selected and the prefix TST1 for the component schema names.

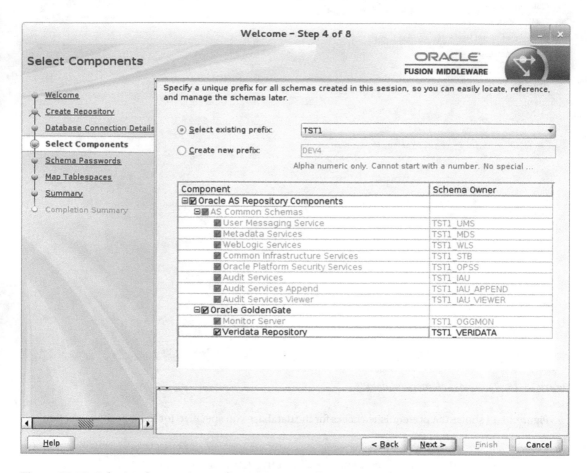

Figure 15-15. *Selecting the repository components to install*

Once you select the repository components and click Next, the installer will pop up a window indicating the prerequisite checks for the selected repository components, as shown in Figure 15-16.

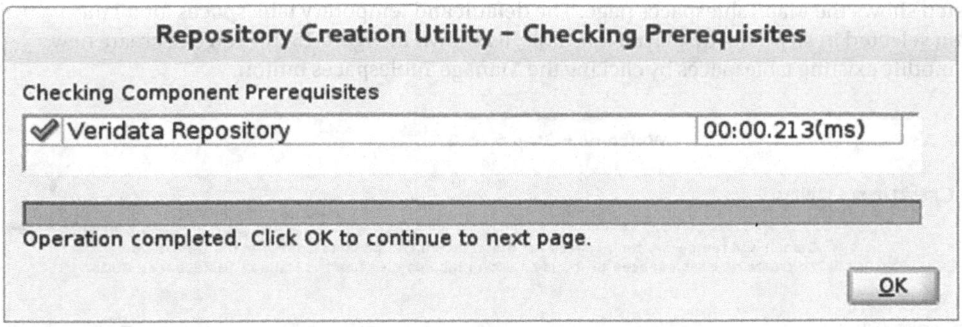

Figure 15-16. *Checking the component prerequisites*

This step will usually take less than a minute to complete. Once the prerequisite checks are complete, click OK to close the smaller window and click Next on the RCU installation screen to continue.

Figure 15-17 shows the Schema Passwords screen. Make sure you have selected "Use same password for all schemas." Provide the schema password and click Next. The password must be at least eight alphanumeric characters with no special characters except $ # . _.

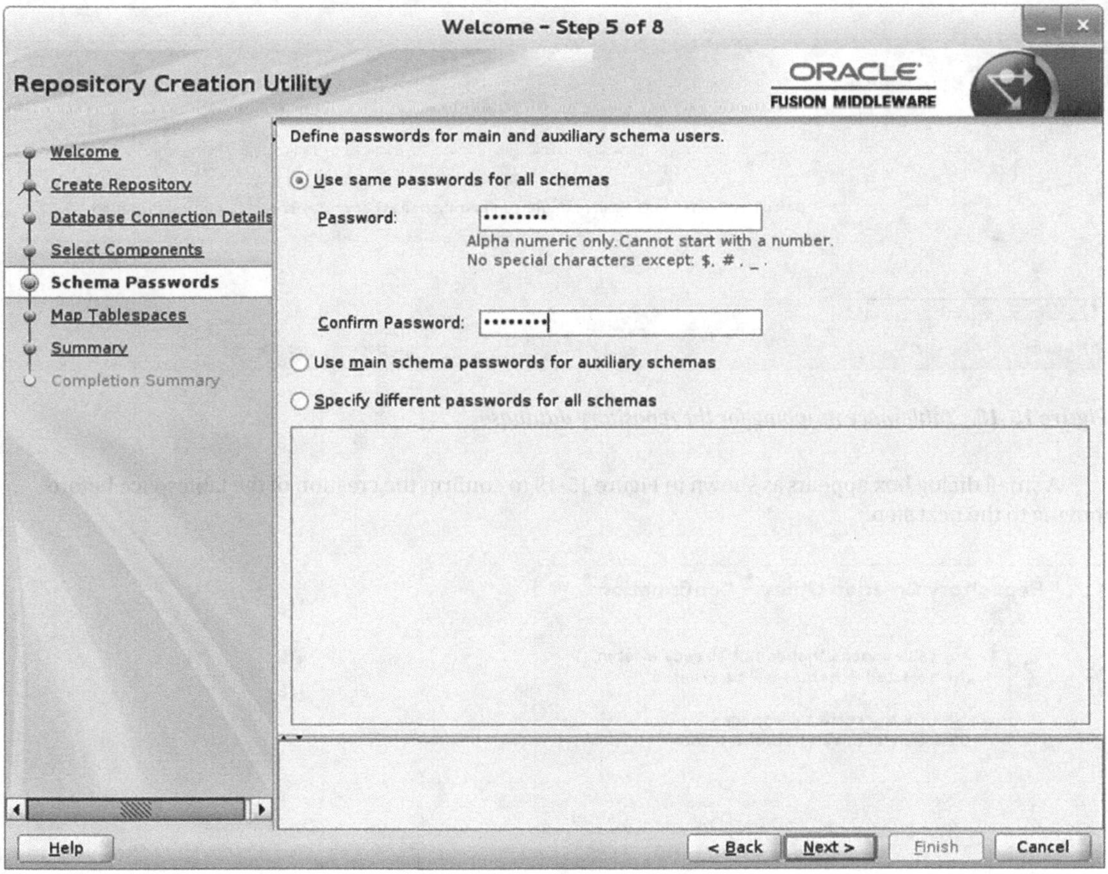

Figure 15-17. *Providing the schema passwords*

The next step shows the Map Tablespaces page. The default and temporary tablespaces for all the components you selected in step 4 are displayed in a table, as shown in Figure 15-18. You can create new tablespaces or modify existing tablespaces by clicking the Manage Tablespaces button.

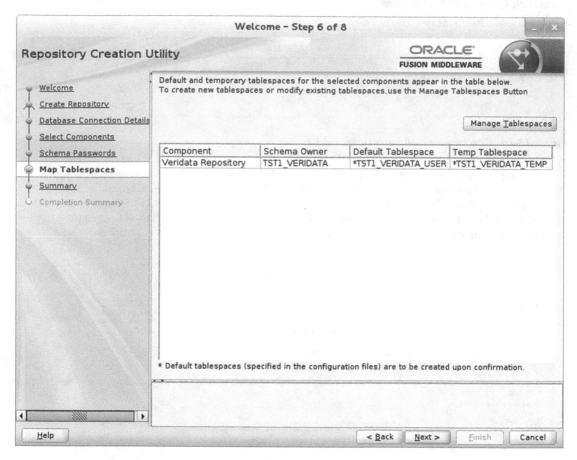

Figure 15-18. Tablespace mapping for the repository database

A small dialog box appears as shown in Figure 15-19 to confirm the creation of the tablespace before moving to the next step.

Figure 15-19. Confirming the tablespace creation

Figure 15-20 shows the creation of the tablespace in progress in the repository database. This usually takes a couple of minutes to complete.

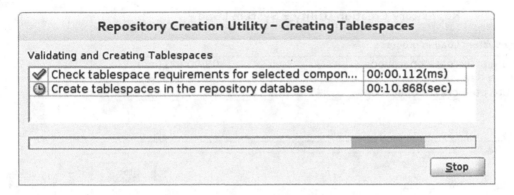

Figure 15-20. *Creating tablespaces in the repository database*

Figure 15-21 shows the repository database summary. Click Create to begin the system load.

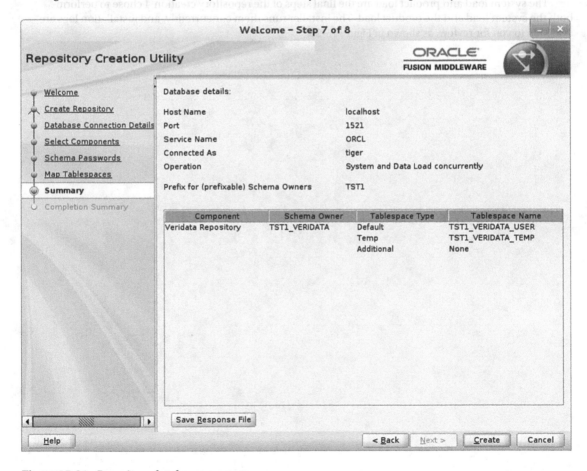

Figure 15-21. *Repository database summary*

Figure 15-22 shows the progress of the repository system load.

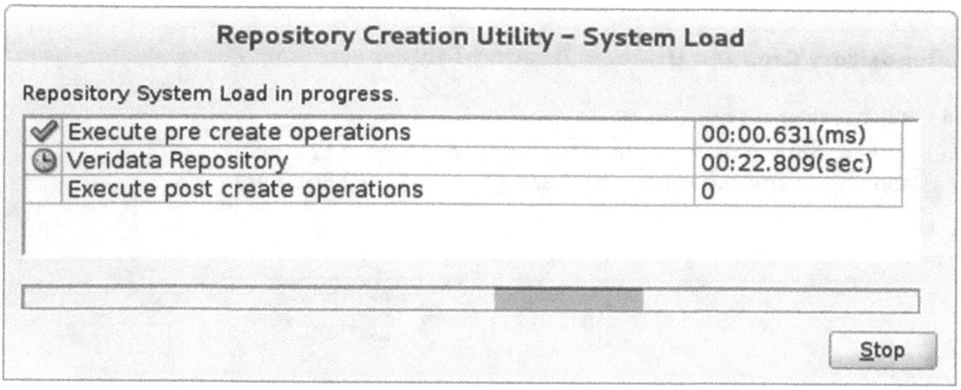

Figure 15-22. *System load progress for the repository*

The system load and product load are the final steps of the repository creation. I chose to perform both the system load and the product load. The installer runs them concurrently, and installation logs are available to you for review, as shown in Figure 15-23.

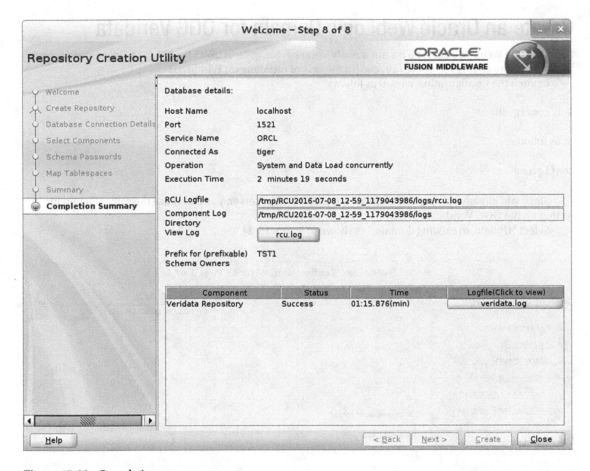

Figure 15-23. Completion summary

Create an Oracle WebLogic Domain for OGG Veridata

Install Oracle WebLogic Server if it's not already installed. Navigate to ORACLE_HOME/oracle_common/common/bin/ and locate config.sh or config.cmd (in the case of installing on Windows).

Launch the Configuration Wizard as follows:

```
$ ./config.sh
```

or as follows:

```
config.cmd
```

Since you already created a domain for the OGG Monitor server, you can reuse the same domain for setting up the OGG Veridata server.

Select "Update an existing domain," as shown in Figure 15-24.

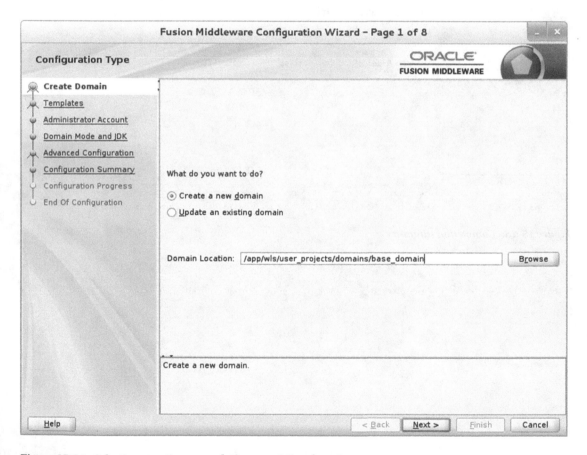

Figure 15-24. *Selecting, creating, or updating an existing domain*

The configuration options change if you select "Update an existing domain," as shown in Figure 15-25.

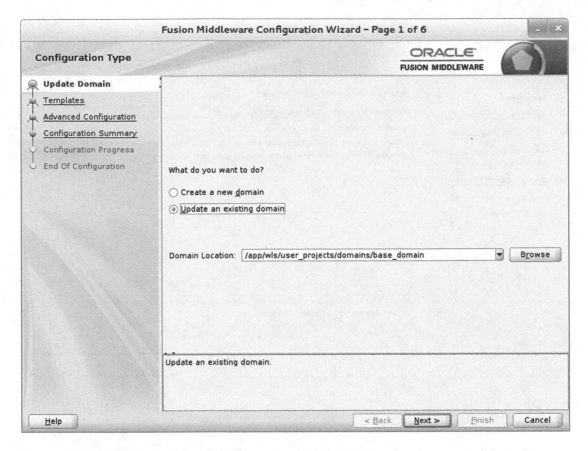

Figure 15-25. *Updating an existing domain*

Figure 15-26 shows a list of templates that you can use to create your new domain. You want your domain to support the Oracle GoldenGate Veridata server, WebLogic Server, and JRF. Select the templates for Veridata, as shown in Figure 15-26.

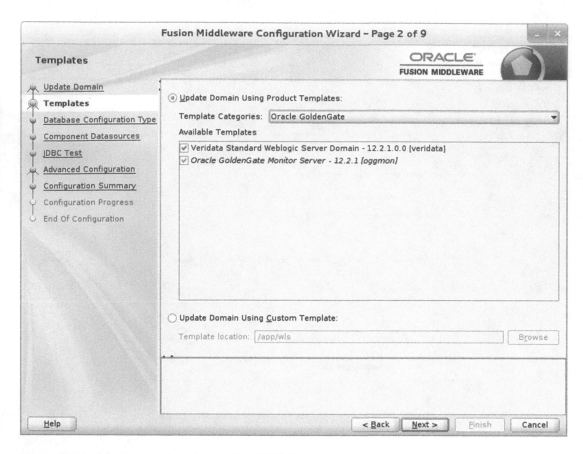

Figure 15-26. *Selecting templates for creating a WLS domain*

The Configuration Wizard offers you two ways to select and configure information for schemas used in your WebLogic domain.

If you select RCU Data, it will allow you to connect to the database to automatically retrieve schema information for the templates you selected in the previous step. Fill in the details for your repository database that you have set up in the previous section in this chapter. Click the Get RCU Configuration button to retrieve the schema information.

Figure 15-27 shows the connection result log for the RCU data.

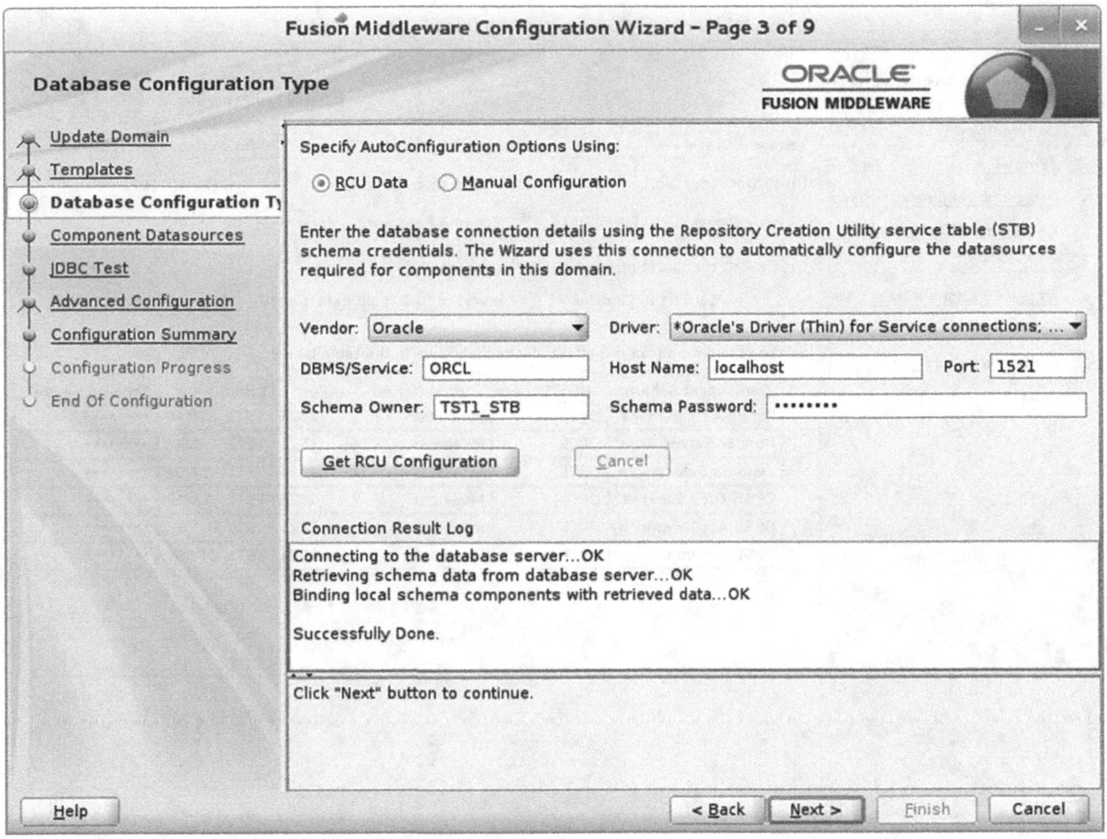

Figure 15-27. *Providing the database type and details*

Figure 15-28 shows the JDBC component schema details. These schemas were created when installing components using RCU. Click Next to continue.

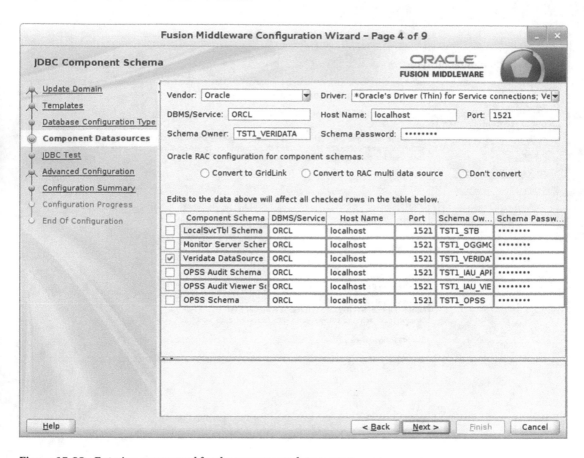

Figure 15-28. *Entering a password for the component data sources*

In this step, you can test the data source configurations for the data sources in the previous screen. Select the check boxes for which you want to test the configuration and click Test Selected Connections. The Configuration Wizard tests connections for each component schema, and the results are displayed in the Status column. Details of the connection results are displayed as shown in Figure 15-29.

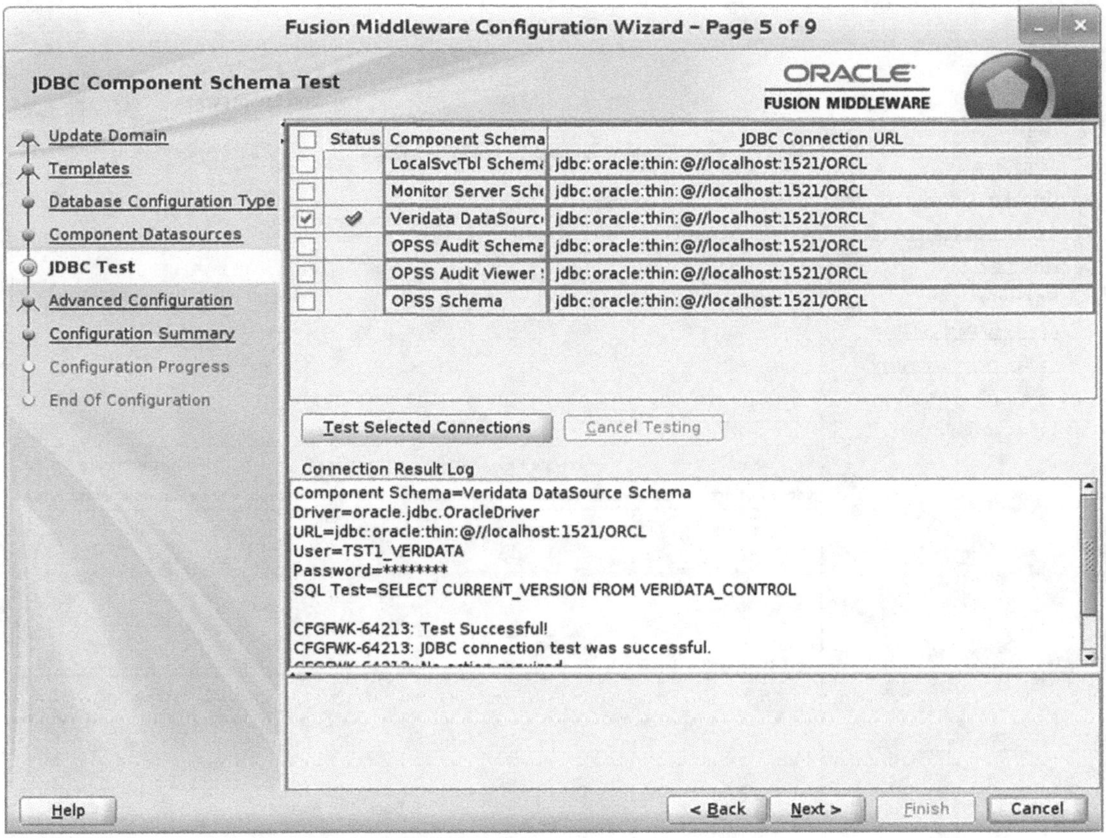

Figure 15-29. *JDBC test for each component schema*

Figure 15-30 shows the key names in the domain and store name. This was configured while configuring the domain for the OGG Monitor server. Click Next to continue.

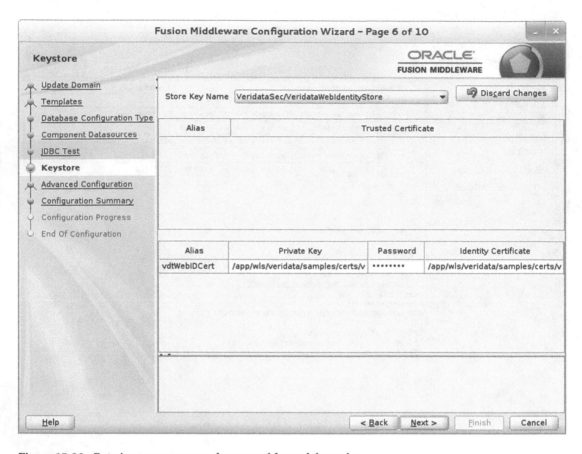

Figure 15-30. *Entering a username and password for each key value*

Figure 15-31 shows the advanced configuration options for the WLS domain. I have selected to configure the settings for the managed server only. The Administration Server and Node Manager options are not available as you have already configured them for the domain.

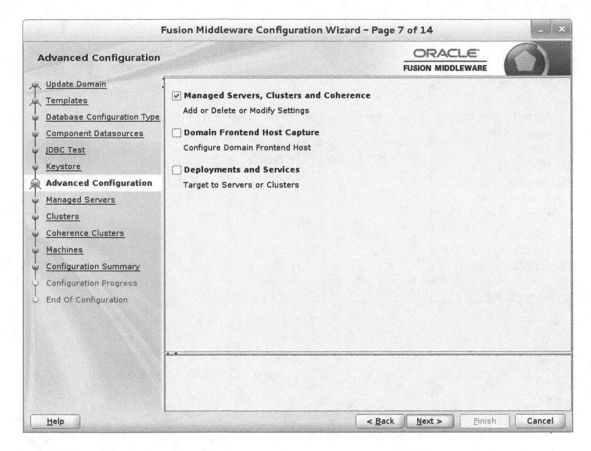

Figure 15-31. *Advanced configuration*

Configure the managed server as shown in Figure 15-32. You can add multiple managed servers in this step. I accepted the default values. MONITORSERVER_server1 was configured in Chapter 13. You will configure VERIDATA_server1 in this section.

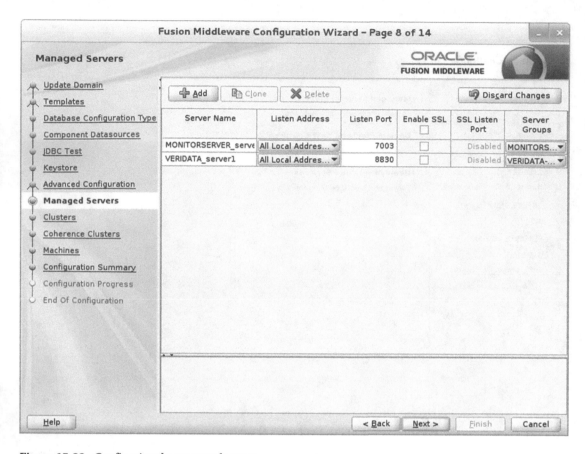

Figure 15-32. *Configuring the managed server*

Figure 15-33 shows the cluster configuration screen. You can add a cluster in this step to group WLS instances to work together to provide scalability and high availability. You do not need to configure clusters. Simply click Next to continue.

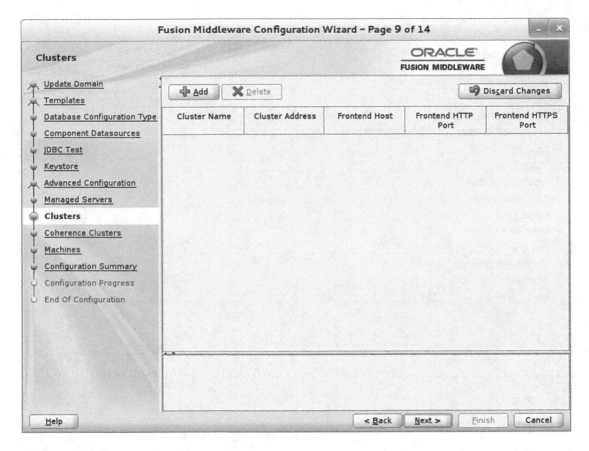

Figure 15-33. *Cluster configuration*

Figure 15-34 shows the coherence cluster details. This screen is shown only if you selected to install coherence during WLS installation. You can either accept the default cluster name or type a custom cluster name. Enter a port to be used for the cluster listen port and click Next to continue.

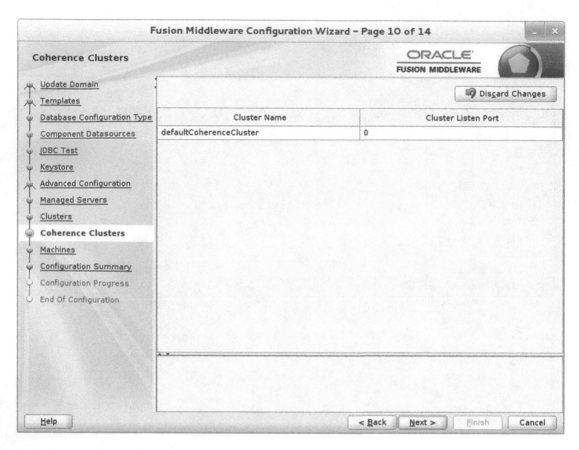

Figure 15-34. *Configuring the coherence cluster*

Figure 15-35 shows the machine configuration screen. Machines are the physical unit of hardware and are associated with the WLS instances that are hosted on them. I added `Machine-1` to host the OGG Veridata server. Click Next to continue.

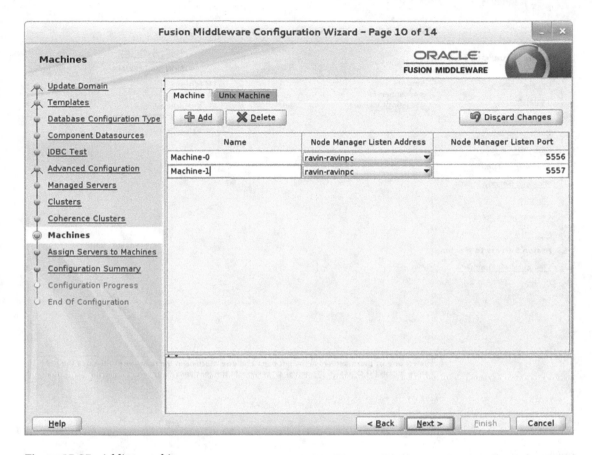

Figure 15-35. *Adding machines*

You can assign servers to machines. You can create a separate machine and assign servers to them or you can have multiple servers on the same machine. Figure 15-36 shows Machine-1, which we created in the previous step for hosting VERIDATA_server1.

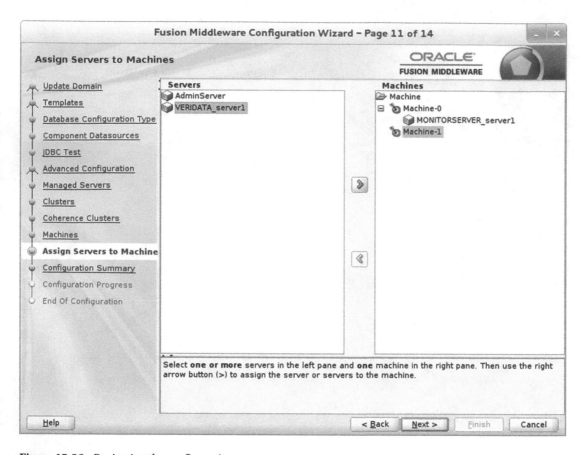

Figure 15-36. *Reviewing the configuration summary*

Figure 15-37 shows the servers assigned to Machine-0 and Machine-1. You can also configure this from the Oracle WLS admin console.

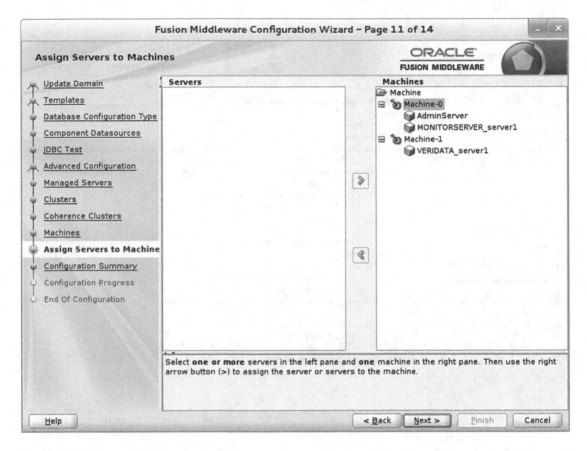

Figure 15-37. *Assigning servers to machines*

Figure 15-38 shows a detailed configuration summary. It provides a summary of all the configurations you have chosen until now. Review the detailed summary before continuing to create the WLS domain. If you want to change some information, click Back to navigate to the appropriate screen and modify the configuration as required.

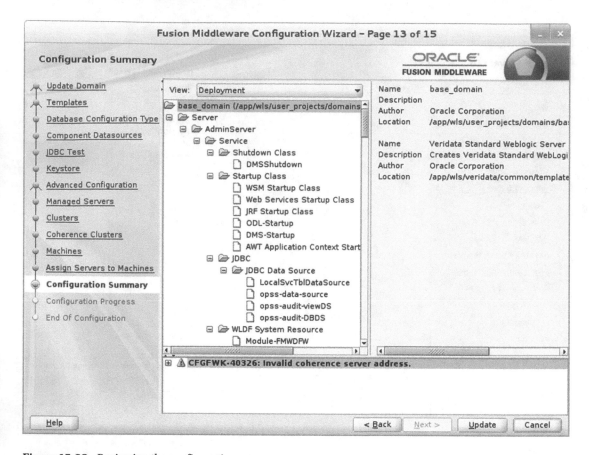

Figure 15-38. *Reviewing the configuration summary*

Figure 15-39 shows the configuration progress. Once the domain has been created successfully, you are pretty much done. Click Next to continue.

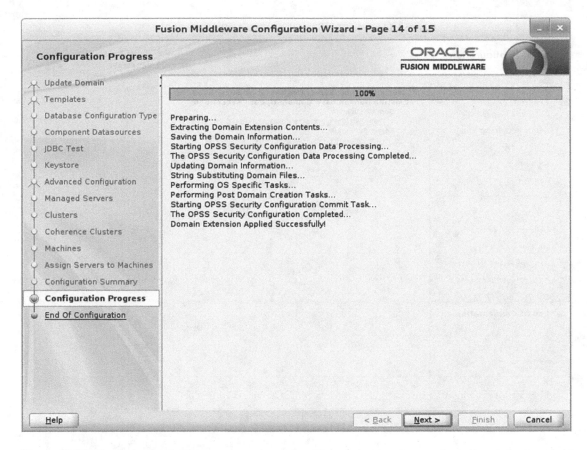

Figure 15-39. *Configuration in progress*

Figure 15-40 shows that the Oracle WebLogic Server configuration succeeded. The existing domain name base_domain was successfully updated with the new configuration. Click Finish to exit the setup.

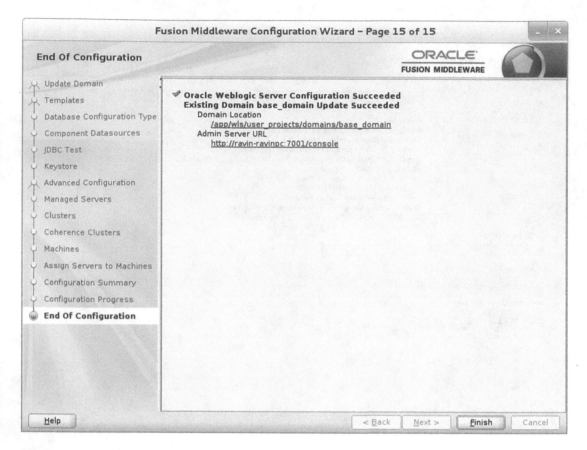

Figure 15-40. *Configuration completed successfully*

Start Veridata Managed Server

The first step to start the OGG Veridata server is to start the WLS server. This is located in the WebLogic domain you created.

```
$ cd /app/wls/user_projects/domains/base_domain
$./startWebLogic.sh
```

If you are using Windows, locate and run startWebLogic.cmd.

```
Enter username to boot WebLogic server:weblogic
Enter password to boot WebLogic server:
```

Enter the username and password for the WLS admin user when prompted.
Notice the startup messages on the screen; starting WebLogic Server may take a few minutes.

```
<19-Jun-2016 11:35:22 o'clock EDT> <Notice> <WebLogicServer> <BEA-000365> <Server state
changed to STARTING.>
<19-Jun-2016 11:35:23 o'clock EDT> <Info> <WorkManager> <BEA-002900> <Initializing
self-tuning thread pool.>

Oracle Coherence Version 12.2.1.0.0 Build 60603
Grid Edition: Production mode
Copyright (c) 2000, 2015, Oracle and/or its affiliates. All rights reserved.

<19-Jun-2016 11:41:44 o'clock EDT> <Notice> <WebLogicServer> <BEA-000365> <Server state
changed to STANDBY.>
<19-Jun-2016 11:41:44 o'clock EDT> <Notice> <WebLogicServer> <BEA-000365> <Server state
changed to STARTING.>

<19-Jun-2016 11:48:51 o'clock EDT> <Notice> <WebLogicServer> <BEA-000365> <Server state
changed to ADMIN.>
<19-Jun-2016 11:48:53 o'clock EDT> <Notice> <WebLogicServer> <BEA-000365> <Server state
changed to RESUMING.>

<19-Jun-2016 11:48:56 o'clock EDT> <Notice> <WebLogicServer> <BEA-000329> <Started the
WebLogic Server Administration Server "AdminServer" for domain "base_domain" running in
production mode.>

<19-Jun-2016 11:48:56 o'clock EDT> <Notice> <WebLogicServer> <BEA-000360> <The server
started in RUNNING mode.>
<19-Jun-2016 11:48:57 o'clock EDT> <Notice> <WebLogicServer> <BEA-000365> <Server state
changed to RUNNING.>
```

Once you have started WebLogic Server, you can navigate to the admin console or use the command line to start the WLS managed server you created for the Oracle GoldenGate Monitor.

For starting the WLS managed server through the command line, use the following:

```
$./startManagedWebLogic.sh MONITORSERVER_server1 http://ravin-ravinpc:7001
```

Enter the username and password for the WLS admin user when prompted.

Log in to the WLS Server admin console using the admin login you created during installation. The URL for the admin console is in the following format:

```
http://ravin-ravinpc:7001/console
```

Figure 15-41 shows the admin console login page.

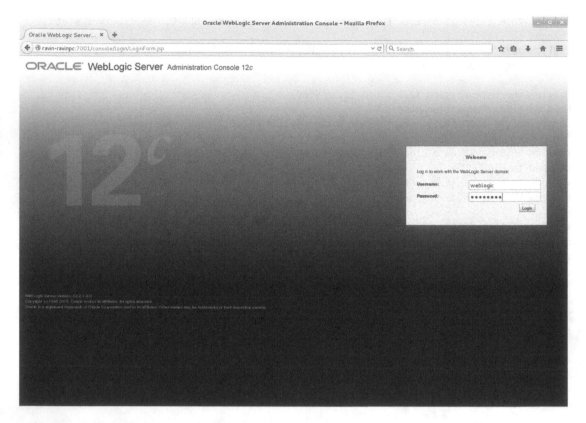

Figure 15-41. *WLS admin console login page*

Expand your OGG Monitor domain under the domain structure and click Servers, as shown in Figure 15-42. Go to the Control tab and select the check box for the managed server you want to start. Click Start. This may take a few minutes.

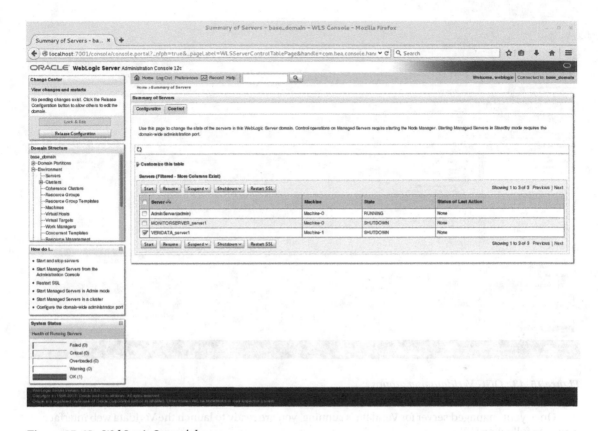

Figure 15-42. *WebLogic Server's home*

The Veridata managed server can also be started with the script veridataServer.sh (or .bat for Microsoft Windows) located in the <DOMAIN_ HOME>/veridata/bin directory. In this example, navigate to /app/wls/user_projects/domains/base_domain/veridata/bin.

On Microsoft Windows command shell:

```
veridataServer.bat start/stop [SERVER_NAME] [ADMIN_URL]
```

On UNIX command shell:

```
veridataServer.sh start/stop [SERVER_NAME] [ADMIN_URL]
```

where SERVER_NAME is name of Veridata Managed Server

ADMIN_URL is Veridata domain Administrator Server. The URL is in the format http://<admin server>:<port>

You can now create users and assign privileges to the users using the Oracle WebLogic administrator console, as shown in Figure 15-43. I am going to use the WebLogic admin user weblogic to log in to the Veridata console.

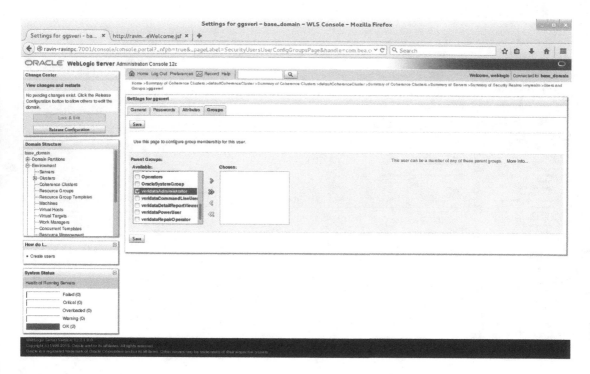

Figure 15-43. OGG Veridata user groups

Once your managed server for Veridata is running, you are ready to launch the Veridata web interface using the following URL:

```
http://hostname:8830/veridata/
```

This will launch the Oracle GoldenGate Veridata login screen, as shown in Figure 15-44.

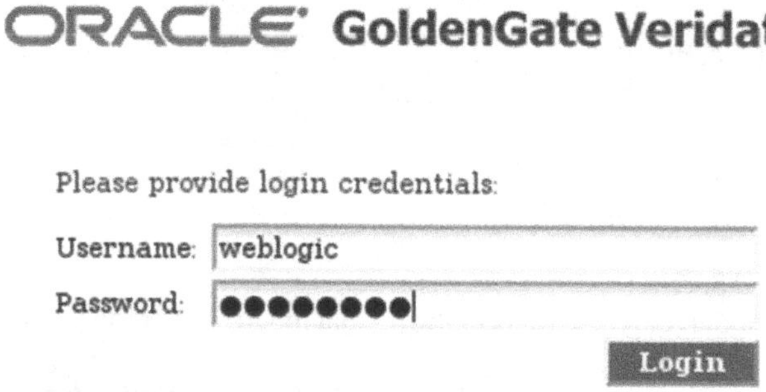

ORACLE° GoldenGate Veridata

Please provide login credentials:

Username: weblogic
Password: ●●●●●●●●

Login

Figure 15-44. OGG Veridata login screen

After the successful login, you are welcomed by the Oracle GoldenGate Veridata home page, as shown in Figure 15-45. At this moment, you do not have any comparable jobs set up. You need to first set up the OGG Veridata Agent for proceeding further with configuring your compare jobs in OGG Veridata.

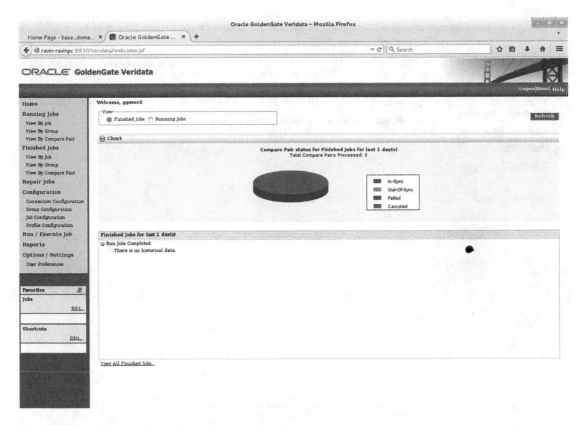

Figure 15-45. *OGG Veridata home*

Install the OGG Veridata Agent

The Oracle GoldenGate Veridata Agent retrieves data from the source and target databases and sends it to the OGG Veridata server. You already have downloaded the Oracle Fusion Middleware 12*c* Media Pack (Oracle Fusion Middleware 12*c* GoldenGate Monitor and Veridata) from the Oracle Software Delivery Cloud site for installing the Oracle GoldenGate Veridata server. Use the same JAR file to install the Oracle GoldenGate Veridata Agent as discussed in this section.

Copy the downloaded files to the OGG Veridata Agent installation directory and launch the installer.

```
$ java -jar -Xmx1024m fmw_12.2.1.0.0_ogg.jar
```

Follow these steps to complete the installation.

Click Next on the Welcome and Auto Updates screens. Select the Oracle Home where you will be installing the Veridata Agent. For this example, you will install the agent in the /app/veriagent directory, as shown in Figure 15-46. For installing the OGG Veridata Agent, you do not necessarily need WebLogic Server and JRF installed in this location. Click Next to continue.

353

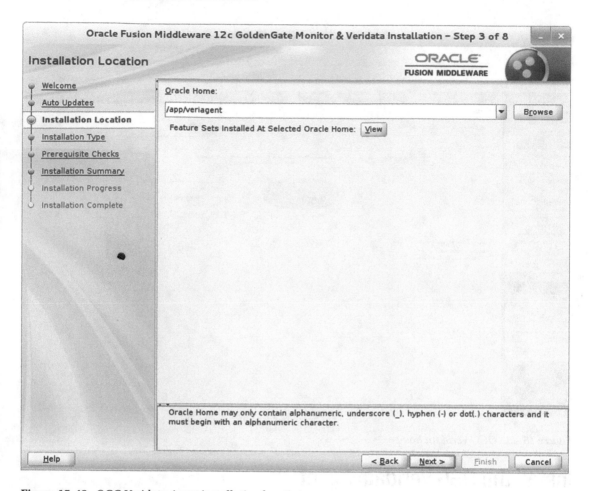

Figure 15-46. *OGG Veridata Agent installation location*

In the next step, you are presented with various installation types for Oracle Fusion Middleware 12*c*. Select Oracle Golden Gate Veridata Agent as the installation type, as shown in Figure 15-47.

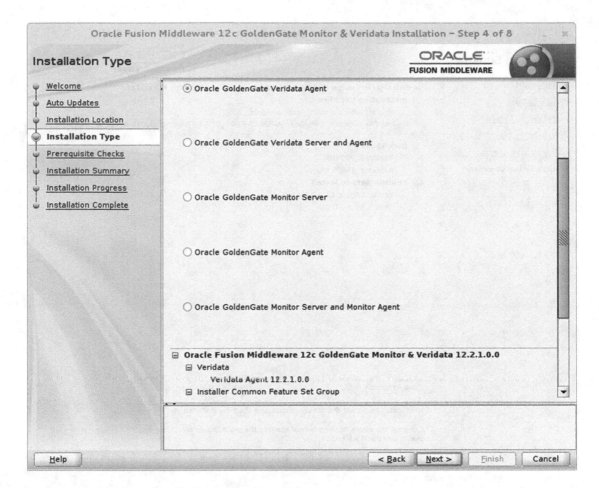

Figure 15-47. Selecting the installation type

The installer performs the prerequisite checks. Click Next to review the installation summary, as shown in Figure 15-48.

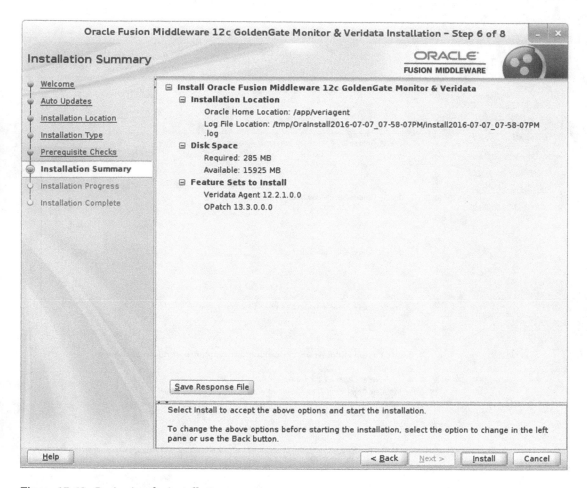

Figure 15-48. *Reviewing the installation summary*

Figure 15-49 shows the installation tasks and their status in progress. Wait until it finishes. This may take up to 15 minutes. You can view the installation messages for the current step by clicking View Messages. You can also view the installer log by clicking the View Log button.

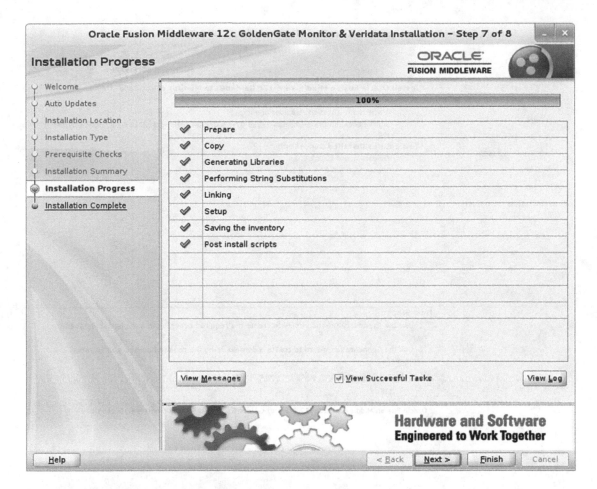

Figure 15-49. *Installing the OGG Veridata Agent*

Figure 15-50 shows that the Oracle GoldenGate Veridata Agent installation has successfully completed.

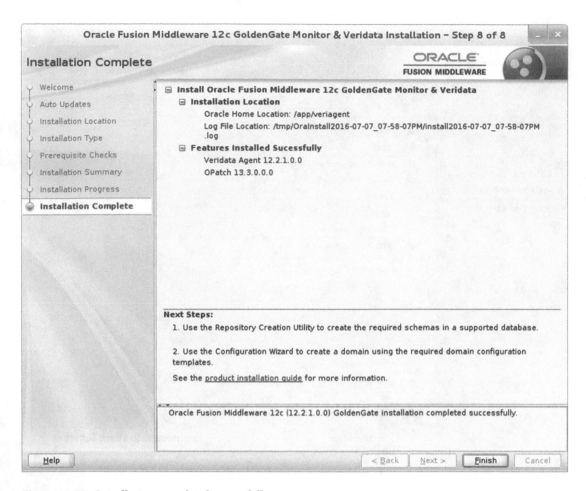

Figure 15-50. *Installation completed successfully*

Deploy the OGG Veridata Agent

At this point, when you have your OGG Veridata server and Veridata Agent installed, you must next deploy the agent to a location outside ORACLE_HOME.

Navigate to <Veridata install folder>/Veridata/agent to locate the agent_config.sh script.

```
cd /app/veriagent/veridata/agent
```

Deploying the Veridata Agent is an easy task; just pass the deployment location as an argument to agent_config.sh. Make sure you are deploying the Veridata Agent outside the ORACLE_HOME location.

- On a Microsoft Windows command shell:

  ```
  agent_config.bat <deployment location>
  ```

- On a Unix command shell:

  ```
  ./agent_config.sh <deployment location>
  ```

- This took less than a minute for me.

```
[oracle@ravin-ravinpc agent]$ ./agent_config.sh /app/ggs/vagent
Successfully deployed the agent.
```

To print the logs onscreen while deploying, run the previous scripts in debug mode. For this, you simply pass an extra argument of true.

- On a Microsoft Windows command shell:

```
agent_config.bat <deployment location> true
```

- On a Unix command shell:

```
./agent_config.sh <deployment location> true
```

Start and Stop the Veridata Agent

It's time to start your Veridata Agent. Since the OGG Veridata Agent can work independently from Oracle GoldenGate, you do not need to configure the agent to communicate with the Oracle GoldenGate instance. Navigate to the directory where you have deployed the OGG Veridata Agent to locate the agent.sh and agent.properties.sample files.

Make a copy of agent.properties.sample as agent.properties. Edit agent.properties to include the server port and database URL for Veridata. The following is the content of the agent.properties file in our demonstration. The file is well-documented with comments. Read through the file and uncomment and set the appropriate properties as per your environment needs.

```
# The server.port property is the port where the Veridata agent listens
# for connection requests.
server.port=7862


# The database.url specifies the JDBC connection URL for the database.
# Samples for all supported databases are shown below.
database.url=jdbc:oracle:thin:@ravin-ravinpc:1521:orcl


# Uncomment the following line to change the connection pool
# size. The Veridata agent uses a separate connection pool
# for each database user.  The default values is 20.
#pool.maxSize=20


# Uncomment the following line to change the maximum number
# of idle connections in the connection pool.  The default value
# is the same as pool.maxSize.
#pool.maxIdle=20


# Uncomment the following line to change the timeout for idle connections
# in the Oracle connection pool.  The value is in seconds.  The default
# value in the Veridata Agent is 300 seconds.
#pool.maxIdleTime=300
```

```
# Uncomment the following line to change the time between checks for
# timeout outs in the connection pool. The value is is seconds.
# The default value in the Veridata agent is one quarter of maxIdleTime.
#pool.checkInterval=75


# Uncomment the following line to change the number of statements
# cached per connection.  The default value is 20.
#pool.maxStatements=20


# The server.driversLocation property is the directory
# containing the JDBC driver jar file(s). The JDBC drivers
# included with the Veridata agent will be retrieved from the
# standard locations.
# The path is relative to the Veridata agent
# deployment directory. OR An absolute path to the directory containing
# drivers can be specified.
server.driversLocation = drivers


# The database.additional.repair.warnings is a list of DBMS specific error
# numbers/codes that should be considered as a warning if it is raised when
# repairing a single row
# The error numbers/codes specified here are checked along with the error
# numbers/codes that Veridata already treats as warning cases.
# The format of the value for database.additional.repair.warnings is a comma
# or space separated list of integers. For instance:
# database.additional.repair.warnings=1400,1407,17266
# database.additional.repair.warnings=1400 1407 17266
# database.additional.repair.warnings=<database.additional.repair.warnings>


# For Oracle uncomment the following line:
server.jdbcDriver=ojdbc7.jar oracle.xdb.jar


#The database.characterSet parameter is used for overriding the source #database character
for comparison.
#The parameter value should be the name of the character set used to encode #the character
data (CHAR, VARCHAR2, CLOB and LONG).
#This parameter should match the "SOURCECHARSET OVERRIDE" in the replicat #parameter file at
the target database.
#This is supported only for Oracle Databases.
#database.characterSet=


# The database.transaction.isolation property controls the
# transaction isolation level used during initial compare.
# The default value for Sybase, DB2, SQL Server and Teradata is
# READ_UNCOMMITTED.  The only value supported for Oracle
# is READ_COMMITTED.  SQL Server versions 2005 above also support
# the value SNAPSHOT which requires that ALLOW_SNAPSHOT_ISOLATION is
# enabled in the database.
#
# Confirm out of sync always uses the READ_COMMITTED
# transaction isolation level.
#database.transaction.isolation=READ_UNCOMMITTED
```

```
#
server.useSsl=false
server.use2WaySsl=false
server.allowTrustedExpiredCertificates=true
server.identitystore.path=./config/certs/serverIdentity.jks
server.truststore.path=./config/certs/serverTrust.jks
# SSL/TLS Advanced configuration
server.identitystore.type=JKS
server.truststore.type=JKS
server.identitystore.keyfactory.alg.name=SunX509
server.truststore.keyfactory.alg.name=SunX509
server.ssl.algorithm.name=TLS
```

Execute the following command to start the OGG Veridata Agent. This is instant and returns no output.

```
$ ./agent.sh start agent.properties
```

A new directory log gets created in the agent deployment location. Navigate to this directory and check the log file to verify whether the Veridata Agent has properly started.

```
[oracle@ravin-ravinpc logs]$ cat veridata-agent.log
[2016-07-08T15:48:57.677-04:00] [veridata] [NOTIFICATION] [OGGV-60150] [oracle.veridata.
agent] [tid: 1] [ecid: 0000LNC3_8^Fw000jzpmZo1NW0Ee000001,0] Configuring logging.
[2016-07-08T15:48:58.704-04:00] [veridata] [NOTIFICATION] [OGGV-60151] [oracle.veridata.
agent] [tid: 1] [ecid: 0000LNC3_8^Fw000jzpmZo1NW0Ee000001,0] Config file for logger is /app/
ggs/vagent/config/odl.xml
[2016-07-08T15:48:59.035-04:00] [veridata] [NOTIFICATION] [] [oracle.veridata.agent]
[tid: 1] [ecid: 0000LNC3_8^Fw000jzpmZo1NW0Ee000001,0] OGGV-60001: Veridata Agent Version
12.2.1.0.0 OGGVDT_12.2.1.0.0_PLATFORMS_151012.2202 built on Mon, 12 Oct 2015 22:25:03 -0700
For Testing Purposes Only
[2016-07-08T15:48:59.047-04:00] [veridata] [NOTIFICATION] [OGGV-60002] [oracle.veridata.
agent] [tid: 1] [ecid: 0000LNC3_8^Fw000jzpmZo1NW0Ee000001,0] Veridata Agent running on
ravin-ravinpc port 7862
```

If you are installing OGG Veridata on the Windows platform, you need to set up OGG Veridata to run as the Windows service after the installation of the OGG Veridata Agent is complete. We will not discussed setting up the OGG Veridata Agent to run as a Windows service in this book. Please refer to the Oracle documentation for details on setting up a Windows service if you need to do so.

Creating and Running OGG Veridata Compare Jobs

Now that you have your OGG Veridata server and agent configured, you'll create your first compare job. Log in to OGG Veridata as the OGG Veridata admin user. The first step toward creating your compare job is to set up the source and target connections to be used for comparison. Under the Configuration menu in the left panel, click Connection Configuration. This will launch the New Connection Assistant, as shown in Figure 15-51. Enter a connection name and description. Click Next to continue.

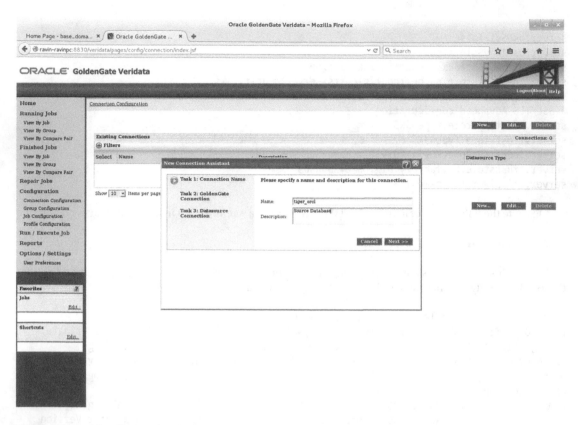

Figure 15-51. *New Connection Assistant*

Next, provide the host machine name, the port on which the OGG Veridata Agent is listening, and the data source type. The port number is the same as you used in the agent.properties file. Figure 15-52 shows the connection details for the host ravin-ravinpc on port 7862 for data source type Oracle.

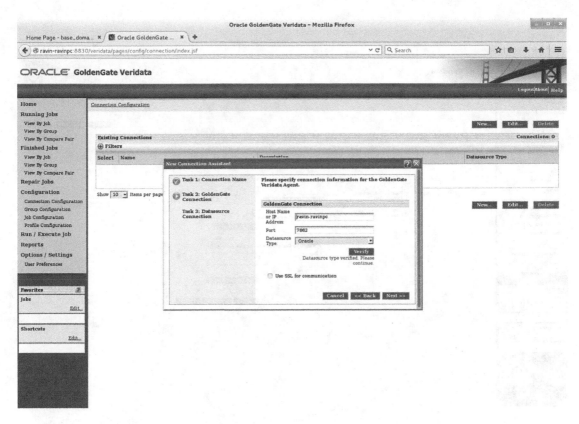

Figure 15-52. *GoldenGate connection details for connection configuration*

Provide the data source connection details as shown in Figure 15-53. This is the database user with which OGG Veridata will log in while executing compare jobs. Click the Test Connection button to validate the connection details.

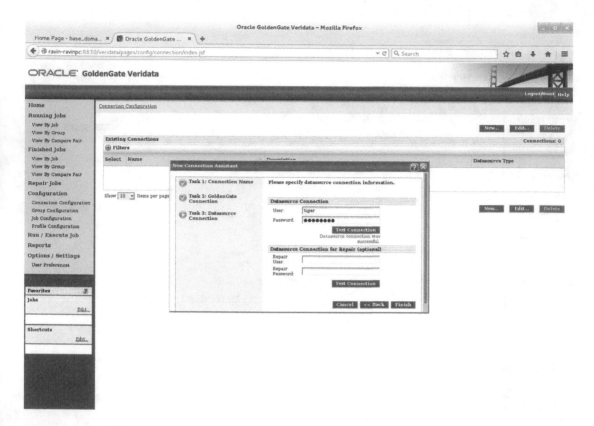

Figure 15-53. *Database connection details*

Click Finish to complete creating your source connection. You will get a success message, as shown in Figure 15-54.

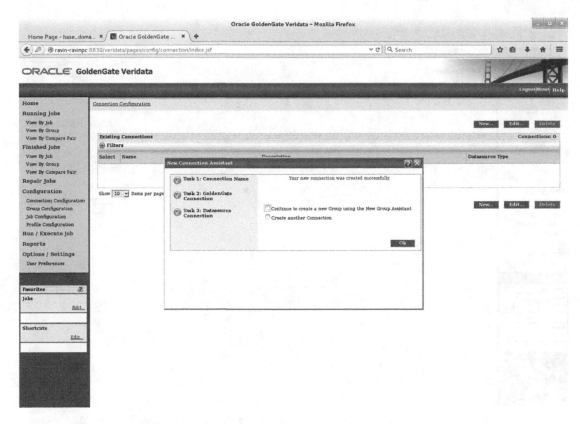

Figure 15-54. *Connection created successfully*

Follow similar steps to configure the connection for the target database. Figure 15-55 shows the connections I configured for running the compare jobs.

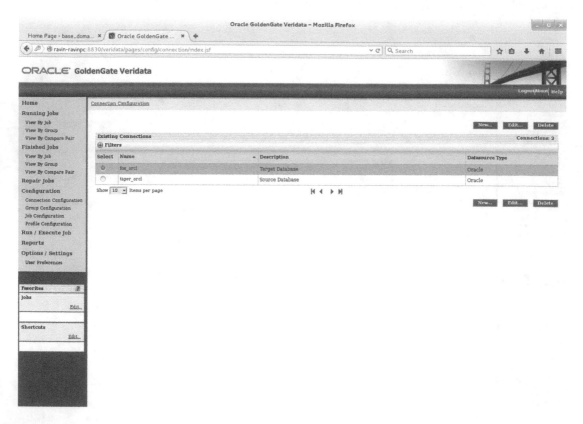

Figure 15-55. *Connection list in OGG Veridata*

Next, you need to create a group that will have the connection instances you created for the source and target. You will also add compare pairs to this group. You can add one or more compare pairs per group. This group will be used while creating the compare job. Click Group Configuration in the left panel menu items. This will open the New Group Assistant, as shown in Figure 15-56. Enter the group name and description. Click Next to continue.

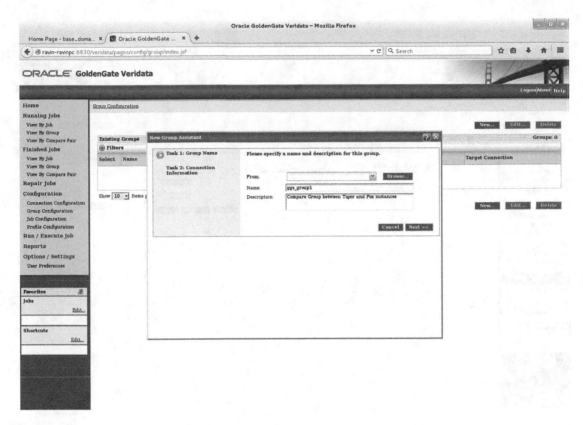

Figure 15-56. *New Group Assistant*

Link the source and target data source connections to the new group, as shown in Figure 15-57.

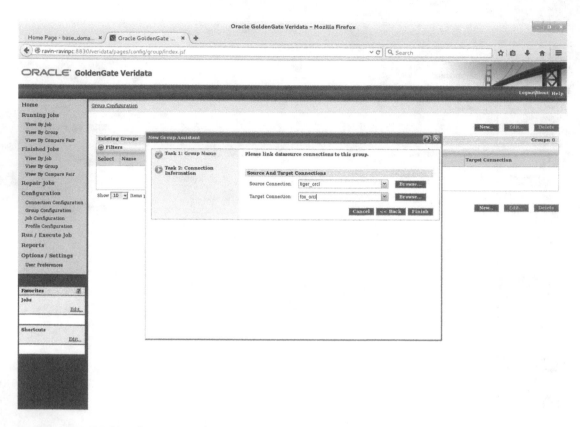

Figure 15-57. *Linking the source and target data source connections to the group*

Click Finish to complete creating the group. Select the check box Go to Compare Pair Configuration and click OK, as shown in Figure 15-58. Compare the pair configuration is the actual place where you defined the tables to be compared.

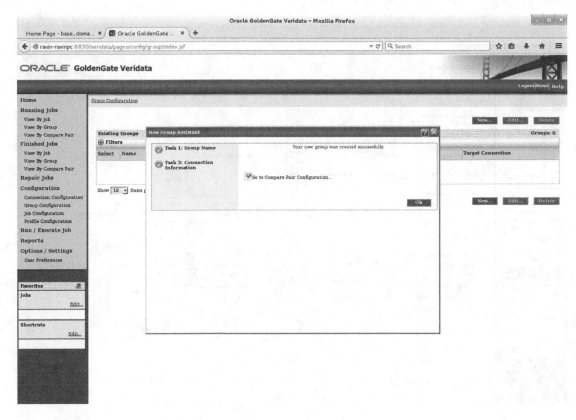

Figure 15-58. *Completing the group creation*

On the Compare Pair Configuration screen, select the source and target data sources and click the Manual Mapping tab, as shown in Figure 15-59.

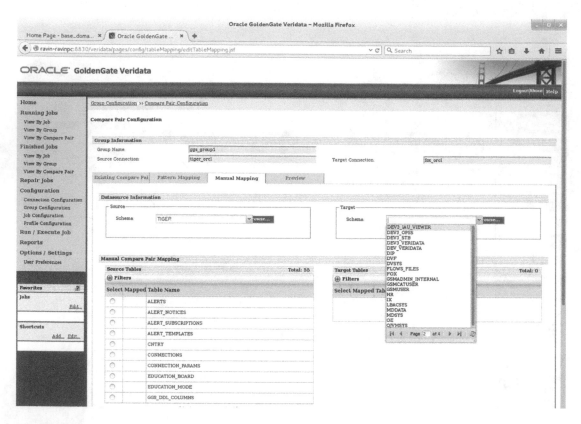

Figure 15-59. *Comparing the pair configuration details*

Next, you also select the database user/schema that owns the tables to be compared. Select the appropriate values from the drop-down lists, as shown in Figure 15-60. Also, select the table names from the Source Tables list and the Target Tables list. Click the Generate Compare Pair button at the bottom of the screen. This will display a message "The compare pair was added to the preview list."

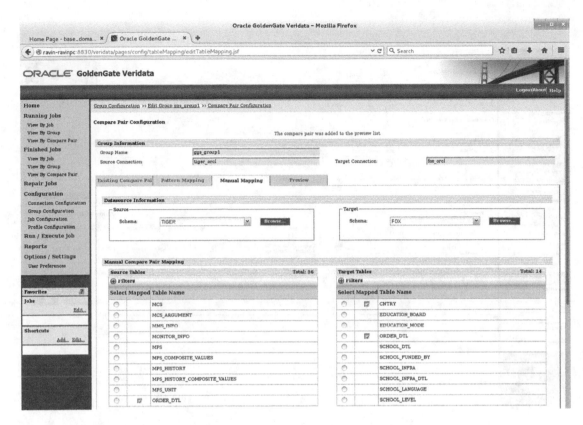

Figure 15-60. Adding compare pairs

Click the Preview screen to preview the compare pairs you have added to the group ggs_group1, as shown in Figure 15-61. Verify the details and click Save.

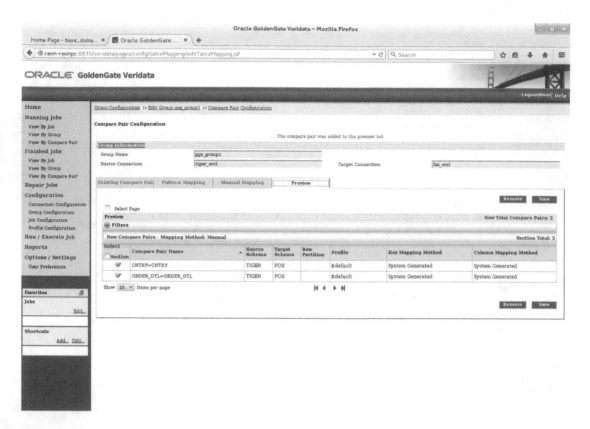

Figure 15-61. *Previewing and saving compare pairs*

On the Compare Pair Configuration screen, click the Existing Compare Pair tab. You need to validate the column mapping for the first time and verify whether there is any change in the structure of tables. The green check mark, as shown in Figure 15-62, indicates that the column mapping was successful. The column mapping failed for the ORDER_DTL table. This was because I intentionally dropped the index on the table ORDER_DTL to demonstrate the failing of the column mapping and its impact on the compare job.

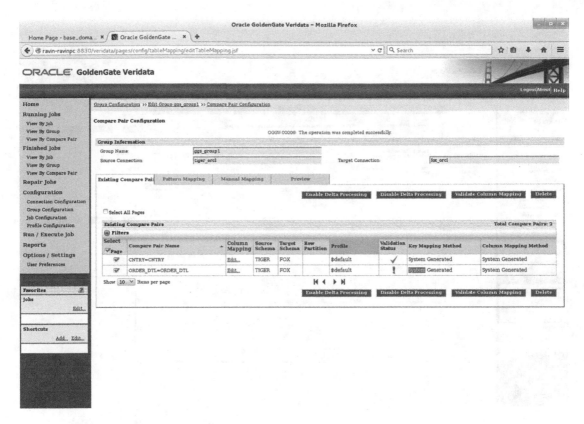

Figure 15-62. *Validating column mappings*

Now that you have your group ready and configured with compare pairs, let's create our first compare job using the New Job Assistant, as shown in Figure 15-63. Click Job Configuration from the menu items in the left panel.

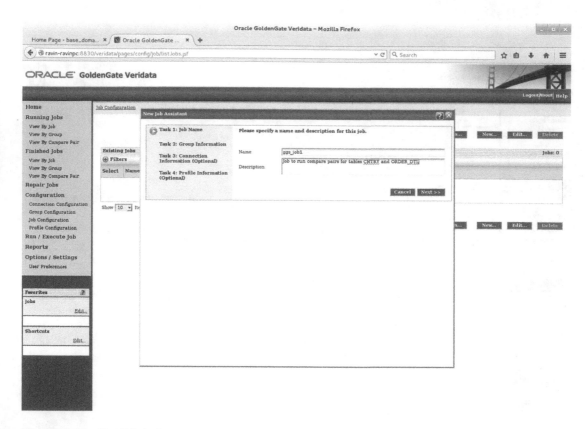

Figure 15-63. *New Job Assistant*

Provide the group information to be linked with this job, as shown in Figure 15-64.

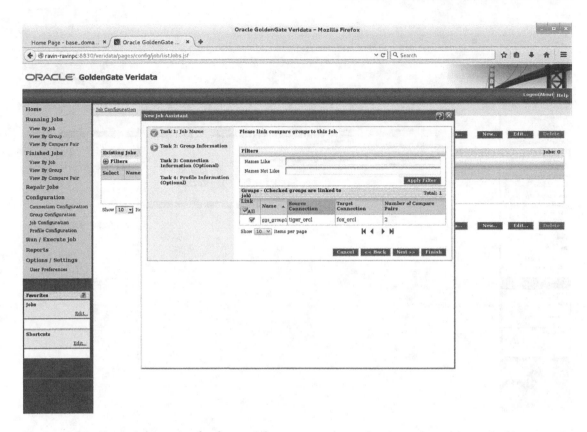

Figure 15-64. *Group information for the new job*

Figure 15-65 shows the connection information for the job. This is optional step, and by default it will pick connection information from the group you linked in with the job you are creating.

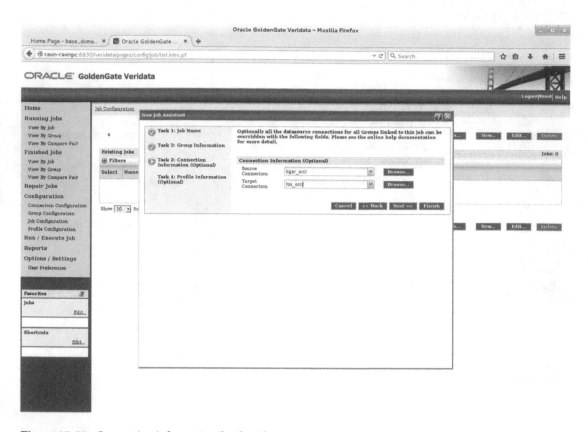

Figure 15-65. *Connection information for the job*

Select profile information from the drop-down, as shown in Figure 15-66. I have chosen the $default profile. Click Finish to complete the creation of the new compare job.

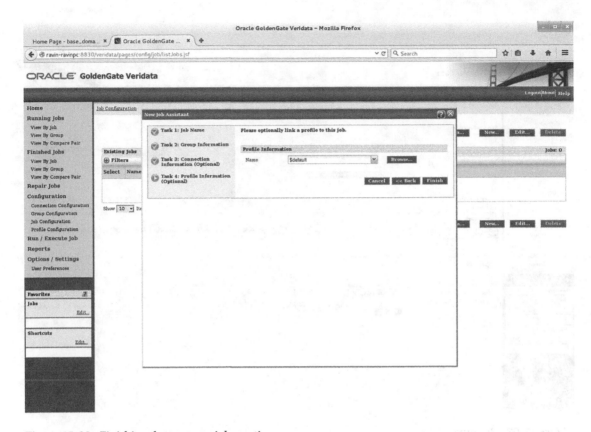

Figure 15-66. *Finishing the compare job creation*

Click Run/Execute Jobs from the menu items in the left panel. You need to click Retrieve Compare Pair List to fetch the compare pairs list associated with this job, as shown in Figure 15-67. Click the Run Job button. This may take up to a few minutes depending on the volume of data in the tables. Please note the column mapping failed for the ORDER_DTL table because of a missing index on the table.

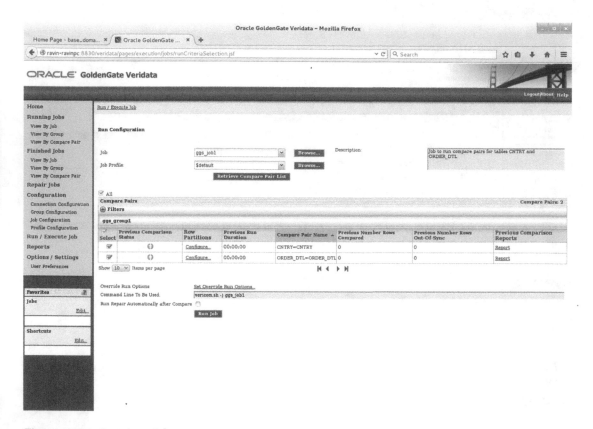

Figure 15-67. *Running a job*

Figure 15-68 shows the compare job is running.

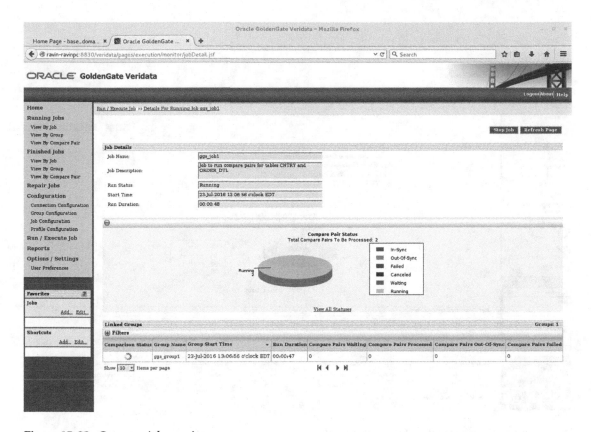

Figure 15-68. *Compare job running*

Figure 15-69 shows the result of the compare job. Click the Report link to view a detailed report of the compare job.

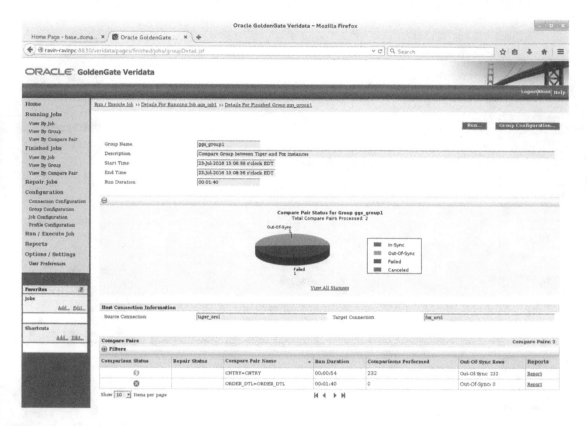

Figure 15-69. *Comparing the job execution result*

You can both view online or download the report for each compare pair. Figure 15-70 shows the report for comparing the ORDER_DTL table.

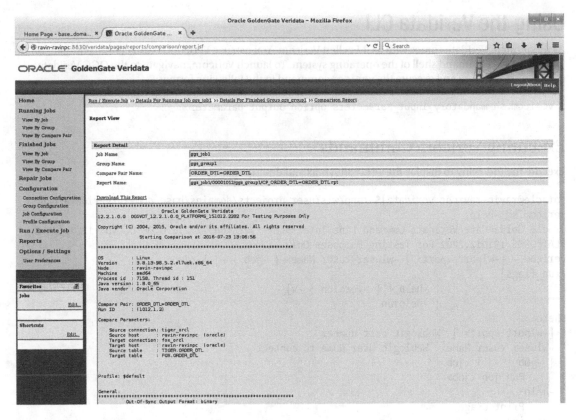

Figure 15-70. *Compare report of a failed compare pair*

Congratulations, you have created and executed your first compare job. Similarly, you can create more compare jobs as required.

Using the Veridata CLI

As mentioned, Veridata comes with a CLI called Vericom. You can use Vericom to run certain comparison tasks from the command shell of the operating system. To launch Vericom, navigate to the OGG Veridata installation directory and execute the vericom command in the following format:

```
$ vericom.sh mandatory_input_parameters option_output_parameter
```

Executing Vericom Commands

Execute the following to display the vericom syntax and descriptions:

```
[oracle@ravin-ravinpc veridata]$ /app/wls/user_projects/domains/base_domain/veridata/bin/
vericom.sh -help
Oracle GoldenGate Veridata Command Line Interface - Version 12.2.1.0.0  OGGVDT_12.2.1.0.0_
PLATFORMS_151012.2202 For Testing Purposes Only
vericom   [-wlport <port> ] -wluser <user Name> { -job | -j } <job>
[run_flags]
                         | -help | { -version | -v}
                         | -helprun
Where:
  [-wlport <port> ]  Weblogic port number
  -wluser <user Name>  Weblogic User Name to connect
  { -job | -j } <job>
       Run job <job>
  -help
       Print usage.
  -version, -v
       Print version.
  -helprun
       Print usage of run_flags
  run_flags
       Flags for running a job or compare pair
```

You can also execute the following to get a complete list of run-related syntaxes for Vericom:

```
[oracle@ravin-ravinpc veridata]$ /app/wls/user_projects/domains/base_domain/veridata/bin/
vericom.sh -helprun
Oracle GoldenGate Veridata Command Line Interface - Version 12.2.1.0.0  OGGVDT_12.2.1.0.0_
PLATFORMS_151012.2202 For Testing Purposes Only
vericom   [-wlport <port> ] -wluser <user Name> { -job | -j } <job>
[run_flags]
                         | -help | { -version | -v}
                         | -helprun
Where:
  [-wlport <port> ]  Weblogic port number
  -wluser <user Name>  Weblogic User Name to connect
  { -job | -j } <job>
       Run job <job>
  -help
       Print usage.
  -version, -v
```

```
        Print version.
  -helprun
        Print usage of run_flags
  run_flags
        Flags for running a job or compare pair

Run Flags Usage:
        [ -g group_name -c compare_pair_name ]
        [ -rP profile_name ]
        [ -rR | -rO ]
        [ -rN number_of_threads ]
        [ -rD number_of_seconds ]
        [ -rC | +rC ]
        [ -rOb | -rOx | -rO2 | -rOO ]
        [ -rOs number_of_rows ]
        [ -rdO | -rdN run_id ]
        [ -pS partition_name
           | -pSq SQL_predicate
           | -pSA1 ascii_start_key
           | -pSA2 ascii_ending_key
           | -pSH1 hex_start_key
           | -pSH2 hex_ending_key ]
        [ -pT partition_name
           | -pTq SQL_predicate
           | -pTA1 ascii_start_key
           | -pTA2 ascii_ending_key
           | -pTH1 hex_start_key
           | -pTH2 hex_ending_key ]
        [ -pq SQL_predicate ]
        [-nw ]
        [ -w | -wp interval ]
        [ -repair ]
        [ -norepair ]
Where:
  -g group_name
        Name of the group. Requires -c.
  -c compare_pair_name
        Name of the compare pair. Requires -g.
  -rP profile_name
        Override the default profile.
  -rR     Review Previous OOS Results.
  -rO     Generate OOS XML from Previous Run.
  -rdO    Do not use delta base from previous run
          for this job. Requires -c.
  -rdN run_id
          Use delta base from run run_id.
          Requires -c.
  -rN number_of_threads
          Override the number of concurrent threads.
  -rD number_of_seconds
          Override the COOS delay for this job.
```

```
-rC       Do not run COOS this job.
+rC       Do run COOS this job.
-rOb      Generate binary OOS for this job.
-rOx      Generate XML OOS for this job.
-rO2      Generate both binary and XML OOS for this job.
-rOO      Do not generate OOS for this job.
-rOs      number_of_rows
          Number of rows in each OOS XML chunk for this job.
-pS       Use named partition on the source.
-pSq      Use SQL predicate on the source.
-pSA1     Use arg as the starting ascii key the source.
-pSA2     Use arg as the ending ascii key the source.
-pSH1     Use arg as the starting hexadecimal key the source.
-pSH2     Use arg as the ending hexadecimal key the source.
-pT       Use named partition on the target.
-pTq      Use SQL predicate on the target.
-pTA1     Use arg as the starting ascii key the target.
-pTA2     Use arg as the ending ascii key the target.
-pTH1     Use arg as the starting hexadecimal key the target.
-pTH2     Use arg as the ending hexadecimal key the target.
-pq       Use SQL predicate on the source and target.
-nw       Do not wait for job to complete; job is submitted in background.
-wp       Wait for job to complete, poll at specified interval.
-repair   Launch a repair job automatically after compare job finishes. ]
-norepair
          Do not launch a repair job automatically, after compare job finishes. ]
```

Vericom Exit Status

After execution, Vericom exits with a numeric status ranging from 0 to 5. Table 15-1 describes the Vericom exit statuses.

Table 15-1. *Vericom Exit Statuses*

Exit Status	Description
0	The command executed successfully.
1	Invalid syntax.
2	Vericom could not locate connection information in veridata.loc or veridata.cfg.
3	Finer details about input errors that mostly include errors or missing flags that run comparisons.
4	The comparison job completed successfully with some rows not in sync.
5	Could not connect to the Veridata server.

Running a Job Using Vericom

In the following example, I executed a compare pair for table CNTRY, job ggs_job1, and group ggs_group1:

```
vericom.sh -j ggs_job1 -g ggs_group1 -c CNTRY=CNTRY -w
Connecting to: ravin-ravinpc:7862
Run ID: (2124, 0, 0)
Job Start Time: 2016-08-27 18:46:17
Job Stop Time: 2016-08-27 18:46:20
Job Report Filename: /app/veridata/data/rpt/ggs_job1/00002124/ggs_job1.rpt
Number of Compare Pairs: 1
Number of Compare Pairs With Errors: 0
Number of Compare Pairs With OOS: 0
Number of Compare Pairs With No OOS: 1
Number of Compare Pairs Cancelled: 0
Compare Pair Report Filename: /app/veridata/data/rpt/ggs_job1/00002124/ggs_group1/CP_
CNTRY=CNTRY.rpt
Number of Rows Compared: 84
Number of Rows In Sync: 84
Number of Rows With Errors: 0
Number of Rows Out Of Sync: 0
Number of Inserts Out Of Sync: 0
Number of Deletes Out Of Sync: 0
Number of Updates Out Of Sync: 0
Compare Pair OOSXML Directory: /app/veridata/data/oosxml/ggs_job1/00002124/ggs_group1
Compare Pair OOSXML Filename:
Job Completion Status: IN SYNC
```

Uninstalling OGG Veridata

For any reason if you want to uninstall OGG Veridata from your machine, it's easy. Here are the steps to completely uninstall OGG Veridata:

1. Stop the Oracle Fusion Middleware servers and processes.

2. Use RCU to remove the schema that you were using as the OGG Veridata DB repository.

3. Run the Oracle Fusion Middleware uninstall program to remove the installed software.

   ```
   On Microsoft Windows command shell:
   deinstall.cmd
   ```

   ```
   On UNIX command shell:
   ./deinstall.sh
   ```

4. Manually remove data in the domain home or application home directories. Some of the data will not be removed by the uninstall program and will require manual cleanup.

Summary

In this chapter, you learned how to install, configure, and use Oracle GoldenGate Veridata. This product was originally offered as an Oracle GoldenGate offering but can compare and fix the data differences regardless of the replication technology you are using between two database instances. It can work with Oracle GoldenGate, Oracle Advanced Replication, Streams, Oracle Data Integrator, customized batch jobs, and any other replication technology that you are using for moving data from one system to another.

You learned about why to use OGG Veridata and how it works. You also created and executed your first compare job.

By now, you have worked on simple to advanced configurations of Oracle GoldenGate and seen product offerings for sustaining and monitoring Oracle GoldenGate. In the next chapter, we will discuss troubleshooting techniques with examples. We will also discuss some of the common issues that you can configure your environment to handle automatically without manual intervention.

■ ■ ■

Troubleshooting Oracle GoldenGate

Oracle GoldenGate is a robust and near real-time replication solution with the capability to replicate millions of transactions in homogeneous as well as heterogonous database configurations. In this chapter, we will focus on identifying failure situations and taking corrective actions to fix the issues.

Types of Failure

Let's first understand the types of failure your OGG replication environment can have.

- *Oracle GoldenGate process failure*: An OGG process failure includes abended extract, data pump, replicat, collector, and manager processes. The abended process has an underlying error that you will learn to diagnose later in this chapter. OGG process failures sometimes are also caused by a corruption of trail files.

- *Problem with the source or target database*: This kind of failure includes failures at the database level that are preventing OGG replication such as tablespace full, archive log destination full, redo log corruptions, missing or no primary or unique keys on the table, database hung issues, and so on.

- *Server storage issues*: Since OGG process and trail files are stored on the server, any issue with server storage can impact your Oracle GoldenGate replication. The most common error is filling up the file system used by Oracle GoldenGate. Corruption of the file system, issues with privileges on the file system to the OGG user, issues with mounting/dismounting of the file system during server maintenance activities, and so on, are a few other server storage issues that can cause your OGG replication to stop.

- *Network issues*: The network provides the communication channel for your source and target OGG processes to communicate. Issues like network failure, network performance degradation, and the port assigned to OGG already in use by another process on the server can also cause OGG replication to halt.

- *User errors (conscious or unconscious mistakes)*: Last but not the least, there are several conscious or unconscious mistakes done by the OGG operator or admin that can also affect your OGG replication. *Conscious* mistakes refer to situations where an intent to fix something caused another issue, while *unconscious* mistakes are the ones where the user accidentally performed an action that negatively affected the Oracle GoldenGate replication. These include manually deleting (or bad shell scripts that deleted) trail files from the source or target OGG instance, performing insert/update/ delete operations directly on the target, forcefully stopping an Oracle GoldenGate process in the middle of a transaction, or killing the OGG process at the OS level.

© Ravinder Gupta 2016

R. Gupta, *Mastering Oracle GoldenGate*, DOI 10.1007/978-1-4842-2301-7_16

Where to Look for Errors?

Issue an INFO ALL command at the GGSCI prompt of your Oracle GoldenGate instance. If one or more of your Oracle GoldenGate processes is stopped or abended (meaning abnormally ended), you need to look at certain log files to identify the cause of the error. The three main log files where OGG writes information and error messages are as follows:

- OGG error log file (ggserror.log)

- Report file of each extract, data pump, or replicat process

- Discard file of each extract, data pump, or replicat process

Let's briefly discuss each of these files.

OGG Error Log File

The Oracle GoldenGate error log file is located in the home directory of your Oracle GoldenGate instance. Each Oracle GoldenGate installation on the server will have its own error log file with the name ggserror.log.

The ggserror.log file will have information like the start and stop of OGG processes (manager, extract, data pump, and replicat). It logs any error messages that caused abrupt termination of any OGG process. In addition to error messages, it logs information messages for logging OGG operations.

Earlier in this book, you learned how to configure the OGG manager process to log lag information by adding parameters such as LAGREPORTMINUTES, LAGCRITICALSECONDS, and so on.

You can view the ggserror.log file from the OGG home using operating system commands or you can issue VIEW GGSEVT at the GGSCI prompt.

By looking at the ggserror.log file, you can identify what error caused the issue and at what time. You can also scan information regarding operations that were performed when or before the error occurred. This file provides a history of error messages that you can scan to understand how frequently the issue is happening like the discard file being filled up every two hours.

The following are a few info, warning, and error information events logged into the ggserror.log file:

```
2016-08-17 08:26:13  INFO    OGG-00963  Oracle GoldenGate Manager for Oracle, mgr.
prm:  Command received from GGSCI on host ravin-ravinpc:13316 (STOP).
2016-08-19 09:05:51  INFO    OGG-00993  Oracle GoldenGate Capture for Oracle, tst7dext.
prm:  EXTRACT TST7DEXT started.
2016-08-21 13:07:23  INFO    OGG-01738  Oracle GoldenGate Capture for Oracle, tst1ext1.
prm:  BOUNDED RECOVERY: CHECKPOINT: for object pool 1: p26416_extr: start=SeqNo: 10557, RBA:
12704272, SCN: 3414.2021339131 (14665039687675), Timestamp: 2016-08-21 13:07:20.000000,
Thread: 1, end=SeqNo: 10557, RBA: 12704768, SCN: 3414.2021339131 (14665039687675),
Timestamp: 2016-08-21 13:07:20.000000, Thread: 1


2016-08-22 06:33:10  WARNING OGG-03504  Oracle GoldenGate Delivery for Oracle, tst7drep.
prm:  NLS_LANG character set AL32UTF8 on the target is different from the source database
character set US7ASCII. Replication may not be valid if the source data has an incompatible
character for the target NLS_LANG character set


2016-08-23 07:56:16  ERROR   OGG-00446  Oracle GoldenGate Capture for Oracle, tst1ext1.
prm:  Could not find archived log for sequence 10445 thread 1 under default destinations SQL
<SELECT name    FROM v$archived_log   WHERE sequence# = :ora_seq_no AND        thread#
= :ora_thread AND          resetlogs_id = :ora_resetlog_id AND         archived = 'YES'
AND          deleted = 'NO' AND         name not like '+%'         AND standby_dest = 'NO' >,
```

```
error retrieving redo file name for sequence 10445, archived = 1, use_alternate = 0Not able
to establish initial position for sequence 10445, rba 51626000.
2016-08-23 07:56:16  ERROR   OGG-01668  Oracle GoldenGate Capture for Oracle, tst1ext1.
prm:  PROCESS ABENDING.
```

OGG Process Report File

Report files are located in the OGG_HOME/dirrpt directory. They contain process-specific logging of activities it has performed since it was started. The report file logs info, warning, and error information specific to the process. A process can have multiple report files in the format <process name><sequence number>.rpt. By default OGG maintains up to ten report files for each process. You can view the report files using operating system commands or you can issue the following command at the GGSCI prompt:

```
GGSCI> VIEW REPORT <process name>
```

In the case of an abended or hung process, you can view the report file to determine what trail file the process was reading or writing when it abended. If the process is hung, you can review the report file to confirm whether the process is performing any activity. Also, while configuring a new manager, extract, data pump, or replicat process, if your process is not starting, you can view the report file to check for any syntax error that is preventing the process from getting started.

Here's an extract from a report file. The file shows the Oracle GoldenGate, database, and operating system configurations in use. It shows the extract parameter file configuration and how the extract parameters are resolved and interpreted by Oracle GoldenGate.

```
***********************************************************************
                 Oracle GoldenGate Delivery for Oracle
   Version 11.2.1.0.3 14400833 OGGCORE_11.2.1.0.3_PLATFORMS_120823.1258_FBO
     Linux, x64, 64bit (optimized), Oracle 11g on Aug 23 2012 20:37:31

   Copyright (C) 1995, 2012, Oracle and/or its affiliates. All rights reserved.

                    Starting at 2016-08-19 07:53:03
***********************************************************************


Operating System Version:
Linux
Version #1 SMP Mon Aug 10 09:44:54 EDT 2015, Release 2.6.32-573.3.1.el6.x86_64
Node: node2-ravinpc
Machine: x86_64
                        soft limit     hard limit
Address Space Size    :   unlimited      unlimited
Heap Size             :   unlimited      unlimited
File Size             :   unlimited      unlimited
CPU Time              :   unlimited      unlimited


Process id: 20537

Description:

***********************************************************************
**           Running with the following parameters             **
***********************************************************************
```

```
2016-08-19 07:53:03  INFO    OGG-03035  Operating system character set identified as UTF-8.
Locale: en_US, LC_ALL:.
REPLICAT TST1DREP
HANDLECOLLISIONS
REPERROR 2291, discard
ASSUMETARGETDEFS
DISCARDFILE /app/ggs/tiger/dirrpt/tst1drep.dsc, PURGE
USERID tiger,PASSWORD *********

2016-08-19 07:53:03  INFO    OGG-03501  WARNING: NLS_LANG environment variable is invalid or
not set. Using operating system character set value of AL32UTF8.
MAP TIGER.ORDER_TST, TARGET FOX.ORDER_TST;

**********************************************************************
**                       Run Time Messages                        **
**********************************************************************

Opened trail file /app/ggs/tiger/dirdat/d1000017 at 2016-08-19 07:53:04

MAP resolved (entry TIGER.ORDER_TST):
  MAP "TIGER"."ORDER_TST", TARGET FOX.ORDER_TST;
Using following columns in default map by name:
  ORDERID, ORDERTYPE, ORDERNAME
Using the following key columns for target table FOX.ORDER_TST: ORDERID, ORDERTYPE, ORDERNAME.

2016-08-22 06:41:06  INFO    OGG-01021  Command received from GGSCI: STATS.
```

OGG Process Discard File

The discard file logs failed operations that were not replicated because of data errors. To create a discard file, include the DISCARDFILE parameter in your extract or replicat process. It is also located in the OGG_HOME/dirrpt directory with a name of the format <group name><sequence number>.dsc. Use PURGE or APPEND with the DISCARDFILE parameter to control how the new discard transactions are written in the existing file or a new file for each time the process is run.

For example, include one of the following in your extract or replicat parameter file:

```
DISCARDFILE ./dirrpt/ettnd001.dsc, APPEND, MEGABYTES 50
```

Or:

```
DISCARDFILE ./dirrpt/rfdld001.dsc, APPEND
```

Or:

```
NODISCARDFILE
```

If a discard file is filled as specified by the MEGABYTES parameter, the process will abend with an error similar to the following:

```
2015-11-28 19:22:17 GGS ERROR 103 Discard file (/app/ggs/fox/dirrpt/rttn0002.dsc) exceeded
max bytes (10000000).
```

You can include the DISCARDFILEROLLOVER parameter in your extract or replicat process to rollover aging discard files using the following command:

DISCARDROLLOVER AT 06:00

Or the following:

DISCARDROLLOVER ON sunday

Or the following:

DISCARDROLLOVER AT 04:30 ON sunday

However, it is important to investigate the reason of failures in the discard file and take corrective actions. Here's an extract from one of the discard files on my machine:

Oracle GoldenGate Delivery for Oracle process started, group TST1UREP discard file opened:
2016-08-16 14:48:17

Current time: 2016-08-16 22:31:38

OCI Error ORA-01403: no data found, SQL <DELETE FROM "FOX"."ORDER_TST" WHERE "ORDERID" =
:b0>
Operation failed at seqno 140 rba 32477764
Discarding record on action DISCARD on error 1403
Problem replicating TIGER.ORDER_TST to FOX.ORDER_TST
Record not found
Mapping problem with delete record (target format)...
*
ORDERID = 29732004
*
Current time: 2016-08-16 22:31:38

Troubleshooting Using the LOGDUMP Utility

LOGDUMP is one of the most important utilities in the Oracle GoldenGate software bundle; it allows you to read through the trail files to look for data corruptions or trail file corruptions. It is useful in investigating data errors you have noticed in one or more of the three logging files discussed in the previous section.

We discussed using the LOGDUMP utility in Chapter 8 of this book. Figure 16-1 shows information in the trail file viewed by using the LOGDUMP utility.

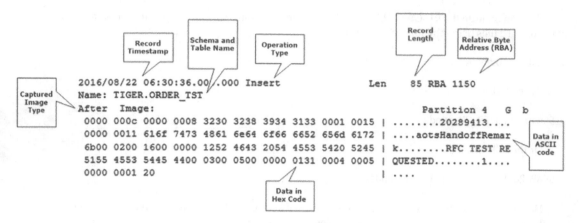

Figure 16-1. *LOGDUMP view of a source trail file*

Troubleshooting Using SHOWSYNTAX

You can use the SHOWSYNTAX parameter in the replicat parameter file to start an interactive session on the replicat to view SQL statements before they are applied. This can help you identify the SQL statement that is causing the replicat to abend.

```
SHOWSYNTAX [ APPLY | NOAPPLY ] [ INCLUDELOB [ max bytes | ALL ] ]
e.g.
SHOWSYNTAX INCLUDELOB 2M
```

The replicat after adding the previous parameter *must* be started from the OS command shell as shown here:

```
replicat paramfile /app/ggs/tiger/dirprm/ettn0001.prm
```

If you tried to start it from the GGSCI prompt, you would get an error similar to the following:

```
2015-11-27 03:56:23 ERROR OGG-01991 Start Replicat from the command shell of the operating
system when using the SHOWSYNTAX parameter.
```

Please note SHOWSYNTAX is not supported by the coordinated replicat.

Finally, if the Oracle GoldenGate error seems to be a bug or you need support from Oracle to resolve the issue, you can reach Oracle Support at http://support.oracle.com.

Performing a Sanity Check

If this is your new installation on the server and you are facing issues with starting up the process, here are few sanity checks you must perform to ensure there are no configuration issues:

- Ensure that the environment variables (LD_LIBARARY_PATH, PATH, ORACLE_SID, ORACLE_HOME, and so on) as discussed in Chapter 3 are set.

- Ensure that the OGG user has read and write permissions on the transaction and archive logs.

- Verify that the build of Oracle GoldenGate is compatible with your system. Execute the following to check the build name and ensure that you have the correct database and OS as indicated in the build name:

```
$ ggsci -v

Oracle GoldenGate Command Interpreter for Oracle
Version 11.2.1.0.3 14400833 OGGCORE_11.2.1.0.3_PLATFORMS_120823.1258_FBO
Linux, x64, 64bit (optimized), Oracle 11g on Aug 23 2012 20:20:21

Copyright (C) 1995, 2012, Oracle and/or its affiliates. All rights reserved.
```

- Ensure that the source and target databases are up and accepting connections.

- Ensure that the manager process is running on both the source and target OGG instances.

- Execute INFO on the extract or replicat process to verify they were created properly and have trails assigned to them.

- Use the CHECKPARAMS parameter in your extract and replicat parameter files to verify the syntax of the parameter file. View the report file; if there are no errors and still the process is stopped, make sure that CHECKPARAMS is removed. The parameter verifies the syntax and reports the error in the report file. It will keep the process STOPPED after verifying the syntax.

- Check the OGG user permissions on the parameter and report files. The user should have at least read permission on the parameter files.

- Ensure the RMTHOST parameter precedes RMTTRAIL in your extract parameter files.

- Database connection parameters (USERID, PASSWORD) must precede TABLE and MAP statements in extract and replicat parameter files, respectively.

Troubleshooting Examples: Issues with the Extract Processes

You must have some sort of monitoring to patrol your Oracle GoldenGate processes and alert you in situations where process are extract hung, abended, or stopped. In this section, we will discuss a few examples of situations when an extract process needs troubleshooting.

Extract Abended Due to Privilege Issue

Here's an example:

```
GGSCI> status extract ETTN0001
EXTRACT ETTN0001: ABENDED
```

In this case, you can either check ggserror.log using the GGSEVT command or check the extract report file. I checked the extract report file and noticed error 501.

```
GGSCI>VIEW REPORT ETTN0001
2015-11-27 15:45:18 GGS ERROR 501 GoldenGate Capture for Oracle, ettn0001.prm: Extract read,
error 13 (Permission denied) opening redo log /app/oracle/ggsdemo/arch/0001_0000000218.arc
for sequence 218.
```

The DBA needs to grant the GG user (in our case TIGER) read permission on the redo logs. Once the permissions are granted, restart the process and check INFO/STATS on the channel to verify whether the channel is working fine now.

Extract Abended/Stopped Due to Disk Space Full

Here's an example:

```
2015-11-28 09:33:31 GGS ERROR 103 Oracle GoldenGate Collector: Unable to write to file
"/app/ggs/tiger/dirdat/t3024841" (error28, No space left on device).
```

Check the available disk space on the file system where trails are being written. You may need to clear old trail files or any old unnecessary files to clean up the space. Once you have enough space, you can restart the process. To prevent accumulation of old processed trail files, use the PURGEOLDEXTRACTS parameter in the MANAGER parameter file.

```
e.g.
PURGEOLDEXTRACTS /app/ggs/tiger/dirdat/*, USECHECKPOINTS, MINKEEPDAYS 3, FREQUENCYMINUTES 5
```

Extract Abended Due to Network Communication Error

Here's an example:

```
2015-11-29 10:14:35 GGS ERROR 112 There is a problem in network communication, a remote file
problem, encryption keys for target and source do not match (if using ENCRYPT) or an unknown
error. (Remote file used is /app/ggs/fox/dirdat/f2000026, reply received is Unable to lock
file "/app/ggs/fox/dirdat/f2000026" (error 13, Permission denied). Lock currently held by
process id (PID) 9257217).
```

Either wait for the lock to be released by itself or kill the OS process and restart the abended channel.

Extract Abended Due to Memory Allocation Error

Here's an example:

```
GGS ERROR 105 malloc 2097152 bytes failed
```

Most often restarting the process fixes the issue. If the problem persists, check the SGA memory or contact Oracle GoldenGate Support.

Extract Abended Due to ORA-03135

Here's an example:

```
GGS ERROR      182 OCI Error describe for query (bad syntax) (status = 3135-ORA-03135:
connection lost contact
Process ID: 10820 Session ID: 3265 Serial number: 1), SQL< SELECT user_id  FROM all_
users  WHERE username = 'TIGER' >
```

Try restarting the extract manually. This could happen when the database server terminates unexpectedly or the server times out the connection. Check if the server session was terminated. Also, verify whether the timeout parameters are correctly set for the database.

Troubleshooting Examples: Issues with Replicat Processes

An OGG replicat with a high lag may be actually hung and not processing any transaction in the trail file. Your monitoring process should not only report abended and stopped channels but also report channels crossing a lag threshold. We will discuss monitoring end-to-end lag replication lag using a heartbeat table in Appendix C of this book. The following are some examples of troubleshooting issues with replicat processes.

Replicat Abended/Stopped Due to Missing Checkpoint Table

Here's an example:

```
GGSCI> status extract RFTN0001
REPLICAT RFTN0001: ABENDED
```

Check the replicat report file and look for GGS ERROR.

```
GGSCI>VIEW REPORT RFTN0001
2015-11-28 12:21:10 GGS ERROR 516 Extract read, Checkpoint table FOX.CHECKPOINT_TAB does not
exist. Please create the table or recreate the RFTN0001 group using the correct table.
```

The error says the checkpoint table is missing. Re-create the checkpoint table. Issue the following command to populate the newly created checkpoint table with the data from the checkpoint file. The convchk utility can be found in the OGG installation directory.

```
convchk RFTN0001 FOX.CHECKPOINT_TAB
```

Start the replicat.

```
GGSCI>START RFTN0001
```

Replicat Abended/Stopped Due to Corrupt Checkpoint Table or Missing Data in Checkpoint Table

Here's an example:

```
GGSCI> status extract RFTN0001
REPLICAT RFTN0001: ABENDED
```

Check the replicat report file and look for GGS ERROR.

```
GGSCI>VIEW REPORT RFTN0001
GGS ERROR 516 Extract read, No data found selecting position from checkpoint table FOX.
CHECKPOINT_TAB for group RFTN0001, key 1285475687 (0x4512053).
```

The error says the checkpoint table is missing data. Truncate the checkpoint table. Issue the following command to populate the fresh data into the checkpoint table with the data from the checkpoint file. The convchk utility can be found in the OGG installation directory.

```
convchk RFTN0001 FOX.CHECKPOINT_TAB
```

Start the replicat.

```
GGSCI>START RFTN0001
```

Replicat Abended Due to Table Structure or Data Inconsistency Error

Here's an example:

```
2015-11-28 20:48:22 GGS ERROR 218 Error mapping from TIGER.SCHOOL_DTL to FOX. SCHOOL_DTL
```

This error usually occurs if there is a difference in table definition. If there is a missing index or column or even if the column order is different on the source and the target, the mapping error happens. To resolve this, you either have to fix the table structure difference on target or make it same as on the source.

For a heterogeneous environment, where the source and target table definition need not be same, the table definition file needs to be regenerated for the replicat group. This is done using the DEFGEN utility discussed previously in this book.

Replicat Abended Due to Error Processing DDL Statement

Here's an example:

```
2015-11-02 11:22:28 GGS ERROR 2001 Oracle GoldenGate Delivery for Oracle, rttn0004.prm:
Fatal error executing DDL replication: error [Error code [1918], ORA-01918: user 'EAGLE'
does not exist, SQL / * GOLDENGATE_DDL_REPLICATION * / alter user eagle account unlock], no
error handler present.
```

The error states that a unlock user DDL is being applied on the target when the user itself doesn't exists. Either create the user and restart the process *or* skip the transaction if the user is not required to be synchronized in target database.

Replicat Abended Due to Table Not Present in Target Schema

Here's an example:

```
2015-11-28 18:29:12 GGS ERROR 101 Oracle GoldenGate Delivery for Oracle, rttn0001.prm: Table
FOX.SCHOOL_LOC does not exist in target database.
```

To resolve this error, you need to create the missing table in target schema. Regenerate the definition file if not using ASSUMETARGETDEFS. You will also need to sync the table before starting the replicat.

Replicat Abended Due to Discard File Full

Here's an example:

```
2015-11-28 19:22:17 GGS ERROR 103 Discard file (/app/ggs/fox/dirrpt/rttn0002.dsc) exceeded
max bytes (10000000).
```

The error says the discard file is full and needs to be cleaned up or the size of discard file needs to be increased. However, it is important to check what has caused the discard file to fill up and take corrective action accordingly.

Troubleshooting Examples: Data Sync Issues

Oracle GoldenGate does not capture a before image for all columns unless instructed to do so by adding GETUPDATEBEFORES in the extract parameter file. It instead uses key column values on the source and target to identify the records to be updated or deleted. There can be instances when even though your replication is working fine, the source and target tables may be out of sync. Some of the reasons that can cause data sync issues are as follows:

- DML transactions performed on the target tables by the database user

- Difference in source and target character sets

- Difference in key columns

- No key columns

- Disk failure

- Long suspended replication because of server or network failures

In Chapter 15, we discussed Oracle GoldenGate Veridata to ensure data integrity. You can use OGG Veridata to identify and repair data synchronization issues. Since OGG Veridata comes with an additional license cost, you can perform the following steps to synchronize data manually.

For synchronizing tables in my original replicat REPCAT01, I will create an additional temporary replicat group REPCAT02.

Edit and comment tables to be synchronized from REPCAT01 and restart the REPCAT01 so that replication on other tables in the replicat continues to happen.

```
GGSCI> EDIT PARAMS REPCAT01
```

```
REPLICAT REPCAT01
PURGEOLDEXTRACTS
ASSUMETARGETDEFS
DISCARDFILE /app/ggs/fox/dirrpt/repcat01.dsc, PURGE, MEGABYTES 599
USERID fox, PASSWORD fox123_
MAP TIGER.ORDER_DTL, TARGET FOX.ORDER_DTL;
MAP TIGER.ORDER_INFO, TARGET FOX.ORDER_INFO;
--MAP TIGER.CUSTOMER_INFO, TARGET FOX.CUSTOMER_INFO;
```

Bounce the replicat REPCAT01.

```
GGSCI> STOP REPLICAT REPCAT01
```

```
GGSCI> START REPLICAT REPCAT01
```

Note the timestamp on the source system.

```
8/22/2016 4:38:30.723920 PM -05:00
```

Ensure that you do not have a long-running transaction on the source database on the table you are going to work. This is required since if you begin a copy while a long-running transaction is already processing, that transaction will not be captured.

Copy the source table directly to the target table using the database utility. I use expdp/impdp for huge tables and a simple select over database link for relatively small tables.

Create replicat REPCAT02 as follows. Make sure you are using an existing trail file that is being used by REPCAT01 and include the HANDLECOLLISION parameter.

```
GGSCI> ADD REPLICAT REPCAT02, EXTTRAIL /app/ggs/fox/dirdat/f1, BEGIN 2016-08-22 04:38:30
```

```
GGSCI> EDIT PARAMS REPCAT01
```

```
REPLICAT REPCAT01
PURGEOLDEXTRACTS
ASSUMETARGETDEFS
HANDLECOLLISIONS
DISCARDFILE /app/ggs/fox/dirrpt/repcat01.dsc, PURGE, MEGABYTES 599
USERID fox, PASSWORD fox123_
MAP TIGER.ORDER_DTL, TARGET FOX.ORDER_DTL;
MAP TIGER.ORDER_INFO, TARGET FOX.ORDER_INFO;
--MAP TIGER.CUSTOMER_INFO, TARGET FOX.CUSTOMER_INFO;
```

Start REPCAT02 and monitor the lag.

```
GGSCI> START REPLICAT REPCAT02
GGSCI> SEND REPLICAT REPCAT02, GETLAG
```

Once replicat REPCAT02 gives you an output showing "At EOF, no more records to process," you can remove HANDLECOLLISION from REPCAT02 and restart it.

You can continue using REPCAT02 or merge the table from REPCAT02 back to REPCAT01. To merge the table CUSTOMER_INFO back to REPCAT01, perform the following steps:

Stop the corresponding extract data pump process, EXTDMP01, so it does not sends any new trail file to the target.

```
GGSCI> STOP EXTDMP01
```

Monitor the lag on REPCAT01 and REPCAT02.

```
GGSCI> SEND REPLICAT REPCAT01, GETLAG
GGSCI> SEND REPLICAT REPCAT02, GETLAG
```

Once you get "At EOF, no more records to process" for both REPCAT01 and REPCAT02, stop both the replicats.

```
GGSCI> STOP REPLICAT REPCAT01
```

```
GGSCI> STOP REPLICAT REPCAT02
```

Uncomment the table from REPCAT01.

```
GGSCI> EDIT PARAMS REPCAT01

REPLICAT REPCAT01
PURGEOLDEXTRACTS
ASSUMETARGETDEFS
DISCARDFILE /app/ggs/fox/dirrpt/repcat01.dsc, PURGE, MEGABYTES 599
USERID fox, PASSWORD fox123_
MAP TIGER.ORDER_DTL, TARGET FOX.ORDER_DTL;
MAP TIGER.ORDER_INFO, TARGET FOX.ORDER_INFO;
MAP TIGER.CUSTOMER_INFO, TARGET FOX.CUSTOMER_INFO;
```

Start EXTDMP01 on the source and REPCAT01 on the target.

```
GGSCI> START EXTRACT EXTDMP01
GGSCI> START REPLICAT REPCAT01
```

You no longer need REPCAT02; delete it.

```
GGSCI> DELETE REPLICAT REPCAT02
```

Troubleshooting Examples: DDL Capture Issue

If this is a new DDL capture setup, ensure that the setup was done properly. Verify that you have included the DDL parameter in the extract parameter file. Ensure you have correctly included GGSCHEMA in the GLOBALS parameter file.

Oracle GoldenGate software comes with two SQL files (marker_status.sql and ddl_status.sql), which you can run as the SYSDBA user to check the status of the DDL setup.

The output of marker_status.sql should look like the following, indicating the marker tables were set up correctly:

```
[oracle@ravin-ravinpc tiger]$ sqlplus / as sysdba

SQL*Plus: Release 12.1.0.2.0 Production on Mon Aug 22 19:15:47 2016

Copyright (c) 1982, 2014, Oracle.  All rights reserved.

Connected to:
Oracle Database 12c Enterprise Edition Release 12.1.0.2.0 - 64bit Production
With the Partitioning, OLAP, Advanced Analytics and Real Application Testing options

SQL> @marker_status.sql
Please enter the name of a schema for the GoldenGate database objects:
tiger
Setting schema name to TIGER
```

```
MARKER TABLE
-------------------------------
OK

MARKER SEQUENCE
-------------------------------
OK
```

Next, execute ddl_status.sql and observe the output.

```
[oracle@ravin-ravinpc tiger]$ sqlplus / as sysdba

SQL*Plus: Release 12.1.0.2.0 Production on Mon Aug 22 19:15:47 2016

Copyright (c) 1982, 2014, Oracle.  All rights reserved.

Connected to:
Oracle Database 12c Enterprise Edition Release 12.1.0.2.0 - 64bit Production
With the Partitioning, OLAP, Advanced Analytics and Real Application Testing options

SQL> @ddl_status.sql
Please enter the name of a schema for the GoldenGate database objects:
tiger
Setting schema name to TIGER

CLEAR_TRACE STATUS:

Line/pos   Error
---------- ----------------------------------------------------------------------
No errors  No errors

CREATE_TRACE STATUS:

Line/pos   Error
---------- ----------------------------------------------------------------------
No errors  No errors

TRACE_PUT_LINE STATUS:

Line/pos   Error
---------- ----------------------------------------------------------------------
No errors  No errors

INITIAL_SETUP STATUS:

Line/pos   Error
---------- ----------------------------------------------------------------------
No errors  No errors

DDLVERSIONSPECIFIC PACKAGE STATUS:

Line/pos   Error
---------- ----------------------------------------------------------------------
No errors  No errors
```
400

```
DDLREPLICATION PACKAGE STATUS:

Line/pos   Error
---------- -------------------------------------------------------------
No errors  No errors

DDLREPLICATION PACKAGE BODY STATUS:

Line/pos   Error
---------- -------------------------------------------------------------
No errors  No errors

DDL IGNORE TABLE
-----------------------------------
OK

DDL IGNORE LOG TABLE
-----------------------------------
OK

DDLAUX     PACKAGE STATUS:

Line/pos   Error
---------- -------------------------------------------------------------
No errors  No errors

DDLAUX PACKAGE BODY STATUS:

Line/pos   Error
---------- -------------------------------------------------------------
No errors  No errors

SYS.DDLCTXINFO  PACKAGE STATUS:

Line/pos   Error
---------- -------------------------------------------------------------
No errors  No errors

SYS.DDLCTXINFO  PACKAGE BODY STATUS:

Line/pos   Error
---------- -------------------------------------------------------------
No errors  No errors

DDL HISTORY TABLE
-----------------------------------
OK

DDL HISTORY TABLE(1)
-----------------------------------
OK
```

```
DDL DUMP TABLES
------------------------------------
OK

DDL DUMP COLUMNS
------------------------------------
OK

DDL DUMP LOG GROUPS
------------------------------------
OK

DDL DUMP PARTITIONS
------------------------------------
OK

DDL DUMP PRIMARY KEYS
------------------------------------
OK

DDL SEQUENCE
------------------------------------
OK

GGS_TEMP_COLS
------------------------------------
OK

GGS_TEMP_UK
------------------------------------
OK

DDL TRIGGER CODE STATUS:

Line/pos   Error
---------- -------------------------------------------------------------------
No errors  No errors

DDL TRIGGER INSTALL STATUS
------------------------------------
OK

DDL TRIGGER RUNNING STATUS
------------------------------------
ENABLED

STAYMETADATA IN TRIGGER
------------------------------------
OFF
```

```
DDL TRIGGER SQL TRACING
------------------------------------
0

DDL TRIGGER TRACE LEVEL
------------------------------------
0

LOCATION OF DDL TRACE FILE
-------------------------------------------------------------------------------
/app/oracle/product/12.1.0/dbhome_1/rdbms/log/ggs_ddl_trace.log

Analyzing installation status...

VERSION OF DDL REPLICATION
-------------------------------------------------------------------------------
OGGCORE_12.1.2.1.0_PLATFORMS_140727.2135.1

STATUS OF DDL REPLICATION
-------------------------------------------------------------------------------
SUCCESSFUL installation of DDL Replication software components
```

Now, note the trace file from the previous output. Stop the extract on the source.

```
GGSCI> STOP EXTRACT EXTDDL01
```

Execute `ddl_tracelevel.sql` from the OGG home directory and set the trace level as 1 when prompted. Start the extract process.

```
GGSCI> START EXTRACT EXTDDL01
```

Issue a DDL statement at the source and check the trace file /app/oracle/product/12.1.0/dbhome_1/rdbms/log/ggs_ddl_trace.log for the DDL operation you performed at the source database.

```
SESS 4294967295-2016-08-09 22:10:44 : DDL : DDL operation [GRANT SELECT, INSERT, DELETE ON
"TIGER"."ORDER_TST" TO PUBLIC ], sequence [25124], DDL type [GRANT] OBJECT PRIVILEGE, real
object type [OBJECT PRIVILEGE], validity [], object ID [], object [TIGER.ORDER_TST], real
object [TIGER.TST], base object schema [], base object name [], logged as [TIGER]
```

This confirms that DDL operations are being captured by the DDL trigger. Next, connect to the database and validate if the DDL operation exists in the DDL history table (GGS_DDL_HIST).

```
select metadata_text from TIGER.GGS_DDL_HIST where seqno=25124;
```

Look for your DDL operation and the immediately following MD_TAB_MARKERSEQNO.
Now, query the GGS_MARKER table to query the record corresponding to the marker sequence you noted earlier.

```
select metadata_text from TIGER.GGS_MARKER where seqno=32129;
```

If you can see your DDL statement, this means a marker was written for your DDL operation to the redo log. You are good until this stage.

Connect to the source Oracle database with the OGG DDL user and issue the following statements:

```
select metadata_text from TIGER.GGS_DDL_HIST where seqno=25124;
select metadata_text from TIGER.GGS_MARKER where seqno=32129;
```

The two statements should return same output as returned when you ran it from the SYS user. However, if you do not get any data, this means the role_setup.sql file you ran during the DDL setup was not run properly. Rerun the script and grant the role to the OGG user. Start the extract EXTDDL01 and monitor it. If the DDL statements are still not captured, contact Oracle Support.

Troubleshooting Examples: Trail Files Corruption

If a data pump extract or replicat process abends with an incompatible record error as follows, this means the trail file has become corrupted:

```
2016-08-20 07:18:25  ERROR   OGG-01028  Incompatible record (101) in ./dirdat/bt000054, rba
2542 (getting header)
```

The record has missed the header and started somewhere in middle. Hence, the record is corrupted. Although rare, there may be situations when a local or remote trail file gets corrupted. Some of the situations when this can happen are as follows:

- Two extract processes overwrote the same trail file.

- An extract process crashed in the middle of writing into a trail and was not able to update the checkpoint file.

- The user mistakenly edited the trail file while trying to view data in it manually.

To confirm if the trail file is corrupt, open the trail file using LOGDUMP and issue a count as follows:

```
Logdump 32 >open /app/ggs/tiger/dirdat/t1000008
Current LogTrail is /opt/app/d1c1d206/ggs/11.2.1.0.3/dirdat/tst0001
Logdump 33 >count
Bad record found at (RBA 1507, format 5.50 Unknown TokenID 64)
 4701 00bd 4800 0039 4504 0041 0058 05ff 02f2 4d38 | G...H..9E..A.X....M8
 3295 8064 0000 0000 0030 a538 0000 0a45 0152 0000 | 2..d.....0.8...E.R..
 0001 464f 5243 4541 5050 2e58 4246 414c 4552 544c | .....TIGER.TSTALERTL
 4f47 5f54 0044 0000 5800 0000 0a00 0000 0000 0000 | OG._T.D..X..........
 a0ae 6000 0100 0f00 0000 0b58 4246 3031 3030 2d31 | ..`........XBF0100-1
 3533 0002 0015 0000 3230 3135 2d31 322d 3136 3a31 | 53......2015-12-16:1
 343a 3330 3a30 3100 0300 0a68 6a68 6a64 6866 6b6a | 4:30:01....hjhjdhfkj
 7364 6866 6b73 646a 6866 646a 6b0a 0a64 6664 0a66 | sdhfksdjhfdjk..dfd.f
 0a64 0a64 ffff 0000 0000 0000 0000 0004 0004 ffff | .d.d................
 0000 0005 0004 ffff 00                            | .........
LogTrail /app/ggs/tiger/dirdat/t1000008 has 4 records
Total Data Bytes            1198
  Avg Bytes/Record           299
Insert                        2
RestartOK                     1
Others                        1
After Images                  3
```

```
Average of 3 Transactions
    Bytes/Trans .....      463
    Records/Trans ...        1
    Files/Trans .....        1
```

If the output contains "Bad record found," it means the trail file is corrupt.

Corrupt Trail on the Source

Situations like a system failure where the extract crashes suddenly while it is in the middle of writing a transaction to the trail and updating checkpoint file results in trail file or checkpoint file corruption. To recover from such a scenario, perform the following actions:

Identify the begin sequence number (BSN) from the replicat process. The BSN identifies the oldest uncommitted transaction held in extract memory. It gives you the recovery point for extract process.

```
GGSCI> info replicat REPCAT01, detail
```

The output contains the following:

```
Current Log BSN value: 1452687
```

If you're using classic capture mode, query the source database to get the sequence number of the transaction log that matches the BSN value.

```
SQL> select name, thread#, sequence# from v$archived_log
where 1452687 between first_change# and next_change#;

NAME                                    THREAD#     SEQUENCE#
------------------------------------    ----------  ----------
/app/oradata/arch1_163_800262442.dbf    1              245
```

Now, reposition the extract process to begin from the BSN value.

- When classic capture is being used:

```
GGSCI> ALTER EXTRACT REPCAT01 EXTSEQNO 245
GGSCI> ALTER EXTRACT REPCAT01 EXTRBA 0
GGSCI> ALTER EXTRACT REPCAT01 ETROLLOVER
```

- When using integrated extract:

```
GGSCI> ALTER EXTRACT REPCAT01 SCN 1452687
GGSCI> ALTER EXTRACT REPCAT01 ETROLLOVER
```

Monitor the extract process.

```
GGSCI> INFO EXTRACT EXTDMP01 SHOWCH
Sequence #: 7
RBA: 0
```

Alter the replicat to begin reading from this trail file.

```
GGSCI> ALTER REPLICAT REPCAT01 extseqno 000007, extrba 0
```

Start the extract and replicat processes.

```
GGSCI> START EXTRACT EXTDMP01
GGSCI> START REPLICAT REPCAT01
```

Corrupt Trail on the Target

When the trail file being processed by the replicat process is corrupt, one of the quickest resolutions is to skip bad transactions and make the replicat start processing from the next good transaction. You will later need to manually sync the missing transaction from the source to the target table.

Identify whether the trail is partially corrupt or completely corrupt. The output of the count command shown earlier gives the number of good transactions in the trail file that can be read. You can use one of the following methods to skip bad transactions:

- Use LOGDUMP to point the replicat to a good RBA.

- Using the SKIPTRANSACTION parameter.

Using LOGDUMP to Point the Replicat to a Good RBA

Execute INFO on the replicat process and determine the last RBA it has processed.

```
GGSCI (node2-ravinpc) 4> info replicat TST7DREP
```

```
REPLICAT    TST7DREP  Last Started 2016-08-19 07:53    Status ABENDED
Checkpoint Lag        00:00:00 (updated 00:00:29 ago)
Log Read Checkpoint  File /app/ggs/fox/dirdat/d7000006
                     2016-08-22 13:20:12.000429  RBA 19429201
```

Open the trail file and navigate to the position indicated by the RBA.

```
$ logdump
Logdump> open /app/ggs/fox/dirdat/d7000006
Logdump> pos 19429201
Logdump> next
```

Scan the trail file until the transaction indicator shows the end of the transaction and note the RBA. The values of TransInd can be interpreted as follows:

```
TransInd    :      .  (x00) : First Statement in transaction
TransInd    :      .  (x01) : Statement in middle of transaction
TransInd    :      .  (x02) : Last Statement in transaction
TransInd    :      .  (x03) : Single Statement transaction
```

Alter the replicat process with the RBA you noted from the logdump output.

```
GGSCI> alter replicat TST7DREP extseqno 000006, extrba 19745683
```

If the replicat is still abended and the report file still indicates an incompatible record in the trail, it means the next transaction in the trail is also corrupt. Repeat the previous steps to skip to the next available transaction. If all records in the trail are corrupt, you can skip the bad trail file and alter the replicat to start with the next available trail file.

Using SKIPTRANSACTION

You may have noticed that skipping transactions using LOGDUMP is tedious. Oracle GoldenGate eases this task by providing the SKIPTRANSACTION parameter for the replicat processes. Issue the following command at the GGSCI prompt to skip the bad transaction and start the replicat from the next transaction.

```
GGSCI> START REPLICAT TST7DREP SKIPTRANSACTION
```

Error Handling in Oracle GoldenGate

Most of the replication errors occur while applying transactions by the replicat process. You can specify the REPERROR parameter in the replicat parameter file to instruct the replicat what to do in the case of a specific replication error.

Table 16-1 lists the options you can use with REPERROR.

Table 16-1. REPERROR Options

Option	Description
DEFAULT	Sets a global response to all errors except those for which explicit REPERROR statements are specified
DEFAULT2	Provides a backup default action when the response for DEFAULT is set to EXCEPTION
{SQL ERROR}	SQL error number
{User Defined Error}	A user-defined error that is specified with the RAISEERROR option of a FILTER clause within a MAP statement
ABEND	Rolls back transaction and abends the channel
DISCARD	Writes error to discard file and continue with next transaction
IGNORE	Ignores the error and continues
RETRYOP	Retries the operation; you can specify the number of retries using the MAXRETRIES option
EXCEPTION	Processes the error as an exception
TRANSABORT	Aborts the transaction and repositions to the beginning of trail
TRANSDISCARD	Discards the entire transaction
TRANSEXCEPTION	Processes every record in the transaction as an exception

For example, use the following reperror format to abend the replicat for all errors except duplicate records that you want to be ignored. For this error to occur in first place, you need to have the primary key enabled on the target table.

```
REPERROR (DEFAULT, ABEND)
REPERROR (-1, IGNORE)
```

Here's another example that instructs you to discard the transaction if any record in the transaction generates error 1403. For other errors, it instructs the default as ABEND.

```
REPERROR DEFAULT ABEND
REPERROR 1403 TRANSDISCARD
```

You can also use REPERROR specific to one MAP statement and also globally for all the tables in the replicat.

```
REPLICAT RFTN0002
REPERROR (DEFAULT, ABEND)
MAP TIGER.TABLEA, TARGET FOX.TABLEA, REPERROR (0001, IGNORE);
MAP TIGER.TABLEB, TARGET FOX.TABLEB, REPERROR (1403, DISCARD);
```

You can also save failed records and error messages in an EXCEPTION TABLE. You can either create a single exception table for all the tables in the replicat or create one exception table for each table being replicated.

Here I am creating only one table for handling exceptions for all the replicated tables for the FOX schema:

```
SQL> CREATE TABLE FOX.GG_EXCEPTIONS
(
REP_NAME VARCHAR2(8 BYTE),
TABLE_NAME VARCHAR2(61 BYTE),
DML_DATE TIMESTAMP(6),
ERRNO NUMBER,
DBERRMSG VARCHAR2(4000 BYTE),
OPTYPE VARCHAR2(20 BYTE),
ERRTYPE VARCHAR2(20 BYTE),
LOGRBA NUMBER  xxx    NOT NULL,
LOGPOSITION NUMBER NOT NULL,
COMMITTIMESTAMP TIMESTAMP(6) NOT NULL,
GGS_FILENAME VARCHAR2(256 BYTE),
CDRFAIL NUMBER,
CDRSUC NUMBER,
CDRDETECT NUMBER
);

Table created.

SQL> CREATE UNIQUE INDEX FOX.EXCEPTIONS_PK ON FOX.GG_EXCEPTIONS
(LOGRBA, LOGPOSITION, COMMITTIMESTAMP);

Index created.

SQL> ALTER TABLE FOX.GG_EXCEPTIONS ADD (
CONSTRAINT EXCEPTIONS_PK
PRIMARY KEY
```

```
(LOGRBA, LOGPOSITION, COMMITTIMESTAMP)
USING INDEX FOX.EXCEPTIONS_PK);

Table altered.

SQL> GRANT DELETE, INSERT, SELECT, UPDATE ON FOX.GG_EXCEPTIONS TO FOX;

Grant succeeded.
```

Now, configure your replicat as follows to handle the exception:

```
GGSCI> EDIT PARAMS RFTN0001
REPLICAT RFTN0001
USERID FOX, PASSWORD fox123_
ASSUMETARGETDEFS
DISCARDFILE /app/ggs/fox/dirrpt/rftn0001.dsc, APPEND
REPERROR (DEFAULT, EXCEPTION)
MAP TIGER.CNTRY, TARGET FOX.CNTRY;

--exception handler
MACRO #exception_handler
BEGIN
-- Using one EXCEPTIONS table for all replicated tables
, TARGET FOX.GG_EXCEPTIONS
, COLMAP ( rep_name = @GETENV("GGENVIRONMENT", "GROUPNAME")
, TABLE_NAME = @GETENV ("GGHEADER", "TABLENAME")
, ERRNO = @GETENV ("LASTERR", "DBERRNUM")
, DBERRMSG = @GETENV ("LASTERR", "DBERRMSG")
, OPTYPE = @GETENV ("LASTERR", "OPTYPE")
, ERRTYPE = @GETENV ("LASTERR", "ERRTYPE")
, LOGRBA = @GETENV ("GGHEADER", "LOGRBA")
, LOGPOSITION = @GETENV ("GGHEADER", "LOGPOSITION")
, COMMITTIMESTAMP = @GETENV ("GGHEADER", "COMMITTIMESTAMP")
, GGS_FILENAME = @GETENV("GGFILEHEADER", "FILENAME")
, CDRFAIL = @GETENV("DELTASTATS","CDR_RESOLUTIONS_FAILED")
, CDRSUC = @GETENV("DELTASTATS","CDR_RESOLUTIONS_SUCCEEDED")
, CDRDETECT = @GETENV("DELTASTATS","CDR_CONFLICTS"))
, INSERTALLRECORDS
, EXCEPTIONSONLY;
END;

MAP FOX.CNTRY #exception_handler();
```

Start the replicat and verify whether replication errors are getting logged into the GG_EXCEPTION table you created in the target schema.

Let's see another example. Here we have one exception table per replicated table. REPERROR (-1, EXCEPTION) means that when you encounter the ORA-00001 error, the exception handler will kick in.

The EXCEPTIONSONLY clause instructs that such exceptions will be logged in the SCHOOL_DTL_ EXCEPTIONS table. This table has all the columns of the SCHOOL_DTL table and some additional columns to log information about row violations in the OPTYPE, DBERR, and DBERRMSG columns.

```
REPLICAT RFTN0003
ASSUMETARGETDEFS
USERID FOX,PASSWORD fox123_
REPERROR (-1, EXCEPTION)
MAP TIGER.SCHOOL_DTL, TARGET FOX.SCHOOL_DTL;
INSERTALLRECORDS
MAP TIGER.SCHOOL_DTL, TARGET FOX.SCHOOL_DTL_EXCEPTION,
EXCEPTIONSONLY,
COLMAP (USEDEFAULTS,
optype = @GETENV ("lasterr", "optype"),
dberr = @GETENV ("lasterr", "dberrnum"),
dberrmsg = @GETENV ("lasterr", "dberrmsg"));
```

For any new GGS error, you can always refer to the OGG Error Messages reference guide, which lists each error number with its possible cause and action.

Summary

This chapter discussed troubleshooting techniques in Oracle GoldenGate. It discussed different types of failures, OGG log files for error diagnosis, the LOGDUMP utility, and SHOWSYNTAX. You then learned about performing sanity checks. The chapter discussed troubleshooting examples for the extract and replicat processes. We also discussed troubleshooting and how to perform corrective actions for issues with data replication, DDL replication, and trail file corruption. Finally, we discussed error handling in Oracle GoldenGate.

In the next chapter, we will discuss the possibility of extending Oracle GoldenGate's capabilities and integrating a relational database with nonrelational and nondatabase systems.

■ ■ ■

Using Oracle GoldenGate Adapters

Up until now we have discussed how to capture data changes in near real-time from supported relational databases and replicate them to other relational databases such as Oracle, Sybase, Microsoft SQL, IBM DB2, and so on. The real-time capture capability for supported database systems can be used and expanded to integrate relational database systems with nonrelational databases and also with nondatabase systems. To extend Oracle GoldenGate to integrate it with nondatabase systems, Oracle GoldenGate provides you with three tools.

- The flat-file adapter
- JMS capture or delivery
- Java APIs

The flat-file adapter lets you write captured data into flat files. These flat files can be actively fed into Big Data systems and other nonrelational database systems. Using JMS capture and delivery, you can publish data changes in the form of JMS messages or capture data changes from JMS messages and write them to the target database. You can also write custom Java handlers to process data changes captured on the source system and apply them to target systems using third-party Java APIs. We will discuss these adapters in this chapter.

Generating Flat Files in Real Time

Oracle GoldenGate can generate a series of sequential data flat files and control files from the transactional data captured on the source system. This capability is effectively used in data warehouse system ETL and legacy applications that consume these flat files in real time.

The Oracle GoldenGate flat-file adapter uses a special type of extract, implemented as a user exit. The extract produces rolling data flat files. The data is formatted by Oracle GoldenGate to the specifications of the target applications either as delimiter-separated values or as length-delimited values. Near real-time data feeds to legacy systems can be achieved by minimizing the elapsed time frame for rolling over batch files.

Oracle GoldenGate is a heterogeneous replication tool, but if your target database is not supported by OGG, the flat-file adapter still can be implemented on the source system to capture transactions in real time and generate flat files. These flat files can be sent across the network using an appropriate file transfer tool like SFTP, data routers, and so on. Figure 17-1 shows the components of Oracle GoldenGate when using the flat-file adapter for generating flat files.

© Ravinder Gupta 2016

R. Gupta, *Mastering Oracle GoldenGate*, DOI 10.1007/978-1-4842-2301-7_17

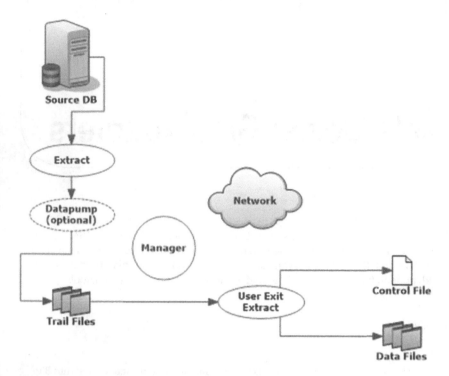

Figure 17-1. *Oracle GoldenGate flat-file adapter configuration*

A writer is configured in the user exit properties file. This writer is responsible for generating data files based on specifications set by other properties in the user exit properties file. It is possible to configure more than one writer in the same user exit properties file. This allows you to generate flat files in more than one format for the same input/captured data.

Here I have specified that I am going to use two writers in my user exit properties:

```
goldengate.flatfilewriter.writers=dsvwriter,ldvwriter
```

dsvwriter and ldvwriter are standard names used for naming your flat-file writer. You can choose any name you want. Each properties setup in the properties file should then be prefixed with the writer name. When your data files are being written, they will have a temporary extension indicating that the file is not yet ready for loading in the target database. Once the temporary file meets the rollover criteria defined in your user exit properties file, it will be rolled over to the specified format.

One control file is also generated per table or per operation type as specified in the user exit properties. However, if your extract process is writing all the data in just one flat file, only one control file for the extract will be generated.

There are two modes of output supported by the flat-file adapter.

- Delimiter-separated values (DSV)

- Length-delimited values (LDV)

Data can be output all to one file, one file per table, or one file per operation code. Here the operation code means insert, delete, or update (I, D, U).

412

Overview of Tasks

The following are the steps you need to follow to generate flat files using the Oracle GoldenGate flat-file adapter:

1. Download the OGG application adapter.

2. Install the OGG application adapter.

3. View the sample files.

4. Create the OGG user and set up the role.

5. Prepare the database for flat-file extraction.

6. Add the checkpoint table.

7. Generate the table definition.

8. Create the flat-file adapter properties file.

9. Create the primary extract.

10. Create the user exit extract.

11. Start the extracts.

12. Verify the flat files.

Downloading OGG Application Adapters

Oracle GoldenGate application adapters can be downloaded from www.oracle.com/technetwork/middleware/goldengate/downloads/index.html. Look for the Oracle GoldenGate application adapters and then click the appropriate version for your operating system environment. For demonstration in this chapter, I downloaded "Oracle GoldenGate Application Adapters 12.1.2.1 for Linux x86-64."

Installing the OGG Application Adapter

The OGG application adapter installation requires first installing the OGG instance and then unzipping the application adapter binaries in the OGG home directory. Assuming you already have your Oracle GoldenGate instance setup, navigate to the OGG home directory and extract the TAR file as shown here:

```
cd /app/ggs/fftiger
tar -xvf /app/downloads/ggs_Adapters_Linux_x64.tar
```

You may also choose to extract the compressed binary into a temporary directory first and then copy the libraries and required files from the temporary directory to the OGG Home directory.

Viewing the Sample Files

The following are the most important files related to the flat-file adapter:

- Shared library (flatfilewriter.dll on Windows, flatfilewriter.so on Unix)

- Sample user exit properties file (ffue.properties)

- Sample extract parameter file (ffue.prm)

413

Navigate to AdapterExamples to view the sample files included with the installation. You can use these files as the baseline for creating configuration files for your flat-file adapter.

```
[oracle@ravin-ravinpc fftiger]$ cd AdapterExamples/
[oracle@ravin-ravinpc AdapterExamples]$ ls -lrt
total 8
drwxr-xr-x. 2 oracle oinstall 4096 Apr  2 2015 jms-capture
drwxr-xr-x. 2 oracle oinstall 4096 Apr  2 2015 java-delivery
drwxr-xr-x. 2 oracle oinstall   57 Apr  2 2015 file-writer
```

Apart from your primary extract parameter file, you need to configure the user exit extract and properties file to configure your flat-file adapter.

The sample contents of the user exit extract parameter file are shown here:

```
[oracle@ravin-ravinpc file-writer]$ cat ffue.prm


-- To setup extract as a pump to read the trail and output flat-files
--   ggsci> add extract ffue, extTrailSource dirdat/tc
--   ggsci> info ffue

Extract ffue

CUserExit flatfilewriter.so CUSEREXIT PassThru IncludeUpdateBefores, PARAMS "dirprm/ffue.
properties"
-- CUserExit flatfilewriter.dll CUSEREXIT PassThru IncludeUpdateBefores, PARAMS "dirprm/
ffue.properties"

SourceDefs dirdef/tc.def

-- Table gg.employees;
-- Table gg.job_history;
Table gg.*;
```

The following is the sample content of the properties file included in AdapterExamples, which you can use to instruct your OGG flat-file adapter to generate flat files.

```
[oracle@ravin-ravinpc file-writer]$ cat ffue.properties
#-----------------------
#LOGGING OPTIONS
#-----------------------
goldengate.log.logname=ffwriter
goldengate.log.level=INFO
goldengate.log.modules=LOGMALLOC
goldengate.log.level.LOGMALLOC=ERROR
goldengate.log.tostdout=false
goldengate.log.tofile=true


#-----------------------
#FLAT FILE WRITER OPTIONS
#-----------------------
```

```
goldengate.flatfilewriter.writers=dsvwriter
goldengate.userexit.chkptprefix=ffwriter_

#------------------------
# dsvwriter options
#------------------------
dsvwriter.mode=DSV
dsvwriter.rawchars=false
dsvwriter.includebefores=false
dsvwriter.includecolnames=false
dsvwriter.omitvalues=false
dsvwriter.diffsonly=false
dsvwriter.omitplaceholders=false
#dsvwriter.files.onepertable=false
dsvwriter.files.prefix=csv
dsvwriter.files.data.rootdir=./dirout
dsvwriter.files.data.ext=_data.dsv
dsvwriter.files.data.tmpext=_data.dsv.temp
dsvwriter.files.data.rollover.time=10
#dsvwriter.files.data.rollover.size=
dsvwriter.files.data.norecords.timeout=10
dsvwriter.files.control.use=true
dsvwriter.files.control.ext=_data.control
dsvwriter.files.control.rootdir=./dirout
dsvwriter.dsv.nullindicator.chars=<NULL>
dsvwriter.dsv.fielddelim.chars=|
dsvwriter.dsv.linedelim.chars=\n
dsvwriter.dsv.quotes.chars="
dsvwriter.dsv.quotes.escaped.chars=""
dsvwriter.metacols=position,txind,opcode,timestamp,schema,table
dsvwriter.metacols.txind.fixedlen=1
dsvwriter.metacols.txind.begin.chars=B
dsvwriter.metacols.txind.middle.chars=M
dsvwriter.metacols.txind.end.chars=E
dsvwriter.files.formatstring=pump_%s_%t_%d_%05n
#------------------------
# ldvwriter options
#------------------------
ldvwriter.mode=LDV
ldvwriter.rawchars=true
ldvwriter.includebefores=false
ldvwriter.includecolnames=false
ldvwriter.files.onepertable=false
ldvwriter.files.data.rootdir=./dirout
ldvwriter.files.data.ext=.data
ldvwriter.files.data.tmpext=.temp
ldvwriter.files.data.rollover.time=10
ldvwriter.files.data.norecords.timeout=10
ldvwriter.files.control.use=true
ldvwriter.files.control.ext=.ctrl
ldvwriter.files.control.rootdir=./dirout
```

```
ldvwriter.metacols=position,timestamp,@TOKEN-RBA,@TOKEN-POS,opcode,txind,schema,table
ldvwriter.metacols.TOKEN-RBA.fixedlen=10
ldvwriter.metacols.TOKEN-POS.fixedlen=10
ldvwriter.metacols.timestamp.fixedlen=26
ldvwriter.metacols.schema.fixedjustify=right
ldvwriter.metacols.schema.fixedpadchar.chars=Y
ldvwriter.metacols.opcode.fixedlen=1
ldvwriter.metacols.opcode.insert.chars=I
ldvwriter.metacols.opcode.update.chars=U
ldvwriter.metacols.opcode.delete.chars=D
ldvwriter.metacols.txind.fixedlen=1
ldvwriter.metacols.txind.begin.chars=B
ldvwriter.metacols.txind.middle.chars=M
ldvwriter.metacols.txind.end.chars=E
ldvwriter.metacols.txind.whole.chars=W
ldvwriter.ldv.vals.missing.chars=M
ldvwriter.ldv.vals.present.chars=P
ldvwriter.ldv.vals.null.chars=N
ldvwriter.ldv.lengths.record.mode=binary
ldvwriter.ldv.lengths.record.length=4
ldvwriter.ldv.lengths.field.mode=binary
ldvwriter.ldv.lengths.field.length=2
ldvwriter.files.rolloveronshutdown=false
ldvwriter.statistics.toreportfile=false
ldvwriter.statistics.period=onrollover
ldvwriter.statistics.tosummaryfile=true
ldvwriter.statistics.overall=true
ldvwriter.statistics.summary.
fileformat=schema,table,schemaandtable,total,gctimestamp,ctimestamp
ldvwriter.statistics.summary.delimiter.chars=|
ldvwriter.statistics.summary.eol.chars=\n
ldvwriter.metacols.position.format=dec
ldvwriter.writebuffer.size=36863
```

Creating the OGG User and Role

You are required to create an OGG user in the database and grant the required privileges to this user, as shown here. If you already have your Oracle GoldenGate user set up, as discussed in previous chapters, you can skip this step.

```
SQL>create user tiger identified by tiger123_;

User created.

SQL>grant connect,resource,dba to tiger;

Grant succeeded.

Set up GGUSER role

SQL>@role_setup.sql
```

GGS Role setup script

This script will drop and recreate the role GGS_GGSUSER_ROLE
To use a different role name, quit this script and then edit the params.sql script to change
the gg_role parameter to the preferred name. (Do not run the script.)

You will be prompted for the name of a schema for the GoldenGate database objects.
NOTE: The schema must be created prior to running this script.
NOTE: Stop all DDL replication before starting this installation.

Enter GoldenGate schema name: tiger
Wrote file role_setup_set.txt

PL/SQL procedure successfully completed

Role setup script complete

Grant this role to each user assigned to the Extract, GGSCI, and Manager processes, by using
the following SQL command:

GRANT GGS_GGSUSER_ROLE TO <loggedUser>

where <loggedUser> is the user assigned to the GoldenGate processes.

Log in to the database as sysdba and grant GGS_GGSUSER_ROLE to the OGG user you just created.

SQL>GRANT GGS_GGSUSER_ROLE TO tiger;

Preparing the Database for Flat-File Extraction

To capture the redo information required for OGG, enable supplemental log data either for the database or
for the set of tables to be replicated.

Enable minimal supplemental logging at the database level.

SQL> ALTER DATABASE ADD SUPPLEMENTAL LOG DATA;
Database altered.

Enable GoldenGate replication.

SQL> ALTER SYSTEM SET ENABLE_GOLDENGATE_REPLICATION=TRUE;
System altered.

Switch the log file.

SQL> ALTER SYSTEM SWITCH LOGFILE;
System altered.

Log in to GGSCI and enable supplemental logging for the GoldenGate table/schema.

GGSCI> DBLOGIN USERID tiger, PASSWORD tiger123_

```
Successfully logged into database
GGSCI> ADD SCHEMATRANDATA tiger ALLCOLS
2016-06-21 16:50:44  INFO    OGG-01788  SCHEMATRANDATA has been added on schema tiger.
2016-06-21 16:50:45  INFO    OGG-01976  SCHEMATRANDATA for scheduling columns has been added
on schema tiger.
2016-06-21 16:50:45  INFO    OGG-01977  SCHEMATRANDATA for all columns has been added on
schema tiger.
```

Adding a Checkpoint Table

Although not mandatory, it is good practice that you add a checkpoint table that will be used during recovery.

```
GGSCI> edit params ./GLOBALS


GGSCHEMA tiger
CHECKPOINTTABLE tiger.checkpointtable

GGSCI> dblogin userid tiger, password tiger123_;
Successfully logged into database.

GGSCI> add checkpointtable tiger.checkpointtable

Successfully created checkpoint table tiger.checkpointtable.
```

Generating the Table Definitions

Even though you don't have a target database where OGG trails will be sent, you still need to generate definition files for the tables for which you are generating flat files. These definition files are used by the user exit extract process for writing appropriate information in flat files and control files. To generate the table definition, create a temporary file called temp01.prm with the following content in the dirprm directory:

```
DEFSFILE /app/ggs/fftiger/dirdef/ettn0001.def
USERID tiger, PASSWORD tiger123_
TABLE TIGER.ORDER_DTL;
```

Save this file and go to the home directory of OGG. Issue the following command to generate the definition file for tables in the temp01.prm file:

```
defgen paramfile dirprm/temp01.prm
```

Creating the Flat-File Adapter Properties File

Here's the content of the ffue.properties file I have used in our demonstration setup. This file is the most important configuration file, which instructs the OGG flat-file adapter for generating flat-file and control files in your required format.

```
#-----------------------
#LOGGING OPTIONS
#-----------------------
--goldengate.log.level=DEBUG
--goldengate.log.tofile=true
#-----------------------
#FLAT FILE WRITER OPTIONS
#-----------------------
goldengate.flatfilewriter.writers=dsvwriter
goldengate.userexit.chkptprefix=fttn0001_
goldengate.userexit.datetime.removecolon=true
#-----------------------
# dsvwriter options
#-----------------------
dsvwriter.mode=DSV
dsvwriter.rawchars=false
dsvwriter.includebefores=false
dsvwriter.includecolnames=false
dsvwriter.omitvalues=false
dsvwriter.diffsonly=false
dsvwriter.omitplaceholders=false
dsvwriter.files.onepertable=true
dsvwriter.files.data.ext=_data.dsv
dsvwriter.files.data.tmpext=_data.dsv.temp
--dsvwriter.files.prefix=TIGER_
dsvwriter.dsv.nullindicator.chars=
dsvwriter.dsv.fielddelim.chars=|
dsvwriter.dsv.fielddelim.escaped.chars=
dsvwriter.files.data.rollover.time=1800
dsvwriter.files.data.rootdir=/app/ggs/fftiger/ffile
dsvwriter.files.data.rollover.size=10000
dsvwriter.metacols.position.format=hex
dsvwriter.metacols=timestamp,position,opcode
dsvwriter.metacols.timestamp.fixedlen=20
dsvwriter.metacols.timestamp.column=MY_TIMESTAMP_COL
dsvwriter.metacols.TKN-SCN.novalue.chars=0
--dsvwriter.dsv.quotes.chars=
dsvwriter.rawchars=true
dsvwriter.metacols.opcode.updatepk.chars=U
dsvwriter.dsv.linedelim.escaped.code=20
--dsvwriter.dsv.linedelim.escaped.chars=-
dsvwriter.dsv.fielddelim.escaped.chars=\n
```

Creating the Primary Extract

We require two extract processes. One extract process captures transactional information from database redo logs and writes them into trail files. The other extract process, which is the user exit extract, will read this trail file data and write it into flat files.

Create the primary extract for the capture as shown here:

```
GGSCI> ADD EXTRACT ETTN0001, TRANLOG, BEGIN NOW
EXTRACT ADDED.

GGSCI> ADD EXTTRAIL /app/ggs/fftiger/dirdat/t1, EXTRACT ETTN0001
EXTTRAIL ADDED.

GGSCI> edit params ETTN0001

extract ETTN0001
EXTTRAIL /app/ggs/fftiger/dirdat/t1, FORMAT LEVEL 3
USERID tiger, PASSWORD tiger123_
TABLE TIGER.ORDER_DTL;
```

You can have multiple primary extracts to distribute tables across multiple capture groups. You need one corresponding user exit extract for each primary extract group.

Creating the User Exit Extract

Create the user exit extract for generating flat files. You need to include the source definition file and properties file in the user exit extract parameter file, as shown here:

```
GGSCI> ADD EXTRACT FTTN0001, EXTTRAILSOURCE /app/ggs/fftiger/dirdat/t1
EXTRACT ADDED.

GGSCI> edit params FTTN0001

extract FTTN0001
SOURCEDEFS /app/ggs/fftiger/dirdef/ettn0001.def
CUSEREXIT flatfilewriter.so CUSEREXIT PASSTHRU, PARAMS "dirprm/ffue.properties"
REPORTCOUNT EVERY 70 seconds, RATE
USERID tiger, PASSWORD tiger123_
TABLE TIGER.ORDER_DTL;
```

Starting the Extracts

Start the primary extract and then the user exit extract.

```
GGSCI> START EXTRACT ETTN0001
GGSCI> START EXTRACT FTTN0001
```

Verifying Flat Files

Monitor the primary and user exit extracts for transactions. Use the INFO and STATS commands to monitor the extracts.

Navigate to the root directory location specified in the ffue.properties file.

```
cd /app/ggs/fftiger/ffile
```

There are three types of files generated for each table. In this example, you have only one table, ORDER_DTL, configured for demonstrating flat-file generation. The following is the file and its contents:

$ cat TIGER.ORDER_DTLcontrol
```
/app/ggs/fftiger/ffile/TIGER.ORDER_DTL_2016-07-15_07-23-21_data.dsv
```

$ cat TIGER.ORDER_DTL_2016-07-16_12-17-26_data.dsv
```
"2016-07-16 12:17:24.|0000000300519d54|U|Trng_Completion|00:01|23:59|1|ALL|2016-07-16
  10:17:19"
"2016-07-16 12:18:25.|0000000300519e3c|U|AUTO|01:00|23:59|1|ALL|2016-07-16 10:18:19"
"2016-07-16 12:18:25.|0000000300519f18|U|Schedule_R1508|10:00|19:00|3|ALL|2016-07-16
  10:18:20"
"2016-07-16 12:19:25.|0000000300519fde|U|Trng_Completion|00:01|23:59|1|ALL|2016-07-16
  10:19:20"
"2016-07-16 12:20:24.|000000030051a0c5|U|SCH_LINUX|00:10|23:55|5|ALL|2016-07-16 10:20:20"
"2016-07-16 12:20:24.|000000030051a1a6|U|AUTO|01:00|23:59|1|ALL|2016-07-16 10:20:20"
"2016-07-16 12:21:24.|000000030051a262|U|Trng_Completion|00:01|23:59|1|ALL|2016-07-16
  10:21:20"
"2016-07-16 12:21:24.|000000030051a349|U|Schedule_R1508|10:00|19:00|3|ALL|2016-07-16
  10:21:20"
"2016-07-16 12:22:24.|000000030051a40f|U|AUTO|01:00|23:59|1|ALL|2016-07-16 10:22:20"
"2016-07-16 12:23:24.|000000030051a4ec|U|Trng_Completion|00:01|23:59|1|ALL|2016-07-16
  10:23:20"
"2016-07-16 12:24:25.|000000030051a5d3|U|Auto|01:00|20:00|12|SAT|2016-07-16 10:24:20"
"2016-07-16 12:24:25.|000000030051a6b0|U|AUTO|01:00|23:59|1|ALL|2016-07-16 10:24:20"
"2016-07-16 12:24:25.|000000030051a76c|U|Schedule_R1508|10:00|19:00|3|ALL|2016-07-16
  10:24:20"
"2016-07-16 12:25:24.|000000030051a832|U|Trng_Completion|00:01|23:59|1|ALL|2016-07-16
  10:25:20"
"2016-07-16 12:25:24.|000000030051a91a|U|SCH_LINUX|00:10|23:55|5|ALL|2016-07-16 10:25:20"
"2016-07-16 12:26:24.|000000030051a9db|U|AUTO|01:00|23:59|1|ALL|2016-07-16 10:26:20"
"2016-07-16 12:27:24.|000000030051aab7|U|Trng_Completion|00:01|23:59|1|ALL|2016-07-16
  10:27:20"
"2016-07-16 12:27:24.|000000030051ab9f|U|Schedule_R1508|10:00|19:00|3|ALL|2016-07-16
  10:27:20"
"2016-07-16 12:28:25.|000000030051ac65|U|AUTO|01:00|23:59|1|ALL|2016-07-16 10:28:20"
"2016-07-16 12:29:24.|000000030051ad42|U|Trng_Completion|00:01|23:59|1|ALL|2016-07-16
  10:29:20"
"2016-07-16 12:30:25.|000000030051ae2a|U|TEST_R1602|00:00|23:00|15|ALL|2016-07-16 10:30:20"
"2016-07-16 12:30:25.|000000030051af0d|U|SCH_LINUX|00:10|23:55|5|ALL|2016-07-16 10:30:20"
"2016-07-16 12:30:25.|000000030051afce|U|AUTO|01:00|23:59|1|ALL|2016-07-16 10:30:20"
"2016-07-16 12:30:25.|000000030051b08a|U|Schedule_R1508|10:00|19:00|3|ALL|2016-07-16
  10:30:20"
"2016-07-16 12:31:24.|000000030051b150|U|Trng_Completion|00:01|23:59|1|ALL|2016-07-16
  10:31:20"
"2016-07-16 12:32:25.|000000030051b237|U|AUTO|01:00|23:59|1|ALL|2016-07-16 10:32:21"
"2016-07-16 12:33:25.|000000030051b314|U|Trng_Completion|00:01|23:59|1|ALL|2016-07-16
  10:33:21"
"2016-07-16 12:33:25.|000000030051b3fb|U|Schedule_R1508|10:00|19:00|3|ALL|2016-07-16
  10:33:21"
```

```
$ cat TIGER.ORDER_DTL_2016-07-16_12-47-30_data.dsv.temp
"2016-07-16 12:33:45.|000000030051b150|U|Trng_Completion|00:01|23:59|1|ALL|2016-07-16
  10:33:25"
"2016-07-16 12:33:46.|000000030051b237|U|AUTO|01:00|23:59|1|ALL|2016-07-16 10:33:26"
"2016-07-16 12:33:46.|000000030051b314|U|Trng_Completion|00:01|23:59|1|ALL|2016-07-16
  10:33:26"
"2016-07-16 12:33:46.|000000030051b3fb|U|Schedule_R1508|10:00|19:00|3|ALL|2016-07-16
  10:33:26"
```

Do not ever change anything in the temporary flat files being generated. You can open them in read-only mode to see what's getting written in them.

Flat-File Adapter Properties

Let's take a look at the commonly used flat-file adapter properties and their usage. These are sufficient for most flat-file configuration requirements. For a complete list of properties available to configure your adapter, you can also refer to the Oracle documentation.

Table 17-1 lists the logging properties that you can use to configure logging information captured by the flat-file adapter.

Table 17-1. *Logging Properties*

Property	Usage	Description
goldengate.log.logname	goldengate.log.logname=writer	Specifies the prefix of the log file name. For example, the file generated in this example will be writer_20100803.log.
goldengate.log.level	goldengate.log.level=ERROR|WARN|INFO|DEBUG	ERROR: Only writes messages if errors occur. WARN: Writes error and warning messages. INFO: Writes error, warning, and informational messages. DEBUG: Writes all messages, including debug ones. The default value is INFO.
goldengate.log.tostdout	goldengate.log.tostdout=true|false	Specifies whether the log information is to be written on standard out.
goldengate.log.tofile	goldengate.log.tofile=true|false	Specifies whether the log information is to be written in the log file.

Table 17-2 lists some generic properties that you can include in your flat-file adapter properties file. If you do not explicitly include a property, the default value of the property is used.

Table 17-2. General Properties

Property	Usage	Description
`goldengate.flatfilewriter. writers`	`goldengate.flatfilewriter. writers=dsvwriter,ldvwriter`	Specifies the name of the writer that will run within the user exit.
`goldengate.userexit.buffertxs`	`goldengate.userexit. buffertxs=true|false`	Specifies whether entire transactions are read before being output.
`goldengate.userexit. chkptprefix`	`goldengate.userexit. chkptprefix=pump1_`	Specifies the prefix for the checkpoint file name.
`goldengate.userexit.chkpt. ontxend`	`goldengate.userexit.chkpt. ontxend=true`	Specifies whether the need to roll files over is checked after every transaction or only when the extract process checkpoints.
`goldengate.userexit.datetime. removecolon`	`goldengate.userexit.datetime. removecolon=true`	Specifies whether a colon is written between the date and time.
`goldengate.userexit.timestamp`	`goldengate.userexit. timestamp=utc`	Specifies whether the record timestamp is output as the local time or Coordinated Universal Time (UTC).
`goldengate.userexit.datetime. maxlen`	`goldengate.userexit.datetime. maxlen=19`	Specifies the maximum output length of a datetime column. Setting `goldengate.userexit. maxlen=19` truncates to a date and time with no fractional seconds. Setting `goldengate. userexit.maxlen=10` truncates to the date only.

Table 17-3 lists properties specific to flat-file configurations. These properties define what should be written in the flat files and in which format. They also control the name and location of the flat files. Substitute `<writer_name>` with the writer name you have defined in the `goldengate.flatfilewriter. writers` property.

Table 17-3. *Format Flat-Files Properties*

Property	Usage	Description
mode	dsvwriter.mode=dsv ldvwriter.mode=ldv	Specifies flat-file format as DSV or LDV
groupcols	<writer_name>.groupcols=true|false	Specifies whether the column name and its before and after values are to be grouped together Examples: When FALSE (default): field1, field1_before, field1, field2, field2_before, field2 When TRUE: field1, field2, field1_before, field2_before, field1, field2
files.onepertable	<writer_name>.files. onepertable=false	Specifies whether data is written one rolling file per table or one rolling file for all tables in the user exit extract process
files.oneperopcode	<writer_name>.files. oneperopcode=true	Creates separate files based on the insert, delete, or update opcodes
files.prefix	<writer_name>.files. prefix=tigerprod_	Specifies the prefix for data files and control files
files.data.rootdir	<writer_name>.files.data.rootdir=/ opt/app	Specifies the directory where flat files will be stored
files.data.ext	<writer_name>.files.data.ext=_ data.dsv	Specifies the extension of flat files after rolling over
files.data.tmpext	<writer_name>.files.data.tmpext=_ data.dsv.temp	Specifies the extension of temporary flat files before rolling over
files.control.use	<writer_name>.files.control. use=true	Specifies whether a control file will be generated
files.control.rootdir	<writer_name>.files.control. rootdir=/opt/app	Specifies the location for storing control files
files.control.ext	<writer_name>.files.control.ext=_ data.control	Specifies the extension of control files
files.formatstring	<writer_name>.files.formatstring= myext_%d_%010n_%s_%	Specifies the format string for creating flat-file names: %s = Schema %t = Table %n = Seqno %d = Timestamp %o = Opcode

The properties in Table 17-4 instruct the flat-file adapter on how and when to roll over data in temporary files to flat files.

Table 17-4. *Properties for Rollover Flat Files*

Property	Usage	Description
files.data.rollover.time	<writer_name>.files.data.rollover.time=10	Number of seconds elapsed after the first record is written to the file for rollover
files.data.rollover.size	<writer_name>.files.data.rollover.size=10000	Maximum number of bytes written in the flat file before rollover happens.
files.data.norecords.timeout	<writer_name>.files.data.norecords.timeout=10	Wait time in seconds from the last record written in the file before rollover.
files.rolloveronshutdown	<writer_name>.files.rolloveronshutdown=true	Specifies what to do with temporary files if the extract process stops.
		When FALSE:
		Empty temporary files are deleted and nonempty temporary files are left as it is.
		When TRUE:
		Nonempty trail files are rolled over.
files.data.rollover.attime	<writer_name>.files.data.rollover.attime=*:00	Specifies a time at which flat-file adapter will roll over all files.
	<writer_name>.files.data.rollover.attime=*:10, *40	*:00 means rollover at every hour.
writebuffer.size	<writer_name>.writebuffer.size=50000	Write buffer size. A higher buffer size reduces the number of system write calls.

Table 17-5 lists the properties for configuring the data format for data captured and written to flat files.

Table 17-5. *Format Data Properties*

Property	Usage	Description
rawchars	`<writer_name>.rawchars=false`	Specifies whether Unicode multibyte data, if present, should retain the binary form or be converted to ASCII before writing in the file.
includebefores	`<writer_name>.includebefores=true`	Whether both the before and after images of data are included. This is only for update operations. The default is `false`.
afterfirst	`<writer_name>.afterfirst=true`	If this property is set to true, it specifies that the after image will be written in the data file. The default value is `false`.
includecolnames	`<writer_name>.includecolnames=true`	If `true`, column names are also written before the column values within double quotes.
diffsonly	`<writer_name>.diffsonly=true`	If `true`, only those column values are written in the file whose before and after images are different. For capturing before images, the `GETUPDATEBEFORES` parameter should be used in the extract parameter file.

Next, I have listed properties for configuring metacols. *Metacols* are not actual table columns but optional columns that you can write in your data files. Before we discuss metacols properties, these are some frequently used metacols:

position: A unique position indicator of records in a trail.

opcode: I, U, or D for insert, update, and delete records.

txind: The general record position in a transaction (0: begin, 1: middle, 2: end, 3: whole).

txoppos: Position of record in a transaction, starting from 0.

schema: The schema (owner) name of the changed record.

table: The table name of the changed record.

schemaandtable: Both the schema and table name concatenated as schema.table.

timestamp: The commit timestamp of the record.

%COLNAME: The value of a data column.

numops: The number of operations in the current transaction. This value will always be 1 if goldengate. userexit.buffertxs is not true.

numcols: The number of columns to be output.

<value>: Any literal value.

Table 17-6 lists the properties and their usage for configuring metacols.

Table 17-6. *Configuring Metadata*

Property	Usage	Description
metacols	<writer_name>.metacols=timestamp,opco de,txind,position,schema,table	Specifies the metacols list to be written in the data file for each record.
metacols. {metacol-name}. fixedlen	<writer_name>.metacols.timestamp. fixedlen=23	Specifies the length limit for each metacol value; characters after the length limit are truncated.
metacols.opcode. insert.chars	<writer_name>.metacols.opcode.insert. chars=INS	Overrides the default character I to identify insert operations.
metacols.opcode. update.chars	<writer_name>.metacols.opcode.update. chars=UPD	Overrides the default character U to identify update operations.
metacols.opcode. delete.chars	<writer_name>.metacols.opcode.delete. chars=DEL	Overrides the default character D to identify delete operations.
metacols.txind. begin.chars	<writer_name>.metacols.txind.begin. chars=B	Overrides the default character 0 to identify the beginning of transactions.
metacols.txind. middle.chars	<writer_name>.metacols.txind.middle. chars=M	Overrides the default character 1 to identify the middle of the transaction.
metacols.txind. end.chars	<writer_name>.metacols.txind.end. chars=E	Overrides the default character 2 to identify the end of the transaction.
metacols.txind. whole.chars	<writer_name>.metacols.txind.whole. chars=W	Overrides the default character 3 to identify a whole transaction.
begintx.metacols	<writer_name>.begintx. metacols="B",numops	Specifies the metacol value to mark the beginning of the transaction.
endtx.metacols	<writer_name>.endtx.metacols="E"	Specifies the metacol value to mark the end of the transaction.

Table 17-7 lists the properties for configuring information in DSV files. These properties are specific to a DSV file writer.

Table 17-7. *Configuring DSV*

Property	Usage	Description

dsv.nullindicator.chars	`<writer_name>.dsv.`
	`nullindicator.chars=NULL`
	`<writer_name>.dsv.`
	`nullindicator.chars=`
		Specifies the character to use for NULL values in DSV files. If you specify no character while setting the property, the NULL values will be kept blank.

dsv.fielddelim.chars	`<writer_name>.dsv.fielddelim.` `chars=|`	The default field delimiter is a comma. You can override it with any character.
dsv.linedelim.chars	`<writer_name>.dsv.linedelim.` `chars=\n`	Overrides the line delimiter. The default is specific to the operating system.
dsv.quote.chars	`<writer_name>.dsv.quotes.` `chars='`	Overrides the quote character (").

dsv.quotes.policy	`<writer_name>.dsv.quotes.`
	`policy={default|none|always|`
	`datatypes}`
		Specifies when to apply quotes. `default`: Only dates and chars are quoted.
		`never`: No metadata column or column values are quoted.
		`always`: All metadata columns and column values are quoted.
		`datatypes`: Only specific data types are quoted. Used with `dsv.quotes.policy.datatypes` to specify specific datatypes.

dsv.onecolperline	`<writer_name>.dsv.` `onecolperline=true`	Forces each column to start with new line; prefixed with its metacols.
dsv.quotealways	`<writer_name>.dsv.` `quotealways=true`	When true, each column is quoted.

Troubleshooting Your Flat-File Configuration

If one or more of your extract processes gets abandoned or shows no transactions, you can follow these steps to troubleshoot any possible error:

1. Check whether the shared library (`.so` or `.dll`) in the extract parameter file is correct and is accessible.

2. Check for the SOURCEDEFS file specified in the extract parameter file. Check whether the name is correct and the file is accessible.

3. Verify your user exit properties file `ffue.properties` is correct and accessible. Also, ensure the path specified in the GG_USEREXIT_PROPFILE environment variable is correct if specified.

4. Verify all the output directories you specified in the user exit properties file exist and have read-write permissions.

5. Check the user exit log file for errors.

6. Set log.level=DEBUG for capturing detail errors in the log file. It is recommended that you remove or comment this property after an issue is identified and fixed to avoid the unnecessary growth of the log file.

OGG for JMS Messaging

Oracle GoldenGate using the Java application adapter libraries can now capture messages from JMS capture and deliver them to supported target databases. It can also capture transactions and publish them in the form of JMS messages to be fed into and processed by the JMS delivery processes on the target system.

This capability of Oracle GoldenGate enables you to integrate transactional systems with Java systems in near real-time.

JMS Delivery

Implementation Overview for JMS Delivery

Let's now discuss the implementation of Oracle GoldenGate for capturing transactions and delivering it to the JMS queue on Oracle WebLogic Server, which is the JMS provider. Here is an overview of the tasks for this implementation:

1. Install the OGG application adapter.

2. Configure the primary extract to capture before images for update operations.

3. Generate the definition file for the tables being captured.

4. Create and configure a data pump extract.

5. Configure the Oracle WebLogic queue (JMS provider).

6. Configure the Java data pump.

7. Configure the OGG Java user exit and JMS handler.

How Does It Work?

The OGG Java adapter is installed on a server running Oracle WebLogic, which is the JMS provider. You can also have other JMS providers like ActiveMQ. The configuration is similar. Ideally, you should install your JMS delivery on a separate data integration server that is different from your source database server. This is because formatting XML messages with the Java adapter is a resource-intensive task and may add additional performance overhead on your database server if running on the same server. Figure 17-2 shows an ideal configuration for JMS delivery where you have implemented JMS delivery on a separate data integration server.

The capture process captures change data directly from Oracle redo logs or archive logs and writes the data into trail files to be sent to the data integration server. The user exit extracts on the data integration server use the definition file and JMS handler to write data in the form of XML messages and send the messages to the JMS provider (Oracle WebLogic server queue). This is then consumed by the JMS consumer process. Figure 17-2 shows the components of Oracle GoldenGate for JMS delivery.

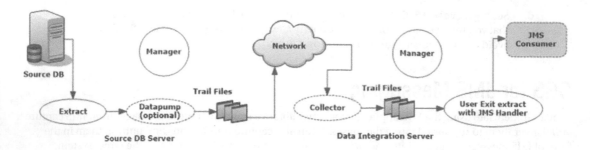

Figure 17-2. *JMS delivery*

Configuring the Primary and Data Pump Extracts on the Source Database Server

Install Oracle GoldenGate and configure your source database for supplemental logging as discussed in previous chapters. You must generate a definition file for tables in your primary extract. This will be used by the user exit extract on the data integration target server.

Enable minimal supplemental logging at the database level.

```
SQL> ALTER DATABASE ADD SUPPLEMENTAL LOG DATA;
Database altered.
```

Enable GoldenGate replication.

```
SQL> ALTER SYSTEM SET ENABLE_GOLDENGATE_REPLICATION=TRUE;
System altered.
```

Switch the log file.

```
SQL> ALTER SYSTEM SWITCH LOGFILE;
System altered.
```

Log in to GGSCI and enable supplemental logging for the GoldenGate table/schema.

```
GGSCI> DBLOGIN USERID tiger, PASSWORD tiger123_
Successfully logged into database
GGSCI> ADD SCHEMATRANDATA tiger ALLCOLS
2016-06-21 16:50:44  INFO    OGG-01788  SCHEMATRANDATA has been added on schema tiger.
2016-06-21 16:50:45  INFO    OGG-01976  SCHEMATRANDATA for scheduling columns has been added
on schema tiger.
2016-06-21 16:50:45  INFO    OGG-01977  SCHEMATRANDATA for all columns has been added on
schema tiger.
```

Create a temporary parameter file temp.prm in the /app/ggs/tiger/dirprm directory on the source machine and add the following entries:

```
DEFSFILE /app/ggs/tiger/dirdef/ue1.def
USERID TIGER, PASSWORD tiger123_
TABLE TIGER.ORDER_DTL;
```

Run the following command from the OGG Home directory /app/ggs/tiger. This will generate the definition file.

```
defgen paramfile dirprm/temp.prm
```

A definition file gets generated at /app/ggs/tiger/dirdef/ue1.def. Add and configure the primary capture extract as shown here:

```
GGSCI> ADD EXTRACT ETTN0001, TRANLOG, BEGIN NOW, THREADS 10
EXTRACT ADDED.

GGSCI> ADD EXTTRAIL /app/ggs/tiger/dirdat/t1, EXTRACT ETTN0001
EXTTRAIL ADDED.

GGSCI> edit params ETTN0001

extract ETTN0001
EXTTRAIL /app/ggs/tiger/dirdat/t1, FORMAT LEVEL 3
RecoveryOptions OverwriteMode
USERID tiger, PASSWORD tiger123_
GETUPDATEBEFORES
TABLE TIGER.ORDER_DTL;
```

Configure the data pump extract to send trail files to the data integration target server, as shown here:

```
GGSCI> ADD EXTRACT PFTXD001, EXTTRAILSOURCE /app/ggs/tiger/dirdat/t1
GGSCI> ADD rmttrail /app/ggs/jms/dirdat/u1, extract PFTND001

GGSCI> EDIT PARAMS PFTND001

EXTRACT PFTND001
USERID tiger, PASSWORD tiger123_
RMTHOST node2.ravin-pc.com, MGRPORT 7809
RMTTRAIL /app/ggs/jms/dirdat/u1
RecoveryOptions OverwriteMode
PASSTHRU
GETUPDATEBEFORES
TABLE TIGER.ORDER_DTL;
```

Configuring Data Integration on the Target Server

Make sure you have installed Oracle WebLogic Server, created the WLS domain, and set up the JMS connection factory and queue on your target server. We already discussed installing WLS and creating the WLS domain in Chapter 13. Refer to the Oracle documentation for creating the JMS connection factory and queue for Oracle WebLogic Server.

Next, create a javaue.properties file to be used by the user exit extract to instruct the Java application adapter for generating JMS messages to be fed into JMS queues.

The content of the javaue.properties file is shown here:

```
### javaue.properties ###
gg.handlerlist=ggsjms1
```

```
### Path to WebLogic jars ###
#gg.classpath=

### JNDI properties
java.naming.provider.url=t3://localhost:7001
java.naming.factory.initial=weblogic.jndi.WLInitialContextFactory
java.naming.security.principal=weblogic
java.naming.security.credentials=ravinder123_

### JMS Handler
gg.handler=ggsjms1
gg.handler.ggsjms1.type=jms
gg.handler.ggsjms1.format=xml
gg.handler.ggsjms1.format.mode=op
gg.handler.ggsjms1.destinationType=queue
gg.handler.ggsjms1.destination=myggsq
gg.handler.ggsjms1.connectionFactoryJndiName=myggscf

### native library config ###
goldengate.userexit.nochkpt=TRUE
goldengate.userexit.timestamp=utc
goldengate.log.logname=cuserexit
goldengate.log.level=INFO
goldengate.log.tofile=TRUE
goldengate.userexit.writers=javawriter
javawriter.stats.display=TRUE
javawriter.stats.full=TRUE
javawriter.bootoptions=-Xmx32m -Xms32m
-Djava.class.path
=ggjava/ggjava.jar:dirprm:/app/wls/domains/base_domain/lib/wlfullclient.jar
```

Make sure you have set up the PATH variable to include the JVM location and set up LD_LIBRARY_PATH to include the path to the Java libraries in your application adapter installation directory.

Create the user exit extract javaue to include the path to the javaue.properties file and definition file, as shown here:

```
GGSCI> add extract javaue, exttrailsource /app/ggs/jms/dirdat/u1

GGSCI> edit params javaue

EXTRACT javaue
SOURCEDEFS /app/ggs/jms/dirdef/u1.def
CUserExit libggjava_ue.so CUSEREXIT PassThru IncludeUpdateBefores
GETUPDATEBEFORES
TABLE TIGER.ORDER_DTL;
```

First start the primary extract and data pump extract on the source database server. Next, start the JMS delivery process. Execute the info and stats commands on the extract processes to monitor the progress of the capture and delivery processes.

JMS Capture

Implementation Overview for JMS Capture

Let's now discuss the implementation of Oracle GoldenGate for capturing transactions from JMS messages, writing them to trail files, and sending the trail files to the target server for the Oracle GoldenGate replicat process to apply into the database. Here is an overview of the tasks for this implementation:

1. Install the OGG application adapter.

2. Configure the Virtual Access Module (VAM) extract.

3. Generate gendef to generate a definition file for the JMS message data.

4. Create and configure a data pump extract.

5. Create and configure the replicat on the target server.

How Does It Work?

JMS messages are read from the JMS producer by the JMS handler portion of the VAM extract. If there is no message to be read, the extract waits for a time specified by the EOFDELAY parameter. If you do not specify this parameter, the default is 1 second. When all messages for a particular transaction are read, the VAM plug-in parses the message in the form of the Oracle GoldenGate trails data format, and the extract process writes it to trail files. If the write to trail is successful, the JMS messages are removed from the JMS queue; otherwise, the extract process abends with an error.

Next, the data pump process picks up a trail file and sends it across the network to the target server where it is collected by the collector process, and the replicat then applies the data changes to the target database. Figure 17-3 shows the components of Oracle GoldenGate for JMS capture.

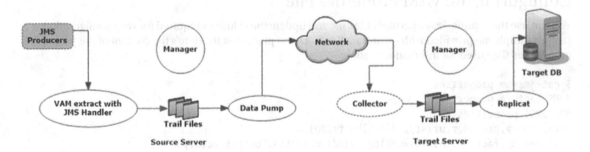

Figure 17-3. *JMS capture*

Navigate to the AdapterExamples/java-delivery directory. You have sample files available here that you can use to baseline your JMS delivery setup.

```
[oracle@ravin-ravinpc java-delivery]$ ls -lrt
total 44
-rw-r--r--. 1 oracle oinstall 1864 Apr  2  2015 tc.def
```

```
-r-xr-xr-x. 1 oracle oinstall 4666 Apr  2  2015 tc000000
-rw-r--r--. 1 oracle oinstall 1040 Apr  2  2015 mgr.prm
-rw-r--r--. 1 oracle oinstall 5383 Apr  2  2015 javaue.properties
-rw-r--r--. 1 oracle oinstall 1301 Apr  2  2015 javaue.prm
-rw-r--r--. 1 oracle oinstall  149 Apr  2  2015 format_tx2xml.vm
-rw-r--r--. 1 oracle oinstall  709 Apr  2  2015 format_op2xml.vm
-rw-r--r--. 1 oracle oinstall  331 Apr  2  2015 defgen.prm
-rw-r--r--. 1 oracle oinstall 2299 Apr  2  2015 capture.prm
```

Configuring the VAM Extract

Assuming that you already have a JMS producer configured from where your VAM extract can pick up JMS messages, let's configure the VAM extract as shown here:

```
GGSCI> ADD EXTRACT jmsvam, VAM
GGSCI> ADD EXTTRAIL /app/ggs/jms/dirdat/v1, EXTRACT jmsvam, MEGABYTES 50
GGSCI> EDIT PARAMS jmsvam

EXTRACT jmsvam
VAM libggjava_vam.so PARAMS(dirprm/jmsvam.properties)
REPORTCOUNT EVERY 5 minutes, rate
GETUPDATEBEFORES
TRANLOGOPTIONS VAMCOMPATIBILITY 1
TRANLOGOPTIONS GETMETADATAFROMVAM
EXTTRAIL /app/ggs/jms/dirdat/v1
TABLE TIGER.ORDER_DTL;
```

Configuring the VAM Properties File

You can use the sample jmsvam.properties file and update the values as required for your configuration. Using a sample file provided with the installation is a good place to start. Here's the content of the jmsvam. properties file I used for this demonstration:

```
$ cat jmsvam.properties
#JMS capture properties
### JNDI properties
java.naming.provider.url=t3://localhost:7001
java.naming.factory.initial=weblogic.jndi.WLInitialContextFactory
java.naming.security.principal=weblogic
java.naming.security.credentials=ravinder123_

gg.jms.destination=GGSQ
gg.jms.connectionFactory=GGSCF
gg.jms.id=time

### Java and WebLogic classpath env settings
jvm.bootoptions=-Xmx512m -Xms256m -Djava.class.path=

## Parser settings
parser.type=xml
xml.sourcedefs=dirdef/t1.def
```

```
xml.rules=tx_rule

### transactions
tx_rule.type=tx
tx_rule.match=/transaction
tx_rule.subrules=op_rule
tx_rule.txid=*txid

### operations
op_rule.type=op
op_rule.match=./operation
op_rule.seqid=*seqid
op_rule.timestamp=*ts
op_rule.schemaandtable=@table
op_rule.optype=@type
op_rule.optype.insertval=I
op_rule.optype.updateval=U
op_rule.optype.deleteval=D
op_rule.subrules=col_rule

### subrules.columns
col_rule.type=col
col_rule.match=./column
col_rule.name=@name
col_rule.index=@index
col_rule.before.value=./before-value/text()
col_rule.before.isnull=./before-value[@isNull=true]/@isNull
col_rule.after.value=./after-value/text()
col_rule.after.isnull=./after-value[@isNull=true]/@isNull
```

Creating a Definition File for JMS Message

Notice the property xml.sourcedefs=dirprm/t1.def specifies the definition file to be used while creating
the JMS message definition file. This file contains information for the table, column, and data types. Use the
defgen utility as discussed earlier in this chapter to generate the t1.def file.

Create a temporary parameter file called temp.prm in the /app/ggs/jms/dirprm directory on the source
machine and add the following entries:

```
DEFSFILE /app/ggs/jms/dirdef/t1.def
USERID TIGER, PASSWORD tiger123_
TABLE TIGER.ORDER_DTL;
```

Run the following command from the OGG Home directory /app/ggs/jms. This will generate the
definition file.

```
defgen paramfile dirprm/temp.prm
```

A definition file gets generated at /app/ggs/jms/dirdef/t1.def.

Next, the utility GENDEF is used to generate the JMS message definition file. This file is then specified in
the data pump extract or the replicat process on the target server. The syntax to generate the definition file
based on settings you specified in the jmsvam.properties file is shown here:

```
gendef -prop dirprm/jmsvam.properties -out dirdef/jmsvam.def
Using property file: ./dirprm/jmsvam.properties
Outputting definition to: ./dirdef/jmsvam.def
Source_file = dirdef/t1.def
```

Configuring the Data Pump Extract

Configure the data pump extract to send trail files generated by the VAM extract to the target server as shown here:

```
GGSCI> ADD EXTRACT pjmsvam, EXTTRAILSOURCE /app/ggs/jms/dirdat/v1
GGSCI> ADD rmttrail /app/ggs/fox/dirdat/f1, extract pjmsvam

GGSCI> EDIT PARAMS pjmsvam

EXTRACT pjmsvam
USERID tiger, PASSWORD tiger123_
RMTHOST node2.ravin-pc.com, MGRPORT 7809
RMTTRAIL /app/ggs/fox/dirdat/f1
PASSTHRU
TABLE TIGER.ORDER_DTL;
```

Configuring the Replicat on the Target Server

Add and configure the replicat parameter file as shown here:

```
GGSCI> ADD REPLICAT rjmsvam, EXTTRAIL /app/ggs/fox/dirdat/f1, NODBCHECKPOINT

GGSCI> EDIT PARAMS rjmsvam

REPLICAT rjmsvam
PURGEOLDEXTRACTS
SOURCEDEFS dirdef/jmsvam.def
DISCARDFILE /app/ggs/fox/dirrpt/rjmsvam.dsc, PURGE, MEGABYTES 599
USERID fox, PASSWORD fox123_
MAP TIGER.ORDER_DTL, TARGET FOX.ORDER_DTL;
```

Next, start your user exit extract, data pump, and replicat processes. You can run the INFO and STATS commands to monitor the progress. Compare and verify the captured and applied data.

Summary

This chapter explores how to extend Oracle GoldenGate and integrate a relational database with nonrelational and nondatabase systems. We discussed how to install and configure the Oracle GoldenGate application adapter 12*c* on the Unix/Linux platform. At this stage, you are now capable of using Oracle GoldenGate to generate flat-file data to be fed into nonrelational database systems like Big Data systems. You also learned how to integrate Oracle GoldenGate with its near real-time capture and apply ability with JMS systems.

In the next chapter, you will implement Oracle GoldenGate using Oracle clusterware for high availability systems hosting mission-critical applications.

PART IV

■ ■ ■

Exploring GoldenGate Possibilities

CHAPTER 18

■ ■ ■

Configuring Oracle GoldenGate HA

Oracle GoldenGate replication is frequently used in mission-critical applications to achieve little downtime in the case of failure. In an Oracle RAC configuration, the database keeps running when one node fails. However, in an Oracle GoldenGate configuration, many critical components may be running on only one server, and if that server in the cluster fails, your OGG replication will be impacted.

To address this and configure OGG high availability (HA), you need to implement Oracle Clusterware. With Oracle Clusterware implemented, if one server fails, OGG can move the processing to another server and thus minimize overall downtime. In this chapter, we'll discuss how to set up Oracle GoldenGate high availability using Oracle Clusterware in a two-node cluster.

HA Using Oracle Clusterware

These are some concepts you should be aware of before you can begin configuring Oracle GoldenGate high availability:

- Oracle GoldenGate runs on one server at any time. Hence, in a high availability configuration, OGG can run in active-passive mode only.

- Each node in the cluster must have identical parameter files.

- If one node fails, Oracle GoldenGate is automatically started on the other node. The processes are started from the point they stopped to maintain data consistency.

- A shared server should be available to store recovery-related files. The checkpoint files and Oracle GoldenGate trails should be stored on this shared system.

- You can install Oracle GoldenGate locally on each node and maintain recovery-related files on a shared location. Alternatively, you can install Oracle GoldenGate on a shared location and register it with Oracle Clusterware.

- Shared file system options from Oracle are Oracle Cluster File System (OCFS2), Oracle ASM Cluster File System (Oracle ACFS), and Oracle Database File System (DBFS). Oracle ACFS is the recommended cluster file system for Oracle Golden Gate binaries and trail files in Real Application Cluster configurations for ease of management and high availability. However, if your Oracle Grid Infrastructure version is older than 11.2.0.3, then ACFS mounted on multiple servers concurrently does not currently support file locking; thus, you need to mount ACFS on only one server.

© Ravinder Gupta 2016
R. Gupta, *Mastering Oracle GoldenGate*, DOI 10.1007/978-1-4842-2301-7_18

Oracle Clusterware for OGG

Oracle Clusterware in a cluster configuration manages node membership and facilitates resource management and high availability. Third-party applications can be registered and managed with Oracle Clusterware. In this chapter, you will see how to register the OGG manager processes as an application to Oracle Clusterware to avail of the benefits.

Oracle Clusterware can be installed as a stand-alone server and manage a cluster of servers and various applications running on these servers. This enables you to install Oracle Clusterware on nondatabase servers as well and include them as part of a cluster of servers.

You may choose to perform a local OGG installation on every server or a single installation on a central shared file system. The recovery-related files should be stored on a shared location. You can use a symbolic link to point Oracle GoldenGate instances on individual servers to generate files on the shared file system.

Oracle Clusterware communicates only to the OGG manager process. If a manager process goes down, Oracle Clusterware will attempt to restart the manager. However, if your extract or replicat processes are down, they have to be started by your OGG manager process. This can be done by including the AUTOSTART and AUTORESTART parameters in the manager parameter file.

If you attempt to stop the manager from the OGG command interface (GGSCI), Oracle Clusterware will attempt to restart it. For any maintenance activity, stop the manager process if required only using Oracle Clusterware commands.

Virtual IP

Oracle Clusterware makes use of virtual IP (VIP) addresses to achieve high availability. The VIP is used to access the server, and if the server hosting the VIP goes down, Oracle Clusterware migrates it to another surviving server. Applications then continue accessing the new migrated server using the VIP.

With Oracle GoldenGate, the manager process is accessed through the VIP. This isolates the OGG manager process from the physical server on which OGG is running.

All the remote extract, data pump, replicat processes, and processes of the OGG Management Pack should communicate to the manager process through the VIP only. It is, however, necessary that this VIP is a fixed IP address over a public subnet. In this example, the fixed IP you are using is 23.2.1.4.

Figure 18-1 shows a RAC configuration with two nodes. VIP 1 and VIP 2 are the virtual IPs to access the nodes that share common storage. The applications can access either of the two nodes using load-balancing software for an active-active configuration of HA. If the applications use only one of the two nodes and the other node is available only during failover, it is called an *active-passive* configuration for high availability.

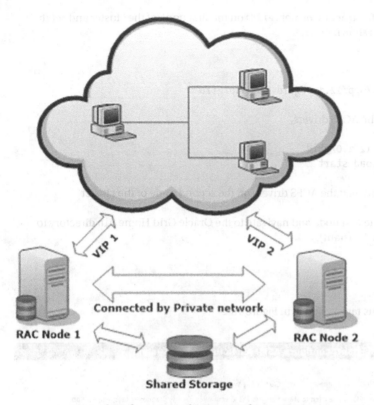

Virtual IP for a 2 Node RAC configuration

Figure 18-1. *Virtual IP for a two-node RAC configuration*

Setting Up the Oracle ACFS File System

Oracle ACFS is the recommended cluster file system for Oracle GoldenGate binaries and trail files in cluster configurations for ease of management and high availability. You must have Oracle Grid Infrastructure installed to configure ACFS. Here are the steps to configure ACFS:

1. Install the Oracle ASM support libraries.

2. Create ASM disks.

3. Install Grid Infrastructure for the cluster.

4. Launch the ASM Configuration Assistant and create the ACFS system.

5. Mount the ACFS file system on each node of the cluster and use the file system.

For this demonstration, I have a two-node source system (rac1-ravinpc and rac2-ravinpc) with Oracle Grid Infrastructure 12c. We will not discuss Oracle Grid Infrastructure software installation in this book. Please refer to the appropriate documentation on installing Oracle Grid Infrastructure and setting up a two-node cluster if you do not have it set up already. Also, I have added an ASM disk group named GGS_DATA for setting up the ACFS file system on it.

Add the fixed IP (23.2.1.4) on the public network in the cluster to the /etc/hosts file on both nodes of the cluster with an alias of ggs-vip.

Next, log in as the Oracle Grid Infrastructure owner (grid) on the first node of the cluster and set the environment to +ASM1 using oraenv as shown here:

```
[grid@rac1-ravinpc ~]$ . oraenv
ORACLE_SID = [RAC1] ? +ASM1
The Oracle base for ORACLE_HOME=/app/12.1.0/grid is /app/grid
```

Log in as the root user and load the ACFS drivers.

```
[root@rac1-ravinpc bin]# cd app/12.1.0/grid
[root@rac1-ravinpc bin]# ./acfsload start
```

Similarly, set the environment and load the ACFS drivers on the second node of the cluster rac2-ravinpc.

Now, log in as the grid user on the first node and navigate to the Oracle Grid Home bin directory to launch asmca (the ASM Configuration Assistant).

```
$ cd /app/12.1.0.2/grid/bin
$ ./asmca
```

Click the ASM Cluster File Systems tab, as shown in Figure 18-2.

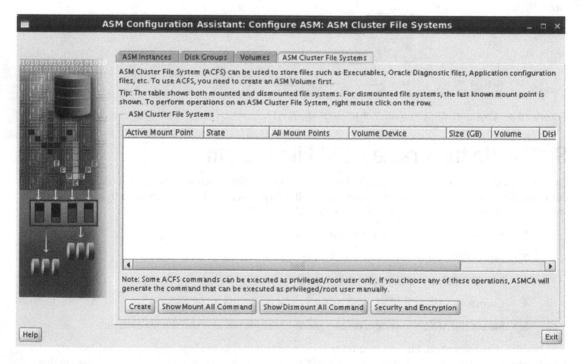

Figure 18-2. ASM Cluster File Systems tab

Click the Create button to create a new ACFS file system. This will open a new window, as shown in Figure 18-3.

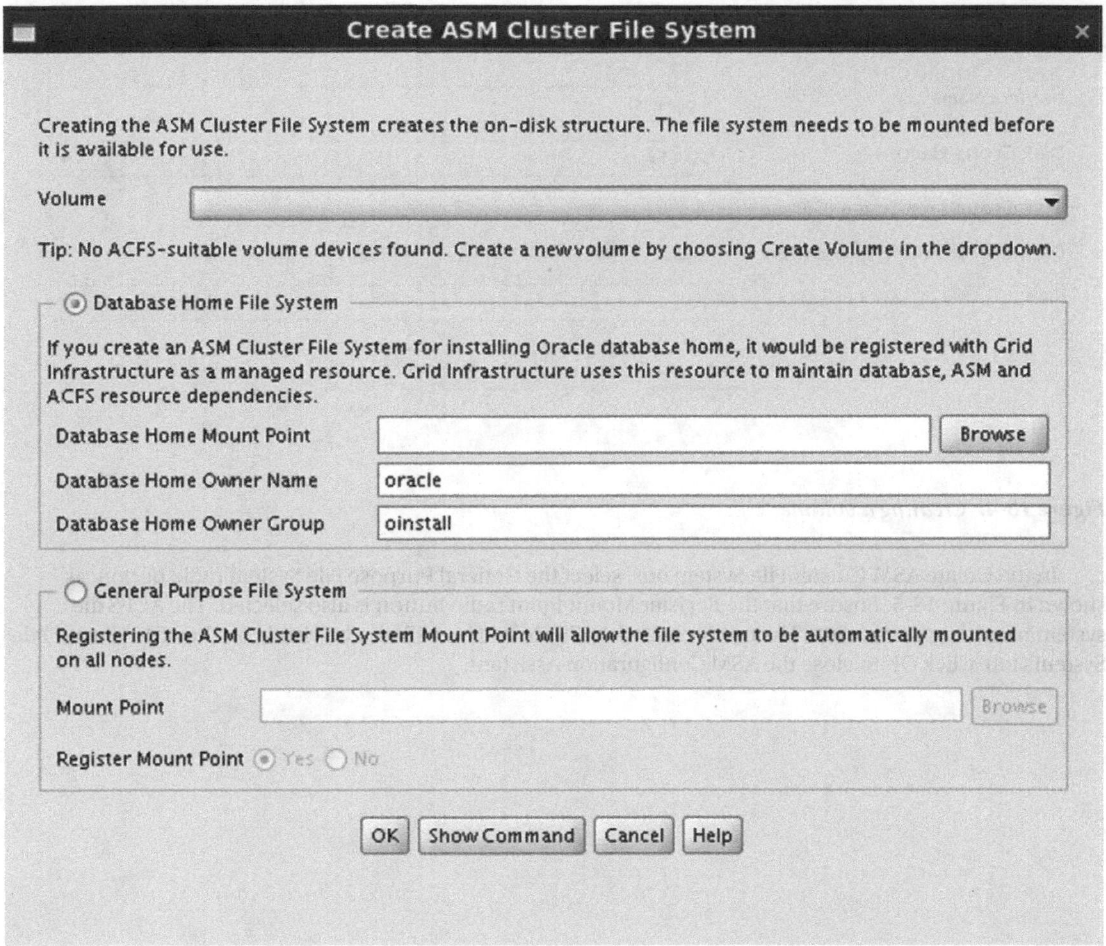

Figure 18-3. *Creating an ASM cluster file system*

From the Volume drop-down, select Create Volume and click OK. This will launch the Create Volume window, as shown in Figure 18-4. Enter the volume name, select the disk group name, and enter the size in gigabytes, as shown in Figure 18-4.

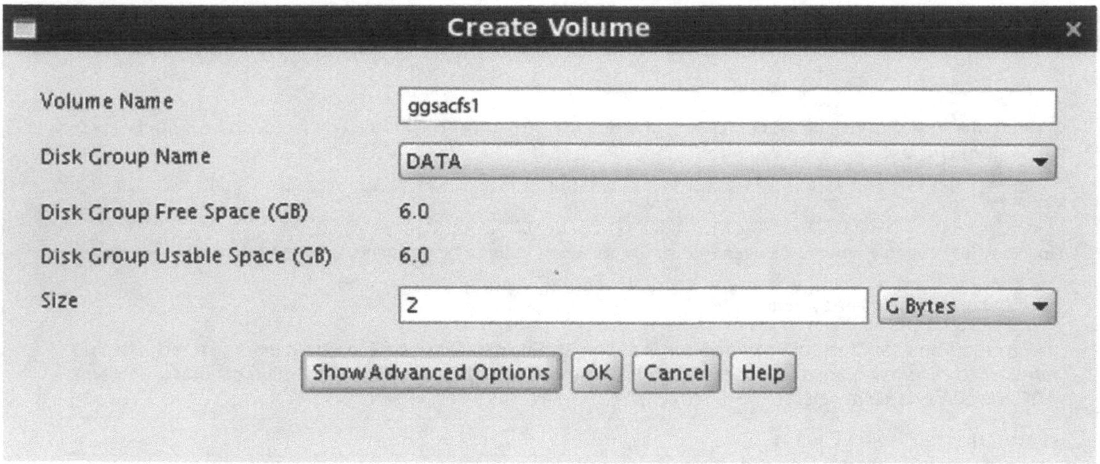

Figure 18-4. *Creating a volume*

In the Create ASM Cluster File System box, select the General Purpose File System radio button, as shown in Figure 18-5. Ensure that the Register Mount Point radio button is also selected. The ACFS file system name is ggsacfs-301. The newly created ACFS file system will also be visible on the ASM Cluster File Systems tab. Click OK to close the ASM Configuration Assistant.

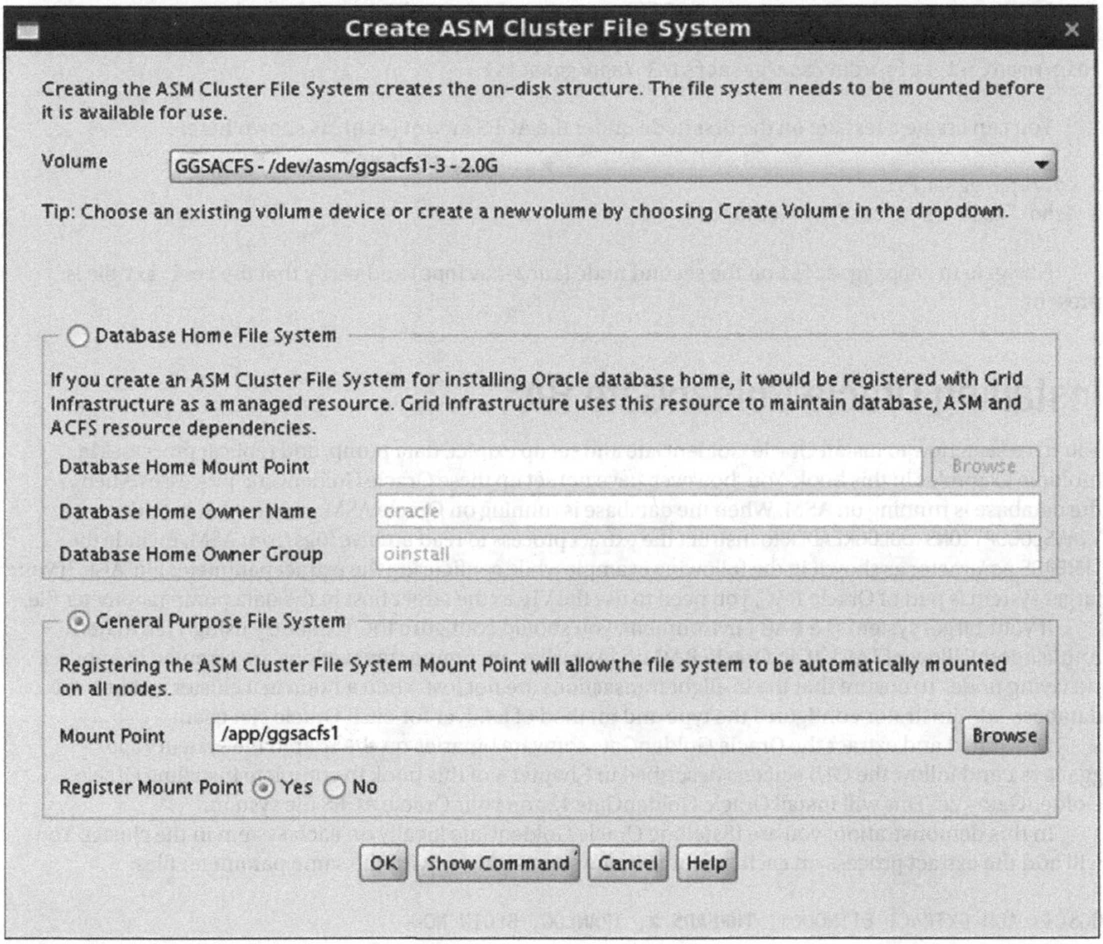

Figure 18-5. *Creating a general-purpose file system*

Log in as root and mount the new ACFS file system on both machines, as shown here:

```
/bin/mount -t acfs /dev/asm/ggsacfs1-3 /app/ggsacfs1
```

You can create a test file on the first node under the ACFS mount point, as shown here:

```
$ cd /app/ggsacfs1
$ echo "this is a test" > test.txt
```

Navigate to /app/ggsacfs1 on the second node (rac2-ravinpc) and verify that the test.txt file is present.

Installing Oracle GoldenGate HA

You have seen how to install Oracle GoldenGate and set up extract, data pump, and replicat processes in multiple examples in this book. You, however, have not set up these Oracle GoldenGate processes when the database is running on ASM. When the database is running on Oracle ASM, you need to include TRANSLOGOPTIONS DBLOGREADER to instruct the extract process to read archive logs from ASM. Include the THREADS parameter as shown in the following example while configuring the extract parameter file. Also, if your target system is part of Oracle RAC, you need to use the VIP as the target host in the data pump parameter file.

If your target system is a RAC environment, you should configure the TNS entry using Transparent Application Failover (TAF). If an Oracle RAC node crashes, incoming transactions are rerouted to another surviving node. To ensure that the in-flight transactions are not lost when a node in a cluster crashes, the database administrator configures the type and method of failover for each Oracle Net client.

Download and extract the Oracle GoldenGate software binaries on the shared file system /app/ggsacfs1 and follow the OUI screens described in Chapter 4 of this book to complete installing Oracle GoldenGate 12c. This will install Oracle GoldenGate 12c on your Oracle ACFS file system.

In this demonstration, you are installing Oracle GoldenGate locally on each system in the cluster. You will add the extract process on each machine in the source cluster with the same parameter files.

```
GGSCI> ADD EXTRACT ETTND001, THREADS 2, TRANLOG, BEGIN NOW

GGSCI> ADD EXTTRAIL /app/ggs/tiger/dirdat/t1, EXTRACT ETTND001, MEGABYTES 100

GGSCI> edit params ETTND001

EXTRACT ETTND001
USERID tiger, PASSWORD tiger123_
TRANSLOGOPTIONS DBLOGREADER, DBLOGREADERBUFSIZE 3000000, ASMBUFSIZE 30000
EXTTRAIL /app/ggs/tiger/dirdat/t1
TABLE TIGER.ORDER_DTL;
```

Add and configure the data pump extract.

```
GGSCI> ADD EXTRACT PTTND001, EXTTRAILSOURCE /app/ggs/tiger/dirdat/t1

GGSCI> ADD RMTTRAIL /app/ggs/fox/dirdat/f1, EXTRACT PTTND001, MEGABYTES 100

GGSCI> edit params PTTND001

EXTRACT PTTND001
```

```
USERID tiger, PASSWORD tiger123_
RMTHOST targetsvr-ravinpc, MGRPORT 7809
RMTTRAIL /app/ggs/fox/dirdat/f1
TABLE TIGER.ORDER_DTL;
```

Create and configure the replicat process on the target server, `targetsvr-ravinpc`.

```
GGSCI> ADD REPLICAT RFDLD001, EXTTRAIL /app/ggs/fox/dirdat/f1, CHECKPOINTTABLE CHECKPOINT,
BEGIN NOW

GGSCI> edit params RFDLD001

REPLICAT RFDLD001
USERID fox, PASSWORD fox123_
DISCARDFILE /app/ggs/fox/dirrpt/RFDLD001.dsc,append,MEGABYTES 200
ASSUMETARGETDEFS
MAP TIGER.ORDER_DTL, TARGET FOX.ORDER_DTL;
```

Start the extract, data pump, and replicat processes.

Configuring OGG HA

Before you can start configuring your environment for high availability, ensure that you are meeting the following listed requirements:

- A minimum of a two-node cluster of servers
- Root access on the servers
- A shared location that is accessible from all servers in the cluster
- A fixed IP over a public subnet to be used as the virtual IP address

In this example, I have installed Oracle GoldenGate instances on each server in the cluster with recovery-related files on a shared location. The following are the steps to achieve high availability in this configuration.

Step 1: Create a Minimum of a Two-Node System with Oracle GoldenGate

This setup has a source configured in a two-node RAC sharing storage with the file system ACFS. I have configured only one extract and one data pump process on the source. For the simplicity of this example, the target is a stand-alone database with one replicat configured on it. I have OGG installed on both nodes with recovery-related files (trails and checkpoint files) on the shared storage.

The manager process has AUTOSTART and AUTORESTART configured to manage restarting the extract and replicat processes.

Next, you need to register OGG with Oracle Clusterware.

Step 2: Create a VIP for the Oracle GoldenGate Application

To create a VIP, you must be logged in as the root user. Navigate to GRID_HOME as the Oracle Home in which Oracle Grid Infrastructure components have been installed (such as /app/12.1.0/grid).

Navigate to the `bin` directory and execute the following:

```
$ cd /app/12.1.0/grid/bin
$ appvipcfg -help
Production Copyright 2007, 2008, Oracle. All rights reserved
Unknown option: help
Usage: appvipcfg create -network= -ip= -vipname=
                        -user=[-group=] [-failback=0 | 1]
                delete -vipname=
```

Now, identify your network number as shown here:

```
$ ./crsctl status resource -p | grep  -ie .network -ie subnet | grep -ie name -ie subnet


NAME=ora.net1.network
USR_ORA_SUBNET=23.2.1.0
```

Here `ora.net1` in `NAME` indicates the network number as 1, and `USR_ORA_SUBNET` is the subnet under which the VIP will be created. Next, create the application VIP for GoldenGate, where `ggs-vip` is the name of the application VIP that you will create.

```
$ ./appvipcfg create -network=1 -ip=23.2.1.4 -vipname=ggs-vip -user=root
```

You can modify attributes for the resource `ggs-vip` as shown here:

```
$ crsctl modify resource ggs-vip -attr "RESTART_ATTEMPTS=3, START_TIMEOUT=300, STOP_
TIMEOUT=300, CHECK_INTERVAL=10"
```

As the root user, run the following command to allow the Oracle Clusterware owner, the `grid` user in this case, to start the VIP.

```
$ /app/12.1.0/grid/bin/crsctl setperm resource ggs-vip -u user:grid:r-x
```

Log in as the `grid` user and start the VIP.

```
$ ./crsctl start resource ggs-vip
CRS-2672: Attempting to start 'ggs-vip' on 'rac1.ravin-pc'
CRS-2676: Start of 'ggs-vip' on 'rac1-ravinpc' succeeded
```

Check the status of the VIP.

```
/crsctl status resource ggs-vip
NAME=ggs-vip
TYPE=app.appvip_net1.type
TARGET=ONLINE
STATE=ONLINE on rac1-ravinpc
```

Now you should be able to ping the VIP from the other nodes. Ping the VIP from `rac2-ravinpc`.

```
ping -c4 23.2.1.4
PING 23.2.1.4 (23.2.1.4) 56(84) bytes of data.
64 bytes from 23.2.1.4: icmp_seq=1 ttl=64 time=0.030 ms
64 bytes from 23.2.1.4: icmp_seq=2 ttl=64 time=0.049 ms
64 bytes from 23.2.1.4: icmp_seq=3 ttl=64 time=0.048 ms
64 bytes from 23.2.1.4: icmp_seq=4 ttl=64 time=0.053 ms


--- 23.2.1.4 ping statistics ---
4 packets transmitted, 4 received, 0% packet loss, time 2999ms
rtt min/avg/max/mdev = 0.030/0.045/0.053/0.008 ms
```

Step 3: Create the Agent Script

At this stage, when you have successfully created the application VIP, you can now create the agent script. This agent script will be used by Oracle Clusterware for resource-specific command executions during normal as well as failover time.

The agent script accepts five parameter values: start, stop, check, clean, and abort. The script is not written to check for abended/stropped extract or replicat processes. This check is not recommended to be part of the agent script used by Oracle Clusterware.

Here are the contents of a sample agent script, gg_agent.sh:

```
#!/bin/sh
GGS_HOME=/app/ggs/tiger
#specify delay after start before checking for successful start
start_delay_secs=5
#Include the GoldenGate home in the library path to start GGSCI
export LD_LIBRARY_PATH=${LD_LIBRARY_PATH}:${GGS_HOME}
#set the oracle home to the database to ensure GoldenGate will get the
#environment settings to be able to connect to the database
export ORACLE_HOME=/app/oracle/product/11.2/db
#check_process validates that a manager process is running at the PID
#that GoldenGate specifies.
check_process () {
 if ( [ -f "${GGS_HOME}/dirpcs/MGR.pcm" ] )
 then
 pid=`cut -f8 "${GGS_HOME}/dirpcs/MGR.pcm"`
 if [ ${pid} = `ps -e |grep ${pid} |grep mgr |cut -d " " -f2` ]
 then
 #manager process is running on the PID - exit success
 exit 0
 else
if [ ${pid} = `ps -e |grep ${pid} |grep mgr |cut -d " " -f1` ]
 then
 #manager process is running on the PID - exit success
 exit 0
 else
 #manager process is not running on the PID
 exit 1
 fi
 fi
 else
```

```
  #manager is not running because there is no PID file
  exit 1
  fi
}
#call_ggsci is a generic routine that executes a ggsci command
call_ggsci () {
  ggsci_command=$1
  ggsci_output=`${GGS_HOME}/ggsci << EOF
${ggsci_command}
  exit
  EOF`
}
case $1 in
'start')
  #start manager
  call_ggsci 'start manager'
  #there is a small delay between issuing the start manager command
  #and the process being spawned on the OS - wait before checking
  sleep ${start_delay_secs}
  #check whether manager is running and exit accordingly
  check_process
  ;;
'stop')
  #attempt a clean stop for all non-manager processes
call_ggsci 'stop er *'
  #ensure everything is stopped
  call_ggsci 'stop er *!'
  #stop manager without (y/n) confirmation
  call_ggsci 'stop manager!'
  #exit success
  exit 0
  ;;
'check')
  check_process
  ;;
'clean')
  #attempt a clean stop for all non-manager processes
  call_ggsci 'stop er *'
  #ensure everything is stopped
  call_ggsci 'stop er *!'
  #in case there are lingering processes
  call_gsci 'kill er *'
  #stop manager without (y/n) confirmation
  call_ggsci 'stop manager!'
  #exit success
  exit 0
  ;;
'abort')
  #ensure everything is stopped
  call_ggsci 'stop er *!'
  #in case there are lingering processes
```

```
call_gsci 'kill er *'
#stop manager without (y/n) confirmation
call_ggsci 'stop manager!'
#exit success
exit 0
;;
esac
```

Save this file either on the node under the same directory so it is accessible by Oracle Clusterware or on shared storage, or both. I saved this file on my shared storage directory: /app/ggsacfs1/scripts/gg_agent.sh.

Step 4: Add a Clusterware Resource for the Oracle GoldenGate Application

As the grid user, execute the following command to add Oracle GoldenGate:

```
$GRID_HOME/bin/crsctl add resource ggsapp -type cluster_resource -attr "ACTION_SCRIPT=/
app/ggsacfs1/scripts/gg_agent.sh, CHECK_INTERVAL=30, START_DEPENDENCIES='hard(ggs-vip)
pullup(ggs-vip)', STOP_DEPENDENCIES='hard(ggs-vip)'"
```

Here, ggsapp is the application name you have assigned with which Oracle Clusterware will identify the Oracle GoldenGate resource. I have chosen hard start and stop dependency for ggs-vip, which means the application ggsapp is always started/stopped whenever the VIP is started or stopped.

If your OGG owner is different from the Oracle Clusterware owner, then you need to execute the following command as the root user, where ggsowner is the OGG owner in your setup:

```
$GRID_HOME/bin/crsctl setperm resource ggsapp -o ggsowner
```

Check if the resource ggsapp is available as the Oracle Clusterware resource.

```
$GRID_HOME/bin/crsctl status resource ggsapp
NAME=ggsapp
TYPE=cluster_resource
TARGET=OFFLINE
STATE=OFFLINE
```

Step 5: Start the Resource Using Oracle Clusterware

As the grid user, execute the following to start the resource:

```
$GRID_HOME/bin/crsctl start resource ggsapp
CRS-2672: Attempting to start 'ggsapp' on 'rac1-ravinpc'
CRS-2676: Start of 'ggsapp' on 'rac1-ravinpc' succeeded
```

Again, check the status of the ggsapp resource.

```
./crsctl status resource ggsapp
NAME=ggsapp
TYPE=cluster_resource
TARGET=ONLINE
```

```
STATE=ONLINE on rac1-ravinpc
```

Stop the ggsapp resource.

```
./crsctl stop resource ggsapp
CRS-2673: Attempting to stop 'ggsapp' on 'rac1-ravinpc'
CRS-2677: Stop of 'ggsapp' on 'rac1-ravinpc' succeeded
```

Check the status of OGG processes on rac1-ravinpc when ggsapp is stopped.

```
GGSCI (rac1-ravinpc) 1> info all
```

Program	Status	Group	Lag at Chkpt	Time Since Chkpt
MANAGER	STOPPED			
EXTRACT	STOPPED	ETTND001	00:00:00	00:00:29
EXTRACT	STOPPED	PTTND001	00:00:02	00:00:27

Start the ggsapp resource again.

```
GRID_HOME/bin/crsctl start resource ggsapp
CRS-2672: Attempting to start 'ggsapp' on 'rac1-ravinpc'
CRS-2676: Start of 'ggsapp' on 'rac1-ravinpc' succeeded
```

Verify the OGG processes status. They should have started automatically on rac1-ravinpc.

```
GGSCI (rac1-ravinpc) 1> info all
```

Program	Status	Group	Lag at Chkpt	Time Since Chkpt
MANAGER	RUNNING			
EXTRACT	RUNNING	ETTND001	00:00:00	00:00:10
EXTRACT	RUNNING	PTTND001	00:00:01	00:00:09

Step 6: Manage the Application

Suppose rac1-ravinpc has a scheduled downtime. You will have to relocate the ggsapp to another available node.

```
[oracle@node1 bin]$ ./crsctl relocate resource ggsapp -f
CRS-2673: Attempting to stop 'ggsapp' on 'rac1-ravinpc'
CRS-2677: Stop of 'ggsapp' on 'rac1-ravinpc' succeeded
CRS-2673: Attempting to stop 'ggs-vip' on 'rac1-ravinpc'
CRS-2677: Stop of 'ggs-vip' on 'rac1-ravinpc' succeeded
CRS-2672: Attempting to start 'ggs-vip' on 'rac2-ravinpc'
CRS-2676: Start of 'ggs-vip' on 'rac2-ravinpc' succeeded
CRS-2672: Attempting to start 'ggsapp' on 'rac2-ravinpc'
CRS-2676: Start of 'ggsapp' on 'rac2-ravinpc' succeeded
```

Check the OGG process on rac2-ravinpc.

```
GGSCI (rac2-ravinpc) 1> info all

Program     Status    Group      Lag at Chkpt  Time Since Chkpt

MANAGER     RUNNING
EXTRACT     RUNNING   ETTND001   00:00:00      00:00:04
EXTRACT     RUNNING   PTTND001   00:00:05      00:00:06
```

Also, check the status of resource ggsapp.

```
[oracle@rac1-ravinpc bin]$ ./crsctl status resource ggsapp
NAME=ggsapp
TYPE=cluster_resource
TARGET=ONLINE
STATE=ONLINE on rac2-ravinpc
```

Step 7: Test the Failover

Let's crash rac2-ravinpc. For this I powered off rac2-ravinpc. The following is the status after the rac2-ravinpc is down.

```
./crsctl status resource ggsapp
NAME=ggsapp
TYPE=cluster_resource
TARGET=ONLINE
STATE=ONLINE on rac1-ravinpc

./crsctl status resource ggs-vip
NAME=ggs-vip
TYPE=app.appvip_net1.type
TARGET=ONLINE
STATE=ONLINE on rac1-ravinpc
```

This shows the ggsapp resource and ggs-vip has been failed over from rac2-ravinpc to rac1-ravinpc. Check the status of OGG processes on rac1-ravinpc.

```
GGSCI (rac1-ravinpc) 3> info all

Program     Status    Group      Lag at Chkpt  Time Since Chkpt

MANAGER     RUNNING
EXTRACT     RUNNING   ETTND001   00:00:00      00:04:10
EXTRACT     ABENDED   PTTND001   00:00:00      00:00:09
```

The manager and the extract process are started, but the data pump extract has been abended with the following error:

```
2015-12-02 16:45:56  ERROR  OGG-01031 There is a problem in network communication, a
remote file problem, encryption keys for target and source do not match (if using ENCRYPT)
or an unknown error. (Reply received is Unable to open file "./dirdat/t1000016" (error 11,
Resource temporarily unavailable)).
```

453

```
2015-12-02 16:45:56  ERROR   OGG-01668  PROCESS ABENDING.
```

Check the status of the OGG processes on rac1-ravinpc.

```
GGSCI (rac1-ravinpc) 17> info all

Program     Status       Group        Lag at Chkpt  Time Since Chkpt

MANAGER     RUNNING
EXTRACT     RUNNING      ETTND001      00:00:00       00:08:18
EXTRACT     ABENDED      PTTND001      00:00:00       00:00:00

GGSCI (rac1-ravinpc) 18> info PTTND001

EXTRACT     PTTND001     Last Started 2015-12-02 18:24    Status ABENDED
Checkpoint Lag         00:00:00 (updated 00:08:24 ago)
Log Read Checkpoint  File ./dirdat/t1000019
                     2015-12-02 18:16:24.415084  RBA 1171
```

Check the status of the OGG processes on the target server, targetsvr-ravinpc.

```
GGSCI (targetsvr-ravinpc) 2> info all

Program     Status       Group        Lag at Chkpt  Time Since Chkpt

MANAGER     RUNNING
REPLICAT    RUNNING      RFDLD001      00:00:00       00:00:05

GGSCI (targetsvr-ravinpc) 3> info RFDLD001

REPLICAT    RFDLD001     Last Started 2015-12-02 20:38    Status RUNNING
Checkpoint Lag         00:00:00 (updated 00:00:07 ago)
Log Read Checkpoint  File ./dirdat/t1000016
                     2015-12-02 18:16:24.422522  RBA 1991

GGSCI (targetsvr-ravinpc) 4> send RFDLD001 status

Sending STATUS request to REPLICAT RFDLD001 ...
  Current status: At EOF
  Sequence #: 16
  RBA: 1991
  0 records in current transaction
```

The replicat process shows it has completed all the data and currently is at the end of the file. Now you will do an et (extract trail) rollover on the source.

```
GGSCI (rac1-ravinpc) 21> alter extract ETTND001 etrollover

2015-12-02 18:34:04  INFO    OGG-01520  Rollover performed.  For each affected output trail
of Version 10 or higher format, after
```

starting the source extract, issue ALTER EXTSEQNO for that trail's reader (either pump EXTRACT or REPLICAT) to move the reader's scan to the new trail file; it will not happen automatically.
EXTRACT altered.

Start the extract to begin writing to a new trail file.

```
GGSCI (rac1-ravinpc) 23> start extract ETTND001


Sending START request to MANAGER ...
EXTRACT ETTND001 starting

GGSCI (rac1-ravinpc) 24> info all

Program     Status       Group        Lag at Chkpt  Time Since Chkpt

MANAGER     RUNNING
EXTRACT     RUNNING      ETTND001     00:00:00      00:00:58
EXTRACT     RUNNING      PTTND001     00:00:00      00:00:08

GGSCI (rac1-ravinpc) 31> info all

Program     Status       Group        Lag at Chkpt  Time Since Chkpt

MANAGER     RUNNING
EXTRACT     RUNNING      ETTND001     00:00:00      00:00:05
EXTRACT     RUNNING      PTTND001     00:00:00      00:00:00

GGSCI (rac1-ravinpc) 32> info ETTND001

EXTRACT     ETTND001     Last Started 2015-12-02 18:35    Status RUNNING
Checkpoint Lag         00:00:00 (updated 00:00:02 ago)
Log Read Checkpoint    File ./dirdat/t1000020
                       2015-12-02 16:45:46.216461  RBA 1111
```

On the target you need to move the replicat to start again from the next sequence since you have performed the rollover on the extracts at the source.

```
GGSCI (targetsvr-ravinpc) 3> stop replicat RFDLD001


Sending STOP request to REPLICAT RFDLD001 ...
Request processed.

GGSCI (targetsvr-ravinpc) 4> alter replicat RFDLD001 extseqno 17 extrba 0
REPLICAT altered.

GGSCI (targetsvr-ravinpc) 5> start replicat RFDLD001
```

Now let's update some data on the source.

```
SQL> select count(*) from ORDER_DTL;

  COUNT(*)
----------
      3500

SQL> begin
  2      for i in 4001..5000 loop
  3              insert into ORDER_DTL values (i, dbms_random.string('U',30),60);
  4      END LOOP;
  5      commit;
  6  end;
  7  /

PL/SQL procedure successfully completed.

SQL> select count(*) from ORDER_DTL;

  COUNT(*)
----------
      4500
```

Let's check whether it is replicated to the target.

```
SQL> select count(*) from ORDER_DTL;

  COUNT(*)
----------
      4500
```

Summary

In this chapter, we discussed how to configure Oracle GoldenGate high availability using Oracle Clusterware and the Oracle ACFS file system in a two-node Oracle source. We discussed how to set up the Oracle ACFS file system and register the OGG manager as an application with Oracle Clusterware. For achieving high availability, you saw how to implement a virtual IP address and tested failover by manually turning off one of the two servers. This configuration is linearly scalable, and you can add more nodes to the configuration.

In the next chapter, we will discuss how to integrate relational database systems with Big Data systems. You will be setting up the Oracle GoldenGate replicat or extract process to capture changes into trail files in a specific format that is read by the Java adapters for Big Data systems.

CHAPTER 19

■ ■ ■

Oracle GoldenGate for Big Data

With the advent of Big Data analytics solutions, organizations are realizing the potential of their data assets by combining structured transactional data with semistructured and unstructured data. Oracle GoldenGate 12c enables customers to enhance their Big Data analytics initiative by incorporating existing real-time architectures into Big Data solutions. GoldenGate can stream transactional data into Big Data systems and keep the Big Data repositories up-to-date with the production systems.

GoldenGate can deliver in near real-time to most popular Big Data solutions including Apache Hadoop, Apache HBase, Apache Hive, and Apache Flume. OGG for Big Data includes OGG application adapters for Java. It further enables a customer's easy integration with additional Big Data systems, such as Oracle NoSQL, Apache Kafka, Apache Storm, Apache Spark, and others.

OGG for Big Data is a key component of Oracle's Big Data integration offering along with Oracle Data Integrator 12c. Figure 19-1 shows Oracle GoldenGate integrating relational database systems with Big Data systems.

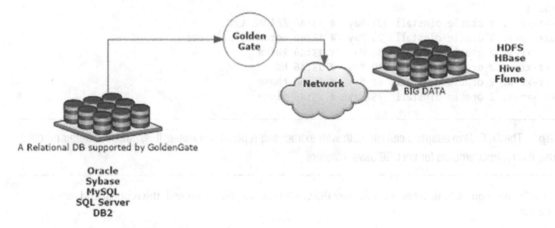

Figure 19-1. *OGG for Big Data configuration*

Let's begin by installing Oracle GoldenGate for Big Data. We will then look at a few of the most popular examples to see how to integrate OGG with Big Data systems.

© Ravinder Gupta 2016
R. Gupta, *Mastering Oracle GoldenGate*, DOI 10.1007/978-1-4842-2301-7_19

Downloading Oracle GoldenGate for Big Data

You can download Oracle GoldenGate for Big Data by navigating to www.oracle.com/technetwork/middleware/goldengate/downloads/index.html. Search for *Oracle GoldenGate for Big Data* for your operating system platform where your OGG instance is running. In this chapter, we will begin by installing and configuring Oracle GoldenGate for Big Data V12.2.0.1.1 on Linux x86-64.

Installing Oracle GoldenGate for Big Data

Extract the compressed .zip file you downloaded and copy the TAR file to the OGG instance home directory. In all the examples in this chapter, my OGG home directory is /app/ggs/tiger/.

```
unzip 122011_ggs_Adapters_Linux_x64.zip
```

Untar the file as follows:

```
cd /app/ggs/tiger
tar -xvf ggs_Adapters_Linux_x64.tar
```

This will create several files and directories specific for OGG for Big Data inside your OGG home directory. Make sure you have Java 7 or higher installed for the OGG adapter for Big Data to run properly.

Navigate to /app/ggs/tiger/AdapterExamples/big-data. This directory contains example parameter files and properties files that you can use as baselines to set up your OGG adapter for Big Data.

```
[oracle@ravin-ravinpc big-data]$ ls -lrt
total 4
-r--r--r--. 1 oracle oinstall 903 May  4 13:46 README.txt
drwxr-xr-x. 4 oracle oinstall  28 May  4 13:46 metadata_provider
drwxr-xr-x. 2 oracle oinstall  80 May  4 13:46 kafka
drwxr-xr-x. 2 oracle oinstall  39 May  4 13:46 hdfs
drwxr-xr-x. 2 oracle oinstall  41 May  4 13:46 hbase
drwxr-xr-x. 2 oracle oinstall  75 May  4 13:46 flume
```

■ **Tip**   The OGG Java adapters can run both with extract and replicat processes. It is, however, better practice to use the replicat process for the OGG Java adapters.

Let's take a quick look at how to configure the OGG Java adapter to run with the replicat and extract processes.

Running the OGG Java Adapter with the Replicat Process

Let's see an example of how to configure the OGG adapter for Apache Flume. We will discuss in detail Apache Flume and how to configure OGG for Apache Flume later in this chapter.

Create a replicat process as follows:

```
GGSCI> add replicat rflume, exttrail /app/ggs/tiger/dirdat/fl
```

Edit the replicat parameter file to include the following parameters:

```
GGSCI> edit params rflume

REPLICAT RFLUME
TARGETDB LIBFILE libggjava.so SET property=dirprm/flume.props
REPORTCOUNT EVERY 1 MINUTES, RATE
GROUPTRANSOPS 10000
MAP TIGER.*, TARGET TIGER.*;
```

Create the flume.props property file to include the following parameters. You can configure parameter values as per your required configuration.

```
[oracle@ravin-ravinpc flume]$ cat flume.props


gg.handlerlist = flumehandler
gg.handler.flumehandler.type=flume
gg.handler.flumehandler.RpcClientPropertiesFile=custom-flume-rpc.properties
gg.handler.flumehandler.format=avro_op
gg.handler.flumehandler.mode=tx
#gg.handler.flumehandler.maxGroupSize=100, 1Mb
#gg.handler.flumehandler.minGroupSize=50, 500 Kb
gg.handler.flumehandler.EventMapsTo=tx
gg.handler.flumehandler.PropagateSchema=true
gg.handler.flumehandler.includeTokens=false
gg.handler.flumehandler.format.WrapMessageInGenericAvroMessage=true

goldengate.userexit.timestamp=utc
goldengate.userexit.writers=javawriter
javawriter.stats.display=TRUE
javawriter.stats.full=TRUE

gg.log=log4j
gg.log.level=INFO
gg.report.time=30sec
gg.classpath=dirprm/:/app/lib/flume/lib/*:

javawriter.bootoptions=-Xmx512m -Xms32m -Djava.class.path=ggjava/ggjava.jar
```

Note the RPC client properties file specification in the flume.props file. Create custom-flume-rpc. properties as follows:

```
[oracle@ravin-ravinpc flume]$ cat custom-flume-rpc.properties
client.type=default
hosts=h1
hosts.h1=ravin-ravinpc:52140
batch-size=100
connect-timeout=20000
request-timeout=20000
```

Here, ravin-ravinpc:52140 is the host and port for my Flume agent.

Running the OGG Java Adapter with the Extract Process

We discussed how to create a replicat process to run the OGG Java adapter for Apache Flume. Let's take a look at configuring the same with an extract process.

Create an extract process as follows:

```
GGSCI> add extract eflume, exttrailsource /app/ggs/tiger/dirdat/fl
```

Edit the extract parameter file to include the following parameters:

```
GGSCI> edit params eflume

EXTRACT EFLUME
discardfile ./dirrpt/eflume.dsc, purge
--SOURCEDEFS ./dirdef/eflume.def
CUSEREXIT libjavaue.so CUSEREXIT PASSTHRU, INCLUDEUPDATEBEFORES, PARAMS "dirprm/flume.props"
GETUPDATEBEFORES
TABLE TIGER.*;
```

Create the flume.props property file to include the following parameters. You can configure parameter values as per your required configuration.

```
[oracle@ravin-ravinpc flume]$ cat flume.props

gg.handlerlist = flumehandler
gg.handler.flumehandler.type=flume
gg.handler.flumehandler.RpcClientPropertiesFile=custom-flume-rpc.properties
gg.handler.flumehandler.format=avro_op
gg.handler.flumehandler.mode=tx
#gg.handler.flumehandler.maxGroupSize=100, 1Mb
#gg.handler.flumehandler.minGroupSize=50, 500 Kb
gg.handler.flumehandler.EventMapsTo=tx
gg.handler.flumehandler.PropagateSchema=true
gg.handler.flumehandler.includeTokens=false
gg.handler.flumehandler.format.WrapMessageInGenericAvroMessage=true

goldengate.userexit.timestamp=utc
goldengate.userexit.writers=javawriter
javawriter.stats.display=TRUE
javawriter.stats.full=TRUE

gg.log=log4j
gg.log.level=INFO
gg.report.time=30sec
gg.classpath=dirprm/:/app/lib/flume/lib/*:

javawriter.bootoptions=-Xmx512m -Xms32m -Djava.class.path=ggjava/ggjava.jar
```

Note the RPC client properties file specification in the `flume.props` file. Create `custom-flume-rpc.properties` as follows:

```
[oracle@ravin-ravinpc flume]$ cat custom-flume-rpc.properties
client.type=default
hosts=h1
hosts.h1=ravin-ravinpc:52140
batch-size=100
connect-timeout=20000
request-timeout=20000
```

Oracle GoldenGate Adapter for Apache Flume

Apache Flume is a distributed database service that can streamline data from various data producers into Hadoop systems. It can also perform real-time analytics on data. You can implement Oracle GoldenGate for Big Data to streamline real-time data into Apache Flume systems.

The Flume channel and sink can be configured to any of the supported channels and sinks. I used the memory channel and HDFS sink for my setup.

The OGG adapter for Flume captures unfiltered operations from source trail files and creates flume events for each operation. The configuration has three main components: the Flume source, the Flume channel, and the Flume sink. Let's discuss each of these briefly.

Flume Source

The Flume adapter uses the Avro RPC client to connect to the Flume source. It picks unfiltered operations from the source trail files and creates Flume events for each operation. When a transaction is committed, these Flume events are flushed to the Flume source. The headers in the Flume events contain the schema and table name.

Flume Channel

Flume channels can be considered passive stores that keep the events until they are consumed by the Flume sink. The Flume adapter will use the memory channel. Memory channels are most suitable for higher throughput requirements at the risk of losing staged data in case of agent failures.

Flume Sink

The Flume sink picks the events from the Flume channel and feeds them into the external repository such as HDFS. My Flume adapter will use the HDFS sink. A directory is created for each table where records are written for the particular table. The directory is structured as follows:

```
HDFS_HOME/SCHEMA_NAME/TABLE_NAME/
```

Make sure the Hadoop instance is reachable by your machine where you are configuring and running the OGG adapter for Flume.

Also, make sure Flume is installed and running. You can have both Flume and the OGG instance on the same server or on a different server. Figure 19-2 shows the components of the Oracle GoldenGate Flume adapter for Big Data systems.

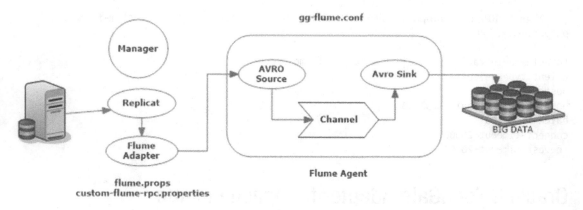

Figure 19-2. *OGG Flume adapter configuration*

Build the Flume Adapter

You need to build a Flume adapter that will be used to stream changes captured in trails to the Flume source. Maven is the recommended utility to build OGG adapters for Big Data systems.

Download and Install Maven

You can build the OGG adapter for Flume using Maven. It is an open source build tool available for download at http://maven.apache.org/.

I have used Maven 3.3.9 for this example. Extract the TAR file at a location where you want to install Maven.

```
tar -xvf apache-maven-3.3.9-bin.tar
```

Set the PATH variable to include the path to mvn in the bin directory.

Pre-checks

These are some of the considerations before you can use Maven to build the Flume adapter:

- If you are using Maven to build the OGG adapter, you need Internet access to connect to the Maven central repository. If your organization uses a proxy server/ VPN to prevent direct connections to the Internet, you need to configure your Maven settings.xml file before starting the build. Refer to the Maven documentation on configuring settings.xml.

- Oracle GoldenGate Java Adapter 12 is built and runs with Java 7. Make sure you are using JDK 7 for building your custom adapter.

- Maven also requires ggjava.jar located in /app/ggs/tiger/ggjava/ggjava.jar. The relative path of ggjava.jar is specified in pom.xml.

Build the OGG Adapter for Flume

Now that you have installed Maven, let's use it to build the Flume adapter. Navigate to the following directory:

```
cd /app/ggs/tiger/AdapterExamples/big-data/flume
```

Start the build using Maven as follows:

```
mvn clean package
```

If you do not have an existing project with a pom.xml file, executing the command will throw the following error:

```
[oracle@ravin-ravinpc flume]$ mvn clean package
[INFO] Scanning for projects...
[INFO] ------------------------------------------------------------------------
[INFO] BUILD FAILURE
[INFO] ------------------------------------------------------------------------
[INFO] Total time: 0.321 s
[INFO] Finished at: 2016-08-03T22:25:50-04:00
[INFO] Final Memory: 6M/100M
[INFO] ------------------------------------------------------------------------
[ERROR] The goal you specified requires a project to execute but there is no POM in this
        directory (/app/ggs/tiger/AdapterExamples/big-data/flume). Please verify you invoked
        Maven from the correct directory. -> [Help 1]
[ERROR]
[ERROR] To see the full stack trace of the errors, re-run Maven with the -e switch.
[ERROR] Re-run Maven using the -X switch to enable full debug logging.
[ERROR]
[ERROR] For more information about the errors and possible solutions, please read the
        following articles:
[ERROR] [Help 1] http://cwiki.apache.org/confluence/display/MAVEN/MissingProjectException
```

I created a demo project with the following command. Make sure your Internet connection is on, as it will download dependencies from the Maven central repository.

```
[oracle@ravin-ravinpc flume]$ mvn archetype:generate -DgroupId=ravin-projects
-DartifactId=ravin-prj1-ggsflume -DarchetypeArtifactId=maven-archetype-quickstart
-DinteractiveMode=false
[INFO] Scanning for projects...
[INFO]
[INFO] ------------------------------------------------------------------------
[INFO] Building Maven Stub Project (No POM) 1
[INFO] ------------------------------------------------------------------------
[INFO]
[INFO] >>> maven-archetype-plugin:2.4:generate (default-cli) > generate-sources
        @ standalone-pom >>>
[INFO]
[INFO] <<< maven-archetype-plugin:2.4:generate (default-cli) < generate-sources
        @ standalone-pom <<<
```

463

```
[INFO]
[INFO] --- maven-archetype-plugin:2.4:generate (default-cli) @ standalone-pom
[INFO] Generating project in Batch mode
[INFO] ------------------------------------------------------------------------
[INFO] Using following parameters for creating project from Old (1.x) Archetype: maven-
      archetype-quickstart:1.0
[INFO] ------------------------------------------------------------------------
[INFO] Parameter: basedir, Value: /app/ggs/tiger/AdapterExamples/big-data/flume
[INFO] Parameter: package, Value: ravin-projects
[INFO] Parameter: groupId, Value: ravin-projects
[INFO] Parameter: artifactId, Value: ravin-prj1-ggsflume
[INFO] Parameter: packageName, Value: ravin-projects
[INFO] Parameter: version, Value: 1.0-SNAPSHOT
[INFO] project created from Old (1.x) Archetype in dir: /app/ggs/tiger/AdapterExamples/big-
      data/flume/ravin-prj1-ggsflume
[INFO] ------------------------------------------------------------------------
[INFO] BUILD SUCCESS
[INFO] ------------------------------------------------------------------------
[INFO] Total time: 17.151 s
[INFO] Finished at: 2016-08-03T22:29:11-04:00
[INFO] Final Memory: 13M/175M
[INFO] ------------------------------------------------------------------------
```

Here's the content of pom.xml:

```
[oracle@ravin-ravinpc ravin-prj1-ggsflume]$ cat pom.xml
<project xmlns="http://maven.apache.org/POM/4.0.0" xmlns:xsi="http://www.w3.org/2001/
XMLSchema-instance"
  xsi:schemaLocation="http://maven.apache.org/POM/4.0.0 http://maven.apache.org/
  maven-v4_0_0.xsd">
  <modelVersion>4.0.0</modelVersion>
  <groupId>ravin-projects</groupId>
  <artifactId>ravin-prj1-ggsflume</artifactId>
  <packaging>jar</packaging>
  <version>1.0-SNAPSHOT</version>
  <name>ravin-prj1-ggsflume</name>
  <url>http://maven.apache.org</url>
  <dependencies>
    <dependency>
      <groupId>junit</groupId>
      <artifactId>junit</artifactId>
      <version>3.8.1</version>
      <scope>test</scope>
    </dependency>
  </dependencies>
</project>
```

Now that I have a pom.xml file for my demo project, let's build the OGG Flume adapter.

```
[oracle@ravin-ravinpc flume]$ mvn clean package
```

The following output shows the Flume adapter was successfully built:

```
[INFO] Building jar: /app/ggs/tiger/AdapterExamples/big-data/flume/ravin-prj1-ggsflume/
       target/ravin-prj1-ggsflume-1.0-SNAPSHOT.jar
[INFO] ------------------------------------------------------------------------
[INFO] BUILD SUCCESS
[INFO] ------------------------------------------------------------------------
[INFO] Total time: 20.278 s
[INFO] Finished at: 2016-08-03T22:58:40-04:00
[INFO] Final Memory: 14M/168M
[INFO] ------------------------------------------------------------------------
```

Configure the OGG Adapter for Flume

Create the flume.props property file to include parameters for Flume connectivity, Flume dependencies, boot options, and other adapter properties. You can configure the parameter values as per your required configuration.

```
[oracle@ravin-ravinpc flume]$ cat flume.props

gg.handlerlist = flumehandler
gg.handler.flumehandler.type=flume
gg.handler.flumehandler.RpcClientPropertiesFile=custom-flume-rpc.properties
gg.handler.flumehandler.format=avro_op
gg.handler.flumehandler.mode=tx
#gg.handler.flumehandler.maxGroupSize=100, 1Mb
#gg.handler.flumehandler.minGroupSize=50, 500 Kb
gg.handler.flumehandler.EventMapsTo=tx
gg.handler.flumehandler.PropagateSchema=true
gg.handler.flumehandler.includeTokens=false
gg.handler.flumehandler.format.WrapMessageInGenericAvroMessage=true

goldengate.userexit.timestamp=utc
goldengate.userexit.writers=javawriter
javawriter.stats.display=TRUE
javawriter.stats.full=TRUE

gg.log=log4j
gg.log.level=INFO
gg.report.time=30sec
gg.classpath=dirprm/:/app/lib/flume/lib/*:

javawriter.bootoptions=-Xmx512m -Xms32m -Djava.class.path=ggjava/ggjava.jar
```

Note the RPC client properties file specification in the flume.props file. Create custom-flume-rpc.properties as follows:

```
[oracle@ravin-ravinpc flume]$ cat custom-flume-rpc.properties
client.type=default
hosts=h1
```

```
hosts.h1=ravin-ravinpc:52140
batch-size=100
connect-timeout=20000
request-timeout=20000
```

Set Up Flume

I have installed Flume at /app/flume/. Navigate to /app/flume/conf/ and create a file if it does not already exist as gg-flume.conf with the following contents. This file sets up the Flume source, Flume channel, and Flume sink. The file will be used to instantiate the Flume agent.

```
a1.channels = c1
a1.sources = s1
a1.sinks = p1
a1.channels.c1.type = memory
a1.sources.s1.channels = c1
a1.sources.s1.type = avro
a1.sources.s1.bind = <MACHINE IP>
a1.sources.s1.port = 41414
a1.sinks.p1.type = hdfs
a1.sinks.p1.channel = c1
a1.sinks.p1.hdfs.path =
/gg/replication/flume/%{SCHEMA_NAME}/%{TABLE_NAME}
a1.sinks.p1.hdfs.filePrefix = %{TABLE_NAME}_
a1.sinks.p1.hdfs.writeFormat=Writable
a1.sinks.p1.hdfs.rollInterval=30
a1.sinks.p1.hdfs.batchSize=10
a1.sinks.p1.hdfs.fileType=DataStream
```

Navigate to the Flume home /app/flume/ and execute the following command:

```
./bin/flume-ng agent --conf conf -f conf/gg-flume.conf -n a1
```

Assuming that you have already installed Hadoop, let's start the Hadoop instance using the following command. Please refer to the Hadoop documentation if you do not have a Hadoop system available.

```
cd $HADOOP_HOME/sbin

./start-dfs.sh
OR
./start-yarn.sh
```

Create the Replicat Process

Create a replicat process as follows:

```
GGSCI> add replicat rflume, exttrail /app/ggs/tiger/dirdat/fl
```

Edit the replicat parameter file to include the following parameters:

```
GGSCI> edit params rflume

REPLICAT RFLUME
TARGETDB LIBFILE libggjava.so SET property=dirprm/flume.props
REPORTCOUNT EVERY 1 MINUTES, RATE
GROUPTRANSOPS 10000
MAP TIGER.*, TARGET TIGER.*;
```

Start the OGG Adapter for Flume

Start the Oracle GoldenGate manager and replicat process.

```
GGSCI> START MGR
GGSCI> START RFLUME
GGSCI> INFO ALL
```

Log in to your Big Data system (Hadoop) and verify the data.

Flume Adapter Properties

Table 19-1 lists some of the most common Flume adapter properties with their usage.

Table 19-1. *Flume Adapter Properties*

Property	Usage Example	Description
javawriter.bootoptions	javawriter.bootoptions=-Xmx512m -Xms32m -Djava.class.path=ggjava/ggjava.jar -Dlog4j.configuration=log4j.properties	Sets boot options. Xms and Xmx set the initial and maximum memory size for the adapter JVM.
gg.handler.name.type	gg.handler.name.type=com.goldengate.delivery.handler.hdfs.HDFSHandler	This property is mandatory for your HDFS adapter.
gg.handler.name.host	gg.handler.name.host=12.12.45.4	IP or host of the machine running the Flume avro source.
gg.handler.name.port	gg.handler.name.port=4524	Port of the machine running the Flume avro source.
gg.handler.name.rpcType	gg.handler.name.rpcType=avro	Flume RPC type value. Should be avro.
gg.handler.name.delimiter	gg.handler.name.delimiter=,	Specifies the field delimiter character. Use , or ; or Unicode format for nonprintable characters. The default delimiter is \u0001.
gg.handler.name.deleteOpKey	gg.handler.name.deleteOpKey=D	Specifies the key that will represent DELETE operations in a DSV file. The default is D.

(continued)

467

Table 19-1. (*continued*)

Property	Usage Example	Description
gg.handler.name.updateOpKey	gg.handler.name. updateOpKey=U	Specifies the key that will represent UPDATE operations in a DSV file. The default is U.
gg.handler.name.insertOpKey	gg.handler.name. insertOpKey=I	Specifies the key that will represent INSERT operations in a DSV file. The default is I.
gg.handler.name.pKUpdateOpKey	gg.handler.name. pKUpdateOpKey=P	Specifies the key that will represent UPDATE operations on the primary key in DSV file. The default is P.
gg.handler.name.includeOpType	gg.handler.name. includeOpType=true	Specifies whether the operation type is to be included in the DSV. The default is true.
gg.handler.name. includeOpTimestamp	gg.handler.name. includeOpTimestamp=true	Specifies whether the operation timestamp is to be included in the DSV file. The default is true.
gg.handler.name.mode	gg.handler.name.mode=tx	The operating mode can be op or tx. If you are grouping your transaction for performance improvement, this should be set to tx.
gg.handler.name.maxGroupSize	gg.handler.name. maxGroupSize=10000	Specifies the maximum number of operations that can be held by an operation group irrespective of the operations belonging to single or multiple transactions. As soon as the operations reach this threshold, the operation group will send a transaction commit. This eventually leads to splitting of transactions across multiple operation groups.
gg.handler.name.minGroupSize	gg.handler.name. minGroupSize=10	Specifies the minimum number of operations that should exist within a group before it can end. This eventually leads to clubbing multiple small transactions into a single group.

Oracle GoldenGate Big Data Adapter for HDFS

Hadoop Distributed File System (HDFS) is a Java-based file system that provides scalable and reliable data storage designed to span large clusters of commodity servers. HDFS, MapReduce, and YARN form the core of Apache Hadoop. Streaming data to HDFS enables the downstream applications to further process data natively on Hadoop.

The OGG Big Data adapter for HDFS provides ready-made functionality to stream transactional data in real time to the Hadoop Distributed File System. The customers can also modify and extend the adapter functionality as per the specific business needs.

Operations are picked from source trail files and written to HDFS. HDFS supports inserts, deletes, and updates (including updates on primary key fields). It, however, does not support TRUNCATE operations. A TRUNCATE statement on the table will make the HDFS extract abend.

A Hadoop single instance or cluster must be installed, running, and accessible to the machine where you will set up the OGG adapter for HDFS.

Hadoop is open source software and can be downloaded from http://hadoop.apache.org. Figure 19-3 shows the components of the Oracle GoldenGate HDFS adapter for Big Data systems.

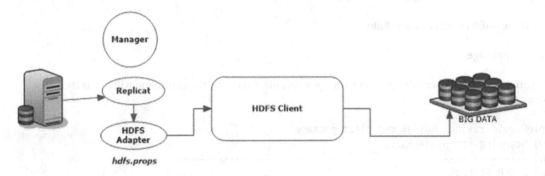

Figure 19-3. *OGG HDFS adapter configuration*

Build the HDFS Adapter

You need to build an HDFS adapter that will be used to stream changes captured in trails to HDFS.

Download and Install Maven

You can build the OGG adapter for HDFS using Maven. It is an open source build tool available for download at http://maven.apache.org/.

I have used Maven 3.3.9 for this example. Extract the TAR file at a location where you want to install Maven.

```
tar -xvf apache-maven-3.3.9-bin.tar
```

Set the PATH variable to include the path to mvn in the bin directory.

Pre-checks

Here are some of the considerations before you can use Maven to build the HDFS adapter:

- Make sure the HDFS client version in /app/ggs/tiger/AdapterExamples/big-data/hdfs/pom.xml is correct before starting the build.

- If you are using Maven to build the OGG adapter, you need Internet access to connect to the Maven central repository. If your organization uses a proxy server/VPN to prevent direct connections to the Internet, you need to configure your Maven settings.xml file before starting the build. Refer to the Maven documentation on to configure settings.xml.

- Maven also requires ggjava.jar located in /app/ggs/tiger/ggjava/ggjava.jar.
  The relative path of ggjava.jar is specified in pom.xml.

- Oracle GoldenGate Java Adapter 12 is built and runs with Java 7. Make sure you are
  using JDK 7 for building your custom adapter.

Build the OGG Adapter for HDFS

Now that you have installed Maven, let's use it to build the HDFS adapter. Navigate to the following directory:

```
cd /app/ggs/tiger/AdapterExamples/big-data/hdfs
```

Start the build using Maven as follows:

```
mvn clean package
```

If you do not have an existing project with a pom.xml file, executing the command will throw the following error:

```
[oracle@ravin-ravinpc hdfs]$ mvn clean package
[INFO] Scanning for projects...
[INFO] ------------------------------------------------------------------------
[INFO] BUILD FAILURE
[INFO] ------------------------------------------------------------------------
[INFO] Total time: 0.321 s
[INFO] Finished at: 2016-08-03T22:35:10-04:00
[INFO] Final Memory: 6M/100M
[INFO] ------------------------------------------------------------------------
[ERROR] The goal you specified requires a project to execute but there is no POM in this
        directory (/app/ggs/tiger/AdapterExamples/big-data/hdfs). Please verify you invoked
        Maven from the correct directory. -> [Help 1]
[ERROR]
[ERROR] To see the full stack trace of the errors, re-run Maven with the -e switch.
[ERROR] Re-run Maven using the -X switch to enable full debug logging.
[ERROR]
[ERROR] For more information about the errors and possible solutions, please read the
        following articles:
[ERROR] [Help 1] http://cwiki.apache.org/confluence/display/MAVEN/MissingProjectException
```

I created a demo project with the following command. Make sure your Internet connection is on, as it will download dependencies from the Maven central repository.

```
[oracle@ravin-ravinpc hdfs]$ mvn archetype:generate -DgroupId=ravin-projects
-DartifactId=ravin-prj1-ggshdfs -DarchetypeArtifactId=maven-archetype-quickstart
-DinteractiveMode=false
[INFO] Scanning for projects...
[INFO]
[INFO] ------------------------------------------------------------------------
[INFO] Building Maven Stub Project (No POM) 1
[INFO] ------------------------------------------------------------------------
[INFO]
```

```
[INFO] >>> maven-archetype-plugin:2.4:generate (default-cli) > generate-sources
       @ standalone-pom >>>
[INFO]
[INFO] <<< maven-archetype-plugin:2.4:generate (default-cli) < generate-sources
       @ standalone-pom <<<
[INFO]
[INFO] --- maven-archetype-plugin:2.4:generate (default-cli) @ standalone-pom
[INFO] Generating project in Batch mode
[INFO] -----------------------------------------------------------------------
[INFO] Using following parameters for creating project from Old (1.x) Archetype: maven-
       archetype-quickstart:1.0
[INFO] -----------------------------------------------------------------------
[INFO] Parameter: basedir, Value: /app/ggs/tiger/AdapterExamples/big-data/hdfs
[INFO] Parameter: package, Value: ravin-projects
[INFO] Parameter: groupId, Value: ravin-projects
[INFO] Parameter: artifactId, Value: ravin-prj1-ggshdfs
[INFO] Parameter: packageName, Value: ravin-projects
[INFO] Parameter: version, Value: 1.0-SNAPSHOT
[INFO] project created from Old (1.x) Archetype in dir: /app/ggs/tiger/AdapterExamples/big-
       data/hdfs/ravin-prj1-ggshdfs
[INFO] -----------------------------------------------------------------------
[INFO] BUILD SUCCESS
[INFO] -----------------------------------------------------------------------
[INFO] Total time: 17.151 s
[INFO] Finished at: 2016-08-03T22:35:18-04:00
[INFO] Final Memory: 13M/175M
[INFO] -----------------------------------------------------------------------
```

Here's the content of pom.xml:

```
[oracle@ravin-ravinpc ravin-prj1-ggshdfs]$ cat pom.xml
<project xmlns="http://maven.apache.org/POM/4.0.0" xmlns:xsi="http://www.w3.org/2001/
XMLSchema-instance"
  xsi:schemaLocation="http://maven.apache.org/POM/4.0.0 http://maven.apache.org/
  maven-v4_0_0.xsd">
  <modelVersion>4.0.0</modelVersion>
  <groupId>ravin-projects</groupId>
  <artifactId>ravin-prj1-ggshdfs</artifactId>
  <packaging>jar</packaging>
  <version>1.0-SNAPSHOT</version>
  <name>ravin-prj1-ggshdfs</name>
  <url>http://maven.apache.org</url>
  <dependencies>
    <dependency>
      <groupId>junit</groupId>
      <artifactId>junit</artifactId>
      <version>3.8.1</version>
      <scope>test</scope>
    </dependency>
  </dependencies>
</project>
```

Now that I have a pom.xml file for my demo project, let's build the OGG HDFS adapter.

```
[oracle@ravin-ravinpc hdfs]$ mvn clean package
```

This output shows the HDFS adapter is successfully built:

```
[INFO] Building jar: /app/ggs/tiger/AdapterExamples/big-data/hdfs/ravin-prj1-ggshdfs/target/
       ravin-prj1-ggshdfs-1.0-SNAPSHOT.jar
[INFO] ------------------------------------------------------------------------
[INFO] BUILD SUCCESS
[INFO] ------------------------------------------------------------------------
[INFO] Total time: 20.278 s
[INFO] Finished at: 2016-08-03T22:39:40-04:00
[INFO] Final Memory: 14M/168M
[INFO] ------------------------------------------------------------------------
```

Configure the OGG Adapter for HDFS

When doing the first-time setup, refer to the sample configuration files that come with software binaries. Create the hdfs.props property file to include the following properties. You can configure the parameter values as per your required configuration.

```
[oracle@ravin-ravinpc hdfs]$ cat hdfs.props
gg.handlerlist=hdfs

gg.handler.hdfs.type=hdfs
gg.handler.hdfs.includeTokens=false
gg.handler.hdfs.maxFileSize=1g
gg.handler.hdfs.rootFilePath=/ogg1
gg.handler.hdfs.fileRollInterval=0
gg.handler.hdfs.inactivityRollInterval=0
gg.handler.hdfs.fileSuffix=.txt
gg.handler.hdfs.partitionByTable=true
gg.handler.hdfs.rollOnMetadataChange=true
gg.handler.hdfs.authType=none
gg.handler.hdfs.format=delimitedtext
gg.handler.hdfs.format.includeColumnNames=true

gg.handler.hdfs.mode=tx

goldengate.userexit.timestamp=utc
goldengate.userexit.writers=javawriter
javawriter.stats.display=TRUE
javawriter.stats.full=TRUE

gg.log=log4j
gg.log.level=INFO
gg.report.time=30sec

gg.classpath=/app/lib/hadoop/share/hadoop/common/*:/app/lib/hadoop/share/hadoop/common/
lib/*:/app/lib/hadoop/share/hadoop/hdfs/*:/app/lib/hadoop/etc/hadoop/:
```

```
javawriter.bootoptions=-Xmx512m -Xms32m -Djava.class.path=ggjava/ggjava.jar
```

Make sure your HDFS Java adapter has the classpath property gg.classpath configured to include the location of your core-site.xml file. The core-site.xml file located at your HADOOP_HOME/etc/hadoop directory contains the connectivity information used by the adapter.

```
gg.classpath=GG_ROOT_DIRECTORY/AdapterExamples/big-data/hdfs/target/hdfs-lib/*
```

The wildcard character (*) is to resolve runtime dependencies of the HDFS adapter on the client JARs.

Set Up HDFS

Assuming that you have already installed Hadoop, let's start the Hadoop instance using the following command. Please refer to the Hadoop documentation if you do not have a Hadoop system available.

```
cd $HADOOP_HOME/sbin

./start-dfs.sh
OR
./start-yarn.sh
```

Create the Replicat Process

You can find the sample parameter file for the HDFS extract process at /app/ggs/tiger/AdapterExamples/big-data/hdfs/dirprm/hdfs.prm.

The sample property file for the HDFS Java adapter is located at /app/ggs/tiger/AdapterExamples/big-data/hdfs/dirprm/hdfs.props.

Copy both the files to /app/ggs/tiger/dirprm and customize them as per your configuration. Create a replicat process as follows:

```
GGSCI> add replicat rhdfs, exttrail /app/ggs/tiger/dirdat/hd
```

Edit the replicat parameter file to include the following parameters:

```
GGSCI> edit params rhdfs

REPLICAT RHDFS
TARGETDB LIBFILE libggjava.so SET property=dirprm/hdfs.props
REPORTCOUNT EVERY 1 MINUTES, RATE
GROUPTRANSOPS 10000
MAP TIGER.*, TARGET TIGER.*;
```

Start the OGG Adapter for HDFS

Start the Oracle GoldenGate manager and replicat processes.

```
GGSCI> START MGR
GGSCI> START RHDFS
GGSCI> INFO ALL
```

Log in to your Big Data system (HDFS) and verify the data.

HDFS Adapter Properties

Table 19-2 lists some of the most common HDFS adapter properties with their usage.

Table 19-2. *HDFS Adapter Properties*

Property	Usage	Description
javawriter.bootoptions	javawriter.bootoptions=-Xmx512m -Xms32m -Djava.class.path=ggjava/ggjava.jar -Dlog4j.configuration=log4j.properties	Sets boot options. Xms and Xmx set the initial and maximum memory size for the adapter JVM.
gg.handler.name.type	gg.handler.name.type=com.goldengate.delivery.handler.hdfs.HDFSHandler	This property is mandatory for your HDFS adapter.
gg.handler.name.HDFSPrefix	gg.handler.name.HDFSPrefix=gg_	Specifies the prefix for all files created in HDFS. The default prefix is gg_.
gg.handler.name.HDFSSuffix	gg.handler.name.HDFSSuffix=.txt	Specifies the suffix for all files created in HDFS. The default prefix is .txt.
gg.handler.name.HDFSFilePath	gg.handler.name.HDFSFilePath	The path location where the files will be written in HDFS. The default location is /ogg.
gg.handler.name.maxFileSize	gg.handler.name.maxFileSize=10m	Specifies the maximum file size created in HDFS. The default is 1g. Use k, m, and g to represent KB, MB, and GB, respectively.
gg.handler.name.fieldDelimiter	gg.handler.name.fieldDelimiter=\u0001	Specifies the field delimiter character. Use , or ; or Unicode format for nonprintable characters. The default delimiter is \u0001.
gg.handler.name.lineDelimiter	gg.handler.name.lineDelimiter=\n	Specifies the line delimiter. The default is \n.
gg.handler.name.writeColumnNames	gg.handler.name.writeColumnNames=true	Specifies whether the column name should be written before their column values in the file in HDFS. The default is true.
gg.handler.name.mode	gg.handler.name.mode=tx	The operating mode can be op or tx. If you are grouping your transaction for performance improvement, this should be set to tx.

(continued)

Table 19-2. (*continued*)

Property	Usage	Description
gg.handler.name.maxGroupSize	gg.handler.name.maxGroupSize=10000	Specifies the maximum number of operations that can be held by an operation group irrespective of the operations belonging to single or multiple transactions. As soon as the operations reach this threshold, the operation group will send a transaction commit. This eventually leads to the splitting of transactions across multiple operation groups.
gg.handler.name.minGroupSize	gg.handler.name.minGroupSize=10	Specifies the minimum number of operations that should exist within a group before it can end. This eventually leads to clubbing multiple small transactions into a single group.

Oracle GoldenGate Adapter for Hive

Hive is a data warehousing infrastructure provided on top of Hadoop for doing summarization and analysis. Oracle GoldenGate can now feed in real-time data to the Hive data store. This provides for agile and cost-effective real-time data warehousing on Hadoop.

Like the Flume and HDFS adapters, the Hive adapter picks operations from source trail files and writes to HDFS. It supports inserts, deletes, and updates (including updates on the primary key fields). It, however, does not support TRUNCATE operations. A TRUNCATE statement on the table will make the Hive extract abend.

A Hadoop single instance or cluster must be installed, running, and accessible to the machine where you will set up the OGG adapter for Hive.

Figure 19-4 shows components of the Oracle GoldenGate hive adapter for Big Data systems.

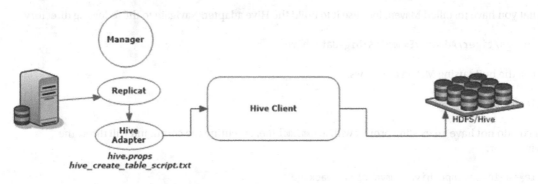

Figure 19-4. *OGG Hive adapter configuration*

Build the Hive Adapter

You need to build a Hive adapter that will be used to stream changes captured in trails to Hadoop.

Download and Install Maven

You can build the OGG adapter for Hive using Maven. It is an open source build tool available for download at http://maven.apache.org/.

I have used Maven 3.3.9 for this example. Extract the TAR file at a location where you want to install Maven.

```
tar -xvf apache-maven-3.3.9-bin.tar
```

Set the PATH variable to include the path to mvn in the bin directory.

Pre-checks

These are some of the considerations before you can use Maven to build the Hive adapter:

- Make sure the HDFS client version in /app/ggs/tiger/AdapterExamples/big-data/ hive/pom.xml is correct before starting the build.

- If you are using Maven to build the OGG adapter, you need Internet access to connect to the Maven central repository. If your organization uses a proxy server/ VPN to prevent direct connections to the Internet, you need to configure your Maven settings.xml file before starting the build. Refer to the Maven documentation on configuring settings.xml.

- Maven also requires ggjava.jar located in /app/ggs/tiger/ggjava/ggjava.jar. The relative path of ggjava.jar is specified in pom.xml.

- Oracle GoldenGate Java Adapter 12 is built and runs with Java 7. Make sure you are using JDK 7 for building your custom adapter.

Build the OGG Adapter for Hive

Now that you have installed Maven, let's use it to build the Hive adapter. Navigate to the following directory:

```
cd /app/ggs/tiger/AdapterExamples/big-data/hive
```

Start the build using Maven as follows:

```
mvn clean package
```

If you do not have an existing project with a pom.xml file, executing the command will throw the following error:

```
[oracle@ravin-ravinpc hive]$ mvn clean package
[INFO] Scanning for projects...
[INFO] ------------------------------------------------------------------------
[INFO] BUILD FAILURE
[INFO] ------------------------------------------------------------------------
```

```
[INFO] Total time: 0.321 s
[INFO] Finished at: 2016-08-03T23:17:20-04:00
[INFO] Final Memory: 6M/100M
[INFO] ------------------------------------------------------------------------
[ERROR] The goal you specified requires a project to execute but there is no POM in this
        directory (/app/ggs/tiger/AdapterExamples/big-data/hive). Please verify you invoked
        Maven from the correct directory. -> [Help 1]
[ERROR]
[ERROR] To see the full stack trace of the errors, re-run Maven with the -e switch.
[ERROR] Re-run Maven using the -X switch to enable full debug logging.
[ERROR]
[ERROR] For more information about the errors and possible solutions, please read the
        following articles:
[ERROR] [Help 1] http://cwiki.apache.org/confluence/display/MAVEN/MissingProjectException
```

I created a demo project with the following command. Make sure your Internet connection is on, as it will download dependencies from the Maven central repository.

```
[oracle@ravin-ravinpc hive]$ mvn archetype:generate -DgroupId=ravin-projects
-DartifactId=ravin-prj1-ggshive -DarchetypeArtifactId=maven-archetype-quickstart
-DinteractiveMode=false
[INFO] Scanning for projects...
[INFO]
[INFO] ------------------------------------------------------------------------
[INFO] Building Maven Stub Project (No POM) 1
[INFO] ------------------------------------------------------------------------
[INFO]
[INFO] >>> maven-archetype-plugin:2.4:generate (default-cli) > generate-sources
      @ standalone-pom >>>
[INFO]
[INFO] <<< maven-archetype-plugin:2.4:generate (default-cli) < generate-sources
      @ standalone-pom <<<
[INFO]
[INFO] --- maven-archetype-plugin:2.4:generate (default-cli) @ standalone-pom
[INFO] Generating project in Batch mode
[INFO] ------------------------------------------------------------------------
[INFO] Using following parameters for creating project from Old (1.x) Archetype: maven-
        archetype-quickstart:1.0
[INFO] ------------------------------------------------------------------------
[INFO] Parameter: basedir, Value: /app/ggs/tiger/AdapterExamples/big-data/hive
[INFO] Parameter: package, Value: ravin-projects
[INFO] Parameter: groupId, Value: ravin-projects
[INFO] Parameter: artifactId, Value: ravin-prj1-ggshive
[INFO] Parameter: packageName, Value: ravin-projects
[INFO] Parameter: version, Value: 1.0-SNAPSHOT
[INFO] project created from Old (1.x) Archetype in dir: /app/ggs/tiger/AdapterExamples/
        big-data/hive/ravin-prj1-ggshive
[INFO] ------------------------------------------------------------------------
[INFO] BUILD SUCCESS
[INFO] ------------------------------------------------------------------------
[INFO] Total time: 17.151 s
```

```
[INFO] Finished at: 2016-08-03T23:17:30-04:00
[INFO] Final Memory: 13M/175M
[INFO] ----------------------------------------------------------------------
```

Here's the content of pom.xml:

```
[oracle@ravin-ravinpc ravin-prj1-ggshive]$ cd ravin-prj1-ggshive/^C
[oracle@ravin-ravinpc ravin-prj1-ggshive]$ cat pom.xml
<project xmlns="http://maven.apache.org/POM/4.0.0" xmlns:xsi="http://www.w3.org/2001/
XMLSchema-instance"
  xsi:schemaLocation="http://maven.apache.org/POM/4.0.0 http://maven.apache.org/
  maven-v4_0_0.xsd">
  <modelVersion>4.0.0</modelVersion>
  <groupId>ravin-projects</groupId>
  <artifactId>ravin-prj1-ggshive</artifactId>
  <packaging>jar</packaging>
  <version>1.0-SNAPSHOT</version>
  <name>ravin-prj1-ggshive</name>
  <url>http://maven.apache.org</url>
  <dependencies>
    <dependency>
      <groupId>junit</groupId>
      <artifactId>junit</artifactId>
      <version>3.8.1</version>
      <scope>test</scope>
    </dependency>
  </dependencies>
</project>
```

Now that I have a pom.xml for my demo project, let's build the OGG Hive adapter.

```
[oracle@ravin-ravinpc hive]$ mvn clean package
```

The output shows that the Hive adapter was successfully built.

```
[INFO] Building jar: /app/ggs/tiger/AdapterExamples/big-data/hive/ravin-prj1-ggshive/target/
ravin-prj1-ggshive-1.0-SNAPSHOT.jar
[INFO] ----------------------------------------------------------------------
[INFO] BUILD SUCCESS
[INFO] ----------------------------------------------------------------------
[INFO] Total time: 20.278 s
[INFO] Finished at: 2016-08-03T23:26:32-04:00
[INFO] Final Memory: 14M/168M
[INFO] ----------------------------------------------------------------------
```

Configure the OGG Adapter for Hive

Create the hive.props property file to include parameters for Hive connectivity, Hive dependencies, boot options, and other adapter properties. You can configure parameter values as per your required configuration.

```
[oracle@ravin-ravinpc hive]$ cat hive.props

gg.handlerlist=hdfs

#Handler Properties
gg.handler.hdfs.type=hdfs
gg.handler.hdfs.rootFilePath=/gg/hdfs/hivemdp4
gg.handler.hdfs.format=delimitedtext
gg.handler.hdfs.format.includeColumnNames=true
gg.handler.hdfs.includeTokens=false

gg.handler.hdfs.mode=tx

#Hive Metadata Provider Properties
gg.mdp.type=hive
gg.mdp.connectionUrl=jdbc:hive2://10.240.118.56:10000/gg_hive
gg.mdp.driverClassName=org.apache.hive.jdbc.HiveDriver

goldengate.userexit.timestamp=utc
goldengate.userexit.writers=javawriter
javawriter.stats.display=TRUE
javawriter.stats.full=TRUE

gg.log=log4j
gg.log.level=INFO

gg.report.time=30sec

gg.classpath=dirprm/:/app/lib/hadoop/share/hadoop/common/*:/app/lib/hadoop/share/hadoop/
common/lib/*:/app/lib/hadoop/share/hadoop/hdfs/*:/app/lib/hadoop/etc/hadoop/:/app/
lib/hadoop/share/hadoop/mapreduce/*:/app/lib/hive/lib/*:/app/lib/hive/hcatalog/share/
hcatalog/*:/app/lib/hive/hcatalog/share/webhcat/java-client/*:

javawriter.bootoptions=-Xmx512m -Xms32m -Djava.class.path=ggjava/ggjava.jar
```

Make sure your HDFS Java adapter has the classpath property gg.classpath configured to include the location of your core-site.xml file. The core-site.xml file located in your HADOOP_HOME/etc/hadoop directory contains the connectivity information used by the adapter.

```
gg.classpath=GG_ROOT_DIRECTORY/AdapterExamples/big-data/hive/target/hive-lib/*
```

The wildcard character (*) is to resolve runtime dependencies of the HDFS adapter on client JARs.

Set Up Hive

When doing the first-time setup, refer to the sample configuration files that come with the software binaries.

The sample parameter file for the HDFS extract process can be found at /app/ggs/tiger/ AdapterExamples/big-data/metadata_provider/hive/hive.prm.

The sample property file for the HDFS Java adapter is located at /app/ggs/tiger/AdapterExamples/ big-data/metadata_provider/hive/hive_mdp_hdfs.props.

Copy both the files to /app/ggs/tiger/dirprm and customize them as per your configuration.

Assuming that you have already installed Hadoop, let's start the Hadoop instance using the following command. Please refer to the Hadoop documentation if you do not have a Hadoop system available.

```
cd $HADOOP_HOME/sbin

./start-dfs.sh
OR
./start-yarn.sh
```

Create a Replicat Process

Create a replicat process as follows:

```
GGSCI> add replicat rhive, exttrail /app/ggs/tiger/dirdat/hv
```

Edit a replicat parameter file to include the following parameters:

```
GGSCI> edit params rhive
```

```
REPLICAT RHIVE
TARGETDB LIBFILE libggjava.so SET property=dirprm/hive.props
REPORTCOUNT EVERY 1 MINUTES, RATE
GROUPTRANSOPS 10000
MAP TIGER.TCUSTMER, TARGET GG_HIVE.TCUSTMER_HIVE, COLMAP(USEDEFAULTS, CUST_CODE2=CUST_CODE,
CITY2=CITY), KEYCOLS(CUST_CODE2);
MAP TIGER.TCUSTORD, TARGET GG_HIVE.TCUSTORD_HIVE, COLMAP(USEDEFAULTS, CUST_CODE2=CUST_CODE,
ORDER_DATE2=ORDER_DATE), KEYCOLS(CUST_CODE2,ORDER_DATE2,PRODUCT_CODE,ORDER_ID);
```

Create Tables in Hive

Unlike the OGG adapter for Flume and HDFS, tables in Hive are not created automatically by the Hive adapter and need to be built manually.

The create table command for creating tables in the GG_HIVE schema is located at /app/ggs/tiger/ AdapterExamples/big-data/metadata_provider/hive in the file sample_hive_create_table_script.txt.

Navigate to $HIVE_HOME/bin and execute the following:

```
./hive
```

Execute the following scripts at a Hive prompt:

```
hive> CREATE EXTERNAL TABLE TCUSTMER(
OPERATION_TYPE STRING,
CUST_CODE STRING,
NAME STRING,
CITY STRING,
STATE STRING,
OPERATION_TIMESTAMP STRING
```

```
)
ROW FORMAT DELIMITED FIELDS TERMINATED BY '\u0001' LINES TERMINATED BY
'\n'
LOCATION '/gg/replication/hive/gg/tcustmer';
hive> CREATE EXTERNAL TABLE TCUSTORD(
OPERATION_TYPE STRING,
CUST_CODE STRING,
ORDER_DATE STRING,
PRODUCT_CODE STRING,
ORDER_ID INT,
PRODUCT_PRICE DOUBLE,
PRODUCT_AMOUNT INT,
TRANSACTION_ID INT,
OPERATION_TIMESTAMP STRING
)
ROW FORMAT DELIMITED FIELDS TERMINATED BY '\u0001' LINES TERMINATED BY
'\n'
LOCATION '/gg/replication/hive/gg/tcustord';
```

Query Hive for Data

Here's how you query Hive for data:

```
hive> select * from TCUSTMER;
hive> select * from TCUSTORD;
```

Start the OGG Adapter for Hive

Start the Oracle GoldenGate manager and replicat processes.

```
GGSCI> START MGR
GGSCI> START RHIVE
GGSCI> INFO ALL
```

Log in to your Big Data system (Hadoop) and verify the data.

Hive Adapter Properties

Table 19-3 lists some of the most common Hive adapter properties with their usage.

Table 19-3. *Hive Adapter Properties*

Property	Usage	Description
javawriter.bootoptions	javawriter.bootoptions=-Xmx512m -Xms32m -Djava.class.path=ggjava/ggjava.jar -Dlog4j.configuration=log4j.properties	Sets boot options. Xms and Xmx set the initial and maximum memory size for the adapter JVM.
gg.handler.name.type	gg.handler.name.type=com.goldengate.delivery.handler.hdfs.HDFSHandler	This property is mandatory for your HDFS adapter.
gg.handler.name.fieldDelimiter	gg.handler.name.fieldDelimiter=,	Specifies the field delimiter character. Use , or ; or Unicode format for nonprintable characters. The default delimiter is \u0001.
gg.handler.name.lineDelimiter	gg.handler.name.lineDelimiter=\n	Specifies line delimiter. The default is \n.
gg.handler.name.rootdirectoryPath	gg.handler.name.rootdirectoryPath=/app/hive	Specifies the root directory in HDFS where directories and files will be created.
gg.handler.name.deleteOpKey	gg.handler.name.deleteOpKey=D	Specifies the key that will represent DELETE operations in the DSV file. The default is D.
gg.handler.name.updateOpKey	gg.handler.name.updateOpKey=U	Specifies the key that will represent UPDATE operations in the DSV file. The default is U.
gg.handler.name.insertOpKey	gg.handler.name.insertOpKey=I	Specifies the key that will represent INSERT operations in the DSV file. The default is I.
gg.handler.name.pKUpdateOpKey	gg.handler.name.pKUpdateOpKey=P	Specifies the key that will represent UPDATE operations on the primary key in the DSV file. The default is P.
gg.handler.name.includeOpType	gg.handler.name.includeOpType=true	Specifies if the operation type is to be included in the DSV. The default is true.
gg.handler.name.includeOpTimestamp	gg.handler.name.includeOpTimestamp=true	Specifies if the operation timestamp is to be included in the DSV file. The default is true.
gg.handler.name.maxFileSize	gg.handler.name.maxFileSize=2g	Specifies the maximum file size created in HDFS. The default is 1g. Use k, m, and g to represent KB, MB, and GB, respectively.
gg.handler.name.mode	gg.handler.name.mode=tx	The operating mode can be op or tx. If you are grouping your transaction for performance improvement, this should be set to tx.

(continued)

Table 19-3. (*continued*)

Property	Usage	Description
gg.handler.name.maxGroupSize	gg.handler.name. maxGroupSize=10000	Specifies the maximum number of operations that can be held by an operation group irrespective of the operations belonging to single or multiple transactions. As soon as the operations reach this threshold, the operation group will send transaction commit. This eventually leads to the splitting of transactions across multiple operation groups.
gg.handler.name.minGroupSize	gg.handler.name. minGroupSize=10	Specifies the minimum number of operations that should exist within a group before it can end. This eventually leads to clubbing multiple small transactions into a single group.

Oracle GoldenGate Adapter for HBase

Apache HBase is a NoSQL database that runs on top of HDFS. It provides quick access to large quantities of sparse data. Users can also perform transactions containing inserts, updates, and deletes. With Oracle GoldenGate for Big Data, transactions can be applied to HBase in real time.

Like the Flume and HDFS adapters, the HBase adapter picks operations from source trail files and writes to HDFS. It supports inserts, deletes, and updates (not including updates on primary key fields). Unlike others, it does support TRUNCATE operations. However, the limitation is that the updates on the primary key fields are not supported. Also, each replicated table must have a primary key.

A Hadoop single instance or cluster must be installed, running, and accessible to the machine where you will set up the OGG adapter for HBase.

Figure 19-5 shows components of the Oracle GoldenGate HBase adapter for Big Data systems.

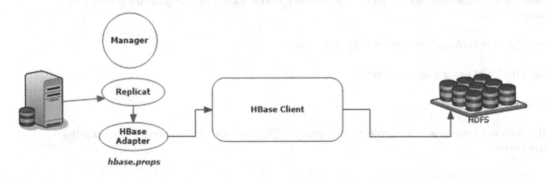

Figure 19-5. *OGG HBase adapter configuration*

Build the HBase Adapter

You need to build an HBase adapter that will be used to stream changes captured in trails to HDFS.

Download and Install Maven

You can build the OGG adapter for HBase using Maven. It is an open source build tool available for download at http://maven.apache.org/.

I have used Maven 3.3.9 for this example. Extract the TAR file at a location where you want to install Maven.

```
tar -xvf apache-maven-3.3.9-bin.tar
```

Set the PATH variable to include the path to mvn in the bin directory.

Pre-checks

Here are some of the considerations before you can use Maven to build the HBase adapter:

- Make sure the HBase client version in /app/ggs/tiger/AdapterExamples/big-data/HBase/pom.xml is correct before starting the build.

- If you are using Maven to build the OGG adapter, you need Internet access to connect to the Maven central repository. If your organization uses a proxy server/VPN to prevent direct connections to the Internet, you need to configure your Maven settings.xml file before starting the build. Refer to the Maven documentation on configuring settings.xml.

- Maven also requires ggjava.jar located in /app/ggs/tiger/ggjava/ggjava.jar. The relative path of ggjava.jar is specified in pom.xml.

- Oracle GoldenGate Java Adapter 12 is built and runs with Java 7. Make sure you are using JDK 7 for building your custom adapter.

Build the OGG Adapter for HBase

Now that you have installed Maven, let's use it to build the HBase adapter. Navigate to the following directory:

```
cd /app/ggs/tiger/AdapterExamples/big-data/HBase
```

Start the build using Maven as follows:

```
mvn clean package
```

If you do not have an existing project with a pom.xml file, executing the command will throw the following error:

```
[oracle@ravin-ravinpc HBase]$ mvn clean package
[INFO] Scanning for projects...
[INFO] ------------------------------------------------------------------------
[INFO] BUILD FAILURE
```

```
[INFO] -------------------------------------------------------------------------
[INFO] Total time: 0.321 s
[INFO] Finished at: 2016-08-03T23:41:10-04:00
[INFO] Final Memory: 6M/100M
[INFO] -------------------------------------------------------------------------
[ERROR] The goal you specified requires a project to execute but there is no POM in this
        directory (/app/ggs/tiger/AdapterExamples/big-data/HBase). Please verify you invoked
        Maven from the correct directory. -> [Help 1]
[ERROR]
[ERROR] To see the full stack trace of the errors, re-run Maven with the -e switch.
[ERROR] Re-run Maven using the -X switch to enable full debug logging.
[ERROR]
[ERROR] For more information about the errors and possible solutions, please read the
        following articles:
[ERROR] [Help 1] http://cwiki.apache.org/confluence/display/MAVEN/MissingProjectException
```

I created a demo project with the following command. Make sure your Internet connection is on, as it will download dependencies from the Maven central repository.

```
[oracle@ravin-ravinpc HBase]$ mvn archetype:generate -DgroupId=ravin-projects
-DartifactId=ravin-prj1-ggshbase -DarchetypeArtifactId=maven-archetype-quickstart
-DinteractiveMode=false
[INFO] Scanning for projects...
[INFO]
[INFO] -------------------------------------------------------------------------
[INFO] Building Maven Stub Project (No POM) 1
[INFO] -------------------------------------------------------------------------
[INFO]
[INFO] >>> maven-archetype-plugin:2.4:generate (default-cli) > generate-sources
        @ standalone-pom >>>
[INFO]
[INFO] <<< maven-archetype-plugin:2.4:generate (default-cli) < generate-sources
        @ standalone-pom <<<
[INFO]
[INFO] --- maven-archetype-plugin:2.4:generate (default-cli) @ standalone-pom
[INFO] Generating project in Batch mode
[INFO] -------------------------------------------------------------------------
[INFO] Using following parameters for creating project from Old (1.x) Archetype: maven-
        archetype-quickstart:1.0
[INFO] -------------------------------------------------------------------------
[INFO] Parameter: basedir, Value: /app/ggs/tiger/AdapterExamples/big-data/hbase
[INFO] Parameter: package, Value: ravin-projects
[INFO] Parameter: groupId, Value: ravin-projects
[INFO] Parameter: artifactId, Value: ravin-prj1-ggshbase
[INFO] Parameter: packageName, Value: ravin-projects
[INFO] Parameter: version, Value: 1.0-SNAPSHOT
[INFO] project created from Old (1.x) Archetype in dir: /app/ggs/tiger/AdapterExamples/big-
        data/hbase/ravin-prj1-ggshbase
[INFO] -------------------------------------------------------------------------
[INFO] BUILD SUCCESS
[INFO] -------------------------------------------------------------------------
```

```
[INFO] Total time: 17.151 s
[INFO] Finished at: 2016-08-03T23:42:18-04:00
[INFO] Final Memory: 13M/175M
[INFO] -----------------------------------------------------------------------
```

Here's the content of pom.xml:

```
[oracle@ravin-ravinpc ravin-prj1-ggshbase]$ cat pom.xml
<project xmlns="http://maven.apache.org/POM/4.0.0" xmlns:xsi="http://www.w3.org/2001/
XMLSchema-instance"
  xsi:schemaLocation="http://maven.apache.org/POM/4.0.0 http://maven.apache.org/
  maven-v4_0_0.xsd">
  <modelVersion>4.0.0</modelVersion>
  <groupId>ravin-projects</groupId>
  <artifactId>ravin-prj1-ggshbase</artifactId>
  <packaging>jar</packaging>
  <version>1.0-SNAPSHOT</version>
  <name>ravin-prj1-ggshbase</name>
  <url>http://maven.apache.org</url>
  <dependencies>
    <dependency>
      <groupId>junit</groupId>
      <artifactId>junit</artifactId>
      <version>3.8.1</version>
      <scope>test</scope>
    </dependency>
  </dependencies>
</project>
```

Now that I have a pom.xml file for my demo project, let's build the OGG HBase adapter.

```
[oracle@ravin-ravinpc hbase]$ mvn clean package
```

The output shows the HBase adapter is successfully built.

```
[INFO] Building jar: /app/ggs/tiger/AdapterExamples/big-data/hbase/ravin-prj1-ggshbase/
target/ravin-prj1-ggshbase-1.0-SNAPSHOT.jar
[INFO] -----------------------------------------------------------------------
[INFO] BUILD SUCCESS
[INFO] -----------------------------------------------------------------------
[INFO] Total time: 20.278 s
[INFO] Finished at: 2016-08-03T23:46:15-04:00
[INFO] Final Memory: 14M/168M
[INFO] -----------------------------------------------------------------------
```

Configure the OGG Adapter for HBase

When doing the first-time setup, refer to the sample configuration files that come with the software binaries. Create the hbase.props property file to include the following properties. You can configure parameter values as per your required configuration.

```
[oracle@ravin-ravinpc hbase]$ cat hbase.props
gg.handlerlist=hbase

gg.handler.hbase.type=hbase
gg.handler.hbase.hBaseColumnFamilyName=cf
gg.handler.hbase.keyValueDelimiter=CDATA[=]
gg.handler.hbase.keyValuePairDelimiter=CDATA[,]
gg.handler.hbase.encoding=UTF-8
gg.handler.hbase.pkUpdateHandling=abend
gg.handler.hbase.nullValueRepresentation=CDATA[NULL]
gg.handler.hbase.authType=none
gg.handler.hbase.includeTokens=false

gg.handler.hbase.mode=tx

goldengate.userexit.timestamp=utc
goldengate.userexit.writers=javawriter
javawriter.stats.display=TRUE
javawriter.stats.full=TRUE

gg.log=log4j
gg.log.level=INFO

gg.report.time=30sec

gg.classpath=/app/lib/hbase/lib/*:/app/lib/hbase/conf/:

javawriter.bootoptions=-Xmx512m -Xms32m -Djava.class.path=ggjava/ggjava.jar
```

Make sure your HBase Java adapter has the classpath property gg.classpath configured to include the location of your core-site.xml file. The core-site.xml file located at your HADOOP_HOME/etc/hadoop directory contains the connectivity information used by the adapter.

```
gg.classpath=GG_ROOT_DIRECTORY/AdapterExamples/big-data/hbase/target/hbase-lib/*
```

The wildcard character (*) is to resolve runtime dependencies of the HBase adapter on the client JARs.

Set Up HBase

Assuming that you have already installed Hadoop, let's start the Hadoop instance using the following command. Please refer to the Hadoop documentation if you do not have a Hadoop system available.

```
cd $HADOOP_HOME/sbin

./start-dfs.sh
```

   OR

```
./start-yarn.sh
```

Create the Replicat Process

The sample parameter file for the HBase extract process can be found at /app/ggs/tiger/AdapterExamples/big-data/hbase/dirprm/hbase.prm.

The sample property file for the HBase Java adapter is located at /app/ggs/tiger/AdapterExamples/big-data/hbase/dirprm/hbase.props.

Copy both the files to /app/ggs/tiger/dirprm and customize them as per your configuration. Create a replicat process as follows:

```
GGSCI> add replicat rhbase, exttrail /app/ggs/tiger/dirdat/hd
```

Edit the replicat parameter file to include the following parameters:

```
GGSCI> edit params rhbase

REPLICAT RHBASE
TARGETDB LIBFILE libggjava.so SET property=dirprm/hbase.props
REPORTCOUNT EVERY 1 MINUTES, RATE
GROUPTRANSOPS 10000
MAP TIGER.*, TARGET TIGER.*;
```

Start the OGG Adapter for HBase

Start the Oracle GoldenGate manager and replicat process.

```
GGSCI> START MGR
GGSCI> START RHBASE
GGSCI> INFO ALL
```

Log in to your Big Data system (HDFS) and verify the data.

HBase Adapter Properties

Table 19-4 lists some of the most common HBase adapter properties with their usage.

Table 19-4. HBase Adapter Properties

Property	Usage	Description
javawriter.bootoptions	javawriter.bootoptions=-Xmx512m -Xms32m -Djava.class.path=ggjava/ggjava.jar -Dlog4j.configuration=log4j.properties	Sets boot options. Xms and Xmx set the initial and maximum memory size for the adapter JVM.
gg.handler.name.HBaseColumnFamilyName	gg.handler.name.HBaseColumnFamilyName=cf	Specifies column family names for HBase tables. The default is cf.
gg.handler.name.HBaseAutoFlush	gg.handler.name.HBaseAutoFlush	If set to false, data is flushed to the HBase region server at the end of each transaction. When true, data is flushed at the end of each operation.
gg.handler.name.mode	gg.handler.name.mode	Operating mode can be op or tx. If you are grouping your transaction for performance improvement, this should be set to tx.
gg.handler.name.type	gg.handler.name.type=com.goldengate.delivery.handler.hdfs.HDFSHandler	This property is mandatory for your HDFS adapter.
gg.handler.name.fieldDelimiter	gg.handler.name.fieldDelimiter=,	Specifies the field delimiter character. Use , or ; or Unicode format for nonprintable characters. The default delimiter is \u0001.
gg.handler.name.lineDelimiter	gg.handler.name.lineDelimiter=\n	Specifies line delimiter. The default is \n.
gg.handler.name.rootdirectoryPath	gg.handler.name.rootdirectoryPath=/app/hive	The root directory in HDFS where directories and files will be created.
gg.handler.name.deleteOpKey	gg.handler.name.deleteOpKey=D	Specifies the key that will represent DELETE operations in a DSV file. The default is D.
gg.handler.name.updateOpKey	gg.handler.name.updateOpKey=U	Specifies the key that will represent UPDATE operations in the DSV file. The default is U.
gg.handler.name.insertOpKey	gg.handler.name.insertOpKey=I	Specifies the key that will represent INSERT operations in the DSV file. The default is I.
gg.handler.name.pKUpdateOpKey	gg.handler.name.pKUpdateOpKey=P	Specifies the key that will represent UPDATE operations on the primary key in the DSV file. The default is P.
gg.handler.name.includeOpType	gg.handler.name.includeOpType=true	Specifies if the operation type is to be included in the DSV. The default is true.

(continued)

Table 19-4. (*continued*)

Property	Usage	Description
gg.handler.name. includeOpTimestamp	gg.handler.name. includeOpTimestamp=true	Specifies if the operation timestamp is to be included in the DSV file. The default is true.
gg.handler.name.maxFileSize	gg.handler.name. maxFileSize=2g	Specifies the maximum file size created in HDFS. The default is 1g. Use k, m, or g to represent KB, MB, and GB, respectively.
gg.handler.name.mode	gg.handler.name.mode=tx	Operating mode can be op or tx. If you are grouping your transaction for performance improvement, this should be set to tx.
gg.handler.name.maxGroupSize	gg.handler.name. maxGroupSize=10000	Specifies the maximum number of operations that can be held by an operation group irrespective of the operations belonging to single or multiple transactions. As soon as the operations reach this threshold, the operation group will send transaction commit. This eventually leads to the splitting of transactions across multiple operation groups.
gg.handler.name.minGroupSize	gg.handler.name. minGroupSize=10	Specifies the minimum number of operations that should exist within a group before it can end. This eventually leads to clubbing multiple small transactions into a single group.

Similarly, you can create and configure the OGG adapter for Kafka using the sample files present at /app/ggs/tiger/AdapterExamples/big-data/kafka/.

Summary

In this chapter, you explored how to integrate relational database systems with Big Data systems. The chapter discussed how to set up the Oracle GoldenGate replicat or extract process to capture changes into trail files in a specific format, which is read by Java adapters for Big Data systems and streamed into Big Data systems. We discussed specific examples for Apache Flume, Apache HBase, Apache Hive, and HDFS.

So far, we have mostly used Oracle Database for demonstrating real-time replication with Oracle GoldenGate. In the next chapter, we will discuss using Oracle GoldenGate for non-Oracle databases in homogenous as well as heterogeneous configurations.

CHAPTER 20

■ ■ ■

Oracle GoldenGate for Non-Oracle Databases

Oracle GoldenGate is capable of capturing and delivering data between a variety of relational, open systems and legacy databases on major platforms. I listed the supported databases in Chapter 1 of this book. This capability allows you to extract and deliver data from/to existing IT solutions without the extra cost of installing new infrastructure. This is also useful in consolidating data in enterprise systems.

Also, OGG for non-Oracle databases can be used in conjunction with OGG for Oracle databases for heterogeneous replication setups. In this chapter, we will discuss the following heterogeneous replications.

- Sybase to Sybase replication

- Sybase to Oracle replication

- MySQL to MySQL replication

- Oracle to MySQL replication

- DB2 to Oracle replication

- Microsoft SQL Server 2005 to Oracle replication

In this chapter, we will discuss how to configure OGG with the assumption that Oracle GoldenGate is already installed on both the source and target databases. For demonstration purposes, I have two tables, ORDER_DTL and BILLING_INFO, created on the source and the target. You will load some sample data in the source and create the initial load extract and replicat processes to push this data to the target. For demonstration in this chapter, I created GGSUSER as the owner of the tables for the GGSDEMODB database, both on the source and target database servers.

Please refer to Chapter 3 for the pre-installation tasks and for how to set up user permissions and database logging, which are required for OGG replication for specific database environments.

OGG for Sybase to Sybase Replication

Let's start the implementation of using OGG for non-Oracle databases by setting up a homogenous replication between two Sybase ASE databases. This demonstration involves Oracle GoldenGate 12*c* on the Unix/Linux platform.

Assuming you have already installed OGG on both the source and the target, configure the manager port on the two systems and start the manager process as shown here:

```
GGSCI> EDIT PARAMS MGR
```

© Ravinder Gupta 2016

R. Gupta, *Mastering Oracle GoldenGate*, DOI 10.1007/978-1-4842-2301-7_20

```
PORT 7809

GGSCI> START MANAGER
GGSCI> INFO MANAGER
```

Next, configure your source Sybase database to set the secondary truncate points. This prevents Sybase ASE from truncating transaction log records.

```
isql> use ggsdemodb
isql> go
isql> dbcc settrunc ('ltm', 'valid')
isql> go
```

You are also required to add supplemental logging for each table being replicated through Oracle GoldenGate, as shown here:

```
GGSCI> DBLOGIN SOURCEDB ggsdemodb, USERID ggsuser
GGSCI> ADD TRANDATA GGSUSER.ORDER_DTL
GGSCI> ADD TRANDATA GGSUSER.BILLING_INFO
```

Set up the initial load extract on the source system to push the existing data in the tables to the target tables.

```
GGSCI> ADD EXTRACT INITEXT1, SOURCEISTABLE
GGSCI> INFO EXTRACT *, TASKS
GGSCI> EDIT PARAMS INITEXT1

EXTRACT INITEXT1
SOURCEDB ggsdemodb, USERID ggsuser, PASSWORD ggsuser4u
RMTHOST node2-ravinpc, MGRPORT 7809
RMTTASK REPLICAT, GROUP INITREP1
TABLE GGSUSER.ORDER_DTL;
TABLE GGSUSER.BILLING_INFO;
```

Add the corresponding initial load replicat process on the target Sybase server, as shown here:

```
GGSCI> ADD REPLICAT INITREP1, SPECIALRUN

GGSCI> INFO REPLICAT *, TASKS

GGSCI> EDIT PARAMS INITREP1
REPLICAT INITREP1
TARGETDB ggsdemodb, USERID ggsuser, PASSWORD ggsuser4u
ASSUMETARGETDEFS
DISCARDFILE ./dirrpt/INITREP1.dsc, PURGE
MAP GGSUSER.ORDER_DTL, TARGET GGSUSER.ORDER_DTL;
MAP GGSUSER.BILLING_INFO, TARGET GGSUSER.BILLING_INFO;
```

Before you can begin your initial load process, set up the regular extract and replicat processes as well. This will allow you to immediately start the extract and replicat processes as soon as the initial load is complete.

Add extract ESYB0001 and configure the parameter file as shown here:

```
GGSCI> ADD EXTRACT ESYB0001, TRANLOG, BEGIN NOW
GGSCI> INFO EXTRACT ESYB0001
GGSCI> EDIT PARAM ESYB0001

EXTRACT ESYB0001
SOURCEDB ggsdemodb, USERID ggsuser, PASSWORD ggsuser4u
RMTHOST node2-ravinpc, MGRPORT 7809
RMTTRAIL ./dirdat/e1
TABLE GGSUSER.ORDER_DTL;
TABLE GGSUSER.BILLING_INFO;
GGSCI> VIEW PARAMS ESYB0001
GGSCI> ADD RMTTRAIL ./dirdat/r1, EXTRACT ESYB0001, MEGABYTES 5
GGSCI> INFO RMTTRAIL *
```

Add the checkpoint table on the target Sybase server as shown here:

```
GGSCI> EDIT PARAMS ./GLOBALS
CHECKPOINTTABLE GGSUSER.GGSCHKPT

GGSCI> DBLOGIN SOURCEDB ggsdemodb, USERID ggsuser, PASSWORD ggsuser4u
GGSCI> ADD CHECKPOINTTABLE
```

Next, add the replicat RSYB0001 and configure its parameter file as shown here:

```
GGSCI> ADD REPLICAT RSYB0001, EXTTRAIL ./dirdat/r1
GGSCI> EDIT PARAM RSYB0001

REPLICAT RSYB0001
TARGETDB ggsdemodb, USERID ggsuser, PASSWORD ggsuser4u
HANDLECOLLISIONS
ASSUMETARGETDEFS
DISCARDFILE ./dirrpt/RSYB0001.dsc, PURGE
MAP GGSUSER.ORDER_DTL, TARGET GGSUSER.ORDER_DTL;
MAP GGSUSER.BILLING_INFO, TARGET GGSUSER.BILLING_INFO;
```

Start your initial load extract process and monitor the transaction statistics on the initial load extract.

```
GGSCI> START INITEXT1
```

Please note that I have not started INITREP1. The initial load replicat process must not be started explicitly. View the INITREP1 report file for the processing status and errors, if any.

```
GGSCI> VIEW INITREP1
```

Once the initial load is complete, you can start the regular extract and replicat processes and stop the initial load process.

```
GGSCI> START EXTRACT ESYB0001
GGSCI> INFO EXTRACT ESYB0001, DETAIL
GGSCI> VIEW REPORT ESYB0001
```

Start the replicat process as shown here:

```
GGSCI> START REPLICAT RSYB0001
GGSCI> INFO REPLICAT RSYB0001
```

Transactions on the source will now start showing up on the target. Once the replicat process has processed the pending trails, remove the HANDLECOLLISIONS parameter from the replicat parameter file.

OGG for Sybase to Oracle Replication

You can synchronize a Sybase source database on the Unix/Linux server with an Oracle target database using Oracle GoldenGate for Sybase and Oracle GoldenGate for Oracle, respectively. Assuming you have already installed OGG on both the source and the target, configure the manager port on the two systems and start the manager process as shown here:

```
GGSCI> EDIT PARAMS MGR
PORT 7810

GGSCI> START MANAGER
GGSCI> INFO MANAGER
```

Next, configure your source Sybase database to set the secondary truncate points. This prevents Sybase ASE from truncating transaction log records.

```
isql> use ggsdemodb
isql> go
isql> dbcc settrunc ('ltm', 'valid')
isql> go
```

You also need to add supplemental logging for each table being replicated through Oracle GoldenGate, as shown here:

```
GGSCI> DBLOGIN SOURCEDB ggsdemodb, USERID ggsuser
GGSCI> ADD TRANDATA GGSUSER.ORDER_DTL
GGSCI> ADD TRANDATA GGSUSER.BILLING_INFO
```

Set up the initial load extract on the source system to push the existing data in the tables to the target tables.

```
GGSCI> ADD EXTRACT INITEXT1, SOURCEISTABLE
GGSCI> INFO EXTRACT *, TASKS
GGSCI> EDIT PARAMS INITEXT1

EXTRACT INITEXT1
SOURCEDB ggsdemodb, USERID ggsuser, PASSWORD ggsuser4u
RMTHOST node2-ravinpc, MGRPORT 7810
RMTTASK REPLICAT, GROUP INITREP1
TABLE GGSUSER.ORDER_DTL;
TABLE GGSUSER.BILLING_INFO;
```

Since you are configuring replication in a heterogeneous environment, you need a definition file on the target to be used by the replicat process. Generate a definition file for the tables in the extract process INITTEXT1 as shown here:

```
GGSCI> edit params temp.prm

DEFSFILE dirdef/ext1.def, PURGE
SOURCEDB ggsdemodb, USERID ggsuser, PASSWORD ggsuser4u
TABLE GGSUSER.ORDER_DTL;
TABLE GGSUSER.BILLING_INFO;
```

Run the defgen utility from your GG_HOME.

```
defgen paramfile dirprm/temp.prm
```

The definition file ext1.def will be generated in the dirdef directory. Copy this definition file in the target's GG_HOME/dirdef directory.

Add the corresponding initial load replicat as shown here:

```
GGSCI> ADD REPLICAT INITREP1, SPECIALRUN
GGSCI> INFO REPLICAT *, TASKS
GGSCI> EDIT PARAMS INITREP1

REPLICAT INITREP1
USERID ggsuser, PASSWORD ggsuser4u
SOURCEDEFS ./dirdef/ext1.def
DISCARDFILE ./dirrpt/INITREP1.dsc, PURGE
MAP GGSUSER.ORDER_DTL, TARGET GGSUSER.ORDER_DTL;
MAP GGSUSER.BILLING_INFO, TARGET GGSUSER.BILLING_INFO;
```

Before you can begin your initial load process, set up the regular extract and replicat processes as well. This will allow you to immediately start the extract and replicat processes as soon as the initial load is complete.

```
GGSCI> ADD EXTRACT ESYB0001, TRANLOG, BEGIN NOW
GGSCI> INFO EXTRACT ESYB0001
GGSCI> EDIT PARAM ESYB0001

EXTRACT ESYB0001
SOURCEDB ggsdemodb, USERID ggsuser, PASSWORD ggsuser4u
RMTHOST node2-ravinpc, MGRPORT 7810
RMTTRAIL ./dirdat/e1
TABLE GGSUSER.ORDER_DTL;
TABLE GGSUSER.BILLING_INFO;
GGSCI> VIEW PARAMS ESYB0001
GGSCI> ADD RMTTRAIL ./dirdat/r1, EXTRACT ESYB0001, MEGABYTES 5
GGSCI> INFO RMTTRAIL *
```

Add the checkpoint table as follows for recovery:

```
GGSCI> EDIT PARAMS ./GLOBALS
CHECKPOINTTABLE GGSUSER.GGSCHKPT

GGSCI> DBLOGIN USERID ggsuser, PASSWORD ggsuser4u
GGSCI> ADD CHECKPOINTTABLE
```

Next, add the corresponding replicat process on your Oracle database server as shown here:

```
GGSCI> ADD REPLICAT RORA0001, EXTTRAIL ./dirdat/r1
GGSCI> EDIT PARAM RORA0001

REPLICAT RORA0001
USERID ggsuser, PASSWORD ggsuser4u
HANDLECOLLISIONS
SOURCEDEFS ./dirdef/ext1.def
DISCARDFILE ./dirrpt/RORA0001.dsc, PURGE
MAP GGSUSER.ORDER_DTL, TARGET GGSUSER.ORDER_DTL;
MAP GGSUSER.BILLING_INFO, TARGET GGSUSER.BILLING_INFO;
```

Start your initial load extract process and monitor the transaction statistics on the initial load extract.

```
GGSCI> START INITEXT1
```

View the INITREP1 report file for processing the status and errors, if any.

```
GGSCI> VIEW INITREP1
```

Once the initial load is complete, you can start the regular extract and replicat processes and stop the initial load process.

```
GGSCI> START EXTRACT ESYB0001
GGSCI> INFO EXTRACT ESYB0001, DETAIL
GGSCI> VIEW REPORT ESYB0001
```

Start the replicat process as shown here:

```
GGSCI> START REPLICAT RORA0001
GGSCI> INFO REPLICAT RORA0001
```

Transactions on the source will now start showing up on the target. Once the replicat process has processed the pending trails, remove the HANDLECOLLISIONS parameter from the replicat parameter file.

OGG for MySQL to MySQL Replication

Let's now see an example to synchronize two MySQL databases on a Unix/Linux server using Oracle GoldenGate for MySQL. Install Oracle GoldenGate for MySQL on both databases. Configure the manager port with an available port as shown here and start the manager process:

```
GGSCI> EDIT PARAMS MGR
```

```
PORT 7811

GGSCI> START MANAGER
GGSCI> INFO MANAGER
```

Next, configure your source MySQL database server to set the secondary truncate points. This prevents MySQL from truncating transaction log records and retains it to be used for replication.

```
isql> use ggsdemodb
isql> go
isql> dbcc settrunc ('ltm', 'valid')
isql> go
```

You also need to add supplemental logging for each table being replicated through Oracle GoldenGate, as shown here:

```
GGSCI> DBLOGIN SOURCEDB ggsdemodb, USERID ggsuser
GGSCI> ADD TRANDATA GGSUSER.ORDER_DTL
GGSCI> ADD TRANDATA GGSUSER.BILLING_INFO
```

Set up the initial load extract on the source system to push the existing data in the tables to the target tables.

```
GGSCI> ADD EXTRACT INITEXT1, SOURCEISTABLE
GGSCI> INFO EXTRACT *, TASKS
GGSCI> EDIT PARAMS INITEXT11

EXTRACT INITEXT1
DBOPTIONS HOST node2-ravinpc, CONNECTIONPORT 3306
SOURCEDB ggsdemodb, USERID ggsuser, PASSWORD ggsuser4u
RMTHOST node2-ravinpc, MGRPORT 7811
RMTTASK REPLICAT, GROUP INITREP1
TABLE GGSUSER.ORDER_DTL;
TABLE GGSUSER.BILLING_INFO;
```

Add the corresponding initial load replicat process on the target MySQL database server.

```
GGSCI> ADD REPLICAT INITREP1, SPECIALRUN
GGSCI> INFO REPLICAT *, TASKS
GGSCI> EDIT PARAMS INITREP1

REPLICAT INITREP1
DBOPTIONS HOST node2-ravinpc, CONNECTIONPORT 3306
TARGETDB ggsdemodb, USERID ggsuser, PASSWORD ggsuser4u
HANDLECOLLISIONS
ASSUMETARGETDEFS
DISCARDFILE ./dirrpt/INITREP1.dsc, PURGE
MAP GGSUSER.ORDER_DTL, TARGET GGSUSER.ORDER_DTL;
MAP GGSUSER.BILLING_INFO, TARGET GGSUSER.BILLING_INFO;
```

Before you can begin your initial load process, set up the regular extract and replicat processes as well. This will allow you to immediately start the extract and replicat processes as soon as the initial load is complete.

Add the extract process as follows:

```
GGSCI> ADD EXTRACT EMYS0001, TRANLOG, BEGIN NOW
GGSCI> INFO EXTRACT EMYS0001
GGSCI> EDIT PARAM EMYS0001

EXTRACT INITEXT1
DBOPTIONS HOST node2-ravinpc, CONNECTIONPORT 3306
SOURCEDB ggsdemodb, USERID ggsuser, PASSWORD ggsuser4u
RMTHOST node2-ravinpc, MGRPORT 7811
RMTTASK REPLICAT, GROUP INITREP1
TABLE GGSUSER.ORDER_DTL;
TABLE GGSUSER.BILLING_INFO;

GGSCI> ADD RMTTRAIL ./dirdat/e1, EXTRACT EMYS0001, MEGABYTES 5
```

Add the checkpoint table for recovery on the target server as shown here:

```
GGSCI> EDIT PARAMS ./GLOBALS
CHECKPOINTTABLE GGSUSER.GGSCHKPT

GGSCI> DBLOGIN SOURCEDB ggsdemodb, USERID ggsuser, PASSWORD ggsuser4u
GGSCI> ADD CHECKPOINTTABLE
```

Add the corresponding replicat process on the target MySQL database server:

```
GGSCI> ADD REPLICAT RMYS0001, EXTTRAIL ./dirdat/e1


GGSCI> EDIT PARAM RMYS0001
REPLICAT INITREP1
DBOPTIONS HOST node2-ravinpc, CONNECTIONPORT 3306
TARGETDB ggsdemodb, USERID ggsuser, PASSWORD ggsuser4u
HANDLECOLLISIONS
ASSUMETARGETDEFS
DISCARDFILE ./dirrpt/INITREP1.dsc, PURGE
MAP GGSUSER.ORDER_DTL, TARGET GGSUSER.ORDER_DTL;
MAP GGSUSER.BILLING_INFO, TARGET GGSUSER.BILLING_INFO;
```

Start your initial load extract process and monitor the transaction statistics on the initial load extract.

```
GGSCI> START INITEXT1
```

View the INITREP1 report file for processing the status and errors, if any.

```
GGSCI> VIEW INITREP1
```

Once the initial load is complete, you can start the regular extract and replicat processes and stop the initial load process.

```
GGSCI> START EXTRACT EMYS0001
```

```
GGSCI> INFO EXTRACT EMYSOOO1, DETAIL
GGSCI> VIEW REPORT EMYSOOO1
```

Start the replicat process.

```
GGSCI> START REPLICAT RMYSOOO1
GGSCI> INFO REPLICAT RMYSOOO1
```

Transactions on the source will now start showing up on the target. Once the replicat process has processed the pending trails, remove the HANDLECOLLISIONS parameter from the replicat parameter file.

OGG for Oracle to MySQL Replication

You have now observed that configuring the Oracle GoldenGate extract and replicat processes on different databases is similar except a few minor differences. Let's now configure real-time synchronization between an Oracle source database and the MySQL target database on the Unix/Linux server using Oracle GoldenGate for Oracle and MySQL, respectively. Configure the manager port with an available port as shown here and start the manager process:

```
GGSCI> EDIT PARAMS MGR
PORT 7812

GGSCI> START MANAGER
GGSCI> INFO MANAGER
```

Log in to the Oracle database at the source and verify whether supplemental logging is already enabled.

```
SELECT supplemental_log_data_min, force_logging FROM v$database;
```

If both of these are already YES, your database is already configured for the logging needed by Oracle GoldenGate. Setting up force logging is optional; you can set supplemental minimal logging and add table/schema-level supplemental logging only from GGSCI. This is especially recommended when only a few tables/schema are to be replicated. It will in turn reduce logging overhead for the entire database. If you have already enabled supplemental logging before the OGG installation, you can skip this step.

Enable minimal supplemental logging at the database level.

```
SQL> ALTER DATABASE ADD SUPPLEMENTAL LOG DATA;
```

Optionally, you can enable force logging for the entire database.

```
SQL> ALTER DATABASE FORCE LOGGING;
```

After changing the logging option, either FORCE logging or MINIMAL SUPPLEMENTAL LOGGING, you must switch the log file.

```
SQL> ALTER SYSTEM SWITCH LOGFILE;
```

Enable GoldenGate replication.

```
SQL> ALTER SYSTEM SET ENABLE_GOLDENGATE_REPLICATION=TRUE;
```

You also need to add supplemental logging for each table being replicated through Oracle GoldenGate, as shown here:

```
GGSCI> DBLOGIN USERID ggsuser, PASSWORD ggsuser4u
GGSCI> ADD TRANDATA GGSUSER.ORDER_DTL
GGSCI> ADD TRANDATA GGSUSER.BILLING_INFO
```

Set up the initial load extract on the source system to push the existing data in the tables to the target tables.

```
GGSCI> ADD EXTRACT INITEXT1, SOURCEISTABLE
GGSCI> INFO EXTRACT *, TASKS
GGSCI> EDIT PARAMS INITEXT11

EXTRACT INITEXT1
USERID ggsuser, PASSWORD ggsuser4u
RMTHOST node2-ravinpc, MGRPORT 7812
RMTTASK REPLICAT, GROUP INITREP1
TABLE GGSUSER.ORDER_DTL;
TABLE GGSUSER.BILLING_INFO;
```

Add the corresponding initial load replicat process on the target MySQL database server.

```
GGSCI> ADD REPLICAT INITREP1, SPECIALRUN
GGSCI> INFO REPLICAT *, TASKS
GGSCI> EDIT PARAMS INITREP1

REPLICAT INITREP1
DBOPTIONS HOST node2-ravinpc, CONNECTIONPORT 3306
TARGETDB ggsdemodb, USERID ggsuser, PASSWORD ggsuser4u
HANDLECOLLISIONS
ASSUMETARGETDEFS
DISCARDFILE ./dirrpt/INITREP1.dsc, PURGE
MAP GGSUSER.ORDER_DTL, TARGET GGSUSER.ORDER_DTL;
MAP GGSUSER.BILLING_INFO, TARGET GGSUSER.BILLING_INFO;
```

Before you can begin your initial load process, set up the regular extract and replicat processes as well. This will allow you to immediately start the extract and replicat processes as soon as the initial load is complete.

Add the extract process as follows:

```
GGSCI> ADD EXTRACT EORA0001, TRANLOG, BEGIN NOW
GGSCI> INFO EXTRACT EORA0001
GGSCI> EDIT PARAM EORA0001

EXTRACT INITEXT1
USERID ggsuser, PASSWORD ggsuser4u
RMTHOST node2-ravinpc, MGRPORT 7812
RMTTASK REPLICAT, GROUP INITREP1
TABLE GGSUSER.ORDER_DTL;
TABLE GGSUSER.BILLING_INFO;

GGSCI> ADD RMTTRAIL ./dirdat/r1, EXTRACT EORA0001, MEGABYTES 5
```

Add the checkpoint table for recovery on the target MySQL database server.

```
GGSCI> EDIT PARAMS ./GLOBALS
CHECKPOINTTABLE GGSUSER.GGSCHKPT

GGSCI> DBLOGIN SOURCEDB ggsdemodb, USERID ggsuser, PASSWORD ggsuser4u
GGSCI> ADD CHECKPOINTTABLE
```

Next, add the replicat process.

```
GGSCI> ADD REPLICAT RMYS0001, EXTTRAIL ./dirdat/r1
GGSCI> EDIT PARAM RMYS0001

REPLICAT RMYS0001
DBOPTIONS HOST node2-ravinpc, CONNECTIONPORT 3306
TARGETDB ggsdemodb, USERID ggsuser, PASSWORD ggsuser4u
HANDLECOLLISIONS
ASSUMETARGETDEFS
DISCARDFILE ./dirrpt/INITREP1.dsc, PURGE
MAP GGSUSER.ORDER_DTL, TARGET GGSUSER.ORDER_DTL;
MAP GGSUSER.BILLING_INFO, TARGET GGSUSER.BILLING_INFO;
```

Start your initial load extract process and monitor the transaction statistics on the initial load extract.

```
GGSCI> START INITEXT1
```

View the INITREP1 report file for processing the status and errors, if any.

```
GGSCI> VIEW INITREP1
```

Once the initial load is complete, you can start the regular extract and replicat processes and stop the initial load process.

```
GGSCI> START EXTRACT EORA0001
GGSCI> INFO EXTRACT EORA0001, DETAIL
GGSCI> VIEW REPORT EORA0001
```

Start the replicat process.

```
GGSCI> START REPLICAT RMYS0001
GGSCI> INFO REPLICAT RMYS0001
```

Transactions on the source will now start showing up on the target. Once the replicat process has processed the pending trails, remove the HANDLECOLLISIONS parameter from the replicat parameter file.

OGG for DB2 to Oracle Replication

I will now demonstrate how to configure OGG replication between a DB2 source database on a Unix/Linux server with an Oracle target database using Oracle GoldenGate for DB2 and Oracle GoldenGate for Oracle, respectively.

Configure the manager port with an available port as shown here and start the manager process:

```
GGSCI> EDIT PARAMS MGR
PORT 7813

GGSCI> START MANAGER
GGSCI> INFO MANAGER
```

Add supplemental logging for each table being replicated through the Oracle GoldenGate GGSCI prompt, as shown here:

```
GGSCI> DBLOGIN SOURCEDB ggsdemodb, USERID gguser
GGSCI> ADD TRANDATA GGSUSER.ORDER_DTL
GGSCI> ADD TRANDATA GGSUSER.BILLING_INFO
```

Set up the initial load extract on the source system to push the existing data in the tables to the target tables.

```
GGSCI> ADD EXTRACT INITEXT1, SOURCEISTABLE
GGSCI> INFO EXTRACT *, TASKS
GGSCI> EDIT PARAMS INITEXT1

EXTRACT INITEXT1
SOURCEDB ggsdemodb, USERID ggsuser, PASSWORD ggsuser4u
RMTHOST node2-ravinpc, MGRPORT 7813
RMTTASK REPLICAT, GROUP INITREP1
TABLE GGSUSER.ORDER_DTL;
TABLE GGSUSER.BILLING_INFO;
```

Since you are configuring OGG replication in heterogeneous environment, generate the definition file for the tables in the extract process. This file will be used in the replicat process.

```
GGSCI> edit params temp.prm

DEFSFILE dirdef/ext1.def, PURGE
SOURCEDB ggsdemodb, USERID ggsuser, PASSWORD ggsuser4u
TABLE GGSUSER.ORDER_DTL;
TABLE GGSUSER.BILLING_INFO;
```

Run the `defgen` utility from your `GG_HOME`.

```
defgen paramfile dirprm/temp.prm
```

The definition file `ext1.def` will be generated in the `dirdef` directory. Copy this definition file in the target `GG_HOME/dirdef` directory. This definition file will be needed by the replicat process for heterogeneous replication.

Add the initial load replicat process on the target Oracle database server as shown here:

```
GGSCI> ADD REPLICAT INITREP1, SPECIALRUN
GGSCI> INFO REPLICAT *, TASKS
GGSCI> EDIT PARAMS INITREP1
```

```
REPLICAT INITREP1
USERID ggsuser, PASSWORD ggsuser4u
SOURCEDEFS ./dirdef/ext1.def
DISCARDFILE ./dirrpt/INITREP1.dsc, PURGE
MAP GGSUSER.ORDER_DTL, TARGET GGSUSER.ORDER_DTL;
MAP GGSUSER.BILLING_INFO, TARGET GGSUSER.BILLING_INFO;
```

Before you can begin your initial load process, set up the regular extract and replicat processes as well. This will allow you to immediately start the extract and replicat processes as soon as the initial load is complete.

Add the extract process as follows:

```
GGSCI> ADD EXTRACT EDB20001, TRANLOG, BEGIN NOW
GGSCI> INFO EXTRACT EDB20001
GGSCI> EDIT PARAM EDB20001

EXTRACT EDB20001
SOURCEDB ggsdemodb, USERID ggsuser, PASSWORD ggsuser4u
RMTHOST node2-ravinpc, MGRPORT 7813
RMTTRAIL ./dirdat/d1
TABLE GGSUSER.ORDER_DTL;
TABLE GGSUSER.BILLING_INFO;
GGSCI> ADD RMTTRAIL ./dirdat/e1, EXTRACT EDB20001, MEGABYTES 5
```

Add the checkpoint table for the recovery on the target database server.

```
GGSCI> EDIT PARAMS ./GLOBALS
CHECKPOINTTABLE GGSUSER.GGSCHKPT

GGSCI> DBLOGIN USERID ggsuser, PASSWORD ggsuser4u
GGSCI> ADD CHECKPOINTTABLE
```

Add the corresponding replicat process as shown here:

```
GGSCI> ADD REPLICAT RORA0001, EXTTRAIL ./dirdat/e1

GGSCI> EDIT PARAM RORA0001

REPLICAT RORA0001
USERID ggsuser, PASSWORD ggsuser4u
HANDLECOLLISIONS
SOURCEDEFS ./dirdef/ext1.def
DISCARDFILE ./dirrpt/RORA0001.dsc, PURGE
MAP GGSUSER.ORDER_DTL, TARGET GGSUSER.ORDER_DTL;
MAP GGSUSER.BILLING_INFO, TARGET GGSUSER.BILLING_INFO;
```

Start your initial load extract process and monitor the transaction statistics on the initial load extract.

```
GGSCI> START INITEXT1
```

View the INITREP1 report file for processing the status and errors, if any.

```
GGSCI> VIEW INITREP1
```

Once the initial load is complete, you can start the regular extract and replicat processes and stop the initial load process.

```
GGSCI> START EXTRACT EDB20001
GGSCI> INFO EXTRACT EDB20001, DETAIL
GGSCI> VIEW REPORT EDB20001
```

Start the replicat process.

```
GGSCI> START REPLICAT RORA0001
GGSCI> INFO REPLICAT RORA0001
```

Transactions on the source will now start showing up on target. Once the replicat process has processed the pending trails, remove the HANDLECOLLISIONS parameter from the replicat parameter file.

OGG for MS SQL Server to Oracle Replication

For the last demonstration example for using Oracle GoldenGate for non-Oracle database configurations, we will discuss how to synchronize a Microsoft SQL Server source database on a Unix/Linux server with an Oracle target database using Oracle GoldenGate for Microsoft SQL Server and Oracle GoldenGate for Oracle, respectively.

Configure the manager process and start it.

```
GGSCI> EDIT PARAMS MGR
PORT 7814

GGSCI> START MANAGER
GGSCI> INFO MANAGER
```

Set the log truncation and bulk copy to false on your source Microsoft SQL Server.

```
isql> exec sp_dboption 'ggsdemodb', 'trunc. log on chkpt.', false
isql> GO
isql> exec sp_dboption 'ggsdemodb', ' select into/bulkcopy ', false
isql> GO
```

Add supplemental logging for each table being replicated through the Oracle GoldenGate GGSCI prompt, as shown here:

```
GGSCI> DBLOGIN SOURCEDB ggsdemodb, USERID gguser
GGSCI> ADD TRANDATA GGSUSER.ORDER_DTL
GGSCI> ADD TRANDATA GGSUSER.BILLING_INFO
```

Set up the initial load extract on the source system to push the existing data in the tables to the target tables.

```
GGSCI> ADD EXTRACT INITEXT1, SOURCEISTABLE
GGSCI> INFO EXTRACT *, TASKS
GGSCI> EDIT PARAMS INITEXT1
```

```
EXTRACT INITEXT1
SOURCEDB ggsdemodb, USERID ggsuser, PASSWORD ggsuser4u
RMTHOST node2-ravinpc, MGRPORT 7814
RMTTASK REPLICAT, GROUP INITREP1
TABLE GGSUSER.ORDER_DTL;
TABLE GGSUSER.BILLING_INFO;
```

Since you are configuring OGG replication in a heterogeneous environment, generate the definition file for the tables in the extract process. This file will be used in the replicat process.

```
GGSCI> edit params temp.prm

DEFSFILE dirdef/ext1.def, PURGE
SOURCEDB ggsdemodb, USERID ggsuser, PASSWORD ggsuser4u
TABLE GGSUSER.ORDER_DTL;
TABLE GGSUSER.BILLING_INFO;
```

Run the defgen utility from your GG_HOME.

```
defgen paramfile dirprm/temp.prm
```

The definition file ext1.def will be generated in the dirdef directory. Copy this definition file in the target GG_HOME/dirdef directory. This definition file will be needed by the replicat process for heterogeneous replication.

Add the initial load replicat process on the target Oracle database server as shown here:

```
GGSCI> ADD REPLICAT INITREP1, SPECIALRUN
GGSCI> INFO REPLICAT *, TASKS
GGSCI> EDIT PARAMS INITREP1

REPLICAT INITREP1
USERID ggsuser, PASSWORD ggsuser4u
SOURCEDEFS ./dirdef/ext1.def
DISCARDFILE ./dirrpt/INITREP1.dsc, PURGE
MAP GGSUSER.ORDER_DTL, TARGET GGSUSER.ORDER_DTL;
MAP GGSUSER.BILLING_INFO, TARGET GGSUSER.BILLING_INFO;
```

Before you can begin your initial load process, set up the regular extract and replicat processes as well. This will allow you to immediately start the extract and replicat processes as soon as the initial load is complete.

Add the extract process as follows:

```
GGSCI> ADD EXTRACT EMSQ0001, TRANLOG, BEGIN NOW
GGSCI> INFO EXTRACT EMSQ0001
GGSCI> EDIT PARAM EMSQ0001

EXTRACT EMSQ0001
SOURCEDB ggsdemodb, USERID ggsuser, PASSWORD ggsuser4u
RMTHOST node2-ravinpc, MGRPORT 7814
RMTTRAIL ./dirdat/d1
TABLE GGSUSER.ORDER_DTL;
TABLE GGSUSER.BILLING_INFO;
GGSCI> ADD RMTTRAIL ./dirdat/e1, EXTRACT EMSQ0001, MEGABYTES 5
```

505

Add the checkpoint table for recovery on the target database as shown here:

```
GGSCI> EDIT PARAMS ./GLOBALS
CHECKPOINTTABLE GGSUSER.GGSCHKPT

GGSCI> DBLOGIN USERID ggsuser, PASSWORD ggsuser4u
GGSCI> ADD CHECKPOINTTABLE
```

Next add the replicat process.

```
GGSCI> ADD REPLICAT RORA0001, EXTTRAIL ./dirdat/e1
GGSCI> EDIT PARAM RORA0001

REPLICAT RORA0001
USERID ggsuser, PASSWORD ggsuser4u
HANDLECOLLISIONS
ASSUMETARGETDEFS
DISCARDFILE ./dirrpt/RORA0001.dsc, PURGE
MAP GGSUSER.ORDER_DTL, TARGET GGSUSER.ORDER_DTL;
MAP GGSUSER.BILLING_INFO, TARGET GGSUSER.BILLING_INFO;
```

Start your initial load extract process and monitor transaction statistics on the initial load extract.

```
GGSCI> START INITEXT1
```

View the INITREP1 report file for processing the status and errors, if any.

```
GGSCI> VIEW INITREP1
```

Once the initial load is complete, you can start the regular extract and replicat processes and stop the initial load process.

```
GGSCI> START EXTRACT EMSQ0001
GGSCI> INFO EXTRACT EMSQ0001, DETAIL
GGSCI> VIEW REPORT EMSQ0001
```

Start the replicat process.

```
GGSCI> START REPLICAT RORA0001
GGSCI> INFO REPLICAT RORA0001
```

Transactions on the source will now start showing up on the target. Once the replicat process has processed the pending trails, remove the HANDLECOLLISIONS parameter from the replicat parameter file.

Summary

The chapter demonstrated how to set up the Oracle GoldenGate extract and replicat processes for Oracle and non-Oracle databases in homogenous and heterogeneous configurations. We discussed how to configure Oracle GoldenGate replication for Sybase ASE, IBM DB2, MySQL, and Microsoft SQL Server.

In the next chapter, we will explore Oracle GoldenGate integration for cloud applications.

CHAPTER 21

■ ■ ■

Oracle GoldenGate for the Cloud

Organizations are increasingly moving toward public cloud computing while at the same time maintaining private clouds (on-premise enterprise systems). If you have applications running on the cloud and you need to connect them to your on-premise systems, you certainly need to keep the data fresh between the two. The challenge posed for doing so is to bulk-load data into the public cloud system and keep it synchronized with the private cloud.

Oracle offers Oracle Data Integrator and Oracle GoldenGate for bulk-loading your enterprise data to the public cloud and keeping it synchronized in real time. This is useful in the initial consolidation of data to the public cloud without interrupting operations. Oracle GoldenGate is SOCKS5 compliant, which is important for replicating the data to and from a cloud database.

The service offering by Oracle GoldenGate for data integration and replication to the cloud is called Oracle GoldenGate Cloud Service (GGCS).

GGCS comes with Oracle Database as a Service (DBaaS) as the cloud database. The on-premise databases supported by GGCS are Oracle Database and MySQL.

GGCS enables you to achieve the following goals:

- You can achieve real-time replication from the on-premise system to the database cloud.

- Since GGCS comes as an Oracle DBaaS, it captures and stores data into the GGCS service trail files and delivers the data to GoldenGate service instances on the target systems.

- You manage and administer GGCS through a centralized web-based portal.

- It supports one-to-one replication between an on-premise system to the cloud and from the cloud to on-premise systems.

- It can also support the bidirectional replication of cloud data into the cloud. However, please note that the CDR capability is currently not supported for bidirectional replication within the cloud.

GGCS Architecture

Oracle GoldenGate Cloud Service is part of the Oracle Public Cloud (OPC). Figures 21-1 to 21-3 show the components and configuration of Oracle GoldenGate Cloud Service. We will discuss these components and how to configure replication in the following sections of this chapter. Figure 21-1 shows how to configure Oracle GoldenGate Cloud Service for an on-premise to cloud replication.

© Ravinder Gupta 2016
R. Gupta, *Mastering Oracle GoldenGate*, DOI 10.1007/978-1-4842-2301-7_21

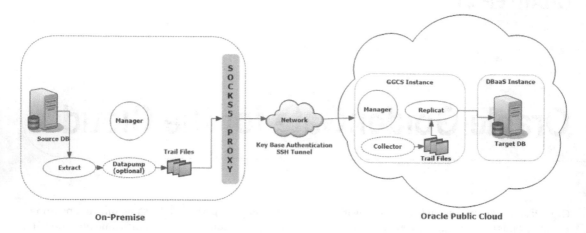

Figure 21-1. *On-premise to cloud replication using Oracle GoldenGate*

Figure 21-2 shows replication within two cloud GGCS instances.

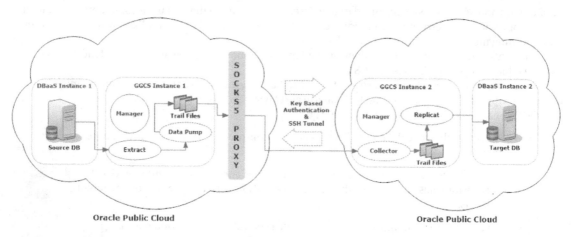

Figure 21-2. *Cloud to cloud replication using Oracle GoldenGate*

Figure 21-3 shows the configuration for a cloud to on-premise replication.

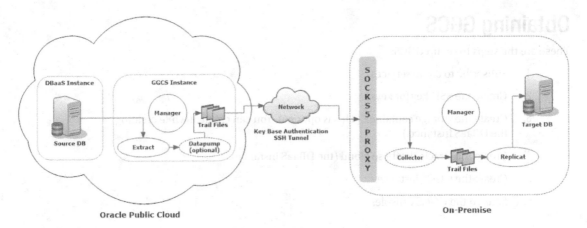

Figure 21-3. Cloud to on-premise replication using Oracle GoldenGate

Components of GGCS

Oracle's GoldenGate Cloud Service has six main components.

- My Account
- My Services
- The GGCS console
- The Oracle database cloud
- The Oracle storage cloud
- The Oracle compute cloud

Let's discuss each of these components briefly.

- *My Account*: You will use My Account to request Oracle GoldenGate cloud services. You can place new orders and request cloud services.

- *My Services*: This is used for administration purposes for your cloud services. It lets you access all of your cloud services and manage them as per your need.

- *The GGCS console*: The web console lets you create service instances and manage them.

- *The Oracle database cloud*: Each GGCS service instance that you create using the GGCS console must have an associated Oracle DBaaS instance. GGCS instances identify a running DBaaS instance for delivering cloud data to the target.

- *The Oracle storage cloud*: This is used for backing up and recovering your Oracle DBaaS instances.

- *The Oracle compute cloud*: GGCS is built on top of the Oracle compute cloud, and GGCS instances are hosted on Oracle compute virtual machines.

Obtaining GGCS

These are the steps to set up GGCS:

1. Subscribe to cloud services.

2. Create the SSH key (or keys).

3. Create the storage container. (This is optional. You can create it while creating the DBaaS instance.)

4. Create the Oracle database cloud (the DBaaS instance).

5. Create the GGCS instance.

6. Launch the GGCS console.

Create the Oracle Cloud Account

Since GGCS works through a centralized web console and is associated with the Oracle public cloud, the first step to obtain GGCS is to create your account in the Oracle cloud.

You can sign in to your existing Oracle account. Navigate to http://cloud.oracle.com.

Click the Free Trial button at the top-right corner. This will take you to the list of cloud services where you can register for a free trial, as shown in Figure 21-4.

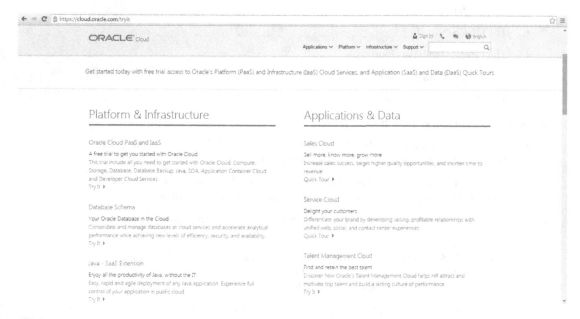

Figure 21-4. *Cloud services available for free trial*

For setting up Oracle GoldenGate Cloud Service, subscribe to the following three services:

- *Oracle Database Cloud Service*: The service creates the database instance to host the replicated data.

- *Oracle Storage Cloud Service*: The service is required for the backup and recovery of replicated data and transactions.

- *Oracle GoldenGate Cloud Service*: The service is required for OGG data replication.

I selected Oracle Database Cloud Service from the list. On the next page, click Start Trial for Database as a Service, as shown in Figure 21-5.

Figure 21-5. *Oracle Database Cloud Service free trial registration*

Once you click Start Trial, you are taken to an online form for a trial subscription, as shown in Figure 21-6.

Figure 21-6. *Trial subscription online form*

Complete the online form and submit it. It will give confirmation of your order for Oracle Public Cloud Services, as shown in Figure 21-7.

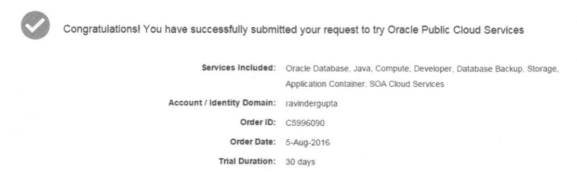

Figure 21-7. *Order confirmation for Oracle Public Cloud Services*

You will receive an e-mail once your request is approved. This may take from a few hours to up to a week. It is suggested that you use your company e-mail while registering for Oracle Public Cloud Services. You can also navigate to the following link for instructions on the trial setup process:

`www.oracle.com/webfolder/technetwork/tutorials/infographics/dbcs_trial_quickview/index.html#`

Once your request is approved, navigate to `http://cloud.oracle.com` and log in with the credentials you received in the e-mail. The e-mail provides you the subscription details and a link to the administrator accounts for My Account and My Services, as follows:

- *My Account Administration*: Sign in to My Account to manage your trials and all your Oracle cloud services.

  My Account URL: `https://myaccount.cloud.oracle.com/mycloud/faces/dashboard.jspx`

  Username: Use your Oracle account username.

  Password: Use your Oracle account password.

- *My Services Administration*: Sign in to My Services to monitor this trial environment, including usage data and status.

  My Services URL: `https://myservices.us.oraclecloud.com/mycloud/ravinderg/faces/dashboard.jspx`

  Identity Domain: ravinderg

Figure 21-8 shows my trial subscriptions in My Account.

Figure 21-8. *Subscription details*

Scroll down to locate the subscription information that you require for setting up GGCS, as shown in Figure 21-9.

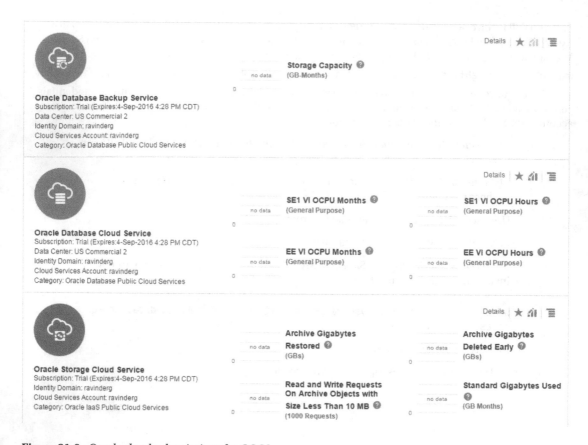

Figure 21-9. *Oracle cloud subscriptions for GGCS*

Similarly, subscribe to the other two services required for GGCS instance setup. Please note Oracle GoldenGate Cloud Service is not available for free trial download, so you need to pay for a subscription as per the pricing shown on the Oracle cloud web site. Figure 21-10 shows the latest pricing information for GGCS while I was setting up this demonstration. Please notice there is no Try It button for this service to subscribe to a trial. You need to contact the Oracle Sales Team to request trials for services not listed on https://cloud.oracle.com/tryit.

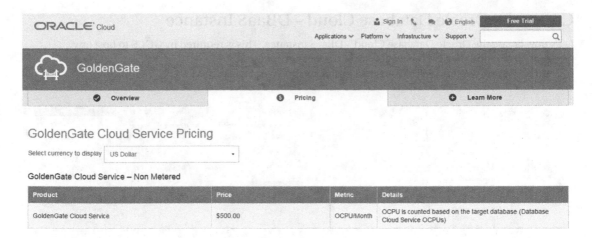

Figure 21-10. *GGCS pricing information*

Create an SSH Key Pair

Open a shell prompt on your machine and execute the following command:

```
ssh-keygen -t rsa -N "some_passphrase" -b "2048" -C "ggcs key 1" -f path/root_name
```

The command instructs you to create an SSH key pair using the RSA algorithm and the passphrase some_passphrase to add an extra level of security when using the SSH key. You can keep it blank if you do not want to set a passphrase. The command instructs you to create a 2,048-bit key (the default key size). The enclose comment ggcs key 1 helps you name your key. Substitute a value of path/root_name with the location of where you want to save your SSH key and the name of your private key.

I executed the following command to create my SSH key pair:

```
[oracle@ravin-ravinpc key]$ ssh-keygen -t rsa -N "" -b "2048" -C "ggcs key 1" -f /app/key/
id_rsa
Generating public/private rsa key pair.
Your identification has been saved in /app/key/id_rsa.
Your public key has been saved in /app/key/id_rsa.pub.
The key fingerprint is:
01:24:b2:8e:42:c7:70:0f:c6:ee:81:05:82:6f:e5:4b ggcs key 1
The key's randomart image is:
+--[ RSA 2048]----+
|oo++..o          |
|o ==+. .          |
| o== .  .         |
|.++oE     .       |
|o.o… S            |
|. . ..            |
|                  |
|                  |
|                  |
+-----------------+
```

This creates two files, id_rsa and id_rsa.pub, in the /app/key directory. You will use these key files for the SOCKS5 proxy and key-based authentication between your on-premise to GGCS cloud.

Create the Oracle Database Cloud – DBaaS Instance

Let's now create the Oracle Database Cloud – DBaaS instance. This is required by GGCS to host any on-premise or cloud data for replication to another cloud instance.

Go to My Services and select your data center, as shown in Figure 21-11.

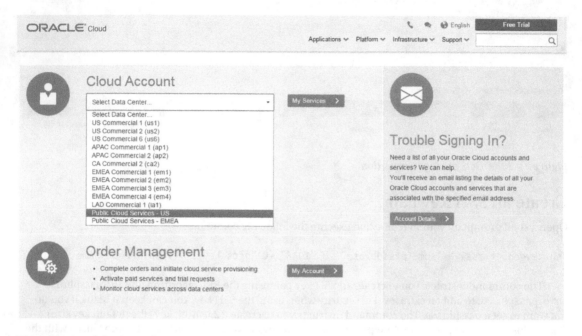

Figure 21-11. *Selecting a data center*

Provide your identity domain for My Services, as shown in Figure 21-12.

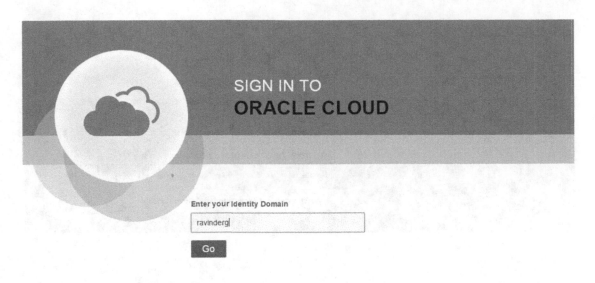

Figure 21-12. *Entering your identity domain*

The next page may ask you to change your password and set your security questions, if you haven't done so already. Figure 21-13 shows the My Services Dashboard.

Figure 21-13. *My Services Dashboard*

Click the menu icon for Database and click Open Service Console. This will launch the welcome page, as shown in Figure 21-14, where you need to click the Go to Console button to launch the service console.

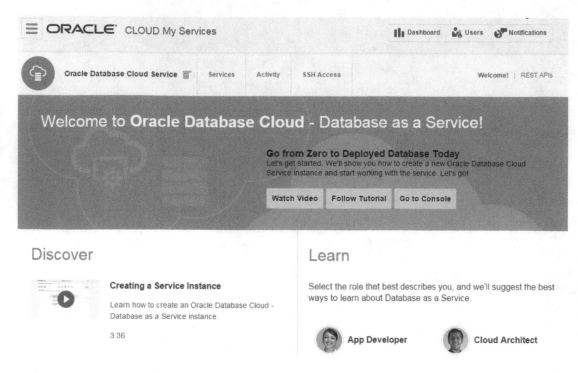

Figure 21-14. *Oracle Database Cloud – DBaaS welcome page*

On the Services console, click the Create Service button to create a new Oracle Database Cloud – DBaaS instance, as shown in Figure 21-15.

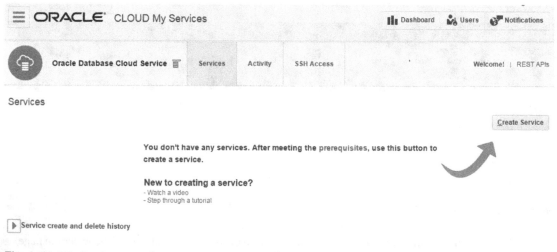

Figure 21-15. *Services console*

Select the subscription type, as shown in Figure 21-16.

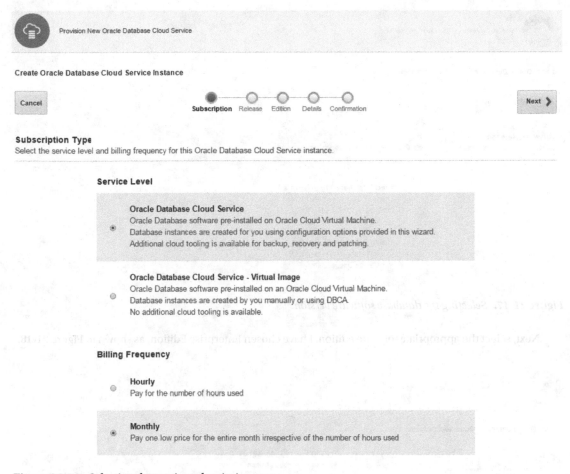

Figure 21-16. *Selecting the service subscription type*

Select the database version that you want to be installed on the instance you are creating. I have chosen to install Oracle Database 12*c,* as shown in Figure 21-17.

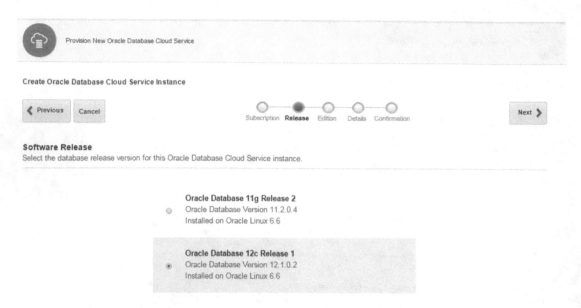

Figure 21-17. *Selecting the database software version*

Next, select the appropriate software edition. I have chosen Enterprise Edition, as shown in Figure 21-18.

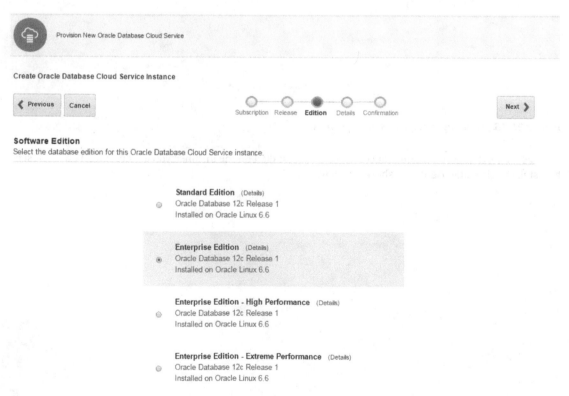

Figure 21-18. *Selecting the software edition*

Next, configure your DBaaS instance. Provide the service name, description, shape, and time zone, as shown in Figure 21-19.

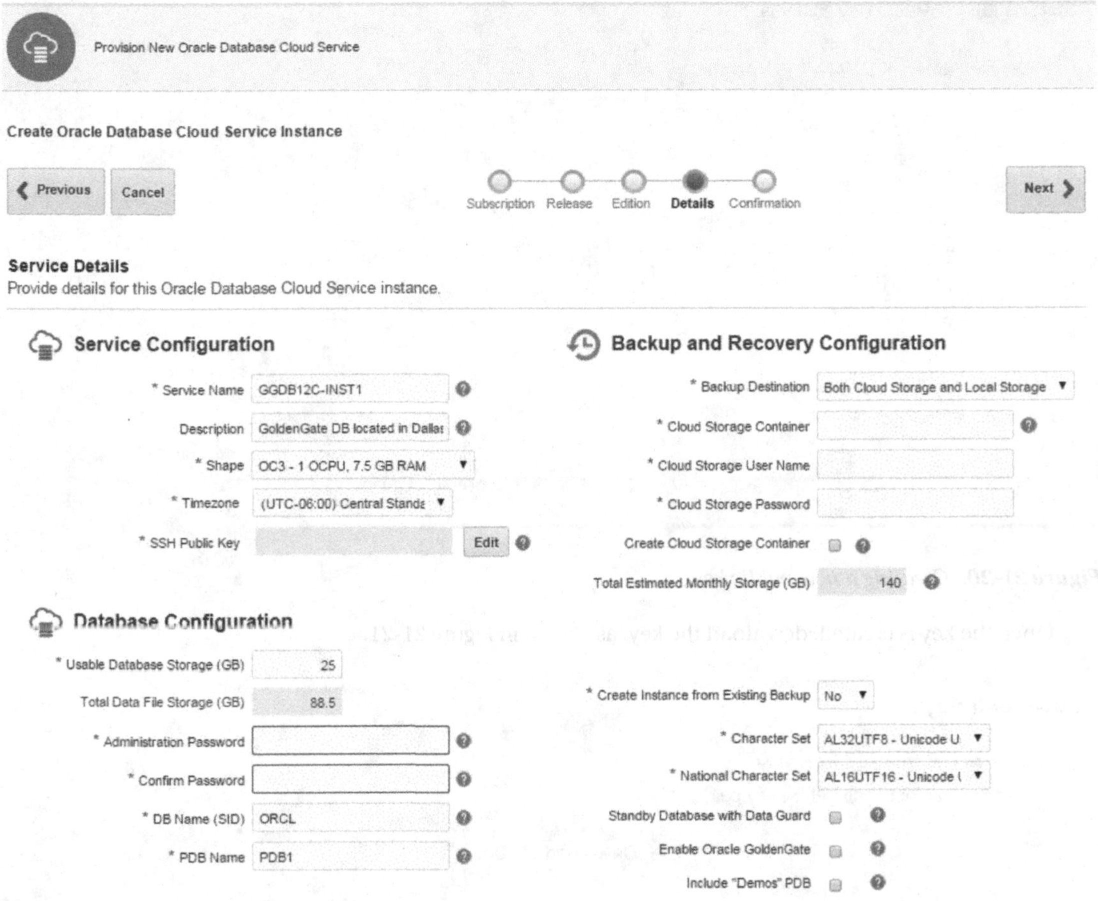

Figure 21-19. *Service configuration*

You should now associating your DBaaS instance with a public key. This will allow you to log in to the associated VM by using a paired private key. Click the Edit button next to SSH Public Key and select Create a New Key, as shown in Figure 21-20.

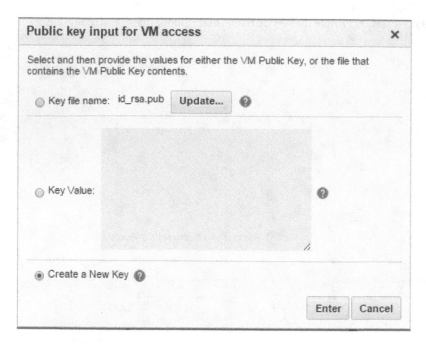

Figure 21-20. *Creating a new public key*

Once the key is created, download the key, as shown in Figure 21-21.

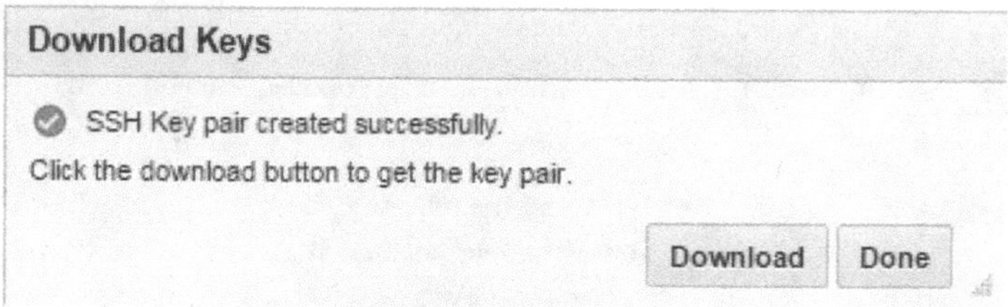

Download Keys

✅ SSH Key pair created successfully.
Click the download button to get the key pair.

Download   Done

Figure 21-21. *Downloading the public key*

Complete the database configuration, as shown in Figure 21-22.

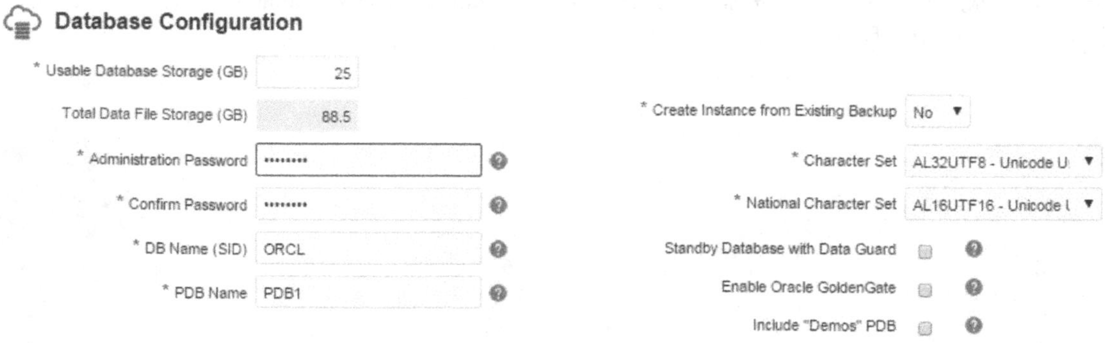

☁ Database Configuration

* Usable Database Storage (GB)	25			
Total Data File Storage (GB)	88.5	* Create Instance from Existing Backup	No ▼	
* Administration Password	•••••••• ❓	* Character Set	AL32UTF8 - Unicode U ▼	
* Confirm Password	•••••••• ❓	* National Character Set	AL16UTF16 - Unicode (▼	
* DB Name (SID)	ORCL ❓	Standby Database with Data Guard	☐ ❓	
* PDB Name	PDB1 ❓	Enable Oracle GoldenGate	☐ ❓	
		Include "Demos" PDB	☐ ❓	

Figure 21-22. *Database configuration*

522

Under Backup and Recovery Configuration, select the check box Create Cloud Storage Container.
Enter the cloud storage container name as **Storage-<identity domain name>/<container name>**.

Next, enter the same username and password that you used while activating the Oracle cloud storage service. The username and password are the ones you received in the trial subscription approval mail from Oracle.

Select the check box Enable Oracle GoldenGate.

Figure 21-23 shows the complete service details for the Oracle Database Cloud – DBaaS instance.

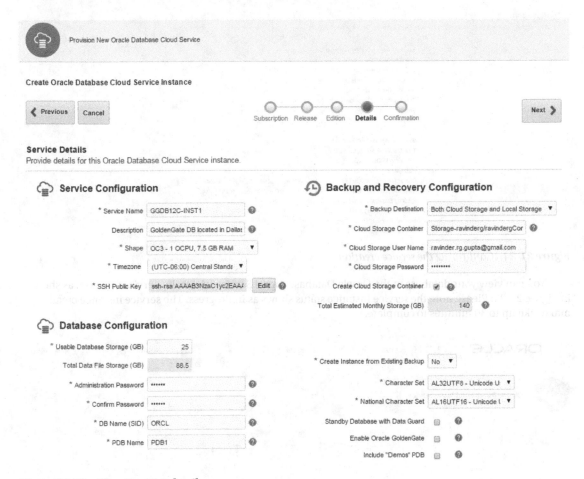

Figure 21-23. *DBaaS service details*

Click Next and review the service instance details. Click Create to create the service instance, as shown in Figure 21-24.

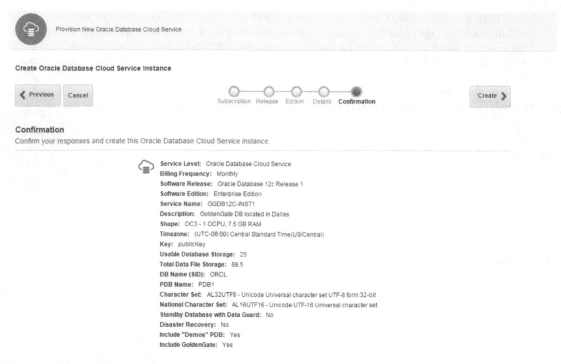

Figure 21-24. *Confirming the service creation*

You can view your database in the Oracle Database Cloud Service under the Services section, as shown in Figure 21-25. Please note the service instance status shows as In Progress. The service instance creation make take up to 30 minutes to complete.

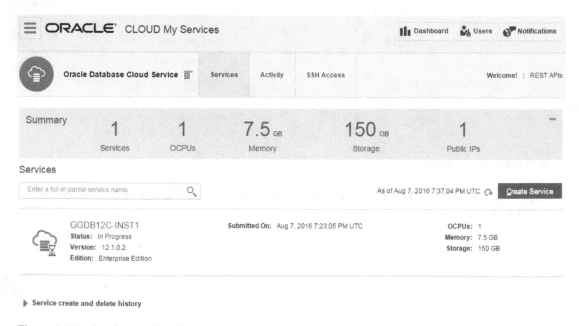

Figure 21-25. *Service creation: In Progress*

It took exactly 30 minutes for the service creation to complete in this demonstration example, as shown in Figure 21-26.

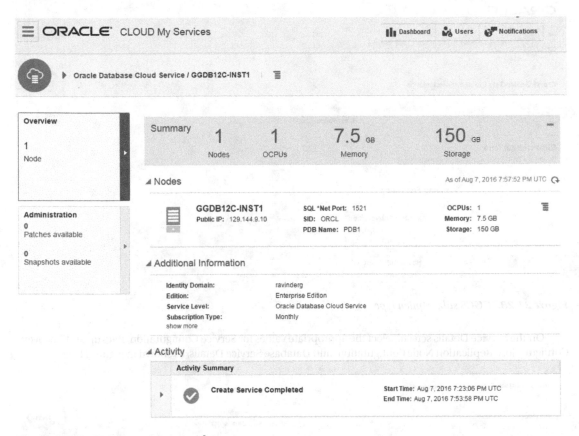

Figure 21-26. *Service creation complete*

Create a GGCS Instance

Navigate to http://cloud.oracle.com, select your data center, and click My Services. Next, in the My Services Dashboard, click GGCS and open the GoldenGate Cloud Service console.

In the GoldenGate Cloud Service console, click Create Service, as shown in Figure 21-27.

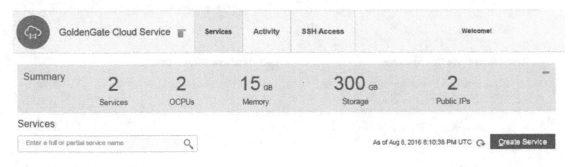

Figure 21-27. *GGCS console*

525

Next, choose your subscription type, as shown in Figure 21-28.

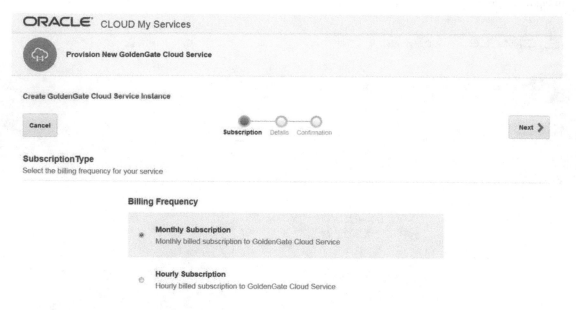

Figure 21-28. *GGCS subscription type*

On the Service Details screen, select the appropriate values for Service Configuration, Backup and Recovery Configuration, Replication Node Configuration, and Database Service Details, as shown in Figure 21-29.

Figure 21-29. *GGCS service details*

Click Next, Confirm, and Create GGCS service instance. The status of the service instance should show "Creating service." Like with the creation of database instance, this too usually takes a while to complete.

You can now launch the GGCS cloud service console again and review the details and status of the services running. You can also delete the instances you created and re-create new ones as per your needs.

SOCKS5 Proxy

Socket Secure 5 (SOCKS5) is an Internet protocol to exchange network data between a client and a server through a proxy server. The SOCKS5 proxy server creates a TCP connection on behalf of the client server. The advantage of the SOCKS5 proxy is that it allows you to deliver data to the cloud without a VPN connection using GGCS. The SOCKS protocol provides additional authentication, which allows only authorized users to access the server.

You can create a SOCKS5 proxy on a Unix/Linux server using the following command:

```
ssh –i <private_key file> -v –N –f -D <Source Server IP>:<Source Server port> <GGCS
User>@<GGCS IP>
```

Here's an example:

```
ssh -N -f -i id_rsa -D 127.0.0.0:1080 ravin@129.144.9.10
```

Test the SOCKS5 proxy using the following command:

```
curl -sSf --socks5 127.0.0.1:1080 www.oracle.com
```

To configure your data pump extracts to send trails to GGCS, use the following in the data pump extract parameter file:

```
RMTHOST <GGCS Server>, COMPRESS, MGRPORT 7840, SOCKSPROXY 127.0.0.1:1080
```

There are two ways you can use a SOCKS5 proxy.

- Creating the SOCKS5 proxy on a local server
- Creating the SOCKS5 proxy on a demilitarized zone (DMZ) server

Creating the SOCKS5 Proxy on the Local Server

In this configuration, the SOCKS5 proxy is created directly on the on-premise source server using the following command:

```
ssh –i <private_key file> -v –N –f -D <Source Server IP>:<Source Server port> <GGCS
User>@<GGCS IP>
```

Here's an example:

```
ssh -N -f -i id_rsa -D 127.0.0.0:1080 ravin@129.144.9.10
```

Figure 21-30 shows the SOCKS5 proxy on the local server.

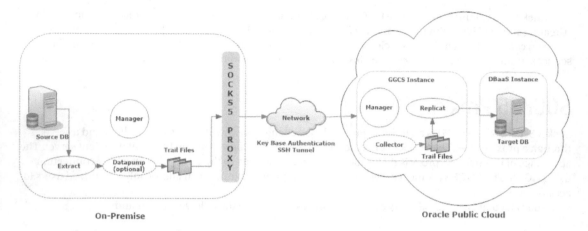

Figure 21-30. *SOCKS5 proxy on the local server*

Creating the SOCKS5 Proxy on a DMZ Server

In this configuration, the SOCKS5 proxy is set up on a DMZ server. A DMZ server is required when your organization's security policies do not allow a direct connection from your organization's LAN or VPN to an outside public network. The external network will have direct access to only the DMZ server and not to the organization's LAN.

First, start the SSH proxy tunnel on the DMZ server as follows:

```
ssh -i <private_key file> -v -N -f -D <DMZ Server IP>:<DMZ Server port> <GGCS User>@<GGCS IP>
```

Here's an example:

```
ssh -N -f -i id_rsa -D 127.0.0.0:1080 ravin@129.144.9.10
```

Add the GGCS server and DMZ server information as follows in the data pump extract parameter file:

```
RMTHOST <ggcs_server>, COMPRESS, MGRPORT 7840, SOCKSPROXY <dmz_server>:1080
```

Figure 21-31 shows an on-premise server connecting to the GGCS server using the SOCKS5 proxy DMZ server.

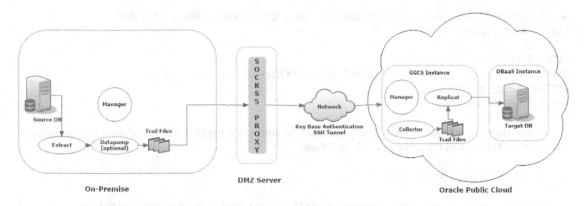

Figure 21-31. *SOCKS5 proxy on the DMZ server*

Replication Configurations Using GGCS

When using GGCS to replicate data to the cloud, there are three replication configurations you can implement.

- On-premise to the cloud

- Cloud to cloud

- Cloud to on-premise

You have already configured the GGCS instance. You can use GGSCI commands to create the extract or replicat processes on the GGCS instance. Let's discuss the steps to set up the replication in the previously mentioned three configurations.

On-Premise to Cloud Replication

The first step for an on-premise to cloud replication is to set up the SOCKS5 proxy. In this example, I am setting up the SOCKS5 proxy on the local server.

```
ssh -N -f -i id_rsa -D 127.0.0.0:1080 ggcs@129.144.9.10
```

Next, create an extract process on the source server as follows:

```
GGSCI> ADD EXTRACT ETTND001, TRANLOG, BEGIN NOW
GGSCI> ADD EXTTRAIL /app/ggs/tiger/dirdat/t1, EXTRACT ETTND001, MEGABYTES 100
GGSCI> edit params ETTND001

EXTRACT ETTND001
USERID tiger, PASSWORD tiger123_
EXTTRAIL /app/ggs/tiger/dirdat/t1
TABLE TIGER.ORDER_DTL;
```

Add and configure the data pump extract.

```
GGSCI> ADD EXTRACT PTTND001, EXTTRAILSOURCE /app/ggs/tiger/dirdat/t1
```

```
GGSCI> ADD RMTTRAIL /app/ggs/fox/dirdat/f1, EXTRACT PTTND001, MEGABYTES 100
GGSCI> edit params PTTND001

EXTRACT PTTND001
RMTHOST ggcs-server, COMPRESS, MGRPORT 7840, SOCKSPROXY dmz-server:1080
RMTTRAIL ./dirdat/f1
TABLE TIGER.ORDER_DTL;
```

For working on the remote GGSCI instance, you can connect to the GGCS instance from the local server using the SSH client and the private key file as follows:

```
ssh -i id_rsa ggcs@129.144.9.10
```

Similarly, you can connect to the remote Oracle Database Cloud – DBaaS instance as follows:

```
ssh -i id_rsa oracle@129.144.9.10
```

Connect to the Cloud DBaaS instance and set up the target user and tables for replication.

```
ssh -i id_rsa oracle@129.144.9.10
>sqlplus /nolog
SQL> connect / as sysdba
SQL> create user ggcs_fox identified by *****;
SQL> grant connect, resource to ggcs_fox;
SQL> exec dbms_goldengate_auth.grant_admin_privilege(ggcs_fox,'apply');
```

Create and configure the replicat process on the GGCS server.

```
GGSCI> ADD REPLICAT RFDLD001 INTEGRATED, EXTTRAIL ./dirdat/f1
GGSCI> edit params RFDLD001

REPLICAT RFDLD001
USERID ggcs_fox, PASSWORD ggcsfox123_
DBOPTIONS INTEGRATEDPARAMS (parallelism 3)
DISCARDFILE ./dirrpt/RFDLD001.dsc,append,MEGABYTES 200
ASSUMETARGETDEFS
REPORTCOUNT EVERY 1 MINUTES, RATE
MAP TIGER.ORDER_DTL, TARGET GGCS_FOX.ORDER_DTL;
```

Cloud to Cloud Replication

Now let's assume you have configured GGCS instances on two different clouds and you want to replicate data from one cloud to another.

Create an extract process on the source cloud GGCS instance as follows:

```
GGSCI> ADD EXTRACT ETTND001, TRANLOG, BEGIN NOW
GGSCI> ADD EXTTRAIL /app/ggs/tiger/dirdat/t1, EXTRACT ETTND001, MEGABYTES 100
GGSCI> edit params ETTND001

EXTRACT ETTND001
USERID ggcsa_tiger, PASSWORD ggcsa_tiger123_
```

```
EXTTRAIL ./dirdat/t1
TABLE GGCSA_TIGER.ORDER_DTL;
```

Add and configure the data pump extract on the source cloud GGCS instance.

```
GGSCI> ADD EXTRACT PTTND001, EXTTRAILSOURCE ./dirdat/t1
GGSCI> ADD RMTTRAIL ./dirdat/f1, EXTRACT PTTND001, MEGABYTES 100
GGSCI> edit params PTTND001

EXTRACT PTTND001
RMTHOST ggcs-server2, COMPRESS, MGRPORT 7841
RMTTRAIL ./dirdat/f1
TABLE TIGER.ORDER_DTL;
```

Create and configure the replicat process on the GGCS server.

```
GGSCI> ADD REPLICAT RFDLD001 INTEGRATED, EXTTRAIL ./dirdat/f1
GGSCI> edit params RFDLD001

REPLICAT RFDLD001
USERID ggcsb_fox, PASSWORD ggcsbfox123_
DBOPTIONS INTEGRATEDPARAMS (parallelism 3)
DISCARDFILE ./dirrpt/RFDLD001.dsc,append,MEGABYTES 200
ASSUMETARGETDEFS
REPORTCOUNT EVERY 1 MINUTES, RATE
MAP GGCSA_TIGER.ORDER_DTL, TARGET GGCSB_FOX.ORDER_DTL;
```

Cloud to On-Premise Replication

You can configure a cloud to on-premise replication in one of these two ways:

- *Cloud to on-premise using a DMZ server*: As discussed earlier, using a DMZ server eliminates the need of a direct connection from a cloud server to a private on-premise network.

- *Cloud to on-premise using a passive extract or passive data pump extract*: The cloud in this case allows a connection directly to a trusted on-premise through specific ports only. The passive extract or passive data pump is stopped and started from the on-premise system.

The configuration in the cloud to on-premise is similar to the configuration in on-premise to cloud using a DMZ server and SOCKS5 proxy. Set up the SOCKS5 proxy as follows:

```
ssh -N -f -i id_rsa -D <dmz-server ip>:1080 ggcs@<cloud server ip>
```

Next, create an extract process on the source cloud GGCS instance as follows:

```
GGSCI> ADD EXTRACT ETTND001, TRANLOG, BEGIN NOW
GGSCI> ADD EXTTRAIL ./dirdat/t1, EXTRACT ETTND001, MEGABYTES 100
GGSCI> edit params ETTND001
```

```
EXTRACT ETTND001
USERID ggcs_tiger, PASSWORD ggcstiger123_
EXTTRAIL ./dirdat/t1
TABLE TIGER.ORDER_DTL;
```

Add and configure the data pump extract.

```
GGSCI> ADD EXTRACT PTTND001, EXTTRAILSOURCE ./dirdat/t1
GGSCI> ADD RMTTRAIL ./dirdat/f1, EXTRACT PTTND001, MEGABYTES 100
GGSCI> edit params PTTND001
```

```
EXTRACT PTTND001
RMTHOST on-premise-server, COMPRESS, MGRPORT 7840, SOCKSPROXY dmz-server:1080
RMTTRAIL ./dirdat/f1
TABLE TIGER.ORDER_DTL;
```

Create and configure the replicat process on the GGCS server.

```
GGSCI> ADD REPLICAT RFDLD001 INTEGRATED, EXTTRAIL ./dirdat/f1
GGSCI> edit params RFDLD001
```

```
REPLICAT RFDLD001
USERID fox, PASSWORD fox123_
DBOPTIONS INTEGRATEDPARAMS (parallelism 3)
DISCARDFILE ./dirrpt/RFDLD001.dsc,append,MEGABYTES 200
ASSUMETARGETDEFS
REPORTCOUNT EVERY 1 MINUTES, RATE
MAP GGCS_TIGER.ORDER_DTL, TARGET FOX.ORDER_DTL;
```

Support for a Non-Oracle Cloud

Besides a great solution for data consolidation in real time for Oracle cloud systems, Oracle GoldenGate also supports Oracle databases on Amazon RDS as a source or target. It enables zero-downtime migration and upgrades, active-active database synchronization, disaster recovery and data protection, and cross-region replication. Amazon RDS customers can use Oracle GoldenGate in various configurations.

Let's discuss some examples taken from the Amazon Relational Database Service User Guide for using Oracle GoldenGate with Amazon RDS.

- An on-premises Oracle source database and on-premise Oracle GoldenGate hub that provides data to a target Amazon RDS DB instance (Figure 21-32)

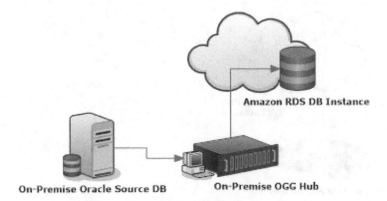

Figure 21-32. *On-premise Oracle DB to Amazon RDS DB instance on the cloud*

- An on-premise Oracle database that acts as the source database and is connected to an Amazon EC2 instance hub hosting Oracle GoldenGate that provides data to a target Amazon RDS DB instance (Figure 21-33)

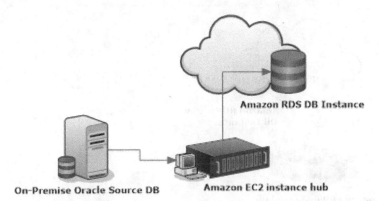

Figure 21-33. *OGG on Amazon EC2 to Amazon RDS on cloud*

- An Oracle database on an Amazon RDS DB instance that acts as the source database and is connected to an Amazon EC2 instance hub that provides data to a target Amazon RDS DB instance (Figure 21-34)

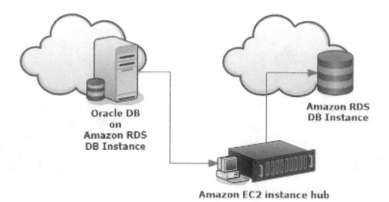

***Figure 21-34.** Amazon RDS to Amazon RDS with OGG on Amazon EC2*

- An Oracle database on an Amazon EC2 instance that acts as the source database and is connected to an Amazon EC2 instance hub that provides data to a target Amazon RDS DB instance (Figure 21-35)

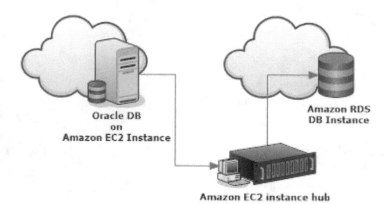

***Figure 21-35.** Oracle DB and OGG on Amazon EC2 with Amazon RDS as target*

- An Oracle database on an Amazon RDS DB instance connected to an Amazon EC2 instance hub in the same region and is connected to an Amazon EC2 instance hub in a different region that provides data to the target Amazon RDS DB instance in the same region as the second EC2 instance hub (Figure 21-36)

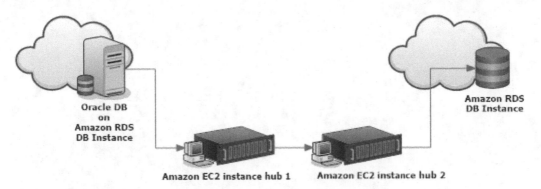

Figure 21-36. *Oracle DB and OGG instances on multiple Amazon EC2 instances*

However, if your business requires complex data transformations before consolidation to and between public cloud and on-premise database systems, then in addition to using Oracle GoldenGate, you need an ETL tool. This is because Oracle GoldenGate can perform only basic row-level transformations. For complex transformations, you can have GoldenGate deliver data to your ETL tool in flat files in real time. Oracle Data Integrator can be used for ETL in conjunction with Oracle GoldenGate to feed data to the staging tables on the target in real time.

Summary

In this chapter, we discussed how to use Oracle GoldenGate Cloud Service for replicating data between on-premise Oracle/MySQL databases and the Oracle public cloud. You created Oracle Database Cloud – Database as a Service instances and Oracle GoldenGate Cloud Service instances. You also created a SOCKS5 proxy on the local and DMZ servers. Oracle GoldenGate also supports some non-Oracle Cloud such as Amazon RDS. We discussed a brief overview of OGG support for Amazon RDS on the cloud.

In the next chapter, you will learn how to install and use Oracle GoldenGate Studio for the quick and easy setup of Oracle GoldenGate replication environments. OGG Studio provides a drag-and-drop interface for configuring OGG replication and is useful to both users new to OGG as well as experienced professionals.

CHAPTER 22

■ ■ ■

Oracle GoldenGate Studio

Oracle GoldenGate Studio is a WYSIWYG, drag-and-drop interface to quickly build and deploy Oracle GoldenGate replication solutions. It provides you with templates to quickly build configurations aligned to best practices. Oracle GoldenGate Studio enables you to perform the following tasks:

- Create and deploy Oracle GoldenGate replication configurations quickly and easily

- Define mappings once and reuse them for deploying at multiple locations

- Perform data filtering and transformation graphically

- Perform drag-and-drop mapping

- Use best-practice wizards for quick and easy configurations

- Export and import Oracle GoldenGate solutions

Architecture

Oracle GoldenGate Studio consists of the following four main components:

- Oracle GoldenGate instance

- Oracle GoldenGate Monitor Agent

- Oracle GoldenGate Studio GUI client

- OGG Studio repository

Figure 22-1 shows the components of Oracle GoldenGate Studio.

© Ravinder Gupta 2016

R. Gupta, *Mastering Oracle GoldenGate*, DOI 10.1007/978-1-4842-2301-7_22

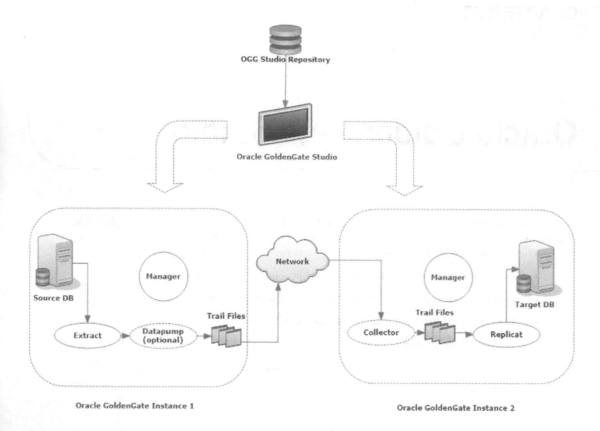

Figure 22-1. *Components of Oracle GoldenGate Studio*

Install and Configure OGG Studio

Let's first install and prepare OGG Studio for building OGG solutions. We will start with installing each of the four components discussed in the previous section.

Install the Oracle GoldenGate Instance

Download the Oracle GoldenGate for Unix/Linux server and perform the installation as discussed in Chapter 4 of this book. Once the installation is complete, log in to the GGSCI prompt and create the data store.

Check to see whether the data store already exists.

```
GGSCI> info datastore
2016-08-14T21:05:00Z  WARNING OGG-06307  Datastore does not exist.
```

If the datastore does not exist, stop the OGG processes and create the data store as follows:

```
GGSCI> stop *
GGSCI> stop mgr
GGSCI> stop jagent
```

```
GGSCI> create datastore
GGSCI> info datastore
GGSCI> start mgr
```

Add the parameter ENABLEMONITORING to the GLOBALS file. Create the GLOBALS file if it does not exist in the agent instance home directory.

```
GGSCI> edit ./GLOBALS
ENABLEMONITORING
```

Install the OGG Monitor Agent

Now that your Oracle GoldenGate Monitor (OGGMON) server is ready, install the OGG Monitor Agent. You can install the OGG Monitor Agent in either OGGMON or OEM mode; however, it is better to install it in OEM mode. If OGGMON mode is used, the agent will keep searching for OGG Monitor, and if you don't have it, it will add warning messages in the log file.

The OGG Monitor Agent installation is discussed in Chapter 13 of this book.

Once you have successfully installed the OGG Monitor Agent, start it. Navigate to the OGG Home and execute the following from the GGSCI prompt.

```
GGSCI> start jagent
```

Check ogg_agent.log in the OGG Agent instance home /logs directory if needed.

Install Oracle GoldenGate Studio

Download the latest OGG Studio binary from the Oracle web site.

```
www.oracle.com/technetwork/middleware/goldengate/downloads/index.html
```

For demonstration in this book, I downloaded Oracle GoldenGate Studio V12.2.1.1.0. Extract the compressed .zip file and launch the JAR as follows:

```
$ export DISPLAY=:0.0
$ java -jar fmw_12.2.1.1.0_oggstudio.jar
```

Figure 22-2 shows the welcome page for the Oracle Fusion Middleware 12*c* GoldenGate Studio installation. Click Next to navigate to the next screen.

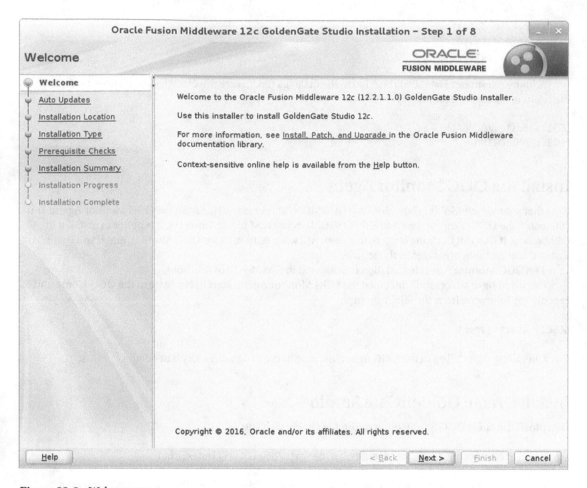

Figure 22-2. *Welcome page*

Next, the installer prompts you to select the Auto Updates and patch options, as shown in Figure 22-3. I chose to skip Auto Updates.

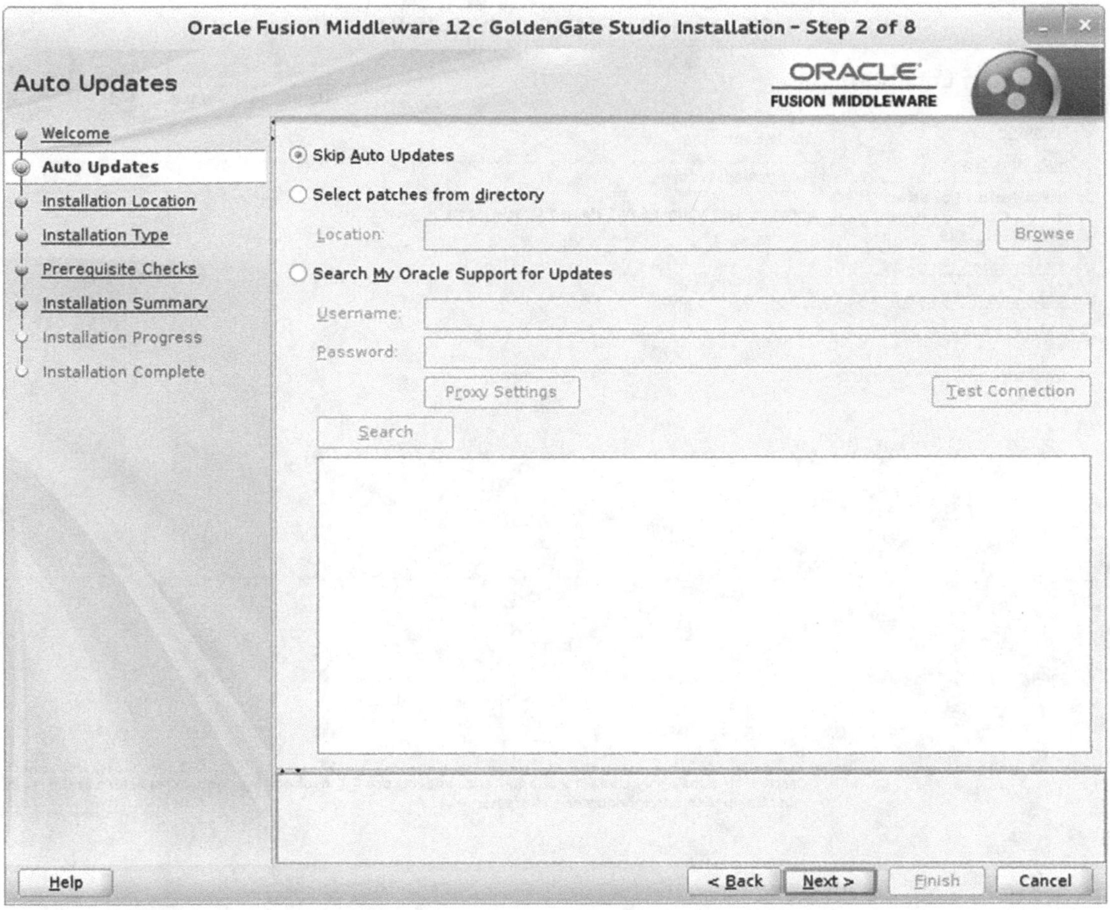

Figure 22-3. *Skipping Auto Updates*

At step 3, select an installation directory where you want to install Oracle GoldenGate Studio. Make sure this directory is empty.

Figure 22-4 shows the installation directory where you will install OGG Studio.

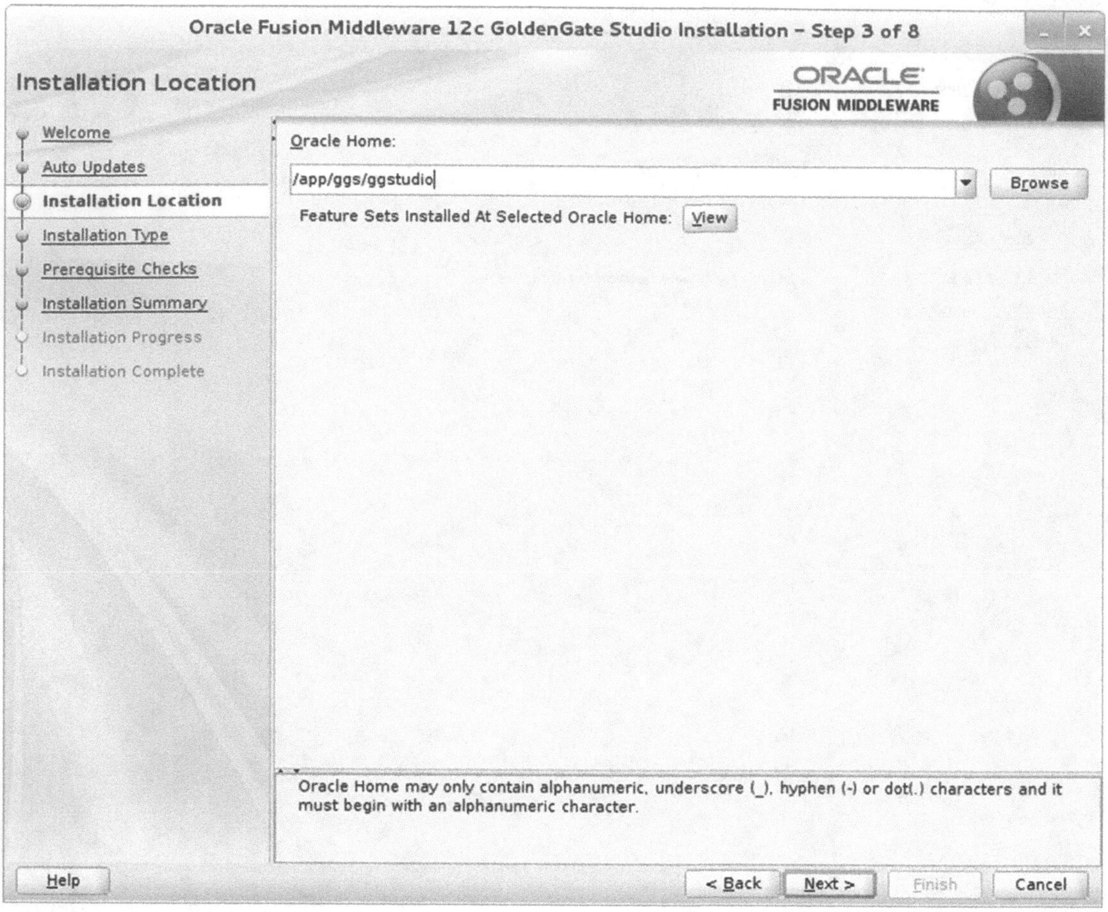

Figure 22-4. *Selecting the installation location*

On the next screen for selecting the installation type, there is only one option, which is preselected, as shown in Figure 22-5. Click Next to continue.

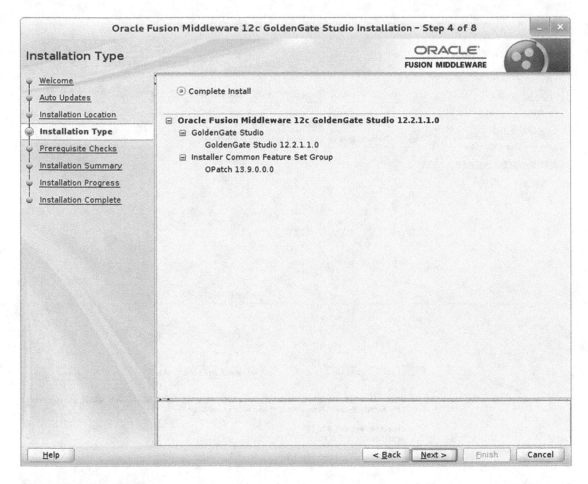

Figure 22-5. Installation type

At step 5, the installer checks for the operating system and Java version prerequisites. I had a slightly older Java version, and hence it gave me a warning, as shown in Figure 22-6. Since this is a minor version difference, I chose to continue the installation. If your Java version is older than Java 1.8, you should abort installation and upgrade your Java version first.

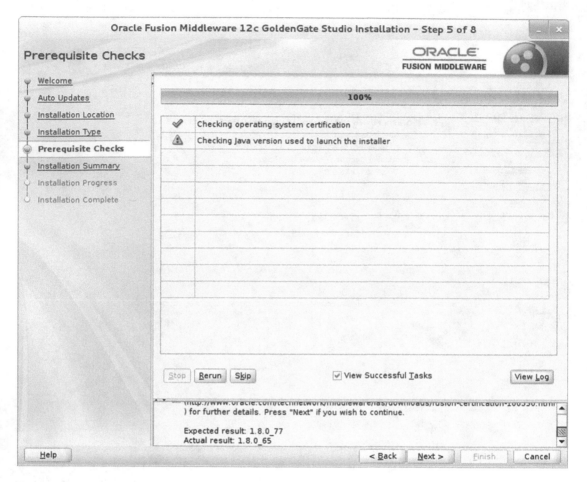

Figure 22-6. *Prerequisite checks*

Review the installation summary on the next screen, as shown in Figure 22-7.

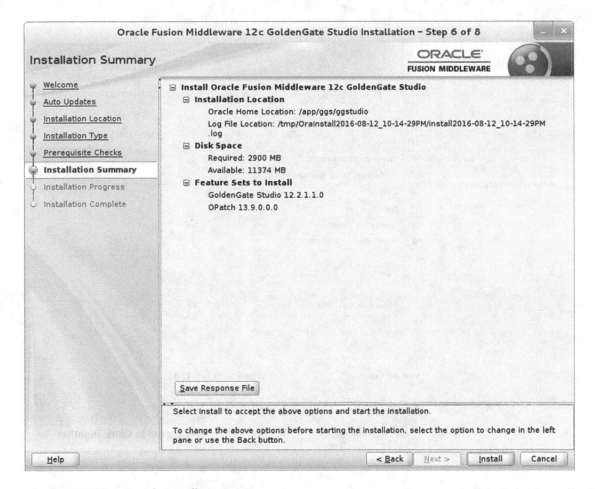

Figure 22-7. *Reviewing the installation summary*

Installation takes approximately five minutes. Monitor the progress of installation, as shown in Figure 22-8.

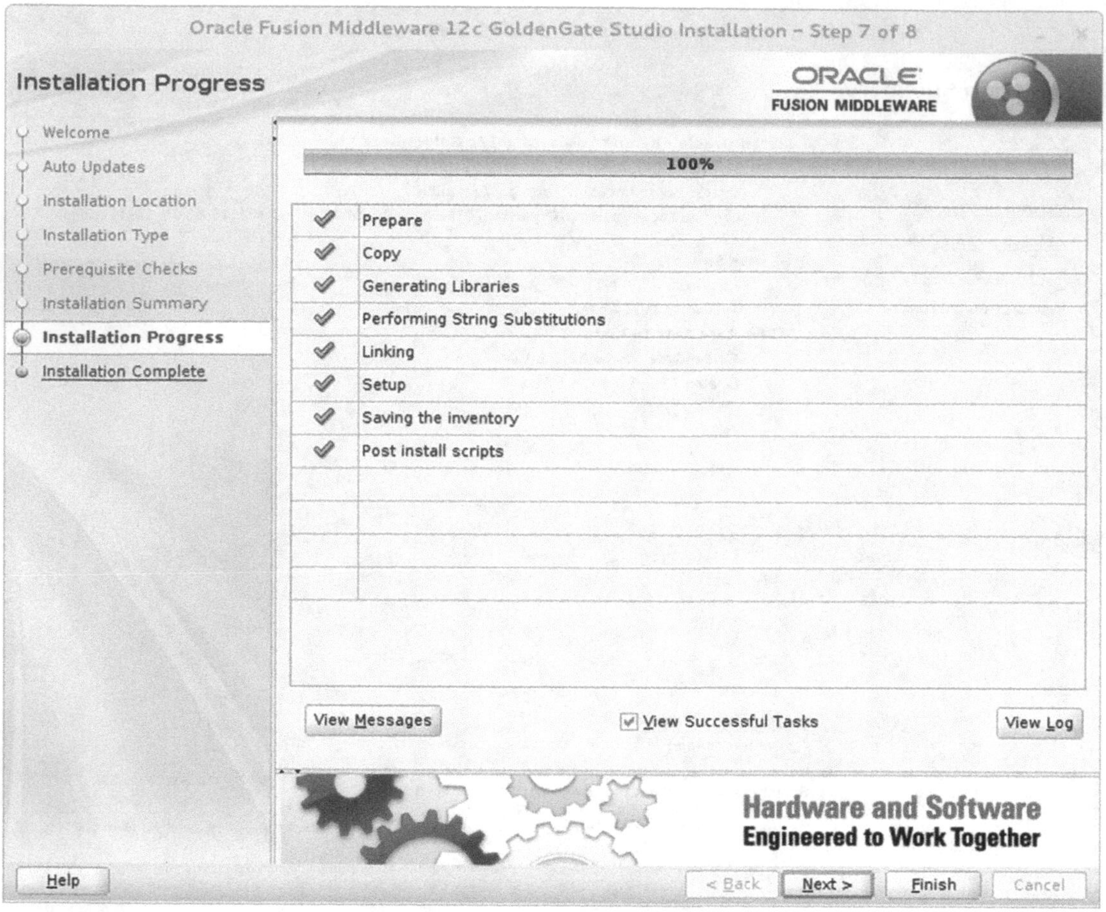

Figure 22-8. *Installation progress*

The installation has completed successfully, as shown in Figure 22-9.

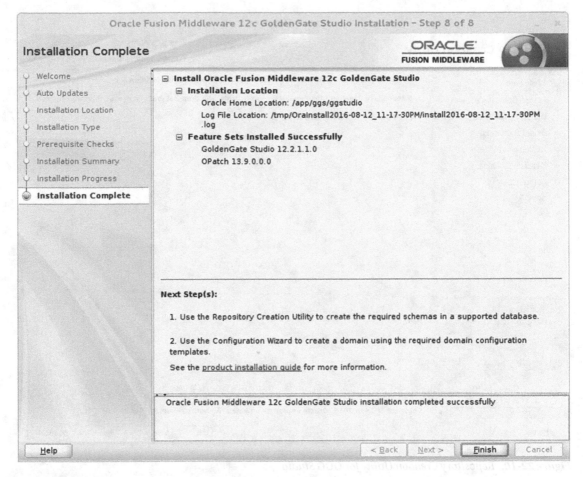

Figure 22-9. Installation successfully completed

You can launch OGG Studio at this stage. However, you need to create the OGG Studio repository to connect OGG Studio to a repository database.

Install the OGG Studio Repository

Navigate to OGGSTUDIO_HOME/oracle_common/bin and execute rcu as follows:

```
$ rcu
```

This will launch Repository Creation Utility, as shown in Figure 22-10. Navigate through the installation screens and create the repository. Click Next to continue.

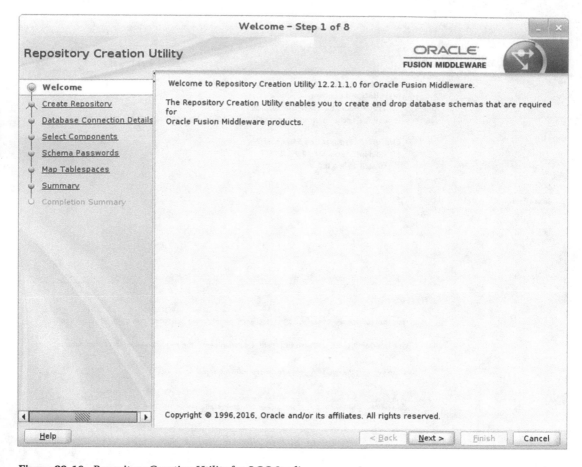

Figure 22-10. *Repository Creation Utility for OGG Studio*

Since you are creating a new repository for Oracle GoldenGate Studio, select Create Repository and under it select System Load and Product Load, as shown in Figure 22-11. Make sure you have DBA privileges to create the repository.

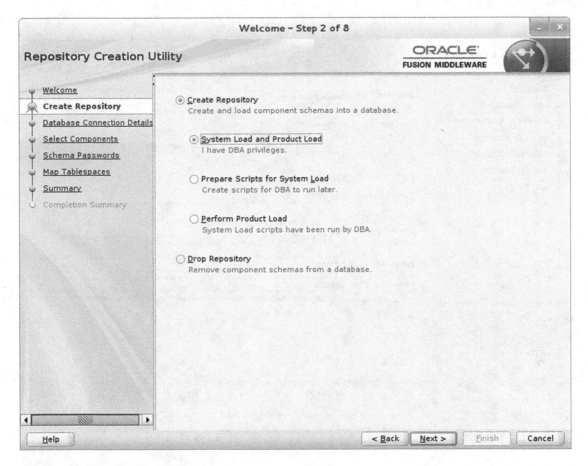

Figure 22-11. *Creating a repository*

Provide the connection details of the database you are connecting to for creating the repository. Make sure the user has the SYSDBA role. Figure 22-12 shows the connection details I used for connecting to the orcl database on ravin-ravinpc.

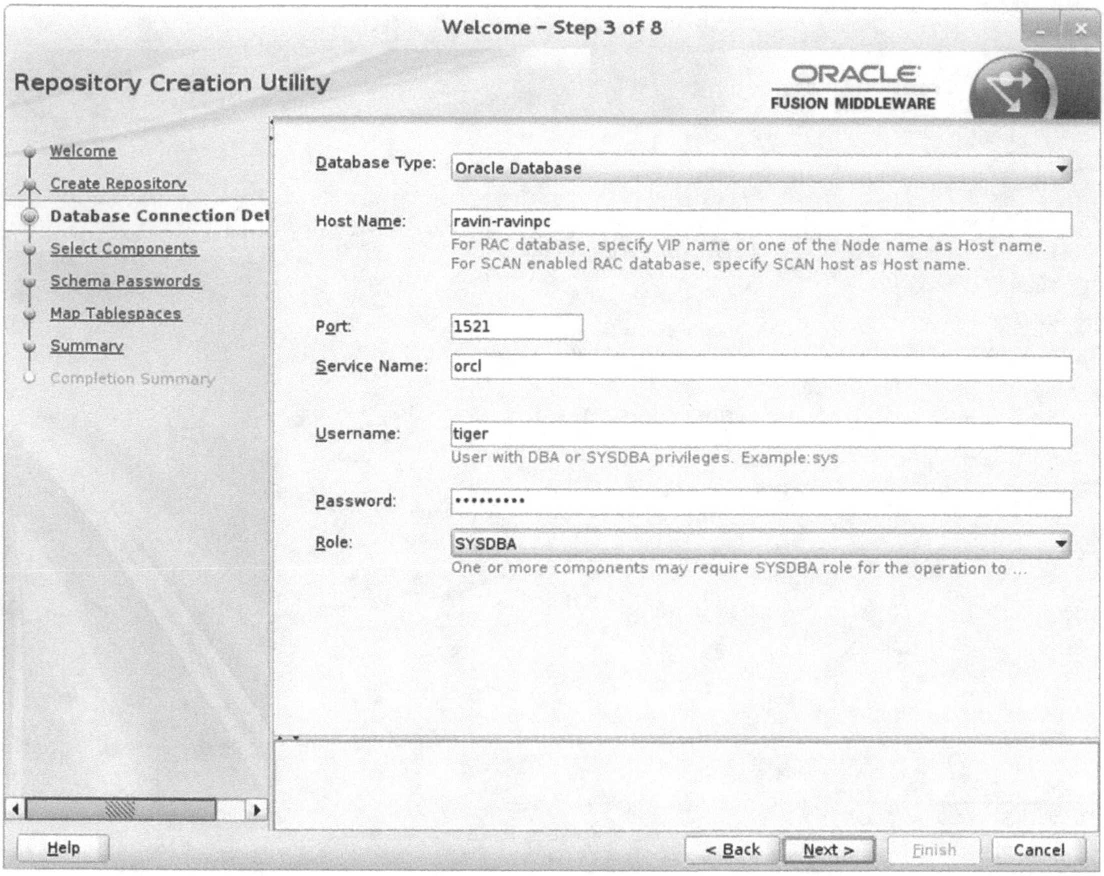

Figure 22-12. *Database connection details*

Figure 22-13 shows the prerequisite checks for the database you specified for repository creation.

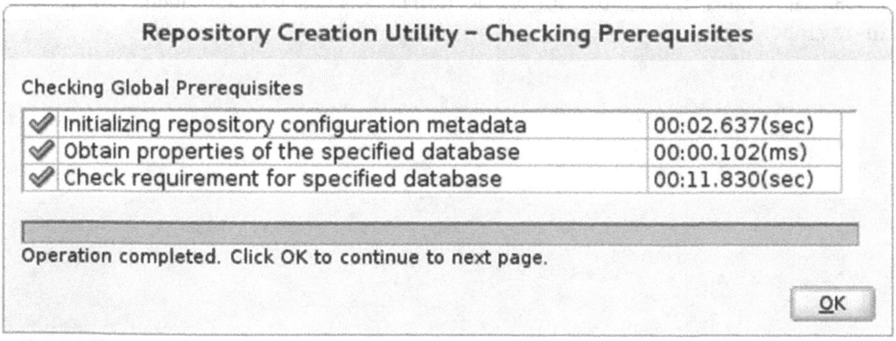

Figure 22-13. *Repository database prerequisites check*

Next, you are asked to select the components to be installed. You must also select a prefix to generate unique names for various schemas that get created with the repository. Figure 22-14 shows the repository components I selected and the prefix TST2 for schema names.

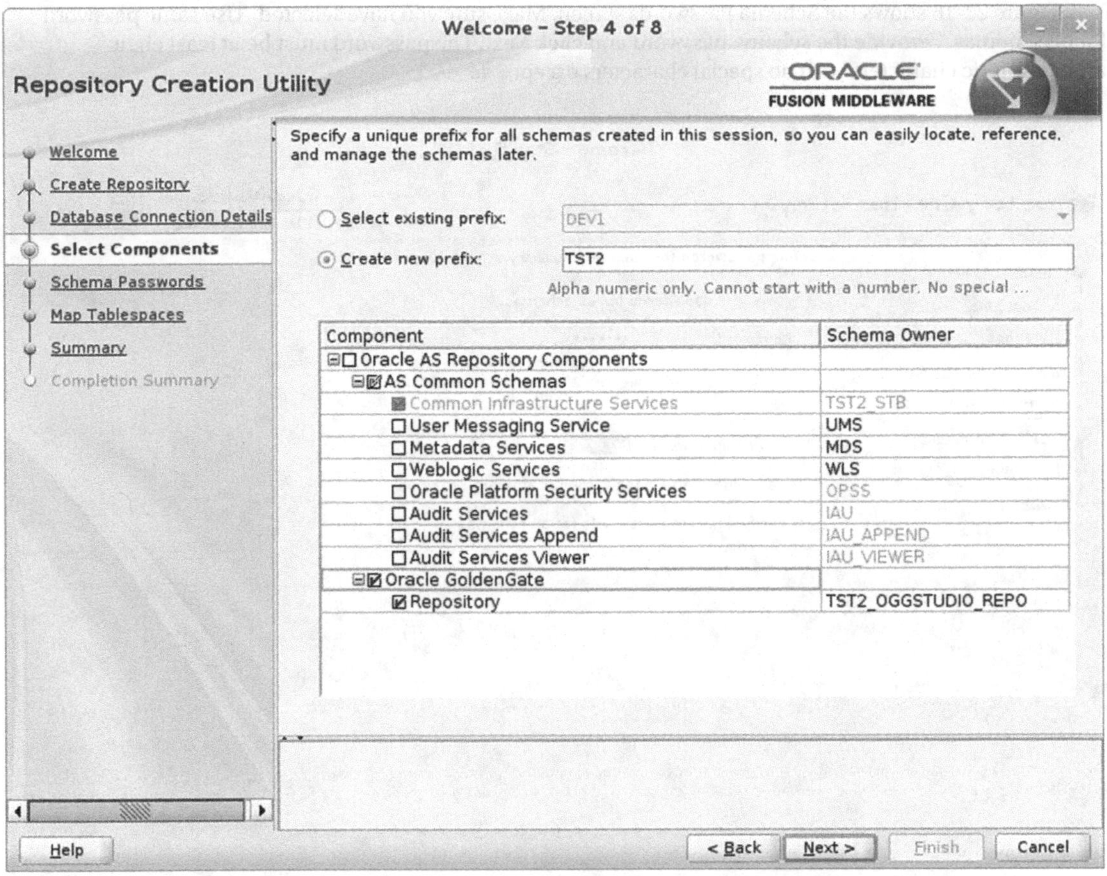

Figure 22-14. *Selecting repository components to install*

Once you select repository components and click Next, the installer will pop up a window indicating the prerequisite checks for the selected repository components shown in Figure 22-15.

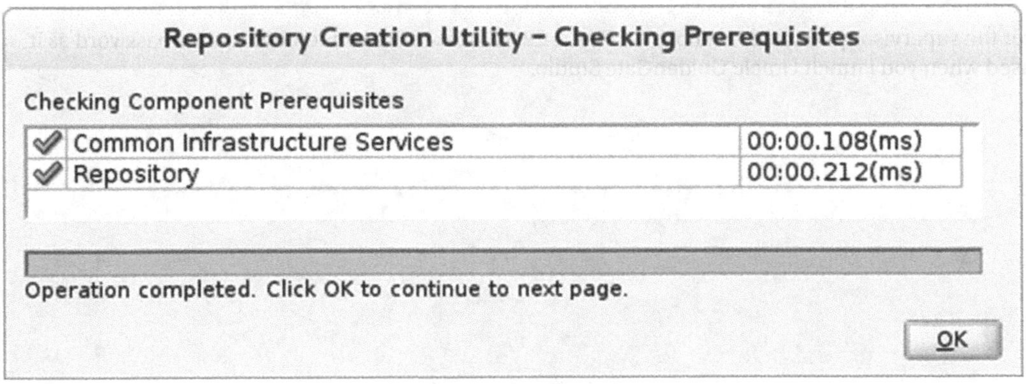

Figure 22-15. *Checking component prerequisites*

Figure 22-16 shows the Schema Passwords screen. Make sure you have selected "Use same password for all schemas." Provide the schema password and click Next. The password must be at least eight alphanumeric characters with no special characters except $ # . _.

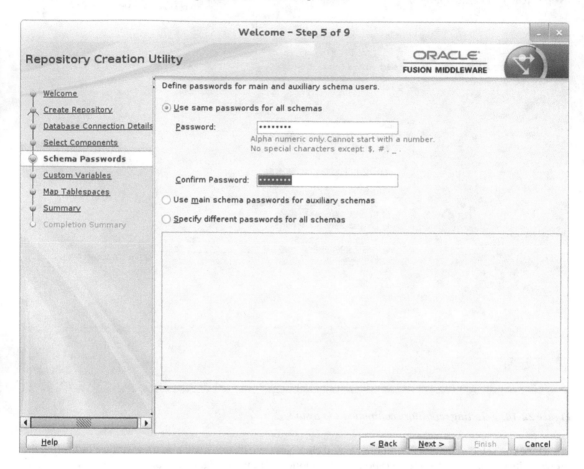

Figure 22-16. *Providing schema passwords*

Enter the supervisor password, as shown in Figure 22-17. Make sure you remember this password as it will be used when you launch Oracle GoldenGate Studio.

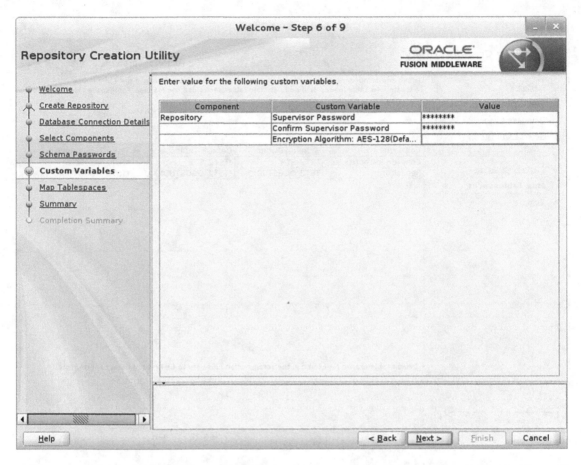

Figure 22-17. *Entering the supervisor password*

The next step shows the Map Tablespaces page. The default and temporary tablespaces for all the components you selected in step 4 are displayed in a table shown in Figure 22-18. You can create new tablespaces or modify existing tablespaces by clicking the Manage Tablespaces button.

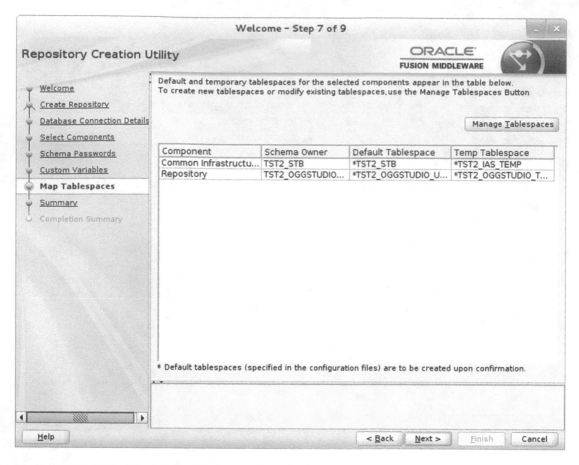

Figure 22-18. *Tablespace mapping for the repository database*

A small dialog box appears as shown in Figure 22-19 to confirm the creation of the tablespace before moving to the next step.

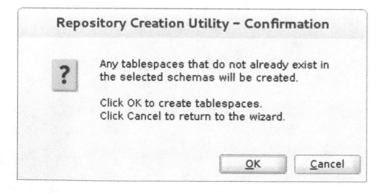

Figure 22-19. *Confirming the tablespace creation*

Figure 22-20 shows the creation of the tablespace in progress in the repository database. This usually takes a couple of minutes to complete.

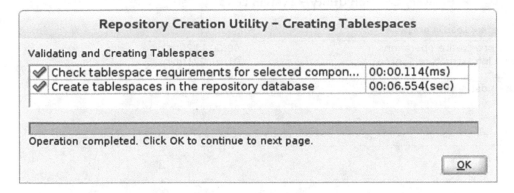

Figure 22-20. *Creating tablespaces in the repository database*

Figure 22-21 shows the repository database summary. Click Next to begin the system load.

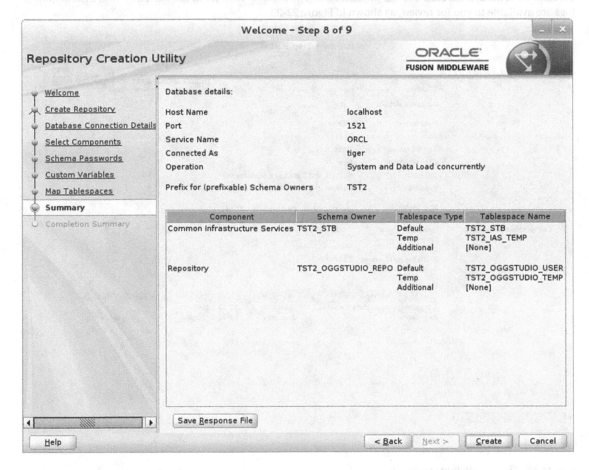

Figure 22-21. *Repository database summary*

Figure 22-22 shows the progress of the repository system load. This step may take up to 15 minutes.

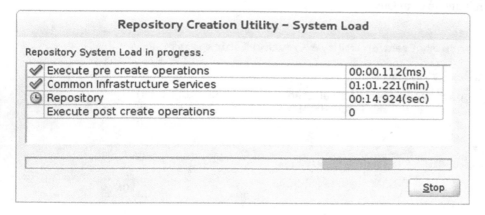

Figure 22-22. *System load progress for the repository*

The system load and product load are the final steps of the repository creation. You can choose to perform both the system load and the product load. The installer runs them concurrently, and installation logs are available to you for review, as shown in Figure 22-23.

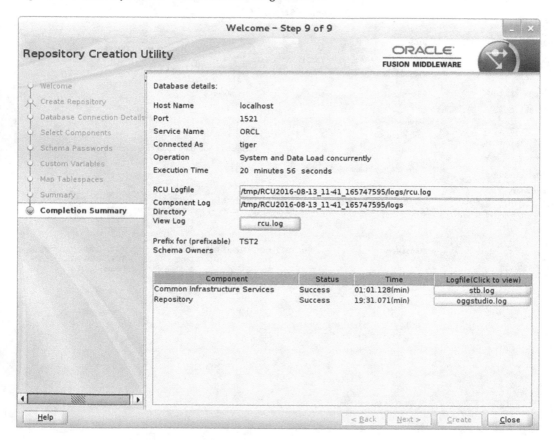

Figure 22-23. *Completion summary*

Launch OGG Studio

Navigate to the $GGSTDIO_HOME/oggstudio/bin directory and launch Oracle GoldenGate Studio by executing the oggstudio file.

```
$ /app/ggs/ggstudio/oggstudio/bin/oggstudio
```

Figure 22-24 shows that Oracle GoldenGate Studio is loading.

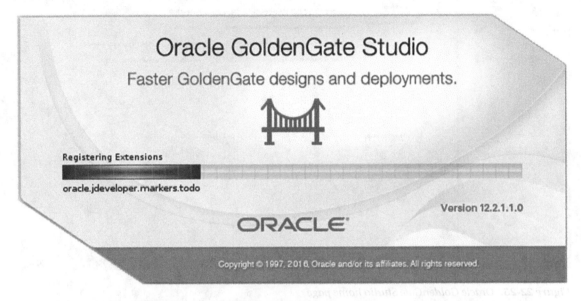

Figure 22-24. *Oracle GoldenGate Studio prelaunch banner*

Figure 22-25 shows the Oracle GoldenGate Studio home page.

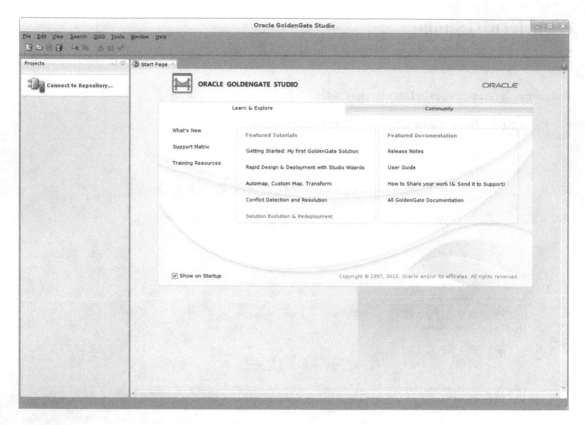

Figure 22-25. *Oracle GoldenGate Studio home page*

Click Connect to Repository in the left panel. A window will pop up so you can set up a new wallet password. This is a one-time setup to keep your Studio and repository credentials encrypted. You can skip this step by selecting "Store passwords without secure wallet," as shown in Figure 22-26.

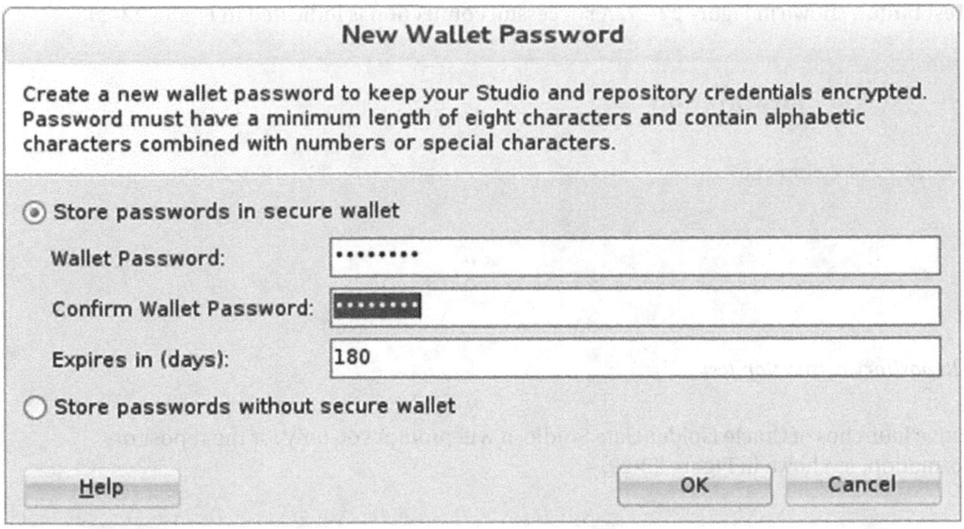

New Wallet Password

Create a new wallet password to keep your Studio and repository credentials encrypted. Password must have a minimum length of eight characters and contain alphabetic characters combined with numbers or special characters.

◉ Store passwords in secure wallet

Wallet Password: `••••••••`

Confirm Wallet Password: `••••••••`

Expires in (days): `180`

◯ Store passwords without secure wallet

| Help | | OK | Cancel |

Figure 22-26. *Setting up the wallet password*

The next screen requests the repository connection information. Fill in the Studio Connection and Database Connection fields, as shown in Figure 22-27.

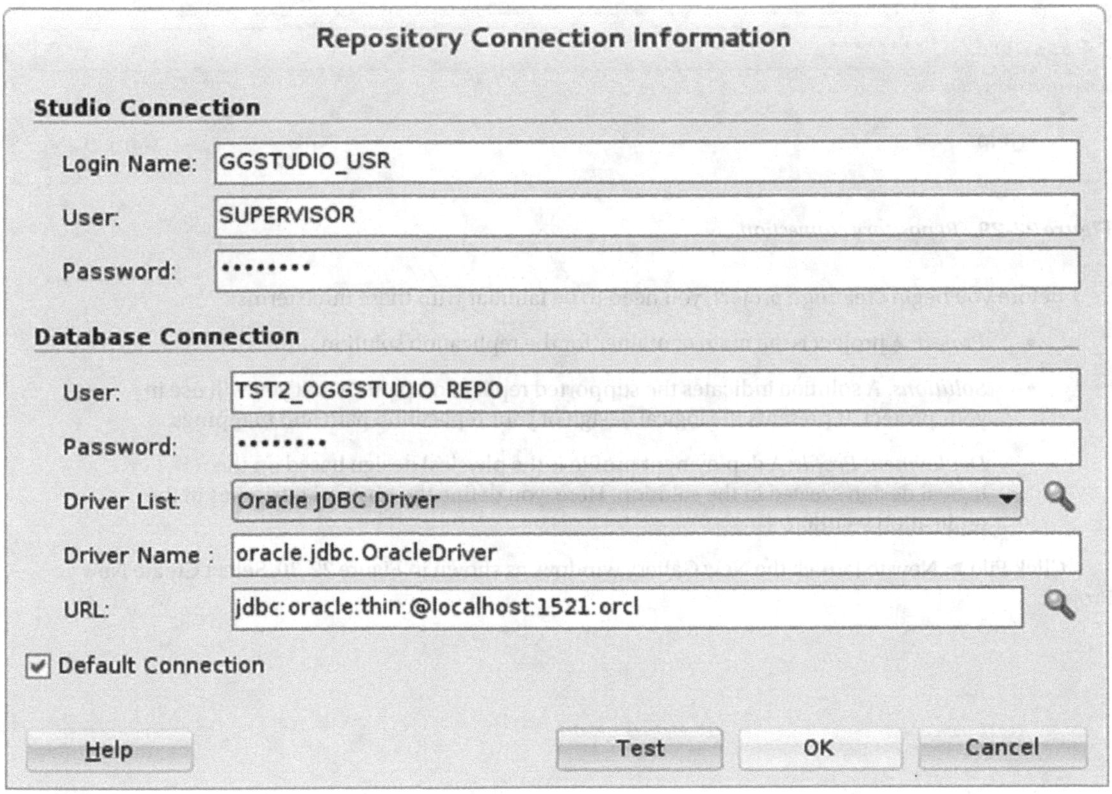

Repository Connection Information

Studio Connection

Login Name: `GGSTUDIO_USR`

User: `SUPERVISOR`

Password: `••••••••`

Database Connection

User: `TST2_OGGSTUDIO_REPO`

Password: `••••••••`

Driver List: `Oracle JDBC Driver`

Driver Name : `oracle.jdbc.OracleDriver`

URL: `jdbc:oracle:thin:@localhost:1521:orcl`

☑ Default Connection

| Help | | Test | OK | Cancel |

Figure 22-27. *Repository connection information*

Click the Test button shown in Figure 22-27. A successful connection is indicated in Figure 22-28.

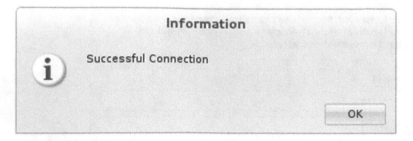

Figure 22-28. *Repository connection test*

In consecutive launches of Oracle GoldenGate Studio, it will prompt you only for the repository connection information, as shown in Figure 22-29.

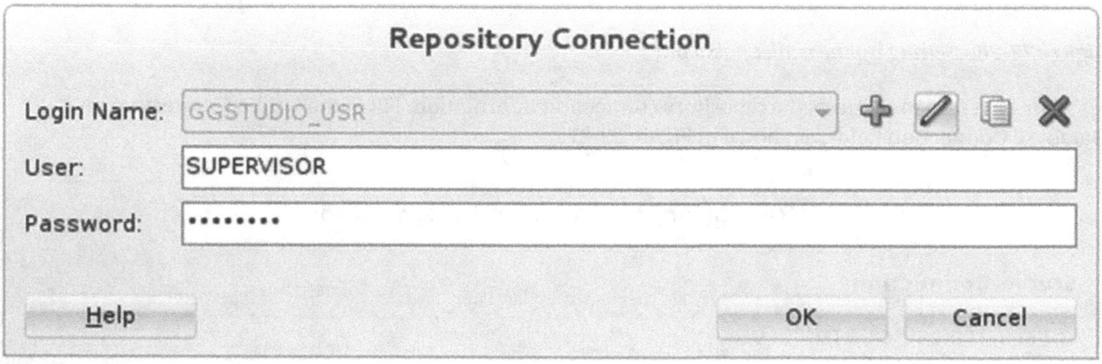

Repository Connection

Login Name:	GGSTUDIO_USR
User:	SUPERVISOR
Password:	••••••••

Help   OK   Cancel

Figure 22-29. *Repository connection*

Before you begin creating a project, you need to be familiar with these three terms:

- *Project*: A project is the main container for the replication solution.

- *Solutions*: A solution indicates the supported replication pattern that you will use in your project. It presents the logical design of your replication path and mappings.

- *Deployment Profile*: A deployment profile is the physical design based on the logical design created in the solution. Here, you define the physical attributes of the replication solution.

Click File ➤ New to launch the New Gallery window, as shown in Figure 22-30. Select Create New Project.

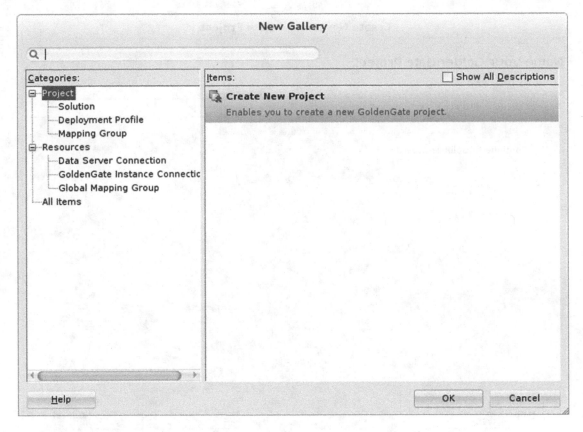

Figure 22-30. *New Gallery window*

The previous step launches the Create New GoldenGate Project Wizard, as shown in Figure 22-31. Name your project and keep the check box Continue to Solution Wizard selected.

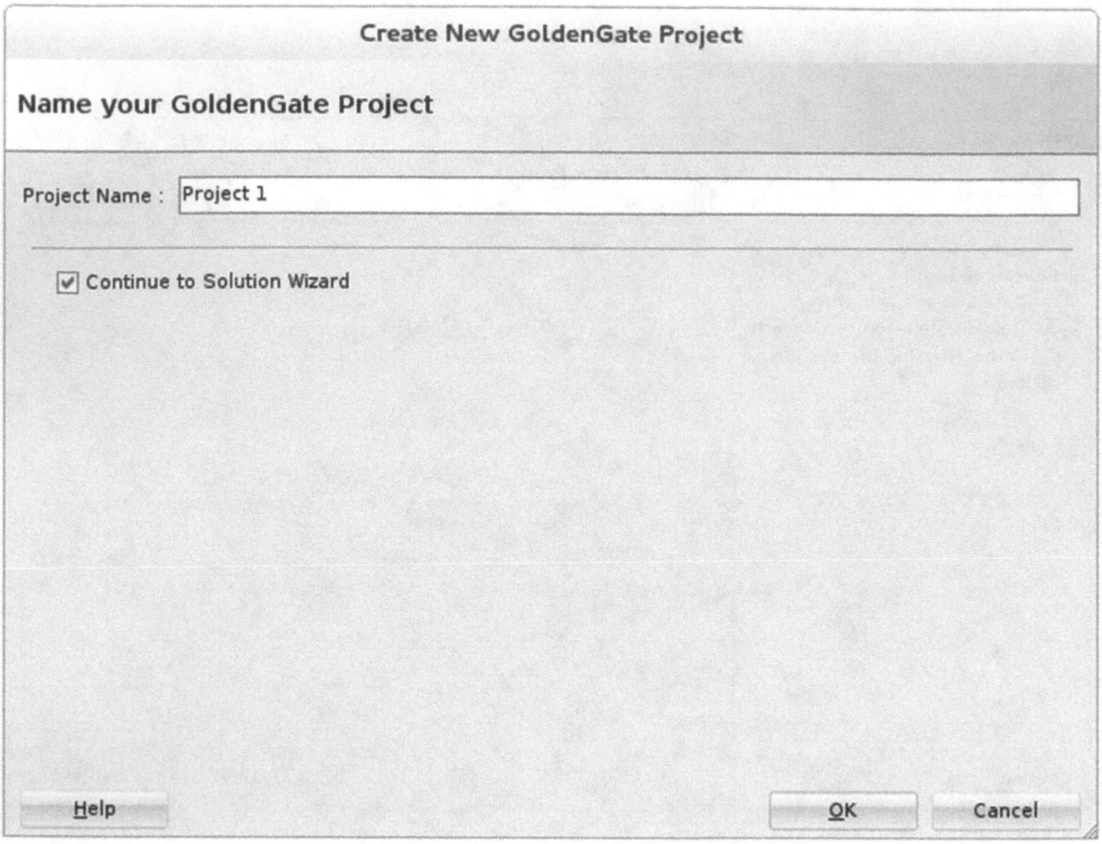

Figure 22-31. *Entering the project name*

In the Create New GoldenGate Project Wizard, enter the solution name and description as indicated in Figure 22-32.

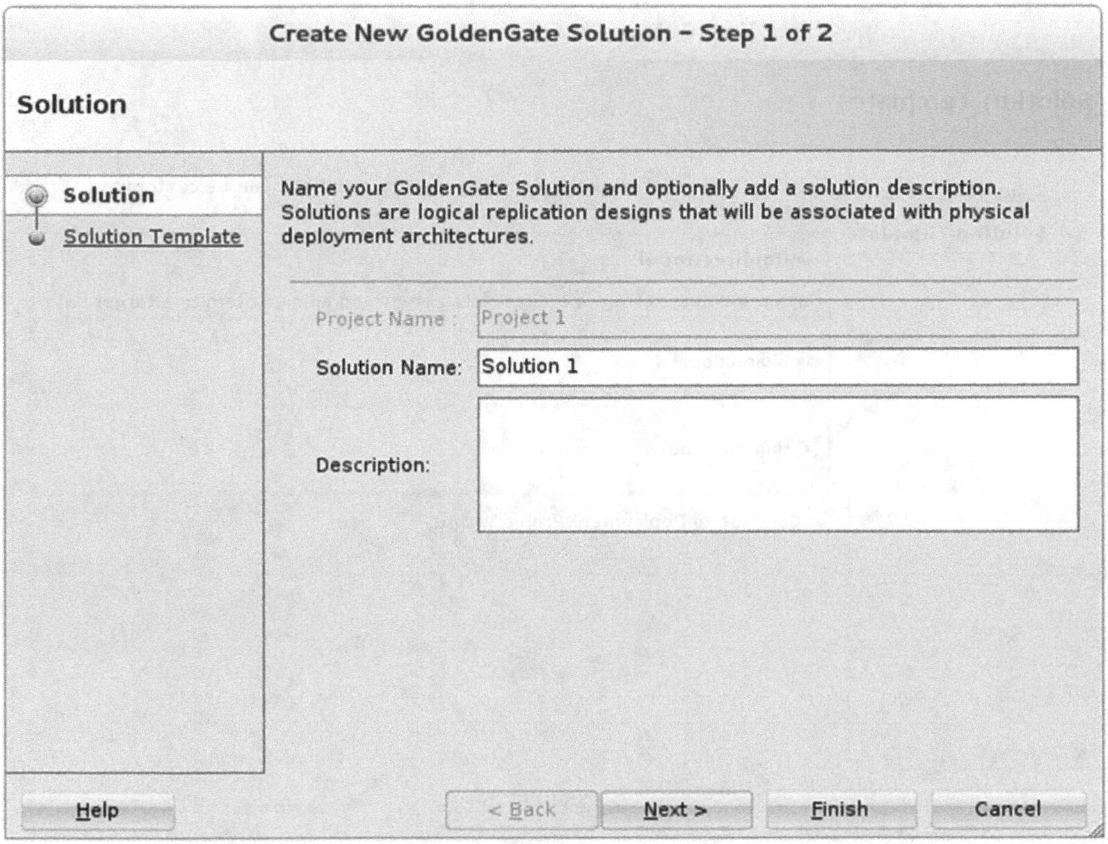

```
┌──────────────────────────────────────────────────────────────────────┐
│              Create New GoldenGate Solution – Step 1 of 2              │
├──────────────────────────────────────────────────────────────────────┤
│  Solution                                                              │
├────────────────────────┬───────────────────────────────────────────── │
│                         │                                              │
│  ◉ Solution             │  Name your GoldenGate Solution and optionally add a solution description.  │
│  │                      │  Solutions are logical replication designs that will be associated with physical  │
│  ◉ Solution Template    │  deployment architectures.                   │
│                         │                                              │
│                         │  ────────────────────────────────────────── │
│                         │   Project Name :  │Project 1              │  │
│                         │                                              │
│                         │   Solution Name:  │Solution 1             │  │
│                         │                   ┌───────────────────────┐  │
│                         │                   │                       │  │
│                         │   Description:     │                       │  │
│                         │                   │                       │  │
│                         │                   └───────────────────────┘  │
│                         │                                              │
├─────────┬───────────────┴──────────────────────────────────────────── │
│  Help   │              < Back    Next >    Finish    Cancel            │
└─────────┴──────────────────────────────────────────────────────────────┘
```

Figure 22-32. *Creating a new solution*

Next, select the solution template. For this demonstration, I have selected Unidirectional Replication, as shown in Figure 22-33.

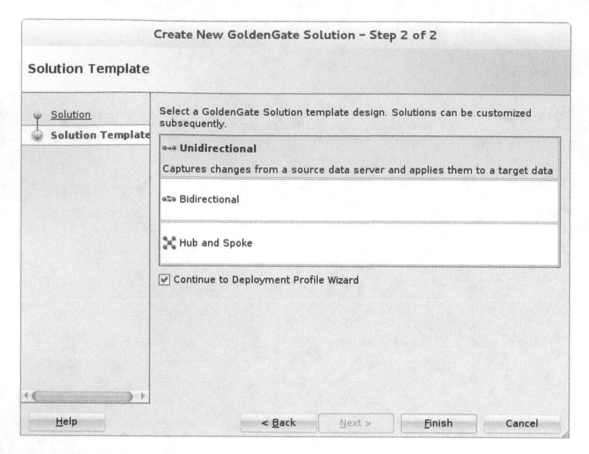

Figure 22-33. *Selecting a solution template*

The next step is to choose a name for the deployment profile for the project you are creating, as shown in Figure 22-34.

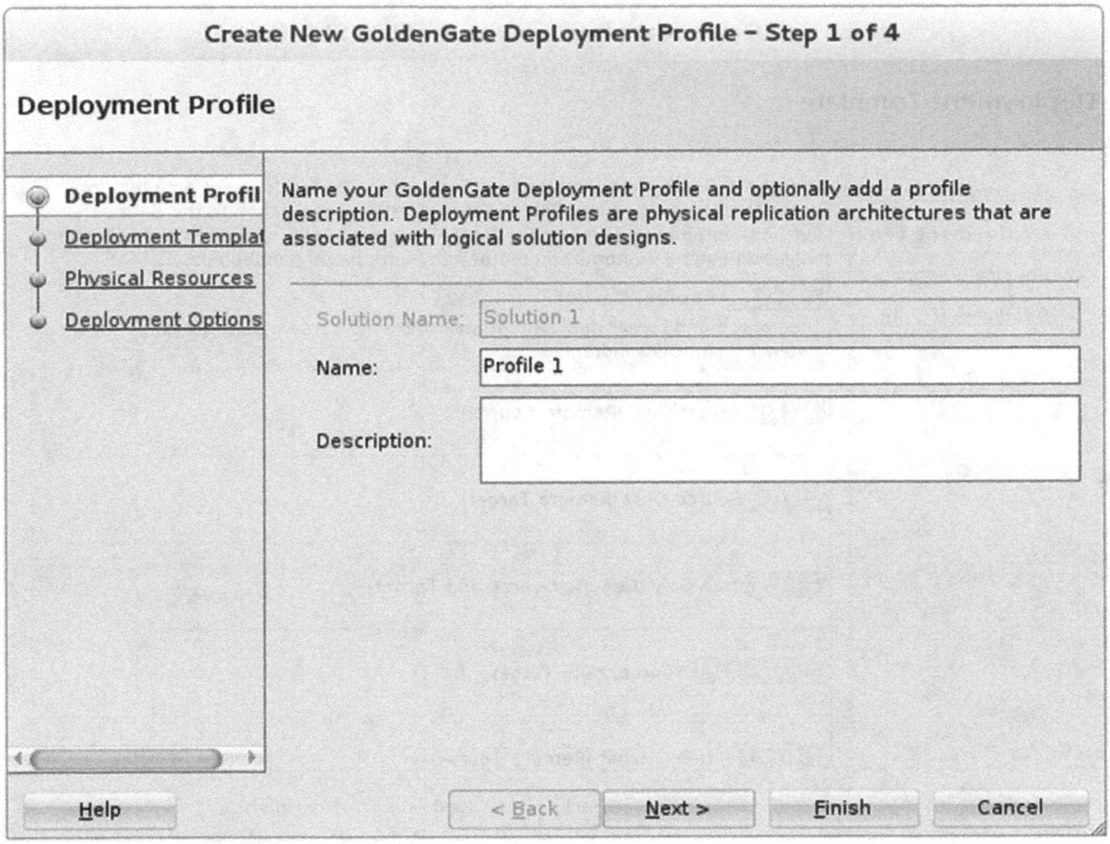

```
Create New GoldenGate Deployment Profile - Step 1 of 4

Deployment Profile

  ● Deployment Profil       Name your GoldenGate Deployment Profile and optionally add a profile
                            description. Deployment Profiles are physical replication architectures that are
  ● Deployment Templa       associated with logical solution designs.
  ● Physical Resources
  ● Deployment Options      Solution Name:  Solution 1

                            Name:           Profile 1

                            Description:



         Help                    < Back       Next >        Finish        Cancel
```

Figure 22-34. Creating a new deployment profile

Select Deployment Architecture Template, as shown in Figure 22-35. The deployment architecture defines the install location of the Oracle GoldenGate instances.

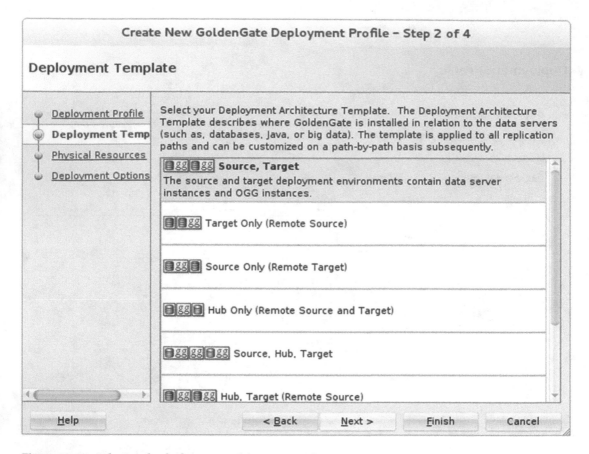

Figure 22-35. *Selecting the deployment architecture template*

As shown in Figure 22-36, the next step prompts you to choose the physical resources for the source and target to indicate the application data server and OGG instance connections. Since you haven't yet created any physical resources, you can click Next without making any selections. We will assign physical resources at a later step.

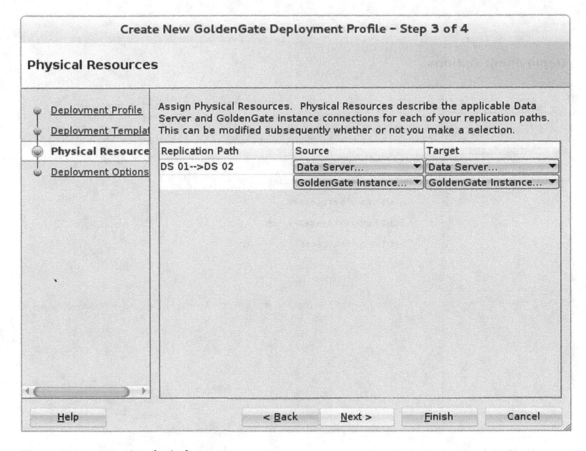

Figure 22-36. *Assigning physical resources*

Next, select the deployment options for deploying your solution. You can skip the initial load and start all the GoldenGate processes if you want to perform these actions manually.

Figure 22-37 shows the deployment options I have selected for the first demonstration.

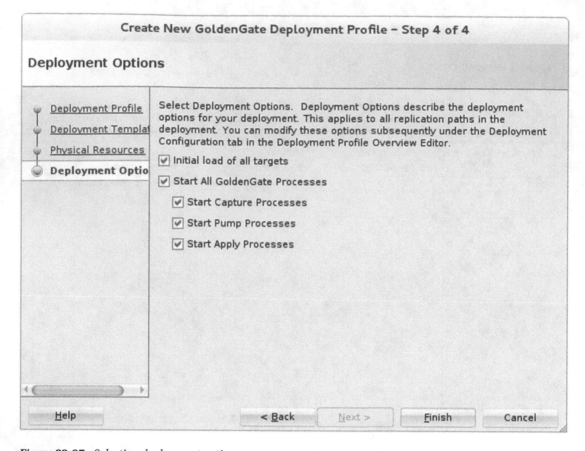

Figure 22-37. *Selecting deployment options*

Click Finish on this screen to complete the initial step for the project creation. Oracle GoldenGate Studio should show the logical design of the solution you are building, as shown in Figure 22-38.

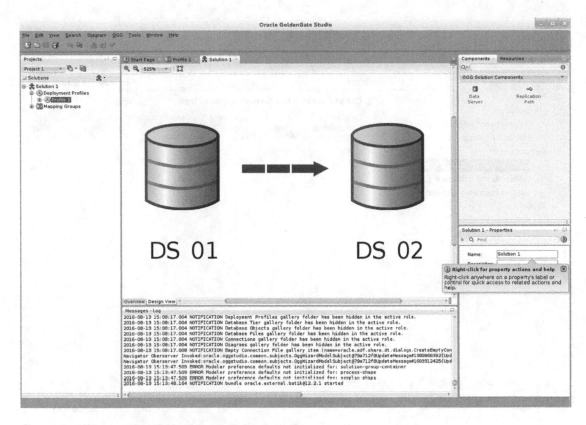

Figure 22-38. *Logical design of Solution 1*

At this stage, you need to create the physical resources to be assigned to Solution 1. Go to the File menu and launch the New Gallery window again. Under Resources, select Data Server Connection, as shown in Figure 22-39.

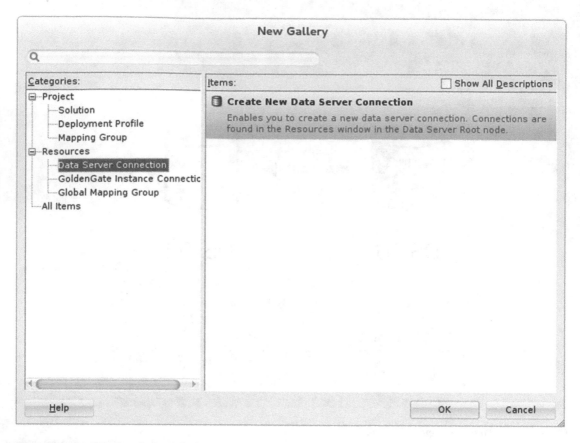

Figure 22-39. *Creating the new data server connection*

Create two data server connections, one each for the source and the target.
Figure 22-40 shows the data server connection for the source.

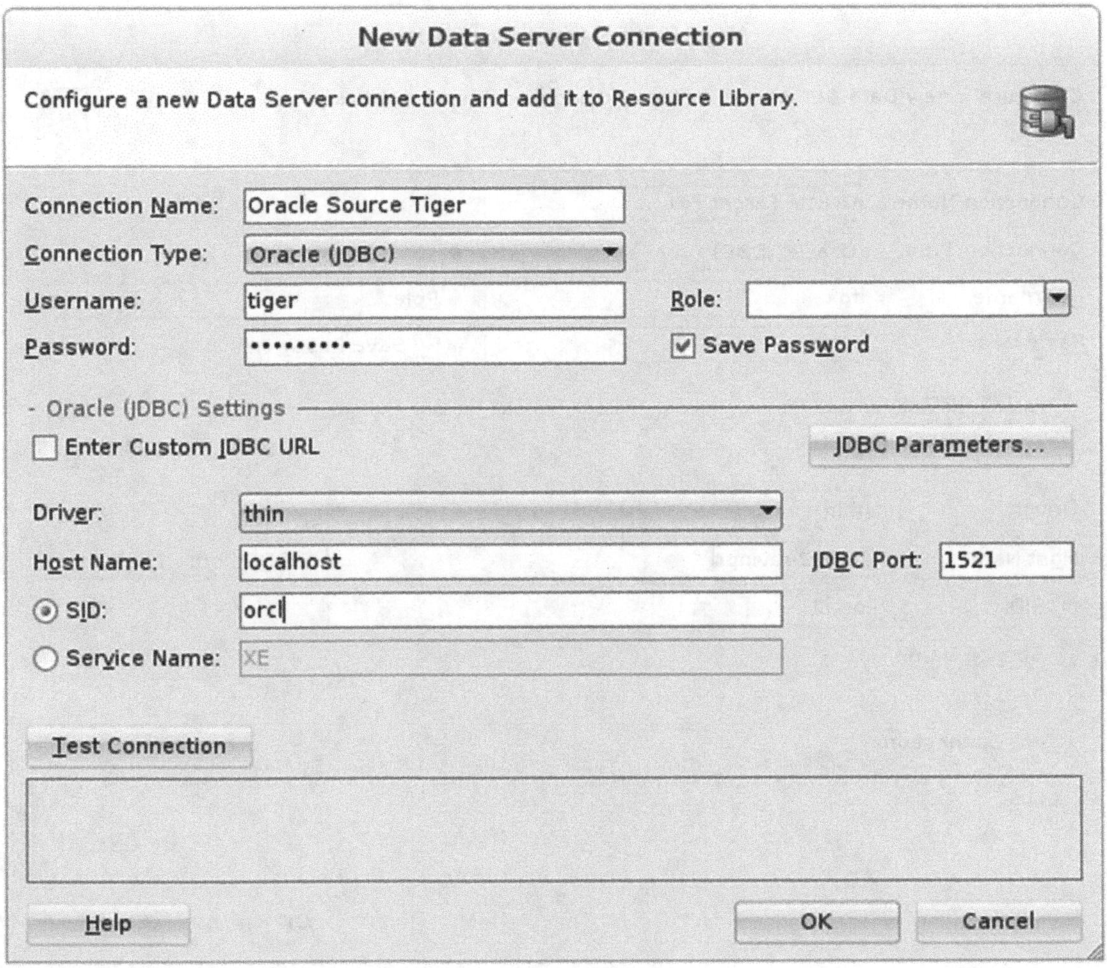

Figure 22-40. *Data server connection for the source*

Figure 22-41 shows the data server connection for the target.

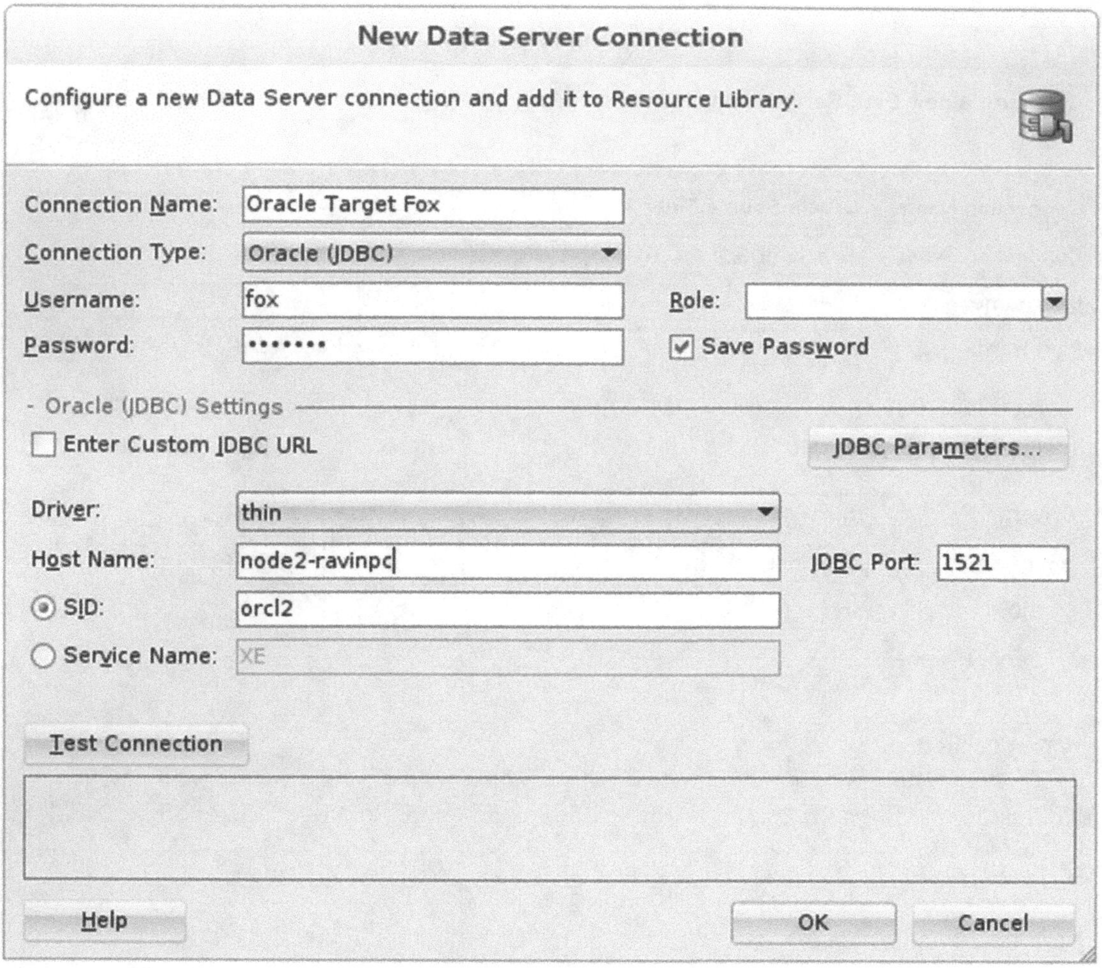

Figure 22-41. *Data server connection for the target*

Next, relaunch the New Gallery window and select GoldenGate Instance Connection under the resources, as shown in Figure 22-42.

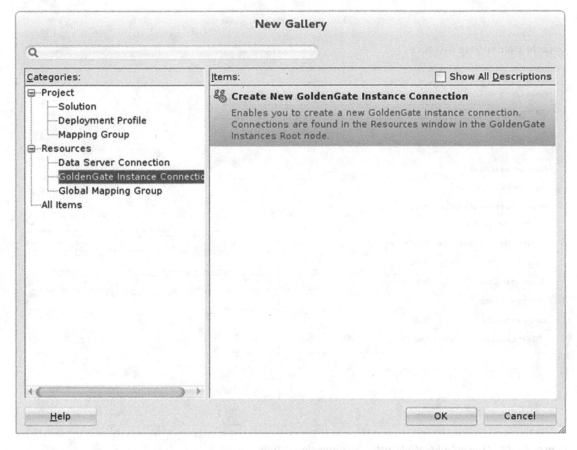

Figure 22-42. *Creating a new GoldenGate instance connection*

Create two GoldenGate Monitor Agent connections, one each for the source and target GoldenGate instances.

The agent username is specified in the Monitor Agent parameter file `Config.properties`.

The agent password is the same password that you configured while running `pw_agent_util.sh` after the Monitor Agent installation.

The agent port is also specified in the Monitor Agent parameter file `Config.properties`.

Figure 22-43 shows the Oracle GoldenGate instance for the source. Similarly, create another instance, called OGG Instance 2, for the target.

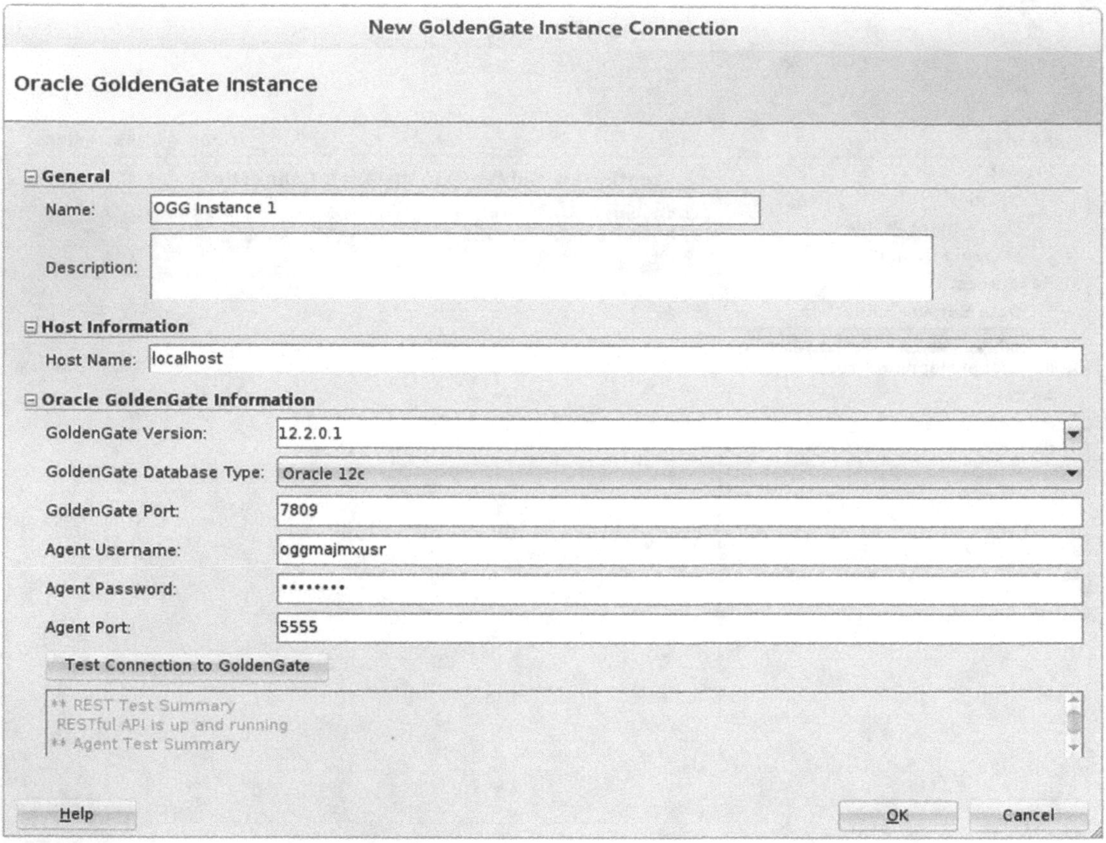

Figure 22-43. *Oracle GoldenGate instance connection details*

The right panel in Figure 22-44 shows the four physical resources you have created.

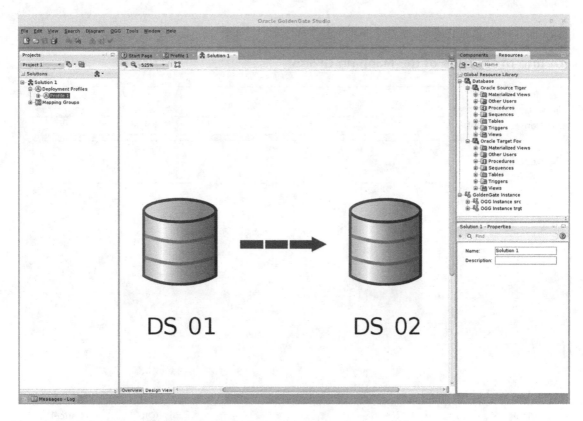

Figure 22-44. *Physical resource as indicated in the right panel*

You can open deployment profile Profile 1 to specify the objects participating in the replication. Just select an object and edit the properties.

Right-click Mapping Groups and select New. This will launch the Create New Mapping Group Wizard, as shown in Figure 22-45.

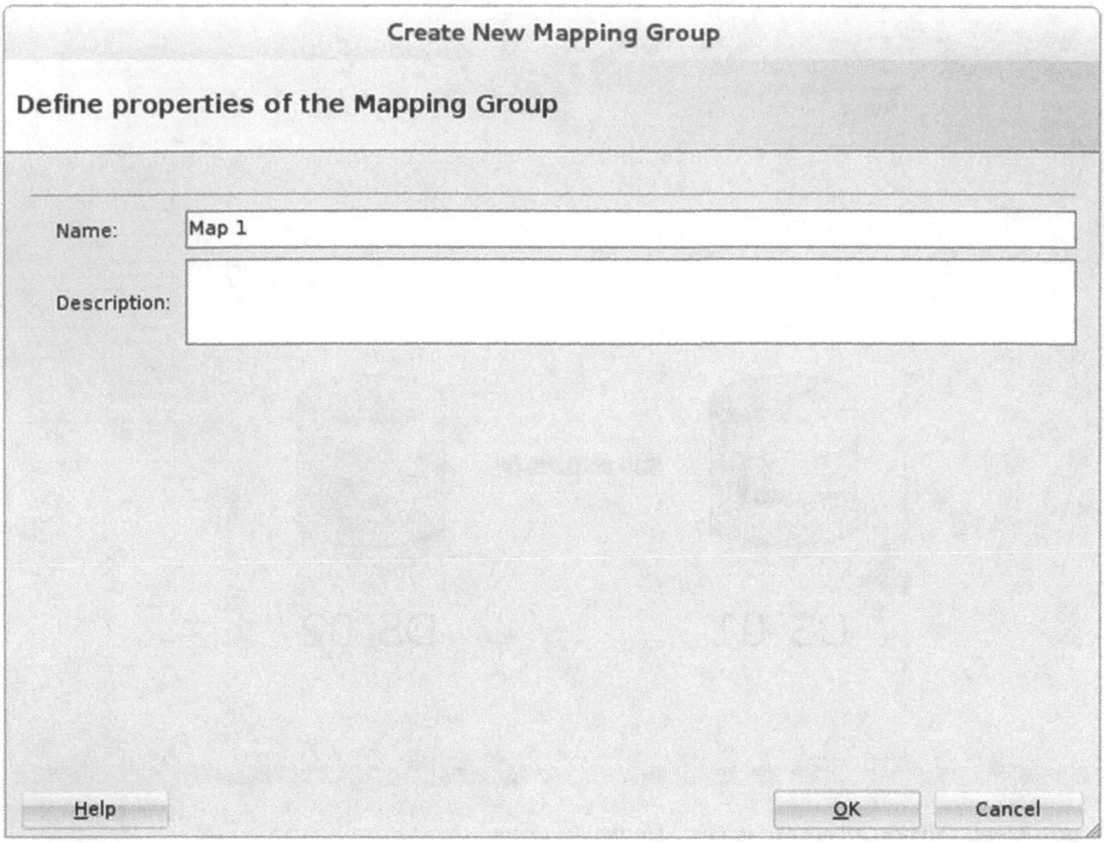

Create New Mapping Group	

Define properties of the Mapping Group

Name: Map 1

Description:

Help   <u>O</u>K   Cancel

Figure 22-45. *Creating a new mapping group*

Select tables to be replicated from the source and target databases. Drag and drop the tables in the mapping area for the source and the target, respectively, as shown in Figure 22-46.

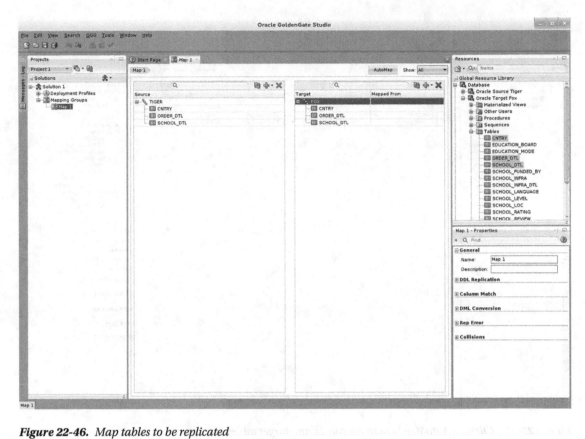

Figure 22-46. *Map tables to be replicated*

Click the AutoMap button, as shown in Figure 22-47. This will map the source tables with the target tables.

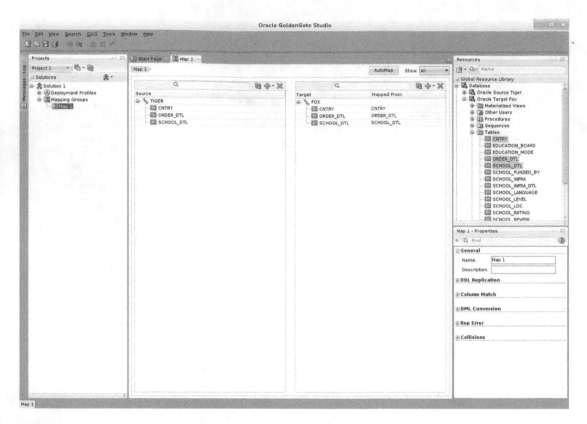

Figure 22-47. *Clicking AutoMap to map the source and target tables*

Next, you need to attach the mapping to Project 1. Drag and drop the mapping on the replication path. It will turn from a black dashed arrow to a red solid arrow, as shown in Figure 22-48. Alternatively, you can click the replication path to select it, and in the Properties panel, click the + symbol to add the mapping.

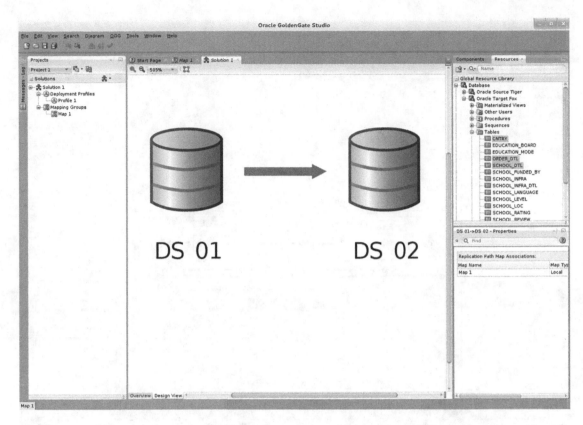

Figure 22-48. *Attaching the mapping to the project*

Select DS 01, DS 02, OGG Instance 01, and OGG Instance 02 one by one. Edit the properties for each of these objects to attach the four physical resources created in the previous steps, as shown in Figure 22-49.

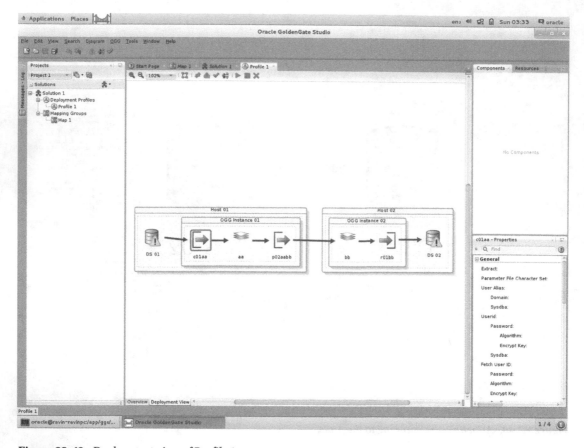

Figure 22-49. *Deployment view of Profile 1*

At this stage, the unidirectional replication solution is fully configured. You can right-click the profile to deploy the GoldenGate configuration online. You can also choose "Generate GoldenGate files…" to save the configuration in the local directory.

Figure 22-50 shows the dialog box that prompts you to generate and save the GoldenGate files in a local directory.

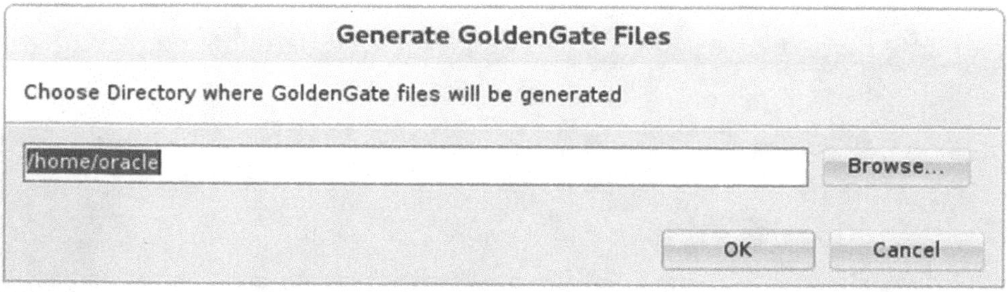

Generate GoldenGate Files

Choose Directory where GoldenGate files will be generated

/home/oracle   Browse...

            OK   Cancel

Figure 22-50. *Generating the GoldenGate files*

Figure 22-51 shows an overview of Profile 1. You can configure the deployment properties and lookup for deployment history and the monitor OGG processes.

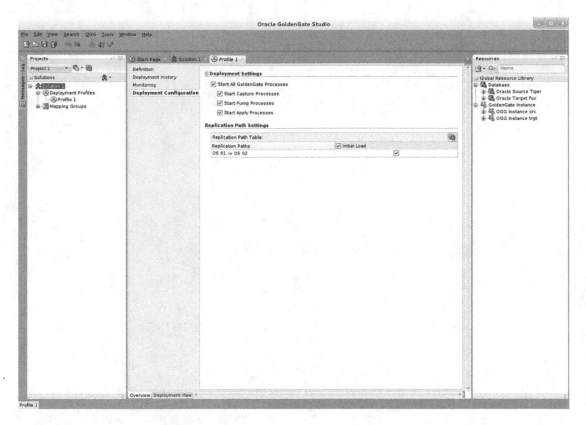

Figure 22-51. *Overview of Profile 1*

The previous demonstration was for a simple unidirectional replication. Oracle GoldenGate Studio allows you to perform advanced replication configurations such as exception handling, conflict detection and resolution, filter and mappings, and so on.

It can allow you to build quick solutions for multiple sources, multiple targets, active-active bidirectional replication, and deploying one solution to multiple locations (development, QA, and production).

Summary

In this chapter, we discussed how to install and configure Oracle GoldenGate Studio. It's a drag-and-drop utility to build quick Oracle GoldenGate replication configurations. The chapter demonstrated how to build a simple unidirectional replication solution using Oracle GoldenGate Studio.

In next chapter, we will discuss how to use the Oracle GoldenGate Reverse Utility to undo database changes to perform selective backouts.

CHAPTER 23

■ ■ ■

Undoing Data Changes

In this chapter, we will discuss how to undo data changes that were replicated from the source database to the target database, using the Oracle GoldenGate Reverse Utility. Although you can use native utilities of a particular database to restore the database to a previous state, like using flashback features in an Oracle database, OGG provides this generic utility that you can use for any supported database to reverse data changes. Also, since the OGG Reverse Utility only backs out changes, it is usually faster than a database restore.

Supported Databases

The following are the databases currently supported by the Oracle GoldenGate Reverse Utility:

- Oracle
- Sybase
- SQL Server
- IBM DB2

Limitations of the OGG Reverse Utility

The OGG Reverse Utility uses a before image to undo data changes on the target database. Although it supports multiple databases, it does not support reversing data changes on a few specific data types for which a before image is not captured.

Oracle Database

The following data types are not supported by the OGG Reverse Utility:

- CLOB
- BLOB
- NCLOB
- LONG
- LONG RAW
- XMLType

© Ravinder Gupta 2016
R. Gupta, *Mastering Oracle GoldenGate*, DOI 10.1007/978-1-4842-2301-7_23

- VARRAY

- Nested tables

Sybase Database

The following are the Sybase datatypes not supported by the OGG Reverse Utility:

- BINARY

- VARBINARY

- TEXT

- IMAGE

SQL Server

The following are the SQL Server data types not supported by the OGG Reverse Utility:

- TEXT

- NTEXT

- IMAGE

- VARCHAR (MAX)

IBM DB2

The following are the DB2 data types not supported by the OGG Reverse Utility:

- BLOB

- CLOB

- DBCLOB

When Do You Need to Use the Oracle GoldenGate Reverse Utility?

The following are a few typical scenarios when you need to undo data changes:

- To undo a replicated transaction (or transactions) committed on the target database

- To roll back the transaction on the target when an accidentally issued transaction on the source is replicated to the target database

- To restore the target database to a state before changes were replicated

How Does It Work?

Figure 23-1 shows the OGG Reverse Utility, which reads specific remote trails and converts them to output trails with undo changes.

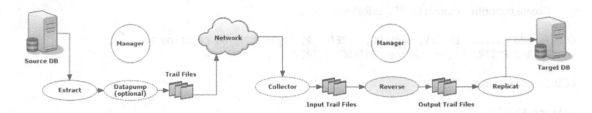

Figure 23-1. *OGG Reverse Utility*

The extract process is started to capture a before image of the transactions on the source. The OGG Reverse Utility reads the transactions from the input trail and reverses the order of transactions. It converts delete operations to inserts and converts insert operations to deletes. For update transactions, a before image is used to convert the update transaction as an after image. Finally, it reverses the begin and end transaction indicators. The output transactions are written to an output trail, which is then read by the replicat to apply the changes on the target database.

OGG Reverse Utility Steps Overview

As discussed earlier, to use the OGG Reverse Utility, you need to set up continuous change extract and replicat processes and a special extract to capture before images. The following are the steps to be performed for undoing data changes using the OGG Reverse Utility:

1. Start the manager on the source and target OGG instances.

2. Create a continuous change extract process and a replicat process on the source and the target, respectively.

3. Note the current time.

4. Start the extract and replicat processes.

5. Perform some transactions on the source table.

6. Note the current time again.

7. Check the target table to verify whether the transactions have replicated.

8. Create a special extract to capture the before images for the previous transactions.

9. Run the special extract process.

10. Use the OGG Reverse Utility to create output trail files that contain undo transactions.

11. Run the continuous change replicat to read the output trails from the previous step and apply the undo changes on the target database.

12. Verify whether the undo changes have been performed.

I performed a few transactions on the ORDER_INFO table on the source database on the ravin-ravinpc server during the following time period:

- *Start time*: 08-AUG-2016 11:00:20

- *End time*: 08-AUG-2016 11:08:35

Create the online extract EXTREV as follows:

```
GGSCI> add extract EXTREV, TRANLOG, THREADS 2, begin 2016-08-08 11:00:20
GGSCI> ADD RMTTRAIL ./dirdat/ee, EXTRACT EXTREV

GGSCI> edit params EXTREV

extract EXTREV

USERID tiger, PASSWORD tiger123_
end 2016-08-08 11:08:35
NOCOMPRESSDELETES
GETUPDATEBEFORES
RMTHOST node2-ravinpc, MGRPORT 7809
RMTTRAIL /app/ggs/fox/dirdat/ee
TABLE TIGER.ORDER_INFO;
```

The BEGIN and END timestamps indicate the time period between which transactions need to be captured along with their before images.

Also, you should register the extract process so you can retain the archive logs required during recovery in case the extract process abends/fails.

```
GGSCI> REGISTER EXTRACT EXTREV, LOGRETENTION
```

Start the extract process and monitor the report file for the end of transactions.

```
GGSCI> start extract EXTREV
```

Create an online replicat REPREV as follows:

```
GGSCI> add replicat REPREV, exttrail /app/ggs/fox/dirdat/rr

GGSCI> edit params REPREV

replicat REPREV
-end 2016-08-08 11:08:35
end runtime
userid fox, password fox123_
ASSUMETARGETDEFS
discardfile ./dirrpt/repcat.dsc, megabytes 10, purge
map TIGER.ORDER_INFO, target FOX.ORDER_INFO;
```

Locate the OGG Reverse Utility from the OGG Home directory for the target OGG instance, as shown here:

```
[oracle@node2-ravinpc fox]$ ls -lrt reverse
-rwxr-x---. 1 oracle oinstall 16100304 Apr 30 19:56 reverse
```

Execute the following to reverse the data changes from the source trails to generate the undo transactions in the output trails:

```
$ /app/ggs/fox/reverse /app/ggs/fox/dirdat/ee*,/app/ggs/fox/dirdat/rr*

Oracle GoldenGate Dynamic Rollback
Version 12.2.0.1.160419 OGGCORE_12.2.0.1.OOGGBP_PLATFORMS_160430.1401
Linux, x64, 64bit (optimized) on Apr 30 2016 16:53:31

Copyright (C) 1995, 2016, Oracle and/or its affiliates. All rights reserved.

Reversed /app/ggs/fox/dirdat/ee000001 to /app/ggs/fox/dirdat/rr000000
Total Data Bytes           83508
Avg Bytes/Record           113
Delete                       320
Insert                       418
Restart OK                     1
After Images                 739
Reversed /app/ggs/fox/dirdat/ee000000 to /app/ggs/fox/dirdat/rr000001
Total Data Bytes            7232
Avg Bytes/Record           113
Delete                        20
Insert                        42
Restart OK                     2
After Images                  64
```

Start the replicat and monitor the replicat process. Ensure that it has picked up the trails and started to apply transactions on the target database.

```
GGSCI> START REPREV
```

Verify the target table data and confirm whether the changes have been undone.

Summary

In previous chapters in this book, you learned how to replicate data in relational, nonrelational, Big Data, and cloud systems. We discussed advanced configurations of Oracle GoldenGate and tools for deploying and monitoring Oracle GoldenGate instances. In this last chapter of the book, we discussed how to undo data changes that were replicated from the source database to the target database, using the Oracle GoldenGate Reverse Utility. We discussed how the Oracle GoldenGate Reverse Utility works and demonstrated it with an example.

PART V

Appendixes

PART V

Appendices

CHAPTER 24

■ ■ ■

Appendix A: OGG Heartbeat and Checkpoints

It is recommended that you implement a heartbeat process in Oracle GoldenGate to monitor the lag between the source and target systems. This can help you identify a lag before it becomes a bottleneck. The heartbeat table also functions as ultimate proof that the GoldenGate replication is working from the source database to the target database. This appendix covers the process of adding and configuring a heartbeat process for Oracle GoldenGate 12.1 and earlier. Although you can still use the same process for OGG 12.2, there is a much simpler method for adding a heartbeat table in OGG 12.2. We will discuss later in this appendix.

Steps to Set Up a Heartbeat Process

These are the steps to add a heartbeat process to your Oracle GoldenGate environment:

1. Add a heartbeat table to the OGG schema on the source database.

2. Add a heartbeat table to the OGG schema on the target database.

3. Add a heartbeat history table to the OGG schema on the target database.

4. Add mapping parameters to each extract, data pump, and replicat process.

5. Create a stored procedure and DBMS scheduler job on the source to update the heartbeat table.

The source table called HEARTBEAT in the source database is updated regularly by using stored procedures and a DBMS scheduler job. The table is added to the extract, data pump, and replicat processes. Each of these processes adds some meta information in the form of tokens; this helps to calculate the lag time of each process.

The table structures, procedure, and trigger code is based on the Oracle documentation about best practices for monitoring lags. You can customize the table structures and associated code based on what suits your environment best.

Create Users

Unless you are configuring a bidirectional replication environment, you should use OGG owner users for the heartbeat setup. In bidirectional replication, the OGG users are excluded from the replication to prevent loopback.

© Ravinder Gupta 2016
R. Gupta, *Mastering Oracle GoldenGate*, DOI 10.1007/978-1-4842-2301-7_24

- On the source database:

```
SQL> CREATE USER TIGER IDENTIFIED BY TIGER123_;
SQL> GRANT CONNECT, RESOURCE, DBA TO TIGER;
SQL> GRANT SELECT ON V_$INSTANCE TO TIGER;
SQL> GRANT SELECT ON V_$DATABASE TO TIGER;
```

- On the target database:

```
SQL> CREATE USER FOX IDENTIFIED BY FOX123_;
SQL> GRANT CONNECT, RESOURCE, DBA TO FOX;
SQL> GRANT SELECT ON V_$INSTANCE TO FOX;
SQL> GRANT SELECT ON V_$DATABASE TO FOX;
```

Create Tables

Create three tables, one on the source and two on the target, as shown here:

- On the source database:

```
CREATE TABLE HEARTBEAT
(
    ID                  NUMBER,
    SRC_DB              VARCHAR2 (30),
    EXTRACT_NAME        VARCHAR2 (8),
    SOURCE_COMMIT       TIMESTAMP,
    TARGET_COMMIT       TIMESTAMP,
    CAPTIME             TIMESTAMP,
    CAPLAG              NUMBER,
    PMPTIME             TIMESTAMP,
    PMPGROUP            VARCHAR2 (8 BYTE),
    PMPLAG              NUMBER,
    DELTIME             TIMESTAMP,
    DELGROUP            VARCHAR2 (8 BYTE),
    DELLAG              NUMBER,
    TOTALLAG            NUMBER,
    UPDATE_TIMESTAMP    TIMESTAMP,
    CONSTRAINT HEARTBEAT_PK PRIMARY KEY (THREAD) ENABLE
);
```

Insert a heartbeat record to the `TIGER.HEARTBEAT` table as shown here:

```
SQL> INSERT INTO TIGER.HEARTBEAT (THREAD)
    SELECT THREAD# FROM V$INSTANCE;
SQL> COMMIT;
```

- On the target database:

```
CREATE TABLE GGS_HEARTBEAT
(
    ID                  NUMBER,
    SRC_DB              VARCHAR2 (30),
```

```
   EXTRACT_NAME        VARCHAR2 (8),
   SOURCE_COMMIT       TIMESTAMP,
   TARGET_COMMIT       TIMESTAMP,
   CAPTIME             TIMESTAMP,
   CAPLAG              NUMBER,
   PMPTIME             TIMESTAMP,
   PMPGROUP            VARCHAR2 (8 BYTE),
   PMPLAG              NUMBER,
   DELTIME             TIMESTAMP,
   DELGROUP            VARCHAR2 (8 BYTE),
   DELLAG              NUMBER,
   TOTALLAG            NUMBER,
   UPDATE_TIMESTAMP    TIMESTAMP,
   CONSTRAINT GGS_HEARTBEAT_PK PRIMARY KEY (DELGROUP) ENABLE
);

CREATE TABLE GGS_HEARTBEAT_HISTORY
(
   ID                  NUMBER,
   SRC_DB              VARCHAR2 (30),
   EXTRACT_NAME        VARCHAR2 (8),
   SOURCE_COMMIT       TIMESTAMP,
   TARGET_COMMIT       TIMESTAMP,
   CAPTIME             TIMESTAMP,
   CAPLAG              NUMBER,
   PMPTIME             TIMESTAMP,
   PMPGROUP            VARCHAR2 (8 BYTE),
   PMPLAG              NUMBER,
   DELTIME             TIMESTAMP,
   DELGROUP            VARCHAR2 (8 BYTE),
   DELLAG              NUMBER,
   TOTALLAG            NUMBER,
   UPDATE_TIMESTAMP    TIMESTAMP,
);
```

Create sequences to be used for inserting into the target tables to uniquely identify rows.

```
CREATE SEQUENCE SEQ_GGS_HEARTBEAT_ID INCREMENT BY 1 START WITH 1 ORDER;

CREATE SEQUENCE SEQ_GGS_HEARTBEAT_HIST INCREMENT BY 1 START WITH 1;
```

Create before insert or update triggers on the target tables.

```
CREATE OR REPLACE TRIGGER GGS_HEARTBEAT_TRIG
   BEFORE INSERT OR UPDATE
   ON GGS_HEARTBEAT
   FOR EACH ROW
BEGIN
   SELECT SEQ_GGS_HEARTBEAT_ID.NEXTVAL INTO :NEW.ID FROM DUAL;

   SELECT SYSTIMESTAMP INTO :NEW.TARGET_COMMIT FROM DUAL;
```

```
SELECT FROM_TZ (CAST (:NEW.CAPTIME AS TIMESTAMP), :NEW.SOURCE_TIMEZONE)
  INTO :NEW.CAPTIME
  FROM DUAL;

SELECT FROM_TZ (CAST (:NEW.PMPTIME AS TIMESTAMP), :NEW.SOURCE_TIMEZONE)
  INTO :NEW.PMPTIME
  FROM DUAL;

SELECT      TRUNC (
                TO_NUMBER (
                  SUBSTR ( (:NEW.CAPTIME - :NEW.SOURCE_COMMIT),
                          1,
                          INSTR (:NEW.CAPTIME - :NEW.SOURCE_COMMIT, ' '))))
         * 86400
       +    TO_NUMBER (
                SUBSTR (
                  (:NEW.CAPTIME - :NEW.SOURCE_COMMIT),
                  INSTR ( (:NEW.CAPTIME - :NEW.SOURCE_COMMIT), ' ') + 1,
                  2))
         * 3600
       +    TO_NUMBER (
                SUBSTR (
                  (:NEW.CAPTIME - :NEW.SOURCE_COMMIT),
                  INSTR ( (:NEW.CAPTIME - :NEW.SOURCE_COMMIT), ' ') + 4,
                  2))
        * 60
       + TO_NUMBER (
            SUBSTR ( (:NEW.CAPTIME - :NEW.SOURCE_COMMIT),
                  INSTR ( (:NEW.CAPTIME - :NEW.SOURCE_COMMIT), ' ') + 7,
                  2))
       +    TO_NUMBER (
                SUBSTR (
                  (:NEW.CAPTIME - :NEW.SOURCE_COMMIT),
                  INSTR ( (:NEW.CAPTIME - :NEW.SOURCE_COMMIT), ' ') + 10,
                  6))
          / 1000000
  INTO :NEW.CAPLAG
  FROM DUAL;

SELECT      TRUNC (
                TO_NUMBER (
                  SUBSTR ( (:NEW.PMPTIME - :NEW.CAPTIME),
                          1,
                          INSTR (:NEW.PMPTIME - :NEW.CAPTIME, ' '))))
         * 86400
       +    TO_NUMBER (
                SUBSTR ( (:NEW.PMPTIME - :NEW.CAPTIME),
                        INSTR ( (:NEW.PMPTIME - :NEW.CAPTIME), ' ') + 1,
                        2))
         * 3600
```

```
        +    TO_NUMBER (
                SUBSTR ( (:NEW.PMPTIME - :NEW.CAPTIME),
                        INSTR ( (:NEW.PMPTIME - :NEW.CAPTIME), ' ') + 4,
                        2))
          * 60
        + TO_NUMBER (
             SUBSTR ( (:NEW.PMPTIME - :NEW.CAPTIME),
                     INSTR ( (:NEW.PMPTIME - :NEW.CAPTIME), ' ') + 7,
                     2))
        +    TO_NUMBER (
                SUBSTR ( (:NEW.PMPTIME - :NEW.CAPTIME),
                        INSTR ( (:NEW.PMPTIME - :NEW.CAPTIME), ' ') + 10,
                        6))
          / 1000000
    INTO :NEW.PMPLAG
    FROM DUAL;

SELECT    TRUNC (
             TO_NUMBER (
                SUBSTR ( (:NEW.DELTIME - :NEW.PMPTIME),
                        1,
                        INSTR (:NEW.DELTIME - :NEW.PMPTIME, ' '))))
        * 86400
        + TO_NUMBER (
             SUBSTR ( (:NEW.DELTIME - :NEW.PMPTIME),
                     INSTR ( (:NEW.DELTIME - :NEW.PMPTIME), ' ') + 1,
                     2))
        * 3600
        +    TO_NUMBER (
                SUBSTR ( (:NEW.DELTIME - :NEW.PMPTIME),
                        INSTR ( (:NEW.DELTIME - :NEW.PMPTIME), ' ') + 4,
                        2))
          * 60
        + TO_NUMBER (
             SUBSTR ( (:NEW.DELTIME - :NEW.PMPTIME),
                     INSTR ( (:NEW.DELTIME - :NEW.PMPTIME), ' ') + 7,
                     2))
        +    TO_NUMBER (
                SUBSTR ( (:NEW.DELTIME - :NEW.PMPTIME),
                        INSTR ( (:NEW.DELTIME - :NEW.PMPTIME), ' ') + 10,
                        6))
          / 1000000
    INTO :NEW.DELLAG
    FROM DUAL;

SELECT    TRUNC (
             TO_NUMBER (
                SUBSTR (
                  (:NEW.TARGET_COMMIT - :NEW.SOURCE_COMMIT),
                  1,
                  INSTR (:NEW.TARGET_COMMIT - :NEW.SOURCE_COMMIT, ' '))))
```

```
                    * 86400
          +    TO_NUMBER (
                  SUBSTR (
                    (:NEW.TARGET_COMMIT - :NEW.SOURCE_COMMIT),
                     INSTR ( (:NEW.TARGET_COMMIT - :NEW.SOURCE_COMMIT), ' ')
                    + 1,
                    2))
              * 3600
          +    TO_NUMBER (
                  SUBSTR (
                    (:NEW.TARGET_COMMIT - :NEW.SOURCE_COMMIT),
                     INSTR ( (:NEW.TARGET_COMMIT - :NEW.SOURCE_COMMIT), ' ')
                    + 4,
                    2))
              * 60
          +  TO_NUMBER (
                  SUBSTR (
                    (:NEW.TARGET_COMMIT - :NEW.SOURCE_COMMIT),
                    INSTR ( (:NEW.TARGET_COMMIT - :NEW.SOURCE_COMMIT), ' ') + 7,
                    2))
          +    TO_NUMBER (
                  SUBSTR (
                    (:NEW.TARGET_COMMIT - :NEW.SOURCE_COMMIT),
                     INSTR ( (:NEW.TARGET_COMMIT - :NEW.SOURCE_COMMIT), ' ')
                    + 10,
                    6))
             / 1000000
      INTO :NEW.TOTALLAG
      FROM DUAL;
END;
/

ALTER TRIGGER GGS_HEARTBEAT_TRIG ENABLE;

CREATE OR REPLACE TRIGGER GGS_HEARTBEAT_TRIG_HIST
   BEFORE INSERT OR UPDATE
   ON GGS_HEARTBEAT_HISTORY
   FOR EACH ROW
BEGIN
   SELECT SEQ_GGS_HEARTBEAT_HIST.NEXTVAL INTO :NEW.ID FROM DUAL;

   SELECT SYSTIMESTAMP INTO :NEW.TARGET_COMMIT FROM DUAL;

   SELECT FROM_TZ (CAST (:NEW.CAPTIME AS TIMESTAMP), :NEW.SOURCE_TIMEZONE)
     INTO :NEW.CAPTIME
     FROM DUAL;

   SELECT FROM_TZ (CAST (:NEW.PMPTIME AS TIMESTAMP), :NEW.SOURCE_TIMEZONE)
     INTO :NEW.PMPTIME
     FROM DUAL;
```

```
SELECT     TRUNC (
               TO_NUMBER (
                 SUBSTR ( (:NEW.CAPTIME - :NEW.SOURCE_COMMIT),
                         1,
                         INSTR (:NEW.CAPTIME - :NEW.SOURCE_COMMIT, ' '))))
         * 86400
       +   TO_NUMBER (
             SUBSTR (
               (:NEW.CAPTIME - :NEW.SOURCE_COMMIT),
               INSTR ( (:NEW.CAPTIME - :NEW.SOURCE_COMMIT), ' ') + 1,
               2))
         * 3600
       +   TO_NUMBER (
             SUBSTR (
               (:NEW.CAPTIME - :NEW.SOURCE_COMMIT),
               INSTR ( (:NEW.CAPTIME - :NEW.SOURCE_COMMIT), ' ') + 4,
               2))
         * 60
       + TO_NUMBER (
           SUBSTR ( (:NEW.CAPTIME - :NEW.SOURCE_COMMIT),
                   INSTR ( (:NEW.CAPTIME - :NEW.SOURCE_COMMIT), ' ') + 7,
                   2))
       +   TO_NUMBER (
             SUBSTR (
               (:NEW.CAPTIME - :NEW.SOURCE_COMMIT),
               INSTR ( (:NEW.CAPTIME - :NEW.SOURCE_COMMIT), ' ') + 10,
               6))
         / 1000000
  INTO :NEW.CAPLAG
  FROM DUAL;

SELECT     TRUNC (
               TO_NUMBER (
                 SUBSTR ( (:NEW.PMPTIME - :NEW.CAPTIME),
                         1,
                         INSTR (:NEW.PMPTIME - :NEW.CAPTIME, ' '))))
         * 86400
       +   TO_NUMBER (
             SUBSTR ( (:NEW.PMPTIME - :NEW.CAPTIME),
                     INSTR ( (:NEW.PMPTIME - :NEW.CAPTIME), ' ') + 1,
                     2))
         * 3600
       +   TO_NUMBER (
             SUBSTR ( (:NEW.PMPTIME - :NEW.CAPTIME),
                     INSTR ( (:NEW.PMPTIME - :NEW.CAPTIME), ' ') + 4,
                     2))
         * 60
       + TO_NUMBER (
           SUBSTR ( (:NEW.PMPTIME - :NEW.CAPTIME),
                   INSTR ( (:NEW.PMPTIME - :NEW.CAPTIME), ' ') + 7,
                   2))
```

597

```
        +    TO_NUMBER (
                SUBSTR ( (:NEW.PMPTIME - :NEW.CAPTIME),
                        INSTR ( (:NEW.PMPTIME - :NEW.CAPTIME), ' ') + 10,
                        6))
           / 1000000
  INTO :NEW.PMPLAG
  FROM DUAL;

SELECT       TRUNC (
                TO_NUMBER (
                   SUBSTR ( (:NEW.DELTIME - :NEW.PMPTIME),
                           1,
                           INSTR (:NEW.DELTIME - :NEW.PMPTIME, ' '))))
        * 86400
        +    TO_NUMBER (
                SUBSTR ( (:NEW.DELTIME - :NEW.PMPTIME),
                        INSTR ( (:NEW.DELTIME - :NEW.PMPTIME), ' ') + 1,
                        2))
          * 3600
        +    TO_NUMBER (
                SUBSTR ( (:NEW.DELTIME - :NEW.PMPTIME),
                        INSTR ( (:NEW.DELTIME - :NEW.PMPTIME), ' ') + 4,
                        2))
          * 60
        + TO_NUMBER (
              SUBSTR ( (:NEW.DELTIME - :NEW.PMPTIME),
                      INSTR ( (:NEW.DELTIME - :NEW.PMPTIME), ' ') + 7,
                      2))
        +    TO_NUMBER (
                SUBSTR ( (:NEW.DELTIME - :NEW.PMPTIME),
                        INSTR ( (:NEW.DELTIME - :NEW.PMPTIME), ' ') + 10,
                        6))
           / 1000000
  INTO :NEW.DELLAG
  FROM DUAL;

SELECT       TRUNC (
                TO_NUMBER (
                   SUBSTR (
                       (:NEW.TARGET_COMMIT - :NEW.SOURCE_COMMIT),
                       1,
                       INSTR (:NEW.TARGET_COMMIT - :NEW.SOURCE_COMMIT, ' '))))
        * 86400
        +    TO_NUMBER (
                SUBSTR (
                    (:NEW.TARGET_COMMIT - :NEW.SOURCE_COMMIT),
                     INSTR ( (:NEW.TARGET_COMMIT - :NEW.SOURCE_COMMIT), ' ')
                   + 1,
                   2))
          * 3600
        +    TO_NUMBER (
```

```
            SUBSTR (
                (:NEW.TARGET_COMMIT - :NEW.SOURCE_COMMIT),
                    INSTR ( (:NEW.TARGET_COMMIT - :NEW.SOURCE_COMMIT), ' ')
                + 4,
                2))
        * 60
      + TO_NUMBER (
            SUBSTR (
                (:NEW.TARGET_COMMIT - :NEW.SOURCE_COMMIT),
                INSTR ( (:NEW.TARGET_COMMIT - :NEW.SOURCE_COMMIT), ' ') + 7,
                2))
      +    TO_NUMBER (
                SUBSTR (
                    (:NEW.TARGET_COMMIT - :NEW.SOURCE_COMMIT),
                      INSTR ( (:NEW.TARGET_COMMIT - :NEW.SOURCE_COMMIT), ' ')
                  + 10,
                  6))
          / 1000000
    INTO :NEW.TOTALLAG
    FROM DUAL;
END;
/

ALTER TRIGGER GGS_HEARTBEAT_TRIG_HIST ENABLE;
```

■ **Note** When configuring heartbeat for bidirectional replication, you need to create all three tables on both the source and target databases.

Add Supplemental Logging

Log in to GGSCI and add supplemental logging for the source HEARTBEAT table.

```
GGSCI> DBLOGIN USERID tiger, PASSWORD tiger123_
GGSCI> ADD TRANDATA TIGER.HEARTBEAT
```

Create a Job to Update the HEARTBEAT Table

Connect as SYSDBA on the source database to create a job in the source OGG schema (TIGER), which calls the stored procedure GG_UPDATE_HB_TAB to update the heartbeat table.

```
CREATE OR REPLACE PROCEDURE TIGER.GG_UPDATE_HB_TAB
IS
    V_THREAD_NUM        NUMBER;
    V_DB_UNIQUE_NAME    VARCHAR2 (128);
BEGIN
    SELECT DB_UNIQUE_NAME INTO V_DB_UNIQUE_NAME FROM V$DATABASE;
```

```
   UPDATE TIGER.HEARTBEAT
      SET UPDATE_TIMESTAMP = SYSTIMESTAMP, SRC_DB = V_DB_UNIQUE_NAME;

   COMMIT;
END;
/

BEGIN
   SYS.DBMS_SCHEDULER.CREATE_JOB (
      JOB_NAME             => 'TIGER.OGG_HB',
      JOB_TYPE             => 'STORED_PROCEDURE',
      JOB_ACTION           => 'TIGER.GG_UPDATE_HB_TAB',
      NUMBER_OF_ARGUMENTS  => 0,
      START_DATE           => NULL,
      REPEAT_INTERVAL      => 'FREQ=MINUTELY',
      END_DATE             => NULL,
      JOB_CLASS            => '"SYS"."DEFAULT_JOB_CLASS"',
      ENABLED              => FALSE,
      AUTO_DROP            => FALSE,
      COMMENTS             => 'GoldenGate',
      CREDENTIAL_NAME      => NULL,
      DESTINATION_NAME     => NULL);

   SYS.DBMS_SCHEDULER.SET_ATTRIBUTE (NAME      => 'TIGER.OGG_HB',
                                     ATTRIBUTE => 'restartable',
                                     VALUE     => TRUE);

   SYS.DBMS_SCHEDULER.SET_ATTRIBUTE (
      NAME      => 'TIGER.OGG_HB',
      ATTRIBUTE => 'logging_level',
      VALUE     => DBMS_SCHEDULER.LOGGING_OFF);

   SYS.DBMS_SCHEDULER.ENABLE (NAME => 'TIGER.OGG_HB');
END;
/
```

Check the Job Status

Verify the job status using the following SQL statement:

```
SELECT OWNER,
       JOB_NAME,
       JOB_CLASS,
       ENABLED,
       NEXT_RUN_DATE,
       REPEAT_INTERVAL
  FROM DBA_SCHEDULER_JOBS
 WHERE OWNER = DECODE (UPPER ('TIGER'), 'ALL', OWNER, UPPER ('TIGER'));
```

Configure the Extract

Create a file heartbeat_extract.prm to be included in the extract parameter file of each extract process in your source Oracle GoldenGate instance.

```
TABLE TIGER.HEARTBEAT,
TOKENS (
CAPGROUP = @GETENV ("GGENVIRONMENT", "GROUPNAME"),
CAPTIME = @DATE ("YYYY-MM-DD HH:MI:SS.FFFFFF","JTS",@GETENV ("JULIANTIMESTAMP")));
```

Include this file in the extract parameter file before or after a TABLE statement, as shown here:

```
include dirprm/heartbeat_extract.prm
```

Configure the Data Pump

Create a file called heartbeat_datapump.prm to be included in the parameter file of each data pump extract process in your source Oracle GoldenGate instance.

```
TABLE TIGER.HEARTBEAT,
TOKENS (
PMPGROUP = @GETENV ("GGENVIRONMENT","GROUPNAME"),
PMPTIME = @DATE ("YYYY- MM-DD HH:MI:SS.FFFFFF","JTS",@GETENV
("JULIANTIMESTAMP"))
);
```

Include this file in the data pump extract parameter file before or after a TABLE statement, as shown here:

```
include dirprm/heartbeat_datapump.prm
```

Configure the Replicat

Create a file heartbeat_replicat.prm to be included in the parameter file of each replicat process in your target Oracle GoldenGate instance.

```
MAP TIGER.HEARTBEAT, TARGET FOX.GGS_HEARTBEAT,
KEYCOLS (DELGROUP),
INSERTMISSINGUPDATES,
COLMAP (USEDEFAULTS,
ID = 0,
SOURCE_COMMIT = @GETENV ("GGHEADER", "COMMITTIMESTAMP"),
EXTRACT_NAME = @TOKEN ("CAPGROUP"),
CAPTIME = @TOKEN ("CAPTIME"),
PMPGROUP = @TOKEN ("PMPGROUP"),
PMPTIME = @TOKEN ("PMPTIME"),
DELGROUP = @GETENV ("GGENVIRONMENT", "GROUPNAME"),
DELTIME = @DATE ("YYYY-MM-DD HH:MI:SS.FFFFFF","JTS",@GETENV ("JULIANTIMESTAMP")));
MAP TIGER.HEARTBEAT, TARGET FOX.GGS_HEARTBEAT_HISTORY,
KEYCOLS (ID),
INSERTALLRECORDS,
```

601

```
COLMAP (USEDEFAULTS,
ID = 0,
SOURCE_COMMIT = @GETENV ("GGHEADER", "COMMITTIMESTAMP"),
EXTRACT_NAME = @TOKEN ("CAPGROUP"),
CAPTIME = @TOKEN ("CAPTIME"),
PMPGROUP = @TOKEN ("PMPGROUP"),
PMPTIME = @TOKEN ("PMPTIME"),
DELGROUP = @GETENV ("GGENVIRONMENT", "GROUPNAME"),
DELTIME = @DATE ("YYYY-MM-DD HH:MI:SS.FFFFFF","JTS",@GETENV ("JULIANTIMESTAMP"))
);
```

Include this file in the replicat parameter file before or after a MAP statement, as shown here:

```
include dirprm/heartbeat_replicat.prm
```

Additional Scripts

Here are few additional scripts that you can use for monitoring and managing your heartbeat process.
Stop the heartbeat.

```
BEGIN
    SYS.DBMS_SCHEDULER.DROP_JOB (job_name    => '"TIGER"."OGG_HB"',
                                 defer       => FALSE,
                                 force       => TRUE);
END;
/
```

Check the current heartbeat.

```
SELECT SRC_DB,
       EXTRACT_NAME,
       CAPLAG,
       PMPLAG,
       DELLAG,
       TOTALLAG,
       UPDATE_TIMESTAMP
  FROM FOX.GGS_HEARTBEAT;
```

Adding the Heartbeat Table in Oracle GoldenGate 12.2

Oracle GoldenGate 12.2 introduced the integrated heartbeat table. It is easy to configure and provides automatic heartbeat transactions every minute. It also includes an auto-purge feature. A heartbeat transaction is replicated from the extract to the data pump and to the replicat. You no longer need to add heartbeat tables to the extract, data pump, or replicat parameter files.

Add GGSCHEMA to the GLOBALS parameter file.

```
EDIT PARAMS ./GLOBALS

GGSCHEMA tiger
ALLOWOUTPUTDIR /app/ggtrails
```

Bounce the manager to make the new GLOBALS file parameter effective.

```
GGSCI> STOP MGR
GGSCI> START MGR
```

Log in to the source Oracle GoldenGate instance from the command prompt and add the heartbeat table, as shown here:

```
GGSCI> DBLOGIN USERID tiger, PASSWORD tiger123_
Successfully logged into database.

GGSCI> ADD HEARTBEATTABLE
2016-08-24 08:54:32 INFO OGG-14001 Successfully created heartbeat seed table ["GG_HEARTBEAT_
SEED"].

2016-08-24 08:54:32 INFO OGG-14032 Successfully added supplemental logging for heartbeat
seed table ["GG_HEARTBEAT_SEED"].

2016-08-24 08:54:32 INFO OGG-14000 Successfully created heartbeat table ["GG_HEARTBEAT"].

2016-08-24 08:54:32 INFO OGG-14033 Successfully added supplemental logging for heartbeat
table ["GG_HEARTBEAT"].

2016-08-24 08:54:32 INFO OGG-14016 Successfully created heartbeat history table ["GG_
HEARTBEAT_HISTORY"].

2016-08-24 08:54:32 INFO OGG-14023 Successfully created heartbeat lag view ["GG_LAG"].

2016-08-24 08:54:32 INFO OGG-14024 Successfully created heartbeat lag history view ["GG_LAG_
HISTORY"].

2016-08-24 08:54:32 INFO OGG-14003 Successfully populated heartbeat seed table with
[GG21CDB].

2016-08-24 08:54:33 INFO OGG-14004 Successfully created procedure ["GG_UPDATE_HB_TAB"] to
update the heartbeat tables.

2016-08-24 08:54:33 INFO OGG-14017 Successfully created procedure ["GG_PURGE_HB_TAB"] to
purge the heartbeat history table.

2016-08-24 08:54:33 INFO OGG-14005 Successfully created scheduler job ["GG_UPDATE_
HEARTBEATS"] to update the heartbeat tables.

2016-08-24 08:54:33 INFO OGG-14018 Successfully created scheduler job ["GG_PURGE_
HEARTBEATS"] to purge the heartbeat history table.
```

Perform the same action on the target Oracle GoldenGate instance. You can also specify values for the heartbeat frequency, retention time, and purge frequency, as shown here:

```
GGSCI> ADD HEARTBEATTABLE, frequency 180, retention_time 15, purge_frequency 2
```

Or as shown here:

```
GGSCI> ADD HEARTBEATTABLE, frequency 120, retention_time 10, purge_frequency 2
```

Log in to the source and target database instances and verify that the following objects have been created. These are the default table names although you can override the default names using the HEARTBEATTABLE parameter in the GLOBALS file.

- Tables:

  ```
  GG_HEARTBEAT
  GG_HEARTBEAT_SEED
  GG_HEARTBEAT_HISTORY
  ```

- Views:

  ```
  GG_LAG
  GG_LAG_HISTORY
  ```

- Procedures:

  ```
  GG_UPDATE_HB_TAB
  GG_PURGE_HB_TAB
  ```

- Scheduler jobs:

  ```
  GG_PURGE_HEARTBEATS
  GG_UPDATE_HEARTBEATS
  ```

Use INFO HEARTBEATTABLE and ALTER HEARTBEATTABLE to view and modify the heartbeat parameters.

```
GGSCI > info heartbeattable
HEARTBEAT table tiger.gg_heartbeat exists.
HEARTBEAT table tiger.gg_heartbeat_seed exists.
HEARTBEAT table tiger.gg_heartbeat_history exists.
Frequency interval: 60 seconds.
Purge frequency interval: 1 days.
Retention time: 30 days.
```

Scheduler updates record in the GG_HEARTBEAT_SEED table. The table is then replicated to the target database. You can query the GG_LAG_HISTORY table in the target database to monitor the lag.

```
SQL> SELECT HEARTBEAT_RECEIVED_TS, INCOMING_PATH, INCOMING_LAG FROM GG_LAG_HISTORY;
```

To delete the integrated heartbeat table, use the following command:

```
GGSCI> DELETE HEARTBEATTABLE
```

OGG Checkpoints

Checkpoints are maintained for each OGG process to aid in the recovery after a failure and to maintain data integrity. Checkpoints are maintained individually for the extract, data pump, and replicat processes.

Extract processes capture the committed changes from redo/archive logs and keep track of the open transactions. It maintains the following four types of checkpoint information:

- *Startup checkpoint*: This is the first checkpoint information when the extract process is started.

- *Current read checkpoint*: This shows information for the current read position of the extract process.

- *Recovery checkpoint*: This shows the oldest open transaction in the database.

- *Current write checkpoint*: This shows the current write position of the extract where it is writing captured information into the local trail files.

Execute the following command to view checkpoint information for a particular extract process:

```
GGSCI> INFO EXTRACT extract_name, SHOWCH
```

The following is sample output of the previous command on extract ETTND001 in the source OGG instance TIGER:

```
GGSCI (ravin-ravinpc) 2> info extract ETTND001, showch

EXTRACT      ETTND001  Last Started 2016-08-10 15:54    Status RUNNING
Checkpoint Lag        00:00:00 (updated 00:00:00 ago)
Log Read Checkpoint   Oracle Redo Logs
                      2016-08-29 12:56:07  Seqno 106863, RBA 1024
                      SCN 3415.2313642031 (14669626957871)

Current Checkpoint Detail:

Read Checkpoint #1

  Oracle Redo Log

  Startup Checkpoint (starting position in the data source):
    Thread #: 1
    Sequence #: 102999
    RBA: 621942800
    Timestamp: 2016-08-10 15:16:54.000000
    SCN: 3412.3864769373 (14658293183325)
    Redo File: Not Available

  Recovery Checkpoint (position of oldest unprocessed transaction in the data source):
    Thread #: 1
    Sequence #: 106793
    RBA: 92417040
    Timestamp: 2016-08-29 09:13:26.000000
```

```
    SCN: 3415.2288070943 (14669601386783)
    Redo File: Not Available

  Current Checkpoint (position of last record read in the data source):
    Thread #: 1
    Sequence #: 106863
    RBA: 1024
    Timestamp: 2016-08-29 12:56:07.000000
    SCN: 3415.2313642031 (14669626957871)
    Redo File: /app/database/oraredo01/orcl/redo_16a.dbf

  BR Previous Recovery Checkpoint:
    Thread #: 0
    Sequence #: 0
    RBA: 0
    Timestamp: 2016-08-10 15:54:46.457843
    SCN: Not available
    Redo File:

  BR Begin Recovery Checkpoint:
    Thread #: 0
    Sequence #: 106793
    RBA: 92417040
    Timestamp: 2016-08-29 09:13:26.000000
    SCN: 3415.2288070943 (14669601386783)
    Redo File:

  BR End Recovery Checkpoint:
    Thread #: 1
    Sequence #: 106847
    RBA: 369596416
    Timestamp: 2016-08-29 12:04:51.000000
    SCN: 3415.2310924285 (14669624240125)
    Redo File:

Write Checkpoint #1

  GGS Log Trail

  Current Checkpoint (current write position):
    Sequence #: 1945
    RBA: 26154763
    Timestamp: 2016-08-29 12:56:14.921105
    Extract Trail: /app/ggs/tiger/dirdat/t1

CSN state information:
  CRC: A6-3B-67-70
  Completed CSN: 14669626957815
  Completed TXNs: 55.19.1716101
```

```
Header:
  Version = 2
  Record Source = A
  Type = 10
  # Input Checkpoints = 1
  # Output Checkpoints = 1

File Information:
  Block Size = 2048
  Max Blocks = 100
  Record Length = 2048
  Current Offset = 0

Configuration:
  Data Source = 3
  Transaction Integrity = 1
  Task Type = 0

Status:
  Start Time = 2016-08-10 15:54:47
  Last Update Time = 2016-08-29 12:56:14
  Stop Status = A
  Last Result = 400
```

A data pump process captures the following three checkpoints. Also, note that the data pump read checkpoints are in local trails and the write checkpoints are in remote trails.

- *Startup checkpoint*: This is the first checkpoint information when the data pump process is started.

- *Current read checkpoint*: This shows information for the current read position of the data pump process in the local trail.

- *Current write checkpoint*: This shows the current write position of the data pump where it is writing captured information into the remote trail files.

Execute the following command to view checkpoint information for a particular extract process:

```
GGSCI> INFO EXTRACT datapump_name, SHOWCH
```

A replicat process captures the following two checkpoints. The replicat reads information from the remote trail files and applies them to the database; hence, it doesn't need a write checkpoint.

- *Startup checkpoint*: This is the first checkpoint information when the replicat process is started.

- *Current read checkpoint*: This shows the position of the last record read in the database including the trail file sequence number and the RBA.

Figure 24-1 shows checkpoint information for the Oracle GoldenGate processes.

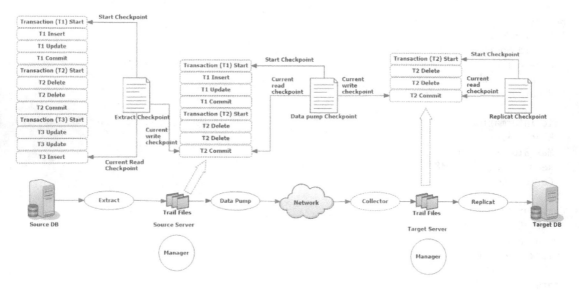

Figure 24-1. *Checkpoints in Oracle GoldenGate*

Checkpoint Storage Location

Extract checkpoints are stored in both the database and the checkpoint file (*.cpe) located in the OGG_HOME/
dirchk directory.

Data pump checkpoints are stored only in the checkpoint files for the particular data pump in the OGG_
HOME/dirchk directory.

Replicat checkpoints can be stored in either database or checkpoint files. The recommended method
for storing checkpoint information for the replicat is by creating the checkpoint table in the target database
as discussed in the next section.

Creating the OGG Checkpoint Table

There are two ways to maintain checkpoints for the OGG target instance, as listed here:

- *Creating the checkpoint table*: This is the default and recommended method for
  maintaining checkpoints for recovering the target.

- *Using checkpoint files*: This is not recommended since a failure to access the file
  system because of a network or server failure would impact the recovery. To use
  this method, specify the NOCHECKPOINTTABLE parameter while creating the replicat
  process.

Let's discuss how to create the checkpoint table. Specify the checkpoint table name in the GLOBALS
parameter file on the target, as shown here:

```
GGSCI> edit params ./GLOBALS
CHECKPOINTTABLE TIGER.GGS_CHECKPOINT_TAB
```

Exit GGSCI and log back in to make the new GLOBALS parameter effective. Log in to the database through GGSCI and add the checkpoint table, as shown here:

```
GGSCI> DBLOGIN USERID FOX, PASSWORD fox123_ GGSCI> ADD CHECKPOINTTABLE
```

To drop a checkpoint table and re-create it, use the following commands:

```
GGSCI> DBLOGIN USERID FOX, PASSWORD fox123_
GGSCI> DROP CHECKPOINTTABLE
GGSCI> ADD CHECKPOINTTABLE
```

Troubleshooting the Checkpoint Table

A bad or missing checkpoint table can be associated with "No data found" and "Table does not exist" errors, as shown here:

```
GGS ERROR 516 Extract read, No data found selecting position from checkpoint table FOX.
GGS_CHECKPOINT_TAB for group REPORA, key 1025454721 (0x4669453).
```

Or as shown here:

```
2016-08-22 17:15:42 GGS ERROR 516 Extract read, Checkpoint table FOX.GGS_CHECKPOINT_TAB does
not exist. Please create the table or recreate the REPORA group using the correct table.
```

To troubleshoot a scenario where an error is related to the checkpoint, follow these steps:

1. Execute INFO REPLICAT replicat_name on the replicat group to verify whether the checkpoint files on the disks are in place and accessible.

2. If the checkpoint table is missing or corrupt, execute commands to drop and re-create the checkpoint table.

3. Resynchronize the checkpoint file with the checkpoint table by executing the convchk utility located in the OGG home, as shown here:

```
$ convchk <replicat_name> <schema_name>.<checkpointtable_name>
```

4. Restart the replicat process and check that the checkpoint information is being captured.

CHAPTER 25

■ ■ ■

Appendix B: Preparing for Interviews

This appendix covers questions and answers that you can use to test your knowledge of Oracle GoldenGate and prepare for interviews.

The Basics

1. What are the different replication topologies supported by Oracle GoldenGate?

Answer: Oracle GoldenGate supports the following replication topologies:

- Unidirectional replication
- Bidirectional replication
- One-to-many replication
- Many-to-one replication
- Peer-to-peer replication
- Cascading replication

2. Why would you prefer Oracle GoldenGate over Oracle Streams?

Answer: Oracle GoldenGate is the strategic solution from Oracle for all replication needs. It not only supports homogeneous but supports heterogeneous environments too. Installing and configuring OGG is simple compared to Oracle Streams. Also, Oracle GoldenGate delivers better performance in high-transaction environments. In addition to Oracle database to Oracle database replication, OGG supports replication between several popular non-Oracle databases and allows you to integrate relational database systems with nonrelational database systems and cloud systems.

In terms of new features, Oracle has stopped adding new features to Oracle Streams and shifted the focus to OGG for all replication needs.

3. What databases does Oracle GoldenGate support for replication?

Answer: OGG currently supports the following database types:

- Oracle Database
- Sybase
- Microsoft SQL Server
- MySQL
- IBM DB2

© Ravinder Gupta 2016
R. Gupta, *Mastering Oracle GoldenGate*, DOI 10.1007/978-1-4842-2301-7_25

- TimesTen

- Teradata

- Informix

- Enscribe

- SQL/MX

However, you cannot install Oracle GoldenGate as the source on DB2 for i and TimesTen databases. You still have the option to send feeds from other supported databases and apply the transactions on DB2 for i or TimesTen databases.

4. Why do you need to configure supplemental logging for replication?

Answer: When a transaction is committed on the source database, by default only the new data (an after image of the affected rows) is written to the redo logs for recovery. To apply the same changes on the target, the trail file should have additional information to identify the before image of key columns. To allow the database to capture and write before images of key columns, supplemental logging is required.

Specifically, in the context of an Oracle database as the source, OGG reads the transaction blocks, which record the redo information for the block. The replicat needs to create SQL statements to apply the captured changes to the target database. The SQL statement should be able to identify the rows to be changed on the target uniquely. Supplemental logging records additional columns for identifying rows uniquely even though the redo block didn't change these columns.

5. What are some key considerations before setting up bidirectional replication using Oracle GoldenGate?

Answer: The following are some key points for bidirectional replication using OGG:

- Both the systems in an active-active replication should have the same time zone. This is required so that timestamp-based conflicts can be resolved.

- The TRUNCATE statement cannot be configured bidirectional. It can, however, be configured to originate from one machine to another but not vice versa. All truncates should originate only from one machine and be replicated to the other.

- If triggers on tables exist and generate DML operations, then in order to avoid conflicts between local DML operations and replicated triggered DML operations, modify your triggers to handle local DML and replicated DMLs. The OGG replicat in integrated mode allows you to handle triggers.

- Do not replicate database-generated values such as sequences to avoid conflicts. You can use even sequences on one database and odd sequences on another to avoid conflicts.

- Tables should have a primary or unique key to identify rows. This will be needed for resolving conflicts.

6. Where can you filter particular column data in Oracle GoldenGate?

Answer: Filtering can be done in the extract, data pump, and replicat processes.

7. Why do you need a data pump if an extract can also send trail files to the target?

Answer: Data pumps are similar to GoldenGate extract processes. These are the secondary extract processes that read from the source trails written by the local extract and that pump them to the target over a TCP/IP network. Having data pumps is not absolutely necessary but is highly recommended.

The following are some of the advantages of having a data pump:

- Protection against losing connectivity to the target system

- Filter and transformation

- One-to-many replication

- Many-to-one replication

8. How is a classic extract different from an integrated extract process?

Answer: In the classic capture mode, data changes are captured from the Oracle redo logs/archive logs. This was the initial capture mode developed and used by GoldenGate Software Inc. The classic capture process is supported for all databases that are supported by Oracle GoldenGate.

Integrated capture mode is specific to Oracle Database 11.2 onward. In the integrated capture mode, the extract process communicates with the database log mining server and receives information in the form of a logical change record (LCR). The database log mining server mines the redo log and captures changes in the form of an LCR.

The following are some advantages of integrated capture over classic capture:

- It supports more Oracle data types compared to classic capture mode.

- The interaction with the database log mining server allows you to switch automatically between copies of archived logs and mirror images of redo logs. This is useful in the case of a disk block corruption of archived/redo logs.

- It supports multitenant container databases containing multiple pluggable databases. This is not possible with classic capture.

- It offers easy configuration for Oracle RAC and ASM.

9. Can you configure multiple extracts to write to the same trail file?

Answer: No, it will either abend with an error that the trail file is locked by another process, or if another extract is not writing to it at the moment, it will overwrite and corrupt the trail file.

10. Can you validate the syntax of parameters used in a parameter file without actually running the process?

Answer: Use the SHOWSYNTAX parameter in the parameter file and start the process. It will report the errors in the report file if there are any.

11. What are the supplemental logging prerequisites for OGG?

Answer: The following supplemental logging is required for OGG on the source where the extract captures information from the redo/archive logs:

- Minimal supplemental logging at the database level

- Object-level supplemental logging (trandata)

12. What are the steps to upgrade a classic capture to an integrated capture?

Answer: The steps to upgrade the extract process are as follows:

1. Stop the extract and register it with the database.

2. Test whether the extract can be upgraded.

3.   Use UPGRADE INTEGRATED TRANLOG to upgrade the extract.

4.   Start and verify whether the extract has been upgraded.

13. What are the limitations with DDL replication in Oracle GoldenGate?

Answer: DDL replication is slightly trickier when compared to replicating data. Some of the important limitations are as follows:

- The maximum length of a DDL statement to be replicated is between 2 MB to 4 MB. If the DDL length exceeds this size, the extract process will issue a warning message and ignore the DDL statement. These ignored DDL statements will be stored in the marker table. The GoldenGate ddl_ddl2file.sql file allows you to dump all the DDL statements at a location specified by the USER_DUMP_DEST directory. You can find this file in your OGG home directory.

- The source and target database objects on which DDL replication will happen should be identical.

- DDL replication is not supported on standby databases.

- DDL replication can be mapped to different object names only by the primary extract process. Data pumps support DDL replication in PASSTHRU mode.

- A DML/DDL operation within a DDL trigger is not captured.

- It is mandatory to use ASSUMETARGETDEFS instead of SOURCEDEFS in the replicat configured for DDL replication.

14. What is the use of DUMPDDL?

Answer: OGG maintains the DDL history table. The DUMPDDL command can be executed in GGSCI to view the contents of the DDL history table. DUMPDDL will dump all the contents of the DDL history table into GGS_DDL_* tables in the database. Since the DDL history table usually has a large volume of data, only the first 4,000 bytes are dumped for performance reasons. The syntax of DUMPDDL is as follows:

GGSCI> DUMPDDL

or as follows:

GGSCI> DUMPDDL SHOW

15. When configuring DDL replication in bidirectional configuration, what DDLOPTIONS should be used in the source and target OGG processes?

Answer: In bidirectional configuration, the extract and replicat on the primary and secondary database servers should have the following parameters:

- Extract on both servers:

   DDLOPTIONS GETREPLICATES, GETAPPLOPS

- Replicat on both servers:

   DDLOPTIONS UPDATEMETADATA

16. How will you configure DDL replication in a heterogeneous environment?

Answer: Each database has its own DDL statement structures and varies in the syntax. Hence, Oracle GoldenGate DDL replication can be configured only between two Oracle databases. Non-Oracle databases are not supported.

17. What is the `GETENV` function used for? Give a few examples.

Answer: It returns information about the GoldenGate environment.
Here's an example:

```
@GETENV ('STATS','TABLE','schema_name.table_name','CDR_CONFLICTS')
@GETENV ('STATS','TABLE','schema_name.table_name', 'CDR_RESOLUTIONS_FAILED')
@GETENV ('STATS','CDR_RESOLUTIONS_SUCCEEDED')
@GETENV ('STATS', 'TRUNCATE')
@GETENV ('STATS', 'DML')
```

18. When do you need `FLUSH SEQUENCE` in OGG?

Answer: `FLUSH SEQUENCE` is executed during the initial synchronization when the extract is started for the first time. It updates the Oracle sequence so that the initial redo logs are available when the extract starts capturing data. This is needed since the redo is not generated until the current cache for the sequence is exhausted.
The syntax to use `FLUSH SEQUENCE` is as follows:

```
GGSCI> FLUSH SEQUENCE schema_name.sequence_name
```

Advanced

19. Are OGG binaries supported on ASM Cluster File System (ACFS) and Database File System (DBFS)?

Answer: OGG can be installed and configured on ACFS, but OGG binaries cannot be stored on DBFS. However, files such as parameter files, trail files, and checkpoint files can be stored on DBFS.

20. What are macros in Oracle GoldenGate? How are they defined?

Answer: Macros in Oracle GoldenGate help to reuse commands and parameters. It is a built-in automation tool that can execute a stored set of processing steps. Macros can be nested among each other and can also be stored in libraries and used via library calls.
You can use macros for extract, replicat, and defgen parameter files. The following is the syntax for defining a macro:

```
MACRO #macro_name
PARAMS (#p1, #p2 ...)
BEGIN
macro_body
END;
```

21. What are the primary components of OGG high availability using Oracle Clusterware?

Answer: The main components of OGG HA are as follows:

- Virtual IP

- Shared storage

- ActionScript (or AgentScript)

615

22. List a few commonly used data filter methods in OGG.

Answer: To filter data, you can use one or more of the following options:

- Use the FILTER or WHERE clause in TABLE/MAP statements

- Use SQLEXEC to execute SQL queries or stored procedures

- Use user exits

23. List data transformation methods in OGG.

Answer: Data manipulation or transformation can be achieved using one or more of the following options:

- Using Oracle GoldenGate conversion functions

- Using user exits from the extract or replicat process to apply a database routine and return results to Oracle GoldenGate

- Using the replicat to deliver data directly to another ETL engine

24. What is a token?

Answer: A user token is information that can be stored to and captured from a user token area in an Oracle GoldenGate trail header. It is typically used to store environment information but can also be used to store any type of information and then used in OGG replication in multiple ways.

Here's the syntax to use the TOKEN option at the source:

```
TABLE <table_name>, TOKENS (<token name> = <token data> [, ...]) ;
```

For example, the following are sets of token values to be written to a trail file header:

```
TABLE TIGER.AUDIT_LOG,
TOKENS (TKN-OSUSER = @GETENV("GGENVIRONMENT","OSUSERNAME"),
TKN-TRANSACTION-CSN =@GETENV("TRANSACTION","CSN"),
TKN-DBNAME = @GETENV ("DBENVIRONMENT","DBNAME"),
TKN-HOSTNAME = @GETENV ("GGENVIRONMENT","HOSTNAME"),
TKN-COMMITTIME = @GETENV("GGHEADER","COMMITTIMESTAMP"),
TKN-REC-FILESEQNO=@GETENV ("RECORD", "FILESEQNO"),
TKN-REC-FILERBA=@GETENV ("RECORD", "FILERBA"));
```

25. What are user exits, and what are they used for?

Answer: User exits are user-defined callbacks to C/C++ functions from within Oracle GoldenGate. These can be called from either the extract or replicat process by using the CUSEREXIT parameter.

User exits can work as an alternative to or can be used along with column conversion functions. The major advantage is that data is processed only once when it is extracted at the source. This is unlike the column conversion functions where data is first extracted and then read again to perform the transformation.

User exits can be used to

- Perform column conversion and manipulation for data transformation

- Repair bad data

- Compute delta information from the before and after update values of any record

- Do complex filtering on extraction and replication of data
- Accumulate statistic data
- Respond to database events

26. What is SQLEXEC used for in OGG?

Answer: SQLEXEC can be used in the extract or replicat parameter file to allow Oracle GoldenGate extract and replicat processes to communicate with the database to execute queries, commands, and stored procedures. This greatly enhances Oracle GoldenGate's capabilities to perform complex processing.

27. What is data loopback in bidirectional replication?

Answer: Imagine a situation where data capture on Machine A is replicated to Machine B and the same transaction on Machine B gets captured by the extract on Machine B and gets replicated back to Machine A. This will lead to an endless loop. This is called *data loopback*.

You must configure OGG bidirectional replication to distinguish between user transactions and local replicat transactions to avoid such data loopback.

28. What are the types of output supported by the OGG flat-file adapter?

Answer: There are two modes of output supported by flat-file adapter, as listed here:

- Delimiter-separated values (DSV)
- Length-delimited values (LDV)

29. What are the different types of flat-file writers in OGG for producing data files?

Answer: There are three flat-file writers.

- dsvwriter
- diffswriter
- binarywriter

30. How can you integrate relational database systems with Java systems?

Answer: Oracle GoldenGate using the Java application adapter libraries can now capture messages from JMS capture and deliver them to supported target databases. It can also capture transactions and publish them in the form of JMS messages to be fed into and processed by JMS delivery processes on the target system.

This capability of Oracle GoldenGate has been enabled for integrated transactional systems with Java systems in near real time.

31. List the key considerations before you start configuring OGG high availability using Oracle Clusterware.

Answer: The following are some key points of consideration when you begin configuring OGG high availability.

- Oracle GoldenGate runs on one server at any time. Hence, in a high availability configuration, OGG can run in active-passive mode only.
- Each node in the cluster must have identical parameter files.
- If one node fails, Oracle GoldenGate is automatically started on the other node. The processes are started from the point they stopped to maintain data consistency.

- A shared server should be available to store recovery-related files. The checkpoint files and Oracle GoldenGate trails should be stored on this shared system.

- You can install Oracle GoldenGate locally on each node and maintain recovery-related files on a shared location. Alternatively, you can install Oracle GoldenGate on a shared location and register it with Oracle Clusterware.

- Shared file system options from Oracle are Oracle Cluster File System (OCFS2), Oracle ASM Cluster File System (OACFS), and Oracle Database File System (DBFS). Oracle ACFS is the recommended cluster file system for Oracle GoldenGate binaries and trail files in Real Application Cluster configurations for ease of management and high availability. However, if your Oracle Grid Infrastructure version is older than 11.2.0.3, then ACFS mounted on multiple servers concurrently does not support file locking. Thus, you need to mount ACFS on only one server.

32. What is GGCS?

Answer: The service offering by Oracle GoldenGate for data integration and replication to the cloud is called Oracle GoldenGate Cloud Service (GGCS).

33. What are the main components of GGCS?

Answer: Oracle GoldenGate Cloud Service has the following six main components:

- My Account

- My Services

- GGCS console

- Oracle database cloud

- Oracle storage cloud

- Oracle compute cloud

34. What is a SOCKS5 proxy?

Answer: Socket Secure 5 (SOCKS5) is an Internet protocol to exchange network data between the client and server through the proxy server. The SOCKS5 proxy server creates a TCP connection on behalf of the client server. The advantage of the SOCKS5 proxy is it allows you to deliver data to the cloud without a VPN connection using GGCS. The SOCKS protocol provides additional authentication that allows only authorized users to access the server.

Oracle GoldenGate 12c

35. What are a few new interesting features in Oracle GoldenGate 12*c*?
Answer: The following are some of the new and significant features added to Oracle GoldenGate 12*c*:

- Support for Oracle Database 12*c* multitenant architecture.

- Oracle Universal Installer support.

- Integrated replicat for Oracle databases.

- Coordinated replicat for non-Oracle databases.

- Inclusion of metadata in trail files such as the table definition record (TDR). Thus, you are no longer required to create definition files containing table metadata at the target system.

- Ease of monitoring channel lags using automatic heartbeat table.

- Improved trail file recovery. In the case of a bad trail file or missing trail files, you can delete the bad trail files and bounce the extract process. This will automatically rebuild the required trail files.

- Support for quick and easy logical design of GoldenGate solutions using GoldenGate Studio.

- Nine-digit trail file sequence to support 1 billion files per trail.

- Expanded heterogeneous support.

- Enhanced security with the introduction of the wallet and master key.

- Support for Big Data.

- Support for private and public cloud systems.

- Repair capabilities in Oracle GoldenGate Veridata.

36. What is a credential store?

Answer: A credential store has been introduced with Oracle GoldenGate 12*c*. It allows you to manage user IDs and passwords in Oracle GoldenGate. You can now store usernames and passwords used in OGG processes in the credential store and can use an alias instead in the extract and replicat processes. The credential store also can be used to store usernames and passwords that you can use for DBLOGIN through GGSCI.

This shields the original credentials to be displayed and provides an extra layer of security. The credential store is implemented as an auto-login wallet within the Oracle Credential Store Framework (CSF).

37. How do you create a credential store in OGG?

Answer: Use the ADD CREDENTIALSTORE command to create a credential store. By default the credential store is created in the OGG directory dircrd.

```
GGSCI> ADD CREDENTIALSTORE
Credential store created in ./dircrd/.
```

The credential store gets created in the dircrd directory in your OGG home. Alternatively, you can specify CREDENTIALSTORELOCATION in the GLOBALS parameter file to create a wallet at another location.

```
$ cd dircrd
$ ls
cwallet.sso
```

38. How will you add a coordinated replicat with a maximum of five threads?

Answer: Execute the following command in GGSCI:

```
GGSCI> add replicat RFDLD, coordinated, EXTTRAIL /app/ggs/fox/dirdat/f1, maxthreads 5
```

Performance and Security

39. What types of encryption are supported in Oracle GoldenGate?

Answer: There are three types of encryption that Oracle GoldenGate can provide for securing information.

- Encrypting passwords used in extract and replicat parameter files

- Encrypting trail files on both the extract and the replicat

- Data being sent over a TCP/IP network for replication

40. I have Oracle GoldenGate configured for Oracle RAC using classic capture processes. How can I increase the maximum size of the read operation into the buffer that holds the results of the read operation?

Answer: Use TRANSLOGOPTION ASMBUFSIZE in the extract parameter file to set the maximum ASM buffer size.

41. Name a few parameters that you can use in the replicat to improve performance.

Answer: BATCHSQL, BATCHTRANSOPS, GROUPTRANSOPS, INSERTAPPEND

42. What is the significance of PASSTHRU in a data pump parameter file?

Answer: A data pump essentially serves the function of reading extract trail files and copying them to the target machine. In some cases, data pumps are also configured to filter some information before actually copying or mapping the source to the target tables when the table names or structures differ.

You can make use of PASSTHRU for tables with no filtering required and when the table structure on the source and the target match exactly. You can define PASSTHRU and NOPASSTHRU in the same data pump as follows:

```
PASSTHRU TABLE TIGER.TABLE1;
NOPASSTHRU TABLE TIGER.TABLE2, WHERE (REGION< 10);
```

In pass-through mode, the extract does not look for table definitions either from the database or from the definition file. This increases the overall throughput.

43. What are the common reasons for the extract process slowing down?

Answer: An extract process can slow down because of the following reasons:

- Long-running batch transactions

- Low-bandwidth network

- Overburdened network

- Long-running and uncommitted transactions writing to dirtmp with insufficient space

44. What are the common reasons for the replicat process slowing down?

Answer: A replicat process can slow down because of the following reasons:

- High volume of transactions on the table

- Table locked on the target database because of blocking sessions

- Missing index on target tables
- Target table that is too large causing increased processing time for update and delete operations

45. An integrated capture with default values has a lag of around 30 minutes. What steps will you take to address this latency?

Answer: Check whether STREAMS_POOL_SIZE is not undersized. For an integrated extract, allocate a sufficient STREAMS_POOL_SIZE value for the database instance and set MAX_SGA_SIZE in the OGG extract parameter file.

Execute the following as SYSDBA:

```
SQL> alter system set STREAMS_POOL_SIZE=3G
```

Add the following to the OGG extract parameter file:

```
TRANLOGOPTIONS INTEGRATEDPARAMS (MAX_SGA_SIZE 2048, PARALLELISM 4)
```

46. When using the integrated replicat, where else other than the OGG report file can you see performance statistics?

Answer: The database AWR reports capture performance statistics for integrated replicat processes.

Troubleshooting

47. What parameter will you use to report long-running transactions to ggserror.log?

Answer: Use WARNLONGTRANS to set a threshold time for open transactions in an extract parameter file as follows:

```
WARNLONGTRANS 1h, CHECKINTERVAL 5m
```

48. What is the difference between RESTARTCOLLISION and HANDLECOLLISION?

Answer: The RESTARTCOLLISION and NORESTARTCOLLISION parameters control whether the replicat applies HANDLECOLLISION logic after the replicat has stopped because of a conflict. When the replicat is started again, RESTARTCOLLISIONS enables HANDLECOLLISIONS only until the first replicat checkpoint is complete. HANDLECOLLISION is turned off automatically after the first checkpoint.

On the other hand, when using HANDLECOLLISION, the replicat will continue to overwrite and process transactions until the parameter is removed from the replicat parameter file and the replicat is restarted.

49. How would you view an encrypted trail file using LOGDUMP?

Answer: Use the LOGDUMP command DECRYPT ON to decrypt the trail file.

50. How will you instruct an extract process to switch and start writing to a new trail file?

Answer: Execute the following command in GGSCI:

```
GGSCI> SEND EXTRACT extract_name, ROLLOVER
```

51. What are the different types of failures in an Oracle GoldenGate replication environment?

Answer: These are the types of failure that impact OGG replication:

- Oracle GoldenGate process failure
- Problem with the source and or target database
- Server storage issues
- Network issues
- User errors (conscious or unconscious mistakes)

52. OGG writes error messages to which files?

Answer: There are three main log files where OGG writes information and error messages.

- OGG error log file: ggserror.log
- Report file of each extract, data pump, or replicat process
- Discard file of each extract, data pump, or replicat process

53. What is REPERROR?

Answer: The REPERROR parameter is used in the replicat parameter file to instruct the replicat what to do in case of a specific replication error.

Oracle GoldenGate GUI Tools

54. What are the installation steps to install and configure OGG Monitor?

Answer: OGG Monitor installation involves the following steps:

1. Install Oracle WebLogic Server 12c with JRF or JDBC.
2. Install the Oracle GoldenGate Monitor server.
3. Create the OGG Monitor repository using the Repository Creation Utility (RCU).
4. Create the WebLogic Server domain using the Configuration Wizard.
5. Configure the OGG Monitor server.
6. Start the OGG Monitor server.
7. Install the Oracle GoldenGate Monitor Agent.
8. Create and configure the OGG Monitor Agent instances.

55. What are the benefits of using the OGG Director?

Answer: The Oracle GoldenGate Director can greatly add to your ability to manage Oracle GoldenGate implementations in your organization. The OGG Director enables you to perform the following tasks:

- Manage and administer Oracle GoldenGate instances remotely
- Issue GGSCI commands remotely from the OGG Director
- Start/stop processes and instances

- Add new extract or replicat processes
- View error and report files for troubleshooting
- Present a graphical view of Oracle GoldenGate implementations in your company network

56. What are the important components of OGG Veridata?

Answer: These are the components of Oracle GoldenGate Veridata:

- Veridata server
- Veridata web user interface
- Veridata repository
- Veridata Agent
- Veridata CLI or Veridata command-line interface

57. What is Oracle GoldenGate Studio?

Answer: Oracle GoldenGate Studio is a WYSIWYG, drag-and-drop interface to quickly build and deploy Oracle GoldenGate replication solutions. It provides you with templates to quickly build configurations aligned to best practices.

Miscellaneous

58. What is the minimum Oracle database version you need to use an integrated replicat in your OGG configuration?

Answer: Oracle Database 11.2.0.4 and above.

59. Can you generate comma-separated values (CSV) files using Oracle GoldenGate?

Answer: Yes, you can use the OGG flat-file adapters to generate delimiter-separated flat files.

60. Can you capture transactions on compressed tables in your source database?

Answer: Yes, OGG 11.2 and higher support capture from compressed tables using the integrated extract process.

61. How do you configure OGG replication when the source and the target OGG are of different versions?

Answer: Use the `FORMAT RELEASE` parameter to generate trail files in a particular release format.

62. How do you delete old trail files in Oracle GoldenGate?

Answer: Use `PURGEOLDEXTRACTS` in the `MANAGER` parameter file.
Here's an example:

```
PURGEOLDEXTRACTS /app/ggs/tiger/dirdat/t*, USECHECKPOINTS, MINKEEPHOURS 2
```

63. The OS patch needs to be applied on the source and target servers that have your OGG set up in a one-directional configuration. Provide the sequence of steps for supporting this maintenance activity.

Answer: Ensure that the extract has processed all the records in the redo/archive logs.

```
GGSCI> SEND EXTRACT extract_name, LOGEND
```

The previous command should show YES; otherwise, wait for some time and check again. Next, execute the following steps in order:

1. Stop the application.

2. Stop the database.

3. Stop the OGG processes on the source.

4. Stop the OGG processes on the target.

5. Apply the OS patch (the SA team performs this step).

6. Start the database.

7. Start the OGG processes on the target.

8. Start the OGG processes on the source.

9. Start the application.

64. What is a checkpoint table?

Answer: Checkpoints are maintained for each OGG process to aid in recovery in the case of failure and to maintain data integrity. Checkpoints are maintained individually for the extract, data pump, and replicat processes.

The checkpoint information can be stored either in the checkpoint files on the server or in a table in the database called a checkpoint table.

65. List some of the database views that you can query to monitor the integrated extract or replicat process.

Answer: Some of the database views for monitoring integrated extract or replicat are as follows:

- DBA_CAPTURE
- GV$GG_APPLY_COORDINATOR
- GV$GG_APPLY_READER
- GV$GG_APPLY_RECEIVER
- GV$GG_APPLY_SERVER
- GV$GOLDENGATE_CAPABILITIES
- GV$GOLDENGATE_CAPTURE
- GV$GOLDENGATE_MESSAGE_TRACKING
- GV$GOLDENGATE_TRANSACTION
- GV$LOGMNR_SESSION
- V$GOLDENGATE_CAPTURE
- V$GOLDENGATE_TABLE_STATS
- V$GOLDENGATE_TRANSACTION

66. List a few things that can cause data inconsistencies between the source and target databases even though you have OGG replication configured.

Answer: In today's increasingly complex IT environment, data distributed across multiple systems is prone to inconsistencies because of several reasons.

- Hardware and network issues such as system failures, disk corruptions/failures, and network failure/glitches can lead to data inconsistencies. These inconsistencies might get introduced after a system is brought back from a failure.

- Errors during the initial load of data before replication can actually be started can lead to data inconsistencies. This may happen based on the initial data migration tool used and the way it handles specific data. Also, sometimes a difference in character sets of two systems may introduce bad characters in the target system during the initial load. These may go unnoticed until you have a transaction that fails because of the inconsistency on the two systems.

- It is extremely important to ensure that the source and target database systems match in terms of table constraints that limit data entered into them. For example, if you have missed the primary/unique constraint or have not enabled a foreign key after the initial load, it may result in duplicates in your target tables when replication is turned on.

- Even though replication is working absolutely fine, transactions on the source can be done in a compromised manner that will prevent it from being captured by the capture process. For example, doing a bulk data load using the NOLOGGING feature in Oracle databases to boost the performance of the load can create problems.

- When replication is unidirectional, the application, users, and DBA on the target machine are not supposed to modify data on the target machine; they still, however, may do it, which may lead to inconsistencies in data.

67. What are the currently supported databases that allow you to use the OGG Reverse Utility?

Answer: These are the databases currently supported by the Oracle GoldenGate Reverse Utility:

- Oracle
- Sybase
- SQL Server
- IBM DB2

68. What parameters will you add to your OGG MANAGER parameter file to report the current lag every hour and write a critical message if the lag exceeds 60 minutes?

Answer: LAGREPORTMINUTES 60, LAGINFOHOURS 1.

69. When configuring replication between two Oracle tables with the same name, same columns, and data types but a different column order, can you consider the two tables identical?

Answer: No.

70. What are the responsibilities of the OGG manager process?

Answer: These are main responsibilities of the OGG manager process:

- Cleaning up old OGG trails
- Starting dynamic processes, such as server collectors, extracts, and replicats
- Error and lag reporting

71. What parameter is used to specify the data source (source trail) for a data pump extract?

Answer: EXTRAILSOURCE.

72. Where is user token information stored?

Answer: In a trail file.

73. You have a replicat group called RFDLD001, and you need to start it with a trail sequence 15 from RBA 215424. What is the command?

Answer: ALTER REPLICAT RFDLD001, EXTSEQNO 15, EXTRBA 215424.

74. How will you restore a corrupt checkpoint table from checkpoint files?

Answer: Use the CONVCHK utility.

75. When using both FILTER and SQLEXEC, by default which option is evaluated first?

Answer: FILTER.

76. What is an extract lag?

Answer: A lag is the difference in time when a change record is processed by the extract and the timestamp of the record in the data source.

77. What is the CHECKPARAMS parameter used for?

Answer: It instructs the process to check the parameter syntax and then stop.

78. What OGG feature provides recoverability without a loss of transactions?

Answer: Checkpointing.

79. Where are Oracle GoldenGate macros defined?

Answer: Macros can be defined inside the parameter file or included in a macro file.

80. You have a system that replicated between a central office and 11 regional nodes. What is the best product you can use to monitor these 13 instances and set up e-mail alerts based on the process status?

Answer: The Oracle GoldenGate Director.

81. How do you add comments in the Oracle GoldenGate parameter files?

Answer: Use the COMMENT parameter or double hyphen (--).
Here's an example:

```
COMMENT this is just a comment statement
```

Here's another example:

```
--this is just a comment statement
```

82. How can you execute a set of GGSCI instructions from a file rather executing each statement individually?

Answer: OBEY file_name.

83. If your source and target do not have primary key defined and you have not used KEYCOLS in your extract and replicat groups, how will the OGG process update and delete statements?

Answer: The first unique key alphanumerically, excluding virtual and nullable columns, will be treated as a primary key. The unique key should also not have a column with a timestamp. If no unique is present, OGG constructs a pseudo-key with all the columns that can form a unique key excluding unsupported columns.

84. Which file contains the list of key values used by the extract for encryptions and by the collector for decryption? Where is it located?

Answer: The ENCKEYS file is located in the OGG home.

85. What is CDR, and what is it used for?

Answer: Conflict detection and resolution (CDR) plays an important role in a bidirectional replication. It ensures any INSERT, UPDATE, and DELETE conflicts between two machines are handled in real time.

86. When is TRANLOGOPTIONS EXCLUDEUSER used?

Answer: It is used to have the extract process avoid capturing DML transactions applied by the replicat process to the database; you have to tell the extract to skip any transactions from a particular user.

87. What is the difference between COLMAP and COLMATCH?

Answer: While COLMAP is used to map columns for a specific table, you can use COLMATCH to map columns for all tables in a particular extract or replicat group.

88. What is COLSTAT used for?

Answer: COLSTAT is a data manipulation function used with the MAP statement in the replicat parameter file for setting the NULL value expression. The COLSTAT function returns an indicator to the extract or replicat process stating that a column is NULL, MISSING, or INVALID.

89. How can you determine whether the parameters for a particular process were recently changed?

Answer: By looking at old report files and comparing the parameters reported in it with the current parameters.

90. What is DEFGEN?

Answer: The DEFGEN utility is used to generate source table definitions in a file called the *definition file*. This file is referred to by the replicat process to map the target table with the source table for replication.

91. What is the difference between ADD SCHEMATRANDATA and ADD TRANDATA?

Answer: ADD SCHEMATRANDATA is used to enable schema-level supplemental logging. The user requires the dbms_streams_auth.grant_admin_privilege privilege to be able to enable schema-level supplemental logging.
ADD TRANDATA is used to enable supplemental logging at the table level.

92. How will you remove unused checkpoint records from the checkpoint table in the database?

Answer: Execute the following command in GGSCI. You must be logged into the database using DBLOGIN prior to running this command.

```
GGSCI> CLEANUP CHECKPOINTTABLE schema_name.checkpoint_table_name
```

93. What is a trace table?

Answer: A trace table is used in a bidirectional replication to identify replicat transactions to extract and hence prevent the extract from capturing them again. The TRACETABLE parameter is required in the extract and replicat parameter files only if an explicit trace table was created using the ADD TRACETABLE command. The default trace table is GGS_TRACE.

Trace tables are required only when using classic replicat. They are not used when integrated replicat is used.

94. What parameter can you use to start an extract when the manager process starts?

Answer: AUTOSTART.

95. Which parameter tells the extract the tables for which changes need to be captured?

Answer: The TABLE parameter in the extract parameter file.

96. For a system that has a firewall controlling the port access, what parameter can be used to control port access for the OGG manager?

Answer: DYNAMICPORTLIST.

97. How can you force the extract to close the current trail file and start writing to a new trail file?

Answer: Execute the following command in GGSCI:

```
GGSCI> SEND EXTRACT extract_name, ROLLOVER
```

98. What image information does the extract store in the trail file based on operation type?

Answer: It stores an after image for the insert and update operations and a before image for the delete operations.

99. How can you schedule for aging discard files and start writing to new discard files?

Answer: Use the DISCARDROLLOVER parameter in extract or replicat parameter files.

100. How can you schedule for aging report files at a particular time instead of waiting until the process restarts?

Answer: Use the REPORTROLLOVER parameter in extract or replicat parameter files.

CHAPTER 26

∎∎∎

Appendix C: Get Certified

This appendix guides you on the path to becoming an Oracle GoldenGate 12c Certified Implementation Specialist. You need to take the Oracle GoldenGate 12c Implementation Essentials (1Z0-447) exam and pass it with a minimum score of 69 percent.

The exam is designed to get you certified by Oracle and recognize your Oracle GoldenGate implementation skills. The exam contains multiple-choice questions with one or more correct answer. The questions range from easy to difficult. The exam also contains several trick questions that test your in-field experience implementing Oracle GoldenGate solutions.

Here are the exam details:

- *Exam number*: 1Z0-447

- *Number of questions*: 91

- *Type of questions*: Multiple-choice questions

- *Duration of exam*: 120 minutes

- *Passing score*: 69 percent

- *Certification name*: Oracle GoldenGate 12c Implementation Specialist

Steps to Get Certified

Here are the steps for getting certified:

1. Check the exam topics.

2. Get trained (through self-study or instructor-led trainings).

3. Get hands-on experience.

4. Take mock exams.

5. Purchase the exam voucher.

6. Register for the exam.

7. Take the exam.

8. View the result.

9. Download the certificate if passed.

Exam Topics

The following are the exam topics for the Oracle GoldenGate 12c Certified Implementation Specialist exam (1Z0-447).

Oracle GoldenGate (OGG) Overview

- Describe an OGG functional overview and common topologies

- Describe OGG Veridata and Management Pack functionality

- Describe the difference between real-time data integration replication and Data Manipulation Language (DML) replication

Architecture Overview

- Describe the OGG components

- Create the two types of capture processes for Oracle databases

- Create the three types of replicat processes

- Explain the difference between an extract and a pump and between local and remote trails

- Configure OGG's process recovery mechanism

Install and Configure OGG

- Download and install OGG and differentiate between various installers (ZIP, OUI, TAR)

- Synchronize the source and target databases with the initial load

- Prepare the database for OGG CDC and check the databases with the OGG schema check script

- Configure the OGG replication component parameter files

- Configure the OGG command-line interface to create OGG processes

- Describe how to identify and resolve issues in a heterogeneous replication and provide appropriate solutions

- Configure OGG utilities

Parameters

- Describe and compare the GLOBALS and MANAGER parameters

- Create solutions using component parameters for replication requirements

- Install OGG parameters

- Explain and identify parameters specific to non-Oracle databases

Mapping and Transformation Overview

- Implement use cases for transformation functions

- Implement macros

Configuration Options

- Describe OGG configuration options (Data Definition Language [DDL] and compression and encryption options)

- Configure OGG event actions based on use cases

- Troubleshoot conflict detection and resolution

- Configure integrated capture, replicat, and deployment options

Managing and Monitoring Oracle GoldenGate

- Manage OGG command and data security

- Implement and troubleshoot OGG monitoring

- Explain the configuration and management of the Enterprise Manager 12*c* plug-in

- Implement and troubleshoot OGG Veridata

How to Schedule an Exam?

Buy an Oracle exam voucher (price: $245) from Oracle University at http://education.oracle.com. The voucher is valid for six months.

Register for the exam at Pearson Vue by visiting http://pearsonvue.com/oracle/.

After completing the exam, visit http://certview.oracle.com to view your result and download the e-certificate. It takes approximately 30 minutes for your exam results to be available in your account.

Good luck!

Index

Get the eBook for only $5!

Why limit yourself?

Now you can take the weightless companion with you wherever you go and access your content on your PC, phone, tablet, or reader.

Since you've purchased this print book, we're happy to offer you the eBook in all 3 formats for just $5.

Convenient and fully searchable, the PDF version enables you to easily find and copy code—or perform examples by quickly toggling between instructions and applications. The MOBI format is ideal for your Kindle, while the ePUB can be utilized on a variety of mobile devices.

To learn more, go to www.apress.com/companion or contact support@apress.com.

Apress®
THE EXPERT'S VOICE™

All Apress eBooks are subject to copyright. All rights are reserved by the Publisher, whether the whole or part of the material is concerned, specifically the rights of translation, reprinting, reuse of illustrations, recitation, broadcasting, reproduction on microfilms or in any other physical way, and transmission or information storage and retrieval, electronic adaptation, computer software, or by similar or dissimilar methodology now known or hereafter developed. Exempted from this legal reservation are brief excerpts in connection with reviews or scholarly analysis or material supplied specifically for the purpose of being entered and executed on a computer system, for exclusive use by the purchaser of the work. Duplication of this publication or parts thereof is permitted only under the provisions of the Copyright Law of the Publisher's location, in its current version, and permission for use must always be obtained from Springer. Permissions for use may be obtained through RightsLink at the Copyright Clearance Center. Violations are liable to prosecution under the respective Copyright Law.

⟨IOUG⟩ *For the Complete Technology & Database Professional*
independent oracle users group

IOUG represents the **voice of Oracle technology and database professionals** - empowering you to be **more productive in your business** and career by **delivering education,** sharing **best practices** and providing technology direction and **networking opportunities.**

Context, Not Just Content

IOUG is dedicated to helping our members become an #IOUGenius by staying on the cutting-edge of Oracle technologies and industry issues through practical content, user-focused education, and invaluable networking and leadership opportunities:

- *SELECT Journal* is our quarterly publication that provides in-depth, peer-reviewed articles on industry news and best practices in Oracle technology

- Our #IOUGenius blog highlights a featured weekly topic and provides content driven by Oracle professionals and the IOUG community

- Special Interest Groups provide you the chance to collaborate with peers on the specific issues that matter to you and even take on leadership roles outside of your organization

- COLLABORATE is our once-a-year opportunity to connect with the members of not one, but three, Oracle users groups (IOUG, OAUG and Quest) as well as with the top names and faces in the Oracle community.

Who we are...

... **more than 20,000** database professionals, developers, application and infrastructure architects, business intelligence specialists and IT managers

... **a community of users** that share experiences and knowledge on issues and technologies that matter to you and your organization

Interested? Join IOUG's community of Oracle technology and database professionals at **www.ioug.org/Join.**

Independent Oracle Users Group | phone: (312) 245-1579 | email: membership@ioug.org
330 N. Wabash Ave., Suite 2000, Chicago, IL 60611

Printed in the United States
By Bookmasters

Printed in the United States
By Bookmasters